WRITING AND COMMUNICATING IN BUSINESS

J. HAROLD JANIS
Professor Emeritus of Business Communication, New York University

Writing and Communicating in Business THIRD EDITION

Macmillan Publishing Co., Inc.
New York
Collier Macmillan Publishers
London

MACMILLAN PUBLISHING CO., INC.
866 Third Avenue, New York, New York 10022

COLLIER MACMILLAN CANADA, LTD.

Library of Congress Cataloging in Publication Data

Janis, Jack Harold, (date)
Writing and communicating in business.

Bibliography: p.
Includes index.
1. English language—Business English. 2. Commercial correspondence. I. Title.
HF5726.J3 1978 651.7′4 77-3867
ISBN 0-02-360300-3

Printing: 3 4 5 6 7 8 Year: 9 0 1 2 3 4

Preface to the Third Edition

THIS edition, like its predecessors, is the distillation of my years of college teaching, my complementary experience as a professional writer for business, and my association with the communication training programs of many business and governmental organizations. I think this information is important to the reader, for it helps to explain the fusion of theory and practice that sets the tone for the book.

When the first edition of this work appeared, it marked a departure from contemporary textbooks on business writing in two ways. First, it treated writing as a form of business behavior; and, second, it broadened the conventional letters-and-reports regimen by bringing new variety and greater intellectual discipline to the basic business writing course. The present edition remains faithful to this concept even while it adapts to the climate of change. There is a new pragmatism in learning and an urgency about the need to sharpen language skills. There is also a fresh commitment to examine the nature and importance of communication in organizations. Happily, as the novelty of communication theory has settled into acceptance, the uses to which it can be put have emerged more clearly. As a result, the ties between rhetoric and communication have been strengthened, and students are showing a bread-and-butter interest in writing and speaking effectively.

What is there, then, in this new edition that can help? Briefly:

- a broad current view of communication within the organizational structure;
- a simplification of the material on the communication process;
- many new problems dealing with communication situations that students can easily identify with;
- new report assignments calling for library research on business subjects;
- the inclusion of a sample library paper to help the student with form and structure;
- a reorganization and infusion of material designed to make the instruction more concrete and better suited to the needs of the nonprofessional writer;
- the addition, in the early chapters, of discussion topics to stimulate thought, develop perspectives, and give the student informal opportunities to speak.

Along with these changes, many new examples and other learning features have been introduced. Among the latter are the section on "Getting Started" at the end of Chapter 1 and the graphic demonstration of methods of organizing data at the end of Chapter 8.

And now, what has not changed? Mainly, it is the aim of equipping students for the writing tasks they inevitably face when they enter the business world. For this, their intelligence demands an explanation of the "why" of what they are asked to do; their energetic spirit requires that they take an active part in the communication experience, whether by writing, discussion, or stand-up speaking; and their interest must be fed by an instructional approach that takes them into the business environment and says, "This is the way it's really done; emulate it, and improve on it if you can."

This text serves those needs. Essentially, it treats the process, language, and practice of communication in organizations. Letters and reports remain the chief vehicles for student writing because they touch most closely on the experience of students and provide the best all-round introduction to communication problems. Still, the contributory roles of other media are shown, and the variety of writing challenges put to students remains at a high level. This diversity is evident in areas ranging from routine letters to job resumes, and it is especially noticeable in the chapters on reports and, later, in those dealing with persuasion, sales writing, and argument. The chapter on "Speech Communication" recognizes the complementary roles of speaking and writing.

Readers wanting to investigate further any of the aspects of communication treated in this text will find it useful to consult the list of "Selected Books for Reference," following Chapter 16. The comprehensive "Manual of Style" closes the book. It supplies a needed reference in matters of English and mechanics. Conveniently placed inside the back cover are a key to the manual and a list of correction symbols.

J. H. J.

Acknowledgments

I OWE a great debt to the many individuals and organizations who gave their assistance:

To my colleagues at New York University: Professor Lawrence D. Brennan for invaluable suggestions regarding general content and arrangement; Professors Ruth G. Batchelor and Kathryn W. Bell for problem material on reports and graphics; and Professors George W. Fluharty and Ralph M. Zink for help with the chapter on "Speech Communication."

To Mrs. Margaret H. Thompson for permission to use, in modified form, the chapter on "Graphic Presentation" that I originally wrote for the *New Standard Reference for Secretaries and Administrative Assistants,* of which Mrs. Thompson is coauthor.

To Miss Karen Burns and the Direct Mail Marketing Association for gracious permission to examine materials useful to me in the chapter on "Sales and Goodwill Messages."

To Mr. Robert W. Keith, vice president of the Manufacturers Hanover Trust Company of New York, for permission to use certain materials for illustrative purposes, and for much encouragement in my writing and teaching activities for the bank.

To the following organizations that, among others, I have served in some communications capacity over the years and that have provided much of the experience and many of the models cited in the text:

American Telephone & Telegraph Company
Chemical Bank
City of New York, Training Division, Office of the Mayor
Federal Reserve Bank of New York
Irving Trust Company
Jamaica Savings Bank
Manufacturers Hanover Trust Company
Merrill Lynch, Pierce, Fenner & Smith
New York Life Insurance Company
Peat, Marwick, Mitchell & Co.
United States Civil Service Commission
United States Life Insurance Company
West Point-Pepperell, Inc.

Finally, to the many other organizations, named and unnamed in the text, for the illustrative material they supplied. I am especially grateful for the courtesies shown by American Airlines, Doyle Dane Bernbach, Inc., Mobil Oil Corporation, and Union Carbide Corporation.

J. H. J.

Contents

1 Communicating in Organizations

If our instant-picture camera works better than theirs, buyers ought to know why. Let's stress convenience and speed.

Please address this letter to Mr. Greystone of Dana Stores: "We welcome your inquiry about our No. 4 grade fiber doormats. . . ."

Senator Hastings tells us nobody can understand this tax form. Isn't there some way the IRS can put it into simple English?

I'm meeting the Pension Committee tomorrow. I must have my proposals ready for distribution and discussion.

Closing the Willamette office isn't going to be easy. What do we tell our workers? What do we tell the community?

THE WORLD of business is a world of action. Products are designed, made, and sold. People are hired. Services are rendered. Policies are devised and implemented. Jobs are learned and performed. Yet there is no practical way in which any of these events can take place without communication.

Communication is the glue that binds the parts of the organization together; it is the open door through which information enters and leaves. Without communication, there can be no organization, and when communication stops, the organization ceases to function.

To most of us, communication is simply writing and speaking. In fact, communication is much more. An organization, for example, operates in an environment influenced by the state of the economy, competition, taxes, politics, public opinion, and government regulation. So, too, within the organization, individuals do their work in an atmosphere controlled by space and time, status, management goals, supervisory discipline, and personal ambition. Communication by these individuals satisfies many needs, takes many forms, requires many skills, and entails many risks and rewards.

Complex? Yes. But not beyond understanding and mastery. So let's begin with an overview of the simpler and more visible aspects of communication, and then proceed to an examination of the role of communication in business and the qualities you will need most as you pursue your goals.

EVERYWHERE, BUSINESS COMMUNICATION

Business communication flourishes wherever business functions must be performed. It is not limited to business enterprises. The same needs for communication are felt and the same means are used in other types of organizations—government agencies, particularly, but also religious and charitable groups, schools and colleges, unions, foundations, museums, and fraternal, business, and trade associations. Private citizens, too, are business communicators, and everyone—the organization and the individual alike—is a receiver of business communications.

We live in a sea of communication. We find it on our doorsteps and in our mailboxes; it is blared over the radio, flashed on television screens, published in newspapers and magazines, enclosed in packages, and spread on boxes, bottles, and cans.

Business communication is the answer to our inquiry and the request to pay a bill. It is the soap coupon, the sale announcement, the charity solicitation, the mail-order catalog, the mortgage contract, the cheesemaker's recipe, and the "thank you" letter from the merchant who sold us our new suit.

As citizens and consumers, we personally contribute to the volume of business communication whenever we send an order, seek information, make a complaint, look for a job, or reserve a hotel room. We also become business communicators when we fill out an advertiser's coupon, enter a jingle contest, draw up a will, sign a lease, claim a tax refund, make application for credit, or report an accident to our insurance company.

In the office or factory, communication gains momentum. Let a sale be consummated, an article manufactured, an instruction given, a policy formulated, a trip taken, money borrowed, a dividend paid, an employee hired or fired—and someone must talk or write about it. The communication takes place in conversations, conferences, and meetings, and in letters, memorandums, reports, manuals, advertisements, press releases, business paper articles, legal documents, and records of all kinds.

We have mentioned the use of communication in public administration. Federal, state, and local governments are composed of innumerable departments, agencies, bureaus, and committees, and literally millions of employees here and abroad. It is hard to imagine activity of such dimensions without a torrent of messages to keep people and administrative units in touch with each other, to preserve and disseminate information, and to give citizens a necessary check on government activities. Big government also means additional checks on the activities of citizens and businesses. Hence there is a corresponding communication flow from business to government. A small army of accountants and lawyers, as well as hordes of executives and lesser employees, spend countless man-hours preparing the reports required by government and answering its inquiries.

KINDS OF COMMUNICATION

The range of communication is perhaps the most clearly conveyed by an examination of the kinds that are employed. A number of classifications may be made.

Classification by Audience

Depending on the number of persons to whom the message is addressed, communication is *interpersonal, group,* or *mass.* Interpersonal communication is the contact between two individuals—for example, writer and reader, speaker and listener, worker and supervisor, salesperson and customer. A sociologist might say that in such communication there is a one-to-one relationship. Group communication involves a number of persons, each of whom retains his identity. The group may be small, as in the instance of the members of a work team or discussion group; or large, as in the instance of a theater audience, a trade convention, or a list of customers. Mass communication consists of messages to large numbers of people through such mass media as newspapers, radio, and television. In this kind of communication, the opportunities for individual identification and participation are minimal.

Classification by Code

Communication may also be classified as *verbal* or *nonverbal.* Writing and speaking use a verbal code, that is, words. Nonverbal communication consists of gestures, actions, pictures, forms of decoration, and other symbolic modes of expression excluding words. Thus one may communicate by manner of dress or grooming, by the thick pile on the office carpet, by a wink or handshake, by tone of voice, and by the promptness with which an appointment is kept. Too often communicators overlook these important influences on their effectiveness.

Classification by Medium

Another way of classifying communication is by reference to the medium employed. *Scribal media,* such as letters and reports, newspapers, magazines, catalogs, and other forms shown in Figure 1-1, communicate principally through the written word. *Aural media,* such as direct voice communication, the telephone, radio, and television, appeal partly or wholly to the ear. *Visual media,* such as pictures, live action, and television are received partly or wholly through the eye. Communication may also take place through the

Abstracts	Job descriptions
Administrative orders	
Advertisements	Laws and bylaws
Agenda	Leaflets
Agreements	Legal briefs
Announcements	Letters
Annual reports	
Applications	Manuals
Arbitration findings	Market surveys
Attitude surveys	Memorandums
	Minutes
Bill enclosures	
Billboards	Orders and order forms
Booklets	
Bulletins	Package copy
Business articles	Performance appraisals
Business and financial news	Plans
	Policy statements
Catalogs	Position papers
Certificates	Posters
Charts	Press releases
Circulars	Procedures
Citations	Programs
Claims	Proposals
Collection notices	Prospectuses
Commemorative literature	
Complaints	Questionnaires
Contracts	
Coupons	Radio and television commercials
Credit forms and letters	Reading rack literature
	Recommendations
Data sheets	Recruitment literature
Direct-mail advertising	References
Directives	Replies to inquiries
Directories	Reports
Dividend notices	Requisitions
	Research studies
Educational literature	Resolutions
Employee publications	Resumes
Estimates	
	Sales presentations
Fact sheets	Schedules
Financial analyses	Signs
Fliers	Specifications
	Speeches
Goodwill literature	Stockholder communications
	Suggestions
Handbills	Summaries
Handbooks	Surveys
Handouts	
House organs	Tags and labels
	Technical papers
Inquiries	Telegrams
Instructions	Training aids
Introductions	
Invitations	Wills

FIG. 1-1. *What business writing includes (a partial list).*

sense of *touch* (tactile communication), *smell* (olfactory communication), and *taste*.[1]

As the descriptions indicate, there is considerable overlapping of the media classifications. A letter or report, though consisting mainly of words, may also appeal to the eye through the letterhead, page layouts, use of charts, and so on. Newspapers and magazines are visual to an even greater extent. Television, motion pictures, and live presentations have a divided aural and visual appeal. Messages sent by telephone, radio, and audio records and tapes can be received only through the ear.

ORGANIZATIONAL USES OF COMMUNICATION

Because it is so pervasive, business communication cannot easily be separated from the other activities of which it is a part. On the management level, communication enters into every movement and decision. Communication is also predominant in supervisory and clerical jobs, where reading, writing or dictating, and talking may take up most of the working day. On all levels of authority and however it is practiced in the organization, communication may be viewed functionally as either internal or external (Figure 1-2).

Internal Uses

When directed to persons within the same organization, communication serves these main purposes:

1. *To keep management informed.* Reports, written and oral, travel up the organizational ladder from workers and supervisors to executives or horizontally from one section or department to another. They are designed principally to give the responsible persons the information they need for making decisions and carrying them out. The reports may deal with financial data, technical developments, production, sales, personnel problems, and similar subjects. Much of the information is obtained with the aid of computers. Management receives other information through procedures set up to receive employees' suggestions and grievances, and through such informal means as casual conversation, hearsay, and rumor.

2. *To coordinate organizational activity.* The interdependence of functions in the organization has already been noted. Through conferences and meetings, members of the management team discuss issues and suggest or formulate policies. When decisions are made, they are transmitted to the various parts of the organization through memorandums, directives, and briefings, and discussed in private conversations and meetings. The purpose is to promote efficiency through informed and united effort.

3. *To instruct workers.* It takes a great deal of communication to keep employees abreast of changes in work rules and to train them to deal with new conditions and job requirements. Labor turnover and the influx of new employees add to the problem. Instructional methods include manuals, charts

[1] To distinguish the class of medium from particular newspapers or magazines, or radio or television stations, the latter are often referred to as *vehicles*.

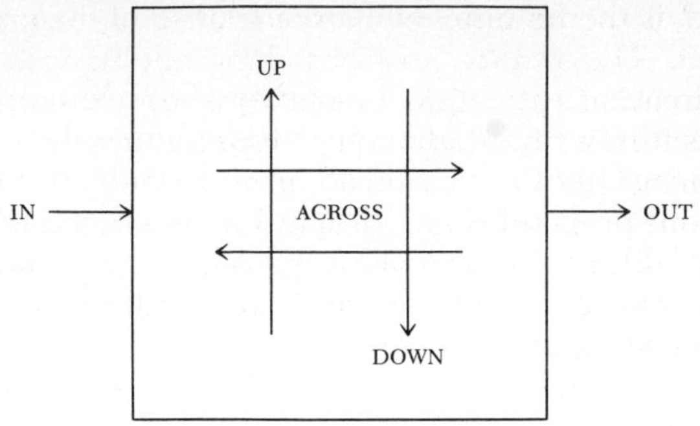

FIG. 1-2. *Communication flow in the organization.*

and worksheets, meetings, and both classroom and on-the-job instruction. The use of motion pictures and videotape is common.

4. *To maintain and improve morale.* Pay and working conditions are also the subject of much communication. Questions relating to these issues are treated through salary and promotion reviews, personal counseling, suggestion systems, and grievance procedures. Still other means are used to help workers develop pride in their jobs and in the company. This part of the program usually depends mainly on keeping employees informed about all aspects of their jobs and their company through bulletin boards, company magazines, annual reports, "family days," plant tours, and direct communications to the workers through letters, meetings, and public address systems.

External Uses

When directed outside the organization, communication has these principal tasks:

1. *To move goods and services.* Personal selling is done in retail stores, by telephone, and by salespersons who call on prospective customers at their homes or places of business. Sales are also made or assisted by mail solicitation, and advertising in newspapers, magazines, and other media. Both oral and written communication is also used to perform such peripheral functions as instructing in the use of a product, extending credit, collecting payment, and adjusting complaints.

2. *To obtain goods and services.* All organizations, whether commercial enterprises or not, spend much of their energies and resources for the necessities of their existence. Among their needs are not only land, buildings, machines, and supplies, but also personnel and professional services, furniture and decorations, food and catering services, advertising, and financing. Contracting for these needs requires some writing, whether in the form of requisitions, bid solicitations, inquiries, formal contracts, or follow-up correspondence, as well as considerable contact in person and by telephone.

3. *To educate and inform.* An important function of the organization is to apprise people of its interests, objectives, and activities. In this way it hopes to create a favorable public climate in which to operate. Public relations, as

the work is called, is the function of every member of the organization and of every department. The public relations department, where one exists, is usually the coordinating agency. Among other duties, it seeks out news of the organization, puts it in writing, and routes it to news media. Many articles in newspapers and magazines are based on material provided in press releases. The public relations program may also sponsor conducted tours of the factory or headquarters building, the loan of company-made educational films, and a speakers' bureau through which company executives are recruited to speak before social and civic groups.

4. *To communicate with stockholders and the government.* Stockholders are a numerous and important force and must receive regular reports regarding financial conditions and operations. Government agencies, too, require many different types of reports ranging from stock registration prospectuses to reports of accidents and potential health hazards. Many companies also have representatives in Washington and in state capitals to inform them of pending legislation and the possible effects on company operations. The same representatives may also serve as lobbyists in promoting their companies' legislative interests.

THE NEED FOR EFFECTIVENESS

With the great volume and utility of communication, new ways are constantly being sought to make it more effective. Greater effectiveness means not only better response, but also a better coordination of communication with the aims of the organization and greater adaptability to change. The need for effectiveness arises especially from these conditions:

1. *Communication's key role in decision making.* Because of the size and complexity of modern organizations and the availability of sophisticated mathematical tools, there is a tendency toward central decision making. The trend is consistent with the view of business as a "system" comprising a number of interdependent functions, none of which can be manipulated without causing consequences to the others. It follows that successful operation of the system depends on a reliable inflow of information to the decision centers and a corresponding outflow of messages to the points at which the decisions must be carried out. Vital to the process is the regulation of the quantity, quality, distribution, and cost of communication within the organization. Since the internal environment is essentially a social one, management must also provide an atmosphere in which people can work harmoniously and efficiently.

2. *Communications's "workhorse" status.* Apart from the purely philosophical considerations that guide management, every organization has mundane work to do, such as financing, buying, hiring, producing, supervising, and selling. These operations involve the use of many kinds of messages and a good deal of exposition and persuasion. Good communication saves time, prevents mistakes, and promotes the objectives of the organization with the least cost and the greatest results. Poor communication defeats those objectives. An example will serve to illustrate the point.

When a policyholder of a large insurance company wrote to cancel his policy, he received a reply that read:

```
Dear Mr. Blaine:

Surrender of the policy is permissible only within the
days attendant the grace period on compliance with the
citation relevant options accruing to the policy.  We
are estopped from acquiescing to a surrender prior to
the policy's anniversary date.  We are confident that
an investigation relevant to the incorporation of this
feature will substantiate that the policy is not at
variance with policies of other companies.

                              Yours truly,
```

The policyholder's reply was much clearer than the letter of the insurance company. He wrote:

```
Gentlemen:

I'm sorry but I don't understand your letter.  If you
will explain what you mean I will try to do what you
ask.

                              Yours truly,
```

Obviously, if the insurance company had written a better letter in the first place, further correspondence would have been unnecessary. As it was, the customer was annoyed, and time and money were wasted—hardly, a satisfactory way to run a business.

3. *Demands of the new media.* In recent years technology has provided great new aids to communication, but not without a price. The computer, for example, is a revolutionary tool in processing quantitative data, but it has not relieved human communicators of performing such data-related functions as selecting, evaluating, deciding, informing, and persuading. In fact, the lightning speed of the computer and the volume of work it can process result in enormous increases in the amounts of data that human communicators must interpret and put to work. Since human communication is, at best, an uncertain and underdeveloped art, the pressure grows for improved performance.

In other ways, too, business is immersed in communication technology. The revolutionary changes in mass communications—including advertising—by motion pictures, radio, and television are an old story. Once office communication was similarly revolutionized by the typewriter, telephone, and dictating machine. But now typewriters are being linked to computer adjuncts to make typing faster and more efficient. The result is a new concept in office communications—"word processing." Meanwhile, messages are being duplicated with increasing fidelity and speed on machines that make every office its own printing house. Such a flowering of communication technology must inevitably have its consequences. Thus the proliferation of paper not only increases costs, but reduces the ability of the hapless recipients to cope with the verbal flood. A related effect is the imposition on the communicator of the need to find ways to combat messages that compete for attention.

4. *Rising costs.* The cost of labor, materials, and overhead has been rising at such a rapid rate that communicators are faced with the necessity of cutting back on message volume and processing information more efficiently. The economies in operations brought by the computer have not significantly affected the cost of communication. A recent figure put the average cost of a business letter at close to $4.00 (it was $2.50 in 1969). One medium-size company sending out three million pieces of mail a year—a not unreasonable figure—budgets a half million dollars for postage alone. The related costs are high, too—for machines, supplies, labor, and overhead. A study would show that many letters, reports, and memorandums are unnecessary; but the greatest savings are usually made through such means as making messages shorter and more effective, reducing the distribution of copies, using standard or printed forms instead of personally dictated messages, and substituting the telephone for written messages where feasible.

If interpersonal communication costs are high, so too are the costs of mass communication. This is used for advertising and public relations and, on a lesser scale, for job recruitment and employee education and morale. When time is sold by the minute and fraction of a minute on radio and television, it stands to reason that a message that can effectively reach as many listeners in thirty seconds as in sixty will save a great deal of money over the length of a campaign. In print advertising, too, the cost per reader or the cost per inquiry can be materially reduced by better writing, better use of type, layout, and illustration, and better timing. Organizations that reach their employees through house publications often find that interest is increased by using fewer words and more pictures, or by changing from a magazine format to a newspaper format. The use of movies, closed-circuit television, and public-announcement sound systems in offices and factories may also help management communicate with employees who cannot be reached effectively by print media.

5. *Competitive and social pressures.* When business goes out to meet its public—its customers, prospective customers, and the community at large—the need for effective communication takes on a special urgency. The impact of advertising costs has already been mentioned. But there are other dimensions to the problem. Competition, for example, is a characteristic of the enterprise system; and the lion's share of the profits goes to those who not only make a better product, but market it most efficiently. Superiority in marketing calls for good communication with both middlemen and consumers. Such communication extends from advertising and selling the product to the other functions that affect the quality of customer relations: credit, shipping, billing, collections, adjustments, and more.

On a still broader level, effective communication must entail a statesmanlike assumption of social responsibility. Today the mass communicator has unprecedented power over the responses of the audience. Sometimes consciously, but sometimes below the level of awareness, consumers are exposed to appeals that affect their wants, their attitudes, their decisions, and their life styles. Through the sender's influence over the communication media, and the selection of material to be communicated, false or misleading information may be transmitted, and competing messages may effectively be prevented from getting through. Public concern over such consequences has led to the organization of numerous citizens' groups, congressional investigations, and independent actions of government agencies.

Whether a balance will eventually be struck between the communicators and their audiences remains to be seen. There is no question, though, that the application of undue pressure at one end inevitably leads to countermeasures at the other end. Of course, the abuses are far more prevalent (or noticeable) in advertising and mass communication than in more restricted spheres like business letters and conferences, but in any case there is a growing awareness of the need for both personal and corporate responsibility in communication matters.

THE BASIC SKILLS: WRITING AND SPEAKING

Organizations, we have seen, have many ways of communicating. For the individual in a managerial or professional position, the need to write and speak effectively is inescapable. As management expert Peter F. Drucker has said, in addressing himself to college graduates:

> If you work as a soda jerker you will, of course, not need much skill in expressing yourself to be effective. If you work on a machine your ability to express yourself will be of little importance. But as soon as you move one step up from the bottom, your effectiveness depends on your ability to reach others through the spoken or written word. And the further away your job is from manual work, the larger the organization of which you are an employee, the more important it will be that you know how to convey your thoughts in writing or speaking. In the very large organization, whether it is the government, the large business corporation, or the Army, this ability to express oneself is perhaps the most important of all the skills a man can possess.[2]

[2] In "How to Be an Employee," *Fortune*, May 1952, p. 126. Mr. Drucker's theme is echoed in *Horizons for a Profession*, a 1967 study conducted by Robert H. Roy and James H. MacNeill for the American Institute of Certified Public Accountants under a grant from the Carnegie Corporation: "To the CPA the ability to express himself well is more than the hallmark of an educated man, it is a professional necessity. Inability to express his findings in understandable, explicit, unambiguous, intelligible English can be self-defeating, potentially misleading, and possibly disastrous to clients, creditors, and investors." *Business Week* has expressed alarm over the slippage of writing ability in the executive suite. In its issue of October 25, 1976 ("Teaching the Boss to Write") it says, "Companies are having to learn to cope not only with supervisors and first-line managers who have trouble communicating, but also with senior research scientists, B-school graduates, and otherwise bright top executives who cannot turn out a clearly written, logically organized interoffice memo—and often do not realize it. . . . Some of those who are most skilled in their own field are among the poorest writers."

Educators and executives undoubtedly share this view. Something more needs to be said, however, both about the relative merits of speech and writing and about the requirements for personal effectiveness in these skills.

Writing and Speaking Compared

Through the years, "put it in writing" has been a common maxim, and faith in writing as a responsible medium has remained undiminished. Even so, the adaptability and speed of speech give it an advantage that writers often wish they could match. A comparison of writing and speaking shows, more particularly, these differences.

CHARACTERISTICS OF WRITING

1. *Writing aids control.* It encourages deliberation and precision in phrasing, fixes responsibility for authorship, permits editing and review, helps to prevent distortion and consequent misunderstandings, and can produce a legally valid record. It also ensures uniformity in instructions, procedures, and other messages that require identical action by many persons.
2. *Writing is mechanically efficient.* Messages can be set down by hand or dictated, and they can be conveniently transcribed, transmitted, filed, and retrieved. Copies in any number are also easy to make and distribute at relatively low cost.
3. *Writing is personally convenient.* The sender can do his writing or dictating at a time that suits him. Conversely, the receiver can put aside a written message until he is ready to give it his full attention. He can also reread it at will and cut out or mark portions for future reference.

For all its advantages, writing can be time consuming in composition, slow in transit, and costly to type or print and deliver. It also requires more formal skills than speaking and much of it is therefore badly phrased and ineffective. Many companies spend large sums to train employees to write and additional sums to hire professional writers and editors. The costs and delays attending the use of letters, especially, is encouraging wider use of the telephone, which provides a remarkably efficient substitute.

CHARACTERISTICS OF SPEECH

1. *Speech is spontaneous.* It requires no preparation and may be engaged in at the moment communication is needed—by telephone, if not in person.
2. *Speech is personal.* The human voice and presence have a personal stamp that is much harder to achieve in writing.
3. *Speech is bimodal.* Meaning may be received not only by the ear, but by the eyes as well. Thus the words and tone of utterance are supplemented by gesture, facial expressions, and the physical environment in which the communication takes place.
4. *Speech has an immediate effect.* There need be no delay between the generation and transmission of the message, on the one hand, and its receipt and the response to it, on the other. Furthermore, with instantaneous response—or "feedback," as the response is called—the speaker can constantly adjust his remarks during delivery to assure a satisfactory outcome.

5. Speech leaves no record. Unrecorded speech is advantageous in many business situations. It permits giving information and exchanging ideas informally or off the record.

It stands to reason that the properties of speech that are advantageous in some circumstances may be disadvantageous in others. Thus the very spontaneity of speech has its dangers when it leads to ill-considered remarks, and the immediate feedback from speech is hardly welcome when the speaker has made a firm decision he does not wish to debate. Similarly, unrecorded remarks have their disadvantages when concrete reference is needed for legal or other purposes.

Developing Competence

To write or speak effectively requires a good grounding in language, but even superior skill with words is useful only if it is applied to the job to be done and adapted to the audience to be reached. Hence the need to center your attention on these three areas of competence: (1) language facility, (2) job proficiency, and (3) human understanding.

1. Language facility. Difficult as your on-the-job problems may be, any task is made easier when you are able to express yourself accurately, when you have a vocabulary suitable to your needs, and when you know the amenities of grammar and sentence structure. Executives are usually found to be very strict about adherence to accepted standards of English, not only because they admire correctness for its own sake, but also because they are much concerned about the impression their messages make on the receiver. Their companies often spend large sums of money to project a desirable impression, but illiteracies work to defeat this objective. Errors in English hurt effectiveness in other ways too, as when they distract the reader or listener, or distort the intended meaning.

The emphasis on English should not deceive us into thinking that possession of the language skills necessarily ensures good expression all the time. The business environment often encourages haste, and one sometimes has to settle for less than his best in order to get the work out. On the other hand, the business communicator often has opportunities to review his work and correct small errors before any serious damage is done. For the fact is that work done in the office usually passes through the hands of a secretary or typist and sometimes through several layers of supervision—a process that gives the communicator the benefit of other people's skills and judgments. No amount of review, however, is going to save the writer or speaker from the embarrassment or jeopardy in which he will be placed by basic deficiencies that should not have been brought to the job in the first place.

Another and often neglected facet of language usage has to do with the connotation, or suggestion, that words carry. In Figure 1-3 you will see what one large bank tells its correspondents about tactless language. In later chapters you will have many opportunities to learn to use words wisely as well as correctly.

2. Job proficiency. Writing and speaking skills cannot be exercised in a vacuum. You must be able to use your writing and speaking skills for the spe-

BETTER LETTERS

Edited by J. Harold Janis

Route to:
Name

Three Enemies of Tact

"Tact," says the American Heritage Dictionary, "is the ability to appreciate the delicacy of a situation and to say the kindest or most fitting thing."

Among the enemies of tact, three come immediately to mind:

1. SUSPICION. A customer writes that his account had been incorrectly charged. The customer's claim is correct. The suspicious writer says, "We have investigated your claim and find you are correct."

The <u>tactful</u> writer says, "We are sorry about the error in your November statement."

2. BLUNTNESS. A customer inadvertently returns a form unsigned. The blunt writer says, "You neglected to sign this form."

The <u>tactful</u> writer says, "Will you please sign the form."

3. NEGATIVISM. A customer opens a new account. The negative writer says, "If any problems should arise in connection with this account, please let me know."

The <u>tactful</u> writer says, "Please let me know whenever I can be of help."

FIG. 1-3. *Advice on using words from one of a continuing series of bulletins for bank correspondents.* [Courtesy of Manufacturers Hanover Trust Company, New York.]

cific business tasks you want to accomplish. If you are a credit correspondent, for example, you must know where to get credit information and how to evaluate it. You must also know how much information you can give to others without betraying confidences or getting your employer into legal difficulties. And you must know what government regulations apply in granting credit and in using credit information. So, too, in marketing, accounting, purchasing, traffic management, insurance, and other fields—every job has particular requirements that control the nature and content of messages that have to be sent. Competence in meeting these requirements is as necessary as language skills. As a matter of fact, practically every employee obtains his job because of his job competence. Unless he is hired primarily for his writing or speaking ability, the test of his communication proficiency usually comes later.

3. *Human understanding.* In addition to language facility and job proficiency, you should have an understanding of human behavior. Writing and speaking are in themselves forms of human behavior, expressing as they do the communicator's response to his environment. Discourtesy in a letter, for example, is not just the result of using the wrong words, but of reacting badly to a situation. If you can understand and control your emotions, you automatically improve the message effectiveness.

Primarily, though you must be concerned with the behavior, or reactions, of the receiver. Certain generalizations about human nature are, of course, possible. Almost everyone responds to considerate treatment. The desire for recognition and appreciation is also universal. So, too, is the desire for security, money, leisure, health, and self-improvement. People are curious, ambitious, gregarious, sometimes timid, lazy, or shy. Still, success in communicating depends largely on the awareness of the motives and feelings of the one individual or class of individual you are addressing, and your ability to fashion the message accordingly. Thus one writer, in recruiting high-school girls for part-time clerical jobs, found the best results, not in the appeal of good working conditions and fair pay, but simply in telling about the other girls from the same schools who were currently employed with the firm. It appeared that the company's greatest obstacle to recruiting had been the fear of both the girls and their parents that the girls would be working in strange surroundings. The knowledge that other girls from the same school would be working with them gave them the assurance they needed. The communicator's skill in this instance came not from any special skill in using words, but from an understanding of the people to be reached.

The Rewards of Proficiency

If a job requires the ability to write and speak, proficiency in these skills offers commensurate rewards. Personal satisfaction rates high among the benefits. Nothing, in fact, is so frustrating as having ideas and not being able to put them accurately into words. Facility of expression, on the other hand, builds self-confidence. It is also a principal means of getting ahead. Our society places a high value on a man's or woman's ability to communicate, and skill in that respect may bring generous rewards in personal recognition and influence. At the same time those who can write or speak well are likely to seek opportunities to exercise that ability in ways that bring them to the attention of others. Many executives owe their positions at least partly to a timely memorandum, a letter, or a report they wrote earlier in their careers.

Just as your ability to communicate is necessary to your own success, so it is necessary to your employer's, who has a special stake in the impressions you make on others. For, symbolically at least, everyone who writes and speaks for the company *is* the company. If your manner of expression shows good judgment and language proficiency, if it does credit to the organization and promotes its objectives, you become much more important to the enterprise than your salary may indicate.

There is still another facet to your activities as a writer or speaker. As we have already pointed out, all communication has consequences to the receiver as well as the sender. By modifying the message so that it minimizes any painful results and improves the beneficial effects, you receive additional satisfaction from your work. If, too, you are conscientious enough to regard your work as a public trust, you may find gratification in the fact that, however limited your contribution, you have a share in those most sublime labors—removing ignorance, spreading knowledge, and promoting human understanding.

GETTING STARTED

If you are going to improve your communication skills, you will need a lot of practice. The projects at the end of this chapter will help you get started. Most of them require you to use some form of written expression. We think it will be helpful, therefore, to brief you on some of the qualities your instructor will be looking for in your work. These qualities will be dealt with in more detail at various points throughout the text, but the suggestions that follow should serve for the present.

What to Do

1. Direct your message to the interests of the reader.
2. Organize your material for effectiveness and ease of comprehension.
3. Be concise, but not at the expense of necessary details or a pertinent illustration.
4. Be courteous and tactful always.
5. Be yourself. Write or speak naturally, simply, and directly; don't resort to stale phrases.
6. Be specific rather than general, concrete rather than vague. Use facts and figures wherever possible.
7. Cultivate clarity in content and language; see that every statement says exactly what you mean.
8. Emphasize the positive (not negative) side of every transaction. For example, tell what *is* your policy rather than what is *against* your policy; tell what you *can* do rather than what you *cannot* do.
9. Use language in ways that are generally acceptable. You needn't be pedantic about your English, but don't be careless either.

A Specific Illustration

To show you how these suggestions work in practice, let's assume that you are writing a course report on consumer protection. To obtain information about the help given the consumer by your own city government, you address a letter to its Department of Markets. The reply you receive reads as follows:

```
Dear ----------:

Acknowledgment is hereby made of your letter of recent
date in re consumer protection.  This is to inform you
that this matter does not come within the jurisdiction
of the Dept. of Markets and you should therefor not
expect us to be of any help.

Hoping this is satisfactory, we remain

                                  Very Truly Yours,
```

If we were to judge this letter by the standards enumerated previously, we would reach these conclusions:

1. The letter is not directed to the reader's interests; it provides no help.
2. No fault can be found with the organization of the letter, nor with its ease of comprehension.
3. The letter is not concise in some of its phrasing (*receipt is hereby acknowledged; this is to inform you that*); it is too concise in that it leaves out information as to where the desired information can be obtained.
4. The letter is discourteous both in its failure to help and in the phrase *you should not expect us to help.*
5. The letter has a number of stale phrases: *receipt is hereby acknowledged; letter of recent date; in re* (Latin for *regarding*); *hoping this is satisfactory;* and *we remain.*
6. The letter is not specific. If the Department of Markets does not have jurisdiction, what department does? Where is it located?
7. The closing paragraph does not make sense in the light of what precedes.
8. The letter is negative in that it tells what the department cannot do in response to the inquiry instead of providing information as to where the desired information can be obtained.
9. The English usage is faulty in these respects: *Dept.* should be spelled out; *therefor* is incorrectly used for *therefore;* and *Truly Yours* in *Very Truly Yours* should not be capitalized.

If the writer could have taken advantage of this kind of criticism before the letter was sent, you would probably have received a letter like this:

```
Dear ----------:

You can probably obtain the information you want from the
Department of Consumer Affairs, Room 80, Municipal
Building, 120 Park Street.  Their telephone number is
555-1234.

Good luck with your report.

                              Very truly yours,
```

The letter now seems to conform in all respects to the prescribed standards. It is directed to the reader's interests; it is well organized, concise, courteous, natural, specific, clear, positive, and correct in its use of language. Only *you* would know for sure if it met your needs.

SUMMARY

Business communication is a pervasive influence in business and on the everyday lives of all citizens. It is worth studying because it plays a key role in decision making, it is necessary to business effectiveness, and it demands understanding if it is to be used wisely.

Communication can be classified as interpersonal, group, or mass; as verbal or nonverbal; and as scribal (written), aural (received by the ear), or visual. Inside the organization, communication is used to keep management informed, to coordinate activities, to instruct workers, and to maintain and improve morale. Directed outside the organization, communication is used to sell goods and services; to maintain contact with suppliers; to satisfy the needs of stockholders, the government, and the public; and to create a favorable climate in which to conduct business.

Commensurate with the great need for communication in business is the value placed on communication effectiveness. For only by being effective can communication smooth the decision-making and administrative processes, while at the same time it meets rising costs. Other burdens on business communication are the pressures it must face both from competition and from a society with its own claims for openness and honesty in business dealings.

The basic tools of business communication are writing and speaking. Writing has important advantages to the organization because it aids control and it is mechanically efficient and personally convenient. On the other hand, it takes time to compose, and it is slow in transit and costly to type or deliver. It also takes a great deal of skill that many communicators do not possess. Speech is the more spontaneous and personal medium; it obtains an added dimension by the presence of the speaker and by the physical environment in which the speech takes place; it can be received and acted on immediately; and it leaves no record. These properties of speech may be advantageous at times and disadvantageous at other times.

To be an effective communicator, you should have facility with language, proficiency in your job, and an understanding of and sympathy for your fellow human beings. You receive your rewards in personal advancement and in the satisfactions that come from self-expression and the opportunity to interact with other people for the good of all.

As you start your writing assignments in the course, you will need to cultivate many qualities, but above all try to be clear and concise, considerate of the reader, and fresh and natural in your choice of words.

TOPICS FOR DISCUSSION

A. The word *communication* was barely heard a half century ago. Today it has become a "vogue" word, with one failure or another attributed to "lack of communication." Can you explain the reasons for the change?

B. Is there a tendency to expect too much from communication? Or is the term used to cover too broad a spectrum of human activities? What social ills, for example, are *not* due to poor or nonexistent communication?

C. Consider the relation of verbal to nonverbal communication in the classroom. Is there too little (or too much) of one or the other? How might a better balance be achieved, and with what results?

D. Consider a major purchase you recently made. To what extent, and in what specific ways, did communication play a part in that purchase? Compare your experience with those of your classmates.

E. In what specific ways could the telephone be useful to an applicant in obtaining a job?

F. Assuming that good English is important to good business communication and considering the importance of business in our society, how do you explain the apparent decline of interest in the teaching and learning of good English in the schools?

G. With your book open to the section of this chapter called "The Organizational Uses of Business Communication," pages 5–7, let each member of the class cite a specific instance of one of those uses with which he or she has personal experience. As a group, try to obtain examples of all of the internal and external uses mentioned.

H. The section "The Need for Effectiveness," pages 7–10, names five conditions that make effectiveness imperative. Let the class be divided into several committees to meet simultaneously, each dealing with a different condition. Under a leader elected by the members of each group, the members will contribute what they know about the subject from personal experience, as, for example, from working at a job, or observing work performed, or participating in some communication-related activity. After fifteen minutes of discussion, the chairpersons will report to the whole class, following which the instructor will call on the class for a general discussion and a summary of the findings. At the discretion of the instructor, this assignment may be announced some days in advance in order to give students the opportunity to recollect their experiences.

I. An investment house brings together each month a panel of nationally known economists who discuss the state of the economy for 40 minutes. The discussions are put on tape cassettes and sold on a subscription basis for $75 a year. Can you suggest any advantages that the tapes might have over a printed format? Any disadvantages?

J. Look ahead to Problem 7, page 20. Apart from Mr. Darvin's poor use of English, how would you account for the apparently poor communication between the customer and the store? What could be done by either or both parties to improve the situation?

K. Analyze each of the following messages from the point of view of the writer's knowledge of human behavior. Offer suggestions for improvement.

Dear Prof:

The flu will keep me out of class for the next week at least.

If you think I'm going to miss anything important, will you write and let me know the assignments.

Sincerely,

John Student

Dear Mr. Smith:

We regret to inform you that your application for employment with this company has been turned down for the reason that you do not meet the high requirements of our personnel.

Very truly yours,

Super Duper Corporation

PROBLEMS

1. Using the *Business Periodicals Index,* which you will find on the reference shelf in your library, take an inventory of the articles that have appeared in the last year under the heading "Communication in Management" and other headings that you will find in the cross references. What particular area or facet of the subject appears to command the greatest interest? Can you explain why? Put your comments in a single paragraph for submission to the instructor.

2. To the best of your ability keep a record of all the business writing that comes to your attention during a single day. Write a paragraph on your findings, indicating whether your awareness of business communication has in any way been heightened by the experience.

3. To demonstrate your ability to express yourself in writing, submit a theme of about 500 words on one of the following topics. Use whatever treatment you consider appropriate to the subject.
   (*a*) The importance of communication in my chosen work
   (*b*) Advertising excesses
   (*c*) Where have all the sales clerks gone?
   (*d*) Why Johnny can't write
   (*e*) Taxation without obfuscation (or: Try—just try—to fill out Form 1040.)

4. At the direction of your instructor, be prepared to step up to the front of the classroom and present in one minute a single idea on the subject of "Why Study Business Communication." Develop a visual aid that will help you put the idea

across effectively in the time allowed. In preparing this assignment, consult Chapter 16, "Speech Communication."

5. Develop a simple two- or three-minute demonstration in the use of some simple gadget or instrument. Be prepared to discuss with the class the utility of the non-verbal modes of presentation you have used.

6. Rewrite the letters in Topic K, page 19, in order to improve the tone.

7. After studying all the information supplied, rewrite the following letter to make it more effective.

```
                                112 Ferry Point Road
                                Harmon Station, MD 21501
                                November 22, 19--

Capital Department Store
200 Charles Center
Baltimore, MD 21201

Gentlemen:

Is this the way you do buisness, paying no attention
to complaints and making threats against innocent
peple.

I payed you're bill months ago, still you keep writting
pay pay or else.  Theres something wrong with your
computter, not with me.  Get off my back or I will make
trouble for you, youll see.

                                 Very truly yours,

                                 Henry Darvin
```

The facts are these: Mr. Darvin bought a table radio on June 16 for $39.50. He brought it back on June 20 with the complaint that the switch was defective. The store replaced the radio, but then mistakenly charged his account $39.50 without crediting him for the return of the first purchase. On July 12, the customer paid the store $39.50 by check and explained in a note on the bill that the second charge for $39.50 was an error. The store, however, kept sending statements with the charge $39.50 on them, the last several accompanied by strong demands for payment.

2
The Concept of Communication

ON ENTERING the office of a friend, a visitor was attracted to a wall sign, intended evidently for employees. It read:

> DON'T JUST WRITE—
> COMMUNICATE!

The visitor pondered the meaning. Isn't writing communicating? Can one write and *not* communicate? Such speculation can be resolved, but only if we understand the *concept* of communication. When is communication achieved? How does it work? What is its special significance in organizations? Here we will try to answer these and related questions.

COMMUNICATION DEFINED

What is communication? The meanings are numerous. Which you choose depends on the context in which you place the word. In one sense, it is the sending and receiving of messages. Thus two individuals are "in communication" with each other when they mutually correspond, telephone, or meet and talk. In a second sense, communication refers to the actual message, as in the phrase "your communication of April 3." In a third sense, communication is the psychic as well as the verbal understanding that exists between sender and receiver. In this respect, it is often observed that certain persons write or speak to each other, but that there is no "communication" between them. Probably this last meaning was in the mind of the executive who posted the sign shown above.

Our own needs will be best served if we define communication as *the process by which messages affect response.* This definition does not exclude any of the meanings already mentioned, but it does force us to take another look at the subject. When someone steps on our toe, we say "Ouch!" When we smell smoke, we look for fire. When a friend extends a hand, we give him ours. These are examples of communication because in each instance the "message" causes something to happen. A written message also causes things to happen. Whether it is a letter, a report, a written procedure, a magazine article, or fiction, it gives the reader pleasure or pain, and makes him think or act. When the response occurs, the message is said to be "getting through"—communicating.

Here three points need to be stressed:

1. *The mere act of writing or speaking is not communicating.* Communication takes place only when the message is received. If the message is not received, there cannot be a response and therefore no communication has taken place. To illustrate, a sinking ship may send a distress signal by wireless, but if the signal is too weak to be heard, there will be no response and therefore there has been no communication. So, too, a writer cannot communicate (except perhaps with himself) through a message that is unmailed, misdirected, or unread. Management, for instance, often frets about the way employees ignore rules and procedures when, in fact, employees do not even know of their existence.

2. *Communication occurs when the message arouses any response, favorable or unfavorable, apparent or not.* A reader may, for instance, misunderstand our instructions and consequently take the wrong action. This is a form of response, though one that we did not desire. In another instance, the fact that we do not receive a reply to a congratulatory letter does not mean that there was no response. The reader was probably very pleased; he just did not have the good manners to express his pleasure to us.

3. *All communication is persuasive.* Whenever any message is perceived by a human being, it alters in some degree the information that an individual possesses and therefore influences him.[1] It may present new information and thus force a reassessment of the information already held, or it may repeat information the receiver already has and thus become a reinforcing agent. In either case, the message causes a change in the receiver. Whether the change favors the sender is not material at this time; the point is that all messages—provided they are perceived—cause changes in knowledge, dispositions, attitudes, beliefs, or actions and may thus be said to be persuasive, whether or not persuasion is the intent of the sender.

[1] Jurgen Ruesch and Gregory Bateson, *Communication: The Social Matrix of Psychiatry* (New York: W. W. Norton, 1951), p. 6.

COMMUNICATION GOALS

Now, bruising someone's toe represents communication of a sort, but it is not entirely analogous to speaking or writing. An important difference is that a misstep and the response to it are involuntary acts, but writing and speaking are deliberate; and being deliberate, they can be directed to particular goals.

Influence: The Main Goal

When we write or speak, we not only expect a response; we try to stimulate and control the response. Our purpose is to direct the receiver's feelings, thoughts, and actions into channels that will help us fulfill the aims we have for ourselves and our organization. In this respect, the question is not only what we want to say, but how we want the reader or listener to react. Effectiveness, not mere telling, is the goal.

Subsidiary Goals

The fact that we aim principally to influence the receiver's response does not preclude our striving for other goals at the same time. These, for instance:

Self-expression. We write to satisfy some creative urge or to find an outlet for our feelings. Even in business we may obtain satisfaction from our ability to put thoughts into words and from the opportunity to express thanks, regret, joy, dismay, or sympathy.

Social interchange. Some of our messages help us to cement friendships and give us a sense of belonging to some group. In this spirit we write to make a luncheon appointment with a friendly competitor, arrange a meeting of the bowling club, or report personal tidbits for the company's magazine.

Personal advancement. All messages are advertisements for ourselves. We use them to improve our immediate situation, cultivate the esteem of others, and achieve status or prestige.

The "Shared Goal"

The goals of the writer or speaker find a parallel in the goals of the receiver. For the reader or listener, too, has needs and desires that he wishes to gratify, and he will as far as possible utilize the message to achieve his objectives. Our message is therefore most effective when it strikes a balance between our aims and the receiver's, and succeeds in satisfying both. This is the principle of the *shared goal.*

A collection letter, for example, is effective to a degree when it results in even a grudging remittance. But the letter is much more effective when it elicits, along with the check, the reader's expressed or felt response, "You've been very considerate. Thanks." Such a response means that we have succeeded in keeping the goodwill of the reader and in making possible a continuance of our relationship with him. The customer, on his part, has also won a point because, in a situation that could have proved embarrassing to him, he was permitted to preserve his self-esteem.

THE COMMUNICATION PROCESS

We have defined communication as a "process." But we have yet to take up the *idea* of process. Let's start with an example.

Like any other literate person, you have undoubtedly on occasion written a letter to your parents or a friend. Ideally, you had a picture of the receiver in your mind as you wrote. You had something to say, of course, but you were also responding to what you believed your reader wanted to know and what he or she felt and understood. Thus you had some imagined guidelines to determine not only what you would say, but how you would frame the message—what words you would use, what attitude you would display. And when you got a reply to your letter, you knew how well you had succeeded in taking your reader's measure.

You were probably not conscious of it at the time, but you were interacting with the reader. Your letter was part of a process, just as the idea of process is part of communication itself. Writing, for example, is not an isolated or arbitrary act. Rather, it has its beginning in some need for expression; the message is fitted to the reader and the requirements of the situation; and the response completes the loop. All communication—verbal and nonverbal—works in a similar way. Every message is part of a continuum, or series of influences, that must be understood if communication is to be understood and carried on effectively.

SOME BASIC MODELS

A common way to show how communication works is to use a model, or simplified representation, of the particular phenomena being examined. The use of several models enables us to view communication from a number of different points of view.

Message-Oriented Model

The most elementary model, and the least satisfactory, views communication as consisting of a source and a message (Figure 2-1). The source decides what is to be said, and the message is the receptacle for the desired statement. This model is message-oriented because the source is concerned only with making a statement. It is entirely one sided. It does not take into account the interests of the receiver or the receiver's capacity to understand the message and be affected by it. An example is provided by the egocentric artist or writer who is so concerned with his own need for expression that he is oblivious to the effect of his work on others.

Receiver-Oriented Model

When a balance is drawn between the needs of the sender and those of the receiver, the result is the receiver-oriented model (Figure 2-2). This model puts the source (now the sender) and the receiver in complementary positions, and each is equally important to the process—the sender by composing the message, the receiver by providing the target audience to which the mes-

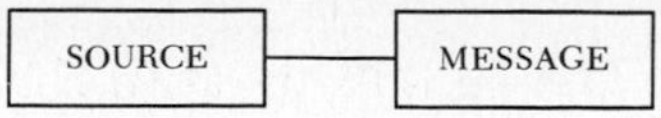

FIG. 2-1. *Message-oriented model.*

sage can be adapted. As we shall see, receiver-oriented communication does not fully achieve the interaction essential to good communication, but it marks a definite improvement over message-oriented communication and probably conforms to most people's ideas of what communication is.

FIG. 2-2. *Receiver-oriented model.*

Response-Oriented Model

A distinct advance over the receiver-oriented model is the response-oriented model (Figure 2-3). Here the sender is shown transmitting a message to a receiver for the purpose of obtaining a response. The response is then used as a measure of the success of the original message and as a guide to fashioning succeeding messages. This process may be carried on indefinitely, with the sender and receiver continually exchanging roles. Stuart Chase once wrote, "Listening is the other half of talking. A message is 50 per cent sending and 50 per cent receiving."[2] The reciprocal relation of "listening" and "talking" is a characteristic of communication at its best.

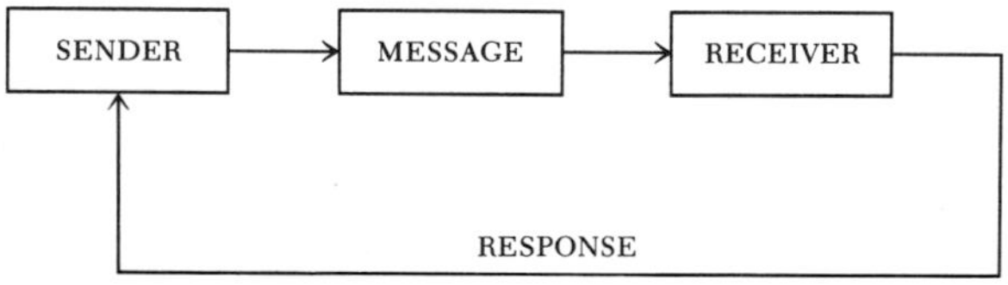

FIG. 2-3. *Response-oriented model.*

THE CONSTITUENT ELEMENTS EXAMINED

So far the constituent elements of the communication process have been identified as the sender, the message, the receiver, and the response. We will now take a closer look at these elements and the parts they play.

The Sender

Guided by the nature of the response desired, the sender fashions the message. In the process he applies his knowledge of the receiver and of the situation, his familiarity with business procedures, and his skill in thinking and

[2] *The Power of Words* (New York: Harcourt Brace Jovanovich, 1953), p. 165.

writing or speaking. All the time, he is influenced by his own feelings and attitudes and by the culture or environment in which he operates.[3]

An illustration can be given. Mary Adams is called on to write an advertisement for a new American car. On the basis of the information she has about the consumer and the car, the copywriter decides to emphasize the performance of the car rather than, for example, its appearance or price. She can write effective copy because she believes thoroughly in the product she is selling and has had considerable experience herself with cars. She realizes, too, that the automobile business is highly competitive, and so she tries to persuade the reader that the car she is advertising will outperform other cars in the same general class, especially foreign cars that have been cutting into domestic sales.

As part of her strategy, the copywriter uses the phrase "Needs half the oil changes of the leading import." When the copy is examined by the advertising agency's review board, however, that phrase is stricken from the ad. Although the advertiser believes it to be true, the variables in such a claim are so unpredictable that it is highly unlikely that the claim could be validly upheld. The uncertainty is increased by the fact that the Federal Trade Commission has recently been bearing down rather heavily on automobile advertising. In other times, the claim would have been used without question, but the climate for advertising has changed. Perhaps there has been too much of it; perhaps too much of it has been misleading; perhaps the consumer did not have the champions he has today. In any event, communicators must be aware of the currents not only in their own organizations and industries, but in society as a whole, and their messages must reflect their sensitivity to them.

The Message

The intelligence transmitted to the receiver is the message. The sender takes a set of related thoughts and finds words for their expression. At the same time care must be exercised that the thoughts so "encoded" are correctly interpreted when they are "decoded" by the receiver. What we have to consider, then, are (1) the content of the message, (2) the language, and (3) the possible distortion of the message by what we shall call "noise."

CONTENT

Insofar as it is possible to distinguish between the content of the message and the language, the content is chosen on the basis of such factors as the writer's purpose, the reader's needs and expectations, the amount of information available, the organization's customs and policies regarding its written communications, the medium that carries the message, and the timing. A few examples will show the influence of these factors:

Purpose. In sales writing, information is carefully selected to influence the reader's purchases, and therefore cannot be expected to be complete or impartial.

[3] This point is the subject of the article "The Writing Behavior of Businessmen," reproduced on pages 114–120.

Reader's needs. In answering inquiries, a credit agency will give much less information to a hotel interested in the financial responsibility of a guest than it would to a company contemplating a major loan to the same person.

Information available. A brokerage house, asked to give an opinion about the securities of a certain company, will have to do much more hedging if information is unavailable or out of date than if it were working from a substantial current file.

Company policy. An industrial firm ensures the receipt of uniform data from each inspector by providing printed forms for its inspection reports.

Medium. A message on a post card must necessarily be short and not confidential. "Please call for the merchandise you left for repair" is more suitable for such a message than "Please call for the diamond bracelet you left for repair."

Timing. June graduations provide the theme of a department store's advertisement featuring gift suggestions.

LANGUAGE

Besides knowing what to say, the writer must find a suitable set of words to give his thoughts expression. The purpose is not only to transmit the message with precision, but to endow it with interest, warmth, conviction, and other qualities conducive to obtaining the desired response. Here is the opportunity for the author's skill and creative instincts to achieve full realization. In the following advertisement for the National Book Committee, Inc., the copywriter clearly shows these qualities.

ABCDEFGHIJKLMNOPQRSTUVWXYZ

Your public library has these arranged in ways that make you cry, giggle, love, hate, wonder, ponder, and understand.

It's astonishing what those twenty-six little marks can do!

In Shakespeare's hands they became *Hamlet.*

Mark Twain wound them into *Huckleberry Finn.* James Joyce twisted them into *Ulysses.* Gibbon pounded them into *The Decline and Fall of the Roman Empire.* Milton shaped them into *Paradise Lost.* Einstein added some numbers and signs (to save time and space) and they formed *The General Theory of Relativity.*

Your name is in them.

And here we are, using them now.

Why? Because it's National Library Week—an excellent time to remind you of letters, words, sentences, paragraphs. In short, books—reading.

You can live without books, of course. But it's so limiting.

With books you can explore the past, guess at the future and make sense out of today.

Read. Your public library has thousands of books, all of which are yours for the asking.

> And add books to your own library. With each book you add, your home grows bigger and more interesting.

Of course, not all writing sounds like that. Some messages are stilted, some are verbose, some are insipid, some are offensive. What makes the difference is the language "behavior" of the writer. This behavior is conditioned by the pressures exerted on him by the organization; but it is also affected by other factors. One of these is the writer's attitude toward the subject of the message, and toward himself and the reader.

With regard to the writer's attitude toward the subject of the message, it is to be expected that one will approach the writing of a letter of condolence or a formal resolution with somewhat different feelings from those that control the writing of a mail-order advertisement, and that the dignity of his language will vary accordingly. The writer's attitude toward himself may be evident in his boasting or timidity, self-assurance or self-depreciation. Thus the salesman who has called on a customer and is uncertain about the impression he has made may reveal his insecurity by writing. "I hope I didn't bother you too much" instead of, "It was good to talk to you the other day." The writer's feelings toward the reader may be expressed by friendliness at the one extreme and hostility or distrust at the other. "We are surprised to hear from you" and "Thank you for writing to us" are two ways of acknowledging a complaint; the difference in attitude is apparent.

Additional factors that control the language of the message are the limits of the writer's vocabulary and his sense of style and usage. An inadequate store of words severely limits the ability to express oneself with precision. Take the sentence:

> An important *point* a man must have to succeed in the job is a knowledge of cost accounting.

How much better that sentence would be—how much more exact—if the writer had used the word "qualification" instead of "point." In other instances a writer misuses the word "forward" for "send"; or dictates "We appreciate your writing in regard to this matter" when the first four words would be sufficient; or writes one sentence of 60 words instead of three averaging out to 20 words; or says, "Your check has been received by us" when "We have received your check" would be more simple and direct. In each instance, the writer has had a choice, exercising it in one way rather than in another. The use of language is full of choices, and the decisions the writer makes determine the manner of the writing—good, bad, or indifferent.

"NOISE"

The fact that a message is sent and received does not ensure that the meaning is preserved during the passage. Audio engineers have for a long time applied the term *noise* to the static, interference, loss of power, or other mechanical condition responsible for distortion of a signal as it travels from one point to another. The word has come into general usage to signify the loss of meaning from any cause during the encoding or decoding process. At the one end, for example, there may be a typographical error, bad enunciation, a wrong word, or an ambiguous sentence. At the other end there may be deficient hearing, bad reading habits, or a weak vocabulary. Even in the best of circumstances, the limitations of words are such that they cannot have precisely the same meaning for everyone. Each person filters them through his own memory and associations and extracts information that is somewhat different in every case. If the gap in meaning is sufficiently wide, serious misunderstanding will result.

An illustration is provided by a letter from a credit bureau. "We are sorry," it said, "that we have been unable to develop any *positive* information about your prospective customer." By positive information the writer meant "any information that can help you." But the reader, taking *positive* to mean "favorable," concluded that the prospective customer was a bad risk—an inference that he later found was incorrect. The deterioration in meaning cost him a big order.

When noise results from the misuse or misinterpretation of language, the term *semantic barrier* is sometimes used to describe the communication deficiency. In Figure 2-4, the vertical line graphically points up the difference that often exists between the encoder's meaning and the receiver's interpretation of a message.

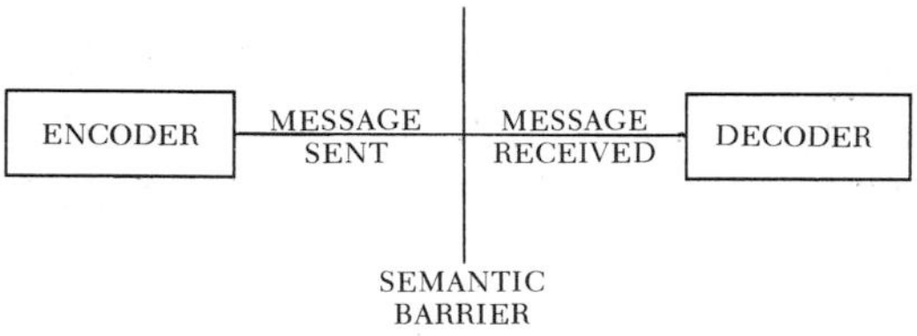

FIG. 2-4. *Model showing how meaning is altered as the message passes from the encoder (sender) to the decoder (receiver).*

The Receiver

Like the sender, the receiver brings to the message his experience, attitudes, knowledge, and communication skills. And these in turn are affected by the environment in which he operates. A worker may not hear the spoken instructions given him because of noise from machinery, or he may not understand what he hears because of inexperience with the terminology. He may be able to overcome these barriers by asking questions. If he feels insecure, however, or is distrustful of management, he may avoid further communication, with the result that the original misunderstanding is turned into errors in job performance. On the other hand, he may understand the signals communicated to him, but decide to ignore them. He will, for example, have no difficulty in understanding the "No Smoking" sign posted directly in front of his workbench. But if the rule is generally violated without penalty, he may feel no pressure to observe it.

The Response

The response to the message tells to what extent the sender has succeeded. Response can be described as either overt or hidden. An *overt response* is one that is manifest. It may be a facial expression, or a gesture, or applause; or it may be an order, a telephone call, a face-to-face reply, a letter, or a coupon returned. A *hidden response* is one that is not apparent to the sender. It may be pleasure, gratitude, anger, resentment, or some other feeling that is not openly expressed, though it may be eventually translated into some overt action. The overt and hidden responses may come simultaneously, but often the overt response is withheld until some later time when it finds expression in, say, new business, a testimonial to a friend, or a decision to buy elsewhere.

Face-to-face communication almost invariably brings some overt response; but this kind of response is less certain in written communication. A writer may try to stimulate a response by asking directly for a reply, as when he writes, "Please let me know if this arrangement is satisfactory." This is a good tactic because it is much easier to deal with a reader (perhaps a customer) when we know how he feels than when we do not. But even when the writer neither seeks nor expects a reply, he will try to couch his message in terms that will produce good feeling rather than bad, for good feeling always brings greater material rewards in the long run.

INTERACTION

Any study of the response in communication must deal with the interaction of the sender and the receiver. For, as we have seen, communication is not merely the sending of messages; it is also "listening"—obtaining clues from the receiver to help us fashion messages that will bring the response we want. Two ways to obtain such clues are embraced in the concepts of *feedback* and *empathy*.

Feedback

The function of the writer as receiver may be contrasted with that of the speaker. The speaker is in continuous communication with his audience. As he talks, they respond, and he regulates his speech accordingly. When people in the back of the room strain to hear him, the perceptive speaker takes notice and speaks louder. If members of the audience appear restive, he may speed up his delivery or relate an anecdote to snap them back to attention. If they heckle him, he may turn conciliatory; if they interrupt his remarks with applause, he may speak longer than he had planned. Thus the speaker's message and the response of the audience—the cause and the effect—are interdependent.

The response that enables the speaker to adjust his message to the audience is called *feedback*. The term has its origin in electronic communication. With the help of a wall thermostat, for example, information about the temperature of a room "feeds back" to the furnace, which responds automatically by turning up the heat or temporarily checking it. The process is repeated whenever the temperature of the room varies from a predetermined level. The importance of feedback, whether to the furnace or to the speaker, is that it permits the source of the original signal or message to adjust instantaneously to faults in the output or effect. As a result, the desired pattern of response may be obtained.

Unfortunately, no exact parallel can be drawn between the feedback available to the speaker and that available to the writer. Usually the writer must complete and send his message before he can get a response. By that time it is too late for him to use the feedback to influence the message. He can use it only as a guide in sending future messages. Thus if the reader's reply shows that he has been offended, the writer in the next message may be conciliatory or contrite, but he does not have the opportunity of the speaker to correct himself as he composes the message. The writer may minimize this disadvantage by submitting the message in advance to the criticism of business associates or experts in the field. Where large numbers of readers are involved, he may send the message to some of them and wait for their reaction before committing himself to the whole audience. Following this principle, a food packer may test the effect of a "double-your-money-back" offer in one medium-size city before advertising it nationally. The response from the sample audience will help determine what alterations in the message are necessary.

Empathy

Whatever the possibilities of feedback in written communication, the chief means of self-correction in the writer lie in his *expectations* of the reader's response. Such expectations are the result of *empathy*, a psychological process by which one person projects himself into the consciousness of another.[4] As Figure 2-5 shows, actual response may be fed back to the writer and influence future messages. Empathic feedback, however, has a direct salutary effect on the composition of the present message.

Empathy is a common human experience. When we select a gift, for example, we seem to sense what will win approval and what will not. The string tie may be just right for Cousin Wilbur, but giving it to Uncle Ned would border on the catastrophic. So, too, when we write. We know intuitively that Mr. A, who keeps ignoring our requests for payment, will answer only when he receives a threat. On the other hand, we can easily predict that Mr. B, who usually pays very promptly, would undeservedly be embarrassed by anything but a gentle reminder.

Invariably our expectations of the reader are affected by what we believe to be his expectations of us. We all have some position or role we must maintain. What a clerk can say or do with impunity may be considered shocking in a college professor. Every company also has an "image" it has created and wishes to preserve through its communications. Its writers must try not to disappoint. The office manager of a highly respected corporation was rightly indignant in commenting on a correspondent's shoddy English. "They may allow that sort

[4] For a detailed treatment of empathy, see David K. Berlo, *The Process of Communication* (New York: Harcourt Brace Jovanovich, 1960), pp. 116–129.

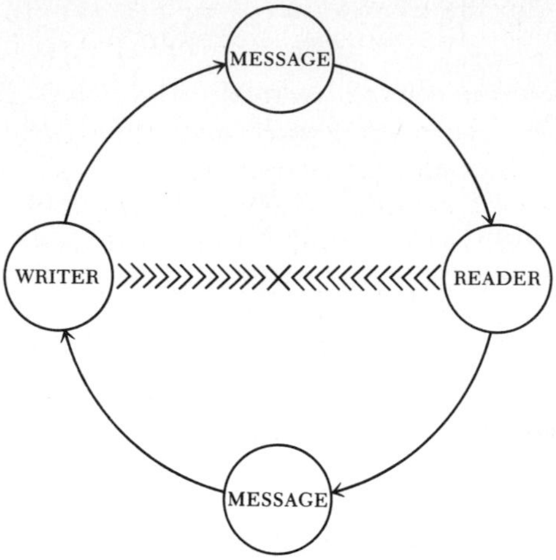

FIG. 2-5. *Two kinds of feedback. Arrows forming circle show how actual response to message is fed back to the writer. Empathic feedback, bypassing message, is shown by arrowheads in horizontal line.*

of thing in the ——— Company," he said, mentioning a disdained competitor, "but our customers expect more of us."

If we are going to write efficiently, we need to sharpen our empathic abilities, our awareness of what the reader senses. One way in which we can enter the reader's consciousness is to make inferences from our own experience. Thus if a customer tells us that she had to wait an inordinate amount of time until a salesman paid attention to her, we can think of the many times we had to wait while one salesman had to cope with a number of customers, or while he was looking the other way, arranging stock, or socializing with another salesman. Knowing how we felt in these circumstances, we are able to sense the customer's feelings and write a suitable apology. In another situation, we may be required to explain our company's stock-purchase plan to employees. By recalling our own confusion and multiplicity of questions when we were first told about the plan, we can anticipate the questions that will be asked and the need for simplicity and detail in answering them.

Many times we have no experience to match the reader's and are therefore unable to make any inferences from them. In those instances and in others we may anticipate the reader's response by putting ourselves in his place. In order to assume the reader's role, we need to know a good deal about both him and the situation. For example:

Is the reader a man or woman?
How old?
How well educated?
What is his position with relation to us and our organization?
What are his business, political, or social connections?
How much does he know about the subject?
Why would he want to know more?

What are his aims, motives, habits?
How has he responded to similar messages in the past?

Some of this information we can surmise from our personal dealings with the reader or learn from correspondence and other communications. A city health department, for example, quickly learns to distinguish between a schoolboy's need in asking for information and a physician's, and it tailors the response accordingly. We have a similar opportunity when we write a report to our employer recommending the replacement of an expensive machine the company had purchased only a year ago. By temporarily taking the part of the reader—"putting ourselves in his shoes" is the popular phrase—we are in a position to understand the questions he would ask about the need for the new machine and to answer those questions in our report.

PSYCHOLOGICAL FACTORS AFFECTING RESPONSE

We have emphasized the role of response in communication and the parts played by feedback and empathy. We have yet to examine the psychological factors that account for the kind of response received. Given the same message, a number of persons will respond in a number of different ways. We are all familiar with the real-life situation in which two witnesses to an accident recount, in contradictory terms, what they saw. Is one lying? Does either have anything to gain from the outcome? Or is each telling what he truly believes he saw? The response to any message involves similar considerations. One customer receives a letter and considers it a favor. Another receives an identically worded letter and considers it an affront. If the difference is not in the letter, can it be in the receiver? What we are suggesting is that the response to any message depends largely on the internal state of the receiver, particularly his perception and motivation. The writer or speaker must understand these factors if he is to be able to influence in a positive way the outcome of his message.

Perception

Part of the meaning of the message comes from the interplay of the receiver's senses on the message, and part of it comes from within the receiver's mind. Two men will read the same menu. Yet the attention of the first will be drawn to the steaks and chops and the attention of the second to the desserts. Perhaps the difference could be attributed to the fact that the first man is hungry and the second is not. If there is a lesson here for a steak house, it is that its advertisements will most likely get attention if they reach the prospective customer when he is hungry.

The influence of the senses and the mind can be demonstrated in still another way. Most of us read at a rate too rapid to permit us to distinguish every word and letter we see. What we rely on is the general configuration of the words and our expectations based on the nature of the text and our experience with language. Thus an author reading proof will often read words that have been omitted by the printer and he will view as correct words that are obviously misspelled. His mind has apparently supplied what his eyes failed to see. Bad proofreading is the result.

The perception and interpretation of a message may be influenced by the particular grouping in which it appears. We are all familiar with the parallel lines that seem to show one longer than the other when in fact they are both the same length. What makes the difference is whether the angles formed at the

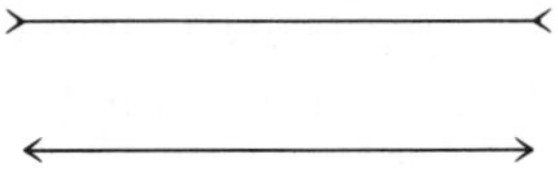

ends are turned outward or inward. A similar phenomenon occurs when readers are shown two identical pictures of a railroad train in a station, the one picture captioned "parting" and the other "arriving." On a scale ranging from *sad* to *happy*, viewers incline toward *sad* in the first instance and *happy* in the second. Other experiments show that a single word—*cold* or *warm*, for example—thrown into a particular context can materially affect the reader's interpretation of an individual's personality or, for that matter, of a company's image.[5] These examples strongly suggest that the way one perceives a message is weighted heavily in the direction of symbols with particularly strong suggestion.

Studies show that our perception of messages is also affected by our beliefs and attitudes. It has been found, for example, that buyers of new cars pay close attention to advertisements for the make of car they have bought but not to advertisements of competing makes. The reason given is that buyers seek confirmation of their original judgment and wish to avoid any dissonant elements.[6] In another instance, a company's stock certificates showed pictures of its plant with smoke billowing from its smokestacks. Years ago, this picture gave a favorable image of industry. Today the company has redesigned its stock certificate to show a smokeless plant in verdant surroundings—an image more consistent with the public interest in antipollution measures. As the examples show, a writer or speaker can benefit by calling forth ideas that are consonant with the reader's or listener's beliefs and avoiding contradictory ideas. We will have more to say about this subject in Chapter 13, "The Elements of Persuasion."

Motivation

Response is related not only to the way people view the world, but also to their needs and drives—their motivation. Some actions are taken to satisfy such elementary wants as the need for food, clothing, and personal comfort. Others are related to the sex drive, to safety and security needs, the need for love and belonging, and the need for self-esteem and self-actualization.

[5] Percy H. Tannenbaum, "The Indexing Process in Communication," *Public Opinion Quarterly*, 19 (1955), 292–302.

[6] A. R. Cohen, J. W. Brehm, and B. Latané, "Choice of Strategy and Voluntary Exposure to Information Under Public and Private Conditions," *Journal of Personality*, 27 (1959), 63.

Maslow believes that there is a hierarchy of needs and that one cannot easily think of satisfying the need of, say, self-esteem until the lower or more basic order of needs is fulfilled.[7]

Businessmen often play skillfully on the motivations of their listeners and readers. Workers may be spurred to produce more, for example, by the introduction of an element of competition—perhaps a contest involving points or prizes. A middle-aged woman debating the choice of a dress examines with special care the one the saleswoman describes as "very youthful." A credit manager succeeds in collecting an old debt when he points out that if the customer delays, he may find it difficult to get credit in the future.

The use of motivation by advertisers is well known. Products are sold not for what they intrinsically are, but for the satisfactions they provide or the needs they fill. Aspirin will relieve a headache; another pill will ease tension, or soothe the stomach, or reduce the discomfort of a cold. Other products promise improved appearance, sexual attraction, the saving of money, personal advancement, a more beautiful home, envious friends. Since some appeals produce better results than others, advertisers are constantly reexamining their markets to uncover new or stronger needs that their products can satisfy. Thus an air conditioner that at one time found its strongest appeal in its "quiet operation," during a later period of high energy costs headlined the claim that it "saves watts."

CIRCUMSTANTIAL FACTORS AFFECTING RESPONSE

Will a letter arriving on Tuesday get more attention than one received on Friday?

Will a blue return card produce more inquiries than a white one?

Will a book review quoted from the *New York Times* sell more books than one quoted from the *Denver Post*?

As these questions suggest, response involves a number of circumstances that operate fairly independently of verbal expression, though not necessarily independent of psychological considerations. These circumstances include (1) the timing of the message, (2) the physical setting in which the message is communicated, (3) the authority for the message, and (4) the previously established rapport between the sender and the receiver.

Timing

Some messages that would be effective if transmitted at one time are ineffective, even detrimental, if transmitted at another time. Thus a letter of condolence or congratulation sent immediately after the event is far more effective than one sent later. So, too, a memorandum about accident prevention gets more attention when it follows an accident than when it precedes one, and a statement of policy about the payment of tuition for employees is better

[7] Abraham H. Maslow, "A Theory of Human Motivation," *Psychological Review*, 50 (1943), 370–396.

issued just before the beginning of the school year than after classes have started.

Occasionally a message is prepared and held for distribution until the propitious time arrives. A retail store, for example, may ask a local newspaper to publish its advertisement for umbrellas only when rain is forecast. In another instance, an airline may avoid unfavorable association by omitting its newspaper advertisements for several days after one of its planes has been involved in a front-page accident. Individuals follow somewhat the same practice when they "lie low," or avoid communication, after some incident in which they have figured unfavorably.

Setting

The reader's response may be affected by the physical environment in which the message appears. In some circumstances, for example, a letter provides a more effective setting than a printed circular, and a handwritten letter gets more favorable attention than a typewritten one. Sometimes an elegant brochure brings better results than a simple folder; at other times an ordinary handbill on coarse paper conveys a sense of immediacy lacking in more pretentious forms. Advertisers in newspapers and magazines inevitably share the prestige and confidence with which the particular publication is regarded. That is one reason why advertising space in the *New York Times* is so avidly sought.

In speech communication, emphasis can be given to a meeting by holding it in the company's boardroom or similarly favored setting. A good restaurant or hotel may serve the same purpose. On the other hand, a chance meeting and conversation in the washroom may more quickly help to solve a knotty problem than a formal meeting arranged by appointment.

Whatever the form or medium used, the response to a written message is sure to be influenced by such factors as type, layout, design, illustration, paper, printing quality, and even the class of postage used. The student submitting a report to his teacher knows the practical value of an attractive cover, good arrangement, and neat typing. Corresponding attention to mechanical details helps bring results in letters and reports written by businessmen.

Authority

The results of a message are closely related to the reader's confidence in the source or encoder and his respect for the authority and integrity of either or both. Thus an opinion expressed by a subordinate may carry little weight, but let a high executive express the same opinion and it is accepted enthusiastically. So, also, the statement of a civic leader commands more attention than that of an obscure citizen, and organizations of high prestige find it easier to attract and persuade an audience than those of poorer reputation. Sometimes, however, an encoder is able to "borrow" prestige by having his message signed or otherwise endorsed by a more important personage—for example, his department head or the president of the company. Similarly, a source that is relatively unknown or obviously biased may increase confidence in the message through the use of an endorsement from a qualified outsider. Testimonial advertising provides a familiar illustration of this technique.

In addition to *employing* authority, a writer may *appeal* to authority. That is, he may deliberately address his message to a person of influence. Thus a customer wishing to make a complaint may address the president of the company instead of risking perfunctory treatment by a subordinate. "Go to the top" is good advice in a number of similar situations. Even when the top man does not personally handle the matter, his authority is a stimulus to the person to whom he refers it.

Rapport

When relations between the writer and the reader have been good—when rapport exists—there is a chance that the reader will respond as the writer desires even when the message itself is less than persuasive. When relations are poor, however, the reader is inclined to adopt a combative attitude. Accordingly, an order from a supervisor whom an employee favors is likely to be carried out promptly and efficiently. But the same order from a supervisor the reader distrusts or dislikes may be received with resentment and carried out indifferently. Similarly, a sales message from a company that has already pleased the reader will get a more ready response than one from a company that has previously given poor service or unsatisfactory merchandise. The need for rapport underscores the point that the last message cannot be much more effective than those that have preceded, for communication is cumulative.

COMMUNICATION IN ORGANIZATIONS

Although our description of the communication process is valid as far as it goes, it does not explain the way communication operates in organizational settings. The models we have shown tend to put the responsibility for results on the sender and the receiver, with emphasis on how these individuals encode and decode messages, how they interact with each other, and how they respond to psychological and circumstantial factors. In organized groups, however, it is not just the individual parties to communication that bear responsibility for the outcome; the burden rests heavily on the organizational structure itself.

Characteristics of Organizations

An organization of whatever kind is a system of overlapping and interdependent groups. Each group has its own immediate goals and methods of reaching them. It demands allegiance from its members and distributes rewards according to their contributions. Some groups represent particular subcultures with their own value systems, for example, engineers, accountants, supervisors, clerks. Other groups develop identity on the basis of sex, age, experience, or tenure. And among all, there exist certain structural relationships: some individuals perform the same tasks, some individuals are responsible to the same supervisors, some individuals have rights and privileges that others do not have, and some individuals are related through friendship and personal trust.

A complicating condition is that the relationships among individuals in the organization are not static, but are constantly changing. Some people are hired; others are promoted, transferred, or fired. New policies and procedures affect some, but not others. And often relationships hinge on the tenuous distinction of who is and who is not informed of organizational changes, developments, and decisions.

What holds such a complex and volatile structure together is communication. In fact, the organization itself is viewed as a communication system, and the communication that takes place within it as "the basic process facilitating the interdependence of the parts . . . the mechanism of coordination."[8] In the following sections we will examine some of the characteristics of communication in organizations and suggest the problems they give rise to.

Directional Flow

It has already been pointed out that messages in organizations flow upward, downward, and across. The direction of the flow has an important bearing on the nature of the communications. For example, there is a tendency to distortion in upward communication because subordinates sense that management likes to hear good news. They are thus likely to leave out of their reports items that may be disconcerting to management. They also, very humanly, build up their own accomplishments and sometimes diminish the accomplishments of their rivals.

Another aspect of the directional flow of communication in the organization is that there is more communication downward than upward. Orders, directions, and information flow down to workers from numerous sources in the management hierarchy, but there is not a corresponding flow of information upward to management. In consequence, management is often isolated from its workers' views and makes decisions without the benefit of knowledge that could be extremely helpful. Many companies try to overcome this dearth of feedback by "open door" policies and suggestion systems through which employees can share their ideas with management. One inhibiting factor in upward communication is the worker's limited view of the company's operations and his consequent inability to speak without evoking a patronizing response from his superiors. But another obstacle is the worker's all-too-frequent lack of the verbal skills needed to present ideas forcefully to management.[9]

Lateral communication between organization members on the same level of authority suffers from other difficulties. Unless committees are set up to encourage cross-fertilization of ideas, for example, there is a good deal of isolation between managers engaged in different types of work, and sometimes the isolation is aggravated by departmental rivalry and the use of specialized

[8] Everett M. Rogers and Rekha Agarwala-Rogers, *Communication in Organizations* (New York: The Free Press, 1976), p. 57.

[9] David J. Lawless, *Effective Management: Social Psychological Approach* (Englewood Cliffs, N.J.: Prentice-Hall, 1972), p. 132.

languages. At one communication conference an engineer from the Bell Telephone Laboratories told of the handicap to both him and his organization caused by his inability to talk with the engineer in the office next door, so different were their technical vocabularies.

Communication Networks

If everyone in the organization communicated freely with everyone else, there would be a chaotic overcrowding of channels. As information theorists would say, unrestricted communication produces noise in the system. The very idea of organization implies a selective approach to what is to be communicated and who are to be the recipients. Lines of communication are drawn and restrictions—formal or informal—are placed on the size of the communication "loop," that is, the circle within which an individual establishes communication channels. An executive, for example, will communicate directly with a few aides and his department heads, and they in turn will communicate with the people in their spheres of responsibility.[10]

The flow of messages within any subsystem is governed by the relationships among the members of the group. These relationships, often referred to as communication networks, take a number of different forms. Leavitt cites the following structures, among others, for a group of five persons.[11]

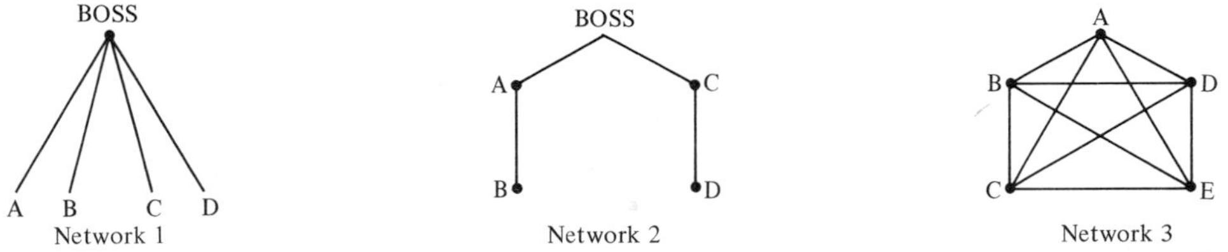

Communication experiments involving these structures provide a number of interesting conclusions.

Communication is faster when, as in Network 1, there is a direct line between the boss, or leader, and his subordinates. The boss may be happy in this arrangement because he has a number of sources of information and can use some as checks against the others. The boss is independent and powerful. The subordinates are in a less satisfying position because they lack effective contact with each other and are isolated from the center of power.

In Network 2, A and C enjoy a direct relationship with the boss, but B and D can communicate with the boss only through A and C. Under this arrangement, it is very likely that those who have the ear of the boss feel more important than those who must go through channels.

Morale is likely to be highest when, as in Network 3, each member of the group can communicate with every other member. Although the leader is A,

[10] Daniel Katz and Robert L. Kahn, *The Social Psychology of Organizations* (New York: John Wiley, 1966), p. 225.

[11] Harold J. Leavitt, *Managerial Psychology*, 3d. ed. (University of Chicago Press, 1972), pp. 189–198.

the network can operate with any other member as leader. Communication is slow here, and there may be confusion at times as messages fly back and forth in a number of different directions. However, because of the plentiful interaction and feedback, creativity is encouraged and the potential for error is minimized.

A fourth network, also cited by Leavitt, provides another opportunity for comment on the influence of group structure on communication.[12]

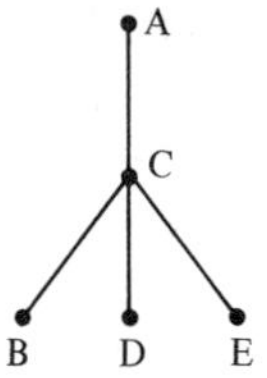

Network 4

Here C may be taken to be a secretary or administrative assistant. He is in a very powerful spot. He has faster access to the internal organization than the boss, and he is also in a position to select the information he transmits upward. March and Simon call such an individual an "uncertainty absorber" for the reason that by reducing the wealth of data pouring in from outside and from below, he gives his boss a smaller body of facts to deal with and thus, in a way, adds to the boss's confidence and efficiency.[13] However, the threat to the boss is apparent if, through oversight or deviousness, his assistant fails to transmit data important to the executive's decisions. Leavitt says that C can end up controlling the organization.

In general, loosely organized groups work slowly, but they have a compensating corrective capacity and high morale. Highly centralized groups, on the other hand, work fast and are easily controlled, but they may be used as a psychological prop by an essentially weak superior. Finally, the differences in group performance are very largely attributable to the degree of feedback available.

The Coding Process

If communication systems make it possible for people to work in concert, information is the raw material from which the systems draw sustenance. This information, however, must be processed efficiently; otherwise the complex relationships that characterize the organization will break down under the overload.

One way to approach the problem is to reduce the amount of encoding. This means "programming" messages that exhibit the same characteristics. Thus standard operating procedures take the place of the repetition of new instructions every time a task must be done. Printed forms to be filled in, like

[12] Leavitt, pp. 195–196.

[13] James G. March and Herbert A. Simon, *Organizations* (New York: John Wiley, 1958), pp. 165–166.

short-answer quizzes, also permit reports of various kinds to be rendered without the need for long exposition. The forms also have the advantage of classifying and arranging the data required so that the information in the reports can be processed most efficiently by computer or otherwise.

Similar efficiencies are achieved by changes in the symbol systems themselves. Tables, charts, and diagrams, for example, are more compact than verbal explanation. Even when words are unavoidable, however, technical terms serve as a kind of shorthand for communication between those who understand the code. Terms can also be invented to serve special needs. For example, it may take a small book to describe an intricate clerical process, but if the word COPIN will immediately and accurately call forth the process, a great deal of description is avoided when references to the process are to be made. Every employee quickly learns the technical language, or jargon, of his organization and applies it often, with considerable advantages in efficiency.

Another aspect of the encoding problem in organizations is the need to reduce the amount of supervision over the writing activities of their members. As long as employees use phrases and forms that the supervisor is familiar with and feels secure in, their supervisor can approve letters and reports quickly. But if employees invent their own phrases and forms of expression, they make the supervisor's task of review more difficult. For the new phrases slow up his reading and, because they are untried, they may in fact have faults of meaning or legal "bugs" that may not be discovered until after the message is sent or acted upon.

Of course, the conformity found in business writing is not always due entirely to legitimate pressures for efficiency or accuracy. Much of it originates in poor learning techniques or in strange ideas about what good style in writing consists of. New correspondents are often encouraged to learn their jobs by examining and imitating letters in the files. In other instances, employees and supervisors alike have preferences for certain clichés and continue to use them even when effectiveness would dictate a fresher style. The reasons may include fear of innovation, desire for approval, laziness, and lack of incentive. However, it should be encouraging to young writers in business to know that both the necessity and tolerance for individual expression increase markedly as one moves up the organizational ladder or into such fields as publicity and advertising.

SUMMARY

Communication is the process by which messages affect response. Controlling the response is the chief goal of the communicator. The receiver shares actively in the process, for he too has goals to fulfill and may use the message for this purpose.

A simple communication model is represented by a sender, a message, and a receiver, with the message serving as the meeting ground for the sender and the receiver. A more advanced model also takes account of the return of the response to the sender. Even this model is incomplete, however, unless it provides for the distortion, or "noise," caused either by mechanical faults in transmission of the message or by the misuse and misinterpretation of language.

An understanding of communication also requires that we pay close attention to the interaction that takes place between the sender and the receiver. This interaction is represented first by feedback, that is, the response returned to the sender, who uses it as a means of determining the effectiveness of his message and correcting any errors. Since feedback is possible only after the message is sent, however, a second kind of interaction—empathy—is also necessary. This is the process by which the receiver anticipates the response, and builds into his message the elements—including content and language—that will produce the optimum results.

The way in which the receiver ultimately responds to the message depends on important psychological and circumstantial factors. In the former category we include the receiver's perception and motivation. Perception is the way in which the individual "sees" the message. Partly it is the result of his sensual acuity, his internal state, and the context in which the message appears; and partly it is the result of his attitudes and beliefs. The receiver's motivation is that want or drive that the communicator taps in order to bring about the desired response. Thus a sales staff may be persuaded to improve their record by the promise of greater material rewards or by an appeal to their spirit of competition.

The circumstantial factors that aid response may include good timing, an attractive physical setting in which the message is communicated, the use of an authoritative medium (like the *New York Times*) or the attribution of the message to an authoritative source, and capitalizing on the previously established rapport between the sender and receiver.

When communication takes place within the organization, there are still other factors that must be considered. Workers who originate and receive messages do not act independently; rather, they are subject to all the pressures that their membership in the group and its subgroups entail—pressures imposed by objectives, values, and allegiances. One factor that influences organizational communication is the directional flow of messages. More messages go down the organizational ladder than up; and the feedback that does reach executives is often designed to protect the sender or spare the feelings of the receiver. The resulting inaccuracies must be reckoned with. Another factor in organizational communication is the relationships or "networks" that exist among members of working groups. In general, loosely organized groups, in which communication is carried on freely among all members, work slowly but have high morale and benefit from plentiful feedback. Highly centralized groups generate less feedback, but they work fast and can be easily controlled.

Organizations encourage systematization of expression in order to promote efficiency. The end desired is not only a reduction in working time, but also freedom from costly errors. Efficiency is also promoted by economy in the use of symbols as, for example, through the use of tables, graphs, blueprints, diagrams, and abstracts of longer communications. The use of trade or professional jargon is another method of achieving efficiency in expression.

Although there is a great need for good writing on all levels, the opportunities for individual expression increase as the communicator moves away from the need for supervision.

TOPICS FOR DISCUSSION

A. Select a written business message, preferably a business letter that you or a friend or parent has recently received, and bring it to class. Be prepared to discuss its effectiveness with relation to the circumstantial factors described in pages 35–37.

B. A municipality has imposed a two-cent tax at the retail level on every product packed in a plastic container. The purpose is to discourage the use of nonbiodegradable materials. In what way has our perception of plastics changed over the years? Of cigarette smoking? Of the use of chemical detergents? Can you suggest other areas—social and material—in which there have been dramatic changes in public perception? How do these changes relate to business communication?

C. Bring an advertisement to class and be prepared to tell what the reader motivation is. Do you consider the motivation effective with relation to the assumed reader, the publication in which the advertisement appeared, and the time of its appearance? Does the class agree?

D. In writing her bank about other business, Mrs. Rath mentioned casually that she was considering opening a savings account. The letter was forwarded to an assistant vice president in the Savings Department, whose reply to Mrs. Rath is given below. What do you think of the reader motivation in this letter? Support your answer by reference to specific words and ideas.

> Dear Mrs. Rath:
>
> Thank you for your letter of May 10 advising that you are considering opening a savings account with us. This information is very gratifying especially in view of the fact that we are now in the midst of making a concerted effort to increase our deposits prior to occupying the quarters in our new building in October.
>
> The building when completed will be 36 stories above the ground and have four basement levels. The Bank will occupy 7 floors plus a majority of the basement space. It will be one of the finest and most modern plants in the entire country when it is completed, and the next time you are in town, we would appreciate the opportunity of showing you around the new building.
>
> When you are ready to open the account, please let me know and I will be very happy to arrange all the details.
>
> Yours very truly,
>
> P.S. We are having our big push during the month of May. Thanks.

E. Many years ago the New York City Council voted to rename two blocks of Leggett Avenue as Jaburg Avenue. The action was supported by a wholesale grocery firm, R. C. Williams & Co., which had its main warehouse on Leggett Avenue. By a quirk of coincidence, the company's chief competitor was Leggett & Company, and R. C. Williams was sensitive about the Leggett Avenue address. Jaburg was the name of the family that controlled R. C. Williams & Co. A reporter for a local newspaper asked for opinions about the proposed change in the street name. The answers follow. Comment on the motivation of each reply.

Henry K. Jaburg, vice president, R. C. Williams & Co.—"We are honored to have the street named after my Uncle Hugo. We felt the name Leggett, which is also the name of one of our competitors, was a bit embarrassing. How would Macy's feel on Gimbel Avenue? I envision a great business boom in the Bronx, thanks to the aggressive leadership of Borough President Lyons who fought to have the name of the street changed."

Joe Greenspan, service station, the Bronx—"Why not rename it Greenspan Avenue. I have been here much longer than the Jaburg people. The other business people on the avenue will not take this lying down, but we will all fight with everything we have to stop this injustice."

Sam Rothberg, restaurant owner, Bronx—"It's a great honor to have the name Jaburg grace our street. Hugo Jaburg rose from a humble beginning to become a great success in business and exemplifies the wonderful opportunities America has to offer to those willing to work for them."

Robert F. Gabriel, company president, the Bronx—"The name Leggett may have been embarrassing to the Jaburg people, but it's going to cost other firms which have been on this street for many years money and customers. We were never notified of a change and will certainly fight it."

Louis Sangillo, truck driver, Weehawken, N.J.—"We truckmen are confused as it is with the East Bronx. Why make it worse. Leggett is a lot easier to pronounce and there are a few people who have an idea of where it is. I would certainly hate to be a new truck driver looking for Jaburg Avenue."

F. Suggest the ways and for what purposes feedback could be employed effectively by the following:

1. The manager of a resort hotel
2. A convention program chairman
3. A store manager
4. The director of an employee letter-writing training program using an instructor from outside the organization
5. The publisher of a new college textbook

G. A critic of the action-reaction (response-oriented) model says that it has a "source orientation" and therefore "emphasizes one-wayness, at the expense of two-way analysis."[14] Feedback, that is, provides the answers the sender (source) seeks and wishes to use, but it does not lead to a genuine receiver orientation or the kind of communication in which the receiver has an equal role.

Comment on the validity of this point of view. Does empathy play any role in compensating for this deficiency, if there is one? Explain.

H. Consider the classroom as an organization. Discuss its operation with respect to such organizational characteristics as goals, relationships within the group, directional flow, communication networks, and the coding process.

I. Refer to Question H, and discuss the organizational characteristics of your college from the same points of view. Do you see any conflict between the goals of the college and those of the classroom? How, if at all, are the relations between instructors and students affected?

[14] Berlo, pp. 115–116.

J. Look ahead to Problem 4 below. What differences would you expect to find in the two messages?

PROBLEMS

1. Draw up a balance sheet of the possible benefits to both writer and reader in each of the following situations:
   (*a*) A landlord sends a letter to tenants of an apartment house asking them not to loiter with baby carriages in front of the house.
   (*b*) The parks department puts up a sign to discourage vandalism.
   (*c*) The publisher of a weekly news magazine asks for prompt renewal when subscriptions are about to expire.
   (*d*) The Community Chest appeals for contributions on the payroll deduction plan.
   (*e*) A student writes to a large company for information to be included in a term report.

2. Using the empathic process, write a 400-word profile, useful to a business writer, about one of the following stereotypes:
   (*a*) The mother of a preschool-age child
   (*b*) The junior credit-department executive of a big-city commercial bank
   (*c*) The small independent farmer
   (*d*) The young sports-car enthusiast
   (*e*) The reader of *Time*

3. Refer to Topic D, page 43. Putting yourself in Mrs. Rath's place, write the kind of letter you would like to receive. You may invent any reasonable details.

4. As an exercise in adapting to different circumstances, compose to the best of your ability two sales messages as follows:
   (*a*) About 150 words (one minute) of a radio commercial urging listeners to obtain a copy of the current issue of *Time* or *Newsweek* at their newsstand. The advertisement will be scheduled for Monday during the 7 p.m. news program.
   (*b*) Copy for a print advertisement of about the same length and for the same purpose as the advertisement described in (a) above. The advertisement will appear in newspapers on Monday morning.

5. Assume that you recently bought from a large department store a digital watch, which stopped running after several weeks. You returned it to the store, where it was replaced by another. This watch, too, stopped running after a few weeks and was returned to the store. The store accepted it with the promise that it would be repaired and returned to you in a week. Four weeks have now gone by without any word from the store. You have telephoned the store several times, but each time the person you spoke to was unable to say what the status of the transaction was and promised to call you back. No one has been in touch with you. You therefore write a letter to the president of the store asking that the watch be returned to you in good condition or that a refund of the purchase price of $79.95 be sent to you. (You need not write this letter unless your instructor so directs.)

   Now describe in a sentence or two your feelings in response to each of the following circumstances; then write a paragraph summing up the lessons in communication that might be learned from this case about the relation between the store's communications and customer's satisfaction.

(*a*) It is two weeks since you wrote and you have not received a reply.

(*b* A week after you write, you receive a printed card that reads, "The matter referred to is being attended to and you will hear from us again soon."

(*c*) A week after sending your letter, you receive a personal reply from the adjustment manager. He says that the manufacturer is swamped with repair orders and it will take about a month for the watch to be returned.

(*d*) Three days after writing your letter, you receive a telephone call from the secretary to the store president. She tells you that a full refund will be mailed to you in the next few days. She also explains that the store has had a number of unsatisfactory experiences with the brand of watch you bought and that the brand is being dropped. You receive the check as promised.

6. Mrs. Frank Dublin of 223 West Street, your city, has written as follows to the Newell Department Store of the same city. As a new correspondent in the Adjustment Department, you are required to write a reply in accordance with the circumstances in *a, b, c,* or *d* below, as your instructor directs. The customer's letter is dated October 9. You are writing on October 11. For assistance with the mechanics of the letter, see Chapter 4.

```
Gentlemen:

In sending you the enclosed check for $45.65, I have de-
ducted 50¢ from the total amount of your October 1 state-
ment.  You charged this amount to me for picking up a
coat which I wanted returned for credit.  I have never
been charged before for returns and I don't see why I
should pay this time.  Please adjust my account accord-
ingly.

                                Very truly yours,

                                Sara Dublin
                                (Mrs. Frank Dublin)
```

(*a*) Your supervisor, for whose signature you are writing this letter, has sent you the customer's letter with this note attached: "Notice about policy on pickups was included in last month's statements. Customers never read their mail. Say 'no' any way you want, but if this customer complains again about pickup charges, you're fired."

(*b*) Your supervisor tells you, "This is a common situation. Here's the way we usually handle it." The letter he gives you reads:

Dear Mrs. __________:

We wish to acknowledge receipt of your letter of recent date objecting to the 50-cent pick-up charge. We have been forced to adopt this policy because of the abuses of many of our customers who take advantage of the return privilege.

We know you will understand our point of view, but there is nothing we can do. Looking forward to your continued patronage, we remain

Very truly yours,

Assume that Mrs. Dublin is one of your better customers. Although the policy has been in force for more than a year, Mrs. Dublin has on several occasions in the past been allowed to return the goods without penalty.

(*c*) Notices about the 50-cent charge were included with the September 1 statements, but Mrs. Dublin was not sent any statement because she owed nothing. Allow the 50-cent deduction this time.

(*d*) The policy of charging for pickups went into effect more than a year ago, when notices were sent to all charge customers. Mrs. Dublin paid the fee several times in the past. Tell her the charge will be put on next month's statement.

3
The Language of Business

THE GOAL of business communication, we have seen, is to obtain a response. Your success as a writer or speaker depends on your ability to predict and modify the receiver's response to suit your objective. The receiver's response, in turn, depends on the meaning the message has for him.

What is meaning? It is the significance one attaches to the message and the symbols that compose it. Some of the symbols consist of words; others are nonverbal. More so than words, the nonverbal symbols are directly related to the things they signify and are therefore less abstract. Thus a photograph of a particular model Chevrolet is less abstract than a verbal description of the same car. Similarly, a bead of sweat on a speaker's brow will communicate his discomfort more concretely than anything he could say. In both instances, the thing we perceive strongly suggests the actual object or phenomenon it stands for. Words, on the other hand, have no relation to the object or phenomenon except through common agreement. The object we take from the library shelf is a *book*, but if we all agreed to call it a *koob* or an *obok*, we would still be able to communicate.

Verbal symbols have their drawbacks. One difficulty is that agreement on the meaning of the symbols is often confined to the dictionary. Among the users of words, meaning is not fixed but varies according to their individual experiences, motives, and feelings. Businessmen, for example, see *surplus* as earnings retained in the business for future use, but many stockholders and employees regard it as an excess of readily expendable funds to which they are entitled. A railroad company uses the term *form of transportation* to mean "ticket," but the traveler takes it to mean "mode of conveyance." No wonder the traveler is confused when he reads, "Our conductor's report states that you traveled from Jersey City to Middletown on Train No. 2325, February 11, at which time you were without any *form of transportation.*"

Another difficulty imposed by verbal symbols is that there are far more thoughts and shades of meaning to be expressed than there are symbols to express them. Even if we could master the whole dictionary, there would still not be enough words to enable us to say with absolute precision all we had to say. Yet individual vocabularies comprise only a small portion of the available word supply, and these are rarely used as skillfully as the language permits.[1] Combining words into phrases and sentences enlarges the opportunities for expression, but it increases the risk of misunderstanding. The executive who wrote, "Mary and I look forward to seeing you at the Horse Show in any event," apparently put all the right words in his omelet; he just did not scramble them well.[2]

In this chapter we will take a closer look at language and meaning. Our aim is to see words in their three dimensions: (1) their relation to things, (2) their relation to feelings, and (3) their relation to each other. In understanding these aspects of language, we will also be learning to use words more effectively.

INFORMATIVE LANGUAGE: WORDS AND THINGS

The difficulties of communication would be considerably lessened if we could always point to the actual objects or events we are referring to. When we use words as substitutes for pointing, we must be sure that the words are informative—that they signify as nearly as possible the things they represent. Students of language use the term *referent* to designate the thing a word stands for. In the instance of the Empire State Building, the structure itself is the referent, and *Empire State Building* is the name or symbol by which we identify it.

The relation between a word and its referent—the thing it denotes—is expressed by the term *denotation.* The denotation of a word is clear or not depending on (1) the accuracy with which the word names its referent, and (2) the extent to which the referent has entered into the reader's experience. Standing alone, the word *bowl* is ambiguous in its denotation because the referent is not clear—*what* bowl? An athletic stadium or a serving dish? Even the term *Revere bowl* will have a clear denotation only for the reader who has seen such an object and knows its name.

Exact Words

As the last example suggests, the more sharply a word brings its referent into focus, the clearer the meaning. Call a horse a *cow,* and you will confuse the reader. Call a horse a *horse* and you will do much better. But if the horse is a small one that pulls a cart for children in the park, you will give a still better

[1] In one study of 67,200 words written by 24 college freshmen, it was found that 96 different words made up 50 percent of the total, and that only ten different words made up 25 percent of the total. The ten words were *the, I, and, to, was, my, in, of, a, it.* See Wendell Johnson, *Your Most Enchanted Listener* (New York: Harper & Row, 1956), p. 110.

[2] Compare: "*In any event,* Mary and I look forward to seeing you at the Horse Show."

idea of the referent if you call it a *pony*. Here we will take up some of the attributes of words that help or hinder exact expression.

FIXED TERMS OF REFERENCE

When an engineer says a pipe is 6.5 centimeters in outside diameter, there is no doubt about the diameter. The doubt would be considerable if he merely said it was "a thin pipe." Characteristic of the language of the engineer and scientist are terms that are as nearly fixed in meaning as any terms can be. Thus carbon dioxide, or CO_2, represents just one combination of elements and no other. In business writing, similar accuracy is possible through the use of signs, letters, numbers, and other fixed terms or identification and measurement, such as centigrade, Fahrenheit, meters, fathoms, knots, miles, yards, tons, dollars, reams, gallons, and quarts. Note the precision of these statements:

> We have your check for $33.16 in payment of our invoice No. 167517 dated November 17, 19—.
>
> Please set this copy in 12-point Bodoni Book.
>
> Flight 407 to Chicago will leave from Gate 39 at 4:15 p.m.
>
> He is 37 years old, a native of Denver, Colorado, with an M.A. degree in sociology from Northwestern University.
>
> We are inquiring about our order No. 4635 A for 24 dozen boxes (5,000 each) of Pal-70 staples in the half-inch size.

DICTIONARY USAGE

Anyone interested in using words accurately will find the dictionary a valuable ally. No dictionary can tell everything about a word, nor can it give assurance that the writer or speaker will make a wise choice. Still, the dictionary is the most authoritative recorder of meaning we have, and to flout its authority is to court both misunderstanding and a loss of esteem.

With respect to meaning, consider the confusion caused by the student who writes, "I have *edited* many financial articles for this report," when he means *studied* or *reviewed*. An office manager who writes that "the *atmospheric conditions* are good for quiet, hard work" seems to be talking about the *climate* when he should be referring to the *atmosphere* in the sense of surrounding influences or environment. A young man does not improve his prospects for a job when his application says, "I am a small but important *clog* in the vast wheel of activity known as the Post Office." Of course, he means *cog*. A retail store executive writes, "Considerable money could be saved through *self-manufacture* of this product." Doesn't he mean, "We could save considerable money if we *manufactured the product ourselves*"?

Apart from the accustomed meanings of words, dictionaries are also important for what they say about the context in which certain words may acceptably be used. *Standard* words are those ordinarily found in the speech and writing of educated persons. Some standard words are more formal than others and some are downright colloquial or informal (compare "*pay* the bill" with "*foot* the bill"). Naturally, a writer or speaker will make a choice on the basis of the kind of communication involved. One would expect a legal document or state invitation, for example, to use more formal language than a simple inquiry or complaint.

As opposed to words in standard usage, words in *nonstandard* usage are not ordinarily considered acceptable by educated persons. Careful writers and speakers make distinctions, for example, between *imply* and *infer;* they do not use *latter* when they mean the *last* of more than two items; and they avoid illiteracies like *suicided, irregardless,* and *disokay.* Some exceptions, of course, are made. Slang, for example, though nonstandard, often carries a certain vitality that makes it suitable for use in advertising and trade talk. Thus "Coke," which started as a slang word for *Coca Cola,* has become a trademarked name for the product, and "specs" is commonly used by builders when they refer to the architects' *specifications.*

AMBIGUITY

An ambiguous word is one that has more than one meaning in the same context. *Hard* has a number of meanings, but it is not likely that one would be confused with another in such phrases as "a *hard* worker," "a *hard* finish," and "a *hard* question." On the other hand, the word *advice* has a double meaning in the sentence, "Our *advice* is that these shares represent a sound investment." The sentence was part of a letter written by a trust company in response to an inquiry from one of its clients. When the customer invested in the shares, only to see the price plummet, he threatened a lawsuit on the ground that the company had used bad judgment. The company's defense? It took no responsibility for the customer's loss, for it was only forwarding an opinion received from other sources. The company, it appeared, used the word in the sense of "information." The customer took it to mean "counsel."

Connecting words are especially prone to ambiguity. A will so confusing that it became the basis of a lawsuit read, "My estate shall be divided equally *between* my brother and my wife's three sisters." The question was whether the brother should get half and the wife's three sisters the other half, or each should receive a fourth of the estate. The surrogate accepted the first interpretation on the ground that if the deceased had wanted each to receive a fourth, he would have used the word *among,* which according to English grammar is customarily used in reference to three or more units.

Since, as, and *while* are other connectives that may cause trouble. "*Since* we increased our prices, sales have fallen sharply" means either, "*Because* we increased our prices, sales have fallen sharply," or "*From the time that* we increased our prices, sales have fallen sharply." The difference can be important. Similarly, *as* may mean either "because" or "during the time that," and *while* may mean either "although" or "during the time that."

ABSTRACTION

The more general or abstract a word is—that is, the more details it leaves out—the harder it is for the reader to associate it with its referent. Some stu-

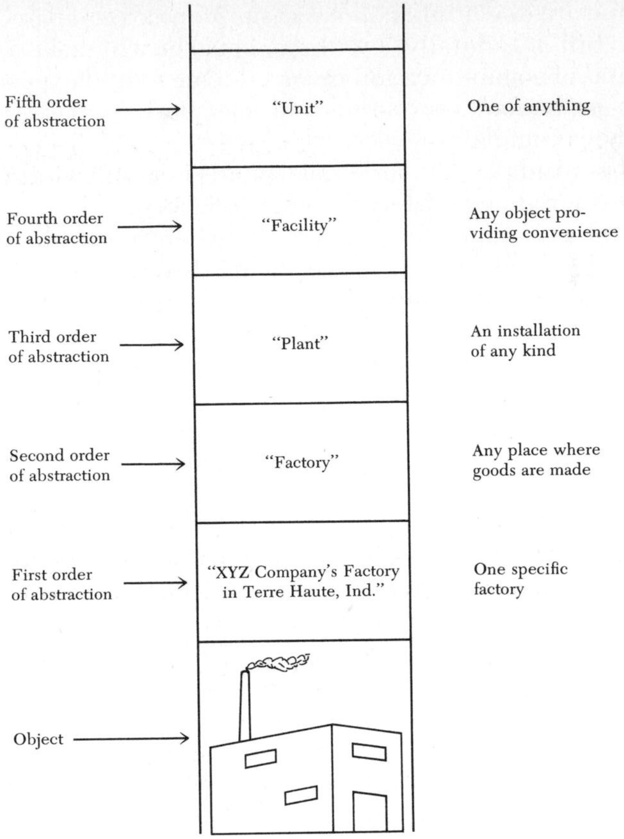

FIG. 3-1. *An "abstraction ladder," showing the dissipation of meaning as language becomes more abstract.*

dents of language use an "abstraction ladder" to classify words according to the degree to which they lose their identifying characteristics. At the bottom of the ladder is the referent. On the rungs, the word symbols are so arranged that they become increasingly abstract as they reach the top. Figure 3-1 illustrates the progressive diffusion of meaning.

All writing represents abstraction to some degree. It would be highly impractical to name every executive of a company every time we wanted to refer to the *management.* By the same token, we find it convenient to use terms like *labor, supplies, expenses,* and *business conditions* without differentiating among the constituents of each group. Nevertheless, abstraction may have its unfavorable consequences. The subject for our abstraction ladder in the diagram, for example, was inspired by a credit agency's report reading, "The company is constructing a new *unit* in Terre Haute." It was impossible even to guess at the kind of *unit* it was. It could have been a factory, a warehouse, or a store.

In another instance, the buyer of a ball-point pen was impressed by the word *Guaranteed* printed on the card to which the pen was attached. When the pen ran out of ink a week later, however, he wondered what the guarantee covered and what adjustment he could expect. He never took the trouble to find out. Nor did he again buy the same make of pen. An oil company found little demand for its *Furnace Efficiency Test* until it changed the name to *Fuel-Saving Test,* a less abstract term. A woman shopping for pound cake passed up one package that listed "butter" as one of the ingredients and bought another with "93-score AA creamery butter."

Understandable Words

Any ideas we may have about the use of exact words must be modified somewhat by the need to use words the reader can understand. There is no question about the exactness of the term *72-point Ultra Bodoni,* but the average reader would probably get more meaning from the less exact phrase, "a heavy type one inch high."

ADAPTING TO SPECIALISTS

The use of specialized terms offers few complications when accountant writes to accountant, mechanical engineer to mechanical engineer, insurance agent to insurance agent, or psychologist to psychologist. For one thing, the use of technical terms makes possible clear and accurate communication with a minimum number of words. Without such terms as *fixed assets, current liabilities,* and *earned surplus,* for example, it would be hard to describe a company's financial position so that an accountant would understand it. Similarly an advertising man uses expressions like *ROP, exposure, Nielsen, split run,* and *halftone* without feeling the need to explain what they mean. Another advantage of using the specialist's language is that it suggests the writer's own authority and thus aids rapport with the reader.

What the writer must avoid is falling into the occupational lingo, or jargon, that is more likely to obscure thought than to reveal it. A memorandum reads:

> It is considered that the increased responsibility assumed will be balanced by the diminished ineffectual intelligence originating in the departmental activities of the various subdivisions delegated under the new setup. Each will be responsible for his own. Pending the reissue of the organizational procedure to be adopted, it will be deemed sufficient for our purposes if uncoordinated activity be confined to those specific groups not immediately concerned and then only on such matters as are not within the scope of the above. Any retroactive action will be considered at a later date.

It is hard, if not impossible, to know what the writer means. The reason is not that the writing is technical, but that it is pretentious. The writer is either showing off or so caught up in the bureaucratic jargon that he cannot express himself simply. In contrast, note this first paragraph from the opinion of a judge of the U.S. Court of Appeals:

> This litigation arises out of an installment contract for the sale of quantities of battery lead by a Canadian seller to a Pennsylvania buyer. The seller sued for

> the price of a carload of lead delivered but not paid for. The buyer counterclaimed for damages caused by the seller's failure to deliver the remaining installments covered by the contract. The District Court, sitting without a jury, allowed a recovery on both claim and counterclaim. The ultimate question is whether the buyer had committed such a breach of contract as constituted repudiation justifying decision for the seller.

Commenting on that paragraph, a critic of legal jargon wrote: "In that one paragraph, you have the entire story of the litigation. There are no 'saids,' there are no 'aforesaids,' there are no 'suches.' There is nothing in that paragraph to throw the reader off. There is no 'in other words,' nor 'it is intended.' It is a perfect example of clear, concise writing. Unfortunately, it is a rare one."[3]

ADAPTING TO LAYMEN

As we have seen, technical terms are useful when they enable people of common interests to communicate with each other clearly and concisely. The use of technical language in messages to nonspecialists, on the other hand, may inspire awe, but it does not usually contribute to understanding. The layman gets more meaning out of words in his own vocabulary. An attorney writes to a client, "Will you please let me know if your father died *testate?*" Since the client is a young man with little experience in estate matters, he would be more certain of the meaning if the sentence read, "Will you please let me know if your father *left a will?*" In another instance the trustee of her husband's estate writes to a widow, "There was a return of 3.68 per cent on the *corpus* of the estate." Aside from the uneasy feeling the word *corpus* gives the widow, the meaning would be clearer if the writer used the more familiar word *principal.*

Writing to customers, a department store executive uses the phrases, "In checking back on the *ledger sheet,* we find," "We have *debited* your account," and "The *arrearage* in your account." But his language would be better adapted to his readers if he said, "In checking back on our *records,* we find," "We have *charged* your account," and "The *unpaid balance* of your account." Or take the case of the insurance company that writes to a policyholder, "Will you please acknowledge payment by *receipting* and returning to us the *voucher* accompanying the check." Perhaps it would not be quite so accurate to say, "Will you please sign the blue slip accompanying the check and return it to us as our receipt," but there is little doubt that such language conforms better to the experience of the average man.

Business executives often overrate the economic understanding of their workers. One study of the language of management revealed that employees were puzzled by such terms as *revenues, excise tax,* and *productivity.* It was suggested that *earnings, sales tax,* and *efficient production* be substituted.[4]

[3] Elliott L. Biskind, "Writing Right," New York State Bar *Journal*, 42 (October 1970), 549.

[4] "Word Impact for Management's Communications," *Research Report of the Public Opinion Index for Industry*, 18 (January 1960).

Any big or difficult words—not only the technical ones—may be out of the reader's range. Some years ago the president of a large savings bank wrote to all his depositors—some 200,000 of them—to ask that they fill out a new signature card which he said the bank needed "in order to *expedite* the service to our customers." During the ensuing week, the bank found it hard to cope with the number of depositors who came in to ask why the card was needed. One man, dressed in a white butcher coat and brandishing the letter, insisted on seeing the president in person. "I've had an account here for eighteen years," he said with some feeling. "You can't *expedite* it now." He thought the word meant "cut off."

It is not to be assumed that you must never use a word you suspect to be outside the reader's vocabulary. If necessary, you can define the term or explain it. As we shall see a few pages farther on, however, even an unfamiliar word may carry the desired suggestion, and that may be enough for your purpose. In other instances, the reader may easily understand the unfamiliar word because its meaning is implicit in the surrounding words, or *context*. It would not be difficult, for example, to guess the meaning of the word *demographer* in the sentence, "*Demographers* frequently have been wide of the mark in forecasts of population growth."

Simple Words

Even when the reader has a specialized knowledge of the subject or a bigger-than-average vocabulary, it should be kept in mind that maximum reading efficiency is usually achieved at a level below the most difficult. Lawyers, doctors, engineers, and scientists, as well as businessmen, seem to agree that much of the writing addressed to them is unnecessarily abstruse. In a letter to the editor of *Jets and Missiles*, a reader cited this sentence from its pages as an example of difficult reading:

> Most refractory coatings to date exhibit a lack of reliability when subjected to the impingement of entrained particulate matter in the propellant stream under extended firing durations.

The editor agreed that the correspondent's suggested revision was an improvement:

> The exhaust gas eventually chews the coating off existing ceramics.

In nontechnical writing, also, there is a strong need for words that are not only exact and clear, but simple and easy to read as well. The reader may understand *conversed with*, but *spoke to* is more alive. *We know* is better than *we are cognizant of*, and *summary* is better than *summarization*. Too much writing in business is characterized by words like *inadvertency*, *subsequently*, and *utilization* when shorter words like *error*, *after*, and *use* carry their meaning faster. Words like *pay*, *meet*, *help*, and *proof* lie idle while readers strain at *remuneration*, *encounter*, *assistance*, and *substantiation*. Some critics say the use of big words indicates a "status complex." It is

"THE FINE PRINT TRANSLATED"

As It Was	*As It Is*
1. In the event of default in the payment of this or any other Obligation or the performance or observance of any term or covenant contained herein or in any note or other contract or agreement evidencing or relating to any Obligation or any Collateral on the Borrower's part to be performed or observed; or the undersigned Borrower shall die; or any of the undersigned become insolvent or make an assignment for the benefit of creditors; or a petition shall be filed by or against any of the undersigned under any provision of the Bankruptcy Act; or any money, securities or property of the undersigned now or hereafter on deposit with or in the possession or under the control of the Bank shall be attached or become subject to distraint proceedings or any order or process of any court.	I'll be in default: 1. If I don't pay an installment on time; or 2. If any other creditor tries by legal process to take any money of mine in your possession.
2. If the company revises this policy form with respect to policy provisions, endorsements or rules by which the insurance hereunder could be extended or broadened without additional premium charge, such insurance as is afforded hereunder shall be so extended or broadened effective immediately upon approval or acceptance of such revision during the policy period by the appropriate insurance supervisory authority.	We'll automatically give you the benefits of any extension or broadening of this policy if the change doesn't require additional premium.
3. Cardholder and any other person applying for, using or signing the Card promise, jointly and severally, to pay to Bank the principal of all loans plus, as provided in paragraph 4, FINANCE CHARGES. Payments shall be made each month at Bank or as Bank may direct, on or before the Payment Due Date, in the amount of (1) the greater of $10 or an amount equal to 1/36th of the Total Debit Balance not in excess of the Maximum Credit on the related Statement Date plus (b) any amounts owing and delinquent plus (c) any excess of the Total Debit Balance over the Maximum Credit.	You must pay us a monthly minimum payment. This monthly minimum payment will be 1/36 of the balance plus, of course, any amounts which are past due, but at least $10. If the balance is less than $10, the minimum payment will be the entire balance. The balance will include the outstanding amount that you have borrowed plus a finance charge.

doubtful whether the satisfaction they give the writer makes up for the hardship they cause the reader.

The following sentence was taken from the market letter of a stock broker:

> Common stocks still have considerable appeal from a longer term viewpoint as media to participate in an indicated ever expanding American economy and a convenient means of maintaining the purchasing power of capital against still pronounced inflationary trends.

A partner in the firm, after attending a company-sponsored class in writing, recast the sentence as follows:

> In the long range, common stocks still look good. They can help the investor benefit from business growth which as yet shows no signs of letup. At the same time they offer a convenient way to keep up purchasing power in the face of still pronounced inflationary trends.

Although both statements occupy about the same space, the first has 19 one-syllable words while the second has 39! Not only brokerage houses, but banks and insurance companies as well, are aware of the verbal barrier between themselves and their customers, and some are trying to remove the barrier by rewriting their contracts and procedures in simple English. Some examples of what can be done in this respect are shown in Figure 3-2.

A fault of many long words is that they are more abstract and therefore more diffuse than their shorter synonyms. *Your communication*, for example, is less precise than *your letter*, *institution* is vaguer than *bank*, and *expedite* is not so sharp as *speed up*. The office manager who sends a memorandum to the building superintendent to "evaluate the condition of the illumination facilities" wants him, more accurately, to "inspect the lights." The reporter who says, "after a comprehensive appraisal of the circumstances," means, more clearly, "after studying the facts." The city official who writes, "Please endeavor to terminate the investigation as expeditiously as possible," could say, more simply, "Please try to complete the investigation as soon as you can."

The last example leads to some interesting reflections. Why not *end* instead of *complete?* The reason is that *end* could mean "to close without finishing." *Complete*, however, carries the suggestion of working to a logical conclusion. Also, why not *inquiry* instead of *investigation?* Here *investigation* is less ambiguous than *inquiry* and therefore preferred to the shorter word. On the other hand, if *investigation* has already been used and the writer wishes to avoid repeating it, *inquiry* would serve as a sufficiently exact synonym. The point is that the length of a word cannot be considered apart from its accuracy.

FIG. 3-2. *Contracts rewritten in simple English: (1) Citibank, New York; (2) Sentry Auto Insurance Company; (3) First National Bank of Boston, Master Charge agreements.* [*As reported in* Time, *September 22, 1975.*]

AFFECTIVE LANGUAGE: WORDS AND FEELINGS

The meaning of words is to be found not only in their relation to their referents, but in their relation to the feelings of the sender and receiver as well. Compare these statements:

1. The meeting will be held on March 5.
2. We would be complimented by your presence at our March 5 meeting.
3. If you want to do the sensible thing, you will attend the March 5 meeting.

The first statement is purely informative. It expresses no feeling and is not likely to arouse any. The second and third statements, on the other hand, are affective. Their language expresses the writer's attitudes and feelings and has a corresponding effect on those of the reader. Thus the second sentence is flattering to the reader and ensures a favorable reception. The third sentence, however, seems to dictate the reader's course of action and implies a lack of confidence in him. The reader is sure to sense the pressure put upon him and respond accordingly. Even if he keeps his resentment in check, he will probably be thinking, "Don't push me. I can make up my own mind." From these examples you can see that affective language offers opportunities for achieving the desired results, but that it also carries with it certain dangers if used unwisely.

Reports and Judgments

One aspect of affective language may be explained by the distinction between *reports* and *judgments*. Reports are statements about things observed or experienced. They can be found true or false by recourse to their referents. Judgments, however, are expressions of opinion arising out of the communicator's own values. That a room is *15 by 20 feet*, that an air conditioner has a *five-horsepower motor*, and that a table is made of *solid walnut* are reports. But that the room is *large*, the air conditioner *weak*, and the table *attractive* are judgments. Actual conditions will support or disprove the reports, but there is no support for the judgments except in the writer's mind. A writer with a different point of view might just as conscientiously have said that the room is *small*, the air conditioner is *adequate*, and the table is *ugly*.

As a rule, you have to be more careful in making judgments than in making reports, for judgments are more likely biased. "You *wrote* us about . . ." is an objective report, but "You *complained* to us about . . ." is a judgment that puts the reader in an unenviable role. "Your *experience*" is objective and neutral, but "your *unfortunate experience*" is a subjective reminder that colors the situation and perhaps makes it worse than it is. So, too, the advertiser who reports the actual weight of his product leaves no room for argument, but the one who calls the box "large" when the consumer's judgment tells him it is small only invites disbelief.

Connotation

The suggestion a word acquires through association is called its connotation. The strength of the connotation varies. *House*—as in "the *house* for sale"—may generally be said to have a weak connotation because it has no significant overtones. *Cottage* is a synonym with considerably more sentiment. Other connotations are conveyed by the synonyms *shack, bungalow, ranch house, residence.* The word *restaurant* also has more affective counterparts in such names as *hash house, steak house, grill, diner, luncheon club, coffee house, casino, tavern, Max's Busy Bee,* and *Le Pavillon.*

The connotation of a word varies from person to person and context to context. *Profit* has a comforting sound to the businessman, but it sometimes irks the consumer and worker who think their share should be bigger than it is. *Competition* may suggest risk to a company's sales manager, better products and lower prices to the consumer, and special exertion to the athlete or to the student trying to obtain a scholarship. *Time and motion study* suggests efficiency to management, but unions see it as a means of exploiting workers. A *loan* suggests expanding business to the banker, but it may connote penury to the housewife and embarrassment to her husband who has to borrow $50 to meet an emergency. The word *foreign* arouses suspicion in the phrases *foreign ideas, foreign goods,* and *foreign agents,* but the stigma is lacking in *foreign car* and *foreign travel.*

Note the differences in suggestion in the parallel statements below:

We admire his *shrewdness*	We admire his *astuteness.*
The group will *eat* together at twelve.	The group will *dine* together at twelve.
Will you please let us know what *you've got on* Bracker & Co.	Will you please let us know *your experience* with Bracker & Co.
He kept a *close watch* on expenditures.	He kept a *vigil* over expenditures.
He *admitted* he had come in late on Tuesday.	He *said* he had come in late on Tuesday.
A *clever* public relations man could *put over* the idea.	A *skilled* public relations man could *make* the idea *succeed.*

FAVOR WORDS

Since some words have a better connotation than others, you can influence response by leaning to words of favorable suggestion. If the reader will not accept anything *foreign,* the same reader often shows a preference for *imported* beer, *continental* clothing, and *French* perfume. A Swiss manufacturer doing business in this country refers to his firm as *international,* a respected designation shared by his American competitors. American manufacturers speak of their *overseas operations* rather than their *foreign subsidiaries.* A foreigner who travels to this country is known most favorably as a *visitor from abroad.*

Sensitive to the implications of the word *profit,* businessmen may prefer such terms as *net income* and *earnings*. A *salesman* is now often called by the more dignified name *representative*. Stock brokerage firms employ *registered representatives*. The *installment plan* meets less prejudice when it is called a *deferred payment plan*. A *credit card* has become a *courtesy card* in some quarters. Employers find that clerks want to be called *secretaries* and that new employees are less easily attracted by the offer of a *job* than by the promise of a *career*.

Many organizations fear prejudice in announcing a *cocktail party*, but they do not hesitate to call the same affair a *reception*. The State Department, with a nice sense of propriety, draws its money for liquor from the innocuously named *representation fund*. Businessmen routinely list expenses for liquor under the general heading of *entertainment of clients*. In advertising over the radio, distributors of soda and other "mixers" preserve the family atmosphere by suggesting the use of the product with "your favorite *beverage*." In family restaurants and hotels, the bar area is often called simply the *lounge*.

Legislators and businessmen who sense that voters would be antagonistic to *price-fixing laws* prefer to call them *fair-trade laws*. *Socialized medicine* and *medical care for the aged* are also opposite sides of the same coin. When Detroit manufacturers considered the appellation *standard* too plain for their lowest priced cars, they changed the name to *de luxe*. The former *de luxe* models became *super de luxe*. *Custom* was another popular name for models made under the ultimate conditions of mass production. When, more recently, fuel conservation became imperative, names like *Fury*, *Duster*, *Stingray*, and *Wildcat*—all suggesting speed and power—were followed by such sedate place names as *Granada*, *Seville*, *Cordoba*, and *Versailles*.

PREJUDICE WORDS

Some words are selected deliberately to arouse the reader's prejudices. "Don't compare it with *ordinary* filters" advertises a cigarette manufacturer, thereby putting the products of all his competitors in an inferior category. A businessman who disapproves a plan may call it a *scheme*, or he may call the originator an *impractical dreamer*. If he frowns on an investment, he may call it a *speculation* or a *gamble*. A business group seeking government support for control of competition proclaimed that "Cutthroat competition is *un-American*." Opponents decried *government intervention* and *monopolistic practices*. Fighting a strike called by the International Electrical Workers' Union, General Electric consistently referred to the group as *Mr. Carey's union* after the name of the president, thus implying that the strike was the will of one man rather than of the entire membership.

It is important to recognize that words do not change the basic nature of a person, thing, or condition, and that the prejudices they arouse may as easily work against the user as for him. Except for the protection offered by the laws of libel and slander, the target of the prejudicial words has little recourse. Businessmen who recognize their social responsibilities use such words with extreme care. The rational reader, on his part, is not misled by mere names. An idea is not necessarily bad because words say so. What is the idea? Let us examine it objectively. The same principle should also apply to our judgment of people. We must not stigmatize a person by some convenient class label, but rather form our opinion of each individual on the basis of his own merits.

POSITIVE AND NEGATIVE WORDS

Whether you say a refrigerator is *half empty* or *half full,* the amount of food in it is the same; the language, however, expresses opposite attitudes.

A correspondent writes:

> *We will have to hold up your order until* you tell us what color you want.

Another correspondent handles the same situation in this way:

> *We will ship your order as soon as* you tell us the color you want.

The difference in attitude is apparent. The first sentence shows the negative or undesirable consequences of the reader's omission. The second emphasizes positive or affirmative action. Generally, the positive approach is likely to be more reassuring, more helpful, and more tactful.

An insurance company wishing to interest employers in providing pension plans for workers writes:

> Most employers accept the fact that the business organization that *lacks fringe benefits* for employees is at a *competitive disadvantage.* High-caliber employees are *difficult to attract* and there is *high turnover* among those hired. The result is *less efficiency* and *less profit.*

This is a discouraging picture and one hardly calculated to kindle the enthusiasm of the reader. Note the difference in tone when the negative words are made positive:

> Most employers accept the fact that the business organization that *provides fringe benefits* for employees *enjoys a competitive advantage.* High-caliber employees are *easy to attract and to hold.* The result is *more efficiency* and *more profit.*

Negative words often reveal some feeling of inadequacy on the part of the writer. The job applicant who says, "Unfortunately, I have no practical experience," advertises the fear that he does not qualify for the position. He would probably improve his chances by leaving out the negative reference and emphasizing his training, education, and personal qualifications. A correspondent writes, "I hope this information is not too confusing." He would have expressed more self-confidence by writing, "If you have any questions, please be sure to let me know."

The person who makes an error is sometimes inclined to magnify the mistake by employing a profusion of words like *inconvenience, loss, delay, suffer, embarrassment,* and *failure.* A simple statement like, "We regret the oversight" is often enough to soothe the victim's feelings and pave the way for constructive action. The same writer seems less reassuring when he says, "We hope there will be *no recurrence of such a delay* in the future" than when he says, "I will see to it that you get *prompt delivery* in the future."

It should not be inferred that there is no place for negative language in business writing. Some ideas are most forcefully impressed on the reader by appeals to fear: the fear of economic loss, the fear of accident or bad health, the fear of offending, and the like. Advertisers often capitalize on these fears by picturing the dreadful consequences of not doing what they recommend. They must be careful, however, lest revulsion against the negative ideas turn into revulsion against the suggested substitutes also.

Freshness

Affective meaning is enhanced by the use of fresh, original language. The reader is easily bored with writing of this sort:

> We wish to announce the opening of a new shop featuring evening dresses. Here quality will be our keynote and you will be sure to find the right style for every formal occasion. See us and be convinced.

What a pleasure, though, to come across writing like this:

> Just opening, a shop for after dark when a husband changes from a company man to a man who wants company. After-Dark is an entire salon built on the idea that night is the important half of the day when a woman ought to beguile like moonglow in clothes that are as flattering as candelight. We believe that a long skirt will do more for the morale of a hostess than success with a soufflé ever could—that brocades or golden lamés will outpull the Late Late Show—and that a husband will always catch the Express if you meet him wearing something extraordinary from the After-Dark Shop of Franklin Simon.

Your own imagination and enthusiasm have much to do with the feeling you engender in the reader. Even when you find your task routine, you can keep your writing fresh by choosing words deliberately instead of accepting the first that come to mind.

AVOIDING CLICHÉS

William H. Whyte, Jr., once parodied the cliché-ridden language of the businessman in a piece called "The Composite Business Speech":

> It is a pleasure and a privilege to be here with you today [the speech begins]. These great annual meetings are always an inspiration to me, and doubly so today. After the glowing introduction by our toastmaster I must confess, however, that I'd like to turn the tables on Chuck. When I say it's about the nineteenth hole and a certain gentleman whose baritone was cracked, those of you who were at the Atlanta conference last year will know what I mean. But I won't tell it. Chuck Forbes is too good a friend of mine and, seriously, I know

full well what a tower of strength his yeoman service has been to the association in these trying times.[5]

The dozen or so warmed-over expressions make the paragraph more amusing than meaningful. Similar clichés can be found in letters, reports, and advertisements. The remedy lies in finding substitute expressions that are more specific, more colorful, or at least less imitative. Compare:

TRITE	IMPROVED
Our competitors are *having a field day.*	Our competitors are invading our territory and taking away our customers.
Sales were *few and far between.*	Sales were slow—only eight orders came in during the first two weeks of the month.
Jones is really *on the ball.*	Jones is bright and adaptable.
The new model is *head and shoulders above* the last one.	The new model costs $30 less than last year's and gives a sharper picture.
They sold out *lock, stock, and barrel.*	They sold everything—stock, fixtures, lease.
As luck would have it, the check arrived on Tuesday.	Luckily, the check arrived on Tuesday.

In letter writing, especially, clichés often acquire a stiff dignity, or stiltedness, as in the phrases, "under date of March 10" (for "on March 10") and "subsequent to receipt of your letter" (for "after receiving your letter"). We will have more to say about such expressions in Chapter 4, "Business Letters."

VIVIDNESS

Deep impressions on the reader's feelings are made by words that create vivid pictures. We are accustomed to imagery in creative and journalistic writing, and get it less frequently perhaps in business writing. Here is a description of a dust storm as reported by *Time* magazine:

> Stagnant air hung heavy and ominous over the parched plains last week. Then a cold front hit, and the year's worst duster began to blow. Winds up to 70 m.p.h. whipped across 120,000 square miles of the Southwest dust bowl, and the earth boiled into black clouds 20,000 feet high in the sky. The dust was so thick that dawn came invisibly; when rain began to fall, tiny mud balls pelted the town of Guymon, Okla. Schools closed, stores shut down and thousands of farm families listened tensely at their radios as their lands and their livelihoods slipped away.

[5] William H. Whyte, Jr., "The Language of Business," *Fortune*, November 1950, p. 114.

The adjectives *stagnant, heavy,* and *ominous* create an expectant atmosphere. Force is applied with the verbs *whipped, boiled,* and *pelted.* Specific figures add conviction: *70 m.p.h., 120,000 square miles, 200,000 feet high.* At the same time, the mood is heightened by the repetitive sounds in such phrases as *hung heavy, parched plains, boiled into black clouds,* and *their lands and their livelihoods slipped away.*

A comparable use of vivid language characterizes the following advertisement for Republic Steel. Note the use of specific detail and the choice of words to suggest the size and strength of the machine. The partiality to words with hard sounds—note especially the number of words with the letter *g*—reinforces the impression of strength.

> WORLD'S BIGGEST SHOVEL MOVES MOUNTAINS IN MINUTES
>
> This gargantuan coal stripper will outstrip all other movable land machines in the world for size and results. Its dimensions are staggering: height—20 stories; weight—14 million pounds; reach—more than a city block. It will be able to pick up 173 tons of material at one bite.
>
> This is an outsize example of the big things being fabricated from Republic steels, present and to come, in the giant world of earth-moving equipment. This very moment hordes of huge, rugged machines are rearranging the face of the earth to meet the changing needs of man. They are doing the world's rough, tough jobs of building roads, mining, logging, clearing land for new homes, buildings, and bridges.
>
> Only the strength of steel has the rugged stamina to stand under the brutal slam of bucket teeth into rock, to support the hoist and sweep of tremendous loads, to gouge great trees out of their sockets. . . .

FIGURES OF SPEECH

Vivid writing generally makes liberal use of *figures of speech.* These are a form of literary exaggeration employing, for the most part, symbolic or imaginative rather than literal terms. When we say "lend a hand," for example, we are not literally asking for the loan of a hand, but only for the help that the hand traditionally symbolizes.

Although there are many kinds of figures of speech, probably the most familiar is the *metaphor,* or comparison of dissimilar things—for instance, the mind of a child is called "a tablet on which nothing is written"; a thermostat is referred to as "the brain of the heating plant." Other common figures of speech appeal to the ear: The *pun* is a play on words ("No business like snow business"). *Alliteration* is the repetition of sound ("Better Buy Birds Eye"). *Onomatopoeia* is the use of a word that imitates the sound of the thing named ("the jingle of the cash-register"; "the whisper-quiet engine").

The most effective figures of speech are apt and original, as in these examples:

The fiery breath of this oxyacetylene flame also helps weld everything from ships to fenders. It slices through thick slabs of metal as if it were cheese and carves jigsaw shapes out of stacks of steel sheets—as many as 100 pieces at a time. (Metaphor and alliteration.)—*Union Carbide Corporation.*

You can't imagine all the stuff that blows, flows, swirls, swims, rushes, roars, gushes and pours through B. F. Goodrich hose. (Alliteration and onomatopoeia.)

It likes to flex those big new muscles! The sweet, smooth and sassy Chevrolet. (Metaphor and alliteration.)

Makes housework click like clockwork. (Metaphor, alliteration, and onomatopoeia.)—*Johnson's Wax.*

Nobody likes a fact man. But there are times when facts—like spinach and taxes—have to be faced with fortitude. (Pun, metaphor, and alliteration.)—*United States Steel Corporation.*

Provides raceways for electric wiring. (Metaphor.)—*Electrunite Tubing.*

LANGUAGE STRUCTURE: VERBAL RELATIONSHIPS

Words, informative and affective, take on additional meaning from the way they are formed and the way they are combined with other words. Through grammatical processes, we can change the form or structure of words so that they denote number (*boy, boys*), possession (*boy's, boys'*), time (*works, worked, has worked*), degrees of comparison (*warm, warmer, warmest*), and other subtleties of meaning. We can also arrange words to form sentences, and sometimes we can change the meaning simply by changing the word order. Thus, "The salesman thanked the customer" means one thing, but "The customer thanked the salesman" means something quite different.

As you can see, we are dealing here with the ground rules of English composition. A reasonably complete representation of these rules, especially designed to help you edit your work, will be found in the Style Manual concluding this book. In the meantime, we shall take this space to discuss some structural attributes of language that have special significance in business writing.

Conciseness

When you take more words than you need to express an idea, you not only slow down reading, but obscure the thought. No reader will take exception to the use of details for purposes of clarification, but he will be disconcerted by the inclusion of obvious or irrelevant details, the repetition of words and ideas, and other failures to come directly to the point. The contrast in the following examples is apparent:

BEFORE REVISION (138 WORDS)

We are offering for your consideration and comments the attached outline which provides for a review of procedures in connection with the authorization and reporting of minor outside plant construction, removal, and rearrangement of work by means of master work orders. These procedures are intended to reduce substantially the number of individual work orders required for small jobs and to expedite minor outside plant work which may be required to complete service orders or to maintain the plant in good working condition.

Under the master work order procedures, both editing and reconciling are usually done as one operation in the Accounting Office, thereby reducing the total all-over time required. A saving in labor cost also accrues to the section responsible for plant engineering, due to the reduction in the number of work orders that must be prepared.

AFTER REVISION (78 WORDS)

We should appreciate your comments on the attached revision of the outline of procedures.

The revision provides for the use of master work orders for small jobs on outside plant. We believe that these orders will speed up the work of the Plant Engineering and Accounting Offices. Plant Engineering will have to prepare considerably fewer work orders and therefore will save in labor costs. In most cases, Accounting will save time by editing and reconciling in one operation.

One reason for the kind of writing in the first column is probably the writer's desire to give importance to what he has to say. In his own mind, at least, wordiness is equated with substance. When the writer relaxes and expresses himself naturally, the chances for concise writing are improved.

Sometimes an excess of words indicates the writer's lack of familiarity with his subject. In these instances, he either fills out a sparse message with wordy phrasing, or quotes his sources verbatim instead of assimilating the details and condensing them to the few essentials the reader needs to know. The following sentence is an example of what happens when a government correspondent cites an official regulation without being sure of its meaning:

> "PA" means that you are classified with those currently serving under absolute or probational appointments in positions held by the employee on a permanent basis, including preference eligibles in excepted positions under appointments without time limitations.

When the writer understands the meaning of the regulation governing "PA" employees, he is more likely to write like this:

You are on the "PA" list because you have a permanent civil service appointment.

A profusion of words may serve as a protective shield. Forced to express an opinion and afraid of the consequences, the writer seeks cover in redundancy. Compare:

WORDY	CONCISE
Our past experience with Mr. Thomas has been of a favorable nature and we are of the opinion that he should be entitled to the usual courtesies ordinarily extended your guests.	Our experience with Mr. Thomas has been favorable, and we believe he is entitled to the courtesies ordinarily extended your guests.
It does not seem likely that any of these developments will be of such a serious or lasting nature as to have other than a transitory adverse effect.	It is not likely that any of these developments will have a lasting adverse effect.

Sentence Length

There is a close correlation between sentence length and comprehension. Short sentences are generally easy to understand because they provide frequent stops and because their structure is necessarily simple. This sentence has 47 words:

> The effect of foreign competition also shows up in the downward trend of steel mill exports which, during the first five months of this year, averaged about 170,000 net tons per month, compared with an average of 225,000 tons per month during the same period last year.

Although this is not a particularly difficult sentence, the idea stands out more clearly when the message is broken up into three sentences of 16, 17, and 16 words each.

> The effect of foreign competition also shows up in the downward trend of steel mill exports. During the first five months of this year, these exports came to about 170,000 tons per month. This compares with an average of 225,000 tons per month during the same period last year.

Actually, even a long sentence can be quite readable if the thought follows a fairly straight line as, for example, when one phrase or clause is added to another to form a coordinate series.

> The functions of the executive committee are to keep in close touch with the actual operations of our affiliate companies, to review annually the budgets of

all affiliates, and to assist the board by conducting worldwide surveys of oil supply and demand.

When, however, the relationship of ideas is complex, with one idea depending on another, and a third perhaps on the second, a long sentence is harder to follow.

> Although some of us who are familiar with the situation have definite reservations about the new procedure, we have to confess that something new has been introduced into the relations between the producers and the operating companies which will have an effect that we have as yet been unable to assess.

The structure of this type of sentence is easily simplified when some of the subordinate elements are separated and put into independent sentences, as shown below:

> Some of us who are familiar with the situation have definite reservations about the new procedure. Still, we have to confess that something new has been introduced into the relations between the producers and the operating companies. What the ultimate effect will be, we have not as yet been able to assess.

A specialist respected for his studies of "readability" recommends that sentences average 17 words.[6] This average can be maintained by varying the length of sentences from a few words to as many as 25 or 30 words. In some circumstances, an average of 20 to 25 words per sentence may be maintained without undue discomfort to the reader. Any sentence of more than 40 words, however, should be suspect. Some of the factors that control the sentence length are these:

1. *Reader's literacy.* The educated reader has more experience with long sentences than the less educated one and is able to extract their meaning more readily.

2. *Kind of message.* Relatively long sentences are characteristic of thoughtful writing. When relationships between ideas are involved and subtle, long sentences are often necessary to accommodate the qualifying phrases and clauses and the details needed to express the desired shades of meaning. Thus sentences tend to get longer as the subject matter becomes more analytical, more deliberative, or more technical.

3. *Effect desired.* Since they provide fewer stops, messages with long sentences read more smoothly than messages comprising a series of short sentences. Long sentences therefore have a legitimate place in messages intended to have a calming or conciliatory effect. The staccato effect of very short sentences, however, is useful in attracting attention and stimulating action.

[6] Rudolf Flesch, *The Art of Plain Talk* (New York: Harper & Row, 1946), p. 38. The Flesch formulas for determining readability are still widely used.

"Voice"

The directness and force of a statement are affected by the "voice" of the verb. A verb is in the *active* voice when the subject performs the action the verb denotes. A verb is in the *passive* voice when the subject is the receiver of the action.

> *Active:* We paid the bill on March 5.
> *Passive:* The bill was paid by us on March 5.

In the first sentence, the subject *we* tells who paid the bill. The subject is therefore said to perform the action of the verb. In the same sentence, the verb carries the action to the object *bill,* which is called the receiver of the action. In the second sentence, the word *bill,* which receives the action of the verb, becomes the subject. As you can see, the active voice provides the simpler and less awkward means of expression. Here are some further examples for comparison:

PASSIVE	ACTIVE
The *customer will be notified* when *notice is received* from our agent.	*We will notify the customer* when *we hear* from our agent.
This matter will be taken up with our Legal Department.	*We will take up this matter* with our Legal Department.
Under this service, *arrangement is made* to hold *securities deposited by you* with us.	Under this service, *we arrange* to hold *securities you deposit* with us.
We will be glad to work with Mr. Snow or any other *person designated by you.*	We will be glad to work with Mr. Snow or any other *person you designate.*

The merits of the active voice should not completely obscure the utility of the passive voice. There are times, for instance, when you want to emphasize the receiver of the action rather than the performer. In that case, you may make the receiver the subject as in the sentence, "*The machine was shipped* from our Muskegon factory on February 24." At other times, the passive voice enables you to be deliberately vague about the performer of the verb action. In the sentence, "*A question has been raised* as to the validity of the current practice," the construction makes it unnecessary to name the person or persons who have raised the question. Again, the sentence, "*Mr. Green is believed to be* considerably in debt," helps protect the source of the information.

Subordination[7]

The flexibility of language is nowhere better illustrated than in the technique of subordination. Without subordination we would have difficulty in

[7] Although our concern in this section is with subordination as a means of achieving connection in sentences, the principle applies also to longer units of composition. It is especially useful

showing the relation of one idea to another because each would have to be expressed as an independent thought. We would have to write like this:

> You are arriving on Thursday. Please let me know.

Although the two sentences are grammatically complete, the relationship is not clear. When, however, we subordinate one statement to the other by means of the conditional *if*, the connection is revealed:

> If you are arriving on Thursday, please let me know.

Subordinate relationships are commonly shown by any of the subordinate sentence elements: subordinate clauses (those beginning with any of the subordinate conjunctions: *if, as, when, while, because, since, although,* etc.), phrases (groups of related words not having a subject and predicate), and individual parts of speech (adjectives and adverbs, for example). Note in the following sentences the differences in the techniques of subordination and the incidental variations in compactness:

always need commas

> I forwarded to our Tax Department the income tax questionnaire *which you received from the State of California.* (Subordinate clause)
>
> I forwarded to our Tax Department the income tax questionnaire *sent you by the State of California.* (Participial phrase)
>
> I forwarded to our Tax Department the income tax questionnaire *from the State of California.* (Prepositional phrase)
>
> I forwarded to our Tax Department the *State of California* income tax questionnaire. (Adjective)

The position of the subordinate sentence elements may seriously affect the sense. A correspondent writes:

> Mr. Dakin had an account at our Main Street store, which was closed in May of last year.

This sentence is intelligible, but it does not say what the writer means. The Main Street store is still open; it is the account that was closed. We can correct the error simply by putting the subordinate clause next to the word it really modifies:

---

when it is taken to mean that subordinate ideas be given less space than more important ones and that they be placed where they will not command more attention than they are worth. In some instances, ideas of minor consequence can be omitted altogether. See "Development," Rule 5, Style Manual.

> Mr. Dakin had at our Main Street store an account which was closed in May of last year.

or

> At our Main Street store, Mr. Dakin had an account which was closed in May of last year.

Although the sentence now says what the writer means, it is somewhat awkward in construction. We can correct the awkwardness by recasting the sentence:

> Mr. Dakin had an account at our Main Street store until May of last year.

Parallel Structure

When ideas are functionally coordinate or equal, their relationship is best shown when they are expressed in parallel structure, that is, in the same grammatical form or pattern. We say, for example, "The flag is red, white, and blue," rather than "The flag is red, white, and also has blue in it." Although not so obvious, a similar difference can be found in these two sentences:

1. These huge antennas are not only required for long-range radar, but also trans-horizon communications, telemetry tracking, and to provide other early-warning alert applications.
2. These huge antennas are required not only for long-range radar, but also for trans-horizon communications, telemetry tracking, and other early-warning alert applications.

The first sentence is confusing because, as the following analysis shows, the elements that should be consistent in structure are not:

1. These huge antennas are
not only — required for long-range radar (verb phrase)
but also — trans-horizon communications (noun phrase)
telemetry tracking (noun phrase) and
to provide early-warning alert applications (infinitive phrase).

The sentence is clarified when the structure is changed so that the coordinate ideas are expressed in similar grammatical form.

2. These huge antennas are required
not only for — long-range radar (noun phrase)
but also for — trans-horizon communications (noun phrase)
telemetry tracking (noun phrase) and
other early-warning alert applications (noun phrase).

Parallel structure helps to give writing consistency, clarity, and force. Since it permits the stringing of any type of coordinate grammatical elements—single parts of speech, phrases, clauses, or whole sentences—it also increases the possibilities for variety and interest. These possibilities are suggested in the following sentences and paragraphs. For the use of parallel structure in larger units of composition, see pages 240–242.

> We know, for instance, that 32 percent of the visitors to the exhibit are under 21; that adults are divided equally by sex; that the great majority, young or older, are curious, alert, and active.

> Bill Peale gave up his sales interest and spent his spare time with his sons. He taught them to ice skate. He took them hunting. He cultivated an interest in their Y activities.

> As with most 3M products, the steps from discovery to market are many and oftentimes strewn with stumbling blocks. What are the product's applications? Its limitations? How can it be produced in quantity, economically? How can it be packaged? How should it be marketed?

> In a series of informative picture essays and an interpretive text of 35,000 words by Edward Seidensticker, you will read the story of Japan before it knew the Western world; come to understand the place of the Emperor in Japanese life; learn about the marvels of Japanese art, and the meaning of Buddhism; and discover the mixture of Oriental and Occidental influences throughout Japan's education, politics, technology and entertainment.

Directness

Eventually, the aim of every writer and speaker must be to communicate in a way that makes comprehension possible with the least strain on the reader or listener. The communicator's awareness of this need is shown in a number of ways that have already been described: being specific, adapting language to the reader, keeping sentences relatively short, favoring the active voice, placing modifiers close to the words they modify, and putting coordinate ideas in parallel structure. The methods also include a number of other techniques that, on the whole, are designed to cut through verbal density of the sort shown below and make the message simpler and more direct.

VERBAL DENSITY

```
     In summary, since no changes in procedure are to be
made at the time of the transplant and since the internal
controls appear to be sound, it is recommended that the
Auditing Department interpose no objection to the move at
the time its concurrence is officially solicited.
```

1. *It and there.* The expletives *it* and *there* usually prevent concise, forceful expression and should be used sparingly.

NOT: *It is* not considered that a detailed examination is necessary.
BUT: A detailed examination is not considered necessary.

NOT: *There are* three basic requirements of the regulation.
BUT: The regulation has three basic requirements.

2. *Proximity of subject and verb.* The separation of the subject and verb by more than a few words may prevent easy comprehension. The fault is corrected by a rearrangement of words and sometimes by the use of two sentences

NOT: *The source and use of funds* available on January 1 of selected years (the date considered to be the approximate seasonal peak of loans and advances outstanding) *are shown* on the following table.
BUT: *The following table shows* the source and use of funds available on January 1 of selected years. The date is considered to be the approximate seasonal peak of loans and advances outstanding.

3. *Which is, that is.* As a rule, the fewer the number of subordinate clauses in a sentence, the better the sentence reads. Words like *which is* and *that is*, which create such clauses, may often be reduced to simple adjectives, participles, or prepositional phrases.

NOT: The program is designed to provide a wide range of services *which are* appropriate to our aims.
BUT: The program is designed to provide a wide range of services appropriate to our aims.

NOT: The foreign exchange position sheets *that are* prepared at the end of each business day have proved to be very helpful.
BUT: The foreign exchange position sheets prepared at the end of each business day have proved to be very helpful.

NOT: An employee does best the work *which is* of greatest interest to him.
BUT: An employee does best the work of greatest interest to him.

4. *Strong verbs.* A single strong verb can often do the work of several weaker words, with improved results.

WEAK	STRONG
made a decision	decided
came to the conclusion	concluded
placed an order for	ordered
showed an increase	increased
be of service	serve

5. *Connecting phrases.* Long connecting phrases slow reading and should be eliminated or reduced to single words where possible.

NOT: The procedure is *in the process of* being reviewed.
BUT: The procedure is being reviewed.

NOT: *During the course of* their research *in connection with* the feasibility of . . .
BUT: *During* their research *on* the feasibility of . . .

. 6. *Rewriting.* Awkward, involved sentences should be reworked until they are expressed in the simplest way.

NOT: Our reply to the manufacturer will incorporate a request that they inform us of any product improvements they have made relevant to the several serious shortcomings in their central dictation system.
BUT: We will ask the manufacturer what they have done to correct the serious shortcomings in their central dictation system.

SUMMARY

Because the response to a message depends on the meaning the receiver attaches to it, the sender has a special responsibility to use language that is accurate, conforms to accepted standards of usage, and is conducive to good feeling and easy comprehension. Words are informative when they bear a close relation to their referents, or the things they stand for. Words are affective when they relate to the feelings of the sender or receiver. Words also take on additional meaning through structure, that is, through their grammatical form and the way they are combined with other words.

To be informative, words should be exact, easily understood by those for whom they are intended, and simple enough to promote maximum reading efficiency. Words are most exact when they represent fixed terms of reference like numbers or technical names. Exactness also requires that the words be used in ways sanctioned by the dictionary, that they be free of ambiguity, and that they be concrete rather than abstract. Whether the receiver is a specialist in some esoteric field of knowledge or a plain citizen, the words used should be part of his working vocabulary. Occupational lingo, or jargon, may provide an effective way to communicate with one's peers, but it should not be used to feed the sender's pretensions. Simple words are usually best because they speed reading as well as understanding, but care should be taken to see that they express the intended meaning accurately.

In using language for its affective value, the sender should distinguish between report (fact) words and judgment words. The latter are usually more biased and are more likely to affect the feelings of the receiver. The receiver's feelings are also affected by the suggestion or connotation of words. In this respect, distinctions are made between words that connote favor (e.g., *fair-trade laws*) and those that connote prejudice (e.g., *price-fixing laws*); between positive, or affirmative, words (e.g., *promptness*) and negative words (e.g., *no delay*). Another factor in the affective use of language is freshness. Words that are original and vivid, or at least natural, lend interest and afford pleasure; those that are stereotyped and dull defeat those objectives.

Language structure is most effective when ideas are expressed concisely, and sentences and paragraphs are kept at reasonable length. Other structural advantages are often obtained by the use of the active voice and parallel structure, by putting related words close together, by using exact connectives, and by reducing complex verbal constructions to simple ones.

PROBLEMS

1. Make the following statements more specific. Invent any necessary details.
   (*a*) We have received your request for our booklet.
   (*b*) Your account is now long overdue.
   (*c*) I'll meet you for lunch tomorrow.
   (*d*) My report is based on several well-known books in the field.
   (*e*) He has an office downtown.
   (*f*) Checks in large amounts should be countersigned by one of the senior officers.
   (*g*) The luncheon prices are very reasonable.
   (*h*) The wheelbase is somewhat shorter than it was on last year's models.
   (*i*) The contents of this book on letter writing are well worth while.
   (*j*) Our new photo-offset machine is a real time saver.

2. In each of the following sentences, one word or expression is faulty. Rewrite the sentences, substituting correct or exact words for the incorrect or inexact ones.
   (*a*) Knowing their strong financial position, we believe you can deal with this company in confidence.
   (*b*) Let me enumerate a little more my civil service status.
   (*c*) Since our last meeting, my impression of your company has advanced even further.
   (*d*) We believe the first two alternatives should be instituted immediately.
   (*e*) Our experience in retailing has given us a large insight into the problems of store location.
   (*f*) In the past ten years this country has witnessed an enormous raise in the demand for educated men and women.
   (*g*) If it were a bonified offer, there would be no question about our accepting it.
   (*h*) We would suggest exchanging from General Dynamics common to Lockheed for better appreciation potential.
   (*i*) Let's put an end to this impractical and exorbitant situation.
   (*j*) This change has been installed to reduce costs.
   (*k*) Thank you for returning the application card regarding your new account.
   (*l*) The signature should be provided on the last line.
   (*m*) As soon as we received this requirement, we complied with it.
   (*n*) Please send us a check for the differential.
   (*o*) You may be sure that in the future your checks will be dispensed to the correct address.

3. The following memorandum is written in very abstract language, with a resulting vagueness in meaning. Recast it in concrete and specific terms. You may make any reasonable assumptions.

```
Memorandum to Mr. Carroll Finney, Section Head
              Emporium Department Store

We have just been contacted by the source of the items we
recently ordered to the effect that the better part of
them will be forthcoming soon.

These are of such a nature that I believe we can reap
considerable benefits in the sales area if we show them
to good advantage where it counts.  Upon their arrival,
therefore, I suggest you take adequate steps to insure
good results.  I should like to be able to communicate to
our senior personnel that all areas have put forth a max-
imum of effort in this regard.

                                 Philip Bentley
                                 Buyer
```

4. In the following sentences, find the nonstandard usages and substitute standard usages for them. See if your dictionary can provide any help.
   (*a*) Miss Thomas sat beside of me at the conference.
   (*b*) Their offer was the best of any we received.
   (*c*) We have the sweaters in a choice of nile green, mauve, and teal blue, but the latter is the most popular.
   (*d*) The return from our investment wasn't near as much as we wished.
   (*e*) He might of won the prize if only he had tried harder.
   (*f*) In addition to my salary, I receive a percent of all sales.
   (*g*) We seldom ever employ non-college graduates for this position.
   (*h*) What kind of a car are you looking for?
   (*i*) It will be alright if you make the exchange any time before January 15.
   (*j*) The clock has the most unique design we have ever seen.

5. List five sentences written in the jargon of some field with which you are familiar (try going to trade or technical publications for your examples). Then rewrite each sentence in everyday terms.

6. The following jargon was taken from the correspondence of a stock brokerage firm. On the basis of what you know about stocks, or can find out about them, try rewriting each sentence so that it would be meaningful to the nonprofessional investor.
   (*a*) These issues are particularly attractive for their semidefensive characteristics.
   (*b*) We are impressed by the secular growth characteristics of every other phase of the product line.
   (*c*) On a structural basis, we suggest you cut back on Detroit Edison.
   (*d*) Operations are apt to be cyclical.
   (*e*) The price of this stock is high statistically.

7. Improve the connotation of the following statements:
   (*a*) You will hear from us as soon as we have investigated your references.
   (*b*) We pride outselves in being an aggressive company.
   (*c*) Because of the uncertainty of the market, we suggest that half of your holdings in this issue be eliminated.
   (*d*) Our informer was George Peabody, who works in the accounting office.

(*e*) Let our truck driver call for your wash this week.
(*f*) We note that this is the first time you have been delinquent in paying a bill.
(*g*) Many employees have been taking advantage of the earlier quitting time to do some shopping on the way home.
(*h*) The work should take merely an hour a week.
(*i*) We regret that our blunder caused you such inconvenience.
(*j*) Elbert Ray, our new president, is the child of the chairman of the board.

8. Rewrite the following negative statements in positive terms:
(*a*) We are sorry to tell you that the alterations will not be completed until Thursday.
(*b*) You needn't worry about experiencing any further delay in getting this shipment.
(*c*) We shall have to delay sending you the shower curtains you ordered until you tell us whether you want green or beige.
(*d*) It is against our policy to carry regular checking accounts with balances under $1,000.
(*e*) We trust that in the future you will not fall behind again in making your payments.
(*f*) We close at 5 p.m. every day.
(*g*) We cannot undertake to answer by mail your request for employment with this company.
(*h*) You will never have reason to regret buying this suitcase.
(*i*) It's a mistake to buy a car without looking into the cost of a personal bank loan.
(*j*) We are sure our customers will not be unduly inconvenienced through the use of our new order forms.

9. Rewrite the following sentences, substituting fresh expressions for the stale ones:
(*a*) If you put off your order, you may miss the boat.
(*b*) Every man has to pull his own weight in this organization.
(*c*) The sudden decline in prices gives us all much food for thought.
(*d*) The company is expanding by leaps and bounds.
(*e*) Our object in stocking the product is to get in on the ground floor.
(*f*) Smith is head and shoulders above any of the other job candidates.
(*g*) Immaculate tailoring is the keynote of quality.
(*h*) Words fail to express our deep appreciation.
(*i*) We waited with bated breath for Jim Oliver to return from his sales trip.
(*j*) David Styles works like a beaver; he's entitled to a raise.

10. Rewrite the following statements in vivid but appropriate language. Take only one sentence for each statement.
(*a*) The accounting department is run very efficiently.
(*b*) Bad weather caused a drop in sales.
(*c*) The Seville is a car that will give you lots of satisfaction.
(*d*) Bermuda is all you could wish for in a vacation spot.
(*e*) Truck trailers tie up city traffic.

11. From current advertisements select and hand in five examples of figurative language.

12. Rewrite the following sentences so that all the verbs are in the active voice.

(*a*) The canceled check was returned by us to you on Tuesday by registered mail.
(*b*) It was intended that the program be administered by the vice president for sales.
(*c*) In order for the effectiveness of the new procedure to be properly evaluated, the help of our customers will be needed.
(*d*) Favorable comment on the company's buying practices has already been made in this report.
(*e*) It should be noted that the shipment will be sent from our Bridgeport factory on September 23.

13. Rewrite the following statements to make them simpler, clearer, and more direct. As necessary, you may delete words, shorten sentences, rearrange the parts, and simplify the vocabulary.
(*a*) If the occasion should arise, please do not hesitate to get in touch with us if we can be of assistance in similar circumstances.
(*b*) According to our files, we do not have any record of having received payment.
(*c*) The personality conflicts that may arise on the job are also factors which the Staff Relations Assistant must mollify or eliminate through the execution of transfers, this being a realm of responsibility difficult to define because of its diversity and varying degrees of significance.
(*d*) We are not satisfied with the adequacy of this arrangement when measured in terms of future needs.
(*e*) Naval stores products are produced from pine stumpage available in Florida, Louisiana, and other areas in the Southeast in decreasing quantities.
(*f*) Another broad facet of external influence upon the operation of our financial institutions is the area of interest rates and Federal regulation.
(*g*) We are of the belief that the system presently in use is basically sound and that the modification of this system in such a way as to provide the controls that are necessary and to eliminate unnecessary duplication of records is all that is needed for improved operations.
(*h*) Utilizing its cash position, the present Reed Division was acquired by Ace in 1976.
(*i*) The payroll is prepared by the secretary from the attendance records.
(*j*) The result would be a more orderly government securities market, which is of prime concern to the Treasury Department and this bank.
(*k*) These rates, which included costs of depreciation of fixed assets, guard services and public health services not previously recognized in the accounts, closely approximated the actual cost.
(*l*) The following is a report indicative of my findings and recommendations.
(*m*) That the policy causes no great problem is supported by the fact that the company states that out of 500,000 mortgages, only three included collateral.
(*n*) It is not considered that a detailed examination is necessary.
(*o*) The first requirement of good internal control is incorporated in the present procedure in that each [State treasurer's] office maintains a list of institutions to be examined and it is the responsibility of the Assistant Chief Examiner in each office to see that the examinations are conducted except in those instances where responsibility has been delegated to a subordinate who is responsible for assigning examiners, as in the case of currency exchanges and credit unions.

14. Improve the following statements by the application of parallel structure:

(*a*) This article will briefly outline the steps an executive may take in (1) analyzing the present operations, (2) find the different data processing equipment applicable to his operations, and (3) the approach to be taken in determining whether an improvement in speed, cost, and in efficiency will result.

(*b*) The purpose of our inquiry is to help devise means of improved internal control, eliminating the duplication of records, provide better information, and it should facilitate audit review.

(*c*) Check each account and making sure that each one is a good risk.

(*d*) In many instances accountants are called upon to handle special work, such as trust accountings, maintenance of profit-sharing and pension fund accounts, a detailed audit of accounts receivable, cash receipts and disbursements, and there are many other such assignments requiring substantial detailed work.

(*e*) This process prevents the tire cord from shrinking as it cools, which would contract the tread grooves.

(*f*) The improperly trained personnel, often inadequate to carry out their functions efficiently, coupled with a lackadaisical attitude toward enforcement policies, indicate the need for a complete reorganization of the office.

15. At the 1933 Chicago World's Fair, Western Union offered visitors a choice of thirty-three standardized telegrams. The two that were most popular (measured in terms of the number purchased and sent), and the two that were least popular, are quoted below. In the light of what you know about language and human nature, which of the following telegrams do you think were the most successful? Which do you think were the least successful? Give your reasons.

(*a*) THE FUTURE OF THE COUNTRY THAT HAS PRODUCED WHAT THIS FAIR COMMEMORATES CANNOT BE IN DOUBT. IT IS AN INSPIRING EXHIBIT.

(*b*) IF YOU WOULD SEE THE DREAMS OF GREAT MEN REALIZED IN THE FULLNESS OF BEAUTY AND USE, DON'T MISS THIS FAIR.

(*c*) MISS YOU AT THIS GREAT FAIR. IF YOU WERE HERE MY JOY WOULD BE COMPLETE. SENDING MUCH LOVE WITH THIS WIRE.

(*d*) MY OLD DOGS GET TIRED BUT IT'S WORTH IT TO SEE ALL THERE IS TO SEE. REGARDS TO ALL.

4 Communicating with Letters

LETTERS are the most personal form of written communication, the most numerous, and the most versatile. They give you the chance to deal with people directly, individually, and with an intimacy not otherwise possible through writing. They also enable you to exert, more fully than in any other written medium, the force of your character and personality.

Letter writing takes up a significant part of business time. A single correspondent—whether an executive or aide—will write often dozens of letters a day to customers, prospective customers, suppliers, credit agencies, employees, government officials, and others. The letters fulfill a variety of business functions, from making inquiries and arranging appointments to selling goods and adjusting complaints. Even when the telephone or in-person conversation is more convenient, the letter is often preferred because it leaves a record for future reference.

Business people customarily dictate their letters. Some employ stenographers, but an increasing number are using dictating machines. Either way, dictation requires a high degree of skill. In machine dictation, especially, the opportunities to make corrections are limited and the dictator must try to be right the first time. Only in the instance of the most important or most difficult letters will the experienced correspondent write a draft by hand or dictate a draft to be typewritten and returned for editing.

Although letters conform generally to the same language requirements as other forms of business composition, they are distinctive in three respects: (1)

their mechanical makeup, (2) their tone, and (3) their structure. These topics are discussed here in detail. At the end of the chapter you will also find a section on letter dictation and some comments on the use of form letters.

Mechanical Makeup

MECHANICAL MAKEUP

Letters are easily identified by their appearance. In addition to the message substance, they consist of certain formal parts prescribed by custom and convenience. These include a heading, inside address, salutation, complimentary close, and signature. The details of these and other physical characteristics vary somewhat according to the preferences of the organization. Some companies, for example, believe the salutation and complimentary close to be superfluous and omit them; but the practice has not caught on. Common styles of makeup are shown in Figures 4-1 and 4-2. Another style, the full block style shown in Problem 15, page 126 is preferred by some organizations because the alignment of all elements with the left margin speeds up typing. The disadvantage is that it makes letters look lopsided.

To ensure uniformity and neatness, large companies publish secretarial manuals that prescribe the style in which their letters are to be typewritten. The rules that follow are not practiced without exception, but they conform to current standards.

General Layout

The standard business letter sheet is 8½ × 11 inches, though smaller sizes are sometimes used for special purposes. A good quality white bond paper is preferred. A printed heading gives at least the sender's name and address and usually includes the telephone number.

The letter is so arranged on the page that the total effect is that of a well-framed picture. The margins should be at least one inch at the sides and bottom—more when the letter is brief. Body copy is usually single-spaced, with double spacing between paragraphs. If the letter is very short, up to seven or eight lines, an employer may prescribe double spacing for the text.

Paragraphs may either be indented five or ten spaces or set flush with the margin to create a block effect. Blocked paragraphs appear to be favored. It is customary to put no punctuation after the lines of the heading and inside address, except for the period to mark an abbreviation.

Neatness requires that the right-hand margin be as even as possible, that the typing impression be uniformly dark, and that corrections be made so neatly that they will not be noticed. The use of white opaquing fluid to paint out errors is generally preferred to erasures.

For insertion in the standard "long" envelope, the regular letter sheet is folded twice horizontally. To fit the standard "small" envelope, it is folded in half horizontally and then twice vertically.

The Heading

If the letter sheet already bears the printed address of the sender, the heading will consist only of the date. This should be placed several lines under the

GARRETT MANUFACTURING COMPANY

350 Park Avenue New York, N.Y. 10022
Tel: (212) 432-5000

Mr. Simon Walters, Secretary
South Carolina Mills, Inc.
Charleston, SC 29410

Dear Mr. Walters:

This letter is an example of the style adopted as standard for the Garrett Manufacturing Company. The margins are adjusted to make the letter appear longer than it is wide and to give it somewhat the same shape as the page itself.

The date is typed on the fourth line below the bottom of the printed heading, so that it ends at the right margin. The inside address is written in block form. Paragraphs are also blocked (not indented). Except for periods to mark abbreviations, no punctuation is used after the lines of the inside address. The salutation is typed at the left margin two lines below the inside address and is followed by a colon.

The complimentary close is begun slightly to the right of the center of the page on the second line below the message. It is followed by a comma. The name of the writer is typed four spaces below the complimentary close and the title or department designation is placed immediately below the name.

Dictator's and transcriber's initials are placed at the left-hand margin, two spaces below the title.

Very truly yours,

Lauren F. Palen
Assistant Vice President

LFP:ms

FIG. 4-1. *Correct form of a business letter.*

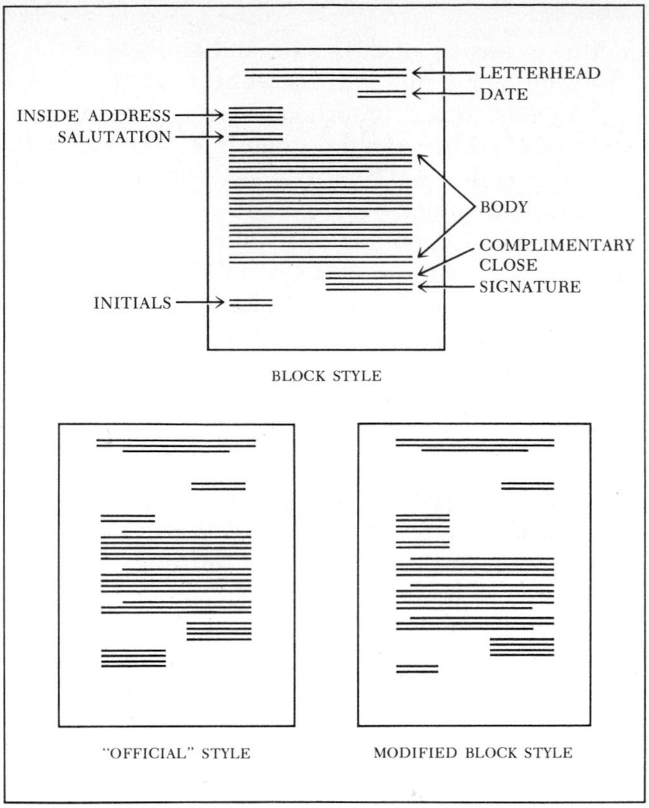

FIG. 4-2. *Common styles of mechanical makeup.*

printed heading. It may be typewritten in dead center or begin at the center or a little farther to the right, but it should not extend beyond the right-hand margin. The name of the month should be spelled out.

If there is no printed address on the letter sheet, the heading will consist of both the sender's mailing address and the date, placed a little to the right of center and arranged in block style as follows. The ZIP code is placed two spaces after the name of the state.

```
475 Ninth Avenue          265 West 16th Street
Chicago, IL  60634        New York, NY  10011
February 25, 19--         August 6, 19--
```

Words like Street and Avenue, and East and West are generally spelled out. Numbered streets up to and including ten are also spelled out. The name of the state, however, is preferably abbreviated to conform to the two-letter codes established by the Postal Service (see Rule 33f, Style Manual.)

Inside Address

The inside address consists of the name and address of the receiver. It is advisable to write the name and address, abbreviating or not, exactly as he signs it or as it appears in the letterhead. An apartment or room number should follow the street address on the same line. The city address and state should be typewritten on the next line. The ZIP code follows on the same line two spaces after the state name.

All lines of the inside address begin flush with the left-hand margin. In ordinary correspondence, the positioning is several lines or more below the date. However, in letters that come outside the usual routine of business (a letter inviting a customer to lunch, a letter of congratulations or condolence, a letter to a high government official)—especially where small stationery is used—the inside address is customarily placed at the left margin several spaces below the signature. In personal letters to friends, it may be omitted altogether.

A title of courtesy (*Mr., Miss, Mrs., Ms., Dr., Professor, Reverend*) should always precede a person's name. (The title *Ms.* is acceptably used in addressing a woman, married or not.) A business or other official title may follow, either on the same line or on the next, depending on the length of the title. These styles are correct:

```
Dr. Ellen Taubman
100 Park Avenue, Room 102
New York, NY  10017

Mr. Cornelius C. Evans
Vice President for Marketing
Dayton Steel Co., Inc.
1200 Buckeye Street
Dayton, OH  45406

Mr. Henry P. Starr, President
Consolidated Electronics
East Lansing, MI  48823

Senator Ann Parsons
United States Senate
Washington, DC  20510
```

Salutation

Letters addressed to organizations begin *Gentlemen* or *Ladies,* or *Ladies and Gentlemen,* depending on the sexual composition of the top management. Letters addressed to both private individuals and those connected with organizations almost invariably begin in the style of *Dear Mr. Jones.* A more formal but rare salutation is *My dear Mr. Jones. Dear Sir* is seldom used except in printed form letters. *Dear Sirs* is archaic. *Dear Ray* would be the correct style in writing to someone you normally call by the first name.

In all ordinary business correspondence, even when the reader is addressed by the first name, a colon follows the salutation. The comma is usually reserved for purely personal letters between friends.

In the instance of public officials and members of the clergy, custom often prescribes special forms of address. You will find a comprehensive list of these forms in *Webster's Third New International Dictionary*.

Body

The typing of the letter text is governed by rules of editorial style covering such matters as spelling, abbreviations, capitalization, underlining, the use of figures and symbols, and the division of words at the ends of lines. Since these rules cover the preparation of not only letters but other kinds of writing as well, they are treated in the Style Manual.

Should a letter require a second page, be sure to carry over at least three lines of the text. Unless special printed stationery is provided for the purpose, you should use a blank sheet of the same quality as the first sheet and type the name of the addressee, the page number, and the date on a single line about one inch from the top, like this:

```
Mr. Thomas S. Farmer          -2-          October 14, 19--
```

Complimentary Close

The complimentary close is placed two spaces below the last line of the text and halfway to the right or directly in line with the date. The most common closes are *Very truly yours* and *Yours very truly.* Note that only the first word is capitalized. *Yours truly* and *Truly yours* are somewhat colder and are seldom used any more. *Sincerely yours, Yours sincerely,* and *Sincerely* are growing in favor. *Respectfully yours, Yours respectfully,* and *Respectfully* are useful when you want to show special deference, as when writing to a high public official or member of the clergy. *Cordially yours* and *Cordially* are correct in writing to someone you regard as a good friend. The complimentary close is usually, but not always, followed by a comma.

Signature

There is much variation in the style of the signature. The full signature includes the company's name, which is typewritten two spaces directly below the complimentary close. If the name is so long that it would overrun the right hand margin, it is centered below the complimentary close. The name, the name and title, or only the title of the signer is typewritten three or four spaces below the company's name and flush with the complimentary close. If the signer has no formal title, his department affiliation may be indicated. The writer signs his name in the space between the lines.

Many companies consider their name in the heading sufficient for purposes of identification and responsibility, and they therefore omit the company name in the signature. Shown here are several acceptable styles:

NO

Sincerely,

Combustion Engineering Corporation

John C. Lyle

John C. Lyle
Field Representative

Very truly yours,

Carolyn Brinckman

Sales Department

Sincerely yours,

Francis T. Payne

Francis T. Payne, Manager

A man's signature is never preceded by *Mr.* or any other title. A woman, however, may do her reader a special favor by putting *Miss, Mrs.,* or *Ms.* in parentheses before her name.

Very truly yours,

(Miss) *Deborah Forbes*

Cashier

Sincerely yours,

Helen S. Patrick

(Mrs.) Helen S. Patrick

Initials, Enclosures, Copies

The initials or name of the dictator followed by the stenographer's initials appear a couple of lines below the signature, flush with left-hand margin. These styles are common:

PST:HR pst:hr PST/HR

Philip S. Throm:HR Philip S. Throm
very Rare HR

If the full name of the signer is used in this position, it is not typewritten under the complimentary close. Sometimes the initials are omitted from the original copy and are placed only on the carbon copies for purposes of record.

When a letter is to be accompanied by a pamphlet, photocopy, or other enclosure, the fact is indicated directly below the initials in the manner of the examples below:

Be consistent don't

Enclosure Encl. 2 enclosures *not good* Enclosures: 2 *correct*
enclosure enc. 3 encs.

if streets & states are written out

Enclosures of special importance are usually listed.

Enclosures: 1. Davis sales contract
 2. List of vendors

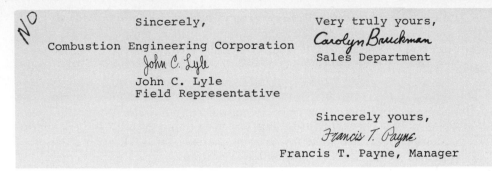

To show that carbon copies of the letter are being sent to others than the addressee, place directly below the typist's initials or the enclosure notice, on all copies or on the carbon copies alone, a notation in one of these styles:

Copy to Mr. Edward Fellows
cc: Mr. Edward Fellows

CC: Ms. Lillian Melman
Mr. Arthur Frank

Special Forms

If you want to address the letter to the company, but bring it to the attention of a particular individual, you will use an "attention line." This is placed two spaces above or below the salutation, and it is either centered or placed at the left-hand margin. These styles are correct:

Attention of the Advertising Manager

Attention of Mr. Samuel Triton

Attention: Mr. Samuel Triton

It is better not to abbreviate the word *Attention.* Since the letter is addressed to the company, the salutation should be *Gentlemen* or, if appropriate, *Ladies*.

Notations like REGISTERED MAIL, AIR MAIL, and SPECIAL DELIVERY are typed in capital and small letters or all capitals, usually with underlining, and placed a couple of lines above the inside address either in the center of the page or at the left margin.

For the convenience of the reader or file clerk, the subject of the letter is sometimes named in a heading placed in one of the positions already recommended for the attention line. A prefacing label is not necessary, but if one is used, the word *Subject*, followed by a colon, is preferred to the Latin *Re* (in the matter of). If the letter you are replying to has a reference or file number to which you are requested to refer, you may treat it in the same way as a subject notation. The example below combines several of the special forms mentioned:

AIR MAIL

Pastor & Crimmons, Inc.
890 West 18th Street
New York, N Y 10013

Attention of Mr. Arthur V. Gold

Gentlemen:

Subject: Caribbean Oil Company

Envelope Address

The envelope address is the same as that prescribed for the inside address, with the added caution to use the two-letter state abbreviation and the ZIP code. The address is positioned somewhat below and to the right of the exact

Dorothy E. Bennett
Hale Manufacturing Company
415 West Main Street
Norwalk, CT 06856

AIR MAIL
SPECIAL DELIVERY

Sales Promotion Department
Barnaby Enterprises
1700 Wilshire Boulevard
Los Angeles, CA 90028

Attention of Mr. Edward M. Cord

FIG. 4-3. *Style of envelope address.*

center of the envelope, as shown in Figure 4-3.[1] Note also in the figure the position of the several notations.

TONE

Because a letter involves you and the reader more personally than other types of business composition, you have a special responsibility to respect the relationship. Like a visitor, you are expected to be considerate of your host and choose your ideas and words accordingly. This is not always easy: you are pressed for time, you are too eager to win your point, you are irked by the reader's behavior. In these circumstances, selfishness, egotism, pomposity, discourtesy, and insincerity have a way of insinuating themselves into the message, and you must guard against them.

The Reader's Point of View

A good letter is reader oriented: it shows an awareness of the reader's aims while at the same time it satisfies yours. Thus it observes the principle of the *shared goal,* which we spoke about in Chapter 2. When the letter is one sided—when it seeks an advantage for you without offering any to the reader or when it expresses your views and feelings without regard for those of the reader—it cannot be considered entirely successful even if the reader eventually takes the action you want.

The writers of the following message are so absorbed in their own interests that they seem to forget about the readers':

We are conducting a campaign to increase our business in the coming year

[1] Bulk mailers, whose mail is most likely to be processed by electronic scanners, should obtain from the Post Office the more specific instructions it has issued for positioning addresses on envelopes.

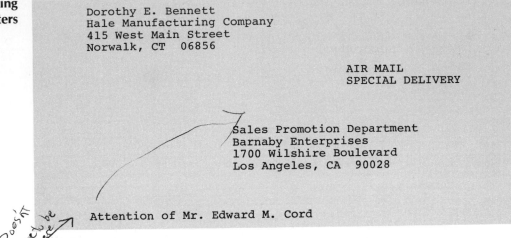

and if everyone will go out and hustle and call the attention of his friends to our service, our goal will be attained. Multigraphing. Addressing. Mailing.

The message is improved when it is directed to the readers' aims:

When you have circular letters to go out, why upset office routine? We'll process them for you, address them, and mail them—probably at less cost than you could do them yourself. And fast! 50 or 50,000 in a single working day. Call 293-4900 for an on-the-spot estimate.

Note also the difference in point of view in these examples:

WRITER'S POINT OF VIEW	READER'S POINT OF VIEW
The new Gridley is the best model we have ever made and stands out among competitive machines for its efficiency and low cost.	We wish we could send you a sample machine so that you could apply it to your own jobs and realize the better methods, greater efficiency, and lower cost it offers you.
We'd appreciate your business now because it's a little slow.	It's a good idea to order the work now when we have lots of time to do the job to perfection.
I need this information for a paper I am writing.	Your marketing record is so outstanding that I feel my paper would not be complete without reference to it.

THE *YOU* APPROACH

The pronoun *you* can be very helpful in directing the letter to the reader's personal interests. Compare:

IMPERSONAL APPROACH	YOU APPROACH
Personal credit can be a person's most valuable and useful asset. Low-cost personal loans permit the purchase of needed goods today—out of current income. They help organize one's financial affairs on a more efficient basis.	Do *you* know that personal credit can be one of *your* most valuable and useful assets. Low-cost personal loans enable *you* to buy the important things *you* need or want today—out of current income. They can also help *you* organize *your* financial affairs on a more efficient basis.
The enclosed pamphlet, "Taxation of Estates and Gifts," spells out the Federal Estate Tax, Federal Gift Tax, and State Inheritance Tax on various estates and gifts.	As an attorney, *you* are undoubtedly required to discuss estate planning problems with *your* clients. We believe the enclosed pamphlet, "Taxation of Estates and Gifts," will be helpful to *you* in such discussions.

A common violation of the *you* approach is writing as if to a crowd instead of to a single person.

MASS APPROACH	YOU APPROACH
We like people to write and ask about our service.	We are glad *you* wrote to ask about our service.
This booklet is designed to help its readers plan better vacations.	This booklet is designed to help *you* plan a better vacation.
We are always sorry whenever our customers fail to get complete satisfaction from our merchandise.	We are sorry that *you* are not completely satisfied with the Auto Toaster *you* bought from us a short time ago.

In their zeal to improve even on the pronoun *you*, some writers follow the practice of punctuating the letter with the name of the reader in this fashion:

We assure you, *Mr. Jones,* that the procedure we suggest . . .

To many readers, the effect seems patronizing. The fault is aggravated when the name is obviously filled in to occupy a space left for the purpose in a printed form letter.

HUMANIZING THE WRITER

While looking for opportunities to use the pronoun *you*, you should not go to an unhappy extreme to avoid the pronouns *I* and *we*. Admittedly, there is some danger that frequent reference to yourself may suggest egotism. On the other hand, *I* and *we* establish better rapport with the reader than the impersonal constructions many writers use either because of false modesty or a desire to evade responsibility. "This is to acknowledge receipt" is a very impersonal way of saying, "I have received." "It is believed" is also much colder than "we believe" and can be justified only when there is good reason to be vague about the identity of the believer. The examples that follow offer further contrasts:

IMPERSONAL	PERSONAL
Reference is made to your letter of	*We* refer to your letter of
There is enclosed a memorandum	*I* am enclosing a memorandum
It is suggested that this department be supplied with	*We* suggest that *you* send *us*
It is the understanding of the writer that	*I* understand that
Notice has been taken of	*We* have noted that

Sometimes a question arises as to which pronoun should be used, *I* or *we*. A satisfactory rule to follow is to use *I* when you refer to yourself and *we* when you refer to your company or to unnamed persons in the company. This practice permits the use of both *I* and *we* in the same letter and even in the same sentence:

I have been looking over the samples of the bindings you sent *us*.

To be sure, a diffident writer or one in the lower ranks may use *we* exclusively and still achieve a reasonably personal effect. A practice to be avoided, however, is using the name of the company or the phrase *our company* when *we* would be simpler and less pompous.

STRAINED	MORE NATURAL
Rawlings & Co. do not manufacture the type of bearing you inquired about.	*We* do not manufacture the type of bearing you inquired about.
Our company has been in business for sixty years.	*We* have been in business for sixty years.
Please mail the card to the *Allyn Corporation* at your convenience.	Please mail the card to *us* at your convenience.

Although *I* and *we* are helpful to the style of the letter, they would be conspicuous and probably monotonous at the beginning of several successive paragraphs. The fault can be remedied by an occasional change of sentence structure.

OVERCONSPICUOUS WE

Dear Mr. Troy:
We have your letter of March 29 in which you object to our notifying Mrs. Pierce of sums we have sent you for the care of her niece, Mary Rover.
We agree that notices of this type should be sent only to you and Miss Rover.
We are sorry about our error and offer our sincere regrets.
Very truly yours,

IMPROVED

Dear Mr. Troy:
We have your letter of March 29 in which you object to our notifying Mrs. Pierce of sums we have sent you for the care of her niece, Mary Rover.
Notices of this type, we agree, should be sent only to you and Miss Rover.
Please accept our sincere regrets.
Very truly yours,

Naturalness

Letters are usually most effective when they sound natural—almost as if the writer were speaking personally to the reader. One way to achieve this effect is to use the personal pronouns *you* and *I*, as suggested in the several pages preceding. Another way is to avoid getting into a verbal rut. Letters are so much a part of business routine and some of the ideas to be expressed arise so often that the temptation to use clichés becomes very strong indeed. Hackneyed or stilted writing is bad in any kind of writing, but it strikes a particularly sour note in what purports to be personal communication.

The hackneyed phrases in the first column below are characteristic of business letter jargon. Some are archaic, some legal-sounding, and others simply overformal. Many, characteristically, come at the beginning and end of the letter and thus weaken the parts that should make the strongest impressions. Note the improvement when the hackneyed phrases are put in everyday English.

HACKNEYED	IMPROVED
Kindly advise	Please let us know
As per your request	As you requested
We deem it advisable	We believe it advisable
The said matter	This matter
Receipt is acknowledged	We have received
We have your letter and thank you for same.	Thank you for your letter.
Your favor of April 6	Your letter of April 6
At your earliest convenience	As soon as you can
Pending receipt of	Until we receive
Please indicate thereon	Please indicate on it
Subsequent to	After
Your letter of recent date	Your recent letter
Hoping to hear from you, we remain,	May we hear from you soon?

The deadening effect of stereotyped language on the whole letter is shown in this example:

> Dear Mr. Grimes:
>
> Pursuant to our understanding with respect to the disposition of your claim, we have approved same for settlement and are enclosing release for your signature.
>
> Kindly execute this release as per instructions, have your signature witnessed, and return in self-addressed envelope.
>
> Assuring you that a check will be mailed to you promptly, we are
>
> Very truly yours,

Here is the same letter written in a fresher, more natural style:

```
Dear Mr. Grimes:

You will be glad to know that your claim has been approved
in accordance with the terms we discussed.

All you have to do is sign the enclosed release in the
presence of a witness and return it in the envelope we
have provided.  Your check will be mailed promptly.

                              Very truly yours,
```

It would be a mistake to assume that the same level of diction is used, or should be used in all letters. In Figure 4-4, you will see samples of writing taken from different files of the same company. The differences in style can be accounted for by the differences both in the nature of the correspondence and in the relations between the writer and the reader.

Courtesy

Courtesy is consideration for others. It therefore encompasses the reader's point of view, which we have already discussed; but it extends further to the active cultivation of good feeling through language techniques.

THE LANGUAGE OF COURTESY

A considerate writer makes frequent use of the terms customarily associated with courtesy, such as those italicized in the sentences below:

Thank you for your check for $104.56.
Many thanks for your order of April 27.
We appreciate your writing to us so promptly.
Please let us know when the goods arrive.
We are sorry that you have not yet received your lamps.
We sincerely regret the inconvenience.
Do *accept our apologies.*

A request can be softened if it is phrased as a question. The question of courtesy, as the construction is called, is usually followed by a period.

wishy-washy

Harsh: Take care of this matter at once.
Softer: *May we ask you* to take care of this matter at once.
Will you please take care of this matter at once.
Also courteous: *Please* take care of this matter at once.

TACT

Every normal reader seeks to preserve and enhance the good opinion he has of himself. Writing that helps him do that has tact as well as courtesy. The following letter was written in response to an oil company's request for a special report prepared by an oil trade magazine:

```
Dear Mr. Beal:

Your request for an inspection copy of the Williston Pe-
troleum Record's special report on Canadian Oil Prospects
has been referred to me, and it is with great regret that
I must advise that we cannot comply.

Our special reports are offered for sale, and we consider
it unfair to our subscribers if anyone can obtain without
cost what others are required to pay for.  We know that
you have long been a subscriber to our magazine and that
by declining to accede to your request we may lose an old
and valued customer.  However, in that case and in the
interests of our subscribers as a whole, we shall have to
accept that penalty.

                                  Very truly yours,
```

The writer's hostility is apparently the result of unwarranted suspicion of the customer, coupled with considerable bullheadedness. The subscriber did not really want anything he was not entitled to and would no doubt have been made considerably happier if the letter had read as follows:

```
Dear Mr. Beal:

We appreciate your interest in our special report on
Canadian Oil Prospects.  Because of the cost of prepara-
tion, there is a nominal charge of $5 for this report.

If you will write or telephone your approval, we'll be
glad to send you a copy with our bill.  We're sure you'll
find the report helpful.

                                  Very truly yours,
```

The danger of tactlessness is greatest in situations to which you or the reader may be especially sensitive—for example, one involving an error, a claim for damage, or the refusal of a request. In these instances, try to soften the hard connotations such as you will find in expressions of suspicion, obligation, and compulsion, and in references to the reader's deficiencies. Compare:

HARD WORDS	SOFT WORDS
You claim	Your letter states
Your letter about the alleged loss of	Your letter about the loss of
You must have misunderstood our instructions.	Our instructions were that
Surely, you must realize	We are sure you realize

FIG. 4-4. *Levels of business-letter usage.*

the you approach

(COLLOQUIAL)

My face is red over the delay in sending you and Ed the tax information I promised. Life has been hectic but not that hectic.

Lunch Friday will be just fine. See you at the Lawyers Club at 12:30.

(INFORMAL)

We have your letter of September 25 requesting information concerning 300 shares of Blanko Corporation that you sent us for transfer. In order to help us identify the item, will you please let us have the name of the person to whom the stock was to be transferred and also the certificate numbers of the shares you sent us. We would appreciate your writing on the enclosed carbon of this letter and returning it to us in the envelope we have provided.

I am sorry about the lost check. If you will complete the enclosed Affidavit, I will be happy to send you our official check for $256.70.

(FORMAL) not really courteous, cold & impersonal

This will serve to introduce Miss——————, who has been in our employ since July 2, 19-- as a typist in our Credit Department. Miss——————, an excellent worker, is leaving our Company on March 22, 19-- to reside in Puerto Rico. Mr. William—————— of the New York Hilton Hotel, one of our valued customers, said you might know of some job opportunities for Miss——————.

With regard to your recent inquiry, Mr. John—————— has been numbered among our depositors since this office opened ten years ago. Mr.—————— maintains a satisfactory personal account on which balances average consistently in four figures, and he is also known to us in connection with several substantial business accounts. On the basis of our experience we have no hesitancy in recommending Mr.—————— as deserving of the usual courtesies.

(OFFICIAL)

As requested in your letter to us of November 28, 19--, all of the $200,000 principal amount of your Corporation's 5% Registered Debenture Bonds due 19-- called for redemption on December 1, 19-- at the principal amount thereof and three months' accrued interest have been presented to us and paid. After such redemption, there remains outstanding $850,000 principal amount.

With further regard to your claim covered by our File No. 1467B, we regret to advise that after due consideration of the circumstances surrounding the accident, the Claim Board has reached the conclusion that we are not justified in making payment in this instance.

We must absolutely refuse	We are sorry we cannot
We are forced to decline your offer.	We appreciate your offer even though we cannot accept it.
You neglected to say	You did not say

The passive voice is also useful in softening statements that might otherwise be tactless. (For the differences between the passive and the active voice, see page 69.)

Active: You failed to sign the card.
Passive: The card was returned unsigned.

Active: You should have sent us the requisition yesterday.
Passive: The requisition should have been sent to us yesterday.

SINCERITY

Deceit is a form of discourtesy because it shows a low opinion of the reader's intelligence. A printed message—an advertisement, for instance—sometimes succeeds in spite of its insincerity because it is impersonal and addressed to a large audience, many of whom may not be very discriminating. In a letter, however, insincerity becomes a personal affront. A letter from a charitable organization begins:

> This is an unusual letter from our Fund Raising Committee. It is *not* an appeal for funds.

Yet after several paragraphs devoted to an account of the success of the previous year's drive, the letter closes with these words:

> Soon the campaign for the new year will be in full swing and we shall ask you to resume your support. If you would like to avoid being bothered by our letters, why not give now? The enclosed envelope is for your convenience.

In another instance, a form letter bearing the printed signature of the president of a mail-order book club begins:

> I am writing to you from the living room of my home.

Even if the man had himself written the original letter under the circumstances described, it was too much to expect an intelligent reader to share the desired intimacy.

Positive Tone

The difference between negative and positive language has already been described (pages 61–62). Your letters will create better feeling and be more persuasive if you lean to positive words. The difference in tone is apparent in the two letters that follow:

NEGATIVE

```
Dear Mr. Brown:

We regret that we cannot comply with your request to
withdraw $50 from your savings account and send you a
check for that amount.

It is a strict rule of the bank that no withdrawals can
be made without presentation of the passbook.

We will have to hold up your request until this rule is
complied with.

                                  Very truly yours,
```

POSITIVE

```
We are looking forward to sending you a check for the $50
you wish to withdraw from your savings account.

Will you please fill out and sign the enclosed withdrawal
slip and return it to us with your passbook.  Your check
will be sent immediately.

                                  Very truly yours,
```

STRUCTURE

A letter is generally designed to achieve a limited, immediate goal in small space. This aim furnishes a guide to the selection and arrangement of the letter's contents.

Structural Qualities

The qualities needed to construct an effective letter are (1) unity, (2) completeness, (3) compactness, and (4) order.

UNITY

The letter should deal preferably with only one subject; otherwise the emphasis is divided and dissipated. Disunity is especially likely to occur when the writer is unable to make up his mind about the primary purpose of the letter. A senior executive, for example, hearing that a company to which he sells has elected a new president, sends the officer a letter of congratulations but uses the same communication to suggest a closer business relationship. As a result, the writer reveals his insincerity, and neither part of the letter accomplishes its purpose. In other situations, there is considerable inconvenience to the reader and a possible delay in the answer if each of the several subjects in a single letter requires action by a different individual or department.

The two ideas in the following message would have been better dealt with in separate letters:

```
Gentlemen:

In looking over our last invoice, No. 129-5465, we note
that you inadvertently added shipping charges of $57.63.
If you will refer to your confirmation of our order of
April 6, you will see that the shipping charges were in-
cluded in the price quoted.

Incidentally, Mr. Hollis asked me to mention that he is
interested in your published announcement of a new line
of floor coverings for hotels and restaurants.  He would
like some more information that he can present to our
commercial customers.

                                 Very truly yours,
```

An exception to the one-message-one-letter rule is usually made when all the matters to be treated are of a strictly routine kind and are to be acted upon by a single person. In such an instance, it is good practice to list and enumerate the several subjects under a unifying statement of this sort:

COMPLETENESS

The letter should include whatever details are needed to produce the response you want. Only a thoughtless writer leaves the reader at loose ends. A city health department, for example, took this way to answer a citizen's complaint about the smoke issuing from a nearby factory:

```
Dear Sir:

We regret to inform you that the smoke nuisance you re-
ported does not come under the jurisdiction of this de-
partment.

                                 Very truly yours,
```

The letter, of course, left the angry citizen wondering just where to write. Couldn't the correspondent have saved everybody's time by simply forwarding the complaint to the department that had jurisdiction?

When letters must serve as lasting formal records, as they often do, completeness may require the inclusion of many specific dates, numbers, names, and other details that may not seem necessary in more ephemeral correspondence. Even when the details seem to encumber the letter, they must at times be tolerated, as in the following example:

```
We received a telephone call today from Mrs. Elizabeth T.
Walsh, 1005 Fifth Avenue, New York, N.Y. 10028, informing
us that she has not received the dividend payable Septem-
ber 10, 19--, on 300 shares of stock in the Altex Corpo-
ration, registered in the following name:

        Mrs. Elizabeth T. Walsh and Frank Dana,
        Trustees under the Will of Samuel H. Farnum
```

In other instances, completeness requires not only that the relevant facts be given, but that there be sufficient reasoning or emotional appeal to help the response to the letter reach its greatest potential. The letter below, entirely factual, limits the attainable response:

```
Dear Madam:

In accordance with our advertised free-trial offer, we
enclose the purchase price of the Fancy-Freez vegetables
you recently tried.

                                      Very truly yours,
```

With the addition of affective language and a sales-directed ending, the letter is allowed to reach a higher objective:

```
Dear Madam:   not good also Dear Sir

Thank you very much for trying the new Fancy-Freez Vege-
table Dishes.

We are happy to refund your purchase price of the vege-
tables with the extra-special touch.  We hope you have
been most pleased with your selections and will tell your
friends about the quality, flavor, and good value of
these New Vegetable Dishes by Fancy Freez.

                                      Sincerely yours,
```

COMPACTNESS

Completeness offers no excuse for wordiness. Because letters are essentially short, even a little padding can be unduly distracting. Words also cost money—in the writer's time, the stenographer's time, and the reader's time. Yet many writers seem to be under some compulsion to fill the letter sheet.[2] Actually, no letter is too short that says all that needs to be said. If the letter sounds abrupt, the fault is that of poor word choice, not brevity.

In comparing the letters below, note that the revised version is only half the length of the original, but with no loss of detail. The difference in effect is apparent.

[2] Some companies have solved this problem by providing half-sheets for letters and even smaller forms for informal interoffice memorandums.

AS ORIGINALLY WRITTEN (102 WORDS)

> Dear Mr. Granger:
>
> We recently learned that you were interested in discussing estate planning with someone in our Estate Planning Division.
>
> I will be happy to sit down with you at your convenience and assist you in any way I can in working out a plan for your estate.
>
> As I indicated to you on the telephone this morning, I will meet with you at your office or, if you would like, we could get together here at my office.
>
> When you can find a suitable time for getting together, please call. Any time which is convenient to you would be fine with me.
>
> Sincerely,

AS REVISED (48 WORDS)

> Dear Mr. Granger:
>
> It was a pleasure to talk with you on the telephone this morning about getting together to discuss your estate plans. When you have set aside a convenient time, won't you call me? I'll be glad to see you either here or at your office whenever you say.
>
> Sincerely,

Details not relevant to the purpose of the message should be omitted. A young man looking for a job writes:

> For three years I worked as a junior accountant for Excelsior Films which, as you probably heard if you looked at your television last week, won seven Academy Awards.

The principal idea has more effect when the sentence is stripped of its irrelevancy:

> For three years I worked as a junior accountant for Excelsior Films.

Some letters can be improved simply by shortening common redundancies. Compare:

WORDY	CONCISE
enclosed herewith	enclosed
attached hereto	attached

placed an order for	ordered
letter under date of	letter of
letter with regard to	letter about
check in the amount of	check for
write your signature on	sign
we wish to state that	(omit)

In striving for compactness, do not make the mistake of leaving out words necessary for courtesy or grammatical completeness. "Received yours of March 12" will pass in a telegram, but a letter will seem more personal if the statement is filled out to read, "I have your letter of March 12."

Understandably, a correspondent may be a bit sensitive about writing a letter consisting of only one or two short sentences. If a short, strictly factual letter does seem abrupt, the addition of a goodwill phrase almost anywhere, but especially in the close, will remove the bluntness. Note the last paragraph in this brief reply to a depositor's inquiry.

```
Dear Mr. Hayden:

The interest paid to your savings account in 19-- was
$27.66.

We're glad to be of help.
                                   Sincerely,
```

For additional help in achieving conciseness, you will do well to review the section "Language Structure: Verbal Relationships" in Chapter 3, pages 65–74.

EFFECTIVE ORDER

The letter should be organized to bring the desired results. This means taking the line of least resistance: starting usually with ideas that interest the reader, following with those that need explanation or reasoning, and closing with a stimulus to action. Note how the following letter leads from what the reader knows to what the writer wants:

```
Dear Mrs. Davis:

We recently had the pleasure of installing carpet
in your home.

Our reputation for high-quality workmanship in the
installation of cut carpet is a matter of pride with
us.  You can help us maintain this standard by giving
us your comments (brief or otherwise) on the work we
have done.

Simply use the back of this letter and return it to
us in the enclosed postage-paid envelope.

                                   Very truly yours,
```

In a situation involving a *yes* or *no* decision by the correspondent, an important question relating to order is at what point in the letter the decision will be communicated. In the *inductive* arrangement, the decision follows the facts or reasons on which it is based. In the *deductive* order, the decision precedes any accompanying explanation. Generally, the inductive order is used when the decision is negative or when there is some other reason for wanting the reader to understand the background for the decision before the decision is announced. The explanation thus serves as a buffer. The deductive order, on the other hand, is appropriate when the decision favors the reader and there is no valid reason for withholding it.

In the following example, the order is inductive (explanation before decision) because the claim is considered unjustified and the action suggested may not be well received by the reader.

```
Dear Mr. Dabny:

We're sorry about the experience you had with the Addex
L53, which you returned to us for replacement.

Although the Addex is guaranteed against defects in
materials and workmanship for 90 days after purchase, the
guarantee does not cover accidents beyond our control.
The smashed case suggests that the instrument was stepped
on or damaged by a heavy blow.

We can replace the case and put the calculator in good
working order for $24.75, payable in advance.  If we do
not hear from you in two weeks, we will return the in-
strument to you.

                                 Sincerely yours,
```

In the next example, the deductive order (decision first) is used because the customer's claim is justified and the action taken is favorable.

```
Dear Miss Egmont:

We're sending you today a new Addex L53 Pocket Calculator
to replace the one you returned to us as defective.

Ordinarily, we expect our products to give good perform-
ance for years beyond the guarantee period.  In this
instance an exception occurred.

We appreciate your patience and are confident you will
have a happier experience with the replacement.

                                 Sincerely yours,
```

With a little experience, you should be able to dictate routine letters with only a mental outline to guide you. If a letter is to be relatively long or complex, however, you will find it helpful to make a few notes in advance of dictation. Here, for instance, is a brief outline for a letter to a supplier who has just given notice that delivery will be delayed:

Acknowledgment
Delay should have been anticipated
Need goods badly—reasons
Competitors getting deliveries
Both of us will lose
Action wanted

Beginning and Ending the Letter

Except for the easily identified mechanical features of the letter, the most distinctive and in some ways the most important parts are the beginning and the ending. Both have functions to perform that contribute enormously to the effectiveness of the letter, and both follow certain formal patterns of composition.

THE BEGINNING

The letter opening, usually comprising the initial sentence or paragraph, serves these purposes:

1. *It introduces the subject of the letter.* The opening may name the subject directly or state the occasion for writing.

> We are writing about the double-pedestal steel desk we ordered last week.
>
> We are glad to give you the information you asked for in your letter of April 16 regarding the financial standing of the ABC Company.
>
> I was interested to learn through the pages of *Sales Management* that you are offering reprints of your series of *Fortune* advertisements.
>
> Last week we ordered by telephone a copy of the *National Exporters' Register.* When it arrived today, we discovered that the Shipping Suppliers Supplement was not included.

In some instances, the letter dispenses with a formal introduction and instead opens with a statement that moves the action sharply forward. Many writers, and readers too, prefer this approach because it saves time and words.

> We have decided that the double-pedestal desk we ordered last week is going to be too large for our purpose and would like to know if you can supply the same type of desk in the single-pedestal style with a 60-inch top.
>
> The ABC Company, about whom you inquired in your letter of April 6, has been a valued customer of ours for the past four years.
>
> Will you please send me a set of reprints of your recent series of *Fortune* advertisements. I saw your offer in *Sales Management.*

On examining our copy of the *National Exporters' Register* which arrived today, we discovered that the Shipping Suppliers Supplement was not included.

The amount of detail in the opening will vary with the degree of formality you wish to establish and the use to which the letter will be put as a source of reference.

Formal: Thank you for your check of March 12 for $146.66 in payment of our invoice No. 3975 covering your purchase of . . .
Informal: Thanks for your check.

2. *The opening establishes contact with the reader's interests.* You may attract attention in the beginning by referring to an experience shared by you and the reader. This point is illustrated in the examples already given as well as in the following:

We welcome your recent *Time* order.

It was a genuine pleasure to welcome you on your visit to Washington Square Village.

We recently noted you had occasion to return an item for refund.

Thank you very much for sending in your registration card for the Taylor binoculars that you purchased recently.

You may also trade on the reader's normal curiosity and other motives. This technique is especially suited to sales and promotional letters.

The Eskimos have no words in their language similar to our two warm and golden words, "Thank you."

What questions would you ask if you could hire a dozen or more of the leading direct-mail experts in the country to help you?

If you would like your supervisors to become better acquainted with management problems and how to solve them, you'll find constructive use for the 16-mm color film, "You Decide."

Especially in the opening, it is a common fault to make a statement that is apparently of less consequence to the reader than it is to the writer.

WE OPENING	YOU OPENING
We are pleased to announce the opening of our new sporting goods department.	With the opening of our new sporting goods department, you'll now find it just as easy to pick up a new putter or fly-rod as to choose a new tie.

For some months we have been trying without success to find a man to fill the job of Presentation Manager.	Because of your many connections in editorial offices, we thought you might know someone who would be qualified to fill a position with us as Presentation Manager.
Our experience with your F45 copper tubing has not been at all satisfactory.	Perhaps you can help us solve a little problem we've been having with your F45 copper tubing.

In striving to engage the reader's interest, the opening should avoid the overgeneral and farfetched. A satisfactory beginning usually comes as close as possible to the central purpose of the letter.

Farfetched: There's something so final about tearing the last page off the calendar . . . it's like putting another year away in the history books. And I guess it's perfectly natural to think how well it went.
Improved: The end of the old year gives us a good opportunity to thank you for the business you sent our way.

3. *The opening helps to form an attitude conducive to favorable response.* The reader's attitude toward the letter and the writer is formed by the tone of the opening. Expressions of appreciation and sympathy—*thank you, we appreciate, I'm sorry*—are often appropriate. Controversial statements and those implying criticism of the reader are generally avoided. It is also desirable in most instances not to begin with a refusal.

QUESTIONABLE TONE	IMPROVED TONE
We have received your order for . . .	We are glad to have your order for . . .
We regret that we cannot allow the discount you took in paying our invoice of October 18.	Thank you for your check tendered in payment of our invoice of October 18. We note that you have taken the discount allowed for prompt payment.
It was a mistake to wait so long before notifying us that the table you ordered a month ago has not yet arrived.	We are disturbed to hear that your table has not yet arrived.

THE ENDING

The close of the letter, usually the last sentence or paragraph, performs one or more of these functions:

1. *It tells the reader what to do.* The close may direct the reader to write, send money, pay a visit, or take any other action the purpose of the letter requires.

May we hear from you soon?

Don't delay. Mail the order card now!

We hope you'll give us the opportunity to serve you again soon.

If you wish delivery before Christmas, we urge you to mail your order today.

We shall expect your check for $19.40 within the next few days.

Please sign your name on the line marked with an "X" and return the card in the envelope we have provided for your convenience.

We suggest you drop in to discuss the matter with us. We shall be looking forward to seeing you.

2. *It tells what the writer will do.*

Now that we know of your interest in the *Bulletin,* we are putting your name on our mailing list and will see to it that you receive all issues as they are published.

I'll see you on Tuesday.

Pending the adjustment, we are glad to send you a duplicate shipment of the missing wrenches. You should receive them in a few days.

As soon as our investigation is completed, we'll write to you again.

You may be sure that we will forward your suggestion to Mr. Gray as soon as he gets back.

Sometimes the action by the writer is contingent on action by the reader.

If you will sign the release before a notary public and return it in the envelope enclosed, we will send you your check promptly.

3. *It builds goodwill.* Whether or not the letter specifies any action, it may close with an expression designed to cement the relationship with the reader. This may be a conciliatory statement, an offer to help, a wish or hope, or an expression of appreciation, regard, or good wishes.

Thank you for your interest in writing.

Please accept our best wishes for your continued success.

We sincerely regret the inconvenience to you.

If there is anything we can do, please be sure to let me know.

We look forward to the opportunity of serving you again soon.

We do appreciate your efforts in our behalf.

We hope this information will be helpful to you.

LETTER DICTATION

"Writing" letters today usually means dictating them either to a stenographer or into a recording machine. The machine is popular with many executives because it permits dictation at their convenience—even after business hours and away from their offices. By either method, letters are produced much faster than if they are first written on a scratch pad. They are also likely to sound more natural because they are spoken, and to be a bit wordier because speech is generally less disciplined than writing. Some businessmen still prefer to write out the more difficult letters, but no one who intends to make a career in business can afford not to develop the ability to dictate letters efficiently. The learning process may be hard and possibly create some personal embarrassments, but you should not flinch from the task, for the results will immeasurably increase your effectiveness.

Of course, you need not plunge into dictation without some warming up. For example, it is always a good idea to study your mail and to plan your projected replies carefully, to get out the relevant files, and to make notes of the things you want to say in the order in which you want to say them. If, during these preliminaries, you think of some special way in which you want to express an idea, you may also write out a phrase or statement and incorporate it into your dictation. When you finally call in your stenographer or take up your dictating machine, you should be completely prepared. Even then, however, you must take into account the necessity of thinking through one idea and expressing it clearly and effectively before you go on to the next. This *think-then-speak* technique is necessary in order to avoid a lot of backtracking and rephrasing—the sort of emending which you can do fairly easily when you write, but which you cannot do without some confusion when you dictate. That is not to say that you cannot make corrections in dictated work. Even machines make allowances for human error and permit you to correct mistakes. Besides, you can always treat the typewritten product of your dictation as a draft on which you can make further corrections. With experience, however, you will need drafts only for the most demanding work.

Dictating to a Stenographer

See that the stenographer is comfortably seated and is ready to give you complete attention. Speak directly to the stenographer, enunciating clearly and maintaining an even rate of speed, never too fast to keep up with. Begin by giving the name, title, and address of the recipient, as well as any special instructions regarding enclosures, number of copies, and special handling in the mail. In dictating names and technical terms, spell out those with which the stenographer may have difficulty and cannot conveniently look up. Also express your preferences, if you have any, with regard to punctuation and paragraphing.

If you are interrupted or lose your trend of thought, you may ask the stenographer to repeat all or part of what you have dictated and then continue from there. If the interruption is to be extended, give the stenographer permission to leave. Always you will get better work and feel more at ease in dictating if you treat your stenographer with consideration and courtesy.

Machine Dictation

Dictating machines range from simple portable models operating on batteries to intracompany telephone systems that carry your dictation to central transcription departments. Instructions for the use of all machines are invariably provided by the manufacturers and are often supplemented by the instructions of the employers. What all machines share in common is an inability to ask questions. When you use them, you must therefore anticipate all the questions the transcriber may have and you must give the information in the order that it is needed. For example, if you want the letter typed on special stationery, you must say so before you dictate the letter, not after. Otherwise, the transcriber won't hear the instructions until after the letter is already typed on the company's regular stationery.

Although no rules will be applicable to all machines and all systems, the following suggestions for machine dictation will be found generally useful:

1. Know your machine and follow the instructions for its use. It's disheartening to dictate a long letter only to discover that it has not been recorded. Other difficulties may be caused by failing to stop the machine or cover the mouthpiece when you interrupt your dictation to talk to a visitor. Any extraneous noises or the failure to speak directly into the mouthpiece will also interfere with clear reception.
2. Modulate your voice so that it is neither too loud nor too soft. The speed at which you dictate is not important as long as you articulate clearly. The operator can adjust the playback to the speed desired.
3. Some machines have indicator slips for leaving special instructions with the operator and marking the places where corrections are to be made. In other instances you are expected to dictate all your instructions along with the letter. Even then, it is usually possible to make changes by talking to the operator in person or by telephone or by leaving a note before transcription begins. The procedures that follow assume that all instructions will be dictated.
4. Start by giving the operator such basic information as:
   (a) Your name, department, location, telephone extension
   (b) Type of message; for example, letter, memo, schedule
   (c) Number of copies needed
   (d) Name and address of addressee, including attention line, if any
   (e) Salutation; for example, *Dear Miss Brown, Dear George, Gentlemen*
   (f) Subject line, if desired
5. Preface corrections or special instructions with the word *correction* or *operator* (or *Miss Jones* or *Mary*) so that the words in the instructions won't be confused with those in the letter. For example:

   Your order will be shipped by March 25 *operator, make that April 8* at the latest.

By keeping the playback a few words ahead of the typing, the operator can conveniently make such corrections.

6. Indicate paragraphing and any special preferences with regard to punctuation, for example, "semicolon," "dash," or "parentheses" and "close parentheses." Your voice inflection may indicate commas and periods, but experience will tell you whether these should be dictated, too.
7. Dictate long or unusual figures by digits. For example, $565.00 would be dictated "five-six-five point double-oh dollars."
8. Spelling can be very troublesome for the operator unless you help.
   (a) Spell out all proper names except the most familiar and indicate initial capital letters with instructions in the style of "Operator, cap J Jacksonville," or "Operator, initial caps Mary Jones."
   (b) Spell out technical and unfamiliar words.
   (c) When sounds may be confusing, use a phonetic key, for example, "V as in Victor."
9. When you get to the end of the letter, indicate:
   (a) The closing; for example, *Very truly yours, Sincerely yours,* etc.
   (b) The signer's name and title
   (c) Enclosures, if any
   (d) Instructions for marking copies
   (e) Instructions for typing the same letter or similar letters for other adressees

A Dictation Model

The following model will give you an idea of how the recording of a dictated letter might sound to the transcriber. What it cannot convey is the voice inflection, which can be as valuable as the instructions themselves in guiding the operator.

Operator, this is William Davidson of the Stock Transfer Department, extension 2204. I have a letter requiring two carbons. Please address the letter to United Guaranty G-U-A-R-A-N-T-Y Company, 100 Maiden Lane, New York, N.Y. Zip Code one double-oh three eight. Attention Mr. Emil E-M-I-L Callmer C-A-double-L-M-E-R, Gentlemen, Subject Associated Metals Corporation.

We have your letter of November sixteen regarding the issuance of a replacement for *operator cap C* Certificate *cap* N oh period *all caps* NCO *space* two nine eight five *B operator B as in boy* for twenty shares of common stock registered in the name of Stephen *S-T-E-P-H-E-N* Dohrmann *D-O-H-R-M-A-double-N. Paragraph.* Both the affidavits and the bond forms should be executed in three counterparts and the bond forms should include as obligees *O-B-L-I-G-E-E-S operator initial caps* Associated Metals Corporation *comma* Merchants Trust Company *comma* and the City Trust and Savings Bank of Geneva *G-E-N-E-V-A comma* New York. *Paragraph.* In addition to the assignment mentioned in your letter *comma,* it is also necessary that you pay *correction operator change that you pay to that we be furnished with* funds to our order in payment of the New York *operator cap S* State stock transfer tax *period.* The tax will amount to sixty-three cents *period.* We must also have a certification of the value of the shares. *Paragraph.* We will be glad to issue a replacement certificate as soon as these requirements are met. Very truly yours, William Davidson, Stock Transfer Department. *Operator, please mark one carbon for Mr. D. R. Troutman at our 60 Broad Street Office, third floor.*

Here is a copy of the letter, as transcribed:

November 19, 19--

United Guaranty Company
100 Maiden Lane
New York, NY 10038

Attention Mr. Emil Callmer

Gentlemen:

Associated Metals Corporation

We have your letter of November 16 regarding the issuance of a replacement for Certificate No. NCO 2985B for 20 shares of common stock registered in the name of Stephen Dohrmann.

Both the affidavits and the bond forms should be executed in three counterparts and the bond forms should include as obligees Associated Metals Corporation, Merchants Trust Company, and the City Trust and Savings Bank of Geneva, New York.

In addition to the assignment mentioned in your letter, it is also necessary that we be furnished with funds to our order in payment of the New York State stock transfer tax. The tax will amount to sixty-three cents. We must also have a certification of the value of the shares.

We will be glad to issue a replacement certificate as soon as these requirements are met.

Very truly yours,

William Davidson
Stock Transfer Department

WD:RH
Copy to Mr. D. R. Troutman

FORM LETTERS

The volume of correspondence and the other pressures of business make it all but impossible for every letter to be a genuinely personal communication.

The drive to systematize correspondence has its dangers, of course. The greatest is that a form letter may not fit the situation in which it is used. Another is that a form may be couched in such general terms or sound so routine that it will fail to establish real rapport with the reader. Still another danger is that the letter will be badly printed and that such filled-in details as the name and address of the receiver will be misspelled or sloppily typewritten.

The truth is that form letters need have none of the disadvantages mentioned and that even a printed letter may perform a completely satisfactory job. Certainly, if there must be a choice, almost any reader would prefer a printed letter or post card, provided it is prompt and fully informative, to a personally dictated letter that is delayed or badly written. Actually, a form letter may do a better job than a personal letter simply because more time can be spent in writing and testing the form letter. And again, there is no rule that says a form letter has to be sloppy or even impersonal in appearance. Before we go further, it may be well to indicate several kinds of form letters from which the sender can choose, beginning with the one that provides the greatest ease of handling.

1. The printed letter (or post card)
2. The letter typewritten personally or by an automatic typewriter from a master or "guide" letter, or made up of paragraphs selected from a set of master paragraphs
3. The letter produced by a computer-directed typewriter from a "bank" of programmed instructions stored in the machine

An increasing number of letters is being produced on typewriters linked to data processing machines. These afford the greatest promise of personalized (rather than personal) treatment of standard letter situations. However, because of cost considerations and ease of handling, the other methods of letter mechanization will continue to be used. The letters typewritten from prepared models can always be individually adapted and preserve their personal appearance. But even printed post cards and letters can have provisions for filled-in data and a system by which only applicable phrases or paragraphs can be checked off. And they can be neat, helpful, and attractively phrased, as the example in Figure 4-5 shows.

A final word in favor of form letters: They are not always, but they can be, infinitely better than a large proportion of the "personal" letters that are now being dictated or copied by unskilled correspondents too busy to care about the reader and too lazy or ignorant to get away from the clichés that have gathered dust in the company's files for decades and longer. When routine correspondence is finally handled both efficiently and effectively through systematization, letter writing may again he raised to the level of art because then correspondents will be left only with the unique situations, each representing a special challenge to their intelligence and verbal skills. There will also be plenty of creative opportunities for writers who work with systems managers to produce truly effective letter forms.

CROSSMARK & COMPANY

620 Fifth Avenue New York, N.Y. 10022
Telephone 947-4000

September 23, 19--

Estimate #3083
Merchandise Tan Briefcase
Cost of Repair $19.50

Mr. M. P. Davidson
1693 Broadway
New York, NY 10001

Dear Mr. Davidson:

The cost of repairing the merchandise which you returned is shown above.

If you wish us to proceed with the work, please sign and return the enclosed copy of this letter to us, as we are waiting for your further instructions.

We will replace the zipper and repair the torn parts.

☐ Charge to my account

☐ Check enclosed

☐ Send C.O.D.

Very truly yours,

CROSSMARK & COMPANY

H. M. Rogers

H. M. Rogers

Accepted. . . . .

SUMMARY

Letters are the most personal form of written communications; they are characterized by their distinctive mechanical makeup, their tone, and their structure. Business letters are usually typewritten in block style (no indentions for paragraphs or other letter parts) on 8½ by 11 inch paper. In addition to the printed heading, they have a date, inside address, salutation (as *Dear Mr. Smith*), body, complimentary close (as *Very truly yours*), and signature. The salutation is usually followed by a colon and the complimentary close by a comma. The envelope address is the same as the inside address; it should include the ZIP code.

The tone reflects the mood of the letter. Tone will be good if ideas are expressed from the reader's point of view, with ample use of the pronoun *you*. The pronouns *I* and *we* will also give the letter a personal touch, though they should not be intrusive. Natural expression should be preferred to the hackneyed, and courtesy, tact, and sincerity should prevail. To obtain the desirable qualities, the writer will lean to expressions like "for your convenience" rather than "our policy requires"; "please let us know" rather than "kindly advise"; and "the card was returned unsigned" rather than "you failed to sign the card."

A well-structured letter deals usually with just one subject, omits nothing essential to achieving its purpose, and observes the principles of conciseness and good organization. The beginning introduces the subject of the letter, establishes contact with the reader's interests, and helps form a receptive attitude. The ending may tell the reader what to do or tell what the writer will do; it may also attempt to build goodwill through a conciliatory statement or an expression of regard or good wishes. Between the beginning and the end, the body contains the substance of the letter, including the data, reasoning, and appeals needed to explain the writer's actions or to move the reader to the desired response. In letters where decisions go against the reader, the "bad news" usually follows the supporting facts or reasons. Where decisions favor the reader, the "good news" usually comes before the explanation.

The customary way to write letters in the office is by dictating them to a stenographer or to record them for transcription. In either case, efficiency requires that you organize your ideas beforehand and enunciate clearly. When the same type of letter situation arises frequently, the use of form letters can save a great deal of time and money without loss of effectiveness.

TOPICS FOR DISCUSSION

A. Writing in the *New York Times*, Richard Sennett, professor of sociology and director of the Center for Humanistic Studies at New York University, expresses the following view:

FIG. 4-5. *A printed form letter with personal signature. The portions blocked off were filled in on a typewriter.*

The oldest meaning of "the public" in English was a synonym for the common good. Gradually, new meanings were added to both "public" and "private" until by the 18th century they indicated a complementary set of social relationships, one intimate and family-centered, the other more impersonal and centered on relations with strangers.

The 18th-century city brought this balance to a civilized high point in the life of the ordinary citizen. Ritualized forms of speech, manners and dressing allowed people to deal easily with strangers and feel comfortable in their presence; for instance, the elaborate compliments that seem, in retrospect, so stilted were for people of the time ways of signaling friendly intentions to strangers by using stock phrases and flatteries that could apply to anyone.[3]

Is the point made by Professor Sennett in any way applicable today? Can you give any examples? Is it conceivable that much of the criticism of stereotyped phrases in business is a result of the misapprehension of the purpose of these phrases—of the role they play in "signaling friendly intentions" to strangers? Can it be that striving to be "personal" in letters to strangers smacks of insincerity? Would any of the letter phrasing in this chapter (or this book, for that matter) support such a view? Be prepared to take a position and to argue it with reference to specific examples of letter language.

B. Although the paper that follows was written some time ago, it still represents accurately the conditions that control the writing of business letters in organizations. Read the article carefully with a view to answering the following questions. Feel free to contribute any of your own views and supportive examples. *And remember: the fact that certain business conditions encourage the use of stereotyped phrases does not necessarily excuse the use of those phrases or make them effective.*

1. How does the organizational status of the correspondent affect his use of language?
2. What is gained by the practice of substituting "new" clichés for "old" clichés, as described here?
3. What are the purposes of stock phrases?
4. When efficiency requires the use of stock phrases, are there any that might be considered superior to others?
5. When, if ever, is vagueness or the use of jargon justified?
6. What parallels might you expect to find between writing for an employer and writing for a teacher? What differences? Following the precedent of this article, how might you explain "the writing behavior of the student of business communication"? Write such a paper if your instructor directs.

THE WRITING BEHAVIOR OF BUSINESSMEN[4]

Anyone who is willing to make the comparison cannot fail to be impressed by the disparity between the "rules" that govern the style of business correspondence and the actual on-the-job performance in almost any large company.

Published advice about the style of business letters is remarkably uniform in

[3] Richard Sennett, "The Coldness of Private Warmth," *New York Times*, January 5, 1977.

[4] By J. Harold Janis, reprinted from the *Journal of Communication*, 15 (June 1965), 81–88.

its insistence on simplicity, directness, and clarity. The following quotations from reasonably current sources may be considered representative:

> Few of us can expect to write with the clarity of a Hemingway or Steinbeck. Who can copy the magic of Robert Frost? Yet each one of us can try to use strong, plain English [1].
>
> Rely on short, simple words. . . . Avoid the "weasel" words and phrases. A "weasel" word is a word that absolves the writer of any responsibility for a conclusion. [3].
>
> A good business letter is clear and unambiguous. Similarly, it is simple and direct. . . . A good business letter is concise. . . . Avoid the stereotyped expressions that were the stock in trade of the old-school business writers. [4].
>
> Why aren't our books and letters and speeches full of racy, colloquial, rhythmical, personal language? Why do we have to be told by books like this that we are stiff and formal and pompous and unnatural? [2]

Such advice is not essentially different from that given to writers outside of business. Echoes will be found in any college handbook of composition. There is also no reason to doubt that writers themselves believe in the rules and wish to abide by them. In business, more so than in the creative arts, the reverence for rules makes the drive to conform especially potent. In any case, the ideal of simple, clear, and direct English has the inherent appeal of efficiency, which businessmen find naturally attractive. If, then, the writing of reasonably literate and knowledgeable businessmen does not at times reflect the desired qualities, can it not be that the qualities are inconsistent with the requirements of the business situation or contrary to the behavioral patterns of the writers?

The Learning Process

Whatever qualities businessmen may say they like in their letters, the business environment often encourages a stereotyped and impersonal style. Partly responsible is the kind of training the businessman receives as an apprentice. The fastest way to teach an employee to write his company's letters is to show him the work of his predecessors and have him emulate it. The procedure is also most helpful to the supervisor, for as long as the employee's letters use the language that has been approved before, it can be approved again. But let the trainee change the phrasing and the work of review is immediately slowed while the reviewer takes the time to interpret the new idiom and look for hidden traps. The consequence is that the apprentice soon learns the value of precedent, and he follows the old forms—however stereotyped or wordy they may be—not because he thinks they are well phrased, but because they are efficient and safe. Even the writer whose formal education has prejudiced him against clichés finds it difficult, if not impossible, to resist the pressure for conformity. At the opposite end, it takes a very trusting and patient and self-confident supervisor to encourage any form of individual expression in work done for him. The number of such supervisors having charge of routine work is bound to be proportionately few.

But even if individuality were permitted by the learning process, it would be considerably restrained by the unique relationship of the writer to his organization and to his immediate superior. Unlike the literary writer, the business writer is not an independent agent. He is always writing not just *to* someone, but *for* someone—his company, his department, his superior. Even when his own signature appears at the bottom of a letter, he is really signing on behalf of his employer. What this relationship does to his writing style is partly evident in the tendency to use *we* instead of *I*, or the passive construction—for example, *consideration has been given*—which eliminates the need for self-reference. The self-effacement of the writer may also be evident in his use of *the writer* or *the undersigned.* These expressions are especially favored in correspondence written for another person's signature. In some instances, the "ghost" is a little embarrassed about using *I* or *we* when he is obviously referring to someone other than himself. In other instances, the signer insists on the use of *the undersigned* as a means of dissociating himself from the actual writer. Whatever the psychology, the situation encourages the less personal forms of reference.

The Uses of Stereotypes

After the letterwriter's apprenticeship, habit takes over. Even when he is at last permitted freedom of style, the correspondent may still find it easier to continue with the stereotypes because they are suited to office conditions. They permit a large volume of correspondence to be handled in rapid time without the need to find new ways to express familiar ideas. The fact that most correspondence is dictated, with little or no opportunity for revision after typing, puts additional pressure on the writer to use the stereotypes in preference to a mode of expression that is more original but less certain in its effect.

From time to time, pressure may be put on the writer or on his department to improve the language of outgoing letters. The remedy usually offered is the substitution of new clichés for old ones. Thus it may be suggested that *at your earliest convenience* be replaced by *as soon as convenient* and *under separate cover* by *separately*. One could, of course, substitute *as soon as you can* or *at your convenience* in the first instance and some phrase like *by third-class mail* or *by parcel post* in the second, but these alternatives require some discrimination and are therefore either not pressed on the writers or are rejected by them as not being in the interests of their personal efficiency. The point is that whatever efforts may be made to individualize routine correspondence, the very nature of the work and the psychology of the writer eventually lead back to the routinization of language.

Observation suggests that stereotyped writing is much less a problem in the higher echelons than in the lower. The acquisition of authority tends to give a man the self-confidence he needs to express himself in a natural and personal way. Furthermore, it is in the responsible positions that the businessman is more likely to be confronted with situations that are individual rather than routine and therefore less susceptible to the use of clichés. Nevertheless, some businessmen in high positions do carry forward the preference for the stereotypes they acquired in their younger days. But the use of these stereotypes by the executive is not to be equated with the use of the same clichés by his subordinates. For authority confers special privilege, and many an executive's bromides have become his distinctive mark of style. One board chairman has broken the spirit of a number of assistants by always tacking on the superfluous and archaic *I remain* to letters prepared for his signature; yet he strongly believes—and who is to deny it?—that the phrase is his personal stamp.

The distinction made between the language of routine and more personal correspondence suggests that a distinction should also be made between formal and informal language. However desirable one may consider the simple and direct approach to letter writing, the fact is that many letters represent a kind of ritual that would lose much of its effect if it were reduced to everyday language. On the face of it, *We wish to advise you* is stilted and superfluous, yet it can lend dignity and importance to an official notification or announcement. Similarly *in the amount of* is a verbose rendering of *of* or *for;* yet in the sentence, "We are pleased to inform you that we have extended your company a line of credit *in the amount of* $100,000," the larger figure and the formality of the occasion both suggest that *in the amount of* is more appropriate than *for.*

Not only are some occasions more formal than others, but some persons and institutions are also more formal than others. One of the delights of receiving a business letter from England is that it *is* different. Even in domestic correspondence, if everyone were to use the same "simple" style, a great blow would be struck at character and diversity. "We have not yet *been favored with a reply* to our letter of January 4" is admittedly archaic, but it says much about the writer that is not altogether unattractive. There is also some question as to whether it is not more considerate of the reader's feelings than "We have not yet *received a reply* to our letter of January 4."

The Question of Effectiveness

Critics often make the point that a fresh style is more effective than a stale one. Few persons would quarrel with that dictum were it to be applied to messages whose effectiveness depends on their persuasiveness—that is, on their ability to arouse the reader to some new thought or action. A great many business letters, however, do not require such persuasiveness. Often they are mere formalities or they deal with repetitive situations that the reader is already familiar with and thoroughly reconciled to. Routine requests and acknowledgements fall into this category. Not only is nothing to be gained in these situations by original treatment, but something may be lost. In one instance, a bank regularly required to write letters acknowledging the receipt of authorized signatures from its corporate customers rewrote its stock letter to conform to current ideas of effectiveness. When several customers to whom the new letter had been sent asked why the signatures had not been acknowledged, the bank went back to its old form. Apparently the letter beginning with the stereotyped *We wish to acknowledge receipt* was more quickly recognized for what it was than the letter that began with the more individualized *We appreciate having.* After the reader has become accustomed to any form letter, a change in language is disturbing because it requires a new orientation to it. Over the long term, however, the repetition of distinctive phrasing will pall or smack of insincerity whereas flat or even stereotyped language will stand up reasonably well. Compare, for example, the effect of the continual repetition of *I'm delighted to have your letter* with that of *We have your letter*.

Another point often overlooked by the cliché hunters is that some words and phrases that may be judged clichés in some instances are, in other instances, quite meaningful and not easily replaced. The phrase *acknowledge receipt of* has already been mentioned. When a writer wants the reader to acknowledge receipt of his letter, a procedure often necessary in legal and quasi-legal correspondence, it is hard to find any other words that would do as well. *Let us know that you have received,* though wordier, is perhaps simpler, but it does not have the official tone of the customary phrase. When the reader responds, he may also say *I have received your letter,* but the idea of tendering the letter as a receipt is more explicitly expressed in *I acknowledge receipt of your letter.* He could, of course, say, in a less conventional way, *Please accept this letter as a receipt for your letter,* but that does not seem to be an improvement on the first statement.

In another instance, a credit man will say, "Mr. Smith is *known to us as* the president of the XYZ Corporation." Why not reduce the jargon to "Mr. Smith *is* the president of the XYZ Corporation?" The reason is apparent: The credit man wants to limit the statement to what he is sure of at the moment of writing; to do otherwise could place either him or the reader in jeopardy. The credit man will also use the phrase *well and favorably known to us* in endorsing a prospective debtor. Wouldn't it do to say *favorably known to us?* The answer is no because the word *well* adds another dimension to the endorsement. Couldn't the writer rephrase the statement so that the endorsement reads, "We have known Mr. Smith for a long time and think well of him?" He could, but it is not likely, no more so than that he would try to find an original way to express a Dun & Bradstreet rating.

The Question of Meaning

That people and situations, not rules, control the style of business letters is further evidenced in the many available examples of effective writing that are not only wordy and stilted, but also vague and ambiguous. In business, more so than in social relationships, communicators have a strong need to protect themselves against the consequences of their own words. Hence they often hedge their statements, or obscure their meaning, or say less than they might. The use of the impersonal *it* and the passive voice is a case in point. When a businessman says, "*It is believed* that the company is readying a new venture," he probably wants to protect himself or his source. Similarly, he may prefer, "We believe that *confidence can be placed in dealings* with this company" to "We believe *you can deal confidently* with this company" simply because the passive statement is less pointed and therefore—at least in the mind of the writer—safer.

Although no one likes to endorse fuzzy writing, inexactness is often necessary when the writer attempts to deal realistically with business situations. Unlike the storyteller, who has the prerogative of creating situations that his skill as a writer permits him to deal with effectively, the business writer must work within the limitations that circumstances impose on him. A credit correspondent, for example, states that a company is opening a new *unit.* He might better have said *store* or *warehouse* or *factory,* except that the information that came to him read *unit* and he could not take it upon himself to interpret the term. *Your recent letter*—more often written as *your letter of recent date*—may seem unnecessarily vague until it is discovered that either the incoming letter was undated or that there has been such a delay in answering the letter that the writer was embarrassed to mention the date. In the circumstances, one could argue against any reference to the incoming letter or for the omission of the word *recent,* but then, of course, the reference would be even vaguer. Phrases like *Thank you for your cooperation* are less specific than they might be but, like many other generalizations, they have the virtue of fitting a number of situations without forcing the hardpressed writer to rephrase the thought each time.

Not less disturbing than vagueness to a critic of style is the jargon of business writers—particularly the pretentiousness that all but obscures meaning. Like many other rhetorical faults, this one is often due to ignorance or carelessness, but another frequent cause is the writer's need to assert himself. Especially in the lower positions, the drive for recognition is strong, and his writing gives the employee one of the few media available to him for self-expression. One brokerage house, well known for its dealings with large numbers of nonprofessional investors, had to give up in dismay its efforts to train its portfolio analysts to write simple English. The analysts had spent a long time acquiring their professional lingo and hoped to put it to use as security analysts—a more advanced position. Giving up their jargon was like giving up their professional status, and they were not going to surrender without resistance. They are still telling lay investors that they *cut back on a structural basis* or that a stock *sells high statistically* or that a *product line* is particularly attractive for its *secular growth characteristics.* There is some question as to whether the forcible imposition of plain English would have produced sufficient gains in overall clarity to offset the losses in morale among a valuable segment of the company's personnel.

Conclusion

This paper started with the premise that there is a wide gap between the criteria of a good business-letter style and the style dictated by circumstances and personal bias. An examination of both the business writer's production and his environment seems to indicate that the rules of rhetoric he is asked to work with are unrealistic in many instances. Anyone seriously interested in improving the style of business writing must therefore attack the problem not only from the literary point of view, but from the standpoint of business behavior as well. Such an approach may well alter many of the fixed views now held regarding an effective business style. We may particularly come to a realization that there is a valuable place in business writing for many of the stereotypes and circumlocutions that are now generally considered undesirable.

REFERENCES

1. Connecticut Mutual Life Insurance Co. *Speak When You Write.* Hartford: The Company, 1961, p. 16.
2. Flesch, Rudolph. *The Art of Readable Writing.* New York: 1949, p. 207.
3. Himstreet, William C. and Wayne M. Baty. *Business Communications: Principles and Methods.* San Francisco: 1961, pp. 18, 30.
4. Smart, Walter K., Louis W. McKelvey, and Richard C. Gerfen. *Business Letters,* 4th ed. New York: 1957, pp. 25, 32, 35.

PROBLEMS

1. Assume that your company publishes an occasional bulletin for stenographers and typists. This consists of a single sheet of double-spaced copy relating to typing and letter layout. Under an appropriate headline, write such a bulletin on the subject of neatness. Try to be interesting and concrete.

2. With the help of *Webster's Third New International Dictionary* and any other sources you need, write the correct form of the inside address and salutation for letters addressed to each of the following:
   (*a*) One of the two United States Senators from your state
   (*b*) Your local Congressman
   (*c*) The Mayor of your city or town
   (*d*) The minister or priest of a local house of worship
   (*e*) The Secretary of Commerce
   (*f*) One of the Justices of the United States Supreme Court
   (*g*) The United States Ambassador to England
   (*h*) The Governor of your state
   (*i*) The Vice President of the United States
   (*j*) The President of the United States

3. Correct the following forms:
   (*a*) 12/22/78; Aug. 29th, 1978; April Tenth, 1978

   (*b*) James F. Pines, Apt. 6D
   39 W. Fourteenth St.
   Toledo, O.
   43624

   (*c*) Gen'l Container Co.
   875 5th Av.
   Milwaukee
   Wisconsin 53210
   Dear Sirs:

   (*d*) Venetian Asphalt Corp.
   Auburn, N.Y. 13021
   Att.: Elbert M. Dale
   Registered Mail

   Dear Mr. Dale,

(*e*) Re: Your letter of Mar. 19th
Mrs Madeline Frost, Director of Personnel Services
Kane Metals, Inc.
Pittsburgh, Zone 53210, Pa.
Dear Madame:

(*f*) Very Truly Yours
West Rochester Manufacturing Company, Inc.
John S. Smith, Sales Mgr.

(*g*) Yours,
Miss Violet Schaeffer
Order Department

4. In each set of examples below, select the statement that you consider most effective. Because the statements are taken out of context, there is not necessarily a single correct answer in each instance. Be prepared, however, to defend your selections.
   (*a*) (1) We are in receipt of yours of the 15th.
   (2) Have received your letter of April 15.
   (3) We have received your letter of April 15.
   (4) We wish to acknowledge receipt of your letter of April 15.
   (*b*) (1) We have your check for $15 and wish to thank you for it.
   (2) Thank you for your check for $15.
   (3) Your check for $15 received and acknowledged with thanks.
   (4) Have received check for $15 and thank you for same.
   (*c*) (1) We sincerely regret the inconvenience.
   (2) We trust there will be no future recurrence of this error.
   (3) We hope you will not be inconvenienced in this manner again.
   (4) Please let us know whenever such an error is made again.
   (*d*) (1) These are our terms and all our customers must live up to them.
   (2) These terms must be enforced because we would lose money if we made exceptions.
   (3) Our terms are the same for all customers.
   (4) Surely you would not expect us to grant special privileges to you.
   (*e*) (1) Trusting we may hear from you at your earliest convenience, we are
   (2) Don't fail to contact us in the near future.
   (3) We hope to hear from you soon.
   (4) We shall appreciate hearing from you soon.
   (*f*) (1) In view of the facts, we are sorry that we are forced to refuse you credit.
   (2) Under the circumstances, you will understand why we cannot ship your order on credit.
   (3) As a result of our investigation, we feel you are not entitled to credit on this order.
   (4) Accordingly, we feel that too much risk would be involved in giving you credit at this time.
   (*g*) (1) These socks won't wear out quickly.
   (2) We guarantee these socks to wear.
   (3) These are very long-wearing socks.
   (4) Six pairs of these socks are guaranteed for one year's wear.

(*h*) (1) Sweat stains under the arms prove that you wore the dress.
(2) The dress was unmistakably worn.
(3) The dress shows signs of wear.
(4) Evidently you wore the dress before you decided to return it.

(*i*) (1) We are always disturbed to get complaints.
(2) Naturally, we don't like to get complaints.
(3) We are sorry to receive even a single complaint.
(4) We don't like to get complaints, but after all mistakes will happen.

(*j*) (1) On September 14 we wrote you that we wanted the meeting held in or near New York.
(2) Under date of September 14, we communicated to you by means of letter our desire to have the meeting held in or in close proximity to the environs of New York.
(3) Writing on September 14, our desire to have the meeting held in New York or close to it was communicated to you.
(4) You were advised in our letter of September 14 that we desired to hold the meeting either in New York or near it.

(*k*) (1) We regret to learn that the garment you bought is not entirely satisfactory.
(2) We regret to learn that the garment you bought is unsatisfactory.
(3) We regret to learn that the garment you bought is not satisfactory.
(4) We regret to learn of your dissatisfaction with the garment you bought.

(*l*) (1) We are compelled to make a charge of $2 per month because it is otherwise unprofitable for the bank to carry your account.
(2) Because of the expense of carrying your account, we will have to charge you $2 a month for service.
(3) So that we may continue to give you the best in banking service, it will be necessary to charge $2 per month.
(4) It is necessary to charge your account $2 per month to compensate for the many services we perform.

(*m*) (1) We are sorry we mislaid your order. You are requested to supply us with a duplicate order as soon as possible.
(2) We are sorry we mislaid your order. May we ask you to send a duplicate as soon as possible.
(3) We are sorry we mislaid your order. You should send us a duplicate as soon as possible.
(4) We are sorry we mislaid your order. We suggest that you send us a duplicate as soon as possible.

5. Assume that you are employed as an office supervisor in the Taylor Department Store in New York City and see the following letter before it is mailed. Rewrite the letter to demonstrate to the correspondent the correct tone and style of letters to customers.

```
Mrs. Samuel M. Stevens
65 Devlin Road
Middletown, PA  19004

Dear Mrs. Stevens:

Acknowledging receipt of your letter of October 22, we
note that you wish us to send and charge to your account
6 sheets and 12 pillow cases as advertised in last Sun-
day's New York Times.  However, you must have misread our
advertisement because these do not come in pale green,
which you ordered, but only in white, orchid, maize, and
pink.

Hoping you will give us further instructions, we remain,

                              Yours very truly,

                              Order Department / put a name in
```

6. Rewrite the following sentences in a more simple and natural style:
   (*a*) In reply to your letter of recent date regarding the name of our dealer in Minneapolis, we wish to advise that the name of said dealer is S. L. Fair & Co., 945 South Broadway.
   (*b*) This is to acknowledge receipt of your letter dated February 15 enclosing copy of the lease we requested in ours of the 10th.
   (*c*) Kindly advise if said premises have been vacated by you as per our agreement and oblige.
   (*d*) Subsequent to receipt of your communication of April 16, we commenced proceedings to effect collection of the accounts hereinbelow set forth.
   (*e*) They deleted our name as Transfer Agent and inserted their own name in lieu thereof.
   (*f*) We are in receipt of your check for $57.15 and wish to thank you for same.
   (*g*) Reference is made to your January account, payment for which has not yet been received by us.
   (*h*) Should you need further information, kindly advise at your earliest convenience.
   (*i*) It has been noted by us that you desire your mail to be addressed to your home in Teaneck.
   (*j*) Assuring you of our desire to be of service to you, we are

   Very truly yours,

7. Improve the tone of the following statements to make them more affirmative or courteous:
   (*a*) You are hereby requested to supply us with the serial number, which you will find on the motor.
   (*b*) Apparently you forgot to sign the authorization form before returning it.
   (*c*) We have notified the mailing department of the delay you experienced and assure you that it will not happen again.
   (*d*) We have your letter about the alleged loss of three stock certificates.
   (*e*) This will acknowledge receipt of your check of November 12 for $20.50 representing the overpayment to you mentioned in our letter of November 10.
   (*f*) Please accept our apologies if our error caused you any inconvenience.

(*g*) It is against our policy to accept goods for refund after ten days of purchase.
(*h*) Please let us know if we have failed to answer all your questions.
(*i*) Your letter neglects to say which of the two accounts should be credited with this payment.
(*j*) Please let us know whether you intend to send us this information.

8. Write a suitable opening sentence for each of the letters described below:
   (*a*) You are answering a letter from a customer who complains that a clerk was rude.
   (*b*) You write to your bank for credit information about the Gigantic Steel Corporation of Fairfield, Ohio, which has placed with you an order for two electronic computers at $100,000 each.
   (*c*) You write to the head of your personnel department asking for a transfer to another department.
   (*d*) You complain to the manufacturer of a fountain pen, for which you paid $22.50, that the ink flows too freely.
   (*e*) You are placing an order with your company's local stationer for six reams of Strathmore "Script" 20-lb. white bond paper, letterhead size.
   (*f*) You write to deny a request for a loan of $100,000.
   (*g*) You are sending within a few days by United Parcel Service a 15-inch silk drum-shaped lampshade, white, to replace one delivered a few days earlier and reported stained on arrival.
   (*h*) You acknowledge a customer's instructions to address all mail to the main office, 4000 Main Street, Cincinnati, Ohio, instead of to the factory in Marietta, as heretofore.
   (*i*) You write to *Burroughs Clearing House*, a business magazine, for a copy of the April issue containing an article entitled "How to Write Better Letters."
   (*j*) For a local sporting goods store, you write a letter to customers calling attention to your spring line.

9. Rewrite the following letter for conciseness:

> Dear Bill:
>
> I have your letter of September 12 concerning the meeting on investments in the Pension Fund. I will be very happy to meet with you any time including Saturday morning. The only problem involved there is that our office is not open then and the person whom I would want to have sit in on this meeting would not be on hand here. Therefore a time during the week might be better.
>
> There is another problem involved for this week and next week. Mr. Gordon is on his vacation this week, and I plan to be away next week, possibly until the following Tuesday. If you could make it here October 1, 2, or 3 we could plan on meeting at that time. Please let me know if that will fit in with your time schedule.
>
> Cordially yours,

Problems

10. Rewrite the following letter so that the ideas are more effectively organized, developed, and expressed:

> Dear Mrs. Farrell:
>
> Enclosed is your check for $51.50 you sent us with your letter of February 20.
>
> You will have to buy the E-Z Broom Vacuum Cleaner from a local dealer because we are the manufacturers and do not sell at retail.
>
> This is in reference to your letter in which you mention that you saw our advertisement in McCalls.
>
> Very truly yours,

11. Assume that you are applying either for transfer to another college or for admission to a graduate or professional school. You require several letters of recommendation. Write a letter to a professor in your present school, asking him or her to write such a letter for you and to send it directly to the Director of Admissions of the school you wish to attend.

12. Write a letter to an officeholder representing your congressional district or other local political unit, and ask him or her to support some particular legislation on behalf of a cause in which you are personally interested.

13. Write a letter to the editor of your local newspaper commenting on, or taking issue with, an editorial that has appeared recently in the same paper.

14. Assume that you are the manager of the Agency Department of the Long Life Insurance Company. You have today (April 18) received the following letter:

> ARTHUR C. JOHNSTON
> Real Estate—Insurance
> 27 Pioneer Road
> Butte, Montana 59701
>
> April 16, 19--
>
> Long Life Insurance Company
> 84 William Street
> New York, NY 10038
>
> Gentlemen:
>
> I've heard some mighty fine things about your company, and so thought it would be smart to handle insurance for you out here. Will you please send me information about types of policies, commissions, etc.
>
> Very truly yours,
>
> Arthur C. Johnston

It is your company's policy not to have more than one agency in towns with a population of less than 50,000. Your contract with the agency remains in force as long as you are satisfied with the volume of business. Butte has a population of less than 50,000. You already have an agency there in the name of James R. Whyte of 650 Main Street. Although you cannot authorize another agency, you will keep Mr. Johnston's letter on file for future reference. Write the letter.

15. The recipient of the following letter had complained that the supposedly chocolate-coated cookies she had bought had little or no chocolate on them. Study the letter from the viewpoints of content, structure, and tone. Do you think it would satisfy the reader? Could it be a form letter? Offer your comments.

> May 11, 19--
>
> Mrs. Carol Rader
> 29 Oak Park Avenue
> Oak Park, IL 60302
>
> Dear Mrs. Rader:
>
> Thank you for your recent letter concerning Goodee Biscuits.
>
> We were indeed sorry to learn of your dissatisfaction. As we are sure you know, we take great pride in the quality of all Goodee varieties. Our products are subject to the most stringent quality controls, with utmost care and attention given to every step in the production and baking processes. Therefore you can appreciate our concern when a product fails to satisfy one of our consumers. Please let me assure you that your letter will be reviewed thoroughly by our production staff.
>
> In appreciation of your comments, we are enclosing a coupon which you may use toward your next purchase of our products. It may be redeemed at your grocer's for the Goodee products of your choice--whether they be familiar favorites or new varieties.
>
> Reports such as yours are always helpful. Thank you again for your interest, Mrs. Rader.
>
> Sincerely,
>
> *Elizabeth Mae Drury*
>
> CONSUMER SERVICES
>
> Elizabeth Mae Drury/drp

16. Dictate on cassette or reel-to-reel tape the answers to Problems 5, 11, 12, 13, and 14, and bring the cassette or tape to class. Put all the instructions for the transcriber on the tape, as demonstrated in this chapter.

17. Assume that your college receives many requests for its catalog of courses. To handle these inquiries most efficiently, write two forms as follows. Assume that in each instance the catalog will be sent separately, but will arrive some days later.
    (*a*) A printed post card with no fill-ins
    (*b*) A facsimile typewritten letter to be filled in by typewriter with the date, inside address, and personal salutation

5
Special Types of Letters (I)

ALL BUSINESSES perform certain functions in common. They order goods, acknowledge the orders of their customers, make inquiries, answer inquiries, seek and supply credit information, collect debts, and make complaints and adjustments. In this chapter and the next we will take up the kinds of letters used to perform these and other necessary tasks. Many of the letters are written frequently enough, with little or no change, to warrant the use of form letters. Others must be completely personal and unique.

"UTILITY" LETTERS

The letters dealt with here are so routine that they sometimes receive indifferent treatment, especially in the use of language that tends toward the stereotyped. Yet they deserve a better fate because collectively they reach a great number of people and, well expressed, can do much to speed results and build goodwill.

Order Letters

Most goods in business are ordered on purchase order forms. These provide space for exact information about the quantity and kind of goods wanted and the conditions of purchase. An order letter should be equally explicit. It should give the quantity, exact name or description, size, model or catalog number, color, price, and possibly the method of shipment and the date wanted. The letter should also indicate the terms of payment, as, for example, "regular terms," "check enclosed," "less professional discount," or "C.O.D." As a final detail, the purchaser should make certain that the name and address and—if different—the shipping address are plainly indicated.

It stands to reason that the more complete and exact an order is, the less follow-up correspondence will be needed and the fewer mistakes will be made. In the following letter, note the use of details and the columnar arrangement.

Gentlemen:

Please fill the following order on your regular terms:

Cat. No.	Description	Price
4562B	1 2-Dr. metal wall cabinet, white	$ 96.00
148-1	1 metal broom closet, white	43.50
5953	1 metal sink cabinet, white	110.75
	Total	$250.25

The customer for whom we are ordering these articles has already torn out the old cabinets and would like to get the replacements in a hurry. Please ship by truck or express.

Very truly yours,

Acknowledgments of Orders

When an order comes from a regular customer and is to be filled promptly and exactly as specified, there is generally no need to acknowledge it by letter, although many companies do so. Even if the letter serves no other purpose, it is useful as a confirmation of the order; it also provides an opportunity to say "thank you," a gesture that is always important in building goodwill.

Gentlemen:

We appreciate very much your order of September 28 for another model M95 Record Control System. You may be sure that your wishes with regard to special accessories and delivery date, as specified in your Order No. A4568-23, will be strictly observed.

You already know from your own experience how useful the M95 can be, but if at any time we can help you in adapting it to your work, you can be sure that a call from you will be answered promptly and cheerfully.

Sincerely,

In the instance of a first order, courtesy and sound policy make a letter of welcome mandatory.

Gentlemen:

We're very glad to have your first order and to extend to you our regular credit terms of 2% 10 days, net 30.

The cabinets are in stock and will be shipped by express today. You should have them by the end of the week. Your customer will find them sturdy, handsome, and easy to install.

Our representative, John Felton, is going to be in your neighborhood in a few weeks, and we're asking him to drop in to see you.

Sincerely,

When, for any reason, an order cannot be filled exactly as specified, a letter is needed to explain why.

Dear Mr. Sells:

Thank you for your recent order for 100,000 letterheads like the sample you sent us. We'll have a proof for you in a few days.

Although this is practically a duplicate of your order of a few months ago, recent rises in the cost of paper and labor make it necessary for us to increase our price 50 cents per thousand, so that the total price will be $1,650. You'll find no change, however, in the good quality and fine service we have always tried to give you.

Sincerely yours,

Dear Mrs. Castle:

Thank you for your order of April 11 for the two-drawer rollaway model Tower office file we advertised in the _Star_ a few weeks ago.

Because of a temporary shortage of stock, we have only the two-drawer stationary model available for immediate delivery. The rollaway model will probably be back in stock in three weeks.

We are going to hold up your order until we can fill it as you specified. If, however, you'd like us to send you right away the model without wheels, please write or telephone our order department.

Very truly yours,

Letters About Remittances

Since, in a sense, money is the lifeblood of business, business is very careful in accounting for it. However, errors—some mechanical, some human—occasionally occur, and letters are needed to explain and to make corrections. In writing these letters, you should be both explicit and tactful, especially when you charge the reader with an error or with a violation of the terms of payment. Correction of your own error is best done promptly and graciously. The letters that follow suggest the proper tone in several different money situations:

```
Gentlemen:

Although we appreciate your check for $311.56, we are
wondering how to reconcile it with our July 1 statement
for $113.56.  The figures were apparently transposed.

We are returning your check and will wait for a new one
in the correct amount.

                                   Very truly yours,
```

```
Gentlemen:

Thank you for your check for $156.80 which you sent us on
February 26 in payment of our invoice of February 10 for
$160.00.

We assume you have taken the 2 per cent discount allowed
for cash.  Since this discount is given only for payment
within ten days, however, we should have received a check
in the full amount.

We like to be meticulous in all our dealings, as we are
sure you do, and we would therefore appreciate a check
for the difference of $3.20.

                                   Very truly yours,
```

```
Gentlemen:

In the November statement, which we mailed to you yester-
day, you will find that we inadvertently credited your
account with $49.53.  The revised statement enclosed
shows your correct balance.

Please accept our apologies.

                                   Sincerely yours,
```

Requests and Inquiries

All businesspeople have occasion, at one time or another, to write for information or ask for some other favor. They may want a copy of a booklet mentioned in the public press, instructions on the use of a product, information for a report or speech, or a free sample. It is to the credit of modern companies that most of them answer such mail promptly, patiently, and cheerfully, even when there seems to be no immediate advantage to them. Still, the quality of the answer often depends on the quality of the request or inquiry. If the information seeker does not state exactly what he wants to know, he is hardly in a position to complain about an answer that does not meet his needs.

This letter is vague:

> Gentlemen:
>
> Please let us know what copying papers you recommend for the Copymaster we own.
>
> Very truly yours,

The letter that follows is more likely to get a helpful answer:

> Gentlemen:
>
> Some months ago our Cleveland office sent us a Model A-100 Copymaster for which they no longer had use. At the time we were told that the Copymaster Clearon paper would give us best results.
>
> We now find that this paper is very brittle and tears easily in normal handling. The printed image also tends to fade when the sheet is exposed to light. It occurs to us that as stationers handling a number of different copying papers, you might know of one we can use with better results.
>
> Any help you can give us will be appreciated. We use about 5000 sheets a month.
>
> Very truly yours,

Many inquiries and requests contain little sales potential. These are addressed not only to commercial houses, but to government and social agencies as well. Some, like the following, are reasonably uncomplicated:

```
Dear Mr. Geist:

I was very much interested in reading about your speech
the other evening at the annual convention of the Ameri-
can Institute of Electrical Manufacturers.  If a copy of
your remarks is available, I'd appreciate having it.

                              Sincerely,
```

```
Gentlemen:

May I have a copy of your newest catalog of educational
materials available without charge for distribution to
high school science students.  Thank you.

                              Very truly yours,
```

Other requests may put the reader to considerable trouble. When you must write such a request, you can improve the chances of getting a complete reply by touching on these points:

1. *Why are you writing?* Unless the reason is obvious from the nature of the request, a company likes to know why it has been selected for the inquiry. Perhaps, it is the biggest in the field, or the best known, or has some special experience. Perhaps it was recommended by a teacher, a customer, a supplier, or some other source.

2. *Why do you need the information?* The reason may give the reader a clue to how much information to send and how thorough or technical it ought to be. A person who writes to a public health agency for information about mosquito control can expect to get one answer if he says he needs the information for his civics class and a different answer if he says he is going to put the information to practical use in his business, home, or community.

3. *What specific information do you want?* Give full particulars. At the same time avoid making requests that are unreasonable in the amount of work they require of the respondent and inconsiderate of his time. Nothing is so annoying as being asked for a lot of information that may not even be useful to the inquirer or that he could get, with a little exertion, from the public library.

4. *Is there any way you can reciprocate?* If the information is going to be incorporated in a report, you may be able to offer a copy of the completed work. In any case, the respondent may feel well repaid if he can be assured that the help he gives you will be spread among others or will serve some useful civic or business purpose.

In addition to considering these questions, you should of course observe the fundamental principles of courtesy, tact, and common sense. You cannot get away from the fact that you are asking a favor and that a person does a favor only because he wants to and expects to derive pleasure from it. The chances are that an inquiry addressed to the company will receive a less enthusiastic reply than one addressed to a single individual, that a processed form letter will generate a weaker response than a personal letter, and that a stilted letter will draw a more perfunctory answer than a warmly human one.

The letter of inquiry that follows embodies many of the suggestions already given:

> Dear Miss Stanton:
>
> Through a business acquaintance, we learned that you have set up a system for dealing with rumors passing among your shop employees. We'd very much like to know the details of your plan and have samples of any forms or letters you use.
>
> As a large company, we believe that the difficulties we have in tracking down rumors and coping with them must be similar to yours, and we hope we can learn something from your experience. We are strong in our belief that workers are happier and produce more when they are fully and accurately informed about their company.
>
> Some time ago we had an outside organization make a study of communication within our company and, in the expectation that it will be of interest to you, we are sending you a copy of their report.
>
> With much appreciation, we're looking forward to receiving whatever help you can give us.
>
> Sincerely,

Letters of Reply

Much of a correspondent's time is taken up answering other people's letters. Sometimes the reply is a simple acknowledgment for purposes of record and has no other value to the reader. Here is such a letter:

> Gentlemen:
>
> We have today received the original copy of the Vanderman contract. Thanks for sending it to us.
>
> Very truly yours,

At other times, the acknowledgment of a letter is less important than a statement of what you are doing about it.

Gentlemen:

In line with your letter of October 4, we have forwarded to Mr. James Ball the executed original and duplicate of the affidavits to be submitted in connection with the audit of the Federal tax return of Joseph R. Tanner.

A conformed copy was also sent to Mr. Ball for his files. The fourth and remaining copy will be retained by us.

Very truly yours,

If there is going to be a delay in attending to a request, the sender should be notified.

Dear Mr. Downes:

Because of the big demand, our supply of the Belmore Sample Book is completely exhausted. We are making up a new stock, however, and we are sure we will be able to send you your complimentary copy in another week or ten days.

Thanks so much for your patience.

Very truly yours,

When a letter requests information, your reply should be gracious and complete. Still, you may try to save your own time by enclosing printed materials or directing the reader to sources where the information is more readily available. The paragraphs that follow suggest some of the possibilities:

> We think you'll find the information you want in an article that appeared in last January's issue of *Holiday*. It's called "Carnivals in the Caribbean" and tells in some detail the part we have played in opening the area to tourist traffic.

> The position you mention is filled only through competitive examinations. For full particulars, please write to the Municipal Civil Service Commission, 295 Broadway, and ask for Circular M45.

> The topic you've chosen for your report is a most interesting one, and we are delighted to send you a copy of "The Story of Rubber," which we hope will give you the information you need.

Do not invite further inquiries unless you really want them. This letter ending keeps the subject open:

> Please let us know if there is any other way in which we can be of help.

The endings that follow are just as courteous but are more likely to close the matter:

> We appreciate the opportunity to be of help.
> Good luck in writing your report.

Many companies develop form letters to handle recurring types of inquiries. Even though they are not personal, readers usually appreciate their promptness and efficiency. This subject was discussed in the preceding chapter.

CREDIT LETTERS

It is estimated that credit purchases are made by some 50 million or more Americans using over 5,000 different credit cards. These figures do not include the literally billions of dollars worth of credit business traditionally engaged in by American companies in supplying their own needs.

The large volume of credit business characteristic of the American economy requires a corresponding volume of letters to keep the credit machinery operating. The credit function is ordinarily placed in the hands of a credit manager, who has special training for the work. In extending credit—that is the privilege of obtaining money, goods, or services on trust—the credit manager looks for certain qualities in the debtor:

1. *The ability to pay.* Such ability may be represented by property, the cash value of life insurance, or other assests. It may also be represented by a business or job that provides regular income. Figure 5-1, taken from a student's report of an interview with a credit manager reveals some of the practical considerations that enter into a particular company's evaluation of a customer's ability to pay.

2. *The reputation of the debtor.* Honesty, of course, is a prime requirement, but this is usually measured by the debtor's past performance in meeting his obligations promptly. Some insight into the latter qualification is given later in this chapter in the section "Collection Letters."

Credit letters are divided between those that make possible the extension of credit and those that seek to collect when financial obligations are not met. All require a great amount of tact and are governed by strong legal and ethical considerations. To be most successful, they must also reflect the credit manager's broad concept of his job, that is, not only to protect his company's assets, but also to promote good relations with customers. The creditor cannot afford to be either so generous as to take undue financial risks or so firm as to discourage worthwhile credit business.

Making Credit Inquiries

When a creditor wants to bring up to date the file on a customer or to obtain information about a prospective customer, information is sought from rating

EVALUATION OF CREDIT DATA

. . . Many early-warning signals exist in the circumstances of employment. One should look carefully at "own business" category if bank references are not the best. It is also wise to pay close attention to a seasonal or unstable employment record, as might be the case with a longshoreman, waiter, or bartender. Applicants whose income is made up entirely of commission should show proof of consistently good earnings over a long period.

Other danger signals concern personal factors rather than commercial ones. These include carrying several credit accounts simultaneously, supporting several dependents on a lower-bracket income, living in a rooming house, hotel, or with friends, refusing to furnish complete information.

FIG. 5-1. *"Problem" applicants for credit. Part of a student's report of an interview with a credit manager.*

books and directories, credit agencies (Dun & Bradstreet, Inc., is the best known), trade associations, the customer's creditors, or the customer himself.

OBTAINING INFORMATION FROM THE CUSTOMER

The creditor may go directly to the customer for bank, trade, or other references, or for a copy of his latest financial statement. Sometimes such information is solicited directly only when the creditor cannot obtain it from other sources. Since the customer may be sensitive about a credit inquiry, the request needs to be diplomatically phrased. It should certainly not suggest that there is anything unusual in the inquiry or that there is any doubt about the customer's ability to qualify for credit. It should, on the other hand, state specifically what information is wanted.

Especially in retail credit, a printed application form is often provided for the reply. An example is shown in Figure 5-2.

BENSON BROTHERS

Boston—New York—Chicago

REQUEST FOR CHARGE ACCOUNT

ACCT. NO. LABEL | R | S | L | DATE | BY | CR. CDS. A B C D E

SPECIAL INSTRUCTIONS

STORE CODE | AUTHORIZED PURCHASERS

COURTESY CHARGES

INTERVIEWER

DATE OF APPLICATION | MO. | DAY | YEAR | PLEASE FILL IN ALL SPACES EXCEPT WHERE SCREENED

MR. / MRS. / MISS | FIRST | MIDDLE | LAST | WIFE'S/HUSBAND'S NAME | SINGLE ☐ DIVORCED ☐ WIDOW(ER) ☐ SEPARATED ☐ | 2

HOME ADDRESS | CITY | ZIP CODE | HOW LONG | OWN ☐ RENT ☐ | 3

PREVIOUS ADDRESS IF LIVING AT ABOVE LESS THAN 3 YEARS | HOW LONG | RESIDENCE PHONE NONE ☐ | BUSN. PHONE | 4

FIRM NAME | ADDRESS | POSITION | HOW LONG | 5

PREVIOUS EMPLOYMENT IF ABOVE LESS THAN 3 YEARS | ADDRESS | POSITION | HOW LONG | 6

FIRM NAME (MRS.) | ADDRESS | POSITION | HOW LONG | 7

8

NONE ☐ | 1 OTHER CHARGE ACCOUNTS — SHOW DEPT. STORES FIRST — SHOW ACCOUNT NUMBERS | 2 | 3

9

4 | 5 | 6

TOTAL

REG. CK. / SPEC. CK. / SAV. | BANK | BRANCH | REG. CK. / SPEC.CK. / SAV. | BANK | BRANCH

PLEASE SIGN ONE OF THE AGREEMENTS ON REVERSE

The application form is accompanied by a short letter:

> Dear Mrs. McCord:
>
> We are pleased that you want to open a charge account at Farnum's.
>
> To make the process as convenient as possible, we are enclosing our regular application form, which we ask you to fill out and mail.
>
> There are so many advantages to having a Farnum charge account that we know you will enjoy it from the start. We on our part will try to make your every purchase a pleasurable experience.
>
> Sincerely yours,

FOLLOWING UP CREDIT REFERENCES

When a name is given as reference, the credit manager or an assistant will follow up usually by letter. He will (1) state his reason for wanting credit information, (2) tell specifically what information is desired, and (3) promise to keep the information in confidence. An offer to reciprocate is implied if not expressed. The letter is invariably accompanied by a postage-paid return envelope. In the experience of some credit correspondents, a personal letter embodying the request for information receives a more willing and thorough response than a form letter. This letter was dictated:

> Gentlemen:
>
> We have recently received an order from the Daly-Smith Corporation of Tulsa, Oklahoma, who have given us your name as a credit reference.
>
> Would it be possible for you to let us know how long this company has been buying from you, what credit limit you have placed on the account, and how much is currently outstanding and past due? We should also appreciate knowing the customer's paying habits and your general impressions of the account.
>
> You may be sure that the information you give us will be held in strict confidence and that we should be glad to return your favor at any time.
>
> Sincerely yours,

Because of the volume of their inquiries, large companies often use printed form letters. The mechanical style of the form letter below is similar to that of

FIG. 5-2. *An application for retail credit.*

the dictated letter, except that the name of the company inquired about is typewritten after the word "Subject."

SUBJECT:

Gentlemen:

Your firm has been given as a credit reference for the above-named company.

So that we will be in a better position to render service to this customer, we would appreciate receiving a synopsis of your credit experience with the account. We are interested in the high credit, pay record, and outstanding balance as well as other pertinent credit information.

Of course, you may be assured of our confidential use of this information and our willingness to reciprocate should the opportunity present itself.

Very truly yours,

In the following letter, a manufacturer seeks information from a dealer who has sent a first order to be filled on credit terms. The tactlessness is self-evident.

TACTLESS

Gentlemen:

We have received your order in the approximate value of $5,000. Unfortunately, however, we have been unable to obtain credit information about you from our usual sources.

Will you please, therefore, be so kind as to forward your latest fiscal statement as well as a list of representative suppliers and the name of your bank. As you have never dealt with us before, it would be against our policy to fill your order prior to the approval of credit.

Very truly yours,

The letter below shows a far better appreciation of the reader's feelings and bodes well for a satisfactory credit relationship.

TACTFUL

```
Gentlemen:

We are pleased to note your confidence in us as evidenced
by your recent order for May 2 delivery.

We would very much like to fill your order on our regular
terms.  So that we may be able to do so, we would appre-
ciate your providing us with information we customarily
require from new customers.  Will you please send us
(1) a copy of your latest financial statement, (2) the
name of your bank, and (3) the names and addresses of
some of your major suppliers.

When the information is in our hands, we will look for-
ward to arranging a credit line to meet your needs.

Thank you very much for your help.

                                Very truly yours,
```

The printed form letter shown below makes answering easy:

```
                      SUBJECT:

Gentlemen:

We have an initial order and are contemplating establish-
ing a line of credit for the subject.

We would appreciate your recording the results of your
experience in the spaces below and returning this letter
to us in the business reply envelope.  Any information
furnished to us will be held in strict confidence.  If we
can be of similar service to you, please do not hesitate
to call on us.

                                Very truly yours,

---------------------------------------------------------
                        YOUR EXPERIENCE

Sold from______________________To_______________________

Highest credit_________________Now owing________________

Terms__________________________Past due_________________

            ( ) Discount
How pays:   ( ) Prompt
            ( ) Slow
```

Replying to Credit Inquiries

Filling out a printed form is the easiest way to handle a credit inquiry. Where one is not provided, the respondent may use one of his own in preference to writing a letter. One large company answers most credit inquiries by filling out the following form, which is rubber stamped at the bottom of the incoming letter. The spaces are filled in by hand as shown.

OWES	2000
DUE	1000
HIGHEST CREDIT	2000
PAYS	Slow – 30 days
ACCOUNT OPENED	Nov. 1975
LAST SALE	June 1977

The same company advises its credit correspondents to use this form even when the inquirer provides another. In this way the company can better control the information given out, a difficult task when correspondents have a large volume of inquiries to handle and may lack experience with the accounts or the mature judgment needed to decide what information the employer would want them to reveal.

A letter written by a credit reference must be framed with extreme care, for it involves the reputation of the subject. Facts are best because they are objective. When opinions are offered, they should be expressed with considerable restraint, as in these statements:

> On the basis of our experience with Blank Associates, we believe they are entitled to your confidence.

> In our opinion, a policy of caution would be justified in any dealings with this company.

Many companies try to limit responsibility for the information they give by printing a "disclaimer" on the letter sheet. This is an example:

> The information contained herein is confidential and is given for your private use without responsibility on the part of this company or its officers.

The following letter represents a favorable but strictly factual reply to a credit inquiry:

> Dear Mr. Teller:
>
> Your letter of June 25 seeks credit information about Ragway Linens, Inc., 1462 Denver Drive, Palo Alto, California.
>
> An account was opened for this company in July, 19--. We have extended credit up to $10,000, the high point being reached in October of last year. We have done little business with the company so far this year, and nothing is outstanding. Our invoices have always been paid promptly.
>
> We hope this information, which is furnished in confidence, will be of some help to you.
>
> Very truly yours,

Following is a favorable reference involving a more complex situation. Note particularly the expression of opinion in the last paragraph.

> Gentlemen:
>
> Your recent letter requests confirmation of a balance due us by the Augustus Contracting Company of Roscoe, New York. The balance you mention, $57,000, is substantially correct.
>
> We do not normally do business with this company directly. In this instance, however, we hold an assignment of receivables due from the Augustus Contracting Company to Superior Builders, Inc., of Hancock, New York, in connection with materials furnished in the Hancock Public Housing Project. The invoices are not yet up for payment.
>
> Several of our dealers have done business with the Augustus Contracting Company since their inception and we have been familiar with the principals. At times in the past we have had reason to place a great deal of confidence in them and this confidence has been justified. Their long and favorable record includes the successful completion of many large construction projects. On the basis of our experience, we recommend them to you.
>
> Yours very truly,

The next letter was written by a big-city bank in response to a request from one of its associated banks in a smaller community. Note the factual basis of the unfavorable statements.

Dear Ms. Charles:

We are pleased to reply to your letter of October 16 concerning the Aspidistra Trading Company of this city. Although the company is not one of our customers, we have had occasion to look into its dealings from time to time, and we were glad to make current inquiries on your behalf.

The company was registered in 19-- by Edward L. Doe, a naturalized citizen. He first entered business on his own account in 19--, when he conducted a retail clothing store in Wilmington, Delaware. After brief periods of employment as a salesman of soap products, he started the Aspidistra Trading Company in 19--.

In addition to acting as brokers in the sale of small manufacturing establishments, the company runs a sort of advertising agency for the properties listed, placing advertisements in newspapers and magazines, and publishing their own catalog. We are told that Doe is a licensed real estate broker in New York and Pennsylvania. He has been a member of a local real estate board since 19--, but in answering inquiries about him, the organization merely states that they have never received any complaints concerning Doe, nor have they had occasion to question his dealings or ethics.

The local office of the Better Business Bureau informs us that there have been some complaints and numerous inquiries about the company. The complainants usually report that although they paid a large advance fee, advertisements for their property were placed in papers of small circulation with low advertising rates. The opinion was offered that the company is more interested in obtaining advance fees than in selling the properties listed. It was strongly suggested that all persons considering business dealings with the company should thoroughly read and clearly understand all the terms of the contract. The company, we were told, appears to hold its clients to the letter of the contract.

The company maintained banking relations for several years with a small uptown bank, but the bank requested the company to close the account in April, 19--, because of unsatisfactory experience. For about a year prior to closing, the account had been overdrawn, and on several occasions the bank found it necessary to return checks because of insufficient funds. The bank had no knowledge of the company's present banking connection, and we were unable to learn it from other sources.

We hope this information will be of help to you and your client.

Sincerely,

Because of the danger that a letter may get into the wrong hands, credit personnel often prefer to use the telephone to transmit unfavorable information. When a letter is used, reference to the name of the subject may be avoided by such a phrase as "the subject mentioned in your letter of September 17." Even so, any letter that can be proved to be defamatory and prejudicial in a pecuniary sense may be subject to the laws of libel. Thus the best legal safeguards for the sender are strict adherence to the truth and the absence of malice.

Granting and Refusing Credit

Letters approving credit express the pleasure of the creditor in opening the account and encourage the customer to use it. In some instances, the letter also defines the credit limit and states the terms of payment. In retail credit, especially, Federal law requires that the terms of payment and interest charges be explicitly stated and agreed to in writing by the customer (Figure 5-3).

The letter that follows welcomes a charge customer to a retail store. It is signed by the president.

Dear Mrs. Alpert:

There's a note on my desk from our Credit Manager telling me that you recently applied for a charge account with Shane's. I know that you'll find it a timesaver and a practical way to buy.

The enclosed credit card is designed to make your shopping most convenient for you. Please sign it immediately and present it to the clerk whenever you make a purchase you wish to charge. Bills are mailed to you monthly, and payment is expected in accordance with the agreement you have signed.

We want you always to get courtesy and good service at Shane's. If we should ever fail in that aim, please let me know immediately.

Thank you for your confidence in us.

Sincerely,

CUSTOMER'S COPY OF AGREEMENT (tear at perforation and retain the bottom portion)

In consideration of Benson Brothers permitting purchases to be charged by me and others authorized by me, I agree:

1. I have the option to avoid a **FINANCE CHARGE** by my payment of the full amount of all purchases within 1 month from the billing date on each monthly statement.
2. If full payment of the "New Balance" shown on my monthly statement is not received by you within 1 month from the statement's billing date, I will pay the cash price of all purchases and a **FINANCE CHARGE** on the "Adjusted Balance" of my account (the "Previous Balance" less "Payments and Credits" shown on the monthly statement). The **FINANCE CHARGE** is determined by applying a 1½% monthly periodic rate (18% **ANNUAL PERCENTAGE RATE**) on the Adjusted Balance up to $500 and a 1% monthly periodic rate (12% **ANNUAL PERCENTAGE RATE**) on any portion thereof in excess of $500, subject to the following exceptions:

Customer's State	Adjusted Balance	Monthly Periodic Rate	ANNUAL PERCENTAGE RATE
Missouri	Over $500	¾%	9%
Pennsylvania	All	1¼%	15%

Each rate is applied to a median amount within a range (not exceeding $10) of balances within which my Adjusted Balance falls. There will be no **FINANCE CHARGE** on Adjusted Balances of $10 or less.

3. I will upon receipt of each monthly statement make a minimum monthly payment of at least 1/5 of my "New Balance", but not less than $50 (or my entire New Balance if less than $50). I understand and agree that you may change the minimum monthly payment schedule upon notice to me.

NOTICE TO THE BUYER:

1. **DO NOT SIGN THIS CREDIT AGREEMENT BEFORE YOU READ IT OR IF IT CONTAINS ANY BLANK SPACE.**
2. **YOU ARE ENTITLED TO A COMPLETELY FILLED IN COPY OF THIS CREDIT AGREEMENT.**
3. **YOU MAY AT ANY TIME PAY THE TOTAL BALANCE OUTSTANDING UNDER THIS AGREEMENT.**

RECEIPT OF FULLY EXECUTED COPY IS ACKNOWLEDGED • RETAIL INSTALMENT CREDIT AGREEMENT

Benson Brothers
750 Fifth Avenue
New York, N.Y. 10022

Date________

Customer's Signature________________

Residence________________

A hotel chain sends the following letter to credit-approved customers:

> Dear Mr. Talbert:
>
> It is a pleasure to send you the Associated Hotels credit card you recently requested. It entitles you to credit privileges at all of our hotels. For your protection, we suggest that you sign your credit card on the back before placing it in your wallet.
>
> It will be to your advantage to mention this card when making reservations and to show it to our room clerks when registering. A friendly welcome awaits you at all Associated Hotels across the nation, and we assure you we will do our utmost to merit your continued patronage.
>
> Sincerely yours,

When credit is refused, a reason is usually given, although the desire for tact and the need to protect information sources sometimes lead to ambiguity and even evasiveness. A writer may attempt to minimize a refusal of credit by making a bid for the customer's cash business. The theory here is that other companies will probably be no more lenient in granting credit and that the customer will have to buy for cash somewhere if he is to fill his needs. The evident desire to hold on to the customer's friendship may be the decisive factor in obtaining the customer's credit business at a later time should he qualify.

In the following letter, a manufacturer writes to a prospective retail outlet:

> Gentlemen:
>
> Much as we would like to ship your recent order on open account, we just haven't been able to get enough information to warrant the extension of credit at this time. We'd like to have another chance to pass on your credit application after we get to know you better.
>
> In the meantime, may we suggest that you accept the shipment on our regular cash terms, which give you a 3 per cent discount. The items you have chosen are all fast movers and should return your investment with a good profit in a month or two. Of course, we'll send a good selection of display materials with your order.
>
> Please write or telephone and we'll have your shipment on its way at once.
>
> Sincerely yours,

A retail store writes as follows:

FIG. 5-3. *A retail credit agreement.*

Dear Mrs. Black:

We appreciate your desire to open a charge account at Paley's.

So far the credit information we have obtained is not sufficiently conclusive to enable us to make a positive decision. Anytime you can add to the information you have given us, we will be glad to reconsider your application.

In the meantime, you may be sure that you are always welcome at Paley's, where we hope you will continue to fill your fashion needs and enjoy our many personal services.

Sincerely yours,

Legal Considerations

In recent years, abuses in the retail credit field have led to Congressional legislation protecting the rights of consumers. Any letters or forms relating to consumer credit must conform to the provisions of the Consumer Credit Protection Act (familiarly called the "Truth-in-Lending Act") and the Fair Credit Reporting Act. The first provides for disclosure to the customer of the exact terms of a charge account or installment purchases; it also requires that the seller inform the customer explicitly of the procedure to follow in case of a

In Case of Errors or Inquiries About Your Bill

The Federal Truth in Lending Act requires prompt correction of billing mistakes.

1. If you want to preserve your rights under the Act, here's what to do if you think your bill is wrong or if you need more information about an item on your bill:
   a. Do not write on the bill. On a separate sheet of paper write (you may telephone your inquiry but doing so will not preserve your rights under this law) the following:
      i. Your name and account number (if any).
      ii. A description of the error and an explanation (to the extent you can explain) why you believe it is an error.

      If you only need more information, explain the item you are
      sure about and, if

FIG. 5-4. *Notice required to be sent to retail credit customers informing them of their rights under the federal Truth-in-Lending Act.*

billing error, and of the seller's obligation to reply (Figure 5-4). The second statute gives the consumer access to information about him in a credit bureau's files and the right to force correction of false information. In addition, it requires that the consumer be told promptly when someone has asked for a report about his character, general reputation, and way of living. Anyone contemplating the use of credit or credit letters should familiarize himself with the exact provisions of both laws. Copies are obtainable from the Board of Governors, Federal Reserve System, Washington, D.C. 20551.

COLLECTION LETTERS

When customers fail to pay their debts on time, the creditor usually writes to obtain collection by mail. Early notices may take the form of a rubber stamped "Past Due" on a customer's regular monthly statement or a printed sticker that serves the same purpose. Often they are printed on a card or small letter sheet. In any event, the message seldom does more than remind the reader of his indebtedness and ask for payment. The language, like the physical makeup of the collection notice, leans to formality. It is often deliberately stilted. The idea is to give the debtor a chance to pay without the embarrassment created by a personal appeal.

Here are some examples of formal collection reminders:

> We invite your attention to the enclosed statement of your account, which has undoubtedly been overlooked. Payment will be appreciated.
>
> Your account is now past due. Please remit.
>
> Our records show a past-due balance of $________ in your account. Your check in payment is requested.
>
> We call your attention again to your account, which is now considerably overdue. Please send us your check at once. We'll appreciate it.

If the debtor does not respond to the formal reminders, they are followed up by personally dictated letters or by form letters that may look personal. The letters may attempt to excuse the reader's inaction on the grounds of oversight, or they may appeal to his sense of obligation or his desire to preserve his credit standing. As a last resort, a threat is made to place the account in the hands of an attorney or a collection agency for further action. The treatment accorded any particular account depends on the debtor's past record. In Figure 5-5, part of the same report quoted in Figure 5-1, some interesting observations are made regarding one company's view of its debtors.

Collection Appeals

With due allowances for individual differences in debtors, most companies use similar approaches in collecting from delinquent accounts. Some common appeals designed to motivate response may be paraphrased as follows:

Good intentions. "We are sure you have overlooked our bill and need only

PROBLEM ACCOUNTS

Why do accounts fall behind? Who are the people who create the problems? They can be put in four main categories:

1. Those who pay slowly; they will complete payment a little behind schedule.
2. Those who pay sporadically; they bring their account up-to-date at various times during the contract period, and lapse back into inactivity from time to time.
3. Those who unexpectedly find themselves unable to pay.
4. Those who have no intention to pay.

The first two categories, while bothersome, are not really bad accounts. They should be made aware that the missing payments have been noted and that regularity of payments is part of the contract. They should not be permitted to rest comfortably in the belief that "dates do not matter."

The third and fourth categories will be easily distinguished from the first two groups because there will be no payments at all. In many cases, these debtors have spent money unwisely. In other instances, they have suffered reversals that were completely unexpected. If a good client is involved, a lenient policy should be instituted. Many times in industry, if a good customer fails to pay a bill, the amount will be written off as a bad debt. Debtors who have no intention of paying are, of course, the worst to deal with. If an account reaches this stage, it is usually turned over to an internal collection department or an outside collection agency.

this reminder to send your check." "If you have already mailed your check, please disregard this letter."

Sympathy. "Although the amount is small, we have many such outstanding accounts, and the aggregate is important to us in paying our own bills."

Courtesy. "If you have withheld payment because of some dissatisfaction with our goods or service, we should appreciate your courtesy in writing to us." "Although we have written to you many times, we have not yet had the courtesy of a reply. If there is some personal reason for not paying, won't you tell us what it is."

Fairness. "In view of the services we have rendered, it is only fair that you pay us what you owe." "In all fairness, you should live up to the terms we agreed on when the account was opened." "It is not fair to give you more time to pay your bills than we give to other customers."

Self-interest. "Any further delay in payment will only make it harder for you to obtain credit in the future."

Fear. "Unless payment is made at once, we shall have to place your account in the hands of our collection agency (or attorney) with instructions to take any necessary means to collect what is due us."

These appeals may be varied in intensity by shifting from the positive to the negative viewpoint, as these examples show:

> *Positive (mild tone)*: Until now you have maintained an enviable credit standing. Why not preserve it by sending us your June payment at once?
>
> *Negative (stronger tone)*: Your failure to send us your June payment is seriously hurting your credit standing.

The time between letters depends on the type of credit risk and the urgency of collection. It may vary from ten days to a month early in the process and a week to two weeks as the effort continues. A creditor is inclined to be patient with customers who have good assets and earning power and a satisfactory record for meeting debts in the past. He is less patient with a customer whose credit record is spotty. A good collection letter is mild or severe in tone, as the occasion requires, but always courteous.

It is important to note that the debtor is protected by law against embarrassment and undue coercion. A collection notice should not be put on a post card, nor should the message threaten to inform other creditors of the customer's delinquency as a means of enforcing payment. The creditor may, however, report the delinquency to a credit agency as part of a regular arrangement with the agency.

Letters to Retail Customers

The following forms and letters will suggest the style and tone of collection letters used in retail trade. They are arranged in the order of increasing urgency, with the impersonal reminders coming first and the emotional appeals following.

FIG. 5-5. *Treatment of debtors. Part of the same report shown in Fig. 5-1.*

1. (Rubber-stamped on monthly statement):

   PAST DUE

2. (Printed on small card):

   May we remind you that payment of your account is overdue.
   Your check will be appreciated.

3. (Printed letter):

> Dear Customer:
> Most of our customers say they appreciate being reminded when their accounts are overdue.
> So we hope you will accept this reminder in the friendly spirit in which it is intended.
> If our letters happen to cross and your check arrives in the next mail, please disregard this notice and accept our thanks for your payment.
>
> Very truly yours,

4. (Filled-in form letter):

> Dear
>
> We have written to you on a number of occasions in the past in connection with delayed payments on your account.
>
> Your past due balance is shown below. We are confident that your sense of fair play will prompt you to send us your remittance promptly so that your account may be brought up to date.
>
> Very truly yours,
>
> Credit Department
>
> Amount Due $________

5. (Filled-in form letter):

should be personal

```
Dear

We again find it necessary to remind you of the past due
balance on your account about which we wrote to you a
month ago.

Unless we receive your payment immediately, we shall have
to refer your account to our Collection Department.

We are certain that you will want to avoid this in order
not to impair your credit rating.

                                  Yours very truly,

                                  Credit Department

Amount Due $________
```

6. (Filled-in form letter—from the Collection Department):

```
Dear

On each of the monthly bills we send to our customers, a
required payment is noted.  In order for a charge account
to be maintained on an up-to-date basis, that payment
must be made within 10 days of receipt of the bill.

We have notified you that your account is behind in pay-
ment.  The amount noted below is still overdue.

Please send us your check immediately.  We would very
much prefer not to move your account to our delinquent
file.

                                  Very truly yours,

Amount Due $________
```

7. (Personally typewritten letter—from the Collection Manager):

> Dear Mrs. Jones:
>
> Your account has been referred to me by our Collection Department for permission to enter suit. Before authorizing such action, I would like to ask you to telephone me.
>
> I am unwilling to believe that you are arbitrarily withholding payment of your account. If present conditions prevent you from making a payment now, why not call and afford me the opportunity of discussing the matter with you.
>
> Where sincere intentions exist, there is always a way to reach an agreement satisfactory to both parties.
>
> Therefore, I shall hold the matter in abeyance for the next five days while I await your reply.
>
> Very truly yours,

8. (Attorney's letter):

> Dear Mrs. Jones:
>
> My client, Shane's Department Store, has referred to me for collection a claim against you in the sum of $115.65.
>
> I would like to ask you to pay this claim either at my office or at the office of Shane's by noon of March 16.
>
> In the event that you fail to do so before that date, I shall take such further steps as my client may instruct me.
>
> Very truly yours,

Letters to Mercantile Customers

After the initial reminders, collection letters to business accounts generally appeal to the reader's desire to protect his credit standing and thus to continue to obtain the goods he needs to stay in business and make a profit. This appeal as well as others will be found in the following representative letters:

1. (Printed form letter):

> Gentlemen:
>
> In expressing our pleasure in the opportunity you have given us to serve you, may we also call your attention to your recently overdue account.
>
> Without doubt, you plan at this time to pay the balance below. Your check in settlement will be appreciated.
>
> Very truly yours,
>
> $______

2. (Typewritten form letter):

> Gentlemen:
>
> May we refer you to our recent letter regarding a balance of $123.44, which appears overdue on our books.
>
> If you cannot arrange to send us a check or money order today, we know you will do so within the next week at the very latest.
>
> Very truly yours,

3. (Typewritten form letter):

> Gentlemen:
>
> If I could call at your place of business today, I feel sure you would be glad to hand me your check for $123.44 in settlement of your long overdue account.
>
> Since it isn't always possible to see our friends in person, I hope you will respond in a similar fashion to this letter.
>
> Please mail your check today, won't you?
>
> Very truly yours,

4. (Personal letter):

Gentlemen:

The National Credit Bureau has requested us today to give them our experience with you. We have not replied to their inquiry because at this time you owe us $123.44 now past due, and we did not care to give them this information until we had taken the matter up with you.

It is their practice to send a second request within three or four days, and if it is possible for you to take care of your account before such time, it will be very much appreciated, as we would like to inform them that you have no past-due items currently outstanding.

Very truly yours,

5. (Typewritten form letter):

Gentlemen:

Without doubt, a good credit standing is one of your most valuable assets, as it enables you to secure merchandise when you desire it and so take care of the requirements of your customers. Your credit standing is good only when you make payments within a reasonable time. It is not good when you do not reply to collection letters from your suppliers and make it necessary for them to refer the accounts to attorneys or others to collect.

As your account is long past due, we believe we are not unreasonable in asking you to send your check for $123.44 before August 15.

We would very much regret it if you did not reply to this letter and thus forced us to take other means to collect what is owing us.

Very truly yours,

6. (Personal letter):

Gentlemen:

Since we can no longer put off action with regard to your account, we are giving you this last opportunity to send us a reply before we take the final steps.

In all the months we have been writing to you, you have not even given us the courtesy of a reply. If you have held off because of lack of funds or other reason, you owe it to yourself and to us to give us an explanation. As you know, there are ways of easing the burden on you through an extension or installment arrangement, but we can make no such suggestion until we know what your circumstances are.

We therefore urge you to write to us at once. A note on the bottom of this letter will do. The alternatives are to send your check for the full balance of $123.44 or face a suit for collection.

Unless we hear from you by September 1, we shall take immediate action on that date.

Very truly yours,

7. (Personal letter):

Gentlemen:

In view of your failure to answer our letter of August 20, we are sorry that we must now take action to collect the balance of $123.44 due us since last May.

If your check in full payment is not received by December 1, the next letter you receive on this matter will be from our collection agency, the National Credit Bureau.

We hope you will spare yourself this permanent injury to your credit standing and the extra cost that legal proceedings will entail.

Very truly yours,

Follow-up Collection Letters

All the letters we have quoted up to now assume that no replies have been received from the debtors. However, "breaks" in the collection system occur frequently, as when a customer writes an excuse for not paying, promises payment at a later date, asks for credit concessions, or makes only a partial payment. All of these instances call for special letters designed to meet the situations and spur the reader to extra effort to pay.

The follow-up letters below are self-explanatory:

Dear Mr. Wallace:

Thank you for your check for $60. There now remains a balance of $127.65 past due.

Although you did not indicate when we may receive the balance, we know you have the matter in mind and will send us an additional remittance soon.

You may be sure that we value your business and hope you will let us fill your orders if there is anything in our line that you require.

Sincerely yours,

Dear Mr. Duffin:

We are pleased to have your letter informing us that it is your intention to settle your overdue balance of $73.50 at an early date.

Although we dislike to press you, your letter is somewhat indefinite. We are therefore going to ask you to mail us your check within the next ten days.

If you have some other plan in mind, please be sure to let us know so that we may act accordingly.

Very truly yours,

Dear Mr. Gross:

We have your letter asking for an extension of time for the payment of your account in the amount of $487.20.

Since we cannot defer indefinitely the payment of the entire amount, we will ask you to send us a check for $100 on June 1 and another check in like amount each month until the amount is fully paid.

We will expect your check for $100 on June 1 as evidence of your good faith. We are sure you will see the advantage of paying in the manner we suggest.

Very truly yours,

In the instance covered by the following letter, the customer's account was not yet past due, but new orders would have pushed the customer's debt over the maximum line of credit established for him.

Gentlemen:

Thank you for your new orders totaling approximately $3,500. Your continued interest in Farnum products is appreciated.

As your records will show, you currently have outstanding invoices of $8,500 against your established credit line of $10,000. In order for us to enter your order for the scheduled delivery date, therefore, it will be necessary for you to send us your check for $2,000; otherwise the shipping date will have to be postponed accordingly.

We will hold your order in the credit department until we hear from you.

Very truly yours,

Unconventional Letters

One reason customers do not pay is that they have not been moved sufficiently. When a collection man believes this to be the case, he may write a "stunt" or humorous letter to stimulate response. Such letters are usually futile in appealing to hardened debtors and they often irritate the thin-skinned ones. Still, many claims are made for their effectiveness.

The following letter, timed to arrive on Lincoln's birthday, had a "Lincoln" postage stamp tipped on in the space indicated.

Dear Mr. Farnum:

Won't you look at this picture of "Honest Abe," and then do with it what he would have done if he owed us $7.56 as long as you do?

Very truly yours,

A rubber band was included in the following letter:

```
Dear Friend:

Here is a common, ordinary, garden-variety rubber band.

Stretch it to here --------------- X

          . . . and it will fly back, good as new.

But stretch it to here -------------------------------- X

          . . . and IT MIGHT BREAK!

Similarly, a credit arrangement--such as the one which
you and I made--has elasticity . . . up to a point.

Seriously, won't you please mail your remittance for
$________ today?

                                Sincerely,
```

A letter from an industrial company bears a drawing of a coonskin-hatted hunter aiming a long rifle. The letter reads:

```
Gentlemen:

We won't really resort to this sort of thing to collect
the $________ balance due us.  But we hope you'll send us
your check anyway.

                                Very truly yours,
```

SUMMARY

"Utility" letters, one of several classes of letters covered in this chapter, are a large part of the routine of every office. Routine though they are, however, they reach so many people and deal with such important matters that they should never be treated in a routine way. Among the utility letters are order letters, acknowledgements of orders, letters about remittances, requests and inquiries, and replies to inquiries. All of these letters have in common the need to be clear and specific. Where the reader is charged with an error in payment, patience and tact are virtues that are returned in goodwill. When the writer has been charged with an error in billing, the reader deserves a fair explanation and, if the complaint is justified, a gracious apology. An inquiry or request that holds no potential benefit to the reader should explain the reason for the request, limit the request to certain necessary specifics, and offer—if possible—to reciprocate. Answers to letters of any kind should be prompt, courteous, and complete, even if that means only referring the reader to enclosures or to other sources where the materials requested can be obtained.

When an answer must be held up until information can be developed, an interim letter will allay the reader's impatience.

Credit and collection letters involve some of the most sensitive feelings of customers. For that reason and because strict laws protect the rights of debtors, the business writer must use extreme caution in phrasing his letters. Credit is based on the reputation of the debtor and his ability to pay. Letters are used to obtain information about prospective debtors and to give information about one's own customers in response to legitimate requests. Information may be obtained directly from a customer or from his creditors. The inquirer should state his reason for wanting the information, state specifically what information he wishes, and promise to keep the information in confidence. In replying, a credit correspondent sticks closely to the facts and uses the utmost restraint in offering any judgment. Unfavorable references are often best communicated by telephone.

When a customer fails to pay promptly, collection letters become necessary. These may at first take the form of simple, printed reminders that payment is overdue, but if they do not bring a response, form letters and then personal letters are used. Generally, there is an increase in pressure as the system progresses. The reminders may lead to appeals to courtesy, fairness, and self-interest. All customers, but business accounts especially, realize the value of a good credit standing, and they may be urged to preserve it by immediate payment. The threat of legal action marks the final stage before the account is turned over to an attorney or a collection agency.

PROBLEMS

1. The MacAdam Department Store, 100 Main Street, your city, has today advertised in the *Daily Gazette* a sale on a Harmony AM-FM table radio at $59.50, reduced from $99. Write a letter ordering one for yourself. You are enclosing your personal check, which should include any local sales tax.

2. You are doing some research on monopolistic practices in the communications industry. To get a corporate view of the subject, especially as it relates to the telephone industry, write to the Public Relations Department, American Telephone and Telegraph Company, 195 Broadway, New York, N.Y., 10007. Ask if they could send you any company press releases or other printed material on the subject.

3. Assume that you wish either to continue your present undergraduate work at another college or to enter a graduate or professional school following completion of your present degree requirements. Write a letter to the Director of Admissions of the school of your choice. Ask for a catalog and application forms. Also take the opportunity to ask about scholarships and tuition aid.

4. The Eureka portable electric typewriter is regularly advertised in *Time* and other national magazines. It is distributed at retail, however, not by the Eureka Typewriter Company, which places the advertisements, but by office appliance dealers throughout the United States. As a sales correspondent for the company you

receive today a letter and a check for $225 from Mr. Russell Thomson of 50 Washington Mews, New York, N.Y. 10011 to cover the purchase of one of the machines. Write to Mr. Thomson, returning his check and referring him to Panora Distributors, 652 Fourth Avenue, New York, N.Y. 10018.

5. Assume that Mrs. Richard S. Travers of 500 Ward Parkway, Kansas City, Missouri 64112, has a charge account at the Blyden Department Store of the same city. On behalf of the store, handle the following correspondence. Use today's date unless otherwise indicated.
   (*a*) Mrs. Travers has sent you a check for $114.65 in payment of her July account of $104.65. Acknowledge the check and tell her she will find a credit of $10 on her next month's statement. Date your letter August 12.
   (*b*) Mrs. Travers has asked you to send a 16-inch gold parchment drum-shape lampshade advertised in a circular sent to her. The price is $24.50. The gold shade is temporarily out of stock. Say you will send the shade when it comes in, probably three weeks from now.
   (*c*) Mrs. Travers has ordered a sterling silver compote dish to be sent as a wedding gift to Mr. and Mrs. David M. Soyer, 1249 Boulevard Place, Milwaukee, Wisconsin 53227. The price of $76.50 is to be charged to her account. Today (November 6) the package is returned to you from the Milwaukee post office with the notice, "Not Known at Address Given." Write to Mrs. Travers for further instructions.
   (*d*) On January 12 Mrs. Travers wrote to say that she wanted a good desk dictionary sent as a birthday gift to her nephew, Ronald Barton, at the University of Buffalo. She asked you to select one that you consider most suitable for college use. You have sent the *Modern Collegiate Dictionary* and charged the customer's account $8.84, which covers the cost of the dictionary and 34 cents postage. Write to Mrs. Travers telling her you chose the *Modern Collegiate Dictionary* because, for example, it is approved by college educators, it is completely authoritative and up-to-date, and it is lighter in weight and has more words and definitions than comparable dictionaries. Date your letter January 17.

6. Assume that you are the head bookkeeper for John Lee & Co., a small advertising agency at 45 Main Street, Peekskill, New York 10566. You have recently received the catalog of Silversmith Brothers, a large stationery house located at 750 Broadway, New York, N.Y. 10045. Write letters to cover the following situations:
   (*a*) You want to order 200 heavyweight manila folders (letter size, 3-tab, Cat. No. 24RE620-S) at $10.00 per hundred, a box of 25 Pendaflex hanging folders (3-position, 3½-inch tab width, Cat. No. 24RS415⅓) at $8.00 the box, and a set of 25 pressboard file guides letter size, (divided alphabetically, Cat. No. 35EM45630) at $6.00 the set.

   A statement in the front of the catalog reads, "A Silversmith Charge Account is easy to open. With your first order, just send us the name and address of your firm, type of business and name and address of your bank." This is your company's first order and you want it charged. Your bank is the Valley Trust Company, Peekskill.
   (*b*) Silversmith Brothers have sent you the legal size manila folders instead of the letter size you ordered (see Problem 6(*a*)) and charged you $11.00 per hundred. Ask them to have their truck make the exchange and to correct the bill.

(c) The catalog offers to accept old typewriters in trade for new ones. You would like to buy a Eureka electric with standard carriage, listed at $525. You have at present a Remington standard, Model KMC, in good condition. Find out what trade-in allowance Silversmith will give you.

7. Assume that you are the merchandise manager for the Gary Department Store in your city. On March 24, you sent an order to the Johnson Knitting Mills, Lancaster, Pa. 17604, for 72 dozen pairs of plain white cotton tennis socks, No. A26B. You would like to change this order so that half is delivered as specified and the remainder divided evenly between red tops (No. A26C) and blue tops (No. A26D). The number on your original purchase order was S5837. Unless Johnson Knitting Mills want you to, you will not make out a revised purchase order. Today is April 1.

8. As sales manager of Johnson Knitting Mills (see Problem 7, above), write a reply to the letter from the Gary Department Store. Since the bordered socks cost $1 per dozen more than the plain, you would like a new purchase order covering the whole transaction. The plain socks will be delivered on April 15, as promised, but there will be a delay of two weeks in shipping the bordered socks.

9. As head bookkeeper of the Jones Machinery Corporation, you have today (September 3) received from J. M. Bramwell & Co. of Carson City, Nevada 89701, a check for $326.34 in payment for your invoice of August 14 for $349.60, representing the purchase of a Fulton Multiple Drill Machine, Model TF. Ask the company to explain the discrepancy.

10. Assume the part of the bookkeeper for J. M. Bramwell & Co. in the situation outlined in Problem 9 above. Write to the Jones Machinery Corporation at 440 Mountain Avenue, Denver, Colorado 80202, saying that the deduction of $23.26 was for express charges, which you had to pay.

11. Again assume your position as head bookkeeper of Jones Machinery Corporation (Problems 9 and 10 above). Reply to the letter of J. M. Bramwell & Co. by pointing out that your regular terms of sale are F.O.B. Factory. These terms (the abbreviation stands for "free on board") mean that the customer must pay the transportation charges from the factory. The terms are printed on all invoices. Ask for a check for $23.26.

12. As assistant treasurer of the Bloomfield Mills, you have today (March 23) received from one of your customers a check for $456.44 in payment of your invoice No. 7775, dated February 28, for $465. 75. The check is dated March 22. Your terms on this transaction, as stated on the invoice, were 2% 10 days, net 30. These terms mean that payment is due in 30 days, but that a 2% discount is given for payment within 10 days. Apparently, the customer—National Dry Goods Stores, Inc., 780 Seneca Street, Buffalo, New York 14215—took the discount of $9.31 even though they paid some 12 days after the expiration of the discount period.

(a) Assume that the customer took a similar deduction several months ago, when they were sent a letter closely modeled after the second one on page 131. Although the letter succeeded in obtaining a check for the balance, you feel that a different letter with a somewhat firmer approach is needed this time. Write the letter.

(*b*) Assume that the customer has just started doing business with you. Write a letter allowing the deduction, but calling attention to the error and asking for strict compliance with your terms in the future.

13. As manager of radio station WROC, you have received the following letter:

> Rockville High School
> Rockville, IL 61101
> March 26, 19--
>
> Station WROC
> Rockville, IL 61102
>
> Gentlemen:
>
> I enjoyed the talk the other evening by David McKee on the cost of election campaigns. Would you have a transcript of his remarks that you could send me? I would find it valuable in teaching my political science courses.
>
> Sincerely yours,
>
> Arthur T. Bryan

(*a*) Write to Mr. Bryan, telling him that the program originated with the American Broadcasting Company network in Washington, D.C., and that you are forwarding his letter there for reply.
(*b*) Write a covering letter to go with Mr. Bryan's request. Address it to the American Broadcasting Company, 4461 Connecticut Avenue, N.W., Washington, D.C. 20005.
(*c*) Mr. McKee's talk was broadcast locally only. You have no transcript of the talk. Mr. McKee is now abroad. Answer Mr. Bryan's letter.

14. Assume that you are the David McKee mentioned in Problem 13 above. Mr. Bryan's letter has been forwarded to you. Write a letter of reply, enclosing a copy of the transcript.

15. Assume that you are the editor of the *Excelsior News*, your company's employee house organ. You have just seen an article, "Industrial Living Together," in the Second Quarter, 1978, issue of *Falco*, a house organ of the Falcon Manufacturing Company. You think that the article, a plea for cooperation between big and small business, would be interesting to your readers. Ask for permission to reprint it, promising to give credit to *Falco* and the Falcon Manufacturing Company. (Authors are not named in *Falco* articles.)Write to Mr. John J. Dingham, director of the company's Department of Communications, 900 Bush Avenue, St. Paul, Minnesota 55102.

16. The following letter, in mimeographed form, was received by the personnel department of a large company. It was not answered.

Find someone's name

Stronger ending
get to the point

Gentlemen:

About six months ago I wrote to a number of companies to obtain information for a thesis on Career Planning which I was preparing at Metropolitan University. Now I would like to develop some of the more interesting parts of this material in more detail.

Results? benefit the Co.

In selecting an employer, a person is interested in the type of work, working conditions, salary, competitive position of the company, and benefits. It is this latter category about which I would like to obtain more specific information.

self addressed envelope would help

Would you please provide me with information, including company literature, regarding the following benefits:

1. Your pension program.
2. Hospitalization and surgical insurance. Is any part of this paid for by the company?
3. Group insurance. Is this company-paid-for?
4. Employee stock purchase plans.
5. Bonus plans.
6. Death benefits aside from group insurance.
7. Sickness and accident payments and allowances.
8. Termination payments.
9. Vacation plan.
10. Educational benefits.
11. Training programs.

Any information you may provide me with will be very much appreciated.

Very truly yours,

D. R. Peterson

(*a*) Explain briefly but specifically what factors in the letter inhibited response.
(*b*) Rewrite the letter so that it is more effective.
(*c*) Assume the position of the reader. Write a reply with which you enclose your company's manual outlining the various employee benefit plans. Ask the reader to arrange to see you personally if he wants additional information.

17. As credit manager of Milady Fashions, a wholesale dress house, you receive an order from Selma's Dress Shop (Miss Selma Ames, proprietor), 750 Canal Street, New Orleans, La. 70119, for two dozen wool jersey dresses in the "Jaunty" line, which you are now featuring in women's magazine advertisements. The order, dated January 12 and asking for "regular terms," is the first from this store. Handle the following letter situations:
(*a*) Selma's Dress Shop is well rated by Dun & Bradstreet. Acknowledge the order and say it will be shipped, as requested, on February 20 by railway express on your regular terms of 2% 10 days, net 30.
(*b*) Dun & Bradstreet has no information about Selma's Dress Shop, which may have only recently opened for business. Write to Miss Ames for credit refer-

ences, including the name of her bank and two or three companies which have extended credit to her recently.

(*c*) Miss Ames refers you to the Southern Bank and Trust Company of 400 Gulf Street, New Orleans, La. 70130, where she says she has maintained a business account for four years. Ask the bank for any information they can provide, including the size and conduct of the account and whether or not the bank has extended any loans.

(*d*) Miss Ames refers you to Mayfair House, Inc., a wholesale dress company located at 1400 Seventh Avenue, New York, N.Y. 10018. Write to the credit manager (name unknown) for a report on his experience with Selma's Dress Shop. Tell what specific information you want.

(*e*) The information you have obtained from Miss Ames's references is unsatisfactory. Write to decline the order. You will, however, be glad to make up the dresses if the customer sends cash now and allows four weeks for delivery. The total amount is $352.80, including the 2% discount.

18. Assume that you are writing for the signature of Mr. Ralph Brinks, credit manager of the Cory Department Store of your city. Mrs. Donald S. Lane of 15 South Tenth Street writes on May 15 asking that you open a charge account in her name. Handle the following situations:

(*a*) You send her the regular credit application form. Write the accompanying letter.

(*b*) Mrs. Lane fills out and mails you the credit application. All the information is in order. Write to tell her that her account has been opened. Enclose a credit card bearing her identification. She is to present it whenever she makes a purchase. Bills are rendered on the first of the month and are payable by the tenth.

(*c*) The information given to you by Mrs. Lane is not satisfactory. She says she has no other charge accounts, but inquiry at your city's Retail Credit Bureau reveals that she has an account at the Madison Specialty Shop, which has been unsuccessfully trying to collect $256 since the first of the year. Deny the account, but try to retain the lady's goodwill.

(*d*) One of the references given you by Mrs. Lane is the Second National Bank in Dayton, Ohio 45408, where she had her home until recently. Write to the bank, asking for their experiences with Mrs. Lane. Ask especially what her monthly balances averaged and whether she was ever overdrawn.

19. Assume that you are the credit manager of Donlon's, a department store in your city. Write the following collection forms to be sent in the order indicated to charge customers rated as good risks.

(*a*) A reminder to be printed on a card (30 days past due)

(*b*) A second reminder to be printed on a card (60 days past due)

(*c*) A letter combining the suggestion of oversight with the request that the store be notified if the customer has any reason for not paying (2½ months past due)

(*d*) A letter appealing to the customer's sense of fairness (3 months past due)

(*e*) A letter incorporating the appeal to self-interest (3½ months past due)

(*f*) A second letter appealing to self-interest (4 months past due)

(*g*) A registered letter (return receipt requested) demanding an explanation or check (4½ months past due)

(*h*) A letter threatening legal action (5 months past due)

20. Assume that you are the credit manager of Donlon's, working with the collection schedule noted in Problem 19 above. Write letters dealing with the following special situations. Assume in each case that the customer lives at 75 Radcliffe Road.
    (*a*) Mrs. James E. Curtis has responded on January 10 to letter (*c*). She writes that heavy Christmas expenses have left her household budget temporarily short. She hopes to pay by the first of the month. Write a reply, stressing Mrs. Curtis's obligation to pay according to the terms agreed on. Say you will expect a check for $95.65 in full payment of her account by February 1 at the very latest. In the meantime, you will tell her, any additional purchases will have to be paid for in cash.
    (*b*) After receiving letter (*f*), Mrs. Minnie Pardee has sent you on July 8 a check for $25 in partial payment of her account, leaving a balance of $124.50. Thank Mrs. Pardee for her check, but emphasize the need to remit the balance. Ask that she send another check for at least $50 by August 1.
    (*c*) Mr. Fred Stoller has sent you a check for $148.90 with a letter, dated August 10, in reply to letter (*e*). He is highly offended by your "nagging" letters and says it will be a "long time" before he buys from you again. Try to smooth things over; you want his future business, even if he is unfair in his criticism.
    (*d*) Mr. Ivan Talbert, who was sent form (*a*), has written on December 17 to tell you that he has not paid up his account for $130 because the overcoat he bought at that price does not fit properly. He says he will send you his check as soon as the alterations are completed to his satisfaction. The coat, he tells you, is still in the hands of your clothing department. After checking, you find Mr. Talbert's facts to be correct. Write to tell him you'll be glad to wait until he is happy with his coat.

21. Assume that you are the credit manager of *News Currents,* a weekly magazine. In response to your Christmas mailing, many regular subscribers ordered gift subscriptions at the special low price of $12 for the year (the regular price is $20). Most of the givers specified that a bill be sent to them for payment after the first of the year. It is now January 10. You have sent out the bills, but you anticipate that many subscribers will put off payment. Write a series of six collection notices, including letters, designed to be spread over a period of six months. Arrange them in climactic order, so that the last message contains a threat.

22. You are the assistant credit manager of the Merit Tire and Rubber Company of Akron, Ohio. Your terms require payment within thirty days. Write the following collection letters to the dealers named:
    (*a*) The Zenith Auto Supply Company of 524 New London Avenue, Bridgeport, Conn. 06611, owes $587.60 for purchases made sixty days ago. You have not received an answer to a reminder mailed ten days ago. The account is generally slow in paying. Your boss, the credit manager, asks you to "light a fire under them."
    (*b*) The Trenton Hardware Company of 758 Broadway, Trenton, New Jersey 08604, placed a first order for $345.50 two months ago. You wrote a letter as soon as the account became due, then telephoned ten days ago. Mr. Arthur Kalb, the proprietor, said he would "surely send a check in a few days." You have not heard from Mr. Kalb since. Write again, asking for full payment immediately.

(*c*) Mr. Kalb (see problem (*b*)) has answered your last letter. He says he was not exactly frank with you. As a matter of fact, he had been in the hospital for two weeks, during which the store was closed. He is now back on his feet and his old customers are coming back. If you will be patient, he is sure he will pay everything he owes. He asks for an extension until October 1. It is now July 9. Sympathize with Mr. Kalb, but ask for a promissory note, payable on October 1, for the full amount.

(*d*) The Ajax Garage, a good customer in Riverview, Virginia 24587, owes $178.90. past due on an invoice dated January 19. It is now March 1. Write a letter, to be enclosed with a statement of the account, asking for prompt payment. You have not written before about this particular invoice.

(*e*) The Ajax Garage (see problem (*d*)) does not reply to your letter of March 1. Write a second letter, dated March 20, appealing to the customer's self-interest.

(*f*) The Ajax Garage (see problems (*d*) and (*e*)) has not answered. It is April 10. Write a letter asking if there is anything wrong.

23. Assume that you are the collection manager for a large weekly news magazine. Your subscribers, who are for the most part financially responsible business and professional people, are regularly invited to renew their subscriptions by returning the reply half of a double postal card. They are billed some weeks later. You have found from experience that tardiness is usually the result of forgetfulness and simple inertia and that an inoffensively humorous reminder brings excellent results when payment has been delayed. Write such a reminder.

6
Special Types of Letters (II)

IN THIS chapter we will deal with complaint and adjustment letters and with a number of different types of official and personal letters that are a normal part of business correspondence. The term "official" is used here to denote letters relating to the responsibilities and ceremonies of office and not to the tone that marks some legal and quasilegal correspondence. (For an example of the latter, see Figure 4-4, page 95.)

COMPLAINTS AND CLAIMS

Not everything is business goes according to plan. When mistakes and accidents occur, when service is deficient and merchandise does not perform as expected, the victim turns to thoughts of reparation. To be sure, the seller is not always at fault. Sometimes goods are lost, stolen, damaged, or delayed while in transit. At other times, the customer himself has used the product improperly or is not familiar with the conditions under which goods are sold. The important point, nevertheless, is that the buyer feels aggrieved.

Normally, one may expect that a reasonable complaint will be adjusted quickly and fairly. When such an adjustment does not appear to be in prospect, it is generally best to address the head of the company, by name if possible. Very often he is glad to get your letter because it gives him an insight into his company's operations that he does not usually get from his company's internal communications system. Even if the one you address is too busy to handle your complaint personally, he can be expected to send it to a subordinate with instructions that the matter be attended to promptly. And such an order from the top carries a great deal more weight than the customer can command on his own.

A claim or complaint should give full particulars. Only then is the recipient able to investigate the matter and determine what adjustment should be made. Temperance and courtesy in stating the claim help also. The writer who sounds like a crank is sure to prejudice his case.

The letter below is unsatisfactory. The information is indefinite and the tone is discourteous.

CRUDE

> Gentlemen:
>
> What kind of outfit are you running, anyway? We place a simple order six weeks ago and we don't even get an acknowledgment. Now you send us a bill, but we've never even seen the goods.
>
> This kind of service we can do without. If you can't get the stuff to us, just cancel our order and we'll go elsewhere--permanently.
>
> Very truly yours,

The letter that follows is more conducive to good results:

COURTEOUS

> Gentlemen:
>
> On March 24 we placed an order (Purchase Ord. No. T1096) for several parts for our Eureka Blowing Machine. Although we received no acknowledgment, we understood that it would take some time to make up the order and we waited patiently. Today we received a bill from you for $70 to cover the cost of the parts, but we still don't have the shipment.
>
> It's probable that you sent the order and that it has not yet arrived. In any case, we'd appreciate your looking into the matter and letting us know where things stand. Of course, we'll have to hold up payment of your bill until we get the parts.
>
> Very truly yours,

Occasionally, the past experience of the reader suggests that a mild tone in the complaint would be fruitless. Even then, it is possible to be firm without being rude. The tone of such a letter is suggested below. Note especially how it obtains the reader's point of view through the appeal to self-interest.

FIRM

Gentlemen:

It is now more than six weeks since we called your attention to the defects in the chair we purchased from you on August 9. Each time we telephone, you promise that you will pick up the chair and make the necessary repairs. So far, the chair is still here. Obviously, it is of no use to us until the springs and webbing are reset.

We cannot understand how your treatment of us in this instance is in any way going to help you get any future business from us or from other businessmen whom we are in a position to influence. On the contrary, you are building up a reservoir of ill will that can only hurt you. And we still have recourse to the Better Business Bureau--and to legal procedures if necessary--to insure that we get the value we paid for.

You can still salvage something from this situation by repairing the chair at once. We'll expect you, without fail, to call for it within the next few days.

Very truly yours,

ADJUSTMENT LETTERS

Nowhere is the character of an organization better demonstrated than in the way it handles complaints and makes adjustments. In recent years the consumer movement has targeted in on this sensitive area of business practice. Many product deficiencies and false claims have been exposed and both the law and public opinion have stimulated greater self-examination by business organizations dealing with the consumer. Some companies have strengthened their guarantees and some have established "hot lines," which provide toll-free numbers for registering complaints. In general, there is a growing trend to compensate for the impersonal nature of a business by giving the consumer full and specific information on what he can expect from a product and a specific name and address where he can make known his dissatisfactions.

Since adjustments are still made largely by correspondence, a company's letters tell a great deal about its business philosophy and breadth of view. Sympathy, let alone generosity, is always desirable, but that sympathy must be even more evident in the tone of the letters than in the actual concessions made. A customer may forgive the denial of a doubtful claim, but he will not tolerate an offensive attitude, even if the claim is adjusted.

Tone of Adjustment Letters

The suggestions that follow should help to ensure good tone in handling complaints of any sort:

1. Be sympathetic. An expression of regret is a normal and courteous response to any reported dissatisfaction, whether or not the fault is yours. It is intended to conciliate the reader, who is undoubtedly upset, for he would not otherwise have bothered to write. You should note that saying you are sorry is an expression of sympathy and should not be confused with an apology, which carries with it an admission of blame. The statements that follow are properly conciliatory.

> We are indeed sorry to learn of your experience at our store last Tuesday.
>
> We can understand your disappointment in not receiving our shipment of October 7.
>
> May we express our sincere regrets over the damage to the painting we recently shipped to you.

Sometimes the conciliatory statement in the opening is varied to express appreciation for the complaint or to tell, without any preliminaries, what is being done about it.

> We appreciate your writing us so promptly about our error in filling your order of May 10.
>
> We are taking immediate steps to correct our error in filling your order of May 10.

The close of the letter may complement, but not repeat, the conciliatory statement in the opening. It may consist of a "thank you," an apology, or some other bid for goodwill.

> Thank you for writing to us.
>
> We're glad we could make this adjustment for you.
>
> Please accept our apologies.
>
> We hope you'll give us another opportunity soon to show you how good our service can be.

2. *Be tactful.* Since the reader already feels put upon, the language you use should not impose any additional strain on the relationship. Note these contrasts:

> *Overly negative:* Please accept our sincere apologies for the inconvenience you suffered. We hope there will be no recurrence of this unfortunate incident.
> *Better:* We are sorry for the inconvenience caused you.
>
> *Suspicious:* We have your letter about the alleged loss of three stock certificates.
> *Better:* We are sorry to learn about the loss of three stock certificates.
>
> *Grudging:* If what you say is true, we suppose we will have to replace the damaged pen.
> *Better:* Of course, we'll replace the damaged pen.

Sharp: You obviously failed to open the package as soon as it arrived.
Better: Apparently, the package was not opened as soon as it was received.

"Buck-passing": The error was due to the carelessness of one of our clerks who failed to follow our rules.
Better: The error is ours, and we're sorry.

Intemperate: We are forced to refuse your claim.
Better: We are sorry that we cannot make the adjustment in this instance.

3. *Be helpful.* The customer has written to you because he wants some form of satisfaction. Replacing lost or damaged goods or offering a refund usually represents the maximum reparation, while a word of sympathy represents the minimum. The reader may also expect some explanation: Why was there a delay in shipment? How could the damage occur? If the product was misused, what is the proper way to operate it or care for it? What must the reader do to locate a missing shipment, or to file a claim with the transportation company, or to obtain a replacement? What can *you* do to help? Finally, what assurance can you give that you fulfilled your obligations or that you will do so in the future? Answers to these questions form an integral part of adjustment letters and help to bring complaints to a satisfactory conclusion.

Interim Letters

Some complaints cannot be immediately resolved because of the time needed for investigation of the facts. In such a case, keeping the reader waiting only increases his dissatisfaction and makes it more difficult to arrive at a reasonable settlement. It is better practice to send an acknowledgment immediately, expressing sympathy for the reader and telling him that you will be in touch with him again as soon as you have looked into the circumstances. This is an example of such a letter:

Dear Mr. Gaines:

We can understand your feelings in receiving our bill for $70 when you still don't have the spare parts you ordered six weeks ago.

You are probably right in assuming that the parts are on their way, but a vacation shutdown in our main plant will prevent us from getting any definite information for a few days. As soon as we have something to report, we'll get in touch with you again.

In the meantime, thanks very much for your patience. Of course, the bill won't become effective until after you receive the shipment.

Sincerely,

Granting Adjustments

When the fault of the seller is obvious and it is certain that the adjustment will be completely satisfactory to the reader, the letter should tell as soon as possible what the adjustment is. Some degree of frankness in explaining the error may be called for here, but not so much as to cause loss of dignity or the respect of the reader. When full reparation is made, an explanation of how the error occurred may not be necessary.

This letter lacks the proper dignity:

```
Gentlemen:

Please forgive us for our stupid error.  We've pulled
some beauts in our time, but this blunder beats them all.

We hope you'll find the corrected bill in order, but we
wouldn't be too sure.

                                    Very truly yours,
```

The letters that follow have better tone:

```
Gentlemen:

If you will return the damaged cylinder to us, we will
replace it immediately with a new one and reimburse you
for the shipping charges.

We sincerely regret the inconvenience to you.

                                    Very truly yours,
```

```
Gentlemen:

Thanks very much for calling our attention to the error
in our May 16 invoice.  A corrected bill is enclosed.

                                    Very truly yours,
```

Sometimes the only adjustment possible consists of an expression of regret and an explanation of what happened. This is especially true when the service, rather than replaceable merchandise, is at fault. If the circumstances were exceptional, the letter should say so and give assurances of better service in the future. It is unwise, however, to promise that "it will never happen again." Almost all mistakes do.

These letters handle their respective situations well:

Dear Mr. Hare:

From your description, it appears possible that the Shaver is out of adjustment or the shearing head is defective.

We suggest that you take or send your Shaver directly to our Service Branch located at 218 East Lexington Avenue, Baltimore, Maryland 21202, and explain the difficulty you are experiencing. Immediate adjustments to the Shaver will be made and the shearing head checked. If it is defective and in need of replacement, a new shaving head will be installed at no charge.

We are certain that when your Shaver is again in your possession, you will enjoy complete shaving satisfaction.

Very truly yours,

Gentlemen:

We regret to learn that the watch we sent you is not the one you ordered and that you lost a sale as a result. You are perfectly right in returning the watch for credit.

The fact is that we were temporarily out of stock on the Ajax model and sent you the Hercules, a companion model, instead. Of course, we should have written you about the switch.

Although we failed you this time, we are sure you've had sufficient experience with us to know that this is not the way we usually handle your orders.

Please forgive us and let us have another chance soon. We do value your business and would like to prove that we deserve it.

Sincerely yours,

Dear Mrs. Hager:

It goes without saying that we feel bad about the discourtesy you experienced in our basement shoe department the other day. At the same time, we appreciate the time and trouble you have taken to write us, for it is through letters like yours that we are able to take corrective measures.

We have always tried to make your shopping at Gordon's a pleasure, and we hope you will find it so in the future.

Thank you again for your most helpful letter.

Sincerely,

It is not unusual to make an adjustment even when the seller is not at fault. The complainant may have had an exceptional experience; he may have misunderstood the terms of sale; or he may deliberately be trying to gain an advantage to which he is not entitled. Still, the seller may feel that there is more business advantage in making an adjustment than in refusing. The company need not, of course, concede the justice of the customer's claim and may even take the opportunity to explain why similar claims of the sort may be denied.

Note in the following letters that although an adjustment is granted, the inductive order is used, that is, the explanation of the facts surrounding the transaction takes precedence over the granting of the adjustment (the conclusion). If the adjustment were granted immediately, there is some danger that the reader would not pay as close attention to the statement of facts.

Dear Miss Ball:

The dress you left for my attention has been carefully inspected.

The material in this dress is silk and the dyes are the conventional dyes used on silk. We do not know what caused the condition you experienced, as there is nothing in the material or dyes that would react on the average person.

However, we realize you cannot wear a dress that would cause a rash and have therefore passed a credit to your account.

Please be assured that we want all of your transactions with us to be entirely satisfactory.

Sincerely,

Gentlemen:

We are sorry to learn from your letter of August 27 that two of the lamps in our shipment of July 12 were received in a damaged condition and that you are returning them for credit.

Ordinarily there would be no question about accepting the return of damaged goods. As you know, however, claims for damage should be made within five days of the receipt of the shipment. A statement to this effect appears on all our invoices. The purpose of the rule is to give us a chance to make a counterclaim on the transportation company which in many cases is responsible for the damage.

Because we understand your feelings, we are going to allow the credit this time. We are sure, however, that you will be willing to cooperate with us by making claims promptly in the future.

Very truly yours,

A common cause of complaints is the customer's unfamiliarity with the proper use of the product or his failure to follow directions. Correct instructions must be included in the adjustment letter.

Dear Miss Heuber:

We are sorry to learn of your very unsatisfactory experience with Super-X Home Dry Cleaner and particularly on your initial use of the product.

Why the Super-X you purchased should have had such decided odor is hard to explain; in fact, most customers whom we have questioned on the subject tell us that they are pleasantly surprised that the odor is so slight. The use of a small electric fan, however, would hasten evaporation and eliminate any dry-cleaning odor in a short time.

It is well known that petroleum products, and especially petroleum solvents, have a deteriorating effect upon rubber materials, and the fact that your garment came in contact with the shower curtain explains the condition about which you write. Although we do not accept any liability in matters of this kind, we certainly recognize that mistakes can occur. If you will purchase a new shower curtain similar to the one damaged, we shall be glad to send you our check in payment, provided you forward us the receipted bill.

We believe the enclosed detailed instructions on dry cleaning with Super-X will be quite helpful to you. Should you have any additional questions you wish answered, Mrs. Mary Hayden, director of our Consumer Service Department, will be glad to answer them for you.

Sincerely yours,

Refusing Adjustments

Some complaints are both unreasonable and costly to adjust, without any compensating benefits to the seller. The result is a denial of the claim. Invariably the reader expects, and should be given, a reason for the refusal. Although a refusal at the beginning of the letter may be diplomatically worded, as the first example below indicates, many good writers prefer to state the facts or circumstances first and deny the adjustment later. Either way, a positive statement in the close should try to salvage whatever goodwill is possible.

Gentlemen:

We wish we could replace the Model S-2 copying machine about which you recently wrote us.

Our records show, however, that this machine was purchased fully 26 months ago and that the guarantee has long since expired.

We notice that you gave up your service contract last July. If you wish to reinstate it, we are sure we can put your copier in good working order. Under any circumstances, we would be glad to talk to you about the purchase of a later model and offer you a fair allowance on the old machine.

Our representative, Mr. Charles Raymond, will be in touch with you very soon.

Sincerely yours,

Dear Mr. Gardner:

We are sorry to learn of your experience with one of our Rayex shirts.

In order to obtain the good looks and wrinkle-free qualities of this shirt, we have had to specify that it be laundered by hand only with the mildest soaps. A label on each shirt bears these instructions.

We can well understand that machine laundering would be injurious to the fabric and seams, and Rayex shirts should never be so treated.

Because no fault in the material or tailoring of the shirt is involved, we regret that we are unable to replace it. We believe, however, that Rayex shirts still deserve your confidence and that, properly laundered, they will give you many, many months of satisfactory wear.

Sincerely yours,

Special Cases

Desirable as clear-cut solutions are, many complaints do not lend themselves to simple concessions or refusals. Sometimes sellers are reluctant to admit to faulty products because the admission may leave them open to lawsuits, or to unwarranted claims from cranks. Often they are legitimately puzzled by the complaints. At other times, a company wants more information from the customer before it makes a decision, or it prefers to have a local dealer or representative look into the matter. In all such cases, the companies may try to act agreeably while at the same time suspending a decision or tactfully evading any direct involvement.

The letter below puts the next step up to the local distributor:

Dear Mr. Mason:

We sincerely regret to learn of the difficulty you are experiencing with the operation and servicing of our Tyros color TV receiver.

We are taking the liberty of referring a copy of your letter to our distributors in Los Angeles, the Champion Sales Company, who are thoroughly familiar with the operation of all our TV receivers and with the TV dealer and service situation in your area. They are therefore in a position to advise you as to the most economical procedure to be followed in restoring your Tyros to normal operating order and keeping it that way. You will undoubtedly hear further from them either directly or through a nearby Tyros dealer or service contractor.

Very truly yours,

The following letter from a food packer is noteworthy for its use of facts. In all, it is a tactful if not completely satisfying reply.

Dear Mrs. Cross:

We are indeed greatly distressed and perplexed by your letter of April 23 in which you tell us of your experience with a can of tomato soup--distressed because of the annoyance caused a good customer of ours, and perplexed because we cannot understand how foreign material of any kind can get into a can in our kitchens.

In view of your constant use of our products we know it is not necessary to tell you that only the highest quality ingredients are used and that they are prepared in accordance with the highest standards known to the culinary art. Tomato soup is made only during the harvesting season from choice tomatoes brought to us daily by the growers. They are graded by Government employees, after which they are taken to the washers. They are washed several times and inspected by trained workers, only the pick of the crop being used.

After the tomatoes are pulped and the skin and seeds separated from the pulp, the other ingredients, such as butter and spices, are blended in nickel kettles. The soup is forced through fine screens having a mesh of 27/1000ths of an inch. This prohibits foreign material of any kind from entering the finished product and also makes the soup thick and creamy. The empty cans, just prior to being filled, are turned upside down and thoroughly sterilized with hot water to prevent contamination at this point. An inspector is stationed at each filling machine to see that the product is normal in every way as the cans are filled.

> It is our aim at all times to maintain the high standard of quality of our products and we are greatly disturbed to receive a single complaint. We have always advertised "your money back if not satisfied," and in accordance with this time-honored custom we are taking the liberty of enclosing 36 cents in stamps--to cover the cost of the soup and the postage--which we trust you will accept in the spirit in which it is offered.
>
> Needless to say, we regret exceedingly that anything has happened that should temporarily cause you to question the quality of our products or the care exercised in their preparation.
>
> Very truly yours,

OFFICIAL AND PERSONAL LETTERS

Many letters in business have no direct relation to ordinary business transactions, but they do have an official or personal mission. Such letters, include introductions and recommendations, congratulatory letters, letters of appreciation, and letters of sympathy or condolence. It should be clear that these letters require very special qualities of expression and that no rules can substitute for the good taste and judgment of the writer.

Official and personal letters in business are usually typewritten in the "official" style shown in Figure 4-2, page 83, with the inside address below the letter to the left instead of above the salutation. Many company officers use smaller-sized engraved stationery for this purpose.

Introductions, Recommendations, and References

Businessmen are often called on to write letters vouching for other persons.

A *letter of introduction* is written to a business acquaintance on behalf of an employee, customer, or other person who desires some help from the addressee. The letter usually (1) indicates the relationship between the writer and the person introduced, (2) tells the reason for the introduction, and (3) courteously asks the reader to help. Following is an example of such a letter:

> Dear Mr. Rose:
>
> This letter will serve to introduce its bearer, Mr. Philip Denton, a Detroit businessman with whom we have had the pleasure of doing business for the past seventeen years.

Mr. Denton is president of Denton Plastics, Inc., a leader in the design and production of molded plastic containers for prepackaged liquid consumer products. He is now visiting the Southwest for a purpose that he will explain to you in person. I am sure you will receive him cordially and give him, to the best of your ability, the help he is seeking.

Sincerely,

A copy of the letter of introduction, with a covering letter, is customarily sent ahead to the person addressed.

Dear Mr. Rose:

Early next month you will receive a visit from Mr. Philip Denton, a very good customer of ours, who would like to establish business connections in your part of the country. Enclosed is a copy of a letter with which we have provided him.

As the letter indicates, we have a high regard for Mr. Denton, and we believe that his plans will be of considerable business interest to you. Any help you can give him will be much appreciated.

Sincerely,

A *letter of recommendation* is an endorsement of an employee or former employee who is looking for another job. It states (1) the reason for the letter, (2) the duties performed by the applicant, (3) the applicant's general qualifications, and (4) the recommendation to the reader.

Dear Mrs. Crawford:

Mr. Nelson F. Connelley informs us that he has applied to your company for the position of trainee in your Management Development Program.

We know Mr. Connelley as a former employee who worked in our Plans Department from the time of his graduation from Bard College in June of last year until he left us about a month ago. Although his duties were mainly clerical, we learned to respect his accuracy, his thoroughness, and his capacity for hard work. We particularly liked his pleasant personality and his ability to get along well with others. We were sorry to see him go, but we understood his desire for a position in a business that could offer more rapid advancement.

We have no hesitation in recommending Mr. Connelley for any responsibilities you may see fit to assign him in the position you have open.

Very truly yours,

A *letter of reference* is different from a letter of recommendation in that it reports rather than recommends. It is useful in answering routine inquiries about former employees who have applied for work elsewhere.

> Dear Mr. Clark:
>
> Mrs. Jane Dammler, about whom you inquire in your letter of September 21, was employed by us from June 26, 19-- until May 30, 19--, when she resigned to remain at home.
>
> Mrs. Dammler served as a Typist Clerk and performed her duties in a satisfactory manner.
>
> We found no reason to question her honesty or integrity.
>
> Very truly yours,

Congratulatory Letters

Occasions for sending congratulatory letters include appointments, elections, promotions, and similar achievements. They are usually short and personal, but the degree of formality depends on the relationship that exists between the writer and the reader. Some varied examples follow:

> Dear Miss Dale:
>
> The news of your recent promotion has just reached us here. My associates and I want to join your many friends in extending our congratulations and our best wishes for your continued achievement.
>
> Sincerely yours,

> Dear Henry:
>
> It was with great pleasure that I noted the change in your title. I hear from some of your associates that you are doing an excellent job in the Pension Trust end of your business, and naturally enough I was delighted to see the new recognition that had come to you.
>
> I hope that all goes well with you at home and that you will continue to prosper.
>
> Cordially yours,

Dear Charlie:

I couldn't have asked for anything better this morning than the news of your promotion. Once again your company's management have proved how astute they are, and they as well as you are to be congratulated.

For you and your family I wish the best of everything in the years ahead.

As ever,

Dear Mr. Dobson:

I was delighted to read in this morning's Times of your election as Treasurer of the Worcester Steel Corporation. This is most assuredly a well-merited promotion and one that must result in great personal satisfaction to you.

Please accept my sincere congratulations and good wishes.

Sincerely yours,

Dear Amy:

The Alumni News tells me that you have been awarded the University's Meritorious Service Medal.

Having had the privilege of working with you for a long time, I want to add my congratulations to the many you will receive. I hope that your usefulness to the University has only begun and that we will all enjoy the benefits of your good health and good works for many years to come.

Cordially,

Congratulatory letters to employees are an important part of an organization's program of good employee relations. Here are two from a company president.

Dear Roy:

This day marks the twenty-fifth anniversary of your association with us. As you join the distinguished company of the 25-Year Club, I want to express to you the appreciation of the whole organization for your loyal service and to extend our wishes for your good health and happiness. We sincerely hope you will be giving us your much-needed talents for a long time to come.

I want formally to present you with your 25-Year Pin, so I've arranged a little ceremony in my office for 3 o'clock this afternoon. Please bring a few of your fellow workers with you to help demolish the cake our commissary has prepared especially for the occasion.

With every good wish for you and your family, I am

Sincerely,

Dear Bill:

Ed Simpson told me of the fine talk you gave the other evening at the meeting of the Metropolitan Association of Cost Accountants.

I want you to know that your participation in affairs of this kind means a great deal to the company in its relations with the professional community.

In accepting any similar engagements in the future, you would be doing me a great favor if you let me know of any personal expenses you incur and of any clerical or other help we can provide.

Best of luck.

Sincerely,

Letters of Appreciation

Anyone who receives a congratulatory letter is obliged to reply. Modesty and simplicity should be the keynote here.

Dear Mrs. Clayton:

Thank you for your kind comments on my talk the other evening. I would like you to know that your generous and encouraging words were very heartening.

Sincerely yours,

Dear Tom:

I'm awfully glad you wrote because a nicer compliment I never received.

May I tell you how deeply I appreciate your good wishes and how fortunate I am to have a colleague as thoughtful as you.

Sincerely yours,

The following letter was written by a worker on special assignment, who was permitted to use the office of an executive during the latter's absence on vacation:

Dear Miss Sampson:

I enjoyed the use of your office and the proximity to the many nice people in Room 1402. Janet Blaise was especially helpful in enabling me to produce a great deal of work I could not have done under other conditions.

Thanks very much for your kindness--and welcome back!

Sincerely,

Letters of Sympathy

It is always considerate to send a sympathetic note to a customer or co-worker who is ill or has suffered some other misfortune. Sometimes, if the circumstances warrant, a facetious or slightly humorous note is permitted to creep in. In any case, the letter should strike as optimistic a note as possible.

Dear Mr. Denton:

I was distressed to learn of your accident when I came to call on you the other day, but it was good to know that you are now over the worst and are progressing toward recovery.

You have, as always, my kindest regards and best of good wishes.

Sincerely,

The letter that follows was written by the vice president of a luncheon club to its president:

Dear Joe:

I was sorry to hear about your accident and hope this letter finds you much improved.

At first I thought the whole incident was part of a well-conceived plot to force me into the presidency of the Club, but on sober consideration I decided you would hardly go to such an extreme.

Do hurry up and get back. All of us at the "round-table" miss you.

Cordially,

Letters of Condolence

The letter of condolence is one of the most difficult to write because the occasion is both sad and solemn and touches on the deepest of human feelings. If it is appropriate, it is well to include other members of your organization or family in the expression of sympathy and to extend sympathy to the family of the deceased or to the organization to which he belonged. If you are writing to the family and there is any service you can perform that might be of assistance, you may tactfully offer to be of help.

Dear Bill:

All of us here at Continental are deeply shocked this morning on learning of Colonel Martin's untimely passing.

He was a staunch friend of ours and an executive whose achievements and personal qualities have left their mark on the American scene.

We send our deepest sympathy to all of the Miller organization and to all members of the family.

Sincerely,

Dear Miss Rhodes:

The news of your father's death was most unexpected, and I know that Don Sheldon, who is away on vacation, as well as other friends of your father's here at Midland, will be deeply saddened to hear of his passing.

Please accept my sincere sympathy and tell us if there is any way in which we can help you.

Sincerely yours,

SUMMARY

This chapter deals with complaint and adjustment letters and with letters that have an official or personal mission outside the ordinary stream of business correspondence.

Because of aroused public feeling, businesses are paying more attention than usual to complaints and are making provisions for handling them through special offices and, in some instances, toll-free telephone numbers. The complainant, on his part, should state the facts fully and courteously, but not without firmness when the situation requires it. The letter sent in reply should be sympathetic, tactful, and helpful, even when an adjustment cannot be made. Attitudes to be avoided are the negative, the suspicious, the grudging, and the sharp. If the fault is the seller's, the correspondent should say so and not try to "pass the buck." The fact that an adjustment is granted, however, does not necessarily mean that the customer is free of blame. In some instances, it is well to explain the facts, and possibly the customer's responsibility, before any concession is made. When the adjustment is refused, it is also well to explain the facts first and close the letter with a conciliatory statement.

A letter of introduction is written on behalf of a friend, employee, or customer who wishes some help from the addressee. It should mention the relationship that exists between the writer and the subject. A letter of recommendation represents an endorsement usually of someone looking for a job. A letter of reference is not necessarily an endorsement, but a statement concerning an employee's or former employee's record with the firm. More personal types of letters, including congratulatory letters, letters of appreciation, letters of sympathy, and condolence letters, benefit from a personal touch in harmony with the nature of the occasion and the relation of the writer to the subject or reader. The letters are quite short.

PROBLEMS

1. Submit a letter of complaint that you would legitimately like to send to some company as a result of an experience you have had with its merchandise or service. Give specific details.

2. Assume that you have written the letter called for in Problem 1, page 161. Five weeks have gone by and you have received neither an acknowledgement of your order nor the radio. You have telephoned the store several times, but each time either the line was busy or the store operator was unable to connect you with the right department. Meanwhile your check has been returned by your bank—it is marked "paid"—and you have still not heard from the store. Thoroughly frustrated and angry, you now decide to write a letter asking for satisfaction. Address the letter to the store manager, Mr. George H. Manley.

3. Take the role of the manager referred to in Problem 2 above. The order in question has been located. The radio was delivered by the United Parcel Service two weeks ago, but it was returned to the store because no one was at home to receive it. A no-

tice should have been left advising the customer to call the store to arrange another delivery date. Apparently something went wrong. Your own people were at fault for not following through and apparently quite careless in handling the customer's telephone calls. Write a letter of apology. Ask the customer to call your office directly (give telephone number and extension) to arrange for delivery.

4. As proprietor of the Esquire Men's Shop in Elkton, Illinois 62634, you ordered six dozen men's hats from the Darby Hat Company of Norwalk, Connecticut 06851, on July 21. Today (September 5) you receive delivery by United Parcel Service. The hats are in three cases, each presumably containing a dozen hats. In the third case, however, you find two empty hat boxes bearing the descriptions 463-7-Seal Brown and 463-7¼-Charcoal respectively. Write to the manufacturer to report that the two hats are missing.

5. Assume that you are the manufacturer mentioned in Problem 4 above. It is now September 8. Write to Mr. Ralph Hinds, the proprietor of the Esquire Men's Shop, telling him that the complete order was shipped. The hats must have been removed while the shipment was in transit, and the cases were then resealed. Ask Mr. Hinds to file a claim with his local United Parcel office. You will, in the meantime, be glad to ship duplicates of the two missing hats if Mr. Hinds so wishes.

6. Assume that you are the adjustment manager of the Conway Furniture Company, a retail store in Louisville, Kentucky. A citywide strike of truckmen has for the past week made it impossible to deliver furniture to your customers. Draft a form letter, to be sent to all affected customers, asking for their forbearance. Deliveries will be made promptly as soon as the strike is over. Any questions regarding deliveries should be directed to Miss Anderson, whose telephone number is 735-6512.

7. Assume that you are a correspondent for the Brown Department Store of Cleveland, Ohio. Write a letter that will satisfactorily handle each of the following situations:
   (*a*) Mrs. James Starr, 29 Overview Drive, Cleveland, Ohio 44130, writes (September 8) that the tea table she ordered has a big scratch on top, the result of careless handling by the delivery men. Tell her that you will send a furniture polisher to repair the damage.
   (*b*) Write a letter to Amalgamated Parcel Company, your delivery agents, telling them of Mrs. Starr's complaint. Ask them to be more careful in the future. Address your letter to Mr. Nathan Farmer, the traffic manager, 285 Huron Street, Cleveland, Ohio 44104.
   (*c*) Your receiving department reports that Carroll & Co., book publishers, from whom you buy regularly, have recently been using flimsy packing materials, a condition that could lead to damage and loss. Write to the publishers at 780 Euclid Avenue, Cleveland, Ohio 44110, suggesting that books need to be protected with corrugated paperboard, not merely paper and twine.
   (*d*) Mr. Sidney Nash, a charge customer of 4575 Farragut Avenue, Cleveland, Ohio 44102, has returned a copy of *Farewell, Love,* by George Tennant. He says the book is obscene, he couldn't leave it around the house where his children would see it, and he doesn't see how a reputable department store could "degrade itself" by selling such trash. The only reason he bought it is that it headed the "best seller" list in the Cleveland *Plain Dealer.* Tell Mr. Nash that store policy forbids the acceptance of returned books for credit, but you will

make an exception in this case. The book, a serious novel by a highly regarded author, is carried in all of Cleveland's public libraries. It cannot, however, be considered "family reading."

(*e*) Mrs. Daniel Meister of 45 Fenton Road, Cleveland, Ohio 44112, called to say that your men were supposed to install her wall-to-wall living room carpet yesterday (Thursday, March 15), but that they had not come yet. The salesman who handled the call, Mr. Charles Ferrin, told her that there had been some mixup because your records showed that the carpet was not supposed to be laid until Thursday, March 22. Mrs. Meister is furious. Try to conciliate her. You do not know how the misunderstanding occurred. The installers will call on March 22 as scheduled.

(*f*) Mrs. Carol Hopkins of 255 East Fourth Street, Cleveland, Ohio 44110, asked you by telephone on November 8 to have picked up a Toast-Rite 4-slice toaster, which she said burns the toast every time. She bought the toaster only a few days ago. An inspection shows nothing wrong with the toaster. The dial controlling the thermostat, however, was set at "Dark," It may be that Mrs. Hopkins does not know that the dial has to be set for the color toast she wants. The dial, which has a small brown knob, is located in the lower right of one end of the toaster, the end bearing the name "Toast-Rite." You are returning the toaster by Amalgamated Parcel Delivery.

8. Assume that you are the production manager of the Calmer Printing Company, 350 Commercial Street, Wilmington, Delaware 19808.

(*a*) The Gibbs Kitchens of Belmar, New Jersey 07719, makers of jellies and jams, have written (July 16) to say that labels included in the last batch you printed for them are not sticking to the jars. They have returned a few samples, but cannot return the remainder of the 10,000 they ordered because they need them for labeling. They have been forced, however, to apply an additional coating of glue to make them stick. They want to know what adjustment you will make and warn you in a somewhat unfriendly tone that unless you can provide better quality in the future, they will have to take their business elsewhere. Write to Mr. Dennis Palmer, the proprietor, explaining that you got the gummed paper stock from your regular source and don't know what could have happened. You have tested the labels returned to you and they are definitely defective. You will ask the Premier Paper Company, your supplier, to look into the matter. In the meantime, you will obtain gummed paper from another source and print a duplicate order of 10,000 labels which you will send by air express within a few days—no charge.

(*b*) Write today (July 19) to the Premier Paper Company, 450 South Street, Baltimore, Maryland, 21217 (Elton Richards, sales manager), telling of the Gibbs Kitchens' experience. Tell them you are returning all of the gummed label stock you have on hand and are also canceling your order of July 5, which has not yet been filled. Ask what the company is going to do.

9. Now assume that you are Elton Richards, mentioned in Problem 8(*b*). Write the following letters to answer the complaint about the nonadhering labels:

(*a*) You do not know what could have happened to the labels. You have asked the factory superintendent to find out what he can. You will write again as soon as you get his report. You are, in the meantine, holding up the order of July 5. Today is July 21.

(*b*) It is now July 26. The factory superintendent cannot find any defect in the adhesive used in manufacture of the labels. In fact, it is only the returned labels, not those fresh from the plant, that will not stick to glass. The superintendent suspects that the labels used by Gibbs Kitchens were subjected to unusual moisture conditions, which resulted in a loss of adhesive power. Ask that this point be explained to the proprietor. In the circumstances, you see no reason for an adjustment or for any further suspension of label orders from the Calmer Printing Company.

(*c*) The factory superintendent reports on July 26 that there was a substitution of materials in the making of the adhesive, with results that were not foreseen. The company will stand the cost of the 10,000 Gibbs Kitchens labels, including the cost of the printing. You will also take back all your label stock in the hands of the Calmer Printing Company and indemnify the company for any further loss. The adhesive is now being made according to the old formula. Ask for reinstatement of the Calmer Printing Company's order of July 5.

10. Assume again your position with the Calmer Printing Company (Problem 8). Follow up your initial reply to the complaint of Gibbs Kitchens, as directed below:
    (*a*) Convey the information given you by Mr. Richards (Problem 9(*b*)). You have already replaced the defective labels without charge, but you want Mr. Palmer to know that the gummed stock was not at fault and there may be some precautions he should take to prevent a recurrence of his experience.
    (*b*) Pass on the information that the defect in the labels occurred in manufacture, as stated in Mr. Richards' letter of July 26 (Problem 9(*c*)). Reassure Mr. Palmer about future orders.

11. As director of customer relations for Diogenes Electric Corporation, you have today received a complaint from Mr. John R. Bass of 2166 West 112th Street, Brooklyn, New York 11223. Mr. Bass says that three out of a package of six Diogenes photoflash lamps failed to work, with a resultant loss of both lamps and film. Write a letter to Mr. Bass reassuring him with respect to Diogenes quality and saying that you are sending him under separate cover a package of six photoflash lamps.

12. The letter that follows was addressed to the president of Stacy's, a large and well-reputed department store in New York City. Assume these facts: The letter, dated March 24, was turned over to you as manager of the Adjustment Service Department. Your investigation shows that the newly selected rug was scheduled for delivery on March 27. It is now April 2. Tell Mrs. Parthos that if she has not yet received it, she should use the back of your letter for her reply. A self-addressed stamped envelope marked for the attention of Miss Edna Crown is enclosed. Make your letter as conciliatory as you can and keep in mind that the president expects a copy and a report from you on the results. Of course, you will look into your store procedures and take any remedial action necessary.

1845 38th Avenue, Apt. 6D
Woodside, NY 11377
March 24, 19--

President
Stacy's Department Store
42nd Street and Fifth Avenue
New York, NY 10022

Dear Sir:

During your Warehouse sale of January 30, I purchased a rug totaling $98.28. It was supposed to be delivered on Friday, February 5--terms C.O.D. for $88.28 (a $10 deposit was originally paid on the day of purchase).

I waited patiently the entire day for the delivery but to no avail--it was not delivered. Since you obviously have many deliveries to make, I did not become alarmed until the end of February.

On March 3, I went to your 7th floor rug department and showed my receipt to two of your customer service representatives. I was informed that my rug had probably been resold, which is why it was not delivered. Your representatives had a copy of my receipt along with a boxful of other receipts of rugs that have never reached their original purchasers. They described what they thought happened. Apparently, during a sale, people rip off the sold tags (attached to rugs) and re-buy them. I can certainly sympathize with Stacy's about this and do not hold you responsible for the actions of others. However, I do feel that rugs that have been sold should be removed from the selling floor and kept in a safe place.

After hearing the sad tale of my missing rug, I bought a similar rug in the amount of $100.35 (my original $10 deposit was carried forward). I could hardly believe my ears when the salesman told me he hoped that the same incident wouldn't happen again. Apparently, the rug would not be removed from the selling floor for a least a week or more and Stacy's was about to have a rug sale. Needless to say, I was shocked and dismayed at the prospect of a similar occurrence.

It is now three weeks since my second purchase and I have yet to receive it. I will wait until this Saturday before I take any other action. If there is a reasonable excuse for the delay I would like to hear about it. I only hope my confidence in Stacy's can be restored by the safe and prompt delivery of my second choice.

Very truly yours,

(Mrs.) Constance Parthos

13. Assume that you are a vice president of the Merchants Bank in Providence, Rhode Island. A customer of yours, Mrs. Elsie Dorp, is going to spend some weeks in Vero Beach, Florida. She has asked you to arrange for check-cashing privileges at a local bank. Write to Mr. Peter Cavendish, president of the Vero National Bank in Vero Beach, asking him to extend this courtesy for checks not exceeding $200 per week for a period of four weeks. Mrs. Dorp is the widow of Charles E. Dorp, formerly chairman of Dorp Enterprises, which is still a highly regarded account of yours. Say you are enclosing a copy of Mrs. Dorp's signature for the bank's records. You would reciprocate the favor.

14. Assume that you are the personnel director of the Hanford Insurance Company. Miss Elinor Hopper, a clerk in your bookkeeping department, is leaving to go with her family to Atlanta, Georgia, where they are taking up residence. She has asked you for a letter of reference, which she can show to prospective employers in Atlanta. Miss Hopper has been in your employ for the past eight months. She is prompt, has a good attendance record, takes orders cheerfully, and gets along well with her fellow workers. However, her work is often inaccurate and lacking in neatness; you are glad to see her go. Write the letter as a favor to Miss Hopper, but make sure you are not doing a disservice to another employer. Address the letter *To Whom It May Concern.*

15. Assume that you have just come across the following news item in the business pages of the *New York Times:*

> Election of William J. Smith, Jr., 40 years old, as president of Smith Textile Corporation was announced yesterday (October 20).
>
> He succeeds his father who will remain as chairman and chief executive officer. The company makes cotton, wool, and synthetic fabrics for use in women's clothing. The company said that William J. Smith, Sr., would continue to shape the policies of the enterprise he founded thirty-six years ago.
>
> The younger Smith was formerly vice president in charge of finance as well as a director. For twenty years he has held accounting and administrative positions. He is married, has two children, and is active in civic and community projects.

On behalf of the Broadway National Bank, of which the Smith Textile Corporation is an excellent customer, write a letter of congratulations to William J. Smith, Jr. The letter will be signed by the president of the Bank.

16. Assume you are the controller of the Channel Radio Corporation, 300 North Main Street, Jacksonville, Florida 32206. At a convention last week of the Controllers Institute of America, held at the Hilton Hotel in New York, you heard a talk by Mr. David Struthers, a friend of yours who is also controller of Bowker & Company, 700 Fairwether Avenue, Atlanta, Georgia 30326. Mr. Struthers spoke on the need for a more scientific approach to company financing. Write a congratulatory letter to Mr. Struthers, addressing him by his first name.

17. Assume the role of Mr. Struthers, mentioned in Problem 16. Write a reply to the letter you have received.

18. Your office supervisor, Mary Durstine, has had a skiing accident and is home with her leg in a cast. She will be away from work for another week or two. Write a letter of sympathy to her at 1256 Dorchester Road, your city. Assume that you are Miss Durstine's superior.

19. Assume that you have just seen in your local newspaper an obituary for a former professor, who died at the age of 45. The professor's instruction and counseling have meant a great deal to you. Write a letter of condolence to the widow, Mrs. Hortense Borden, of 235 College Road, your city.

7
Job Applications

SOONER or later, almost everyone writes a job application. This may consist of a letter or a resume, or both. Letters are also used for follow-up after the interview.

Your first task in offering your services is to give careful consideration to your qualifications and the needs of the prospective employer. One mistake that many applicants make is not having a sufficient appreciation of their assets. The employer to whom you write is interested in your educational and job achievements, of course, but he is also interested in your personal qualities: your industry, willingness to learn, ability to work with others. The good application mentions such qualifications as well as the more routine ones.

The immediate purpose of the job application is to obtain an interview during which you and the employer can get better acquainted. Only after the interview can you expect to be offered a job. The application, however, is your introduction. If it does its work well, it "presells" you and creates a favorable climate for the interview. In this respect, writing for an interview has a great advantage over walking in "cold." You will find, in fact, that a good application can influence the entire course of your career.

THE RESUME

A standard part of the job application, the resume is a formal outline or list of your qualifications. Other names for the resume are *data sheet* and *fact sheet*. The resume is usually accompanied by an application letter. In some circumstances, you may be asked to submit a resume after the job interview. In any case, it is advisable to prepare a resume as soon as you have decided to look for a job. Even if you never have occasion to mail it, you will still find it useful as an inventory of your qualifications to keep in mind during the interview or to have for reference when you are filling out the application blank provided by the prospective employer.

Mechanics

The resume is usually typewritten or duplicated in such a way that it looks typewritten. A printed appearance, however, is not necessarily detrimental; it is expected that the applicant will use the same resume in applying to a number of prospective employers. The only precaution to observe in this respect is to be sure that the printed resume is up to date. An old resume brought up to date with additions made in ink or on the typewriter gives the unfortunate impression that the applicant is perpetually unemployed. Neatness, accuracy, and correctness in spelling and punctuation are always extremely important.

Many employers prefer that the resume occupy but a single side of a standard letter sheet. By judicious editing and arrangement, even the applicant with a great many qualifications should be able to compress the resume into that space without crowding. Good margins and orderly grouping and alignment of material will help ensure an attractive appearance.

The title "Resume," "Personal Resume," or "Data Sheet"—if a title is used at all—appears at the top of the sheet. It is followed by the applicant's name, address, and telephone number, prominently displayed. The remainder of the sheet is characterized by a series of topics, each followed by a relevant statement, in abbreviated form, of the applicant's qualifications. Phrases rather than full sentences are used, and the listing of data is common. There is no complimentary close or signature at the bottom. A sample resume is shown in Figure 7-1.

Content

The employment data are classified under such headings as the following:

Job Objective
Education
Business Experience
Extracurricular Activities
Personal Data
References

The *Job Objective* tells what job you want. This topic can pose a difficult problem if you do not know precisely what you are qualified to do. The employer, however, likes to consider the application in terms of a specific job opening. For that reason, you should name some job, however general the description may be. Acceptable objectives might include, for example, "Junior Accountant," "Sales Trainee," "Executive Training Program," "Advertising Copywriter," "Expediter," and "Personnel Assistant."

Under *Education*, you should list in order—beginning with the last—the schools you have attended, with the dates and the diploma or degree earned. If you have a college degree, it is usually not necessary to include the lower schools unless you think the information will be helpful to the reader in judging your scholastic preparation or character. There will probably be some

RESUME

Stephen R. Baumer
1477 Henry Hudson Parkway
Riverdale, New York 10062

Tel.: (212) 439-4504

Age: 21
Height: 5 ft. 9 in.
Weight: 175 lbs.
Marital Status: Single

Objective

Registered Representative

Education

Bachelor of Science with specialization in finance, New York University, College of Business, 19--

Major Courses

Corporate Financial Management
Banking and Financial Markets
Investment Principles and Analysis
Money and Capital Markets

Experience

Summer 19--. Bache and Company, 36 Wall Street, New York. Order clerk. Aided in preparation of charts and statistical surveys.

Summer 19--. Merrill Lynch, Pierce, Fenner & Smith, 1 Liberty Plaza, New York. Recorded and checked authenticity of expenses incurred at branch offices.

University Activities

Banking and Finance Club
Tau Delta Phi Fraternity (Social Chairman)
Intramural Sports
President, Junior Investment Group

Hobbies and Interests

Stamps, sports, politics, the stock market

Reference

Dr. Ernest Bloch, Professor of Finance
New York University
College of Business
Washington Square
New York, N. Y. 10003
(212) 598-1212

advantage in naming completed college courses or programs relating to your job objective and in noting any special honors or other academic achievements.

Since the scholastic record does not tell everything about your years at school, you should include under *Extracurricular Activities* or similar title some details about your participation in school affairs, including clubs, fraternities, sports, and school politics. This information will help to suggest the scope of your interests and your qualities as a person. If you name more than one school, credibility will be strengthened if you show the extracurricular activities for each school individually.

Almost any kind of *Business Experience* is helpful when you apply for a job. Such experience may have been picked up informally through part-time work in a principal's office or through volunteer work for a club or charity organization. Other experience is more formal: summer jobs, full-time jobs, Saturday and evening jobs. In presenting formal business experience, you should arrange the jobs in inverse chronological order, so that the most recent job is listed first. You should also include the names and addresses of the companies for which you worked and give a brief description of your duties.

If you have been in the military service, you should include—preferably under a separate heading—any details of your duties that are relevant to the job you want. For example, your military work may have required qualities of leadership or some specialized business skills your prospective employer can utilize. You should at least mention your highest rank, branch of service, and dates.

Personal Data may include age, height, weight, marital status, and personal interests and hobbies. This information, or as much of it as you think it advisable to give, may be listed in the upper right-hand corner of the resume or near the end. Part of the skill in writing any resume is the selection of details, and at no time are you put to a more severe test of judgment than in deciding what personal information to give. If you earned any part of your tuition, say so, and tell how much, as one-quarter or one-half. One applicant for a sales job showed excellent sense when he included the following facts under the heading, "Miscellaneous":

> *Hobbies*—reading, woodworking, photography, and golf. Aptitude tests showed I am best fitted for contact work (sales or personnel activity). *General health*—excellent. *Willing to travel?*—yes. *Father's occupation*—salesman.

Your *References* are the names of individuals who are personally acquainted with you and are willing to vouch for your ability or character. Probably the most important persons you can name are those under whom you have worked. Others include teachers, clergymen, and friends of the family. Unless the names are such as to carry some weight with the reader, the references do not have to be included in the original application, although you will have to provide them some time before you start to work. Except in the in-

FIG. 7-1. *A sample resume.*

stance of former employers, permission should be sought in advance for the use of names as references. The resume should include their titles and business connections, addresses, and telephone numbers, including area code.

THE APPLICATION LETTER

Far more than the resume, which is apt to be conventional, the job-application letter permits you to show in full measure the force of your intelligence and personality. It gives you a better opportunity to demonstrate your creativeness in dealing with facts, your ability to relate ideas, and your skill in choosing words. It also provides a better mirror of your sincerity and innate tact and courtesy. When the employer asks for a resume, he does not of course rule out an accompanying application letter. Employers, in fact, sometimes use the term "resume" when they mean any type of application, including the letter.

Application letters are either *solicited* or *unsolicited.* The solicited letter is sent in response to a help-wanted advertisement; the unsolicited letter is sent on your own initiative. Both types of letters have their advantages and disadvantages. The solicited letter is directed to a job opportunity that is currently open and is written with a knowledge of the requirements stated in the advertisement. Unfortunately, many other applicants will also read the advertisement and respond to it; competition is therefore likely to be keen.

The unsolicited letter is written to a company that you select. Since no position has been advertised, none may be available. On the other hand, this type of letter is relatively free of competition and therefore receives good attention. Even if a suitable job is not currently open, the letter may pave the way for employment at some future time. Another point: You need not confine your application to a single company. You may write to 25, 50, or 100 companies and be in a position to choose your job after the replies have come in and the interviews have been held.

The differences in composition between the two types of letters are slight. The solicited letter may begin with a reference to the job advertisement, whereas the unsolicited letter must achieve contact with the reader's interests in some other way. Also, the solicited letter must be specifically directed to the job advertised and address itself to the requirements stated or implied in the advertisement. The unsolicited letter, on the other hand permits you to name the job you want and to exercise considerable freedom in stating your qualifications.

Either type of letter may constitute the complete application, but an accompanying resume is usually expected by the prospective employer. The letter should never be a rehash of an accompanying resume, but should concentrate on the more important qualifications or those that seem particularly apt. The letter may expand a point for emphasis and omit some of the other details that are already well covered in the resume. Most important, the letter should take advantage of the opportunity to show your ambition and enthusiasm—qualities that the resume conveys less effectively.

The letter sent with a resume need not be long, but it should be adequate to the task of favorably impressing the reader. The following letter, intended to accompany the resume in Figure 7-1, sounds perfunctory.

INADEQUATE

Dear Mr. Garson:

Will you please consider the enclosed application for a position in your Sales Department.

As my resume indicates, I am majoring in finance at New York University, from which I will graduate this June. I also have some experience in working for Wall Street houses.

I would appreciate an interview so that I may present my qualifications in person.

Sincerely yours,

The letter in Figure 7-2 is somewhat longer, but more specific and persuasive.

The structure of the application letter follows a functional pattern. The letter (1) attracts attention, (2) describes your qualifications, (3) settles any anticipated doubts, and (4) asks for the interview.

Securing Attention

Since the application letter gives the employer his first impression of you, it should be a model of good form and appearance. The letter should be typewritten on plain white bond paper in the weight and size of a regular business sheet. Do not use social stationery or printed stationery. As shown in the sample letters, the heading should consist of your address and the date. In addressing a newspaper box, use the salutation *Gentlemen.* The form of the inside address in the solicited letter in Figure 7-3 is correct. If you can secure the name, it is usually better to address an unsolicited letter directly to the individual who will consider your application than to a department or company alone (Figure 7-4).

To improve the chances that your letter will be read, confine it to one page. Varying the paragraph length will also add visual interest, but avoid paragraphs that exceed ten or twelve lines. Pay close attention to typographical neatness and accuracy.

The letter opening should be free of the clichés that make so many job letters dull. These openings are unoriginal and weak:

> Having seen your advertisement in the *Springfield News,* I thought I would write.

1477 Henry Hudson Parkway
Riverdale, NY 10062
April 23, 19--

Mr. George D. Garson, Vice President
Henderson & Company
40 Wall Street
New York, NY 10005

Dear Mr. Garson:

I'd like to work in your Sales Department, where I believe my four years of college study and several summers' work in the investment business will be an asset to you.

At New York University I have close to an A average in my many finance courses, and I have an equally good record in economics, psychology, and business communication. My experience in financial work was obtained in the past two summers. First with Bache and then with Merrill Lynch, I learned about the day-to-day operations of a large investment firm, and I also gained some of the sense of excitement and enthusiasm that I know will serve me well in my profession.

Anyone who wishes to sell securities must, of course, have a capacity for making friends. In addition to the many friends that have come to me through my family and off-campus activities, I believe I have achieved some success as a student leader at New York University (see enclosed resume).

After the normal training period, I expect to take the examination for Registered Representative. Won't you see me and judge my qualifications for yourself.

Sincerely yours,

Stephen R. Baumer

Stephen R. Baumer

FIG. 7-2. *Letter accompanying the resume in Figure 7-1.*

[redacted]

[redacted]

STREET ADDRESS

CITY & STATE ZIP CODE

TELEPHONE NUMBER

ADDRESS CHANGE? PLEASE PRINT CORRECT ADDRESS ABOVE.

UNION HOSPITAL
500 LYNNFIELD ST.
LYNN, MA. 01904

TO AVOID ADDITIONAL **FINANCE CHARGE** PAY "NEW BALANCE" BY DUE DATE ▷ 04/20/80

▼ FOR INQUIRIES, PLEASE REFER TO ADMISSION NUMBER AND PATIENT NAME

ADMISSION NUMBER	PATIENT NAME	CARRIER NUMBERS	SERVICE OR DISCHARGE DATE
9-23706-6	OBRIEN KATHRYN	25	12/27/79

DATE	DESCRIPTION	AMOUNT
	PREVIOUS BALANCE	.00
12/27/79	OUT-PATIENT SERVICES	125.50

WE HAVE CHANGED OUR COMPUTER SYSTEM AND
ASK YOUR UNDERSTANDING AND COOPERATION.
YOUR INSURANCE CARRIER HAS BEEN BILLED.
IF PAYMENT HAS NOT BEEN CREDITED, PLEASE
CONTACT YOUR INSURANCE COMPANY.
IF PAID RECENTLY...DISREGARD THIS NOTICE
PROMPT PAYMENT WILL BE APPRECIATED.

FINANCE CHARGE IS COMPUTED ON THIS AMOUNT ▶
YOUR **FINANCE CHARGE** IS COMPUTED BY A "PERIODIC RATE" APPLIED TO THE ADJUSTED ACCOUNT BALANCE, WHICH IS THE PREVIOUS BALANCE LESS CURRENT PAYMENTS AND/OR CREDITS.

ADJ. ACCOUNT BALANCE	FINANCE CHARGE	NEW BALANCE
.00	.00	125.50
PREVIOUS BALANCE	AGREEMENT AMOUNT	ANNUAL PERCENTAGE RATE
.00	FULL	.00000 %

PERIODIC RATE(S) .00000 %

BILLING DATE 04/05/80

RETAIN THIS PORTION. PAYMENT RECEIVED AFTER BILLING DATE WILL APPEAR ON NEXT STATEMENT.

DETACH AND RETURN THIS PORTION WITH PAYMENT.

PREVIOUS BALANCE	
.00	125.50
AGREEMENT AMOUNT	DUE DATE
FULL	04/20/80
ADMISSION NUMBER	DISCHARGE DATE
9-23706-6	12/27/79

PLEASE PAY THIS AMOUNT

ENTER AMOUNT PAID

PATIENT NAME
OBRIEN KATHRYN

UNION HOSPITAL
500 LYNNFIELD ST.
LYNN, MA. 01904

RESPONSIBLE PARTY

RICHARD OBRIEN
45 WHITMAN AVENUE
MELROSE MA 02176

PLEASE SHOW ADDRESS CORRECTION ON REVERSE SIDE.

170 Harper Road
Bedford Hills, MA 01417
February 17, 19--

S 4967
The New York Times
New York, NY 10036

Gentlemen:

As a major in marketing research at Boston University, I believe I possess the qualifications needed for the position of part-time interviewer in your organization.

I am a Junior, twenty years old, and have completed, with consistently high grades, courses in marketing methods and policies, consumer research, psychology, and statistics. My class schedule allows me to work after one o'clock every weekday afternoon except Monday, and all day Saturday.

In the past I have found my experiences in dealing with other people very fruitful. For the past two summers I worked as a waitress in the Hyannis Inn, Hyannis, Massachusetts. Early last winter I was employed as an interviewer for the Boston University School of Public Health Survey in the Beacon Hill area. I enjoyed working on this project and received invaluable training at the same time.

With my background and professional interest in the subject, I am sure I can quickly adapt to your own requirements. You will find me thorough and accurate. Both Dr. Sylvia Gael, associate professor of economics at Boston University, and Dr. Harold Keyes, professor of marketing, are familiar with my work and have consented to vouch for me.

At your convenience, I would like to have a personal interview with you. You can reach me at the above address or leave a telephone message for me at TRemont 6-9856.

Very truly yours,

Harriet E. Black

Harriet E. Black

FIG. 7-3. *A solicited application for a part-time job.*

24 Olive Street
St. Davids, PA 19087
May 16, 19--

Mr. Arthur Dolber
Director of Personnel
Fair Department Store
100 Market Street
Philadelphia, PA 19140

Dear Mr. Dolber:

A graduating senior at Temple University, with a strong background in retailing, I would like to be considered a candidate for your executive training program.

I am twenty-one years old. In preparation for my degree in Business Administration, I took courses in retail selling, textiles, and store operations, as well as the more general courses in economics, marketing, and psychology. Through the Retailing Club, I also added considerably to my knowledge by visits to manufacturers, retail stores, and buying offices.

At present I am employed part time by Temple-Roth, Inc., an importer of toys. I sell to wholesale and retail establishments through our showroom. I also fill in as an accounts receivable bookkeeper. Prior to my employment at Temple-Roth, I worked part time for Prior and Company, certified public accountants, and Superior Mills, Inc., manufacturers of men's sportswear.

My varied experience and keen interest in retailing will, I believe, make me a valued member of your staff. May I ask for an interview so that you may further judge my qualifications for your training program. My phone number is (215) 555-5790.

Sincerely,

Jeffery Farmer

Jeffery Farmer

FIG. 7-4. *An unsolicited letter of application.*

> In reply to your advertisement in the *Oregonian,* I present my qualifications below.
>
> With this letter I wish to apply for a position in your company as a collection correspondent.

One of the best ways to open a letter of application is to point up your most important qualification for the job. It is not really necessary to mention the job advertisement when the newspaper address on your letter makes it plain that your letter is a reply to it. Should you, in other circumstances, think it desirable to allude to the advertisement in your opening, try to put the reference in a subordinate position. The openings that follow should attract favorable attention:

> I believe that my three years of experience as an athletic counselor at Camp Winnipeg for Boys qualifies me for the position of senior counselor at your camp.
>
> As a scholarship student in economics and a prospective June graduate I should very much like to be considered for the position of research assistant that you have advertised in this morning's *Post.*
>
> For the past two years I have earned my way through college by doing advertising production work. I am sure that my knowledge and enthusiasm would be an asset to your advertising department.

In writing the unsolicited letter of application, you may also attract attention by telling why you wish to work for the company you are writing to or by capitalizing on some news event.

> My friends in business told me that your company has one of the best sales staffs in the computer field. Because I believe I would make a worthy addition to this staff, I should like to be considered a candidate for your sales training program.
>
> I was interested to learn from a recent article in the *Leader* that your company is planning to open a branch office in Arlington. Since you will need a staff of high caliber, may I offer my services as rate analyst in your insurance department.
>
> In view of the current seasonal upturn in business with its resultant work for the accountant, you will find it necessary before the end of the year to consider certain additions to your staff. To meet such a situation, I should like to offer my services as a semisenior accountant. The summary below will give you an idea of my background and experience.

Describing Your Qualifications

The body of the letter should fulfill the promise of the opening. The selection of details and the emphasis you give any particular point will depend largely on the requirements of the job and the contents of the resume if one is included. On the whole, though, the letter should present your qualifications in an orderly manner and in a way that highlights your achievements and shows how they will help you perform the job you are applying for. Even when your education or experience is not directly related to the job, you may still be able to capitalize on it. Here are two examples, the first from an application for a sales position, the second from an application to enter a company's management training program.

> Last summer I worked as a waiter at a nearby summer resort. What I learned there about human relations and the need to please the patron will, I am sure, be helpful to me in dealing with your customers.
>
> As a camp counselor I was in charge of eight adolescent boys on whom I used all the arts of discipline and motivation, with considerable success. I have no doubt that I will be able to adapt similarly to a supervisory position in business.

A cardinal principle of application letters is modesty. Although you are writing about your own fitness for the job, you should repress any temptation to boast or exaggerate. These statements are bad:

IMMODEST

> Having taken courses in retailing for two years, I can show you how to cut your inventories and increase your sales.
>
> A study of your organization convinces me that I meet all the requirements of your sales personnel.
>
> With this application, your quest for a marketing research assistant is ended.

Equally bad is a negative approach or disparagement of your qualifications. It is well to keep in mind that your letter is expected to give the best impression of yourself that is within your power to create and that, so long as you stick to the truth, you do not have to say anything that will detract from that impression. Statements like the following weaken the letter:

NEGATIVE

> I regret that I do not have any practical experience in the real estate field.
>
> I was just an average student, but I managed to graduate in 19— with a bachelor's degree.
>
> Because I am poor in mathematics, I decided that actuarial work was not for me, and I switched to salesmanship.

The hardest qualifications to project are the intangibles. If an advertisement should ask for a "young woman with tact," it would be relatively simple for any applicant to say, "I have tact." Much more convincing, however, is the statement that demonstrates the point through the use of specific details:

> As the principal's secretary I was required to meet with parents and answer the telephone. This experience helped me develop poise and tactfulness, especially when the principal was away from his desk and I had to resolve many delicate situations myself.

A great value of the letter is that it enables you not merely to name your qualifications, but also establish their relationship through a narrative approach. Note how the "storytelling" technique in the following examples invests the application with interest and persuasiveness.

> Last fall I worked for R. H. Macy & Co. in White Plains as a salesman and ski mounter. My work consisted of not only selling merchandise, but mounting bindings to skis and controlling ski-equipment inventories for the sporting goods section. For the past two summers I have worked for the Garden Hardware Company of Port Chester as a truck driver and stockman. In this position I was responsible for making up orders for delivery on my route. I also did general stock work in the warehouse.

> My participation in my college chapter of the Society for the Advancement of Management has given me an opportunity to see at firsthand how an organization functions. As a member of the group's executive board, I have assumed some of the direct responsibility for carrying out the organization's objectives. Last year I was membership chairman, and our membership drive was so successful that I was awarded a Hamilton wristwatch for my efforts.

> After completing my studies in the best-known high school in Cyprus, Pan-cyprian Gymnasium, in 19—, I was offered a job in the Letter of Credit Department of the Bank of Cyprus, Ltd., Nicosia. I started as a file clerk, and at the time I left the job in 19— in order to continue my studies in the United States, I had the responsibility for checking all the commercial documents for both import and export transactions. Moreover, because of my knowledge of the Greek, English, and French languages, I had been able to assist in handling the foreign correspondence in my department.

> I am now attending Northwestern University, from which I will graduate in June with the degree of Bachelor of Science. My major is finance. The work I have taken includes investment analysis, security analysis, corporate financial management, present-day banking methods, security market fluctuations, and the money market. Along with my courses in finance, I have studied accounting for three years, completed all the business law courses offered on the undergraduate level, and have at the same time taken the full liberal arts program open to business majors.

> My public accounting experience consists of over three and a half years with certified firms in the capacity of junior and semisenior accountant. As a result of this experience, my knowledge of accounting principles, auditing proce-

dure, and business practice is extensive and practical. It has been my good fortune to work under men who have insisted that their clients should receive the highest type of accounting service. With them, there was no compromise with thoroughness, accuracy, or the correct application of principles. Needless to say, the lessons I learned and the experience I acquired during the course of my work with them have been invaluable.

Clinching Your Case

Telling the employer that you have the qualifications for a job does not necessarily imbue him with confidence in you. He may have some doubts or some lingering questions that will have to be answered to his satisfaction before he agrees to see you.

We have already mentioned the advisability of using specific details. These are important in allaying any suspicion that you are bluffing. It is far less convincing to say, for example,

> I am a college graduate

than to say

> I was graduated from Hofstra College in June 19— with the degree of Bachelor of Science in business administration.

It is less convincing to say

> I have experience in advertising production work

than to say

> For the last two years I worked as an advertising production assistant for the Dayton Glass Company. In this capacity, I kept production schedules, ordered artwork and plates, read proof, and met all closing dates for our advertising in national magazines. I also had charge of the production and mailing of all the company's direct advertising to dealers and consumers.

Another way to help make your letter persuasive is to include as references the names, addresses, and telephone numbers of persons who will speak up on your behalf. Here is an example of the way references may be treated in the letter:

> If you wish to know more about the way I discharged my duties with the Grandview Furniture Company, you may get in touch with my immediate superior there, Mr. Jeffrey Crown, Manager of the Order Department. His telephone number is 765-4302. For information regarding my character and scholastic abilities, I refer you to Professor William S. Baxter of the Marketing Department of Concordia College, Stowe, Vermont.

If you have a letter of recommendation, you may send a copy, but do not send the original. Another procedure is to give the name of the writer of the recommendation as a reference in your application and then bring the original letter with you when you are granted an interview.

Should you have some special skill that can be exhibited by means of samples, you may bring the samples with you. This suggestion would apply to such evidence as a designer's sketches, an advertising writer's copy scrapbook, or an architect's blueprints. Anyone who applies for a job as typist or correspondent may expect, of course, that the application letter will be examined for competence in typing or letter writing.

"Sensitive" subjects in the letter of application include those relating to salary and the reason for leaving the last job. With respect to salary, it is usually best not to initiate the subject yourself. On the other hand, you cannot ignore the question of salary if it is raised in the job advertisement. Then, if you are uncertain about what salary to ask for or believe that mentioning an exact figure will put you at a disadvantage, you may cover the subject in one of these ways:

> Until such time as I can prove I am worth more, I should be willing to start with you at the salary you customarily pay for this position.
>
> I shall be glad to discuss the matter of salary with you at our interview, after you have had a better opportunity to judge my worth.

You do not have to give a reason for leaving your last position, but if you do, it must be both an honest reason and one that will not reflect unfavorably on you. Such reasons as the fact that you were unhappy with the work, that you had a disagreement with the management, or that you felt you were underpaid or otherwise not appreciated are usually not received with sympathy by the prospective employer. More acceptable are affirmative reasons like the following:

> I left this job in order to be free to seek another one that would give me experience in my chosen career of banking.
>
> Because I think I have gone as far as I can in my present position, I would now like to work for a larger company where my advancement will be commensurate with my proven ability.
>
> Although I like my present job, my employer is moving the Philadelphia operations to Atlanta, and I will therefore want to continue my career in this city with another good company.

Asking for the Interview

The final step in the letter of application is the request for an interview. If you can be reached by telephone, be sure to give the complete number. It is not necessary to enclose a return addressed envelope, but some writers of unsolicited letters say they get more replies that way. It is probably better not to put a stamp on the return envelope, however, because it may suggest coercion. These closings are well phrased:

> May I have the opportunity of seeing you in person so that I may discuss this application with you in detail. My telephone number is 556-5678.
>
> Of course, the best way for you to judge my qualifications is to talk with me in person. I should be glad to call for an interview at any time that is convenient to you.
>
> If you have an opening at present or expect to have one soon, I should very much appreciate hearing from you. I am enclosing an addressed envelope for your reply.

Follow-up Application Letters

An employer will often answer an unsolicited letter of application even when no job is available. If you receive an answer and wish to maintain contact with the employer in the hope that a job will develop later, you may acknowledge the answer somewhat in these terms:

> Dear Miss Sumter:
>
> I appreciate your answering my letter regarding a position in your Credit Department.
>
> Although I am naturally disappointed that you have no opening at present, I should very much like to be kept in mind in case you should later need a person of my qualifications. You may be sure that I will always consider it a privilege to work for a company as well-regarded as yours.
>
> Thanks again for your courtesy.
>
> Sincerely,

Another opportunity to write to a prospective employer is afforded after the interview. If the employer has left the decision open, usually on the ground that he has other applicants to see, you may conceivably help your chances by writing a letter of this kind:

```
Dear Mr. Fenton:

It was kind of you to give me so much of your time today.
The interview left me more desirous than ever to work for
your company.

After you have interviewed the other candidates, I hope
you will return to my application and consider me well
qualified for the position of management trainee.  In ad-
dition to my education and experience, I can assure you
that I will bring to the job all the energy, enthusiasm,
and intelligence of which I am capable.

I am looking forward to hearing from you.

                                 Sincerely yours,
```

SUMMARY

Job applications made in writing customarily employ a resume and a letter. The resume is a kind of fact sheet, consisting of the specific but abbreviated record—in topical form—of your job objective, education, business experience, and such personal data as age, marital status, and hobbies. The resume may be duplicated and used without change in applying for positions with a number of companies during the period in which the resume is still current.

The application letter, which is individually adapted to each addressee, should have the resume as an enclosure. A solicited letter of application is an answer to a help-wanted advertisement. In addition to any other data it contains, it should address itself specifically to the qualifications mentioned in the advertisement. An unsolicited letter of application is one written to a prospective employer of your own choice. The letter should capitalize on any relevant information you have about the company, and otherwise should concentrate on your qualifications for the job for which you are applying.

Application letters follow the pattern of securing attention, describing your qualifications for the job you want, settling any doubts about your past record and your potential for success, and asking for an interview. A further opportunity for contact with the prospective employer through correspondence may develop after the receipt of a reply saying there are no openings or after an indecisive interview. Always you enhance your chances for success when your letters are physically attractive, fresh (not stale), sincere, and—without rehashing the resume—pertinent in their details.

PROBLEMS

1. Assume that you are about to embark on a job-seeking campaign. Write a resume that you can enclose with your letters of application. Use facts only.

2. Write an unsolicited letter of application designed to accompany the resume mentioned in Problem 1. Address your letter to a specific company.

3. Write an unsolicited letter of application for a part-time, summer, or full-time job—whichever your present circumstances permit. Address your letter to a company of your choice. Use facts only.

4. Look through the help-wanted advertisements in your local newspaper until you find an advertisement for a job you are qualified to fill. Write the letter of application. For your instructor's information, attach the advertisement to the top of your letter.

5. Assume that your have received a response to a letter of application you wrote to Mr. Robert T. Benhil, personnel director of the Claremont Corporation. Mr. Benhil asks you to come in for an interview during the Easter vacation. Today is Saturday, and you are about to leave to spend the vacation at home, too far away to permit you to make the interview. Write a letter to Mr. Benhil (assume his address), telling him that you will telephone for an appointment as soon as you return.

6. Assume that you have just had a job interview with the Mr. Benhil mentioned in Problem 5 above. Mr. Benhil said he would need a few more days to come to a decision. Write a follow-up letter that will tactfully try to influence the decision in your favor.

7. Assume that you are applying in person for the job of your choice at Kelsey and Company, a large industrial firm. While waiting to be interviewed, you are asked to take a half hour to write your autobiography, which will become part of your application. Write the autobiographical statement.

8. Assume that you received an answer to an unsolicited letter of application for a position in the management training program of International Industries, Inc., 339 Michigan Boulevard, Chicago, Illinois 60619. The letter, signed by William C. Griffin, vice president for personnel, said that there was no opening for a person of your qualifications. It is now six months later. You have in the meantime obtained a temporary position as a clerk at Brown's Department Store. Write to Mr. Griffin, reiterating your desire to join the International organization.

9. The following advertisements appeared in *Business World*, described as "a career magazine for young people." Prepare a written answer to one of them.

   (a) But Dr. Milliken!
   I thought the orbitals have rotational symmetry about the axis of the molecules!

   You've met George before. The guy with all the answers. We feel the same way you do about him. But let's face it, he's often right. Koppers isn't looking for wise guys like George. But you don't have to be a wise guy to speak up when you think you're right. Sometimes, what it takes to get ahead is a little impatience. Koppers is after impatient young graduates. We have more job openings than we can fill, and we need young graduates to help us fill them—permanently. Answer this ad if you answer this description: anxious to test your knowledge and ability, impatient to learn and grow in your profession, at home with fresh ideas. We want chemists, chemical engineers, civil engineers, mechanical engineers, metallurgists, metallurgical engineers, electrical engineers, business majors, liberal arts majors and MBA's. Afraid you might get into something you won't like? It's not likely at Koppers. We do all sorts of things with plastics, wood, metal and chemicals. Koppers supplies more than 270 products and services to some 40 industries. Interview us. Write R. A. Dingman, Koppers Company, Inc., Koppers Building, Pittsburgh, Pa. 15219. Koppers has always been an equal opportunity employer.

(*b*) Is that face in the mirror asking disturbing questions about your career?

Then it's time you looked into a future as a Bache Representative—and the outstanding career benefits it presents.

• At the above average earning potential.

• At the compensation plan that gives you ample incentive at the start and does not change as your volume increases.

• At the assurance that the business you build is yours, not to be arbitrarily split when it reaches substantial levels.

• At the peace of mind you'll feel in knowing your future won't require moves to one new location after another.

• At the advertising, promotion and research support available. The prestige office you'll work in.

• At the fact that there's no travel involved.

• At the outstanding training you'll get right in your area to qualify you for this new career. And the fact that you'll be paid while training, to help make the transition easier.

If this sounds like the opportunity that "face in the mirror" has been urging you to find, now's the time to do something about it. If you're a hard worker—if you've had some college and business or sales experience—and if you can demonstrate success in previous work—this could put an end to those disturbing career questions.

To discuss the possibilities of becoming a Bache Representative simply contact the Manager of the Bache office in your area. You'll find us listed in both the white and the yellow page telephone directories. Do it today.

Bache & Co., Inc.
Members: All Leading Exchanges. Founded 1879

100 Gold Street, New York, N.Y. 10038
An Equal Opportunity Employer

(*c*) If you have brains and aren't afraid to use them, think twice about a career in insurance.

Dull old insurance?

No, today's challenging, changing new world of insurance. Today as never before, insurance needs men who want to be involved.

Involved in new and better ways of serving the personal insurance needs of families, from the ghetto to the penthouse.

Involved in the corporate protection problems of industry, from the company-down-the-street to America's biggest blue chips.

We're Marsh & McLennan, industry's leading insurance brokers. Because we serve nearly every industry from aero-space to oceanography, you will enjoy variety unequalled in almost any other field. Because we have a need for many talents (we even have a nuclear engineer and a sea captain on staff), your initiative and imagination are more important than your kind of degree.

Extra added attractions: competitive starting salary. Unlimited opportunity. Outstanding benefits. Offices around the world.

If you're planning for tomorrow, call Marsh & McLennan today. Contact Richard A. Lommel, 1221 Avenue of the Americas, New York, N.Y. 10020.

(*d*) What are you looking for . . .
involvement?
commitment?
growth?

Then consider retailing as Macy's sees it. Not just a rapidly expanding people-to-people business, but deep community involvement. A business that deals not in remote abstractions, but the very hopes and dreams of people. A business that not only provides personal satisfactions and rewards (and provides them fast), but also stretches your mind.

If this describes the career you're looking for, Macy's needs your talents, your imagination, and your help. And we would like to talk to you. Soon.

Why not write to us now? We think that you will be even more interested in our story than you realize!

Macy's is an equal opportunity employer, of course.

For information on interviews for careers in advertising, buying, control, finance, merchandising, operations, personnel, and store management, write to:

Vice-President-Executive Development, Corporate Personnel
R. H. Macy & Co., Inc., 151 West 34 Street, New York, N.Y. 1001

(Stores in New York, New Jersey, California, Georgia, South Carolina, Missouri, Kansas, and Ohio.)

10. Answer any employment advertisement in a current issue of *Business World* or *College Placement Annual.* One or both may be obtained from your college placement office. Hand in the advertisement (or a copy of it) with your assignment.

8 Organizing Information

A LARGE part of business writing consists of explanation, instruction, and straightforward description. Questions that are answered by such writing include What is it? What materials, equipment, or ingredients are needed? How is it made? How does it work? What is the correct procedure? What happened? What should we do? What is the rule or policy?

Informative writing, as this kind of writing may aptly be called, is not confined to any one audience or medium. The information may be intended for workers or executives, technicians, buyers, government officials, plant visitors, students, or any other individuals or groups that may have an interest in the organization and its products or services. The information may be found in a report, memorandum, or letter; in a handbook, guide, procedural manual, or catalog; in a newspaper, magazine, or broadcast advertisement; in a speech or other presentation.

Although the main purpose is to explain or instruct, it is not unusual for informative writing to have a strongly persuasive point of view. Thus a set of safety instructions for workers may be accompanied by a warning about the dangers of ignoring them, and a description of a company's plants, products, or processes may have a considerable sales bias. What we are concerned with here, however, is not so much persuasion as exposition, not so much "selling" ideas as organizing and developing them.

The importance of organization in written composition may perhaps be shown by analogy. When a knowledgeable viewer examines an oil painting, he can undoubtedly obtain some meaning from a close examination of the colors and brush strokes. It is not until he steps back, however, that he sees the larger significance of the artist's work. So it is with writing. Words and sentences have meaning for the reader, it is true; but the larger meaning is indicated by the pattern of the whole composition. Only through familiarity with the overall plan can the reader see the relationships of the parts to the whole and to each other.

DIVISION OF MATERIAL

The assistant looked confused. "I'm trying to get this training program straight in my mind," he said. "It's not so complicated," his supervisor assured him, "when you consider that it has just three parts: first, the recruitment of participants; second, the group instruction; and, third, the on-the-job follow-up." In dividing the subject, the supervisor was employing the first principle of good organization.

All plans and ideas except the most rudimentary consist of a body of interconnected parts. These parts need to be exposed and the relationships between them established. A necessary step in this direction is the division of material. From the writer's point of view, the division—also called *analysis*—serves two purposes. First, it suggests the specific areas, kinds, or parts that need investigation. Second, it helps to organize logically the data obtained. Common methods of dividing material are (1) classification, (2) partition, and (3) enumeration.

CLASSIFICATION

Classification is a systematic process of dividing material into kinds or classes. If you were asked to organize the following "information"

d 4 * c b # 3 a 1 e @ 2

you would probably begin by separating the data into letters, numbers, and arbitrary symbols thus:

dcbae 4312 *#@

By keeping the related kinds of data together, you reduce confusion.

This process is perhaps more aptly demonstrated by reference to a simple government classification of commercially sold dressings for food. This classification accounts for two kinds of dressings:

I. Spoon-type dressings
II. Pourable-type dressings

Subclassifications of both types of dressings represent a further division of the subject:

I. Spoon-type dressings
   - Salad dressing
   - Mayonnaise
   - Sandwich spread
   - Refrigerated dressing
   - Other

II. Pourable-type dressings
   - French dressing
   - Oil and vinegar
   - Cheese
   - Low calorie and dietetic
   - Other

If you wish to proceed with the classification, you can take any of the subcategories and divide them into smaller categories. In that way you can classify salad dressings according to the seasonings used and the amount of salad oil they contain in proportion to other ingredients, and you can classify cheese dressings according to the kind of cheese they contain. The point is that any class of objects presumes several or more subclasses.

To cite another example, *cars* may be divided into passenger cars and trucks. Passenger cars, in turn, may be divided into low-priced, medium-priced, and high-priced cars. In another category, passenger cars may be divided into sedans, convertibles, hardtops, and station wagons. In still other categories, we may divide them into foreign and domestic; small, compact, and full-sized; 4-cylinder, 6-cylinder, and 8-cylinder; standard shift and automatic shift; and so on.

To understand the advantage of any classification, you need only take individual items or characteristics and run them haphazardly together as we did the letters, numbers, and signs in the first example. The choice for the writer, then, is between classification and chaos.

Rules of Classification

The effective use of classification is governed by these rules:

1. *Only one basis of classification should be used at one time.* You may, for example, classify cars according to make, function, price, model, place of origin, size, number of cylinders, or type of shift; but you should not mix your categories by classifying cars as, say, foreign cars (place of origin), domestic cars (place of origin), and trucks (use). You may, however, make one classification of passenger cars (foreign and domestic) and another of trucks.

2. *The basis of classification should serve your purpose.* In reporting on the selection of profitable sites for shopping centers, you may consider classifying them by location, size of trading area, and population served. On the other hand, a classification according to annual precipitation or height above sea level would seem to have no real significance.

3. Classifications should not overlap. Bank accounts, for example, should not be classified as individual, joint, trust, and checking accounts, because checking accounts may be either individual or joint. A better classification would be according to type of service (savings and checking) or name (individual, joint, and trust).

4. Essential classes should not be omitted. The division of an art collection into paintings, drawings, and sculptures will be incomplete if the collection also includes prints, furniture, glassware, and ceramics. The degree of completeness depends on the limits you have set on your classification. Thus a study of a graphic arts collection will be confined to photographs, prints, drawings, and paintings, and a report on sculptures will exclude everything else.

Classification in the Composition

The examples that follow show the use of classification in actual composition. Note particularly how the orderly division of the subject into classes—and, in the second example, subclasses—aids understanding.

> Much oil and gas came to the surface of the earth ages ago and was lost. But not all escaped—much of it was caught in subterranean traps formed by the buckling and folding of the earth in early geologic time. These traps are of three major kinds. All of them consist of layers of porous rock covered by layers of nonporous rock.
>
> For example, porous rock into which oil originally moved may have been folded upward, producing a subterranean formation shaped like an upside-down bowl or saucer. Oil and gas may collect at the top of such an inverted bowl and be kept from escaping by an overlying nonporous layer. This kind of trap is known as an anticline.
>
> A second kind of oil trap [called a fault, is formed at a] break in layers of rock. The rock on one side of the break has slipped up or down so that an uptilted end of a porous layer is thrust against a nonporous layer and thereby sealed.
>
> In a third type of oil trap, buried sandstone that may once have been an old beach tapers off like a wedge, ending between layers of rock that are not porous. Here the oil moves through the sandstone until it can go no farther and collects to form an oil field. This type of accumulation is called a stratographic trap.—*Exxon Corporation*

> Although there are more than 1,000 kinds of trees in the forests of the United States, only about 100 have commercial value; that is, they are suitable for manufacturing into lumber, paper, and other products.
>
> About 40 of the commercial species are softwoods, and the rest are hardwoods. Softwood trees are usually evergreen; that is, they keep their leaves the year round. Another name for softwoods is conifers. The word refers to the cones in which the seeds of most softwood trees develop. Coniferous, or softwood, trees also have needle-like or scale-like leaves.
>
> Most of our building materials and wood for pulp and paper come from

Douglas fir and white fir, hemlock, cypress, redwood, western cedar, larch, the spruces and 11 different kinds of pine trees—shortleaf, longleaf, loblolly, slash, ponderosa, northern white, Idaho white, sugar, lodgepole and jack pine.

Hardwoods have broad leaves and with few exceptions are deciduous trees; that is, they shed their leaves every autumn. Oak is the most important commercial species. Others are gum, yellow poplar, maple, tupelo, beech, cottonwood, birch, basswood, aspen, ash, hickory, walnut, sycamore, magnolia, willow, pecan and cherry.—*American Forest Products Industries, Inc.*

Grouping Homogeneous Units

Classification entails not only the splitting of a subject into its constituent classes but, conversely, the combining of homogeneous units and subclasses into larger groupings. A stockbroker, for example, undertakes to analyze a client's portfolio consisting of nine different stocks. In reporting on these, he can treat each stock independently, making respective recommendations to buy, sell, or hold. A better procedure, though, is to group the issues into two or three main categories like this:

I. Growth stocks
II. Defensive stocks
III. Speculative stocks

One advantage of such grouping is that it permits the reduction of a confusing number of individual items to a manageable few. Another advantage is that it permits the writer to show relationships that would not otherwise be apparent. In the portfolio analysis, for example, the grouping would help to point up any imbalance of funds invested in one stock to the disadvantage of others in the same group, or any imbalance in one group to the disadvantage of the other groups. The abbreviated analysis that follows will make this point clear:

> Your holdings of Consolidated Chemical, Meadow Drugs, Dolphin, and Fairview are in line with your objective of long-term growth. We believe that the amount invested in the last, however, is relatively too small to be of significant value in a portfolio the size of yours and we therefore suggest the sale of this issue, with reinvestment of the proceeds in Dolphin, a good stock which is also insufficiently represented.
>
> Montana Utilities, Superior Gas, and L. D. Packing Corporation are defensive stocks and therefore not subject to wide fluctuations. Giving you good income, they have a potential for moderate growth over the long term and provide a balance for the more volatile growth stocks. We recommend retention.
>
> Harbor Trucking and Temple Manufacturing are speculative stocks with a poor record and unknown prospects. They may return considerable profit at some uncertain time in the future, but they are not in keeping with your objective and we would suggest you sell them. The cash proceeds should then be used to extend further your holdings of Dolphin.

PARTITION

Some subjects lend themselves not so much to a division into classes as a division into parts. Thus while such concepts as clothing and cars are subject to classification, *a* coat or *a* car cannot be divided into any more subclasses. Each, however, can be separated into its components, as shown below. This process is called partition.

COAT A	CAR A
Shell	Frame
Lining	Engine
Fasteners	Body

Perhaps the type of partition most familiar to writers is that which separates a message into (1) an introduction, (2) a body, and (3) a conclusion. Partition is also used to detail the parts of an investigation, procedure, process, plan, or proposition. If you are planning a description of the commercial canning of fruits and vegetables, you may start with this partition:

I. Preparation for canning
II. Blanching the raw food
III. Filling the cans
IV. Hermetic sealing
V. Heat processing
VI. Cooking
VII. Labeling and casing

Eventually, you will also have to take each part and divide it further, as this example shows:

I. Preparation for canning
  A. Cleaning the raw food
  B. Sorting and grading
  C. Trimming and cutting
  D. Inspection

Some Practical Considerations

It is worth noting that you cannot go very far in partitioning a subject without at the same time using some form of classification. In the outline immediately above, for example, "Preparation for canning" has certain distinguishable parts or steps, but these have had to be identified and classified as belonging to the first stage of your subject and not to any of the others. Thus while the actual division of a subject into its parts is partition, any grouping or subgrouping of the parts is, as we have already seen, classification.

Another point worthy of mention is that partition, like classification, needs a consistent basis, plan, or point of view. The "Canning Procedure," for example, is here analyzed as an industrial process, and in other circumstances it could be analyzed as a project for the housewife, but there would be inconsistency and confusion if no distinction were made between the two operations.

How to Use Rubber Cement	
Topic	*Explanation*
1. Use	1. Limited to joining paper surfaces.
2. Tools needed	2. (a) Small brush (b) Eraser made from dried and balled rubber cement.
3. Work surface	3. (a) Old newspaper is best. (b) Do not let cement get on varnished surfaces.
4. Safety precautions	4. (a) Keep can tightly closed when not in use—fumes are noxious. (b) Work in room with window open. (c) Do not work near open flame—cement is flammable.
5. Applying the cement	5. (a) Cement one surface for temporary bond; both surfaces for permanent bond. (b) Apply sparingly with brush. (c) After bonding paper, remove surplus cement with cement eraser or by rubbing with fingers.
6. Thinning the cement	6. If cement becomes thick and unworkable, add rubber cement thinner and mix thoroughly.

FIG. 8-1. *Diagrammatic analysis of a task.*

Similarly, you could profitably describe the industrial process from the point of view of either the observer or the operator, but not of both simultaneously.

Partition of a subject implies a careful examination of all the parts or steps so that none that is important to the reader's understanding will be omitted. This point has special application in telling how a task is performed. If the writer has performed the task himself, he has a tendency to slough over the details, which *he* takes for granted but which the reader cannot. Let us say that you want to give instructions for using rubber cement. Having had considerable experience with this product, you may feel that the instructions are almost too simple to write down: All the user has to do is apply the cement and press together the surfaces that are to be bonded. Some reflection, however, will reveal that the amateur needs to know a good deal more. He may ruin a table surface if he is not careful. He may be overcome by the fumes. He may find the cement too thick to work with. The diagrammatic analysis in Figure 8-1 suggests a satisfactory treatment of the subject.

Examples of Partition

A common type of partition is the job analysis, which divides a job into its parts to permit classification of employees for job determination. In the following example, the work of an investment research specialist in the personal trust division of a large bank is broken down into these duties:

INVESTMENT RESEARCH SPECIALIST

1. Prepares knowledgeable, incisive, and imaginative recommendations of the investment merits of industries, companies, and securities presently or potentially represented in trust portfolios.
2. Upon request, offers investment advice of a respected quality to investment officers, banking officers (for customers or to value collateral), and to the Correspondent Bank Portfolio Department.
3. Supervises a section of analysts, usually recent college graduates, teaching investment and analytical techniques and developing a high order of potential for later assignments in research or portfolio management.
4. Possesses a thorough knowledge of accounting, tax law, and investments, a unique knowledge of the industries in which he specializes and is completely informed on relevant economic, financial, and technical developments.
5. Fully understands his responsibilities and acts as an effective member of the management of the Bank in relationships with staff members, customers, corporate officials, and the community. In this role, participates in the activities of business, social, civic, or charitable organizations.

The technique of dividing a subject into its parts is also evident in the following description of a large company's Supplementary Compensation Plan. It is directed to employees.

SUPPLEMENTARY COMPENSATION PLAN

In addition to your regular salary, you will also share directly in the profits of the company through our Supplementary Compensation Plan. Thus you will have a greater stake in the continued success of your company.

Membership. All employees on the payroll at the end of the year, together with those retiring during the year, will be eligible to participate.

Contribution by the Company. A formula has been worked out to determine the total supplementary compensation to be paid each year. This is obtained by multiplying the company's net operating earnings, after deduction of all applicable taxes, for the year (as they would be reported to the stockholders if no provision for supplementary compensation were made) by 1/100 of 1% for each full $10,000 of such earnings. For example, if such earnings should be $12,000,000, they would be multiplied by 12%, and the total supplementary compensation would be $1,440,000. . . .

Cash Election. During the first three years of employment you will be paid your share of supplementary compensation in cash—thereafter you may continue to receive your share in cash or elect to have all or one half of your share for that year contributed to the trust fund. If you choose cash, your supplementary compensation will be paid to you as soon after the close of the year as is practicable. If you choose to participate in the trust fund, that part of your share will be credited to your account in the trust as soon after the close of the year as is practicable.

Individual Shares. The share allocated to each employee will be the proportion which the total basic salary paid to him during the years bears to the total basic salaries paid to all eligible participants in the same period. Income such as overtime pay, commissions, bonuses or extra compensation in any form will not be included in computing the employee's share.

Participation in the Trust. All regular full-time employees who have completed 3 years' service by the end of any year will be eligible to participate in the supplementary compensation trust.

ENUMERATION

In many instances the division of material does not require the formal procedures already prescribed for classification and partition. Instead, you may simply enumerate, list, or name the points you want to make. The enumeration does not have to divide the subject into all its classes or parts, but only into those you consider essential for your purpose. Thus you may list the highlights of a report, the distinctive features of a plan, the advantages and disadvantages of a course of action, the principal categories of a subject.[1]

Here, for example, the Treasury Department enumerates the main kinds of interest and dividend income subject to Federal income tax. The list is not complete, but it is serviceable.

The principal categories of interest and dividend income which are subject to Federal income tax are:

1. Dividends from corporate stock, both common and preferred.
2. Dividends of building and loan associations, savings and loan associations, and credit unions.
3. Dividends of mutual investment funds or investment trusts.
4. Interest on bonds, notes, or other obligations of corporations.
5. Interest on United States Government bonds, notes, or other obligations (including interest on E, G, and H savings bonds).
6. Interest payments made by banks, individuals, life insurance companies, and mutual savings banks.

Another example of enumeration comes from an article on good dress by a men's style consultant. Following some formal exposition on the choice of fabric, color, and style, the author throws in a number of miscellaneous points. In this instance, enumeration serves as a useful way of dealing with details that are not easily classified.

[1] Note that *enumeration* is here used to denote an informal method of dividing data. Enumeration, in the simple sense of numbering a series of related points, is of course employed in all kinds of expository writing, including classification and partition.

Some extra tips: Business suits should be devoid of fancy or extra buttons, breast pocket flaps, sleeve patches, jacket belts, leather ornamentation, cowboy yokes and color stitching.

Center and side jacket vents are both acceptable but heavy men, particularly those with big behinds, look much better in suits with side vents.

Double breasted suits look fine on thin men but on heavy men they are terrible.—*John Molloy, Men's Fashion Consultant*

SYSTEMS OF ARRANGEMENT

Good organization presumes not only a logical division of material, but also an arrangement that fills the need for consistency, clarity, and convenience to the reader. In writing a guide for visitors, for example, we may undertake to describe our company's headquarters by separating the subject into its parts; but even after we have made the division, some questions would remain about the order in which the parts should be mentioned. Let us jot down the main topics in the order in which they may first occur to us:

I. Dining and recreational facilities
II. Clerical offices
III. Service and maintenance division
IV. Corporate offices
V. Reception
VI. Research laboratories

Although this division may be complete, it is apparent that no thought has been given to arrangement. For one thing, we may reasonably ask whether we do not give undue prominence to "Dining and recreational facilities" by mentioning them first. We may also ask why the initial topic is not "Reception," for that is the area where visitors to headquarters would normally begin a tour of the building. By the time we have finished our examination of the outline, we might well decide that this is a better order:

I. Reception
II. Corporate offices
III. Research laboratories
IV. Clerical offices
V. Dining and recreational facilities
VI. Service and maintenance division

The formal ways in which the parts of a composition may be arranged are numerous. Many are only corollaries or opposites of others. Here we shall attempt to classify some of the arrangements that should prove most useful.

Order of Time

In the description of steps, events, circumstances, or any other type of progression, the clock and the calendar are the writer's natural allies. For the best arrangement will usually be chronological, that is, in the order of occurrence. A program or agenda will be arranged in this way. So will the minutes of a meeting, a salesman's daily report on the calls he has made, an executive's diary, the instructions for operating a machine, and the write-up of a procedure or a manufacturing process from raw materials to finished product. In some instances, the chronological order is reversed, and events are recounted backward in time. This is common practice in job resumes, where the applicant lists the jobs he has held, beginning with the present or last one.

The following paragraphs use the chronological order to provide biographical data about Thomas L. Phillips, a leading American executive:

> Born in Turkey in 1924, of a Greek mother and English father, Mr. Phillips has spent most of his life in conservative New England. After garnering his bachelor's and master's degree at the Virginia Polytechnic Institute, Mr. Phillips joined the herd of Raytheon's electronics engineers in 1948. He rose quickly on a combination of engineering expertise and managerial flair to head the company's most important division, missiles and space, at the age of 36. There he fathered Raytheon's two most successful military efforts—the Sparrow air-to-air missile and the Hawk missile.
>
> Mr. Phillips was also in the right place at the right time when a Raytheon management shakeup created a vacuum for a new executive vice president, then the company's No. 2 man. Three years later, at 40, Mr. Phillips took the title of president, and four years after that became the company's chief executive officer, the No. 1 spot. Just a year ago, he also got the title of chairman.—*Adapted from the* New York Times.

In the next sample, a process is described in the order in which the various operations take place.

> To prevent destructive rust and corrosion, the body is dipped a total of seven times in special cleansing, rinsing and coating baths. The entire lower third is immersed to a depth of 11 to 15 inches, assuring thorough and uniform application of the protective coatings to both interior and exterior surfaces. Protection for the upper body is provided during the dipping procedure by a series of six high pressure sprays.
>
> In the first stage the body is dipped for three full minutes in a tank of alkaline cleaner. The second and third dips are hot, clear rinses. Then the body is lowered for one minute in a special chemical solution that deposits a protective coating of a high purity phosphate. This is followed by two more rinsings. The body is then dried and cooled to room temperature.
>
> After the seventh and final dip in a newly developed zinc-rich emulsion primer, the inner surfaces of the sills are coated with a high melting point wax. Then the body is dried again, wet sanded (by hand), primed for the second time, and painted. Each coat of the Lustre-Bond finish enamel is oven-baked and carefully inspected.—*Ford Motor Company*

Order of Space

In dealing with areas, dimensions, and parts, the description of the various parts may be arranged in the order of east to west, north to south, top to bottom, outside to inside, or in any other spatial progression consistent with the purpose. The details of a truck route may simply follow the road map. The description of a printed form will proceed from left to right and top to bottom, the normal reading order. A study of the potential national markets for a product may move from the largest to the smallest within contiguous states or sections of the country. The description of a house may take the route of the guest inspecting the premises: first floor, basement, garage, backyard. In other descriptions, movement can be keyed to the prominence of the details. Thus the description of a window display will probably move from the foreground to the background, or from the center of interest to the periphery. Similarly, the description of a tool, machine, or appliance may proceed from the features that are most likely to catch the eye (the housing or case, for example) to the smaller parts and those that are concealed from view.

The following description of a company's new offices begins on the upper work levels and takes the reader down to the first floor, out into the garden, then to the underground facilities:

> Two great work areas, the second and third levels of the building, are unobstructed by permanent partitions except for the cores which enclose the mechanical services. The work spaces are of clear span construction, completely flexible in layout. A system of movable panels and partitions, unique in its simplicity, was designed especially for us. They provide enclosed space where required and can be readily moved as future needs indicate. The panels, of bright color, banks of files and plant boxes serve to divide and add variety to work units. Traffic between the floors is by escalators. The floors are pierced by four large garden courts, each beautifully landscaped, so that all work locations are close to the outdoors, seen through large windows, green-tinted to reduce the heat of the sun. On the second level individual insurance is processed; on the third level, group insurance.
>
> The first level houses general departments, such as personnel, the library, tabulating and printing, which serve the insurance departments above. Relatively constant in their space requirements, these first level functions could have their necessary permanent space divisions and accessible locations without adversely affecting the essential flexibility of the main work areas. Also on this level are the employee facilities: the lounges and game room for off-hours recreation, the health and hygiene services of the medical department, a store and cafeteria kitchens. The cafeteria itself is in a one-story wing, cantilevered over a reflecting pool on the south side of the main building.
>
> To the south of the building is a carefully landscaped terrace. This, as well as the courts, is the work in an Oriental tradition of Isamu Noguchi. South of the terrace are lawns and a four-acre pond, visually pleasing and serving as an emergency water supply and accumulation point for spent water from the air conditioning system. Beyond the pond are three large monuments of red granite, also the work of Mr. Noguchi. Related in character to ancient monuments in England and on Pacific islands, they are his conception of a family group, appropriate symbolism for a life insurance company. Below the ground level of the building are the mechanical services of the building itself, the

supply and mail rooms, an auditorium to serve as the company's conference center as well as for recreation purposes, bowling alleys and barber and beauty shops.—*Connecticut General Life Insurance Company.*

Order of Importance

Ideas may be arranged in the order of ascending or descending importance. Thus, if the message details the reasons for a desired course of action, a strong climax is assured if they are presented progressively, with the strongest reason given last. So, too, a survey of a company's competition may dispose of the smaller competitors first and then take up the threat of the bigger rivals. In the description of a book or the summary of an article, on the other hand, it may be found desirable to state the most important ideas first, even if this means a departure from the plan followed by the author. Work rules and statements of policy may also begin with the most important points because the reader is likely to pay the closest attention at the beginning.

The use of the descending order of importance is shown in the following extract from an exposition on the advantages of issuing convertible preferred stocks in corporate acquisitions:

> [In acquiring a company] a buyer is frequently limited to the use of convertible preferred or common. With this choice, preferred can offer the issuer several advantages.
>
> Foremost is the fact that, if convertible preferred designed to sell at a premium over its conversion value is used, rather than common, fewer common shares will ultimately be issued. . . .
>
> Convertible preferred also permits the buyer to meet the seller's dividend objectives without altering its own dividend policy. . . .
>
> Another feature of convertible preferred is its potential for minimizing the voting power of a company's stockholders. This can be important on occasion, particularly if the seller is closely held.
>
> A final argument in favor of convertible preferred has considerably less to recommend it, although it figures prominently in the thinking of many acquisition minded companies, many investors, and much of Wall Street. This is the proposition that convertible preferred adds leverage to the common because earnings per common share are computed after deducting only the preferred dividend from net income. . . .—*Anthony H. Meyer, Irving Trust Company*

In the following paragraph, the order of ascending importance is signified by the phrase, "The best evidence," which introduces the final argument.

> As *The Wall Street Journal* points out, price controls and allocations on refined oil products are demonstrably unnecessary, especially at a time when there is no shortage of refined products or of refining capacity. By stifling normal forces of competition and the free movement of prices, these controls are creating economic distortions for which the consumer ultimately has to pay. They are complicating countless investment decisions. The best evidence that these controls are not needed and that the marketplace itself is the best

possible controller of prices is the fact that gasoline is selling for *less* than the government's price controls permit. Strong competition and the forces of supply and demand have compelled oil companies to forego price increases that are permissible under the law.—*Mobil Oil Corporation*

Order of Familiarity

Since the reader presumably does not know as much as you about the subject of the message, it is usually advisable to begin with ideas that are familiar to him or at least easy to understand, and then work into ideas that he may find harder to grasp. Advertising writers consistently begin with a "point of contact"—a headline or introduction that makes allusion to the known interests or desires of the reader before touching on the details relating to the advertised product. Similar patterns are used in other kinds of writing, also. An article on modern art begins with a discussion of representational art before burdening the reader with the less easily understood nonobjective art. A report on office duplicators takes up the simple hectograph before proceeding to the more sophisticated types.

In explaining computer logic to the layman, IBM provides an analogy with a light switch, a device that is familiar to everyone.

> Computer logic circuits are based on some very simple concepts. They utilize some of the same rules of logic used to design home lighting circuits—the rules of Boolean algebra, invented by a nineteenth-century English mathematician named George Boole.
>
> A simple example is a light that can be turned on or off at either end of a room. Every time you flip that light on or off you are operating a logic machine, working on Boolean algebra and making the light circuit operate in basically the same way as an adding circuit in a digital computer.
>
> A Boolean proposition is either true or false and these two conditions can be represented by any two-state (binary) device, such as a simple on-off switch, relay, vacuum tube, or transistor. Boole devised a set of algebra-like rules of manipulating true-false propositions, using the three fundamental connectives: OR, AND, and NOT.

The explanation continues by taking up in turn the OR, AND, and NOT functions in terms that are still understandable, but more demanding of the reader's attention and intellect.

Orders of Support

Many types of data inevitably lead to some generalization or conclusion. This is especially true of a comparison, a study of advantages and disadvantages, a report of an experiment or investigation, or a statement of reasons for or against a proposition or course of action. Two general methods of arrangement are used in these instances. The first begins with a statement of the conclusion and follows with the supporting data; the second method presents the data and then the conclusion drawn from them. The first method is sometimes called the deductive order; the second, the inductive order. These are only literary terms, however, and are not to be confused with the inductive and deductive methods of reasoning (Chapter 15).

Below is a short example of the deductive order, with the supporting data following the conclusion:

> More than any other professionals over the past decade, doctors have been subjected to a host of controls that radically diminish their much-vaunted independence. These controls, established under federal legislation, include health planning agencies (to limit new hospital construction) and professional standards review organizations (physican panels to monitor the performance of other doctors in hospitals). In addition to the headline-grabbing spate of malpractice suits against individual doctors, recent court rulings holding hospital trustees personally responsible for malpractice by doctors in their hospitals further intensify the pressure toward greater accountability for the medical profession.—Business Week

An instance of the inductive order is provided by this paragraph from a management report. Here the conclusion follows the data.

> You have already investigated the Holley X-100 Computer for possible application to loan control and accruals. According to the information made available to us by the manufacturer, an average of 15 to 25 seconds would be required to complete each loan transaction. Using an average of three transactions per minute, over eight hours daily would be needed at 100 per cent efficiency to handle all the loans discussed in Section III of this report, without equivalent controls and analysis. Therefore we do not recommend this machine for the indicated purpose.

A common variation of the orders of support is the order of cause and effect. Here a prescribed effect either follows or precedes a statement of the cause. The ideas in the following paragraph move from cause to effect.

> . . . . The shock absorbers on most domestic cars devote 90 per cent of their capability to absorbing bumps—compression of the springs—and 10 per cent to the opposite movement, the extension of the springs as the wheel that has hit the bump returns to its normal position. The result of this arrangement is a soft ride on paper-smooth pavement, and a tendency to go out of control on rough surfaces. In severe cases, as under hard braking on uneven surfaces, such an arrangement can lead to "axle tramp" in the suspension (usually in the rear, where the weight of the entire axle is below the springs). When this happens, a kind of cyclical bounce is set up in the wheel. Since the wheel can only provide braking force when it is in contact with the road surface, and since the wheel is bouncing wildly, braking capacity is severely reduced. (Axle tramp is also what causes the washboard effect commonly found in gravel road surfaces and in asphalt paving near stop signs.)—*John Jerome in* The Death of the Automobile

Other Orders

In addition to the orders already described, there are others that can be very useful in various types of exposition.

Order of acceptability. When some conclusions and recommendations are likely to be less acceptable than others, it is psychologically effective to move from the most acceptable to the least acceptable. Hopefully, agreement with the initial points will serve to abate the objections to the others.

Order of utility. In every document there are some kinds of information that must take precedence over others either to make comprehension easy or to serve otherwise the convenience of the reader. Sometimes the order is prescribed by management in order to maintain consistency or to make comparisons easy with other reports in the same series.

Psychological order. When favorable action is desired, the writer may follow a pattern often used in selling. In this arrangement, the writer attracts attention, motivates the reader, instills conviction, and stimulates action, in that order.

Parallel order. In a comparison of two or more things, consistency requires that the components receive parallel treatment. Thus if the present procedure is examined for ease of control, effective performance, and cost, any procedure with which it is compared should be examined for the same features in the same order.

Another type of parallel order might be called *pairing*. Examples would include such arrangements as question and answer, problem and solution, before and after, cause and effect, and need and fulfillment.

OUTLINING

When the message covers more than a few simple points, the outline provides a systematic approach to planning and writing. It shows the division and arrangement of ideas in skeletal form and makes possible the correction of faults in organization before the actual writing takes place.

Using an Outline

Ordinarily, an outline is prepared for the writer's use exclusively. At times, however, it must be exhibited to others—a teacher, an employer, a client—as evidence of work done or as a kind of blueprint for examination or discussion before the actual composition begins.

The outline from which the draft of your paper is written is called the working outline. As you write, you will be constantly testing the soundness of the working outline, and you will make whatever changes in content and order you feel are necessary to produce the desired outcome. At the same time you should try to avoid the stiffness that results from adhering too closely to the enumerated phrases or sentences of the outline and try instead to achieve a natural flow of thought and language. The final outline, if one is required, is the outline of the finished paper.

Outline Arrangement

Although the general arrangement of the outline will vary with the type of composition—letter, report, procedure, and so on—you will do well to assume that the main parts will consist of an introduction, a body, and a conclusion. These names may not actually be used in the outline and, in fact, the "body" may well encompass not one but a number of divisions. Still, the initial tripartite scheme forms a concrete base for a more specific structure. How this development takes effect is demonstrated below in an outline for a business article. Here the term "Introduction" is retained, the body consists of Sections II, III, and IV, and the conclusion takes the title of "Summary." On pages 242–245, you will see how the first two sections of the outline and part of the third have actually taken form in the finished article.

TOURIST DESTINATION DEVELOPMENTS

Topic statement: Tourist destination developments offer individual investors and large-scale developers a practical alternative to resort communities.

I. Introduction
  A. Increasing interest in the concept of tourist destination developments
    1. By individuals seeking vacation and retirement homes
    2. By land developers and hotel firms
  B. Current examples: Disney World, Florida; Vail, Colorado; etc.
  C. Tourist destination development defined
II. Factors favoring tourist destination developments
  A. From viewpoint of individual investors
    1. Community stability maintained
    2. Environment protected
    3. Crime and social turmoil minimized
    4. Investment of individual home owners protected
  B. From viewpoint of large-scale developers
    1. Rising inflow of capital
    2. Long-term nature of projects
III. Project evaluation
  A. Developer's record in similar ventures
  B. Market analysis
    1. Demographic factors
    2. Demand
      a. Expected utilization
      b. Stability of demand
  C. Example: Results of earlier study
IV. Community relations planning
  A. Impact on local economy
  B. Integration into the community
  C. Assurance of quality of concept and design
V. Summary

Rules for Outlining

To be most helpful, the outline should be constructed in accordance with these rules:

1. Show the logical relationship of ideas by their rank. An outline that gives unequal parts the same weight or tries to link unrelated parts can hardly qualify as an outline. The outline on the left below is confusing because it does not equate the present system with the proposed system signified in the title. It also lists the parts of the subject as if all were of equal rank. The outline to the right corrects these faults.

POOR

Proposed Mechanization of Bakery Order Procedure

- I. Present method described
- II. Need for change
- III. Store processing
- IV. Office procedure
- V. Bakery platform handling
- VI. Weekly processing
- VII. Cost comparisons
- VIII. Other considerations

IMPROVED

Mechanization of Bakery Order Procedure

- I. Present method
  - A. Description
  - B. Need for change
- II. Proposed method
  - A. Daily processing
    - 1. At store
    - 2. At bakery
      - a. Office
      - b. Shipping platform
  - B. Weekly processing
- III. Cost comparisons
- IV. Other considerations

2. Follow a consistent numbering scheme to show the relationship between the parts. Our sample outline in the second column above uses numbers and letters. Another system employing decimals is popular among scientists and engineers:

```
1. ______________________________
        1.1 ____________________
        1.2 ____________________
                1.21 ____________________
                1.22 ____________________
                1.23 ____________________
                        1.231 ____________________
                        1.232 ____________________
        1.3 ____________________
                1.31 ____________________
                1.32 ____________________
2. ______________________________
        2.1 ____________________
        2.2 ____________________
3. ______________________________
```

3. Eliminate single subtopics. The division of a topic naturally presumes two or more subtopics. If you cannot create additional subtopics, incorporate the idea of the single subtopic into the main topic by some modification of phrasing. A single subtopic is permissible when it is used to signify an example.

FAULTY	IMPROVED
I. Number of machines in operation A. Five	I. Five machines in operation

II. Trouble reported
  A. Frequent breakdowns
	II. Trouble reported
	  A. Overheating
	  B. Cycle uncompleted
	  C. Damaged electrical connections

ACCEPTABLE

A. Institutional advertising
  1. Example: Xerox Corporation

4. Maintain reasonable consistency in phrasing topics and subtopics. Use phrases or complete sentences, but not both. Also see that phrases are grammatically parallel, avoiding whenever possible the switching from one type of construction to another.

Inconsistent: II. Incoming Section
  A. Receives and routes securities
  B. Transferring securities
  C. Other functions

Improved: II. Incoming Section
  A. Receiving and routing securities
  B. Transferring securities
  C. Other functions

5. Apportion space in the outline approximately as you will in the report. It is bad practice to exaggerate the importance of minor topics by dividing them into an inordinate number of subtopics. Leave the details for the composition.

METHODS OF DEVELOPMENT

A list of topics, however well organized, does not make a composition. The reason is not only that the form is unacceptable, but that there is not enough explanation to make the ideas fully intelligible. In spite of the merits of brevity, ideas can be so compressed that they have no real significance for the reader. The art of composition requires that the writer provide sufficient details and make clear their relation to each other. Let's begin with a simple statement:

The nearest thing to an automatic stocking device is gravity feeding.

The unsophisticated retailer to whom that statement is addressed may understand the individual words, but the full meaning of the sentence will probably escape him. What is an automatic stocking device? How does gravity feeding work? The statement calls for definition of terms, for explanation and example. These are but some of the methods by which ideas are developed and clarified.

Definition

When you find it necessary to use a word not in the reader's vocabulary or a familiar word in a special sense, you may clarify the term by defining it. The definition, in turn, may consist of one or more synonymous expressions, or a short definition or explanation. Sometimes, as in the last definition directly below, it also tells what the term does not represent:

> In electric furnaces huge sticks of *graphite, a highly refined form of carbon,* are suspended from the top of the furnace into the hearth.

> The home builder asks the mortgage broker to obtain for him a commitment by *an institutional lender—a bank, insurance company, or the like*—for the loans with which the home buyers can finance their purchases

---

> One of the basic ingredients is *phenol. Perhaps you know this product better as carbolic acid, an old-time household disinfectant.*

> Checks should never be *postdated, that is, written with dates, days or weeks ahead.*

> Last year, according to *Variety,* foreign motion pictures achieved a gross of $14,824,975. *And by "gross" we mean in movie parlance not what exhibitors take in at the box office, but what they pay to distributors.*

In other instances a formal definition is given. This follows the order of (1) the term defined, (2) the class to which the word belongs, and (3) the distinctive characteristics which set the word apart from all other words in the same class.

TERM	CLASS	DIFFERENTIATION
Communication in industry (is)	the exchange of information	among the personnel of an organization and between the organization and the public, particularly those segments of the public with which the industry works, lives, or maintains business relations.
The term *passenger deficit* (refers to)	the amount	by which revenues from railroad passenger-service operations fall short of covering operating expenses, taxes, and net rents assigned or apportioned to this service.

Salad dressing (is)	an emulsified semisolid food	prepared from edible vegetable oils, acidifying ingredients, and one or more egg-containing ingredients, and cooked starchy paste prepared with food grade starches.

Details

A word, a definition, or an assertion—any idea, in fact—can be clarified by the addition of related or supporting particulars. In the following examples, several different kinds of details are used.

DETAILS OF OPERATION

Each tanker is driven by a great turbine engine capable of developing 19,000 shaft horsepower. The turbine rotates a single screw, a propeller with blades twice the height of a man, that can move the ship at top speeds of 17 knots. A throttle control lever on the bridge controls speed much as an accelerator pedal in an automobile. The vessel runs on heavy fuel oil known as Bunker C, but an automatic system carefully mixes air and fuel in the boiler to effectively reduce the discharge of black smoke from the stack. Both the boiler management and bridge control of the propeller are features of a central operations system that upgrades the ship's over-all efficiency.—*Exxon Corporation*

DETAILS OF CONSTRUCTION AND UTILITY

Of all the plastics, vinyls are probably the most versatile. Perhaps you never noticed it but no matter how you travel—by car, by train, or by plane—you are protected by shatterproof glass, thanks to a plastic that Union Carbide chemists developed. Sandwiched between the two sheets of glass is a thin vinyl plastic which, if the glass happens to break, holds razor-sharp pieces in place so that there is no dangerous shattering. Vinyl plastic, in rigid form, becomes unbreakable phonograph records; semirigid, it serves as scuff-resisting flooring; flexible, it becomes raincoats or shower curtains; and, as a liquid, protective coatings for everything from milk containers to dams.—*Union Carbide Corporation*

HISTORICAL DETAILS

The "role-playing" technique has a sound clinical history. Its founding dates back to Vienna in 1911. Dr. J. L. Moreno's arrival in 1925 dates its entry into this country. In 1933 it was first used by Macy's to train sales personnel and it has found many applications in the department store field since.—*The* New York Times

FACTS AND FIGURES

To supply a 100,000 barrel per day refinery (which would furnish less than 1% of our current needs) with 25 gallon per ton shale would require mining and processing 168,000 tons per day of shale and disposing of 158,000 tons of dry powdery residue—which swells on processing and therefore occupies a larger volume than that mined. Since a very large coal mine handles about 20,000 tons per day, the equivalent of at least 8 large coal mines would be needed to supply one modest refinery.—*Dr. Lewis D. Conta, University of Rhode Island*

DETAILS OF METHOD

The method—called postinflation—is disarmingly simple. A hot nylon cord tire, fresh from the mold, is inflated with air. It then cures under pressure at close to the dimensions it would achieve in service. This prevents the cord from shrinking as it cools, which would contract the tread grooves. The result is that when the tire goes into service on the highway the cord isn't forced to "grow" back to service dimensions. This growth puts a strain on rubber that can cause cracks in the tread channels, make small cuts bigger and hasten ply separation.—*E. I. du Pont de Nemours & Company, Inc.*

Examples or Instances

Often the best way to explain a point is to provide an example or instance. In the following paragraphs, a bank explains the operation of a "check-credit" account:

Let's say that on May 1 your application for CHECK-CREDIT of $1,200 is approved at your local State Trust office. You are then notified and sent 10 checks with your name imprinted on each check.

For the first month you do not use any of the $1,200 credited to your CHECK-CREDIT account. Since you made no loan on your account, there is no charge.

On June 10 you pay an insurance premium or perhaps you buy a hi-fi set, and pay by writing a check on your account for $288. This is your only use of CHECK-CREDIT during June. In July you are mailed a notice stating that your payment for July is $24 (one-twelfth of the $288 credit that you have used) plus interest and insurance charges. The statement also shows that you have used $288 of your $1,200 maximum credit. This means you have an available credit as of June 30 of $912 in your CHECK-CREDIT account. After your July payment of $24 is received, your available credit balance increases to $936 . . . and the amount of credit you have used is reduced to $264.

So you see, your CHECK-CREDIT is truly a revolving account—the regular monthly payments reducing your loan and at the same time increasing the amount you have for future use.

The following paragraph graphically illustrates what happens when force is exerted on a crack in metal:

Once a crack is well started, it takes very little force to carry it through to a complete fracture. Since the force depends on the length of the crack, a specific case must be examined in order to state how much force is involved. For example, consider a plate of steel that is six inches wide and a quarter of an inch thick. Suppose that it has a two-inch crack running into one side. Then the force required to make the crack run the remaining four inches would be only about 400 pounds. Without the aid of the crack it would require a force of 500,000 pounds to pull the plate apart if it were made of the best commercially available steel and a force of 10 million pounds if it were made of ideal steel. It is a large leverage effect like this that makes it possible for a relatively small force to crack an entire ship in two.—*John J. Gilman in* Scientific American

Comparison, Contrast, and Analogy

Many subjects can be clarified by comparisons that point up similarities and differences.

Modernization and mechanization are eliminating many of the back-breaking and time-consuming functions of the bricklaying trade. . . . Bricks are delivered by trucks in packages of 216 bricks each. The old-fashioned method was to deliver the bricks loose. This resulted in many of them being chipped or broken.

The traditional method required the bricks to be loaded on wheel-barrows, which carry only fifty bricks. On this job the Dennings Point Brick Works bind the bricks with metal tapes. They are picked up from the pallets and delivered to the bricklayers by fork lifts and motorized buggies.—*The* New York Times

The underlying principles of the Copyflex process parallel those of photography. They involve exposure of sensitized copying material to light and subsequent development of the latent image resulting from the exposure. But with Copyflex the copying is accomplished entirely inside the machine without the fuss and muss, the time, and the expense that accompany conventional photographic processes.—*Charles Bruning Company, Inc.*

A fuel cell is an electrochemical device in which energy, derived from a chemical reaction maintained by the continuous supply of chemical reactants, is converted to electricity. This means that, like the common battery, a fuel cell converts chemical to electrical energy. But the fuel cell has two major differences:

(1) The fuel is obtained from outside the cell, and only as needed to meet load demands. *It is not stored in the cell.*

(2) The products of the reaction are dissipated and the cell, therefore, remains invariant. That is, *no change takes place* in the electrodes and the membrane-electrolyte.—*General Electric Company*

Analogy helps the reader's understanding by relating an unfamiliar idea to a familiar one.

The way the blast furnace works is very simple. If you blow air on a fire or fan it, it burns better because it gets more oxygen. Centuries ago men learned that by blowing air on a mixture of iron ore and charcoal in a furnace, they could make the charcoal burn with enough heat to form a semi-molten, spongy lump of iron, mixed with slag. Iron in this form had to be reheated and hammered a number of times to drive out impurities before it could be shaped into useful objects.—*United States Steel Corporation*

The following example explains the term *active circuit element* by drawing an analogy between the intelligence and power in speech and the same qualities in electrical signals:

> To explain active circuit elements, we must distinguish between the intelligence and the power of a signal.
>
> For example, a spoken word has the same meaning whether it is spoken or shouted. If the word can be heard above the background noise, the intelligence has been transmitted. The intelligence in speech comes from the brain.
>
> The power in the speech comes from the muscles in the lungs, throat and mouth. To transmit the intelligence over long distances the speaker has to shout. The intelligence could be transmitted even further than the power of any person to shout by having repeaters properly spaced, people who could listen to the sound and then repeat it.
>
> The repeater's function is not intelligent. His work is to repeat exactly the intelligence he hears. However, he does add new power to the signal. This addition of power comes from his own body and not from the signal he heard.
>
> The control of local power to augment the power of an intelligent signal is just what an active circuit element does.
>
> In the electrical case, the intelligence has been converted from mechanical power (sound) to electrical power, or fluctuating electrical currents. These electrical signals can be transmitted over wires, by telephony or telegraphy, or be broadcast as fluctuating waves as in radio or television.
>
> The signal on the receiving end, as long as it is strong enough to be detected (heard) above the random electrical noise, contains the intelligence, but usually is too weak to run a loud speaker or to make a picture on a television screen. The signal is, however, strong enough to control the receiver's local power—supplied by a battery or the power mains—to increase or amplify the signal to the point where it can actuate the speaker or light on the screen.
>
> Thus the intelligence comes from the signal, and the power from a local source of electricity.
>
> The electrical device that makes it possible to control intelligently a non-intelligent source of power is an active circuit element.—*Bell Telephone Laboratories, Inc.*

Causes and Effects

Many statements involve a form of reasoning that relates causes and effects.[2] We have an economic recession. What caused it? What are its manifestations? Brand loyalty is decreasing among consumers. Why? Among what products and producers is the decline felt most? Drought grips the Midwest. What meteorological conditions brought it on? What will happen to crops, to farm prices, and to the consumer if the drought continues? The following ex-

[2] See also "Orders of Support," pp. 226–227, and "Causal Reasoning," pp. 462–463.

cerpt from a report on the status of the professions explores the causes and effects of the changing relationship particularly between lawyers and their clients.

> The technological revolution is forcing a fundamental revision of the professional's relationship to his client. Typically, the professional serves a particular, individual client. A deeply rooted assumption of the professional's work was that in helping his client he was not harming the rest of society. The classic statement of Lord Brougham that the advocate "must go on reckless of the consequences [though he may] involve his country in confusion for his client's protection" was hailed as the highest expression of the lawyer's calling because it was assumed that devotion to duty would not generally result in such dire consequences.
>
> Today that assumption has collapsed. In working for large institutions, from corporate law departments to research laboratories, professionals help to set in motion events that spread far beyond those who come into immediate contact with their clients. Mass production of complex but defectively designed machinery can injure millions. And complex business institutions can multiply the effects of fraud, seriously injuring people who have no direct connection with it.
>
> To contain the effects of individualism, "we are learning that we can't solve 20th and 21st Century problems of foreseeing consequences and preventing them with a horse-and-buggy model of personal responsibility," as Yale Law School Professor Geoffrey Hazard Jr. puts it. In Hazard's words, "Professionals are the knowledge holders, and they must perform the task of social coordination."
>
> But the duty of being society's intermediaries means that when things go wrong they will be blamed. Society is increasingly charging professionals with the job of preventing harm, at the risk of their own necks. Professionals, that is, are now being held responsible for the acts of their clients.
>
> Such responsibilities cause great strain to the professionals and to society. The professional is no longer sure just who his client is. And those who must use professionals to sort through the regulatory maze are discovering that "their" lawyer or accountant has become society's policeman. Privileged communications are in jeopardy of being subpoenaed by an angry litigant, the cost of doing business skyrockets, and what society gains in safety it may lose in innovation.[3]

CONNECTING THE PARTS

If you have done the preparatory work conscientiously, you begin writing with the data already in your possession and a well-conceived plan for presenting the message. The reader, on the other hand, knows nothing of your intentions except what is revealed to him in the composition. If you are sensitive to his needs, you will provide whatever signals are needed to acquaint

[3] "The Troubled Professions," *Business Week*, August 16, 1976, pp. 126–27.

him with the plan of the message and to help him relate and connect the various parts. Here we shall be concerned with the nature of these signals.

Titles, Headings, and Subheadings

Although the author's outline is often artfully concealed in other types of discourse, in explanatory writing there is much to be said for letting the skeleton show. This is done by the use of informative (rather than literary) titles or headings and subheadings. The reader is thus immediately acquainted with the subject and its parts and knows what to expect from each part. It is assumed that the reader already has a special interest in the subject and that you do not have to inveigle him by reaching out beyond its immediate boundaries. Even without the text and pictures, the following headings give a good idea of the plan and content of a booklet of the American Smelting and Refining Company:

ASARCO Products and Processes
  The Sources
  The Processes
  The Products
ASARCO Looks Ahead

"Feedforward"

You are already familiar with the term *feedback*. Sometimes the word *feedforward* is used to describe an introduction, foreword, topic sentence, or prefatory statement of any kind that tells the reader what lies ahead and, in some instances, how the material is organized. The introduction to the report beginning on page 325 performs such a purpose. So, too, does the topic statement below, in which the writer projects the plan he will follow in describing how transatlantic cables are laid.

> A convenient way to cover our subject is to begin at the cable terminal building (near where the cables come ashore—or put to sea, if you will), and continue down to the shore and on through the water to the deep ocean floor, stopping to consider each of the possible hazards we find along the route.—*Eldon Nichols in* Bell Telephone Magazine

The topic sentences that follow show other possibilities:

> There are three important reasons why Shell is so widely used. (The reasons follow.)
>
> When we started, we projected our needs into the future and we agreed on some fundamental principles. (The principles are explained.)
>
> The program consists of two plans—a Savings Fund Plan and a Retirement Thrift Plan. (The two plans are detailed in turn.)
>
> Liquid fuels offer many unique advantages. (The advantages are named.)

Haynes wrought alloys start in the melt shop. (A chronological description of the melting process follows.)

Transitional Sentences

Some topic sentences point in two directions: they remind the reader of what has been said and prepare him for what is to follow. They are called transitional sentences because they bridge the gaps between ideas. Note in the passage that follows how the underscored sentence brings the two parts of the message together. The arrows show the direction of the references.

> Federal funding of $10 billion for rapid transit systems is currently being considered in Congress. Spending, which has been at the rate of about $200 million a year, would be increased to $1 billion . . . under terms of this legislation. These funds will be matched in varying proportions by local as well as state governments.
>
> ↑ <u>Helpful as this much-needed Federal financial support will be, a balanced transportation system can only come about when all modes of transport are treated alike.</u> → The serious deterioration brought about by insufficient funding of public transportation systems and the steadily increasing traffic congestion are evidences of the need for an all-encompassing "Transportation Trust Fund." Such a program would provide balanced financing and permit the tailoring of transportation facilities to meet local problems.—*General Electric Company*

Transitional Words and Phrases

Ideas may be joined and their relationship shown by means of transitional, or connecting, words, and phrases.

RELATIONSHIP	CONNECTIVES
Addition	and, also, too besides, furthermore, moreover first, second, third, etc. one, another finally, in conclusion
Example	for example, for instance to illustrate
Cause and effect	because, since, thus for this reason therefore, consequently, accordingly
Comparison	similarly, in the same way likewise, in a like manner
Contrast	but, however, in contrast on the other hand in spite of

Repetition of a key word or a pronoun substitute may also help to tie together the parts of the message. In this respect, words like *this, that, these, those,* and *such* are especially useful. Note the patterns of repetition in the following passages. The repeated or synonymous words are indicated by identical numbers.

As a rule (1), sick leaves are not granted to part-time workers. In those cases where an exception (2) is considered desirable, requests (3) should be made to the Supervisor for approval by the Department Head. Such requests (3) should be accompanied by adequate information to support the need for an exception (2) to the policy (1).

Sound (1) has two (2) fundamental characteristics—frequency (3) and intensity (4). Both (2) are important in determining whether sound (1) is pleasant and helpful, or harmful and unwanted.

Frequency (3) . . . . (Paragraph follows.)

Intensity (4) . . . . (Paragraph follows.)

Parallel Structure

Next to topic and transitional sentences, probably the most important literary device for associating ideas over a broad area of the composition is parallel structure, a subject we have already had occasion to mention (pages 71–72). Through the repetition of grammatical structure, this technique makes apparent the intrinsic relationship in a paragraph or in a whole section.

In the larger units of composition, parallel structure should be evident in the uniformity of the language used in headings and subheadings. Thus the steps fundamental to the concept of "management by objectives" are developed by the American Management Association in six sections labeled as follows:

A concept of leadership
Establishment of a decision-making process
Definition of results desired
Specification of means to be employed
Individual accountability
Control

The parallel structure (all of the heads are noun phrases) shows that the parts named are coordinate.

Numbering the items in a parallel list emphasizes their relationship. This device is especially helpful when the numbers indicate consecutive steps.

> As soon as we receive from Johnson, Higglesbee, and Davis the securities mentioned in your letter of July 9, we shall proceed as follows:
> 1. Advise you of the securities received.
> 2. Sell the securities at the best available market prices.
> 3. Remit the proceeds to your account with Barclays Bank Limited.

Through the use of parallel structure, the relationship of any series of short coordinate elements is quickly established. Note how the parallel structure contributes to the interest and readability of the following passage:

> The executive searcher keeps a long list of names of men who might just fit into a given corporate slot and he spends a lot of time putting it into shape. This is how a man gets on that list whether he wants to or not:
>
> *He makes speeches* and gets the publicity that goes with them.
>
> *He becomes a panel member* at professional meetings and seminars. The program usually gives a biographical summary of the panel members.
>
> *He becomes an officer of his professional association or trade society.* As such, executive recruiters call him for suggested candidates and eventually they might become interested in him personally.
>
> *He develops a specialty* and has it publicized. In this age of the "gimmick," a new approach to something gets noticed by the press and trade association literature.
>
> *He gets appointed* to the middle management courses at the better known graduate schools. Executive recruiters consider these men "comers" in their fields and keep tabs on them.
>
> *He keeps active* in his school alumni group. Members of these groups are always "sourced" for suggested candidates for top positions.
>
> *He serves as an official* of the Federal Government. A two-year tour of duty is well spent in Washington, D.C. More and more top companies take former Washington officials into top management positions.
>
> *He doesn't get fired.* Nothing turns away an executive recruiter faster than a firing—no matter what the cause!—[italics added] *Charles E. Murphy in* World *(Peat, Marwick, Mitchell & Co.)*

Topic sentences in parallel structure help to relate a series of paragraphs.

> Democracy is not an easy job. Democracy depends on each of us.
>
> *It is up to each of us to learn about candidates.* What are their experiences, philosophies and abilities? Do they live up to their commitments? Are their ethical standards exemplary and do they have the courage of their convictions?
>
> *It is up to each of us to learn how to be effectively involved in the processes of democracy and to seek out opportunities to become involved.* We cannot wait to be asked, for we may not be. And we mustn't be afraid of the small causes. While we cannot all have a measurable impact on the ultimate solution

of the world's major problems, we can all contribute to improving the quality of the life we share.

It is up to each of us to insure that our government respond to the needs and aspirations of the people. It is one thing to criticize public officials to our heart's content while watching the evening news. We will help them do a proper job, however, only by becoming personally involved, earning influence and communicating our views to others in the community.—[italics added] *Gordon L. Hough in* Bell Telephone Magazine

THE METHODS OF ORGANIZATION APPLIED

The writer, we have seen, has at his disposal a considerable arsenal of methods and techniques through which he can bring order into the composition. All that remains is the application of the means to the desired end. The process is demonstrated in the following section of the article outlined on page 229. In the running commentary, you will find a guide to the movement of ideas and the principal methods of organization and development used.

TOURIST DESTINATION DEVELOPMENTS[4]

The spread of affluence, the increase in leisure time, early retirement, and an almost universal mobility have created a surge in tourist destination developments. The following article explores this trend in the resort world and discusses some of the factors to be considered in gauging the prospects of such a project.

[Topic (general) statement] Individuals seeking vacation homes, retirement homes and tax shelters—as well as land developers and hotel firms—are increasingly interested in a tourism concept that is not particularly new but is responsive to current social and economic trends in the United States. [Specific illustrations] Called the tourist destination development, it can be seen in action at Disney World, Florida; Vail, Colorado; Ka'u, Hawaii; Pinehurst, North Carolina; Sun Valley, Idaho; and sundry other places.

[Definition] The tourist destination development is defined as a recreation-oriented community that has adequate isolation, either as a result of location or size, to ensure that the character of the project can be controlled and that the project is self-contained recreationally, socially and economically. It is developed under a comprehensive master plan by a single developer group. The tourist destination development generally includes a major recrea-

[4] Copyright 1972 by Peat, Marwick, Mitchell & Co. Reprinted by permission of the publisher from the house magazine, *World.*

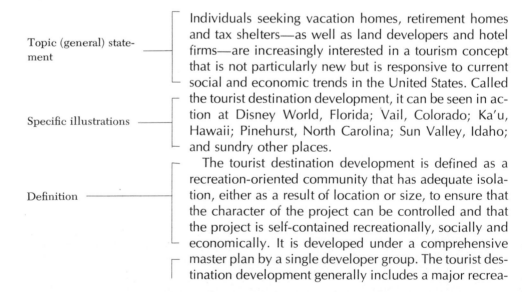

Descriptive details

tional feature (ski slope, beach, lake, amusement park), ancillary recreational facilities (golf, tennis, pools), hotels, and land or, commonly, condominium sales programs.

Factors favoring tourist destination development

Topic sentence

From the investors' standpoint there are several factors that favor the tourist destination development over the more traditional resort community. The primary one is developer control. In a successful resort community each landowner is almost compelled to develop land to the highest use; the governmental agencies involved generally tax the property to the point where the owner has no choice, and his concern with the total community is overridden by his own economic needs. In almost every resort community—Waikiki, Miami, Acapulco, for example—the result has been overdevelopment with an eventual erosion of values.

Factors favoring destination developments contrasted with disadvantages of other types of communities (underscoring added to show connection of main points)

Greed has produced the same result in many tourist destination developments, but at least in these developments the mechanisms are there to avoid overdevelopment, and mitigating forces are operative. In addition to the stability and predictability inherent in a carefully planned and controlled development there are other potential benefits.

There is the matter of the environment. Pollution, noise, and crowding are very much a part of life in major metropolitan centers. A destination resort development, since it has the size necessary to create a relatively self-contained system, can control its pollution levels through a careful plan developed by an interdisciplinary team. This plan, when implemented under close control of the developer, can assure a healthy ecological balance within the project. With this balance assured, the desirability of the project both as a vacation spa and home site is enhanced for the present and can be insured for the future.

Then there is the matter of fear. Although only a small number of people actually experience street crime, the general atmosphere of fear in the cities is real. The tourist destination development can offer, to those who seek it, a socio-economic haven in much the same way as does the five-acre zoned tract in suburbia. In a resort city, the vacationer or retiree may well encounter all of the social problems that made his life tense at home. In a destination resort, he can bask in secure isolation with his mind turned off to the problems of society. The tourist destination development is defensible from the impact of social turmoil in a way that no resort in a National park or city can ever be.

Conclusion of factors favorable to individual investors

Finally, a home or condominium in such a resort is a potentially good investment. The ads proclaim, with a good deal of validity, that in the face of population growth, land—a nonexpanding commodity—can only increase in value. "Own a piece of a major tourist destination development and have your own cash flow, tax shelter, and capital gains package plus a vacation and retirement retreat," they say. This has not proven universally true but for projects with solid inherent or created value it will be true over the long pull.

Topic sentence leading to factors favorable to large-scale developers

Causes and effects

The tide of economic factors is also running with the tourist destination development. The capital requirements for these large projects demand that partners such as insurance companies, wealthy individuals, or real estate syndications participate in the development. Land development really became a boom business when the stock market again proved vulnerable to a downturn, when interest rates fell and money was drawn from other areas into real estate. Real estate investment trusts, insurance companies, and certain large corporations are forcing money into the real estate market and helping to generate the funds needed. Further, large corporations and individuals who are major landowners are seeking better uses for their own real estate. The land involved, whether earmarked for new towns, industrial parks or resorts, lends itself to "planning." The large corporations and the large investors are used to staff planning studies prepared in great detail. The officers and the boards feel consistently more comfortable with a complete plan—such as those provided by destination resorts—as unaffected as possible by outside variables.

Transitional sentence—negative elements suggested

Supporting details

The fact that such stellar participants are on the roster of a project is reassuring, but it is no guarantee of the project's success. These investors and corporate developers are inclined toward investment in developments that follow a proven pattern. Many such developments, stamped out of an apparently safe cookie cutter, are real estate counterparts of those forgotten entrants in the Marilyn Monroe look-alike contests of the Fifties: they have copied a successful model, but lack the real substance in terms of location, dramatic appeal and vitality, to ever succeed themselves. For many of these large investors the long-term nature of the real estate commitment often appears to have been overlooked in favor of short-term profits and tax benefits. Indeed, tax considerations have outweighed other factors in far too many real estate-related ventures. However, the element of concern for investors is that so much money and so many investors are planning their way into the market that the supply of industrial parks, new towns, and resort areas being developed could easily exceed the demand for the next several years.

Project evaluation

Start of an enumeration of clues to success

The problem of the investor is to determine which of these many projects will succeed. His first clue in the project's probability of success will be found in the track record of the land developer *in this type of development. . . .*

SUMMARY

It is natural for a writer to be concerned with details, but first he should consider the overall organization of his composition. Otherwise the meaning of the details is likely to be lost to the reader as he struggles to fit the pieces together.

Good organization consists of (1) dividing the subject into its parts, (2) arranging the parts in a systematic fashion, (3) developing each part in turn, and (4) providing the connective tissue that will draw all the parts and details together.

Classifying the data for a composition will result in a proper grouping, which in turn will permit the labeling of major parts. The most generally applicable partitioning consists of a division into an introduction, a body, and a conclusion. The logic of each subject, however, will determine what particular division and subdivision should be made. In some parts of a composition, a loose enumeration or listing of points is helpful.

Both the major and minor divisions of the composition lend themselves to particular systems (or combinations of systems) of arrangement. Some of the most useful are the order of time, or chronological order; a logical arrangement in space, for example, up, down, and across; the order of importance; the order of familiarity; the inductive (facts → conclusion) and deductive (conclusion → facts) orders; and "pairing" (cause and effect; question and answer; problem and solution; etc). Methods of developing ideas include the use of definitions, details, examples or instances, and comparison and contrast.

Connection is achieved, overall, by a proper use of introductions, headings, and subheadings. These help the reader develop expectations which the writer is under obligation to fulfill. Additional help in relating ideas may be given the reader through the use of connecting words and phrases, topic and transitional phrases, and parallel structure. The last consists of the repetition of grammatical structure, and often includes the repetition of words, in order to show the relation of coordinate ideas (e.g., *They came, they looked, they bought.*).

PROBLEMS

1. Be prepared to comment on the organization of the following passage, with special reference to the way the ideas are divided, arranged, developed, and connected.

> Conservation is generally regarded as a negative factor in our lives. We think of it in terms of deprivation and a return to the hardships of our forefathers. *In a society which has been as wasteful as ours, however, major savings are possible without a loss in the quality of life—and in some respects may even result in an improvement.* Other civilized countries get along with far less energy per capita and still enjoy a pleasant and comfortable way of life.
>
> There is, moreover, a definite and important positive side to conservation. A unit of energy saved is better than a new unit produced for at least three reasons; 1) it avoids depleting our precious and vanishing resources, 2) in most cases, it costs less, and 3) it produces more jobs.
>
> The first statement is self-evident. The question of cost has been investigated in several specific cases, and these studies have indicated that a sum of money invested in conservation in a wide range of applications will save more energy than can be produced by the same investment in oil wells, coal mines, power plants, or other energy producing alternates. One such study, for example, demonstrated that the capital cost of installing solar hot water heaters would be about $^1/_5$ that of generating an equivalent amount of new energy from gas and electricity in the same ratio as now used to produce hot water.
>
> With respect to employment possibilities, energy generating activities such as exploration and drilling, and the construction of major power plants are capital intensive, low labor type operations. Furthermore, much of the labor involved is highly skilled and specialized. Conservation activities, on the other hand, such as insulating buildings, and building and installing storm windows or solar collectors are labor intensive and employ ordinary craftsmen rather than skilled technicians. *Thus for the same investment, conservation measures will in general save more energy and produce more jobs than energy generating activities.*[5]

2. Systematically organize the information in each of the following sets, using only the terms in the problem:
   (*a*) nuts, scratch pads, paper clips, hinges, pocket calendars, screws, cellophane tape, bolts, plastic wood
   (*b*) pedestals, chair, top, legs, cushion, desk, seat, back, drawers, casters

3. Break down into the various steps the registration procedure at your school or college (or hiring procedure at your office or plant). Arrange and number the steps progressively.

[5] From Lewis D. Conta, "Our Nation's Energy Policies: Are We on the Right Track?" Beta Gamma Sigma Invited Essay, n.d.

4. Systematically divide and subdivide any three of the following classes:
   (*a*) Advertising media
   (*b*) Residential buildings
   (*c*) Office machines
   (*d*) Dictation methods
   (*e*) United States mail

5. After some reflection, but without any formal investigation, list the main parts of each of the following subjects:
   (*a*) Improving the office environment
   (*b*) Operating an automobile
   (*c*) Studying efficiently
   (*d*) Using the library
   (*e*) Planting a lawn

6. Make an enumeration of three of the following topics:
   (*a*) Qualifications of a receptionist
   (*b*) Advantages of working for a large company
   (*c*) Hints for saving on personal income taxes
   (*d*) Reasons for the decline of passenger travel on railroads
   (*e*) The broadening effect of travel

7. In one paragraph of about 250 words write a description of your college building or campus, or the building or plant in which you work.

8. Following the order of descending importance, write a short description of the administrative organization of your college or company.

9. Exclusively on the basis of information in *Who's Who in America,* write a short biography (about 200 words) of some leading businessman. The biography is to be used in the printed program of a dinner honoring the man for his business achievements. For the name of a high business official, consult the business pages of your local newspaper, a business periodical, or *Poor's Register of Directors and Executives of the United States and Canada.*

10. Using the deductive order, write a paragraph in praise of supermarket grocery chain stores.

11. Using the inductive order, write a paragraph stressing the need for a new or bigger or better-stocked college library.

12. Assume that a visiting friend from out of state has asked you to map out a day's tour to the principal points of interest in your city or one nearby. Draw up an itinerary in outline form, allowing time for the various stops.

13. Proceeding from the familiar to the unfamiliar, write an exposition (about 500 words) of one of the following subjects:
   (*a*) High performance cars (or cars of some other class)
   (*b*) Instant-picture cameras
   (*c*) High-fidelity sound systems
   (*d*) Slide projectors

(*e*) Fishing tackle
(*f*) Garden tools

14. Using the order of cause-to-effect or effect-to-cause, write a paragraph on one of the following subjects:
(*a*) The rise of the automobile
(*b*) The long-term employment outlook
(*c*) The trend in college enrollments
(*d*) Prospects of the electrical power industry

15. Assume that you have been engaged by the United Postage Meter Company to make a series of case studies of United Postage Meter installations of various types and sizes. With this purpose in mind, you have gone to Brewster, Massachusetts, to visit the Lawson Hardware Company, which installed a United Postage Meter, Model H, in April of last year. You have come away with these notes, which you are asked to arrange in the form of a logical and coherent outline:

Meter resulted in 25% decrease in amount of postage used, as compared with previous year.

Before installation, there was no check on stamps taken by employees for personal use; accounting difficult and inaccurate.

Postage meter does away with loose stamps.

Company mails 100 to 150 pieces daily.

1,000 to 5,000 pieces mailed regularly at end of month.

Handling of mail not previously centralized; each department handled own mail.

Since installation, office boy handles all mail himself; means saving in time for other employees.

Machine saves at least two hours' time in getting out big end-of-month mailings which used to cause confusion and delay, upset office routine.

Postage cost before installation was $10,400 annually.

Many employees had access to stamps; that fact no longer true.

Postage meter makes accounting of postage easy and accurate.

60 employees on Lawson payroll.

16. Define in a single sentence each of the following terms:
(*a*) Mortgage
(*b*) Ledger
(*c*) Rayon
(*d*) Hardtop convertible
(*e*) Letterpress printing
(*f*) Dais
(*g*) Seminar
(*h*) Letterhead
(*i*) Preferred stock
(*j*) Laminated wood
(*k*) Ring binder

Problems

17. Write an extended definition (about 300 words) of one of the following terms. You may use definition, details, examples, or comparison and contrast to make your explanation clear to the layman. Name your sources of information.
    (a) Automation
    (*b*) Mutual funds
    (*c*) Staff organization
    (*d*) The flexible work-week
    (*e*) Cable TV

18. For a popular audience, describe in about 500 words one of the following processes, or one authorized by your instructor.
    (*a*) Water-color painting
    (*b*) Working with clay
    (*c*) Photo-offset printing
    (*d*) Making a linoleum block print
    (*e*) Copper etching

19. Write a paragraph beginning with one of the following sentences. Use the method of development named in the parentheses.
    (*a*) Stereo represents a definite advance over hi-fi in sound reproduction. (Comparison and contrast)
    (*b*) A cardinal principle of business writing is adaptation to the reader. (Examples)
    (*c*) The modern shopping center offers convenience geared to the age of the automobile. (Details)
    (*d*) Living on an allowance is excellent training for any prospective businessman. (Analogy)
    (*e*) One of Frank Lloyd Wright's architectual innovations was the "curtain wall" construction, characteristic of so many of our newer office buildings. (Definition and contrast)

20. Assume you are the chief employment counselor for the American Personnel Service, an employment agency. Write a statement of 500 words, suitable for publication in pamphlet form, about the job opportunities in business for majors in one of the following fields or any other in which you have a personal interest.
    (*a*) Insurance
    (*b*) Economics
    (*c*) English
    (*d*) Marketing
    (*e*) Government
    (*f*) Accounting
    (*g*) Law

21. For the kind of organization named in the assignment, write the copy for a "service" booklet (about 1,000 words)—part of the company's continuing public relations program—on one of the following topics. Concentrate on giving the reader valuable, unbiased information organized for his convenience and interesting to read. There is to be no suggestion of "selling."
    (*a*) For a chain of service stations: Car care
    (*b*) For a loan company: Choosing a new car
    (*c*) For a large men's (or women's) clothier: The art of dressing well
    (*d*) For a bank: Personal finance

(*e*) For a travel agency: What it costs to travel
(*f*) For a florist: The care of household plants
(*g*) For an advertising agency: Advertising in a foreign land
(*h*) For a department store: Selecting a rug or carpet

22. Draw up a set of instructions on one of the following topics:
(*a*) How to change a tire
(*b*) How to place long-distance telephone calls
(*c*) How to wash dishes by hand
(*d*) How to change a typewriter ribbon
(*e*) How to drive a car

23. Express in one or two paragraphs the gist of each of the tables on page 251. In each instance progress from the general to the specific and use any other techniques of order or connection the material suggests. The idea is to communicate the substance and significance of each table without necessarily giving every statistic. (Both tables are from the *Pocket Data Book, USA 1971*, published by the U.S. Department of Commerce.)

24. For the employees' manual of the Broadway Bank and Trust Company, write a set of rules governing benefits under the company's Tuition Refund Plan. Be guided by the information that follows:

The policy of reimbursing full-time employees for tuition at local educational institutions was approved in principle by the Board of Directors. The details were discussed at a meeting of the Personnel Committee, consisting of Mr. Scott (director of personnel), Mr. Gordon (vice president in charge of bank operations), and Mr. Truitt (treasurer). Assume that you were also present.

Mr. Scott proposed that a limit of $900 per year (12 months) be placed on the amount refunded to any one employee. Mr. Gordon raised a question about the conditions under which refunds would be made. It was decided not to reimburse an employee for any course that he failed, or for any course in which he received a D. On the other hand, the employee was to receive a 100% refund for an A, 75% for a B, and 50% for a C. Arithmetical grades would be translated into equivalent letter grades for evaluation purposes. Where no grades were given in a course, the employee would have to present some evidence of satisfactory completion. The amounts reimbursed were not to include fees other than tuition, and there was to be no allowance for books.

Mr. Scott asked how an employee was to apply for a refund. Mr. Gordon suggested that he be required to show his official transcript upon completion of the semester's work. The suggestion was approved. Mr. Truitt thought an employee ought to give the bank advance notice of his intention to apply for a refund; otherwise, he might find himself in the position of taking courses which the bank did not approve and of being refused a refund.

At this point there was a long discussion of the kinds of courses that ought to be approved. Mr. Gordon expressed the opinion that any course given by an accredited institution be acceptable. Mr. Truitt, supported by Mr. Scott, thought there ought to be some limits. The Personnel Committee, they held, could hardly justify the use of the bank's funds for courses in the rhumba or basket weaving. Although Mr. Gordon was skeptical that such courses would be given by an "accredited" institution, he modified his proposal so that refunds would be given for courses related to the applicant's present or future work with the bank. It was also agreed to

Table 1 U.S. Population and Area From 1790

Data 1790–1970 for census dates (Apr. 1 for 1930–70).

Year	Resident population: Number (1,000)	Resident population: Percent increase over prior year shown	Resident population: Per square mile of land area	Area (1,000 sq. mi.): Land	Area (1,000 sq. mi.): Water
1790	**3,929**	(X)	4.5	865	24
1800	**5,308**	35.1	6.1	865	24
1810	**7,240**	36.4	4.3	1,682	34
1820	**9,638**	33.1	5.5	1,749	39
1830	**12,866**	33.5	7.4	1,749	39
1840	**17,069**	32.7	9.8	1,749	39
1850	**23,192**	35.9	7.9	2,940	53
1860	**31,443**	35.6	10.6	2,970	53
1870	**39,818**	26.6	13.4	2,970	53
1880	**50,156**	26.0	16.9	2,970	53
1890	**62,948**	25.5	21.2	2,970	53
1900	**75,995**	20.7	25.6	2,970	53
1910	**91,972**	21.0	31.0	2,970	53
1920	**105,711**	14.9	35.6	2,969	53
1930	**122,775**	16.1	41.2	2,977	45
1940	**131,669**	7.2	44.2	2,977	45
1950	**151,326**	14.5	42.6	3,552	63
1960	**179,323**	18.5	50.5	3,541	74
1970	**203,185**	13.3	57.4	3,541	74

X Not applicable.

Source: U.S. Bureau of the Census.

Table 2 Household Ownership of Cars and Appliances

Income level	Total households	Percent of all households owning—: One or more cars	Two or more cars	Television sets: Black and white	Television sets: Color	Clothes dryers	Air conditioners [1]
1960							
All households	**51,820**	**75.0**	**16.4**	**86.7**		**17.4**	**12.8**
ANNUAL INCOME							
Under $3,000	14,175	44.2	3.9	68.1		10.0	4.6
$3,000–$4,999	11,917	79.1	10.7	90.7		12.3	9.1
$5,000–$7,499	12,398	91.7	19.7	95.7		23.4	14.6
$7,500–$9,999	5,208	95.1	31.4	96.3		30.9	20.3
$10,000–$14,999	3,175	95.4	42.7	97.0		38.6	27.5
$15,000 and over	1,333	94.2	58.8	98.2		50.3	42.2
1969							
All households [2]	**63,297**	**79.6**	**29.3**	**77.4**	**37.8**	**40.8**	[3] **20.5**
ANNUAL INCOME							
Under $3,000	11,126	42.5	4.5	77.3	13.1	11.8	[3] 10.1
$3,000–$4,999	9,367	69.2	13.3	78.5	24.0	22.5	[3] 14.4
$5,000–$7,499	11,874	86.4	22.1	77.5	34.2	33.9	[3] 20.2
$7,500–$9,999	9,629	91.6	34.7	75.6	45.5	49.7	[3] 25.4
$10,000–$14,999	11,771	95.9	48.4	76.9	53.3	62.9	[3] 28.5
$15,000 and over	6,980	96.2	63.1	78.5	64.4	75.0	[3] 31.2

[1] Room and central systems. [2] As of March 1970. [3] Data for 1967.

Source, tables 277 and 278: U.S. Bureau of the Census.

include any courses required for the Bachelor's and Master's degrees in fields related to banking, but that elective courses would be carefully scrutinized for their relevancy. The Committee was skeptical that candidates for a Doctor's degree could qualify under the plan, but they did not rule out the possibility. They also felt that approval should not be given for courses in typewriting and stenography or for those included in the category of "personality improvement" unless the employee's supervisor submitted a recommendation in writing. Mr. Scott said he would not like to see an employee paid to go through law school only to quit the bank later to become a lawyer. After some discussion, the Committee felt that law school courses could be approved only when there was intention to use the knowledge on behalf of the bank.

Employees were to be asked to fill out a form to be provided by Mr. Scott's office and submit it to Mr. Scott a week before registering for any course for which a refund of tuition was desired. The Personnel Committee would indicate its approval or disapproval of the course before the registration date.

Mr. Scott expressed concern about the fact that employees had to put up their own money for tuition without any hope of getting it back for five or six months. If, he said, the bank really wanted to encourage further education among its employees, it would make loans available to those who needed them. After some discussion, it was decided to make no-interest loans for tuition out of the bank's Welfare Fund. The loans would be liquidated by the end of the semester through weekly payroll deductions.

Mr. Truitt said he had been giving some more thought to the term "accredited institution." He pointed out that the City Institute of Public Speaking, as an example, was not accredited, and yet many of the people in the bank could probably benefit from the instruction. Mr. Gordon agreed in principle, but felt that such an institution had no measurable controls like examinations and grades and that similar courses in any of the local colleges would probably hold students to stricter standards of performance. Mr. Truitt and Mr. Scott nodded in agreement.

Mr. Truitt wondered if there wouldn't in some cases be a conflict between work and school. He pointed out that some graduate courses begin at 4:30 p.m. The bank office hours were 9 a.m. to 5 p.m. It was unanimously agreed that employees would not be permitted to take courses that conflicted with working hours. No employee could check out before 5 p.m. for the purpose of meeting a class.

When no further discussion developed, Mr. Scott turned to you with the suggestion that you prepare a statement of the bank's Tuition Refund Plan for the employee's manual, a loose-leaf book (page size 8½ × 11 in.) with information about hours, absences, vacations and holidays, suggestion system, pension plan, profit sharing, etc. Mr. Gordon added that the statement ought to include some remarks about the bank's interest in the education and advancement of its employees and should encourage employees to take advantage of the plan. He also suggested that you "spell out" in some detail the nature of the courses that would be approved for refunds. In answer to your questions, you learned that the bank employed 2,400 men and women; that Tuition Refund Plans were operating successfully in many other companies, large and small; that employees attending school under the plan sometimes put pressure on their teachers for higher grades to enable them to qualify for refunds; that it was expected that some men and women would obtain jobs with the bank to take advantage of the Tuition Refund Plan, then quit when they had taken all the courses they wanted; that the experience of other firms had been that labor turnover is less among participants in the Tuition Refund Plan than among nonparticipants doing the same kind of work.

9 Communicating with Reports: First Steps

An executive can deal effectively in person with only a relatively few individuals. That means that many responsibilities must be delegated to others and that lines of communication with the executive must be kept open. The larger the organization, the more people are involved in providing information and the farther messages must travel. In such a situation written reports provide a convenient way of communicating information about specific areas of business activity. These reports may originate inside the organization or outside, and they can travel up or down the organizational hierarchy or across departmental lines.

If reports are well written, they tell the same story to everyone who reads them and are not easily subject to misinterpretation. They provide useful or necessary information, put abstract ideas into concrete form, focus attention on problems, and stimulate administrative action. From the writer's point of view, reports serve as evidence of work done. They are therefore an especially important means of expression and a path to recognition for anyone whose work is largely meditative, supervisory, administrative, or otherwise intangible.

With the massive increase in the complexity of business over the past several decades, the need for written reports has also increased and brought additional responsibilities to their writers. The complexities require specialists to deal with them. The specialists must communicate their findings to management. But the latter do not possess the particular expertise of the specialists;

and so, unless the specialists are also excellent reporters, it is difficult for them to make their findings clear and persuasive. What seems to be a growing gap between the specialists and management can only be filled by a better appreciation by both sides of the need for more expertness in the preparation of business reports.

KINDS OF REPORTS

Functionally, most reports may be divided into two classes: informational and analytical. *Informational reports* are usually confined to facts and observations. Examples are financial statements, minutes of meetings, abstracts and digests of published material, and records of all sorts: attendance, performance, inspection, and so on. *Analytical reports* not only give the facts, but also attempt to evaluate them. They may include recommendations for action. Examples of such reports include surveys of the market for new products, studies of efficiency, and examinations of proposed policies or procedures with a view to their adoption.

When analytical reports consist principally, if not entirely, of recommendations, they are sometimes called *recommendation reports*. Included in this category would be an advertising agency's suggestions for a new advertising campaign for one of its clients, a labor arbitrator's proposals for settling a strike, and a government commission's plan for redeveloping a slum area.

In addition to being classified by function, reports may also be grouped according to their destination as either internal or external. Internal reports are prepared for the information and use of management. External reports are intended principally for the information of stockholders, customers and prospective customers, government agencies, and the public. Also in this category are the public reports of government and social agencies and trade associations.

Other classifications of reports are made according to their source or frequency of appearance, and by their length, degree of formality, or physical form. Thus there are auditors' reports, laboratory reports, salesmen's reports, inspectors' reports; there are annual reports, semiannual and quarterly reports, monthly reports, weekly reports, and even hourly reports; there are short reports and long reports, informal reports and formal reports, letter reports and memorandum reports. Some reports are handwritten; others are typewritten, or printed on office duplicating machines or letterpress. Some are held together with a paper clip; others are elaborately bound between stiff covers.

PREPARING TO WRITE

Like any other work, report writing turns out most successfully when some advance planning has been done. After all, a report is not something that comes off "the top of your head." The finished product must represent careful investigation, sound thinking, and logical organization, as well as good writing. For this reason, you must give more than ordinary attention to the preliminaries. Without a well-conceived plan, you will waste time and risk an ineffectual report. With a good plan, you will conserve your energies and improve the prospects of writing a report that will make the impression you want. The principal steps preparatory to writing are these:

1. Analyzing the problem
2. Defining the scope of the report
3. Obtaining information
4. Organizing the data

ANALYZING THE PROBLEM

Reports differ so widely in mechanics, content, and spirit that some guides are necessary to help you arrive at a clear concept of your task. Even if you are given the topic to write on, you will undoubtedly have many questions. These may pertain to the length of the report, the extent of the coverage, the formality of the appearance and style, the level of language difficulty, and the point of view. To resolve these and other questions, the points you will need to consider are (1) the purpose of the report, (2) its precedents, (3) its significance, (4) its intended readers, and (5) the practical restrictions on your efforts.

Purpose

The most helpful guide to the kind of report you will write is the purpose it will serve. Is the purpose only to convey information? Is it to offer the reader the benefit of your judgment and advice? Or is it to urge a course of action that will further your own interests? Each of these purposes influences the content and tone of the report in different ways.

The informational report suggests a reliance on facts and the need for enough data to serve the reader's needs. The other types of reports require that facts and judgments be carefully balanced to conform to the situation. If you have a reputation as an expert, for example, your knowledge of the facts will pretty much be taken for granted and you may lean heavily on your conclusions. With less authority, however, you will be expected to rely to a greater extent on the facts. Even when your purpose is to promote a product or service, you must offset your natural bias with enough objective recital of the facts to enable the reader to form a conclusion on his own. Otherwise the "report" becomes a tract.

Precedents

Many reports are of a kind that have been done many times before in the same organization. This is usually true of financial statements, annual or quarterly reports, minutes of meetings, and other reports that a business requires as a matter of routine. In such instances, you may find a former report that you can use as a model. Sometimes a company standardizes certain types of reports by providing printed forms on which they are to be submitted. In still other instances, problems of format and arrangement are solved by a company manual which prescribes the manner in which reports are to be set up.

Whenever reports become routine, there is danger that only passing attention will be paid to them or that important information that does not fit the format will be left out. On the other hand, routine reports develop among their readers certain expectations with regard to their content, organization, and language. A newcomer who changes a routine report in any of these respects may therefore meet considerable resistance unless the changes are first discussed and cleared with his principals.

Significance of the Report

When precedents or instructions are not available, it makes good sense to relate the amount of research, the length of the report, and the time spent in writing it to the importance of the subject and the use to which it will be put. Many reports represent simply routine record-keeping. Others are "feeders" intended to be combined with other information into a larger report for which another person will take responsibility. Some reports arise out of special or compelling circumstances that make them important. Others are important because they state or affect company policy. In each case, study of the significance of the report will help determine the kind of effort called for.

Prospective Readers

The reader's interest in the subject and how much he already knows about it will strongly influence you in determining the content and language of the report. Similarly, your attitude toward the reader will depend on his relation to you and whether he is within the organization or outside. A report intended for an immediate superior or for a person whose rank in the organization is equivalent to yours may be quite informal. A report that will travel up to the division chief or president will be less so. An external report to stockholders, customers, or the public may have considerable bias in favor of management.

The problem of adaptation is further complicated when a report written for one person or group is intended to be distributed also to others whose background and technical knowledge are different from those of the primary audience. This is often a problem in corporate annual reports, which are written primarily for stockholders but which may also be distributed to security analysts, employees, and the public. Adapting even to stockholders alone is difficult because of the disparity in their financial knowledge and interests. Institutional investors, for example, are much more sophisticated than small stockholders in their attitude toward their securities and they look for more detailed information.

Practical Restrictions

The kind of report you write will depend to a great extent on the time you have to prepare it, the amount of data available, and the assistance with which you are provided. A report that must be done overnight is not usually expected to treat its subject as thoroughly as it would if a week or a month were allowed. A report that can draw from a large body of information is likely to be longer than one that has to depend on a few readily available facts. With assistance in tracking down information and preparing tables and visual aids, you may also be able to make a much more complete and effective report than if you have to rely entirely on your own resources. One reason that reports written in large companies are often so much fuller and more attractive than reports written by private individuals is that big companies are customarily well equipped to render assistance in research, chart making, typing, and even binding the finished reports.

DEFINING THE SCOPE OF THE REPORT

While you are turning over in your mind the preliminary details already mentioned, you will probably be thinking of the specific subject area the report will cover. Certainly, before you go digging for material in earnest, you should set up certain limits within which you will work to fulfill your objective. A brief illustration will show the need for this step.

Suppose that you have been asked to make a study of the new passenger cars and to recommend the make and model best suited for use by your company's salesmen. With a confusing variety of makes, models, sizes, and prices to choose from, you have the immediate problem of deciding how many of the new cars you will include in your formal investigation. To study and report on all would take an inordinate amount of time. Nor is the reader likely to appreciate your efforts if he has to go through a bulky report to get at the essential facts.

A little thought will show the desirability of limiting the report to the few models from which a choice would most likely be made. In deciding which models to concentrate on, you may reason from the circumstances that your salesmen travel long distances and carry bulky sample cases, that the company is economy-minded and wants the most transportation for the money, and that the factor of prestige is of little consequence. These facts may lead to the preliminary conclusion that the car your company eventually purchases will have to qualify on particular grounds of price, size, durability, and economy of operation. Further, you may find through a quick survey of all the new cars that only a half dozen meet the criteria you have set. You are now ready to circumscribe the area of your full-scale investigation and your final report. In your report you will undoubtedly tell what reasoning led you to confine your study to the few cars you chose, but the limits you have set will enable you to go thoroughly into the merits of these cars without wasting your time or the reader's.

Limiting the Topic

Just as bad as covering too much territory is covering a subject too scantily. This fault often occurs when, given the choice, you take a topic that is too big for your purpose, your time, or your inclinations. A wiser course is to cultivate a small area in detail. There is little merit, for example, in giving token treatment to "Government Legislation of Railroads," when the problem at hand calls for a close analysis of "Pending New York State Legislation Affecting Commuter Railroad Lines." "Automation in the Office," also, is apt to be less immediately useful as a topic than the more specific "Application of Data Processing Techniques to Inventory Control."

Although the selection of a title in advance does not necessarily control the content of a report, a good working title can have at least a salutary effect on the writer. The titles that follow are recommended for the specific way in which they limit the subject:

Analysis of Procedures for Assisting Workmen Injured on the Job
Meeting the Competition of Captive Finance Companies in the Consumer Credit Field
Proposed Relocation of Warehouse Facilities
Effects of the Consolidation of Tabulating Equipment at the Peoria Office
Evaluation of Procedures—Traffic Payment Department
Improving Control of Fee Collections

Sometimes, for reasons of interest and brevity, the title of a report intended for an audience of disparate interests is rather general. This for example:

Mental Health

In such an instance, it is often helpful to the writer as well as the reader to add a subtitle containing a statement of limited subject, in this fashion:

An account of some instances of the assistance given by the Ford Foundation for mental health research.

The Preliminary Outline

A useful adjunct to the specific title or statement of limited subject is an informal outline that briefly notes the chief points the report will cover. This is not to be confused with the comprehensive outline that customarily follows the gathering of the data and immediately precedes the writing of the report. Rather, the preliminary outline is simply a guide for the investigation and for further thinking about the subject.

The pattern that follows offers a starting point for the writer of almost any formal report:

Introduction
  What is the origin, nature, purpose, etc. of this report?
Body
  What do the facts of the investigation show?
Conclusion
  What is the significance of the facts?
  What, if anything, should be done?
  How should the recommendations be carried out?

As you begin thinking about the body, you will probably find that you can expand that part of the preliminary outline with a tentative list of subtopics, as this example shows:

Body
Present practice
Proposed practice
Anticipated effects

OBTAINING INFORMATION

After you have given some thought to your subject and to the definition of the area the report will cover, the need for specific data will become apparent. Sometimes the information you require is already stored in your head, the result of past observations and experiences. More often, however, you have to go to other sources. Finding the information you need is a real challenge. Many reports are ineffective, and some never even reach the writing stage, simply because the writer failed to see the right people, consult the right documents, uncover the right figures, or get the right answers. The sources of information are many, but they might as well not exist if you do not know where they are or how to use them.

Another point to keep in mind is that a great deal of investigation these days is done on a sampling basis. That is, only a small percentage of a total group is interviewed or sent questionnaires and, from the results, conclusions are drawn statistically about the whole group. This method materially reduces the cost of investigation, but unless the sample is large enough and truly representative of the whole group, the results will be worthless.

Still another word of caution should be voiced with respect to the need for accuracy and completeness in the data you obtain. Accuracy requires that the sources of information be authoritative and up-to-date. Completeness requires that you obtain enough relevant information to support valid conclusions and, further, that you do not overlook adverse data.

The following review of information sources is only suggestive. Those who write reports in business are, as a rule, already familiar with the sources available to them. However, it is often helpful for the reporter occasionally to go to an unexpected source. Thus, if he is accustomed to depending solely on his experience and in-house contacts, he may find that a trade association report or some current book in the field will give him valuable support.

Personal Experience

Many reports are based on firsthand knowledge. They may involve an experiment you conducted, an inspection or investigation or other type of job you performed, your observation of a procedure or event, or your dealings with other persons. Information of this sort is valuable only to the extent that (1) the conditions under which you have made your observations are scientifically valid, (2) you have observed accurately, and (3) you have promptly and accurately recorded the details, including names, dates, amounts, equipment, sequences, reactions, and the like. Only the first point needs to be explained. For an example of scientific validity, let us say that a report undertakes to compare the performance of two machines. Unless both are given the same work to do and unless both are operated by persons of equal skill under comparable conditions, the results would have little meaning.

Company Records

Since so much of a company's activities finds its way into written documents—computer printouts, letters, reports, contracts, advertisements, transcripts of talks—you may find all the information your report requires on the company's premises. With the assistance of a modern copying machine, you can copy the pertinent material and return the originals to their source.

Interviews

Some information can best be obtained by talking to people. The reports of a personnel interviewer follow his meetings with job applicants. A salesman bases his reports on his conversations with customers and prospective customers. A credit investigator and claims adjuster similarly obtain much of their information from interviews. Other, less routine reporting may require interviews also. Thus an investigator may seek the opinions of consumers or question senior employees about long-forgotten details, or solicit ideas in person from co-workers. Interviews may be conducted by telephone, but personal contact has obvious advantages where more than routine answers are desired. Notes should be taken during an interview, if feasible, or set down immediately afterward. As an alternative, the interview may be tape recorded.

Questionnaires

When it is necessary to obtain uniform information from a number of people, you may assemble a list of questions and have identical copies made. You can then ask the questions in person, marking the answers on the forms, or you can give or mail the forms to the respondents to fill out themselves. Questionnaires to be submitted to a large number of people may be first tested on a small percentage of the list—perhaps 5 or 10 per cent. The sampling permits discovery of flaws in the questions before the questionnaire is broadcast to the whole list.

To be of value, questionnaires must be skillfully formulated. Guiding principles include the following:

1. Questions should be clear. The question, "Do you attend the legitimate theater regularly?" is not clear because the reader has no way of knowing what "regularly" means. A prospective purchaser, asked for an expression of opinion on (1) which manufacturer makes "the best riding car" and (2) which makes "all things considered, the car with the most comfortable ride," would have considerable difficulty in distinguishing between the two questions.

2. Questions should be arranged or split in a way that makes them easy to answer and tabulate. "Open" questions, like "How much interest do you have in news of the theater?" permit too much variety in the answers to make tabulation possible. The following treatment, however, satisfactorily solves the problem:

How much interest do you have in news of the theater?

A great deal . . . . ☐
Moderate . . . . ☐
Little . . . . ☐
None . . . . ☐

3. Leading questions should not be used. These are questions that suggest the answer desired or make it embarrassing for the respondent to answer truthfully. Often they employ prejudicial words.

LEADING QUESTIONS (TO BE AVOIDED)

Do you believe in the American system of free enterprise?
Do you read the *New York Times?*
Do you approve of the sale of trashy magazines in neighborhood stores patronized by children?
Would you prefer to buy your groceries from
☐ a chain store that pays profits to stockholders?
☐ an independent local grocer?

4. Personal questions should be avoided. These include questions about sex, religion, politics, and income. An occasional exception is made in confidential questionnaires from trusted sources and in questionnaires that do not require the name of the respondent.

5. Since questionnaires represent an imposition on the time of the respondent, every effort should be made to keep them as short as possible.

Mail questionnaires are usually accompanied by a letter asking the reader for his cooperation. The letter in Figure 9-1 followed by a few days a post card telling the reader to expect the questionnaire. The post card developed anticipation and the letter itself is so flattering in its implication that any reader would probably find it difficult not to respond.

Library Sources

Much if not all the information you require may reside in books, magazines, newspapers, and pamphlets. The biggest help in finding these sources is an easy acquaintance with the library catalog and the reference alcove. You should also search the library shelves for books in your field of interest. Many books have bibliographies either in an appendix or after each chapter; and sometimes references are included in the author's preface. These should lead to other works that may produce the information you want.

Dear TIME Reader:

Please do us a favor.

As I mentioned in my earlier note to you, we feel it is extremely important to ask people like you, familiar with TIME, to help us learn more about our readers and their interests. Your reply--which will help us form a composite picture--will, of course, be completely confidential.

Because our sample of subscribers is small, each and every answer is important to the reliability of the results of the survey. So, I hope you will send us your answers in the enclosed, stamped reply envelope, today if possible.

And many thanks for your cooperation.

Sincerely,

FIG. 9-1. *Letter accompanying a mailed questionnaire.*

The summary of reference books that follows is not intended to take the place of personal search, but it may provide a start.

GENERAL BIBLIOGRAPHICAL GUIDES TO BUSINESS INFORMATION

Two of the most generally useful guides to business information sources are Edward T. Comans, Jr.'s *Sources of Business Information* (University of California Press) and H. Webster Johnson's *How to Use the Business Library, with Sources of Business Information* (South-Western Publishing Co.). Bibliographies in specific areas of business, such as real estate, building construction, and business trends and forecasting are covered in the growing number of volumes included in the *Management Information Guide Series*, published by the Gale Research Co., Detroit.

ENCYCLOPEDIAS, DICTIONARIES, AND ATLASES

Although the best-known encyclopedia is the *Encyclopaedia Britannica*, others like the *World Book Encyclopedia*, *Collier's Encyclopedia*, and the *Encyclopedia International* often make up in clarity and simplicity what they lack in detail. *Webster's Third New International Dictionary* and the *Random House Dictionary of the English Language* are the leading American unabridged dictionaries. A great deal of miscellaneous information can also be found in the smaller *Webster's New Collegiate Dictionary*, the *American Heritage Dictionary*, the *Random House College Dictionary*, and *Webster's New World Dictionary*. An excellent atlas for business use is the *Rand McNally Commercial Atlas and Marketing Guide*.

ANNUALS

Probably the handiest all-around reference books are the *Information Please Almanac* and the *World Almanac and Book of Facts*. Another invaluable annual is the *Statistical Abstract of the United States*. Published by the U.S. Bureau of Foreign and Domestic Commerce, it has summaries of all the important figures relating to population, production, and consumption. The *Economic Almanac*, published biennially by The Conference Board, performs a similar service.

BIOGRAPHICAL DICTIONARIES

Who's Who in America contains biographies of about 40,000 notable living Americans, among them many businessmen and scientists. *Biography Index* is a reference to biographies in books and magazines. *Current Biography* gives biographies of people in the news. Biographies of notable figures of the past will be found in *Dictionary of American Biography* and *Who Was Who in America*. Examples of specialized biographical dictionaries include *Who's Who in Commerce and Industry, Who's Who in the East, Who's Who in Law*, and the official *Congressional Directory*.

GUIDES TO BOOKS, PERIODICALS, AND PAMPHLETS

The *United States Catalog* of books in print (1900–1933) and the *Cumulative Book Index* (1928 to date) provide help in finding names of books, authors, and publishers. *Books in Print* is a handy annual reference to all books currently published. One volume lists books by title, and another by author. Two additional volumes, *Subject Guide to Books in Print*, complete the set. For a list of soft-cover editions, see *Paperbound Books in Print*.

Lists of periodicals will be found in the *Union List of Serials in Libraries of the United States* and *Ulrich's Periodicals Directory*. *N. W. Ayer's Directory of Newspapers and Periodicals*, issued annually, includes circulation figures and advertising rates. The *Gebbie Press House Magazine Directory* lists some 4,000 company-sponsored publications. The *Vertical File Index* lists and describes pamphlets as they are issued.

GUIDES TO MAGAZINE AND NEWSPAPER ARTICLES

The *Reader's Guide to Periodical Literature* lists general magazine articles by author and subject. The *Business Periodicals Index* and the *Applied Science and Technology Index* (both successors to the *Industrial Arts Index*) are, as the names suggest, more specialized. Other specialized indexes include *Engineering Index, Agricultural Index*, and *Art Index*. Also helpful are the annual or semiannual indexes of specific publications. Perhaps the most widely used in business are the *New York Times Index* and the *Wall Street Journal Index*.

BUSINESS DIRECTORIES

For the names of associations of all sorts see the *Encyclopedia of Associations* published by the Gale Research Co., Detroit. Useful directories of individuals in business include *Poor's Register of Corporations, Directors, and Executives of the United States and Canada, Rand McNally's Bankers Directory,* and the *Directory of Directors in the City of New York.* Many trades and industries have their own "Who's Who" of leaders in their respective fields. Leading directories in publishing and advertising are the already mentioned *Ayer's Directory of Newspapers and Periodicals,* as well as the *Standard Directory of Advertisers,* the *Standard Directory of Advertising Agencies* (including the names of their clients) and the *Standard Rate and Data Service,* whose numerous volumes cover all advertising media.

General business and industrial directories include *Thomas Register of American Manufactures, MacRae's Blue Book,* the *Fortune Directory of the 500 Largest Industrial Corporations,* Dun & Bradstreet's *Million Dollar Directory,* listing all firms with a net worth of over $1,000,000, and another Dun & Bradstreet publication, the *Middle Market Directory,* which lists American businesses having total assets of $500,000 to $1,000,000. Financial information about specific companies can be obtained from *Moody's Investor Services* and *Standard and Poor's Corporation Services.*

REPORTING SERVICES

A great deal of information on business topics ranging from collective bargaining to taxes and legislation affecting business can be obtained from volumes in the reporting services of Prentice-Hall (P-H), the Commerce Clearing House (CCH), and the Bureau of National Affairs of Washington, D.C. (BNA). Some representative services include *Federal Tax Service* (P-H), *Real Estate Service* (P-H), *Wills, Estates, and Trust Service* (P-H), *Food, Drug, Cosmetic Law Reports* (CCH), *Utilities Law Reports* (CCH), and *United States Patents Quarterly* (BNA).

GOVERNMENT PUBLICATIONS

For a general survey of government publications see *Government Publication and Their Use* by Lawrence F. Schmeckebier and Roy B. Eastin (Washington, D.C.: The Brookings Institution) and *U.S. Government Serials and Periodicals* by John L. Andriot, in three volumes (McLean, Va.: Documents Index). Government bibliographies include *United States Department of Commerce Publications* (supplemented annually) and the *Catalog of United States Census Publications.* State publications are listed in the *Monthly Checklist of State Publications* issued by the Superintendent of Documents, Government Printing Office, Washington, D.C. Particular government publications of special value to business users include the *Statistical Abstract of the United States,* the *Survey of Current Business* (monthly), *Economic Indicators* (monthly), the *Congressional Record* (daily proceedings of both houses of Congress), and the *Congressional Directory.*

Compiling a Bibliography

The most efficient way to begin research, using published sources of information, is to compile a bibliography of the books, periodicals, and pamphlets you will want to consult. Each source should be entered separately on a 3- by 5-inch index card, as shown in Figure 9-2. If you include the library call number, you will avoid having to look it up again later. You may also add a note on the special value of the source for your purpose. The bibliography cards should be filed alphabetically by author and title. (See the Style Manual, Rule 35, for the correct form of bibliographical data in footnotes and formal bibliography.)

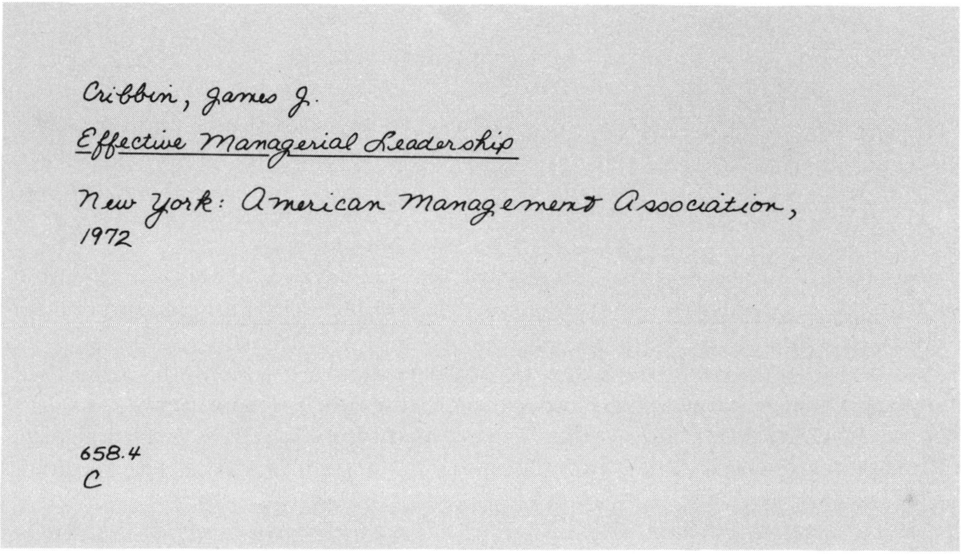
Cribbin, James J.
Effective Managerial Leadership
New York: American Management Association,
1972
658.4
C

FIG. 9-2. *Bibliography card.*

Note Taking

When a bibliographical source has information that will be useful in the actual writing of the report, the taking of notes becomes necessary. Like the bibliographical references, the notes may be placed on 3- by 5-inch cards, although the 4- by 6-inch and larger size cards are sometimes more practical for this purpose.

Probably the most satisfactory notes are those that put briefly and in your own words the substance of the original material (Figure 9-3). If, however, there is the possibility that you will be quoting the author directly in the report, copy that portion of the source material verbatim and put it in quotation marks (Figure 9-4). If you leave out any part of a direct quotation, indicate the omission by a series of periods (see Style Manual, Rule 19*c*). Always be sure to note the page numbers of any material you quote or paraphrase so that you will have them for use in your footnotes.

Treat only one topic on a card. If you fill one side of a card, and have more to

Performance Review

Measures employee against his own job standards as well as against performance of his peers, with whom he is competing. Also serves to recognize good performance, analyze past failures, and discover worker's feelings about his job, co-workers, superiors, and the organization. Differs from a development review, which is geared primarily to improvement of employee and is noncompetitive.

Cribbin, pp. 196-197

FIG. 9-3. *Note card (summary of text).*

write, continue the notes on another card, carefully labeling and numbering it so that you can easily refile it if it becomes separated. File all note cards under subject headings.

Not only library work, but any type of investigation may entail a great deal of note taking. When extensive notes are required, as in reporting the writer's firsthand experiences and observations, they are customarily put on a large pad of paper of letter or legal size. Experienced writers start a new page for

Development Review

"The development review... is an outward sign of the firm's desire to help him [the employee] become more effective, even if he leaves the organization. It endeavors to help him capitalize more fully on his strong points and remedy weak ones. Coaching (p. 196)/ and perhaps even counseling play a key role in the interaction."
(p. 197) —Cribbin

FIG. 9-4. *Note card (direct quotation).*

each phase of the subject and note the subject at the top. Pages are consecutively numbered.

ORGANIZING THE DATA

When you complete your investigation and note taking, you are ready for another crucial step: organizing the material in such a way that it will fulfill the original aim of the report. Because the principles of organization apply also to writing other than reports, this subject was treated earlier (Chapter 8). However, we will here make some observations that apply particularly to the organization of reports.

Assimilating the Data

A recommended preliminary is letting the notes simmer for a short time while you give some thought to their relevance and their significance. During this period of contemplation, you will find that some facts assume greater importance than others and that probably some of your research was a waste of time. Part of the report-writing game is having the courage to throw away the work of many hours or days when information turns out to be insignificant or irrelevant. At this point you may also discover that you need more information on a heretofore neglected aspect of the subject or that you have to find a figure or check on a specific point.

Sometime during the process of assimilation a broad pattern should emerge, a kind of framework on which you can hang the many bits and pieces of information in an orderly fashion. If you worked from a preliminary outline, the emerging pattern may be the same or may follow it very closely. You need then only enlarge the outline to accommodate the details. If, however, you had no preliminary outline or your findings suggest that a different treatment would be preferable, you must continue to work on your material until you have found the most effective arrangement.

General Arrangement

The thinking that controls the development of a report is usually inductive. That is, it leads from a consideration of the data to the formation of conclusions and recommendations. You may begin with a hypothesis, or tentative conclusion, but you must be willing to discard that hypothesis if the findings lead in some other direction. In this way, the objectivity of the report is preserved.

Just as the thinking that goes into the report is inductive, so is the writing of the draft. Following an introduction, which acquaints the reader with the purpose and scope of the report and provides any other information necessary to the reader's understanding of the report, you will set down in rough form your data and the conclusions leading from them. After editing, the report may be presented in the same order: facts, then conclusions. *However, it is not unusual for a somewhat different order to be followed in the final draft.* In fact, there is a marked trend today to present the conclusions and recommendations after the introduction and before the presentation of data. In some instances, the conclusions and recommendations are only summarized before the presentation of data and then presented in full at the end of the report.[1]

The reason for putting conclusions and recommendations at or near the beginning is to allay the impatience of the reader to whom that part of the report is the most important. Especially in a long report, it seems inconsiderate to withhold the conclusions until the very end, even though it is possible for the reader to find them on his own. In some instances a writer will deliberately withhold his conclusions until the end even at the risk of inconveniencing the reader. That is probably the best course to follow when the conclusions are likely to meet with antagonism if stated at the beginning. By stating his facts first, the writer can make his case and perhaps ensure the reader's receptivity to the conclusions. In Figure 9-5 you will see a number of basic report formats in which the conclusions and recommendations occupy varying positions. These formats also suggest a number of different methods of handling the body material.

A.

I. Introduction
II. Discussion
III. Conclusions

B.

I. Statement of the problem
II. Recommendations
III. Supporting data

C.

I. Introduction
II. Analysis of problem
III. Proposed solution
IV. Anticipated results
V. Recommendations

D.

I. Background
II. Faults of present system
III. Alternatives
IV. Recommendations
V. Conclusion

E.

I. Introduction
II. Recommendations
III. Background
IV. Present procedure
V. Proposed procedure
VI. Conclusions

F.

I. Introduction
II. Summary of conclusions and recommendations
III. Investigative data
IV. Conclusions
V. Recommendations
VI. Exhibits

FIG. 9-5. *Some basic report formats.*

[1] The writer is cautioned against *drafting* the report with the conclusions and recommendations preceding the supporting data. When this is done, objectivity is endangered because the writer is then tempted to "justify" the conclusions in the body instead of presenting the investigative data objectively. Wherever the conclusions and recommendations are placed, they should be treated as the consequences of the facts and their analysis, and not as preconceptions for which support has been found.

Outlining

A formal written outline is not absolutely necessary for the writing of a report, but the absence of one presumes a greater capacity for order and detail than most writers claim. The biggest advantage of the written outline is that, like a map, it shows you the road to your destination and enables you to check now and then to make sure you are still on course.

The principles of outlining have already been explained in Chapter 8. An outline of the report reproduced in Figure 10-10, beginning on page 304, is shown below. You will note that the conclusions and recommendations ("Summary Opinion") are summarized directly following the introduction and that each part of the body section has the same inductive pattern: facts fol-

```
            OPERATIONAL AUDIT OF THE CAFETERIA UNIT

                       EASTWOOD BRANCH

  I.  Introduction

        A.  Background: Mandated contributions of re-
            ceipts to operating costs

        B.  Purpose of audit
             1.  To review procedures
             2.  To suggest changes that might contribute
                 to operating efficiency

        C.  Sources of information
             1.  Interviews with staff members
             2.  Personal observation

 II.  Summary opinion
        A.  Time of personnel improperly allocated
        B.  Physical layout inefficient
        C.  Disproportionate share of costs borne by
            company

III.  Observations and recommendations

        A.  Cost of service
             1.  Five-year comparison
                   a. Increased labor costs
                   b. Increased food costs
             2.  Recommendation:  Reduction in personnel

        B.  Meat and poultry quotations
             1.  Cost control through menu planning
             2.  Quarterly bidding by vendors
             3.  Recommendation: Weekly bidding

        C.  Allocation of time
             1.  Understatement of workers' time
             2.  Recommendation: More accurate time allo-
                 cation procedures
```

```
        D.  Serving line layout
              1.  Cashier required to help out in service
                  area
                    a.  Register unattended
                    b.  Loss of serving efficiency
              2.  Recommendation: Reversing flow of traf-
                  fic to put cashier closer to service
                  area

        E.  Special events
              1.  Charging procedure upsets pricing
                  formula
              2.  Recommendation:  Changing accounting
                  procedure to preserve balance between
                  company subsidy and prices paid by
                  employees

        F.  Manual of procedures:  Updating needed

EXHIBITS

   I.  Organization Chart, Cafeteria Unit

  II.  Expenses and Receipts, 1972-1978

 III.  Telephone Record of Meat and Poultry Quotations

  IV.  Suggested Change in Serving Line Flow
```

lowed by a recommendation. The outline for a report of a different kind accompanies the library paper shown in Figure 10-11, pages 324–334.

SUMMARY

Reports are written to give the reader information he needs to form judgments and make decisions. An informative report is confined to facts and observations, whereas an analytical report also attempts to evaluate the data and possibly make recommendations. You should not write a report until you have analyzed the problem, defined the scope of the report, and obtained and organized the necessary information. In your preparation be guided by the purpose of the report and the use to which it is to be put. Consider also the prospective readers of the report, the precedents that have been established for similar reports in the organization, and such practical restrictions as the amount of time and data available. It is usually better to cover a limited topic thoroughly than to skim the surface of a bigger subject. A preliminary outline will help to guide you in your research.

Information for a report may be obtained from personal experience and observation, company records, interviews, questionnaires, and library sources. Interviews and questionnaires are often done on a sampling basis, which requires that the sample be large enough to yield valid results. Questions should be clear, unbiased, phrased and arranged for easy tabulation, and—with some exceptions—free of intrusion on the respondent's personal affairs.

Library sources include encyclopedias, dictionaries, and atlases; annual reference books; biographical dictionaries; guides to books and periodicals and to articles in newspapers and magazines; and government publications. During the research process, you should compile a bibliography, using a file card for each entry, and take notes on cards or paper, making sure to treat only one topic on a single card or sheet and carefully noting the source and page numbers. The final step before writing the first draft is making a comprehensive outline of the whole report.

PROBLEMS

1. Explore the library materials available on the life and the contributions to American business or industry of one of the individuals listed below. Then (a) develop a topic for a research paper on the basis of your interests and the materials available; (b) compile bibliography cards for five books or shorter works on the topic you have chosen; and (c) write a brief paper in which you propose the topic and suggest a possible line of development.
   (*a*) John Jacob Astor
   (*b*) Andrew Carnegie
   (*c*) James B. Duke
   (*d*) Henry Ford
   (*e*) Henry Clay Frick
   (*f*) Andrew W. Mellon
   (*g*) J. Pierpont Morgan
   (*h*) John D. Rockefeller
   (*i*) Charles M. Schwab
   (*j*) Cornelius Vanderbilt

2. List a half dozen recent articles for a bibliography on one of the following topics:
   (*a*) Status of Federal legislation for the protection of consumer interests
   (*b*) Trends in urban or suburban shopping malls
   (*c*) Television advertising techniques
   (*d*) Airport safety precautions
   (*e*) New developments in accounting standards and practices

3. Using the subject cards in your library's catalog, compile a set of a half dozen bibliography cards consisting of the most promising material on one of the following topics:
   (*a*) Employment of minorities and women
   (*b*) New sources of energy
   (*c*) Controlling store thefts by employees and customers
   (*d*) Regulation of consumer credit
   (*e*) Investing in real estate

4. Paraphrase the following passages, as you would in taking notes for a report.

   (a) My concern is that the American public, growing increasingly distrustful of business, will disregard logic and will not leave the definition of corporate responsibility and the power to exercise it in the hands of the owners of the business and their representatives—the existing kinds of boards of directors. Indeed, a tide of sentiment seems to be running that government should insist that certain kinds of people participate in corporate decision-making at the highest level. These would be people drawn from outside the business community. Because businessmen are automatically suspect, the direction of corporations would be invested in others, without regard for their qualifications for business, but simply because they claim to espouse social responsibility. Unfortunately, the government at some point may yield to such public suspicion and mandate a broadened representation in the governance of the corporation. It may take the form of government-appointed directors or representatives, of workers or consumers, or some combination. Should such greater public governance happen here—as it already has elsewhere—it will be tragic for our free economy, and indeed for all who live within it.[2]

(*b*) In today's housing recovery there is a noticeable difference in the health of different sectors. The single-family-detached market is doing quite well, while multifamily construction—five and more units—continues to lag.

The single-family detached home has made a remarkable comeback after being written off by many observers in the early 1970s as uneconomical and inconsistent with a new life-style that supposedly was sweeping the country. These observers also argued that a mobile, young population and smaller average household size, as more people decide to live alone, would help boost demand for multifamily housing. So, too, would relative increases in transportation and energy costs, though it might take many years before the greatest impact of these forces would be felt. The fact remains that most families apparently continue to want to own their own home and a plot of open space.[3]

5. For the Traffic Department of your city, make careful observations of the density and flow of traffic, vehicular and pedestrian, around your campus or business district at various times of the day. Look for significant details. Record your experience in a set of notes, which you are asked to submit—after editing—to your instructor.

6. Assuming that you work in an employment agency, conduct a job interview with a schoolmate or friend with regard to a position he would like to fill. Submit:
   (*a*) A raw set of notes taken at the time of the interview.
   (*b*) An outline for an informational report to be placed in your files for reference.

7. Assume that you are the director of the placement office of your college. You believe it will help student job applicants to know the preferences of personnel managers with respect to the form and content of written job applications.
   (*a*) Draw up a questionnaire that will best serve your purpose.
   (*b*) Write a letter designed to accompany the questionnaire.

8. Mr. Thomas Smith, manager of the Brunswick plant of Cummings, Inc., has asked

[2] Thomas A. Murphy, Chairman of General Motors, speaking at the National Honoree Luncheon, of Beta Gamma Sigma, Las Vegas, Nevada, April 23, 1975.

[3] *Monthly Economic Letter*, Citibank (New York: January 1976), p. 12.

you to determine the feasibility of providing free parking facilities for all plant employees. The plant operates on a day shift only with 1500 employees.

Before you shop around for lots in the vicinity of the plant and within easy access to the employees' routes of travel, you will have to determine the number of employees wishing to take advantage of such facilities. You will also have to determine, in case only limited space is available, what employees should be given preference. If adequate space is found, should any employees have reserved places?

Construct a questionnaire, including a covering letter, to be sent to all employees in the plant to determine the number of employees who would benefit from the proposed free parking facilities. The results of your questionnaire should tell you:

(1) How the employees now commute to and from the plant
(2) Whether or not these commuting habits change with the seasons or with the weather
(3) Whether or not these commuting habits would change if free parking facilities were available
(4) Whether or not car pools are now being used
(5) Whether or not there are any handicapped employees now commuting
(6) Any other information you feel is vital to the problem

9. Assume that you work for the Department of Licenses of Metropolitan City. From the following disorganized statement, make a topical outline for a report to the Commissioner:

The Department of Licenses consists of a Main Office and seven District Offices.

Four years ago, a uniform loose-leaf procedure manual was adopted for all offices. Since that time changes in the manual have been issued in the form of procedure bulletins, not designed to fit the manual.

Six months ago a management consultant recommended that the sending out of these bulletins be discontinued in favor of issuing new pages in the manual to accommodate the changes, but nothing has been done. Mr. Darrell Forster, the Commissioner of Licenses, has now asked you to look into the situation. You agree with the consultant's recommendation and believe the time has come to put it into effect.

Your own investigation has revealed many faults in the present system:

(1) The Chester District Office files the bulletins under several different headings, but it is often necessary to look under more than one heading to find a given bulletin.
(2) There is no way of "killing" obsolete bulletins.
(3) Procedure bulletins received in the District Offices are issued by six different individuals in the Main Office and some are even received from other District Managers.
(4) The Colby District Office has started a partial index because the bulletins often deal with a number of different subjects.
(5) Confusion in finding specific procedures is rampant.

Recommend that all changes in District Office procedures be routed through Mr. Charles Boling of the Main Office, who will serve as a central clearing agency for changes. Mr. Boling will coordinate any new instructions with existing procedures and release them in the form of additional papers or pages for substitution in the loose-leaf procedure manual.

10. National Business Publications is an association of publishers of business newspapers and magazines. Some time ago it appointed a Committee on Advertising Sales to discover ways in which a salesman can use his company's business-paper advertising to his best advantage. Inquiries on the subject were sent to a number of top-notch salesmen. Eleven answers were received. The Committee on Advertising Sales now wishes to prepare for the guidance of other salesmen a distillation of the experiences reported. The tentative title of the report is "How a Salesman Can Use His Company's Business-Publication Advertising."

Guided solely by the salesmen's replies, which are quoted below, write an outline for the National Business Publications' report:[4]

THE REPLIES

"Before I make a swing through my territory, I pick out reprints of suitable ads and send them along with a reproduction of my own picture on a note sheet on which I write each prospect about when I'll be in town and that I'll call him for an appointment. Sometimes I add a note, perhaps right on the reprint itself, pointing out something the ad says that I want him particularly to notice because I want to bear down on that point when I see him."

"I carry a complete line of reprints and I know pretty well which one helps me the most in nailing down certain points so I can snatch one out of my brief case any time I need it so the prospect can see what I'm talking about in addition to hearing me say it."

"After each sales call I always write a little personal note thanking the man for the interview and attaching an appropriate reprint or two, maybe checking off some of the points in the ads to remind him of what we talked about."

"Sometimes when I'm showing reprints of our ads to a prospect or a customer, I show him a list of the trade papers they run in and tell him about the terrific response we're getting from the advertising. I don't lay it on too thick, but sometimes he gets the point that a lot of companies are buying our equipment and getting its advantages. Some of those companies are competitors of his and he doesn't want to be the only one in the business using an inferior product."

"The roughest part of selling our service is getting an interview with a top management man in a good company. Analyzing my volume-cost breakdown, it was obvious that I wasn't making enough presentations to warm prospects. I set out to mail no less than 50 advertising reprints each week but am stepping up the pace to double that figure.

"I take the reprint or tear sheet, put Rightman's name across the left-hand corner in longhand, and enclose it in a good quality envelope (I use Southworth Bond—cost 1¢ more each but the crispness and crinkle seem to add to the importance of the contents). I put no return address on the envelope.

"These are addressed to my prospects, in each case starting with the top man. If, after a few weeks the president hasn't returned the coupon, I go back

[4] The quotations are from a survey made by *Printers' Ink*. Used by permission.

through my list again (my list shows the names and dates of all reprints sent out) and mail to the next executive at that firm.

"My returns (coupons sent in asking for the analysis offered in the ad) have been better than 6%. My last 5 or 6 sales have been to principals who wrote in response to my reprint mailings, and there are at least 6 or 8 other firms that have had a presentation as a result of the mailings and are still very much alive for future business.

"Compared to the telephone, this approach has many aspects I like. Prospects receive the analysis and a letter from New York, and both of them give a far better impression than anyone could get across in just the first sentence or two on the phone. The ad reprint offers him something of value 'free for nothing,' and he can read its 'sell' copy at his own leisure and pace. I have yet to find a single prospect who received the analysis who was not favorably impressed with it and so had an open mind for what follows when I arrive."

"When I do my case planning before making calls, I first figure out the main points I want to get across on that call and then go through my collection of ad reprints and pick out ads that do a good job of illustrating or dramatizing the main points I want to register. I use the suitable ones as sort of sales aids during my call and then sometimes leave them to help keep the impressions alive after my call."

"Sometimes I ask a customer's or prospect's opinion of our advertising. I'll go through some reprints with him and try to get him to tell me if he finds the information interesting and useful and what else he might like to see in the ads or what he thinks other men with job responsibilities like his might like to know about our product if they were interested at the time they saw one of our ads. This I usually do only with customers or prospects that I've gotten to know pretty well. I found that it not only helps register points about our product with them, but every now and then we get a darn good idea that I pass along to the advertising department."

"I try to set up a schedule of reprint mailings to go out between one sales call and the next. Even in cases where I know he has gotten reprints from headquarters, I'll put reprints in my follow-up and send him another one every week or so with a very brief note reminding him of one or another of the sales points I tried to get into his head when I was there last."

"I hit on an idea by accident. I'd forgotten to take reprints one time and during the call I had the feeling I wasn't getting my basic idea across. Since I didn't have a reprint with me I looked around the prospect's office and saw a copy of one of the magazines our advertising appears in. I picked it up and opened to our ad and said, 'Look, here it is right in your own magazine and here's the illustration that shows how this feature works.' The man responded so well, maybe because he saw the story right there in his own magazine that he reads all the time and has respect for, it helped me almost as much as if it was a third party telling it. So now, even though I carry reprints, I always look around the prospect's office and if I spot a business paper that has our ad in it, I'll pick it up and talk from that. If not, I'll use a reprint, although where it's possible I carry copies of recent issues with our ads in them and use those in preference to reprints. That's pretty hard to do because we're in so many magazines, but you'd be surprised how often I find the trade paper I'm looking for, or if it isn't in his office sometimes I'll ask and he'll have his secretary get it."

"I study my competitor's advertising and whenever I can find a reprint of one of our own that does a better job on the same ideas, I send that along to him, usually after a sales call because it's during the sales calls that I begin to get some idea of how much of the competitor's story he believes and what kind of impression competitive advertising is making on him."

"My company sends out reprints to my customers and prospects right from headquarters, but they always attach a note or card with my name on it. However, there are a few key companies in my territory that I've asked headquarters to keep off the master promotion list because I always want to send individual reprints myself with suitable notes that help me make my main points."

10
Putting Reports in Final Form

If you have followed the instructions in the preceding chapter, you are now ready for the climactic step in the preparation of the report—the actual composition. This step is initiated with the writing of a draft of the entire report and is concluded with the final typing and proofreading of the finished product.

If you can use a typewriter, you will probably find it most satisfactory to type the draft on letter-size sheets, leaving wide margins and space between the lines for corrections and insertions. Otherwise, you will write out the draft by hand on a legal-size pad. The draft will conform to the outline you are presumably working from, with the headings and subheadings of the report paralleling the topics and subtopics of the outline.

When the draft is completed, you should lay it aside for a few days, if possible, so that you may come back to it with a fresh mind. Then you will read it through to make sure that it is complete, orderly, and well-reasoned. You may decide that here and there a point needs strengthening, perhaps through rephrasing or through the addition of details. In other instances, you may find minor points that can stand deletion or condensation. This is the time, also, to see that spelling, grammar, and punctuation are correct, and that the phrasing is clear and concise. Such attentions are required by any kind of writing; the report, however, imposes special problems in both the treatment of the data and the language.

TREATMENT OF DATA

As you work from the outline, you will become increasingly aware that it is just the dry bones of the report. To flesh out the skeleton, you will have to draw on the information you have collected in your research, going back to your notes and your other stored experiences. At the same time, you will have to apply your imagination and skill to the problem of molding the data into the shape you desire.

Use of Details

General terms weaken a report because they do not provide an adequate basis for analysis and decision making. If your research has been thorough, you should be able to supply specific details. Compare:

GENERAL	SPECIFIC
Only a small number of the final assembly items in stock account for a major portion of sales revenue.	At present there are approximately 450 final assembly items in stock. Nineteen of these items accounted for 76 per cent of the sales revenue during the first quarter of the fiscal year.
During the year, our employees actively supported our safety program.	The Pensacola plant continued to operate under an effective safety program. During the year it passed 17,106,186 man-hours without a lost-time accident.
Higher costs are being offset by a vigorous cost reduction program and constant efforts to improve production methods.	For the entire year the cost reduction program achieved savings of $7,000,000. These savings were made in such ways as (1) improved mechanical methods of material handling, (2) more efficient layout of equipment and utilization of floor space, (3) improved maintenance to reduce time equipment is shut down, and (4) more effective processes and formulations.

Interpretation of Data

Even specific details can be singularly uninformative. What gives them meaning is the way you select and relate them and generalize from them. By the time you start writing, you have probably already arrived at certain conclusions and subconclusions. In an analytical report especially, but in many primarily informational reports as well, it is your function to point up the significance of your data by drawing inferences. The details in the first paragraph below would be meaningless without the statement of cause and effect in the second paragraph.

The volume of current documents relating to accounts payable transactions consists of approximately 1,000 invoices for which 350 checks are written and

1,200 accounting distributions are made each month. The checks are made payable to an estimated 250 suppliers. Thus some suppliers are receiving more than one check per month. Of the 1,000 invoices, about 10 per cent are subject to discount on ten-day terms while most of the remaining 90 per cent are payable net in thirty days.

The present method for processing accounts payable documents involves accumulating invoices for approximately one week, writing checks for the accumulated invoices and recording the accounting distribution as the checks are written. This handling method fails to provide a systematic correlation of transactions with accounting periods. There is also the possibility of paying suppliers earlier than is necessary and writing several checks to one supplier during a month when one check would suffice.

In the following passage, also, note the use of reasoning to support the prediction regarding the growth of multi-family dwellings in and around the New York Metropolitan Area:

The Regional trend of housing construction indicates that a large proportion of the Regional housing stock will consist of multi-family or apartment units. The major share of future population growth which is expected to occur within the Core and the more densely inhabited Inner Ring counties will probably reside in medium and high density housing units. The Outer Ring suburban counties will also continue to show substantial gains in the construction of apartments. As the amount of developable land diminishes throughout the Region, the demand for multi-family housing will push hard against existing single family zoning provisions in almost every portion of the Region. Land scarcity and its increasing cost is the key factor in the trend towards multi-family housing, and results from factors such as the rapid increase in households, the major job concentration in the Region's Core, and limitations of the commuter transportation network.—*Port of New York Authority*

Persuasiveness

Closely linked to the use of details and the interpretation of report data is the quality of persuasiveness. Any link between cause and effect, any attempt to explain the significance of a fact or figure, tends to increase confidence in the report. Confidence may also be developed by the amount and kind of data presented, the credibility of the data sources, and the promises of savings or other improvement implicit in the recommendations.

Inimical to confidence is any omission of essential data or the glossing over of contrary evidence. Thus a report that recommends costly "improvements" without first showing the faults of the present system will raise doubts about the need for change. So, too, a report that predicts a dramatic increase in the volume of company records and advocates a doubling of filing space to take care of the projected increase will raise considerable skepticism if it does not also explore the possibility of using microfilm or other new space-saving filing technology.

Because of the need for objectivity in a report, one may rightfully question the use of persuasion to influence the response. A defense of the practice may be made as follows: The reporter, in engaging in his investigation, does not set out to find support for any point of view; his mission is solely to discover the facts and to draw valid conclusions from them. Once he has made his investigation and reached his conclusions, however, he is interested in having his findings accepted by the reader, first, because he would not be discharging his responsibilities if he did not present the case as persuasively as the facts warranted and, second, because he will lose status if his findings do not win the support of his superiors. So, then, the reporter must take the role of an objective investigator and analyst and at the same time try as hard as he can, within the limits imposed by his position of trust, to win acceptance of his work.

The report shown in Figure 10-10 (pages 304–323) is notable for its use of reasoning to instill conviction. This is especially evident in the section on "Special Events" (beginning on page 9 of the report), where the analyst shows how a charging procedure upsets the pricing formula for meals served to employees. The reasoning used here shows keen perception and is therefore convincing.

The report from which the following excerpt is taken gains persuasiveness from the reference to the demonstration and testimony by prospective users of the device in question.

> Miss Dorothy Mazzoli, account representative of the vendor, demonstrated the capabilities of the verifier adapter to the satisfaction of those present. Mrs. Daly was able to perform normal key punching and verifying operations with little instruction from Miss Mazzoli.
>
> The device allows an 029 key punch to perform all of the functions of an 059 verifier with one exception. The 059 automatically verifies leading zeros on fields that are so identified on the program control card. These zeros must be verified by individual key strokes when the verifier adapter is installed. Miss Davison indicated this would not be a major problem.

In another report, the following section is particularly disarming because the writer seems to have explored a number of avenues of inquiry that, if not considered, could be detrimental to the success of the policy the reporter has advocated.

> I have looked over the Securities and Exchange Commission and New York Stock Exchange rulings and our own company's general policy on credit extensions and have verified that nothing in the proposed system would violate any of them. I have also spoken to our cash clerks and have their word that the plan is feasible.

```
If the proposed system is accepted, there will be an
added expense of sending telegrams to customers.  We will
also have to allow some of the cash clerks to work over-
time to keep up with the added bookkeeping.  I feel, how-
ever, that both of these expenses will be liberally
repaid by the reduction in outstanding debits.  We are
now being charged 7¼ per cent interest on our net debit
by the Home Office.  If, as I believe, the new system re-
duces our debits, our interest charges will also be re-
duced.
```

Human Interest

Many reports are intended for audiences with only a limited technical interest in the subject. It is essential that these reports, especially, engage their readers with details and sidelights of broad appeal. In the following excerpt from a report to stockholders, the use of a direct quotation, including an apt analogy, adds interest, and the figures in the last paragraph dramatize the success of the company's objective.

> When building in developing countries, an objective is to put operating responsibility into the hands of local nationals as quickly as possible. It's not uncommon for a plant to be built in an area where every employee must be trained in a skill for which he has had little or no background. Abilities in cutting cane or planting rice—or tending goats—are of little value in the operation of a modern electrode plant.
>
> "They're diligent and eager to learn," says an engineer who has served at a number of overseas facilities. "But you just have to realize that often there is little in their background to prepare them in modern mechanical skills.
>
> "Put it this way. It's like going into an area where people have played soccer all their lives, and try to organize a first-rate basketball squad. What is amazing is that in a comparatively short time, we find we have skilled welders and pipefitters and operators who work as though they'd been doing it all their lives."
>
> The proof: less than one in 200 of Union Carbide's more than 43,000 overseas employees is an American.

Through the use of an example, the following paragraphs from a government report gain points for both persuasion and interest.

> Generally speaking, those who proclaim with vehemence that railroads are "shackled" with the "heavy hand of regulation" and who demand more freedom of managerial discretion for railroads are the ones who protest most vigorously when action is taken by railroads to improve their income or cut down expenses. Apparently, their reaction depends on whose ox is gored.
>
> On one occasion, for example, a parking charge of $5 per month was imposed by a railroad for the use of space near the stations for the convenience of commuters. Letters of indignation and protest came from the staffs of brokers, bankers, advertising agencies and national periodicals. Their sentiments did

not correspond with previously expressed statements, editorials and propaganda from their own organizations that railroads would have no problems if they were given more freedom to exercise their own judgment. In fact, these people were disappointed to learn that the Commission could not interfere. Unless their announced philosophy is supported by consistent positive action, the prospect of a quick solution to the commuter problem is extremely dim.—*Interstate Commerce Commission, Docket No. 31954*

LANGUAGE

The language of the report must be carefully selected, not only to clarify ideas, but also to influence the attitude of the reader toward the report and you.

Self-Reference

Writing a report almost invariably raises questions about the degree to which you inject yourself into the narrative and the way you refer to yourself when the need arises. Will you refer to yourself as *I* or *we*, or *the writer*, or will you avoid referring to yourself altogether? Much depends on the nature of the report, your position with relation to the reader, the traditions of your organization, and your own feelings about yourself.

In an informal report written as a letter or memorandum, the use of the pronoun *I* gives the report a commendable directness.

> When *I* called on Mr. Crawford, he told *me* he had received many complaints about the new gaskets.
>
> If the rim of the loading pit was widened about two inches, less refuse would fall to the ground as the trucks are loaded. *I* would also suggest that the cleats in the pit be lowered about two inches to permit the corresponding lowering of the cans into the pit.

A formal report often employs the pronoun *I* when the writer holds a position of some authority. He may be the president of the company, a department head, a public official, or a recognized authority in his field.

> *I* concur heartily with the unanimous recommendation of the State Conference Board of Farm Organizations as to the need for more agricultural research, including laboratory facilities with climate control. *My* financial program will include funds for the establishment of a model climate control project.
>
> On behalf of the Board Directors, *I* am pleased to express our appreciation for the cooperation of our customers and the loyal service rendered by our employees.

A report written jointly by a group or on behalf of a group will refer to the signers, as *we, the Committee, the Commission, the Board, etc.*

> *We* have stated on many occasions that *we* would not impair safety, or reduce standards of service, or cut service merely to keep down operating costs.

> *The Committee* is unanimously of the opinion that all concessions should be let as the result of competitive bidding, except under special circumstances which should be carefully regulated.

In other formal reports, the writer may refer to himself as *we* or—less personally—as *the writer, the investigator, the analyst,* or *your reporter.* He can also avoid the issue by using such impersonal constructions as *investigation showed* and *it is fair to conclude.* In this respect, the use of the passive voice is helpful. Compare:

> *Personal:* I believe
> *Impersonal:* It is believed

> *Personal:* We propose three flexible alternatives
> *Impersonal:* Three flexible alternatives are proposed

A legitimate reason for avoiding the use of *I* or *we* is the desire to preserve an atmosphere of objectivity, though it must be admitted that these personal pronouns give the style a smoothness and simplicity not otherwise possible. Compare:

> *It is recommended* that a program be undertaken to train all supervisors in cost conservation techniques.
>
> *The writer recommends* that a program be undertaken to train all supervisors in cost conservation techniques.
>
> *We recommend* that a program be undertaken to train all supervisors in cost conservation techniques.
>
> *I recommend* that a program be undertaken to train all supervisors in cost conservation techniques.

Word Choice

The fact that the subject of a report is somewhat formidable occasionally encourages the writer to adopt an equally formidable vocabulary. Whatever the author's desire to impress the reader with his fund of long words, the reader's interests require clarity and reading ease. These qualities are best obtained when the language is concrete. Even if words cannot always be simple, they can be exact and alive. The following writing is unnecessarily heavy because of the number of long and abstract words:

> The attainment of organizational goals is the sum of the efforts of individual segments of the organization. Responsibility reporting is one approach to obtaining information on the progress of individual units toward the attainment of overall organizational goals.
>
> Extensive operations due to decentralization or large-scale centralization require a focusing of management attention on the individual units. Utilization of

personnel, equipment, and funds is the measure of the success of the organization.

The language in the following statement is more definite and more meaningful:

> During the past ten years there has been a steady increase in the indirect cost of doing business throughout American industry. This fact has caused alarm particularly among those manufacturers who are forced to meet the competition of European and South American producers. The managements of European enterprises have somehow been able to operate their plants at a much lower ratio of indirect salaries and expenses to direct cost than their American counterparts, enabling them to capture an increasing share of the American markets on the basis of lower selling prices.
>
> Realizing the seriousness of the situation, many domestic companies have reexamined their organizational structures and operating costs with a view to reducing the cost of their products and securing for themselves a better competitive position. One of the more productive tools for this purpose is responsibility reporting. This is a method by which indirect expenses may be effectively controlled by pinpointing these expenses at specific individuals in charge of definite subdivisions of the business.

A report intended for general distribution must necessarily be written in plain, nontechnical language. The following paragraphs are part of a report on the Bell Telephone System's role in moon exploration.

> The moon is not a friendly place for a pilot. As the Apollo 8 astronauts uneasily observed, . . . the surface of the moon is almost colorless and offers none of the floral contrasts of light and dark we are familiar with on earth. To cut the chances of pilot error, astronauts at least would have to see craters and other large features on the moon in relief, by shadows. Mission planners therefore decided that a landing should be made just after dawn on the lunar surface when the sun was between 6 and 20 degrees above the horizon. They chose lunar dawn so the astronauts would not remain on the lunar surface into the lunar night, and because at dawn the sun would be at the astronauts' back rather than shining in their eyes.
>
> Although there are desirable lighting conditions on any particular landing site only one day in the lunar month, there are eight days in each month when lighting is suitable for a landing at some point along the 90-degree-wide Apollo Zone. If only one landing site per mission were picked, landing opportunities would be limited to one day a month. Because problems in the countdown or illness among the astronauts could force a delay of a full month, it made sense to take advantage of the eight-day "landing window" by picking more than one possible landing site for the early missions. . . . Bellcomm people working on landing site selection realized the full implications of the fact that moving the launch day entails moving the landing site.

Sentence and Paragraph Structure

A ponderous style is often the result of poor planning of sentences and paragraphs. If the structure is verbose and involved, it slows down reading and makes comprehension difficult. Business and professional people, no less than mass audiences, respond favorably to writing that is considerate of their energies. Even if an executive *must* read a badly written report, he is likely to resent the imposition.

The style of the following paragraph makes for hard reading. The two sentences have 38 and 28 words respectively, and both are excessively involved.

> The company expedites the sale of farm fence throughout its marketing area by promoting and encouraging the conservation of soil resources by means of crop rotation and better land use, both of which are facilitated by stockproof fencing. The flexibility of the company's facilities, which is a basic requirement for the manufacture of steel and wire to precision specifications has been developed over a long period.

Following is a much more readable paragraph from a report on a related subject. The five sentences average 18 words. All are reasonably simple in structure:

> Our program for improved methods took another major step forward with the start of construction on a 3,000-ton per day self-fluxing sinter plant at Chicago. This plant will be large enough to process about 80 per cent of our iron ore needs for the Chicago facilities. Ground for the plant was broken before the strike closed our Chicago operations. It is expected to be in production late next year. Self-flexing sinter is a combination of fine iron ores and limestone, and is much superior to available natural ores as a blast furnace feed.

The paragraphs below are taken from the draft of a report on cost control. Their wordiness and lack of organization hide the sense.

> The basic objective of the program is to assist management in reducing and controlling clerical costs. Broadly speaking, reduction in clerical costs is achieved through simplication of the operations performed and measurement of the work involved in daily routines. In this manner, unnecessary work is eliminated and substandard employee efficiency is highlighted together with the reasons for such inefficiency.
>
> Since the program is designed to provide a continuing mechanism for achieving performance improvements and maintaining good levels of performance, the savings achieved will be obtained every year in the foreseeable future. In this manner, the program affords management the means of insuring continued clerical cost control and counteracts the tendency on the part of supervisors to increase staff after completion of a "one shot" staff reduction program.

Since the program has been viewed in terms of long-range planning by management, no major emphasis has been placed during installation on improving performances in areas where efficiency is below standard. After installation of the incentive system, certain supervisors immediately set about improving performance through training and regulation of work flow while others made little or no attempt to correct the conditions leading to inefficiency. The control and reporting system will provide the basis for future evaluation of the performance of supervisors with regard to proper planning and scheduling of work flow. Other benefits are development of a sound on-the-job training program and maintenance of effective levels of clerical productivity.

Note the conciseness and increased clarity after revision. The enumeration helps considerably.

The basic aim of the program is to reduce costs by simplifying work and measuring and improving individual efficiency.

Properly administered, the system will ensure good performance and continued savings for years to come. It is designed incidentally to counteract the tendency of supervisors to increase the staff following a "one-shot" staff reduction program.

In line with our objective, efforts are being made to help supervisors in these areas:

1. Plan and schedule work flow.
2. Develop an on-the-job training program.
3. Maintain effective levels of clerical productivity.

So far the cooperation of supervisors has not been uniform. However, the program's control and reporting system provides the basis for rating them on their performance in the future.

Tone

A report is most persuasive when it treats its subject in a calm and rational manner. In Chapter 3 we discussed the difference between reports (facts) and judgments and between informative and affective language. In the interests of objectivity, the reporter is cautioned to back judgments with facts and to use informative rather than affective words. He is also well advised to maintain a detached point of view while he examines the evidence and arrives at valid conclusions. This is not a formula for dullness. Any reporter with a proper enthusiasm for his subject, an imaginative mind, and proficiency in language should—if he has done the necessary investigating—be able to write interestingly. He should also realize that interest is not only what the writer puts into the report, but what the reader brings to it. The following paragraphs show how the positive qualities mentioned can be combined to produce a report that is both convincing and interesting:

The future of the Ace Chemical Company depends on a successful continuing research program. Throughout the company, management personnel with

> whom we spoke recognized this factor and its importance from both a short-term and long-term standpoint. Our own experience and observations confirm the significance of this function in the chemical industry.
>
> Statements of responsible leaders among such outstanding companies as Du Pont, Union Carbide, and Allied Chemical describe the very high percentage of profits resulting from products that were developed in the last ten to fifteen years. Recognition of the importance of research is evident in the sizable research budgets of these companies. It appears that 3 per cent of sales is usual among industrial chemical companies, and the drug companies exceed that figure with expenditures as high as 8 per cent of sales.
>
> It follows, therefore, that an industrial chemical company must match this research effort simply to maintain its position. To do less is to risk the comparatively rapid obsolescene of its product line and the resultant loss of sales and earnings. In the case of Ace Chemical, its present size and goals of expansion demand a greater than "average" effort in research.

In contrast, emotion-laden words and unsupported assertions reveal the reporter's bias. Writing like the following may confirm the belief of sympathizers in the cause, but is less effective in convincing those on the sidelines:

> The low tariff policies followed by the U.S. under the Trade Agreement Act have finally caught up with us. Foreign manufacturers, paying wages far below even the U.S. legal minimum wage, and insuring high productivity by using the latest, most efficient machinery in many cases provided by the Marshall Plan and subsequent giveaway programs, are able to best American manufacturers in our home market as well as abroad—wherever there is enough labor employed to make a significant difference in the cost of the finished product. There is no other conclusion to draw from these data.
>
> Now the Administration proposes drastically to accelerate this frightening trend by the immediate further reduction and eventual elimination of import duties on most manufactured products. To accomplish this, various arguments are used—some uninformed, some purposefully misleading.

In reports of less public significance, the writer sometimes colors his findings by similar displays of prejudice or partiality:

> It is obvious that these employees have been getting away with murder for a long time. They come in when they like, loaf all day, and then expect a full day's pay.

> The results of the experiment were absolutely amazing. Housewives everywhere told us that Duro-Suds were the best detergent they had ever tried. We are certainly encouraged about the prospects for repeat sales.

Here again are examples of a report style that avoids extremes of feeling, gives a balanced treatment, and emphasizes facts and reasons:

The recent demonstrations by the United Workers Union, in protest against shift changes, have ended. While the problems with the Union have not been fully resolved, I am pleased to report that there have been some tangible, long-range gains for the Company in the events thus far. For the first time, picketing and other Union activities in violation of an existing agreement have been stopped by a court order. The firm stand taken by the local management with respect to the new working schedules has further strengthened the Company's right to assign the working forces to meet the workload.

The truck performed best in District 38 where the volume of refuse is heavy and is put out for collection in large cans. While working in this district, the truck ran three loads a day. The truck was less efficient in District 40 where there are many small houses and refuse is put out in small pails and paper bags. Here it ran only two loads a day.

In some months more errors were made in the air-conditioned area than in the non-air-conditioned. At the same time, there was an average 0.9 per cent decrease in errors per person per month in the control area—a figure which is for all practical purposes identical with the average in the test area and does not permit reaching any definite conclusions. In this particular operation, accuracy is more important than production. If an employee has an abnormal number of errors per year he is assigned to less exacting duties, so it is safe to assume that all employees keep their errors to a minimum and that the percentage of errors, regardless of working conditions, is fairly constant.—*General Services Administration*

Mr. Blair was absent on January 29 and February 1 because of a virus infection, on June 24 to attend his brother's graduation from college, on October 25 for a cold, and on December 7 for food poisoning. During the past year, also, he has been between five and twenty minutes late to work on an average of twice a month. On several occasions he had to be spoken to about wearing sports shirts while on duty and once for reporting for work without a jacket. To his credit, he is extremely friendly in greeting customers—his fellow workers are especially conscious of this fact because his voice carries well—and we have been able to trace several new accounts to recommendations of customers he serves regularly.

CONCLUSIONS AND RECOMMENDATIONS

For many reports, the conclusions and recommendations are the writer's most important contribution. These should follow logically from the data and not encompass more than the purpose of the report or the facts warrant. They will be even more convincing if they are stated with restraint. The business reader usually responds well to the force of reason and logic, but he does not want to be pressured into accepting ideas for which he has not been adequately prepared. Phrases like "It is obvious that," "You must," and "No other course is open to us except" are usually indicative of forced and inadequately supported conclusions. A more rational approach is suggested by such phrases as these:

> We believe that . . .
> On the strength of the evidence, it seems fair to conclude that . . .
> The facts point to . . .
> A careful study of the alternatives leads to the following recommendations.

The following conclusions were excerpted from a report inquiring into the possible use of regional bank depositories by a large chemical company (for other parts of the same report, see Figures 10-2 to 10-9). In effect, the conclusions summarize and emphasize the practical significance of what has already been covered extensively in the body of the report.

CONCLUSIONS

Regional depositories are used effectively by many large companies. As this study shows, the main advantages of the plan are (1) improved cash flow, (2) faster credit approval, (3) reduced clerical work, and (4) better customer relations. The most serious objection to the plan comes from companies with a high volume of checks in small amounts, a condition that results in costly service charges unless large compensating balances are kept on deposit. In the case of Ace, however, billings are in sufficiently large amounts to present no problem in this regard.

There is no general system that will fit all companies. For that reason all the banks that offer the plan make it flexible and in most instances tailor it to fit the exact needs of each company. Care must be taken, however, to avoid making the plan too complicated and costly.

Institution of the plan at Ace would require some internal changes. They would consist of planning some way to indicate on the invoice where the check should be mailed, planning for receipts of remittance advices and posting by Accounts Receivable, and arranging for the proper reports to be made to the Treasurer and the Accounting Department.

When recommendations are offered, it is usually necessary to show the reader how they will bring about the desired results. The recommendations quoted below perform this task.

RECOMMENDATIONS

The present procedure and forms are adequate to provide for the accountability of returned goods transactions. However, a few minor revisions can simplify the procedure and reduce the paperwork. The changes we recommend are listed below:

1. Customer service should retain one copy of the receiving report at the time of preparation rather than routing its copy through the sales office and production control.

2. The sales office should prepare the typed credit memos directly from the receiving report copy or from customer correspondence and forward all four copies of the credit memo to accounting. The receiving report copy can be retained by the sales office in lieu of the credit memo notice now being retained.

3. Accounting should verify that the credit memo is issued for items originally purchased by the customer by checking the billing or accounts receivable files. An audit of each transaction can be performed at any time by matching the credit memo with the receiving report copy on file in receiving.

4. Credit memos should not be prepared for goods returned for repair or exchange because such transactions do not reduce the customers' liability to the company. Physical inventory records can be accurately maintained for exchange transactions by reducing the inventory from the receiving report copies and requiring customer service to prepare a production report on repaired items going back into inventory as replacement for the items sent to the customer in exchange.

The recommended revisions of the returned goods handling procedure will reduce the handling required to complete each transaction and eliminate the credit memo form prepared by the sales office. They will also permit verification of the accountability for each transaction in all of the major functions attending the processing of returned goods.

"PACKAGING" THE REPORT

In writing a report, you should keep in mind its ultimate form. There are certain minimal requirements. The report should look attractive, and the physical parts should be arranged for the greatest convenience to the reader. Where possible, data should be put in tables, graphs, maps, and other visual forms; and headings and subheadings should serve as guides to the text. The report may also call for such adjuncts as a title page, a letter of transmittal, and a bibliography. The collective components of reports may be classified as the preliminaries, the text, and the reference matter.

Preliminaries

The introductory parts of reports vary widely in kind and content. These are the most common:

COVER

A cover not only enhances the appearance of the report, but also protects the pages from soiling or crumpling. The cover should contain at least the title of the report. It may also bear the name and title of the writer, the name of the organization for whom it was prepared, and the date. If a clear plastic cover is used, the title page should show through (Figure 10-3).

LETTER OF TRANSMITTAL

The letter of transmittal formally conveys the report to the person who authorized it or is expected to act on it. As an introductory letter it may include data that would otherwise be placed in a preface or introduction (Figure 10-1). As a "covering letter" it may serve simply as a record of the submission of the report (Figure 10-2).

TITLE PAGE

The title page again names the report and may also include any of the other information indicated for the cover (Figure 10-3).

TABLE OF CONTENTS

The table of contents lists, with page references, the prefatory material that follows it as well as the parts of the text and the bibliography, appendices, and exhibits (Figure 10-4).

SUMMARY OR ABSTRACT

For the convenience of the reader, many long reports contain a summary or abstract of the principal findings. The abstract should reflect the tone of the text and maintain the same perspective (see "Abstracts," page 357).

PREFACE

The preface, if one is used, may tell how the report came about, what use is expected to be made of it, and who helped in its preparation. Occasionally, the preface consists of an appreciation of the report contributed by some person, not the writer of the report, with a particular interest in the subject.

Text

The text will usually include all the substance represented in the formal outline of the report.

INTRODUCTION

Unless the material has already been covered in the letter of transmittal or the preface, the introduction will indicate the auspices of the report, its purpose and scope, problems encountered, sources of information, methods of re-

May 8, 19--

Mr. Alfred C. Congers, Treasurer
Protective Insurance Company
400 Madison Avenue
New York, NY 10022

Dear Mr. Congers:

This report, undertaken at your request, represents my analysis of all the check forms currently used throughout the company.

The objective of the analysis was to determine any deficiencies in the present forms and propose recommendations for new forms. Cost reduction was to be a prime consideration.

For my study, I relied chiefly on personal interviews with check vendors, check users, and our Purchasing Agent. In addition, I examined our Purchasing Department files for information relating to check specifications and costs, and our inventory control records for figures on check consumption.

As the report shows, a saving of $12,000 a year can be effected in processing and printing checks through standardization of the design and format.

Should you have any questions about the contents of this report, I shall be glad to discuss them with you at any time.

Very truly yours,

Walter North

Walter North

WN:djd

search, cooperating agencies, and the like. It may also summarize the conclusions and recommendations or give them in full. (Figures 10-5 through 10-7.)

BODY

The body describes the results of the investigation and provides support for the conclusions and recommendations. It usually constitutes the bulk of the report. (Figures 10-8 and 10-9.)

CONCLUSIONS AND RECOMMENDATIONS

Analytical reports invariably offer the writer's conclusions based on his study of the data presented in the report. The conclusions are supplemented in many instances by specific recommendations for action. If the conclusions and recommendations have already been stated fully in the introduction, they are omitted here.

Reference Matter

In addition to the parts already described, many reports include related material for reference purposes.

APPENDIX

Research data too detailed or abstruse for inclusion in the body of the report may be included in one or more appendixes. Occasionally, the main text of the report consists wholly of the writer's conclusions, while all of the data are appended. This system appeals to the reader who is not particularly interested in the details of the investigation but wants the assurance that the spadework has been done and that he can refer to the facts if his curiosity is sufficiently aroused.

EXHIBITS

When tables, charts, and graphs are limited in number, they are best placed in conjunction with the related text. When, however, there is danger that the exhibits will swamp the text, those that can be conveniently separated should be placed in the back of the report. A distinction should be made between "spot tables," which are an integral part of the text, and "reference tables," which appear independently on the text pages or in the appendix. The reference tables as well as other independent exhibits should be referred to in the text and be labeled and numbered. For assistance in preparing tables and charts, see Chapter 12, "Graphic Presentation."

Bibliography

The bibliography is a list of books, articles, and other reference sources used in researching the report. The documentation of specific statements in the text should be made in footnotes. For the mechanics of the bibliography and footnotes, see Style Manual, Rule 35.

FIG. 10-1. *Letter of transmittal that doubles as an introduction to the report.*

In Figure 10-10 (pages 304–323), you will find an example of a complete business report with appended exhibits. The organization of this report was discussed on pages 269–270. Figures 10-2 to 10-9, already referred to, contain parts of a longer and more comprehensive report. They will be found on pages 296–303.

THE LIBRARY PAPER

The point was made earlier that many business reports require library research, and some guides to the use of library sources were offered. In the writing of such a report, the question of whether you will refer to yourself in the first person is not likely to come up because you are dealing exclusively with materials supplied by others. In other respects, the style and tone of the library report do not differ materially from those of other long-form reports. It is inevitable, however, that documentation with footnotes and a bibliography will play a more important role. Another point to keep in mind is that some of the formats suggested for internal business reports will not apply; however, any logical organization based on the general order of introduction-body-conclusion is sure to be satisfactory.

Many business students have limited personal experience in business and may find it difficult to obtain the information required for reports on the internal operations of an organization. For that reason, they may wish to demonstrate their report writing skills by developing a library paper. Part of such a paper is shown in Figure 10-11 on pages 324–334.

SUMMARY

Using the outline as a guide, the writer should compose a draft of the report and then, if possible, put it aside for a few days before editing it for content and phrasing.

The report should be specific in its use of detail, and an attempt should be made to draw inferences from the facts so that their significance will be apparent. Although the reporter's role is not that of an advocate, he must be persuasive in his logic and use of data; otherwise, his report will not win acceptance and he will lose the confidence of the reader. Interest in reports intended for a general readership can be heightened through human sidelights, the translation of statistics into familiar terms, and the use of apt quotations and concrete examples.

In an informal report or in one coming from a recognized authority in the field, the use of the pronoun *I* is recommended for its directness. Reports written on behalf of a committee will often employ the pronoun *we*. In other reports, especially investigative reports written for one's superiors, the writer may also refer to himself as *we* or, less commonly, as *the writer* or *the analyst*. Or he may avoid references to himself entirely by using the passive construction as in, "The recommendation is made that . . ." In other respects, the language should be specific and reasonably simple for the audience intended. Sentence and paragraph length should be controlled and the structure concise and coherent. The writer's bias, if he has any, should not be evident in the language or in the slanting of data; instead, the presentation should be balanced and impartial. Any conclusions and recommendations should be the objective outgrowth of the investigation, as reported, and not a reflection of the writer's sympathies. Depending on its length and degree of formality, the finished report may have, in addition to an introduction, body, and conclusion, such features as a cover, letter of transmittal, title page, table of contents, summary or abstract, preface, and an appendix, exhibits, and a bibliography. Although reports should be developed inductively (facts to conclusion), it is now common to serve the reader's convenience by putting the conclusions and recommendations, or a summary of them, ahead of the supporting data.

Some accommodations in arrangement have to be made for the paper based on library research, as opposed to firsthand investigation, but the same objective tone is generally maintained. The library paper also requires close attention to documentation in the form of footnotes and a bibliography.

SAMPLE REPORTS

The sample reports are Figs. 10–2 to 10–9, pages 296–303, Proposed Use of Regional Bank Depositories by Ace Chemical Company (selected pages); Fig. 10–11, pages 304–323, Operational Audit of the Cafeteria Unit, Eastwood Branch, Consolidated Machine Company; and Fig. 10–12, pages 324–339, Advertising's Golden Decade, 1919–1929 (library paper; part of body omitted).

NOTE: *Problems for Chapter 10 begin on page 335.*

FIG. 10-2. *Transmittal letter of the "covering" type, p. 296.*

FIG. 10-3. *Title page of a business report, p. 297.*

FIG. 10-4. *Table of contents, p. 298.*

FIG. 10-5. *First page of introduction, p. 299.*

FIG. 10-6. *The introduction continued. Note the typographical treatment of the direct quotation, p. 300.*

FIG. 10-7. *The introduction concluded, p. 301.*

FIG. 10-8. *A page of the report body. Note the use of the side head, p. 302.*

FIG. 10-9. *The body continued. Here a second side head and an enumeration add attractiveness to the display, p. 303.*

FIG. 10-10. *An analytical report, complete with exhibits, pp. 304–323.*

FIG. 10-11. *Part of a report based on library research. Footnotes and the bibliography are included, pp. 324–339.*

Ace Chemical Company

Nashville, Tenn. 37203

October 27, 19--

Operations Section
Finance Department

Mr. Arthur M. Curtis, Treasurer
Ace Chemical Company
Nashville, TN 37203

Dear Mr. Curtis:

In line with our various discussions and your memorandum of April 24, I am pleased to submit my report on the "Proposed Use of Regional Bank Depositories by Ace Chemical Company."

I shall be glad to discuss with you any aspect of the report and, should you wish, implement it with a concrete plan for carrying out the recommended procedures.

Sincerely yours,

David T. Smith

David T. Smith

DTS:gb

FIG. 10-2.

PROPOSED USE OF REGIONAL BANK DEPOSITORIES

BY ACE CHEMICAL COMPANY

By

David T. Smith

Operations Section
Finance Department

October 27, 19--

FIG. 10-3.

CONTENTS

FIG. 10-4.

I

THE PROBLEM AND ITS SIGNIFICANCE TO THE COMPANY

Several months ago the Ace Chemical Company found that under the present method of handling cash receipts it was taking from three to five days to list checks, reconcile the cash report, prepare the checks for deposit, and deposit the checks to its account at the bank. This delay was in addition to mailing time for checks sent from all parts of the country.

Immediate steps were taken to correct the situation, and the delay was cut somewhat. It is a fundamental fact that money from receivables cannot begin earning until it becomes a deposit in the bank. For that reason, float time and clerical time must be held to an absolute minimum.

The system now in use is the result of several refinements put into effect during the past few months, but it is essentially the same as it has been for the past twenty-five years. Lengthy delays have been eliminated, but money is still kept out of the banks one or two days longer than necessary. Since it will be difficult to achieve further speed in handling by present

FIG. 10-5.

methods, an alternate method of handling should be examined.

A system that is being used by more and more business firms today is a banking service known as the Lock Box or Post Office Box Collection Plan. In a letter dated April 21, 19--, Mr. R. M. Collins, vice president of the Farmer's National Bank of Cleveland, wrote as follows:

> Corporate executives have recognized the value of a lock box operation as an additional source of funds for investments or for meeting obligations. The concept of a lock box operation is not new, having come into being almost fifty years ago on a rather crude scale compared to present-day practices. In recent years lock box operations have come into their own and today are accepted as an excellent means of speeding up the collection of checks, providing additional working cash, and reducing clerical work in the preparation of deposits.

At the start, some firms designated a single bank, often in or near the city in which the home office was located. The single-bank method had two great disadvantages. First, little or no time was saved in the process, so that the speed-up in cash flow was negligible. About all that was gained was the convenience of having the bank receive and process the customer's remittances. Second, a single bank handling all the receivables found itself so burdened with volume that the company was required to carry heavy compensating balances, offsetting any tangible gains in availability of funds.

FIG. 10-6.

Experience has demonstrated that best results can be obtained from the Lock Box Plan only when it is employed on a <u>regional</u> basis. Should Ace adopt a regional plan for handling deposits?

That is the problem toward which this report is directed. The purpose is to examine carefully the present method of cash handling and explore the alternate method of using Regional Depositories. Specific recommendations will be offered.

Information for this report was obtained from several banks in each region, which were able to describe the plans they offered. Through questionnaires and personal visits, companies already using the plan gave the benefit of their experience with the system.

FIG. 10-7.

III

PRESENT METHOD OF HANDLING DEPOSITS

As already noted, the present method of check and deposit handling has been in use for many years. Several working groups are involved and some duplication exists. The working groups are the Mail Department, the Cashier, the Credit Department, the Accounts Receivable Department, and the Local Bank. The entire procedure can be followed through an examination of the work done by each group in turn.

Mail Department

All mail is picked up at intervals during the day by Company trucks at the local post office. The mail is brought to the mail room and sorted. Any envelope which is marked to the attention of an individual is sent to him unopened. All mail addressed to the Company is opened and the contents scanned.

Any check contained in an envelope addressed to the Company is removed and placed in an alphabetical sorting bin and set up in strict alphabetical order. Any check reaching an individual is sent back to the mail room to be recorded on the cash report.

6

FIG. 10-8.

After the checks have been set up, they are then listed by typewriter on a Cash Report showing date of check, company name, detail, if any, and amount of check (Figure 2). An adding-machine tape is run on both the checks and the listing to verify the total. This Cash Report is prepared to give copies to the Accounting Department, Accounts Receivable, Cashier, and Credit Department.

The completed Cash Report is distributed, giving the Cashier all the checks with his copy of the report, and furnishing Accounts Receivable all accompanying detail with their copy.

<u>Cashier</u>

On receipt of the Cash Report and accompanying checks, the Cashier must look at each check for the following:

1. Is the check postdated?
2. Who is the payee?
3. Is the check signed?
4. Do the written and figure amounts agree?

The amount of each check is then compared against the adding-machine tape prepared by the Mail Department, and the total of that tape proved against the total shown on the cash report.

The Cashier must then stamp the Company endorsement on each check with the bank stamp, validate a deposit slip which was prepared with the cash report, and add any additional checks being sent to the bank for deposit. In preparing the deposit, the Cashier will assist Accounts Receivable by verifying details which ap-

FIG. 10-9.

OPERATIONAL AUDIT

OF THE CAFETERIA UNIT

EASTWOOD BRANCH

Conducted by
Leonard R. Williams
Senior Analyst

Consolidated Machine Company

June 25, 19--

 FIG. 10-10 (*beginning*).

Contents

FIG. 10-10 (*continued*).

OPERATIONAL AUDIT OF THE CAFETERIA UNIT

EASTWOOD BRANCH

Purpose and Scope

The Cafeteria Unit of the Eastwood Branch is required to generate at least half of its operating costs from receipts, a policy that prevails at the Main Office and at all Branches which offer food service. As a rule, the Cafeteria Unit produces slightly more than half of its operating costs from receipts, so that the contribution of the Branch is slightly less than 50 per cent. Naturally, any changes in operating costs will alter both the cost to the employees and the net cost to the Branch. It is the responsibility of the Cafeteria Unit to provide the best service possible by assuring that the quality of food is high and, at the same time, to set the prices charged for food so that they are sufficient to return 50 per cent of the costs.

The purpose of the Operational Audit was to review the present procedures and to suggest changes, if feasible, that might contribute to an improvement in operating efficiency. The report is based on interviews with mem-

1

FIG. 10-10 (*continued*).

bers of the unit and its management, a review of the unit's records, and observations of its operations. Full cooperation was obtained from all concerned.

Summary Opinion

The results of the audit indicate that the personnel of the Cafeteria Unit have been performing their duties in a very capable manner, in keeping with the unit's stated policy goals. The quality of the food is high and the pricing structure is in general conformity with Branch policy. Several matters were reviewed, however, which seem to warrant attention. The functional time allocation did not precisely reflect the actual time spent by employees on cafeteria matters. This came about because of a shift in assignments due to the prolonged absence of the Unit Head in the early months of this year. The Unit Head has since returned, and operations have returned to normal. Also, in the absence of the Unit Head, the procedure for obtaining quotations on the prices of meat and poultry was changed; in fact, it was improved by soliciting more frequent bids, resulting in a reduction of total food costs. The physical layout of the cafeteria line could be changed in order to better utilize the time of the cashier and at the same time facilitate surveillance of the cash register. Finally, the accounting procedure employed for special events,[1] both

---

[1]Employee functions, company meetings, community affairs.

FIG. 10-10 (*continued*).

at the Branch and Head Office, tends to reduce the amount charged employees and increase the subsidy paid by the Company. It is not suggested that this procedure be changed; it is merely reviewed in this report so that if the procedure is thought to need refinement, steps can be taken to change it.

Observations and Recommendations

The Cafeteria Unit, which is under the direct supervision of the Chief of the Service Division, is part of the Personnel and Service function. The unit is composed of a Unit Head, who is also the cook, an Assistant Cook, a Lunch Room Attendant, and part-time personnel, usually four persons, borrowed from other areas of the Branch who assist in preparing and serving meals and in cleaning up after meals (see Exhibit 1). The Unit Head, in addition to her duties as cook, is also responsible for the preparation of menus and the ordering of food and supplies.

Cost of Service

The number of meals served annually has fluctuated with the general trend in the number of persons employed by the Branch. Meals served have increased from 43,116 in 1972 to 49,154 in 1977 (see Exhibit 2).

The Unit's operating costs have shown a rather constant rate of increase. Total costs rose from $46,692 in 1972 to $57,854 last year, an average increase of some $2,232 a year. As a consequence, the net expense to the

FIG. 10-10 (*continued*).

Branch has risen steadily from approximately $22,005 to $27,584 in the five-year period.

The largest component of expense, somewhat exceeding salary expense, has been the cost of food, which accounts for slightly more than half of the Unit's expenditures. Food costs increased from $23,464 in 1972 to $29,192 in 1977, a gain of 24.4 per cent. The average number of employees working in the cafeteria was virtually unchanged for this period, up 9% from 4.10 in 1972 to 4.47 in 1977, but salary liabilities rose from $21,275 to $26,654, an increase of 25.3 per cent.

Total operating costs have increased by 24 per cent over the past six years, which is reflected in the average cost per meal. From 1972 to 1977, the cost per meal rose from $1.08 to $1.17, a rise of 18 per cent. Despite the upward pressure on costs, some reductions have been possible. The average cost per meal, for example, was reduced by $.03 last year.

It is conceivable that further reductions in the average cost per meal may have been possible in the early months of 1978, if an unusual circumstance had not prevailed. It was necessary for the Unit Head to enter the hospital for an operation which was followed by a long period of convalescence. She was absent from the middle of January until the end of May. While she was absent, she was carried on the payroll and a temporary replacement was hired. This lifted the number of Cafeteria employees from 4.47 last year to 5.55 employees through

FIG. 10-10 (*continued*).

May, 1978. As a consequence, the average cost per meal for the first five months of 1978 rose to $1.23. This increase might have been even higher had there not been an offsetting reduction in the cost of food. Total food costs were down approximately $775 for the five-month period, compared with the same period a year ago.

Meat and Poultry Quotations

The absence of the Unit Head resulted in some changes in the normal procedures of the Unit. As has been noted, it is the responsibility of the Unit Head to plan the menu and order the necessary food and supplies. During the absence of the Unit Head, the task of pricing and ordering supplies was assumed by the Chief of the Service Division. During the period that the Chief handled this activity, the cost of food was reduced by some $775 as compared with the same period last year. The lower costs appear to have resulted from the Chief's aggressive purchasing policies.

According to the Unit's manual of procedures, bids on meat and poultry are to be obtained on a quarterly basis. The Chief improved on this system and shopped for prices on a weekly basis. When the cook prepared the weekly menu to determine the quantities of the various items needed, she submitted the list to the Chief. He then telephoned three vendors and received quotations on the items. After a comparison of prices, he placed orders for the items at the best price. Although this is

FIG. 10-10 (*continued*).

not the usual procedure of sending out regular quarterly requests for bids, it is apparently effective and has made reductions in cost possible. It is suggested that the Service Division continue the practice of seeking more frequent bids, if not on a weekly basis, at least on a monthly basis, rather than only four times a year.

While the Chief was handling the ordering of cafeteria needs, he kept only temporary notes of the quotations he received. If a question were to arise in the future about the propriety of some of those bids, there would be no permanent record of the quotations received. It is therefore suggested that a more formal method be used to record the quotations received over the telephone from vendors. A suggested form for this purpose is shown in Exhibit 3. Such a form would provide a permanent record of all quotations and, should it be necessary, the prices could be checked at a later date. In addition, instead of being reviewed quarterly, the quotations could be reviewed on a weekly or monthly basis in the normal continuous audits of expenses.

Allocation of Time

During the long absence of the Unit Head, the Chief of the Service Division was required to devote more than his normal time to the operation of the Cafeteria Unit. His functional time allocation records, however, did not reflect the additional time spent. While discussing the allocation of his time in the course of the operational

FIG. 10-10 (*continued*).

audit, the Chief conceded that he was probably spending 10-12 per cent of his time on cafeteria matters rather than the 4-5 per cent reflected in his time allocation. He explained that he felt that the absence of the Unit Head was an unusual circumstance and that the additional time that he spent on cafeteria matters would raise the Unit's salary expenses inordinately when it could least afford such a raise. He therefore maintained his time allocation at its normal level rather than raising it. Such an increase might have necessitated a rise in the cost of employees' meals.

It is recognized that the intention of the Chief was to preserve the current pricing structure of meals, but the effect has been to somewhat distort the actual cost of the Cafeteria Unit and the other units under his supervision. <u>It is therefore recommended that the time allocations in the future be made to reflect the actual time spent in the particular function</u>. The amount of time allocated to cafeteria matters might also be adjusted slightly for the remainder of the year so that the annual figures will more closely reflect the actual time spent on Cafeteria Unit matters. The Unit Head has returned to work and the temporary cook has left, so that the increase should have no adverse effect on prices.

<u>Serving Line Layout</u>

During the audit, it was observed that the cashier was often called on to perform duties in the kitchen or

FIG. 10-10 (*continued*).

behind the serving line. When this occurred, it was necessary for her to leave the register unattended. Having completed her work in the kitchen or in the serving area, or when an employee had passed through the serving line, the cashier returned to the register. In the course of a lunch period, from 10:45 a.m. to 1:30 p.m., the cashier spent considerable time commuting between the register and the kitchen.

The manager of the Service Division is aware of the time and energy lost in this situation and has undertaken an investigation of ways to remedy it. The ideal solution would be to position the cash register behind the serving line so that the cashier could operate the register and also assist in serving food. Towards that end an estimate has been obtained on the cost of placing the coffee urns in the position now occupied by the register (see Exhibit 4). The cost of repiping the urns was found to be quite high. In addition, placement of the urns outside the kitchen would require cafeteria personnel to leave the kitchen area to make coffee. There is also the possibility of spillage, or even burns, if the employees served themselves. Finally, there is very little room for the register on the counter at the end of the serving line because of the placement of the Levelator containing cups and the compartment holding cold drinks.

A possible solution to this problem would be to reverse the flow of employees in the serving line and reposition the register in the area now occupied by the

FIG. 10-10 (*continued*).

serving trays. The trays could then be placed in the area where the register is now located. The cashier would then be behind the serving line at all times and would be available to ring up sales and assist in food service. In this way, the register would never be left unattended as it is now.

The position of the register as herein described might be slightly less convenient for those employees who purchase only a beverage because they would have to walk from the end of the line where the beverages are served to what is presently the beginning of the serving line. However, this minor inconvenience should be weighed against the benefit derived from the position of the register behind the line where the cashier can easily assist in serving food.

It is suggested that the Cafeteria Unit continue efforts to solve the problem caused by the present position of the cash register and the need for the cashier's assistance behind the serving line, giving consideration to the suggestion stated above, or any other plan which would achieve the same end.

Special Events

In addition to its primary responsibility for preparing meals for all Branch employees, the Cafeteria Unit is frequently called on to provide meals for special events, such as United Fund drives, company symposia, and certain employee functions. On such occasions, the en-

FIG. 10-10 (*continued*)

tire cost of the event, labor, food and supplies is charged to the sponsoring function of the Branch; for example, Public Relations or Personnel. The amount expended for the event is reflected in the Unit's expenses, and the amount charged for the event is entered as a receipt. The receipts for special events, which are equal to the actual cost of these events, are therefore included with all other receipts. This practice, which is essentially the same as the procedure at the Main Office, raises an interesting question. First, should special events be considered as part of the normal operating expenses of the Cafeteria Unit, and, second, is the distortion of the 50 per cent formula caused by this practice the best acceptable procedure? An illustration of the results caused by the current accounting procedure may be helpful in understanding the question.

If the normal operating expenses of the Cafeteria Unit for a particular month are $4,500, at least 50 per cent, or $2,250, must be generated from receipts. The employees would therefore be expected to pay at least that amount at the cash register. If, during that same month, there were special events costing $500, those expenses would be added to the normal expenses for a total of $5,000. The share normally required from employee receipts would then be, theoretically, at least $2,500, up $250 from normal expectations. As was explained above, however, the sponsoring units would be charged at full cost for the special events and the collections made by

FIG. 10-10 (*continued*).

the Cafeteria would be included in its other receipts. Since the Cafeteria Unit would have received $500 of its $2,500 requirement, the employees need contribute only $2,000, rather than $2,250 as they would have if there had been no special event. The Branch maximum contribution, on the other hand, is raised from $2,250 to $2,500. If special events in the same month had cost $1,000, employees would have had to contribute $1,750 and the Branch's share would have been raised to $2,750. In effect then, as the cost of special events rises, the employees' contribution decreases and the Branch's share increases.

For purposes of discussion, a different accounting procedure which would more clearly distinguish between ordinary operating expenses and those for special events is outlined below. This procedure would require the segregation of normal operating expenses and those incurred for special events. The offsetting credit to the cafeteria from the sponsoring function would wash out the cost of the event so that it would not appear in the cafeteria's normal operating costs. The normal operating expenses would appear by themselves and the cost of special events would be segregated so that the impact of the latter on the relative contributions of the Branch and the employees can be clearly seen.

In May, 1978, for instance, operating costs for the cafeteria were $5,984. Receipts were shown as $2,426 from the cash register and $710 from other sources, pri-

FIG. 10-10 (*continued*).

marily special events, for a total of $3,136. Calculated according to the current procedure, the receipts amounted to 52.41 per cent of total costs. The Branch's contribution was therefore $2,848 or 47.59 per cent of total costs. If the same month's costs were calculated without special events, the situation would be quite different. Receipts for special events were $710, an amount equal to their cost. If the cost of special events were subtracted from the total cost, ordinary operating expenses would have been $5,274. Thus, the cash register receipts of $2,426 would have been 46 per cent of the normal operating cost. The Branch contribution of $2,848, therefore, would have been 54 per cent of ordinary operating costs, $211 more than 50 per cent of ordinary operating costs permitted in the basic policy formula.[2]

If 1977 expenses and receipts were calculated by segregating expenses and receipts for special events, the Branch's contribution of $27,582 would have been equal to 49.55 per cent of normal operating expenses, rather than 47.68 per cent of operating expenses as the records reflect. If this same procedure were applied to the first five months of 1978, the Branch's contribution, $13,067.22, would equal 52.33 per cent of ordinary operating expenses, rather than the 49.35 per cent of expenses that the records currently reflect. Calculated

---

[2]Minutes, Board of Directors meeting, March 27, 1970: "Accordingly, the Board will offer no objection to the Company's absorbing up to one-half the cost of operating its cafeteria."

FIG. 10-10 (*continued*).

without special events, the Branch would have paid $583.42 more than its share would have been with special events. Without special events, therefore, the Branch's contribution would have been in excess of 50 per cent in the absence of a rise in prices charged for food.

Discussion of the accounting practices currently in use for the Cafeteria Unit does not imply that they are acting improperly. As was mentioned above, this procedure is substantially the same as that employed at the Main Office. Although this method of accounting may on occasion increase the cost to the Bank, it does tend to hold down the cost of meals to employees which is an important fringe benefit. This discussion is meant merely to point out the situation so that, if the current procedures are thought to need refinement, steps can be taken to change them.

Manual of Procedures

In the course of the audit, the Cafeteria Unit's manual of procedure was reviewed and found to be adequate, and prepared in accordance with Operating Bulletin No. 12. It is suggested, however, that the manual be amended to reflect any changes in operating procedures, in particular the procedure adopted for soliciting quotations by telephone, or otherwise, from food vendors.

FIG. 10-10 (*continued*).

EXHIBITS

FIG. 10-10 (*continued*).

Exhibit I

CAFETERIA UNIT, SERVICE DIVISION

EASTWOOD BRANCH

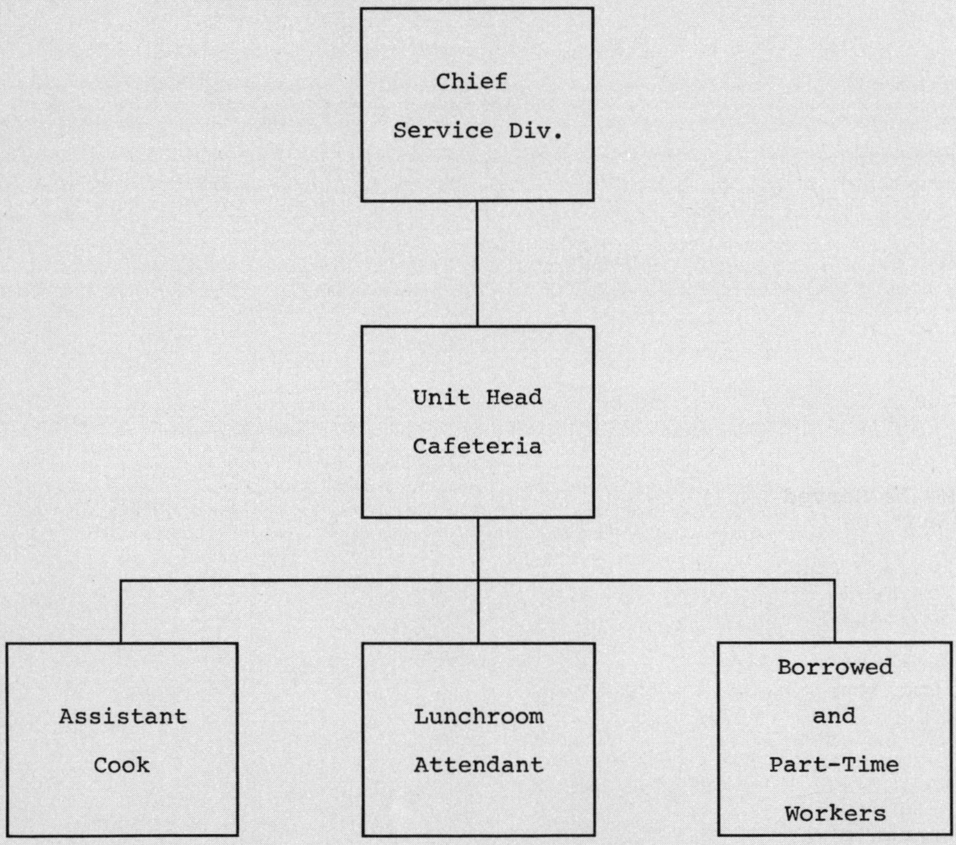

FIG. 10-10 (*continued*).

Exhibit II

CAFETERIA UNIT

EXPENSES AND RECEIPTS

Year	1978*	1977	1976	1975	1974	1973	1972
Salary Liability (Dollars)	14,023	26,654	25,402	24,502	22,919	22,238	21,275
Cafeteria Employees	5.55	4.47	4.28	4.29	4.12	4.16	4.10
Food (Dollars)	11,413	29,192	29,213	25,770	24,846	25,989	23,464
Other (Dollars)	1,041	2,008	1,989	1,531	1,556	1,624	1,953
Total Cost (Dollars)	26,478	57,854	56,604	51,803	49,321	48,851	46,692
Meals Served (Number)	21,528	49,154	47,045	44,706	45,340	48,372	43,116
Average Cost Per Meal (Dollars)	1.23	1.17	1.20	1.16	1.08	1.03	1.08
Receipts (Dollars)	13,411	30,270	29,216	27,218	25,597	27,110	24,687
Net Expense to Branch (Dollars)	13,067	27,584	27,388	24,585	23,724	22,741	22,005
Branch's Per Cent of Total Cost	49.3	47.7	48.4	47.5	48.1	45.6	47.1

* First five months

FIG. 10-10 (*continued*).

Exhibit III

TELEPHONE RECORD

OF

MEAT AND POULTRY QUOTATIONS

QUANTITY	DESCRIPTION	VENDORS 1.	2.	3.	4.	VENDOR SELECTED (INDICATE NO.)

SIGNATURE OF INDIVIDUAL ACCEPTING QUOTATIONS	DATE

FIG. 10-10 (*continued*).

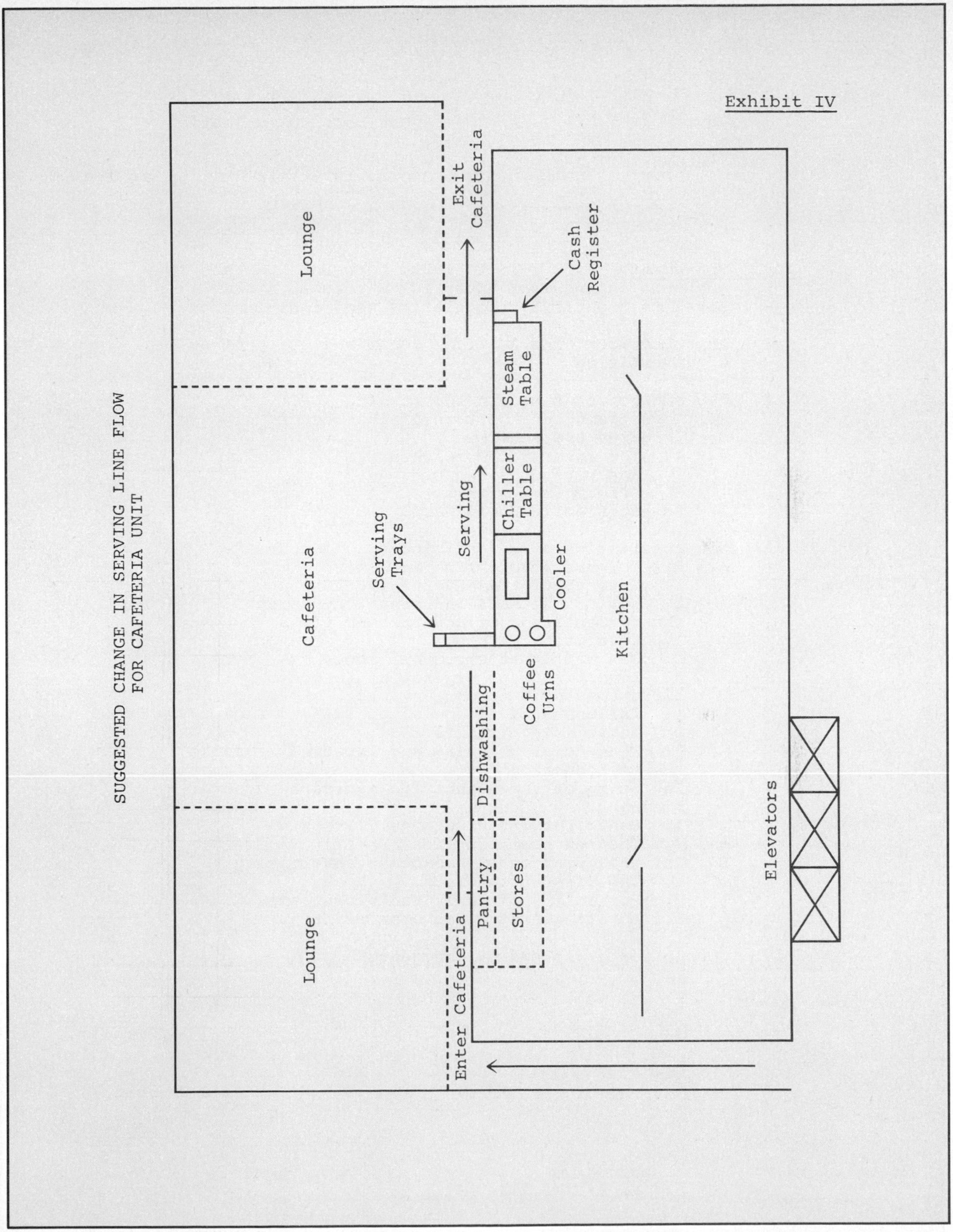
SUGGESTED CHANGE IN SERVING LINE FLOW
FOR CAFETERIA UNIT
Exhibit IV
Lounge
Exit
Cafeteria
Cash
Register
Steam
Table
Chiller
Table
Serving
Serving
Trays
Cooler
Cafeteria
Coffee
Urns
Kitchen
Dishwashing
Pantry
Stores
Lounge
Enter Cafeteria
Elevators

FIG. 10-10 (*concluded*).

Marian Seymour
Business Communication

ADVERTISING'S GOLDEN DECADE: 1919-1929

Outline

Topic Statement: From 1919 to 1929, between a war and an economic depression, advertising reached a new level of creativity, popularity, and influence.

I. Introduction: The American dream and the promise of advertising

II. The emergence of modern advertising
   A. Advertising at the turn of the century
   B. Excesses and reforms
      1. The role of the "muckrakers"
      2. The Pure Food and Drug Act
      3. Reform from within
   C. Advertising in World War I

III. Characteristics of advertising's golden decade
   A. Rise of the advertising agencies
      1. Effects of the advertising contract
      2. New advertisers and creative talent
   B. The fermentation of advertising ideas
      1. Creativity in copy
      2. Sex and other emotional appeals
      3. Advertising of cigarettes to women
   C. Improvements in typography, art, and printing
      1. Influence of the new typography
      2. Advertising artists
      3. Four-color printing and improved magazine reproduction
   D. Beginning of the scientific approach to advertising
      1. Contributions of Claude C. Hopkins
      2. The new psychology
   E. The inauguration of broadcast advertising
      1. The first broadcasts
      2. Popularity of early radio programs
      3. Advantages of radio over print

IV. Conclusion: The end of innocence

FIG. 10-11 (*beginning*).

ADVERTISING'S GOLDEN DECADE: 1919-1929

Introduction

This paper celebrates a remarkable era in the history of advertising. It is the decade following World War I, when the printed word reached a new level of popularity and influence, and advertising found ways to capitalize on its power to an extent never before tried.

The desire for beauty, success, and social acceptance were always part of the great American dream. Through ingenious use of words, pictures, and emotional appeals, advertising sought to make the dream come true for the masses. The dream persists, and the products that promise the reality have multiplied. But times have changed, and advertising will never again be created with the same innocence and blind enthusiasm. This is the story of advertising's wonderful years and the factors that contributed to their significance.

The Emergence of Modern Advertising

Modern advertising is generally conceded to have had its beginning at the end of the last century. It was then that advertising became an important part of our print culture--no longer simply a medium for commercial announcements, but a powerful tool for exercising control over people's thoughts and actions.[1]

---

[1]George French, 20th Century Advertising (New York: D. Van Nostrand, 1926), p. 17.

1

FIG. 10-11 (*continued*)

The growing volume of advertising and the recklessness of its claims, especially in the field of patent medicines, did not escape exposure by the "muckrakers," a new breed of socially conscious investigative journalists. Although politics and business were the general targets of such writers as Lincoln Steffins (The Shame of the City) and Ida Tarbell (History of the Standard Oil Company), advertising was the more particular subject of sensational stories in McClure's, the Ladies Home Journal, and other responsible magazines of the period. As early as 1892, the Ladies Home Journal had already, in fact, refused to accept advertising for patent medicines.[2]

As a result of the public outcry, Congress passed the Pure Food and Drug Act in 1906. Even before that, however, a large measure of self-control was being exerted by the advertising industry itself. In 1903 the Scripps-McRae newspapers appointed a "censor" to monitor their advertising and reject the false and objectionable. Following the founding in 1896 of what is now the Advertising Club of New York, a union of local advertising clubs into the Advertising Federation of America added furthur strength to the promotion of ethical standards.[3] The legal means for the enforcement of these standards was supplied in 1911 by the trade publication Printer's Ink when, after many years of informal persuasion, it

---

[2]James Playsted Wood, The Story of Advertising (New York: Ronald Press, 1958), pp. 322-327.

[3]Frank Presbrey: History and Development of Advertising (New York: Doubleday, 1929), pp. 542-550.

FIG. 10-11 (*continued*).

drew up the Printer's Ink Model Statute, which was eventually adopted by 43 states.[4]

By the time of America's entry into the First World War in 1917, then, advertising had overcome the worst of the criticism directed at it and set a course for stable growth. The war, however, had the effect of rocketing advertising almost overnight to new heights of influence and respectability. It became not only a prime medium for government propaganda, helping, for example, to promote voluntary food rationing and registration for the draft; it also provided the platform from which commercial advertisers could promote their wares. Thus Kodak urged, "Ask your soldier boy to send pictures to you." Aunt Jemima advertisements had soldiers saying, "Aunt Jemima rings the bell for me." And with a picture of men in the trenches, Prince Albert proclaimed its tobacco "The National Joy Smoke."[5]

<u>The Golden Decade</u>

When the war ended in 1919, the impetus it gave to advertising was sustained, and from that time to late 1929, when the stock market crashed and the Great Depression set in, advertising enjoyed an unprecedented era of growth, creativity, and sophistication. In terms of expenditures alone, advertising billings rose from some-

---

[4]Wood, pp. 332-335.

[5]Ibid., pp. 355-357.

what over $2 billion in 1919 to close to $4 billion in 1929.[6]

Many factors contributed to the development of advertising during that period. Among these, and perhaps most important, were (1) the rise of the advertising agencies, (2) the fermentation of advertising ideas, (3) improvements in typography, art, and printing, (4) the beginning of the "scientific" approach to advertising, and (5) the inauguration of broadcast advertising.

1. The Rise of the Advertising Agencies

The Twenties marked great advances in the prestige of advertising agencies and in their creative productivity. Three of the largest and most venerable agencies were N. W. Ayer & Co. in Philadelphia, J. Walter Thompson in New York, and Lord and Thomas in Chicago. Ayer had given the advertising profession "the advertising contract," an agreement between agent and advertiser to work together for an extended period at a stated commission. This replaced the disorderly competitive bidding system through which advertising wholesalers, competing against each other, sold blocks of space in newspapers and magazines.

At first it was proposed that the commission be paid by the client, but after resistance from the rest of the industry, a fifteen per cent commission based on the cost

---

[6]Ibid., p. 365.

FIG. 10-11 (*continued*).

of the space was eventually assumed by the media with which the advertising was placed. The commission system became the single most important stabilizing force in the advertising business.[7]

Ayer, well organized and financed, enjoyed a roster of prestigious clients some of whom it continued to hold for as long as a half century or more. It also attracted some brilliant talent. Among its copywriters of the period was Raymond Rubicam, who wrote for Steinway the advertisements describing the piano as "The Instrument of the Immortals"; for E. R. Squibb & Son a noteworthy series of institutional advertisements, "The Priceless Ingredient"; and for the International Correspondence Schools a series remembered for the headline, "The University of the Night." Rubicam and another Ayer employee, James Webb Young, left in 1923 to form their own agency, Young and Rubicam, where they continued to produce distinguished advertising for such clients as General Foods (particularly Maxwell House Coffee), Johnson & Johnson, Spalding, and Cluett, Peabody & Co. (home of "the Arrow collar man").[8]

During the same period J. Walter Thompson was headed by Stanley Resor, where he became instrumental in wooing housewives away from bars of laundry soap to Lux soap chips and flakes. He was also the first, through the

---

[7]Dorothy Cohen, Advertising (New York: John Wiley), pp. 57-58.

[8]Wood, pp. 462-467.

FIG. 10-11 (*continued*).

Ford Motor account, to promote the idea of the two-car family. Scott Paper became a client in 1927 and, under Resor's influence, cut the number of its products and the prices as well; sales volume soared.[9]

Meanwhile, the head of the Lord and Thomas operation in Chicago was Albert D. Lasker, a man of remarkable energy and ideas. Aided particularly by copywriters John E. Kennedy and Claude C. Hopkins, Lord and Thomas became a leader in creative merchandising and marketing. Lasker was first impressed by Kennedy when he overheard his remark that advertising was "salesmanship in print." Hopkins was later hired for his success in using "reason why" copy, a rational type of advertising message that had not been tried before. Hopkins also espoused the idea that if you want to sell, you had to sell to the millions, a philosophy that Lord and Thomas practiced earnestly. Their advertisements for Sunkist oranges, Palmolive soap, Kleenex, and Pepsodent, among other products, made the names familiar to all.[10]

2. The Fermentation of Advertising Ideas

A characteristic feature of the copy of the time was its length. The copywriters contributed both their ideas and their verbal skills to make the advertisements effective, and they enjoyed enormous prestige. Claude Hopkins had already initiated the change to hard copy. Now there

---

[9] Ibid., p. 458.

[10] John Gunther, Taken at the Flood: The Story of Albert D. Lasker (New York: Harper's, 1960), pp. 66ff.

FIG. 10-11 (*continued*).

was added the impact of "the story line." A classic example was John Caples' advertisement for the U.S. School of Music, "They Laughed When I Sat Down at the Piano But When I Started to Play--." Caples was soon to be lured from the Ruthrauff and Ryan agency to Ted Bates & Co., for whom he was to have the opportunity to write the hard-hitting "copy-tested" ads for which the agency is still renowed.[11]

Another characteristic of the advertising copy in those days was the emergence of the sex appeal. Woodbury and Palmolive were leaders in this innovation. Earlier advertisers had been content to stress brand identification, as in the insipid, "Good Morning. Have You Used Pears' Soap?" which filled the billboards and magazines. Woodbury, on the other hand first shocked and then titillated readers with the slogan, "The Skin You Love to Touch," and Palmolive found the same magic in the phrase, "Keep That Schoolgirl Complexion."

It was not long before more daring appeals were being tried. Many combined the sex appeal with the appeal to fear, and women were chosen as vulnerable targets. Listerine's "Often a Bridesmaid but Never a Bride" became part of our folklore. Slightly earlier, the deodorant Odorono had also appealed to fear with the advertisement beginning, "Within the Curve of a Woman's Arm--a frank discussion of a subject too often avoided," and

---

[11]Martin Mayer, Madison Avenue (1958; rpt. New York: Pocket Books, 1959), pp. 41-42.

FIG. 10-11 (*continued*).

including the statement, "You may offend without knowing."[12]

In Pepsodent, Claude Hopkins literally found riches in the common name he gave to the plaque formed on teeth. He called it "film," and it was thus described in a 1928 advertisement:

> Run your tongue across your teeth and you will feel a slippery viscous coating. That is film.
> It clings to teeth so stubbornly that brushing alone will not remove it successfully. It gets into crevices and stays.
> Stains from food and smoking are absorbed into film and make teeth "off color" and dingy.
> Germs breed in film by the millions. And they with the tartar film develops into, are the chief cause of pyorrhea.
> Film invites the acids of decay.
> Thus, before new ways were found to remove it, tooth and gum disorders were on the increase.[13]

The remedy, of course, was Pepsodent, the "dental science discovery" that "acts to crudle the film" and "harden gums." It is doubtful that such advertising would be permitted today. An interesting footnote is that Hopkins, having secured a financial interest in Pepsodent beforehand, made--by his own report--over a million dollars from his success with its advertising.[14]

A daring innovation of the Twenties was the advertising of cigarettes to women. Cautiously, Chesterfield led the movement with its billboard showing a man smoking and a woman companion saying, "Blow some my way."[15] Lucky Strikes followed with "Reach for a Lucky instead

---

[12]Julian L. Watkins, The One Hundred Greatest Advertisements (New York: Dover, 1959), pp. 36-73 passim; Mayer, p. 61; Wood, pp. 384-385.

[13]Claude C. Hopkins, My Life in Advertising (New York: Harper's, 1936), p. 155.

[14]Ibid., p. 159.

[15]Wood, pp. 376-377.

FIG. 10-11 (*continued*).

of a sweet"--seeking to persuade women that smoking would help them keep their figures trim. After that, the dam broke. Soon society leaders and Metropolitan Opera divas were competing for the privilege of endorsing Lucky Strikes. And with these advertisements, the stage was set for the proliferation of testimonial advertising.[16]

3. Improvements in Typography, Art, and Printing

Even with the introduction of radio advertising in the mid-Twenties, the emphasis on copy was aided by artistic and technical advances in the presentation of the printed word. Typography, which had already achieved distinction in book production at the hands of such masters as William Morris, Bruce Rogers, and John Fass, broke new ground in advertising with refinements in lay-out, decoration, and type design.[17]

. . . .

Conclusion

Advertising's golden decade came to an abrupt and dramatic halt on October 29, 1929, with the stock market crash. Advertising expenditures, which had reached a peak of $4 billion annually declined to $1.3 billion in 1933. Advertising was eventually to recover its eco-nomic position and to become even more ubiquitous with the coming of television. But it was not to regain the unencumbered freedom it enjoyed in the Twenties. That was a time when advertising attracted a large group of educated and talented workers with unquestioning belief in what they were doing; and through their labor, fore-

---

[16]Gunther, pp. 163-169.

[17]French, pp. 44-46; Douglas C. McMurtrie, The Story of Printing and Bookmaking (New York: Oxford University Press), pp. 451ff.

sight, and enthusiasm, advertising became a respectable profession and an indispensable adjunct to modern mass marketing. Those who lived through the times may wonder now at the naiveté of a public that accepted so uncritically the blatant appeals to their emotions and the promises that no deodorant, mouthwash, soap, or toothpaste could ever fulfill. The most that can be said is that advertising enlivened the period and offered to the insecure the hope that all things were possible.

BIBLIOGRAPHY

Cohen, Dorothy. Advertising. New York: John Wiley & Sons, 1972.

French, George. 20th Century Advertising. New York: D. Van Nostrand, 1926.

Gunther, John. Taken at the Flood: The Story of Albert D. Lasker. New York: Harper & Row, 1960.

Hopkins, Claude C. My Life in Advertising. New York: Harper & Row, 1936.

__________. Scientific Advertising. New York: Crown Publishers, 1923.

Hotchkiss, George B., and Franken, Richard B. The Measurement of Advertising Effects. New York: Harper's, 1927.

Mayer, Martin. Madison Avenue. 1958; rpt. New York: Pocket Books, 1959.

McMurtrie, Douglas C. The Story of Printing and Bookmaking. New York: Oxford University Press, 1943.

Poffenberger, Albert T. Psychology in Advertising. New York: A. W. Shaw, 1926.

Presbrey, Frank. History and Development of Advertising. New York: Doubleday, 1929.

Watkins, Julian L. The One Hundred Greatest Advertisements. New York: Dover Publications, 1959.

Wood, James Playsted. The Story of Advertising. New York: Ronald Press, 1958.

FIG. 10-11 (*concluded*).

PROBLEMS

1. Write a library paper on one of the topics suggested in Problem 1 or 2 on page 271. Use at least six different sources of information. Provide appropriate footnotes and a bibliography.

2. Write a library paper on one of the following topics, or on some other topic approved by your instructor.
   (*a*) The American economy following the Civil War
   (*b*) Recent trends in fringe benefits for workers
   (*c*) The development of the modern supermarket
   (*d*) Ethical standards in the executive suite
   (*e*) The future of low-cost urban housing

3. The business manager of a university in the Middle West is making a survey of food services at other universities. He has asked you to write a description of the service, as it is observable to the patron, in the cafeteria of your college. He wants a strictly factual report on the kinds of food served, including menus and prices; the physical arrangements for serving and dining; and the flow of traffic. Write the report in the form of a letter to Mr. William Guest, Business Manager, Lansing University, Lansing, Michigan, 48901.

4. A businessman of your acquaintance is considering extending operations to another city of medium size. He wants to have, in several pages, a concise summary of the city's economic life, including population, industries, recreational facilities, transportation, communications, climate, natural resources, history, etc. For this survey, choose a city of about 250,000 to 750,000 population. Assume that a letter of transmittal, which you need not write, will be appended. At the conclusion of your report, list your sources of information.

5. Assume that you are working for an employer who wants you to keep him abreast of news in one of the following fields:
   (*a*) Retail marketing
   (*b*) Corporate finance
   (*c*) Government actions affecting business
   (*d*) Economic trends
   (*e*) Science in industry
   Keeping his requirements in mind, consult newspapers and business publications for the last three months. Then submit a report for the period. Include a letter of transmittal addressed to Mr. Dunbar S. Barney, Vice President, the Grayson Corporation, 500 Canal Street, Houston, Texas 77004.

6. Writing of yourself in the third person, make an objective analysis of your job qualifications and the market for your services. Then address to yourself a formal report containing your analysis together with a comprehensive plan for finding a job. You may consult Chapter 7 before tackling this assignment, but keep in mind that your report is to include a *plan*, not a resume or application letter.

7. You are working for the foreign department of a large bank. Your immediate supervisor is soon to leave on a business trip to South America. He is going to visit Argentina, Brazil, Venezuela, Chile, and Bolivia. As part of his preparation, he has

asked for reports on general economic conditions in these countries. After due investigation, address a letter report to him on conditions in the one country you may assume has been assigned to you. Address your report to Mr. Bernard Quinlan, Vice President, Chicago International Bank, 80 Great Lakes Boulevard, Chicago, Illinois 60011.

8. For an assumed employer, who is contemplating purchase for general office use, write an informational report to guide him in the selection of one of the following machines. Investigate various leading brands before you write your report.
   (*a*) A photocopy machine
   (*b*) An electric typewriter
   (*c*) A dictating machine
   (*d*) A duplicator for manifold copies

9. From personal experience only, write a report on the efficiency with which the work in some office or plant is being done. Choose preferably some limited operation as, for example, the mailing department, accounts receivable section, credit department, maintenance division, etc. Include your recommendations for improvement.

10. With your special training or interest in the subject area as background, write an analytical report on one of the following topics:
    (*a*) The recent market action of the stock of three competitive companies listed on the New York Stock Exchange
    (*b*) A current advertising campaign in print
    (*c*) The programming policies of a local television station
    (*d*) Customer relations at a local supermarket
    (*e*) Policing on your college campus
    Address your report to some person, real or assumed, who would have a practical interest in your findings.

11. For a local specialty shop that you know reasonably well, write a report on one of the following subjects:
    (*a*) The use of letters to increase business from present customers
    (*b*) Methods of building a selected mailing list of prospective customers
    (*c*) Methods of developing telephone and mail-order business

12. For the president of a service or manufacturing company that you know, write a formal report on one of the following subjects. The report should be based on investigation of external sources, leaving to the reader the determination of specific applications in his business.
    (*a*) Form letters: kinds, uses, advantages and disadvantages
    (*b*) Customers' complaints: Policies governing them and methods of handling
    (*c*) Recruiting and training future business executives
    (*d*) Employee profit-sharing plans
    (*e*) Establishing an employee house organ
    (*f*) Proven employee-relations techniques
    (*g*) Staggering the work hours in downtown offices
    (*h*) Solicitation of charitable contributions from employees
    (*i*) Methods of correspondence supervision and training
    (*j*) Modern trends in providing for office dictation and transcription

13. Assume that an executive in some exisiting organization has asked you to investigate some aspect of communication or business procedure that may have considerable significance for his organization, and to submit to him a written report of your findings. The investigation may take the form of personal experience, experimentation, interviews, or library research. In any case, choose a topic of sufficiently limited scope so that it can be covered in depth in a report of about 10 to 12 pages, including any documentation and exhibits.
   (*a*) Submit, in memorandum form addressed to the instructor, a proposal for the report stating the following:
      (1) Title and business connection of the executive asking for the report
      (2) Subject of the investigation and the purpose to which the report will presumably be put
      (3) Prospective sources of information
      NOTE: For the form of a memorandum, see Chapter 11, "Shorter Reports: Special Types," pages 340–343.
   (*b*) After approval of the memorandum described in (*a*) above, write and submit the formal report, including a letter of transmittal, introduction, body, and conclusion and/or recommendations.
   (*c*) For this report assignment, the following topics are suggested, although you may choose another of special interest to you.
      (1) An analysis of your school's bulletin, with recommendations aimed at making it more helpful to students and more valuable as a showcase for the school's offerings
      (2) A formal proposal for a new course, new program, or some other improvement in the curriculum of your school
      (3) A study of the informational content of the advertising of some important consumer product (e.g., a car, an air conditioner, a television set)
      (4) A study of a particular communication activity (e.g., employee relations, consumer relations) in a specific organization
      (5) The treatment of current social problems in company annual reports (e.g., ecology, health hazards, fair employment practices, strikes, inflation, taxes)
      (6) The use of audiovisual techniques in a company's training program
      (7) Effects of the consumer movement on advertising strategy
      (8) Content analysis of the employee house organ of a particular company
      (9) Methods of a particular company in dealing with adverse public opinion
      (10) Modern methods of systematizing business correspondence

14. Hudson Textiles, Inc., a large manufacturing company with 12 plants throughout the nation and its head office in New York, will pay full tuition refunds to employees who have completed one year's service and who are matriculated in a degree-granting institution. At the present time, 44 of the 200 eligible employees in the New York office take advantage of this benefit.

   A recent survey showed that over the past four years, an average of 75 per cent of those obtaining a college degree at company expense quit Hudson within one year and 12 per cent quit before attaining a degree. The company is expanding each year and needs college-trained personnel for middle-management positions not only in the New York office, but also in the various plants throughout the country. Thus, Hudson not only pays college tuition for lost employees, but is forced to hire college-trained personnel at substantially higher wages to fill middle-management positions and to train these employees who have no company experience. At present more than three-quarters of the existing middle-management positions are filled with employees having fewer than four years with Hudson.

Assume you have been asked by the President, Mr. Thomas J. Robertson, to come up with some recommendations to ease this problem. Mr. Robertson has made it perfectly clear to you that Hudson is more than willing to pay tuition under the refund plan as an employee fringe benefit and as an incentive to ambitious employees to go to college. However, the plan was originally designed to combine business experience with formal education for the benefit of the company that pays the bills. As the situation stands, Hudson is paying the bills but is not benefiting.

Assume also that you have collected data by conducting a series of personal interviews, at Hudson's expense, with a sample of 100 employees in the New York office (44 student employees, 50 nonstudent employees, and 6 recent college graduates). All of the student employees and the 6 graduates indicated that there is no periodic review made of their academic progress or achievements and no recognition given in the form of raises or promotions based on academic achievement. They also said that some supervisors were not even aware of the fact than an employee in their charge was attending school. Ten of the 44 student employees felt that their supervisors were holding them back from promotion because they were attending college. When asked if they thought it company policy to fill middle-management positions from the outside, 30 of the student employees said "Yes"; 48 of the nonstudent employees said "Yes"; and only one of the college graduates said "Yes."

A review of written exit interviews of lost employees indicated that 86 per cent of these ex-employees felt payment of tuition was not enough and 92 per cent said they had received no recognition in the way of promotion after they had received their degrees. These ex-employees revealed a feeling of bitterness toward Hudson because "outsiders" with college degrees held management positions.

All of the employees and ex-employees interviewed indicated that the Personnel Department has seemingly been totally unaware of the fact that they were attending college (or had graduated from college). One ex-employee's statement seemed to reflect the general feeling about the Personnel Department: ". . . The (Personnel) Department was unresponsive to my qualifications and to my desire to stay with Hudson and to grow with the company."

You are to write a report to Mr. Robertson, clearly defining the problem and all of its implications to the company, using the information given to you but presenting it logically and in your own words. Before you present your data, tell how you secured it and why you chose this particular way of collecting data. Why was it necessary to interview the nonstudent employees? State specifically the questions you asked the employees. Present the data clearly, draw your conclusions from the data, and state your recommendations to Mr. Robertson.

15. Reilly and Baker, Inc., sells and services swimming pools. Their ten salesmen check in at the office at 9 o'clock each morning. They call on customers and canvass prospective ones from 10 until 3:30, at which time they return to the office to write up the deals they have completed and to enter new names and pertinent information in their prospective-customer file. Nine stenographers are employed to help the salesmen do the paper work connected with the completion of the deals.

    After a salesman has tentatively completed a deal, the customer's credit must be checked before the final contract can be signed. In his hurry to write out the contracts, a salesman sometimes gives the stenographer incorrect or insufficient information to make a credit check, or he may give her the name of another customer. After she has worked on the credit check, she finds her time has been wasted and she has to start all over. (The next day when Mr. Reilly or Mr. Baker finds out the cause of the delay in making the credit check and in closing the deal, he is sharp with the salesman, who, in turn, is sharp with the stenographer.)

Five o'clock comes and goes; the salesmen have written up the deals in longhand, recorded the names of prospective customers in the proper file, and gone home; and the stenographers are busily completing credit checks and typing contracts in order to have the material ready for the salesmen to pick up at 9 o'clock the next morning. Seldom do the stenographers complete their work before 6:30; more often they do not leave the office until 7:30 or 8:00.

Because of the dissension, the long hours of overtime, the rush of work after a day of waiting, there has been a 100 per cent turnover of the nine stenographers during the past ten months.

Mr. Baker has asked you to find ways of reducing this high turnover of office help.

Before you write your memorandum report to Mr. Baker giving the details of the problem and your recommendations for alleviating the present undesirable situation and thus hopefully reducing the high turnover, consider the pros and cons of the following questions:

Would it be practical to open the office late, perhaps at noon?

Could only one or two stenographers check in at 9 o'clock?

Could the salesmen notify the stenographers during the day of deals completed so that they could get started on the credit checks?

Could the salesmen use portable dictaphones to record the information of deals at the time they are with the customers so that the stenographers could get to work on the contracts as soon as the salesmen return to the office at 3:30? (Mr. Baker has indicated his willingness to buy five such dictaphones.)

Should extra part-time stenographers be hired for the busy hours?

Could the contracts be delayed 24 hours so that the stenographers could work on them during the day while the salesmen are out of the office?

Write the report to Mr. Baker.

11 Shorter Reports: Special Types

IN DEALING with reports so far we have assumed the need for considerable research and writing. Actually, the number of long reports in the organization is likely to be few in proportion to the number of short reports. These short reports may be less demanding of the writer's time, but collectively they assume a greater diversity of form and engage the talents of many more people. They also do most of the things that long reports do: provide information, analyze situations, and make recommendations. Generally, they are part of the daily working routine or have some other immediate application, but like the longer reports, they still require close knowledge of the subject and reach maximum effectiveness only when they are well organized and clearly expressed. Furthermore, there are so many of these reports to be read and digested in any large organization that proficiency in writing them becomes a highly prized talent among staff members. Many employees gain recognition and promotion as a result of their reports. In a large number of organizations, special training programs are developed to improve the quality of reports.

PHYSICAL CHARACTERISTICS

Short reports vary widely in their mechanical makeup. Many special-purpose reports, like that shown in Figure 11-1, are transmitted on printed forms that call for specified details to be filled in. Other special-purpose reports may have only a uniform heading and general instructions followed by a space for the report itself. An example of such a form will be found in Figure 11-2.

When routine internal reports do not fit any of the classifications for which the specialized forms are provided, they are usually typewritten on interoffice stationery, as shown in Figures 11-3 and 11-4. Reports submitted on such sta-

INTERVIEW REPORT

Applicant's Name: ______________ Date: ______________
University & Degree: ______________ Name of Interviewer: ______________

APPLICANT RATING

Indicate your rating of the applicant by circling the appropriate numerical rating — For example: Average — (3)

	Excellent	Above Average	Average	Below Average	Poor
1. ABILITY (Scholastic achievement, level of interview responses)	1	2	3	4	5
2. MOTIVATION (Work habits, quality standards, initiative and perseverance)	1	2	3	4	5
3. PERSONALITY (Social sense, friendliness, persuasiveness)	1	2	3	4	5
4. CHARACTER (Candidness, intellectual honesty, moral and ethical standards)	1	2	3	4	5
5. SPECIAL FACTORS (Appearance, manners, physical condition special accomplishments)	1	2	3	4	5
6. RATING FOR POSITION AS: ______________	1	2	3	4	5

PLACEMENT:
What type of work does applicant want to do?
What is applicant's geographical preference?

SPECIAL INFORMATION:
Class Standing: High School ______________ College ______________
Campus Achievements:
Test Scores:

REMARKS:
Use other side for any additional comments or information

FIG. 11-1. *A special-purpose report form calling for specified details.*

tionery are often referred to as "memorandum reports." They may consist of one or of several or more pages. Plain unprinted paper is generally used for all pages after the first.

For short typewritten reports going outside the organization—for example, credit reports, business proposals, and estimates—the company's regular letterhead and regular letter makeup are customarily used, although special stationery may be provided in some instances. Reports set up as letters are sometimes referred to as "letter reports."

Although they seldom have a cover, title page, or table of contents, short reports may have any of the other features of long reports. These include heads and subheads, footnotes, tables and graphs, and other exhibits. In the interests

SUGGESTION FORM

REFERENCE No.________ (LEAVE BLANK)

CONTROL № 3194

PLEASE PRINT IN PENCIL OR TYPE YOUR SUGGESTION - INCLUDE PRESENT METHOD, IF ANY, IN PROPOSAL

NOTE IF ADDITIONAL SPACE IS NECESSARY USE A SEPARATE SHEET OF PAPER.
DO NOT WRITE BELOW THE DOUBLE LINE OR ON THE BACK OF THIS FORM.

3620 7-60

DO NOT REMOVE THIS STUB

REFERENCE NO.________ (LEAVE BLANK)

CONTROL № 3194

BRANCH TEL. NO.
OR
M. O. DEPT. EXT.________

DATE________

IF YOU WISH TO IDENTIFY YOURSELF TO THE SECRETARY OF THE COMMITTEE, FILL IN YOUR NAME BELOW. YOUR IDENTITY WILL NOT BE REVEALED TO THE MEMBERS OF THE COMMITTEE. THIS STUB WILL BE SIGNED BY THE SECRETARY AND RETURNED TO YOU AS AN ACKNOWLEDGEMENT.

____
SECRETARY OF COMMITTEE

PRINT NAME ________

BRANCH OR DEPT. ________

CONTROL № 3194

DATE________

THIS IS YOUR RECORD.
DETACH AND RETAIN IT
FOR FUTURE REFERENCE.

OFFICE CORRESPONDENCE

DATE________________

TO________________ SUBJECT________________

FROM________________ ________________

MEMORANDUM

DATE

TO OFFICE

FROM OFFICE

SUBJECT

INTERNATIONAL INSURANCE AGENCY, INC.

DATE

TO

FROM

SUBJECT

FIG. 11-3. *Samples of printed memorandum forms.*

of conciseness and readability, extensive use is also made of the enumeration and listing of coordinate details.

ORGANIZATION

Short reports are often less formal in structure than their longer counterparts, but they still require some kind of identification or introduction, some body material, and—as often as not—conclusions or recommendations.

Unless the subject is already announced in a subject line, the introduction will identify the subject of the report and, as the need requires, the authoriza-

FIG. 11-2. *A special-purpose report form allowing for individual discretion in phrasing.*

CONSOLIDATED AIRLINES
Chicago

April 15, 19--

To: O. A. Ewald
S. Kolinski
L. J. Maybury
D. B. Raines
R. G. Ratcliffe

From: R. C. Beggs, Manager, T.O. Administration

Classification of Offices

You will recall that during our last TOA meeting I mentioned that the method of classifying reservations offices had been slightly revised. We all agreed . . . .

INTEROFFICE COMMUNICATION

October 18, 19--

Memorandum to Mr. Arthur Cutler:

Your plan for the November 1 mailing looks fine. Please check with me when the results come in.

James E. Finch
James E. Finch
Vice President--Sales

JEF:hs

FIG. 11-4. *These memorandum forms give more typing flexibility because only the heads are printed.*

tion for the report, its purpose and scope, and the sources of information. Historical or other background material may be added.

The body contains the substance of the data to be transmitted. It is organized chronologically, inductively, or according to some other logical scheme, depending on the nature of the material. Conclusions and recommendations may be added, though there is a strong trend toward stating or summarizing these immediately after the introduction. Tables and other exhibits may be integrated into the text or appended to it.

LANGUAGE

The language of short reports runs the gamut from the very formal to the very informal, and from the stereotyped to the conversational to the slangy. As in writing longer reports, you must consider such factors as the precedents for the kind of report you are writing, the preferences of your superior, the audience to be served, the nature of the subject, and your own rank or authority. The various short reports in this chapter will show the diversity of styles used and serve as a rough guide to the new writer. Generally, however, the writer who is uncertain of the style to be used is best advised to follow these rules:

1. Avoid the stereotyped in favor of a natural but not necessarily colloquial level of diction.
2. Use trade or professional jargon only when it represents a common language between you and the reader.
3. Be restrained in (but do not necessarily avoid) using the personal pronoun *I* or in otherwise referring to yourself.
4. Unless your personal opinions are desired, concentrate as objectively as you can on the conditions you are reporting.
5. Avoid superlatives and other extremes of language.
6. Write as simply and as clearly as you can, no matter what your subject or your audience.

MEMORANDUMS

We have already defined the term "memorandum report" as representing any report written on memorandum (interoffice) stationery. Although most interoffice correspondence can probably be classified as memorandum reports, some memorandums are not reports at all, but inquiries, requests, "thank you's," and other communications of the kind that are often sent outside the organization as business letters. Here, for example, is a memorandum that may be classified as a request:

```
Dear John:

To help us plan our work schedules in an orderly manner,
will you please let me have a vacation schedule for em-
ployees of your section for the period June 1 to Octo-
ber 1.

                              Irving Ghent, Manager
```

The answer, shown below, is also a memorandum, although it more nearly conforms to the definition of a report. The vacation schedule was attached.

```
Memorandum to Mr. Irving Ghent, Manager

Here is the vacation schedule you asked for in your mem-
orandum of April 20.  All employees taking their vaca-
tions from June 1 to September 1 are included.  You will
not find the names of Joe Keene and Mary Carlock because
```

they are taking their vacations in May. My name is not included because, as you know, I am taking my vacation from September 15 to September 30.

John Carey, Assistant Secretary

Enclosure

REPORTING ON METHODS AND PROCEDURES

One of the most common types of reports is the analysis of a method or procedure. Emphasis in these reports varies between showing the inadequacies of the present system and showing the merits of the proposed system. When awareness of the inadequacies of the present system is weak or nonexistent, the analyst will often take a large part of the space to detail the inadequacies. In the report reproduced in Figure 10-10 in the preceding chapter, each section following the introduction and summary may be considered a self-contained shorter report in which the details of a present inadequacy are a necessary prelude to the recommendation for improvement.

When, however, the need for improvement is already known to the reader, the analyst can put the emphasis on the savings or other advantages resulting from the proposed system. Two short reports in which this pattern is followed are shown below.

April 7, 19--

To: Mr. D. R. Chattaway

From: E. M. Dalton

Subject: Improving copy service through the B-B Total Copy System.

Background

In an attempt to reduce copying costs and improve service, a new quick copy system will soon be introduced on a trial basis. The cost of convenience copying (essentially Xerox copying) has risen from $67,000 annually to $114,000 annually over the last three years. In addition, increasing demands for offset copying have caused a heavy backlog of work; consequently, it sometimes takes a week or longer to obtain offset copies. Management became concerned with these developments and authorized a study of all copying operations. The study recommended testing a new quick copy system, the B-B Total Copy System, to determine if it would help solve our copying problems. Below are outlined (1) a description of the system's capabilities, and (2) a plan for testing and implementing Company-wide use of the new system.

I. Capabilities of the B-B Total Copy System

A. Cost per copy

The major advantage of the B-B Total Copy System is a low cost per copy. A recent Company study has shown that the average per copy cost for Xerox copies is 3.5¢. Several users of the B-B system have reported average costs for copy of .5¢. If only 25 per cent of all Xerox copying were diverted to the B-B system, annual savings would amount to over $22,000.

B. Fast Service

The productive capacity of the B-B system will enable the Duplicating Division to offer four-hour offset service, on a normal basis, and while-you-wait service for emergency needs. (Copies are produced at a rate of 150 copies per minute.) As an illustration of the system's capability, a copy center at the University of Wisconsin reports that it is able to maintain four-hour service while producing 275,000 copies per month, representing 743 jobs from 3,744 masters.

C. Good Quality

The quality of copy produced on the B-B system surpasses the quality of any other electrostatic system.

II. A Plan for Testing the B-B Copy System

A. A survey will be conducted to determine each department's convenience copying requirements, specifically: the number of originals, the number of copies, quality requirements, and time frame for copying.

B. From the information obtained in the survey, we will select specific departments or jobs and recommend that the work be tried on the quick copy system. Preference will be given to jobs that are very costly to produce with convenience copiers. The Duplicating Division will also select certain work for production on the automated equipment. By controlling access to the equipment during the test period, we will be able to evaluate properly the system's reliability, quality and productivity. After testing, a final decision will be made to purchase or return the equipment.

C. If the equipment is purchased, guidelines for its Company-wide use will be established; and a handout will be distributed explaining the new system's capabilities and recommended usage.

To: Mr. Hotchkiss Date: May 10, 19--

From: T. Cady Subject: Cost analysis of DLB 750 Terminals

In response to a memorandum dated May 4, 19--, from Mr. Jones, Manager of the Information Processing Department, a cost examination was undertaken in the Teleprocessing Division. The purpose of this study was to determine whether it will be more efficient to lease or purchase the six DLB 750 terminals now in use.

After thorough investigation, it is recommended that the terminals be purchased instead of leased.

The costs of the two proposals for the period June 19-- to June 19-- were examined. The results indicated that if the equipment is leased for the three years, an overall cost of $12,960 will be incurred. If the equipment is purchased, the cost would be $10,212 including maintenance for three years. These figures show a cost advantage of $2,748. A breakdown of the costs is shown in Table I.

The $2,748 savings derived from purchasing the terminals indicate that it will be to the Company's advantage to take this alternative.

/Attachment/

TABLE I: COST ANALYSIS

	3 Year Cost
Leasing cost	
6 Terminals @ $60 per month per terminal	$12,960
Purchasing cost	
6 Terminals @ $1500 per terminal	$ 9,000
6 Terminals @ $ 350 monthly maintenance per terminal	756
6 Terminals @ $19 repair service charge per terminal x estimated number of service calls	456
	$10,212
Monetary savings if terminals are purchased	$ 2,748

PERIODIC REPORTS

Some short reports are issued at regular intervals to keep the reader abreast of a continuing situation or of the activities of some person or organizational unit. Such reports may be issued as frequently as every hour. Others are made daily, weekly, monthly, or over longer periods. In addition to providing current data, the periodic report may refer to conditions noted in the last report and make a projection into the future. It is not uncommon for the writer also to attempt an interpretation of the data, including causes and effects. The periodic report that follows combines several of these features:

October 1, 19--

From: H. S. Canby, Service Department
To: Regional Operations Officer

Subject: Service Report, Denver

Continued improvement has been apparent since my report of July 1, 19--, and it is now evident that we are successfully meeting our assigned workload with a greater degree of regularity. An increasing efficiency in man-hours is shown by the following table:

Actual Man-Hours Expended Per Servicing

	Service Check	Periodic Check
July	11.4	174.3
August	10.7	165.0
September	10.3	142.4

The steady trend toward improvement is attributable to many things, but notable among them are these:

1. Staffing--now have a full headcount.
2. Training--intensified program to increase knowledge and skills, thus permitting new hires to become productive.
3. Discipline--logical policies have been consistently applied in a reasonable but firm manner to achieve compliance.
4. Communications--more attention has been devoted to informing our people and gaining an understanding of them.
5. Morale--all of the foregoing factors have helped to improve the morale and increase cooperation of the working force. There seems to be a growing recognition and appreciation of the necessity of the Company's action concerning shift assignments.

The number of formal grievances going to the Adjustment Committee has increased slightly since the last quarter, from 19 to 22. We are, however, heartened rather than disheartened by this fact because it at least indicates a willingness on the part of our people to abide by this legal procedure for the treatment of their protests.

PROGRESS REPORTS

When a long-term project is undertaken, the progress report enables management to keep in touch with the developing situation. Perhaps a building or repair program has been started, or an automatic system is being installed, or a new plan of operation is undergoing tests. The report may include a chronology of the progress made since the last report; a description of materials, equipment, and personnel used in the program; an account of any special problems or difficulties and the actual or proposed solution; and an estimate of what further steps must be taken to ensure completion of the project.

A familiar type of progress report is illustrated below:

Memorandum to Mr. J. V. Carr:

You will be interested to know the results to date of our offer to provide our dealers with novelty promotional pieces.

Since our mailing on August 13, we have received 112 orders totaling 176,493 pieces. Of the 26 items in the novelty catalog, our dealers ordered 21.

As you can see by reference to the attached table, bookmatches led in volume with 96,000 pieces, but the number of orders was about equal to the number received for the sewing kit, pencil sharpener, billfold, and ball pen.

Items for which no orders were received are the fly swatter, letter opener, stamp case, mechanical pencil, and paper weight.

From the results so far, two conclusions are possible: (1) dealers have no outstanding preferences among the items offered, and (2) our list of 26 items was long enough and varied enough to allow dealers a sufficient choice.

John A. Carroll
Sales Promotion Department

INSPECTION REPORTS

Quality control of products and services is made possible by inspection reports. These are sometimes part of the operating routine and at other times set in motion by complaints. Unless an inspection is routine, the reporter will usually set forth the circumstances that gave rise to the inspection as well as the specific findings. If the reporter has authority to act, he will also indicate how he followed up or solved the problems his investigation revealed. In other instances, he may suggest a solution or leave the remedy entirely to other agencies. Many inspections, of course, result in positive findings and require no further action.

Inspection Reports

Necessarily, the inspection report will be adapted to the audience—technical in language if it is addressed to the specialist, nontechnical if it is addressed to a layman whose complaint resulted in the inspection.

The report that follows was made by a city health department inspector:

```
SUBJECT:  Harbor Water Survey, Pier 126, Lower Bay

An investigation made on September 12 last, at the re-
quest of the Department of Docks, disclosed the above
premises to consist of a ship repair yard, shops, piers,
and drydocks.  Water from the Narrows is used on the
piers as a fire supply and for washing ships.

Harbor water is obtained from two four-inch standpipes
located on the pier.  These standpipes are overboard suc-
tion lines for portable pumping equipment.  A portable
4½" x 7½" x 12" duplex steam or compressed air driven
pump is connected to the standpipe when salt water is
needed.

No cross connections to the city water supply were found.

                                Henry Rawlings
                                Staff Inspector
```

The reports below are excerpted from the weekly inspection log of an industrial firm:

```
Toggle Switches

Orders of 12 Series toggle switches, involving about
2,000 switches, have been rejected through sample inspec-
tion for loose common terminals.

New riveting punches for the Lansing riveters have elimi-
nated the loose rivet problem for the future and have
also made a considerable improvement in the appearance of
the rivet job.

Samples of switches with the loose riveting have been
sent to our testing laboratory to determine the effect,
if any, that the loose riveting may have on temperature
rise and resistance.
```

```
5B65-RS

Again we had trouble with the last order.  It seems that
the leaf spring is the culprit.  The spring is so con-
structed that, in order to hold all the characteristics,
excessive adjusting is required.  Jim Haddock came over
with a new spring die.  We built ten pieces and these
look very good.  Let's hope the new die will continue
producing springs of good quality.
```

946-G

Production is having problems on the thru bolt which holds the basics in place. Either the bracket is too long or the screw is too short. There doesn't seem to be enough thread left to secure the nut properly. Four washers are being used as spacers. Ted Reames was called in on this problem and is checking into it.

INQUIRY REPORTS

Since business decisions must be based on sound information, the gathering of data becomes itself an important part of the decision-making process. When a report is based on inquiries made outside the writer's normal channels of communication, it may be termed—for want of a better name—an inquiry report. Unlike other investigatory reports, the objective here is simple reporting rather than technical examinations, measurements, or recommendations for action. To protect himself and assure the reader of the value of his information, the reporter should specify his sources. He should also be sure to present his data clearly, completely, and objectively.

The following report treats separately the information received from three different sources. In the interests of accuracy and objectivity, the investigator uses direct quotations reconstructed from his notes.

For: John R. Silverman, Vice President, in response to request from client.

From: Andrew Waite, Credit Department

Subject: Quality and prospects of New York mink market with particular regard to the impact of imported pelts and second pelting.

Source No. 1. Mr. Arnold E. Everett
Executive Vice President
Metropolitan Auctions, Inc.
960 West 29th Street

Telephone inquiry
January 5, 19--

"The first pelting for mink is in November; the market opens in late December and is in full swing by early January. This year the two most popular domestic colors, pastel and natural dark brown, opened 20 to 25% off last year's prices. The lighter colors, however, have remained firm or are off no more than 5%. The price difference can be explained by the bad season which furriers experienced last year, and to some extent by the influence of imported pelts and foreign buyers.

"The Scandinavian market opened in early December and was characterized by a determination to sell at almost any price. American buyers were able to purchase at prices up to 25% off from last year's levels. The imported pelts have affected the New York market in a curious way;

our bread-and-butter colors, pastel and natural dark brown, are off, but buyers from abroad have been purchasing quality pelts in New York, thus supporting the prices of such colors as sapphire, tourmaline, white, and argenta.

"Since the New York market opened somewhat off, many breeders who had kept their best animals for breeding purposes have decided to cut back on the size of their herds. If there is a second pelting, or some of those breeder animals are killed, the skins will be introduced to an already weak market and the price could be further damaged."

Source No. 2. Mr. Henry S. Fuller
Controller
Northwest Fur Sales, Ltd.
690 West 26th Street

Telephone inquiry
January 5, 19--

"This year, as has been the case for several years, fur production is up 18 to 20%. The North American pelt is still the finest in the world, but there is some influence by the European market which opens earlier.

"Our market opened generally lower than last year--about 18%. Our best colors, those most marketable in the United States, are off 20%; the white mink has dropped 30% from last year's level. However, platinum, argenta, and sapphire are at the same level or slightly higher than they were a year ago. Our auctioneers tell me that in the last week there has been an upturn in the market, and buying seems more determined. It is really too early to tell about the fate of the mink market in New York, however. Furriers had a bad year, and unless the economy in general picks up, there is no reason to expect an improvement in the fur market. After all, mink is a luxury item and if people don't have the money or if the prices are too high, then nobody buys and nobody makes.

"The second pelting involves the breeder animals, and sometimes prices on those pelts are off up to 20%. It is too early to tell, however, whether there will be much of a second pelting in the current season."

Source No. 3. Mr. Ira Wolf
Sales Manager
Benjamin and Goldstein, Inc.
870 West 31st Street

Personal visit
January 6, 19--

"Mr. Benjamin is pessimistic about the fur market in the coming year because of the general conditions of the economy. On the other hand, I feel that the market for mink has started off at a sane level and historically that has meant a good season for the furriers."

SUGGESTION REPORTS

Suggestion systems are by now a standard part of the operating program of almost all large organizations and many smaller ones. Employees are encouraged, usually by means of money prizes, to submit in writing any ideas that could result in benefit to the company. The suggestion should of course be clearly described and include a statement of the savings or other advantages that will accrue to the company if the suggestion is adopted. The following suggestion report was submitted on the form shown in Figure 11-2:

> I suggest that colored tissue paper be supplied typists for making any extra carbon copies of outgoing letters not needed for filing.
>
> Many times the extra copies--which are now typed on white tissues and are not distinguishable from the file copies--land in the file basket and are automatically filed. This practice not only wastes the file clerk's time, but also increases the bulk of our files without any compensating advantages. If the colored tissues are used, they can be thrown away after they have served their purpose without anyone's worrying about whether they belong in the file.

RECOMMENDATION REPORTS

Although suggestion reports are entirely voluntary and may come from any source, recommendation reports are part of the responsibilities of planners and administrators. Such reports may recommend promotions and increases in salary, organizational changes, new purchases, and changes in production or marketing procedures. Many recommendations originate with suppliers, management consulting firms, and advertising agencies, which are invited to study a specific problem and recommend a course of action. A recommendation report will usually cover these topics:

1. The need or problem that gave rise to the recommendation
2. The recommendation, including complete description and details
3. Factual and logical support of the recommendation
4. A request for action

The following letter report was written to a customer by a telephone company representative. It covers all of the points mentioned above.

> Dear Mr. Smith:
>
> This will confirm our recent conversation regarding the proposed installation of the new 50-line Key-Lite dial system.

As you know, your present telephone service, which is manually operated, requires all calls to be handled by an operator. All outgoing calls, incoming calls, and intercommunicating calls (other than the 11 stations linked on a separate intercom) require operator assistance.

The installation of a dial telephone system will handle automatically all calls within your plant and also permit outside calls without the assistance of an operator. The Toll Diversion feature (optional) will allow your operator to supervise and record all calls outside the Metropolitan Area and assist in administrative control. This will increase the efficiency of your administrative personnel and reduce the work load of the operator considerably. The only duties remaining for your operator will be to screen and distribute incoming calls.

Using the Key-Lite switchboard, the operator can connect calls and ring extensions at the touch of a button, and will no longer have to disconnect incoming calls, as this is done automatically when the extension user hangs up. Your present paging system may be incorporated into this dial system, and by dialing a predetermined code any extension user may page directly over his telephone.

Further efficiencies in operating costs can be made by utilizing the operator's time for other duties.

An estimate of additional cost for the proposed dial system is enclosed.

If you desire any further information regarding this dial system, please call me at 297-3372.

Very truly yours,

PROPOSALS

When a new plan or proposal is being considered in business, a draft of the proposal must be drawn up for approval. The draft must be complete in every detail; otherwise unanswered questions may result in a denial or a delay in taking action. Clarity is also aided by logical organization and the use of topical headings. In the following report, the directors of a company's Quarter Century Club, made up of senior workers, propose the establishment of a scholarship fund. The plan is to be submitted to the membership for discussion and a vote.

Preamble

The Board of Governors of the Quarter Century Club of Allied Insurance Company and a substantial number of the Club's membership favor the establishment of a Scholarship Fund, sponsored by the Club and intended to provide scholarship awards to the sons and daughters of the Company's staff.

Those advocating the adoption of the plan are influenced by the increasing number of Company parents who wish to make possible a college education for their children and by the mounting costs of tuition, board and lodging at our institutions of higher learning.

Underwriting

The proponents of the plan feel that the Fund should be established primarily from voluntary contributions by the members of the Quarter Century Club. However, donations will be welcomed from any others on the Company's staff who are interested in participating, or from anyone else. The costs of underwriting the selection of the applicants will be borne by the Quarter Century Club.

Contributions

The minimum amount necessary for the operation of the Fund is estimated at $3,000 annually. To assure this sum, it would be necessary for 80 per cent of the Club's membership to contribute at least $10.00 each per year. It is to be understood that any who wish to subscribe more may do so. Payments would be requested in late Spring, or approximately six months after the collection of Club dues. It is anticipated that the Company will allow payroll allotments (minimum $1.00 per pay) for those who prefer that means of contributing. The possibility that subscriptions to the Scholarship Fund will constitute a proper deduction for income tax purposes is being explored.

Administration

The Fund will be administered by three Trustees, one of whom will always be a member of the Board of Governors of the Quarter Century Club, one an officer of the Company (Vice President or higher rank), who is not a member of the Club, and one an independent person who is not an employee of the Company. It is intended that the first Trustees be Arthur K. Fellows, Foster M. Pease, Jr., and Waldo S. Blore.

Selection

Awards will be based on competitive examinations prepared and graded by the Educational Testing Service or other similar independent organization chosen by the Trustees of the Fund, except that personality and leadership will be given equal consideration when test results are apparently equal.

Awards

It is proposed that two scholarship awards be made annually in the sum of $3000 each--one to a son and the other to a daughter of a regular employee with a minimum of 5 years of service (including officers under the rank of Vice President) of the Allied Insurance Company. Children of such employees who have retired under the Company's Retirement Plan or have died while in the

Company's employ will be eligible. It will be a requirement that the award be used for first-year college level, but the choice of institution and course of study is to be made by the recipient (provided the institution is fully accredited). It is hoped that later on, if the amount of available money should permit, the size and number of awards may be increased. Awards not used within one year will be reconsidered at the discretion of the Trustees. The amount of the award will be paid directly to the college or university, to be applied against the tuition fees of the recipient for the first year's work. Awards will be limited to one per family and a recipient of a scholarship from the Fund will not be eligible for the competition in subsequent years.

ABSTRACTS

No administrator can do all the reading he should without employing some shortcuts. A common practice is to insist that any reports submitted by subordinates carry an abstract at the beginning. The abstract is a brief summary that retains the sense of the original. It is a customary part of scientific and technical papers. Often a top executive will instruct an assistant to abstract books and articles that have information of importance to him. If only part of a book or article contains material of interest, only that part need be abstracted.

The principal aim in abstracting is to reduce the substance without distortion or change in emphasis. The point of view of the original should also be retained. If the original is written in the first person, for example, the abstract should be written in the first person. The abstract should not contain such expressions as "The author says that." In effect, the abstract *is* what the author says. Attention to the style in other respects is not especially necessary unless the style holds the key to the sense. Thus if the writer has expressed an idea sarcastically, the abstract would have to make clear the author's intent.

The following report is an abstract of an article on job-seekers over 40 years old:

Men over 40 with considerable administration skill are being bypassed by American industry for younger men with much less experience. The reason usually given is that the older workers do not "fit into" the company's pension plan. This idea is refuted by the U.S. Department of Labor as well as responsible business leaders, especially since--to mention one of several points--benefits from most private pension plans are based on years of service. With the balance of available qualified personnel shifting from the younger to the older men, business can no longer afford the luxury of its prejudice against age. Nor can it afford other prejudices that keep the older men out of the jobs they deserve--prejudices based on religion, appearance, physical defects, club and school ties, and marital status.

MINUTES

The official reports of meetings are called *minutes*. They constitute the record of motions offered and acted upon and reports submitted. The thoroughness with which minutes are recorded varies considerably from organization to organization. In the instance of government and corporate bodies and other units that have strong legal obligations, verbatim reports are often taken and transcribed for the record. In other instances, notes are taken by the recording secretary and his minutes are read, corrected, and approved at the next meeting or they are submitted to a minutes committee for such action.

When legal considerations are relatively unimportant, the minutes are somewhat less formal and become mainly the means by which the accomplishments of a meeting are summed up both for those who were present and those who could not attend. At a minimum, minutes show the following:

1. The name of the organizational unit (e.g., the Finance Committee)
2. The kind of meeting (e.g., luncheon, special, regular)
3. The time, place, and date of the meeting
4. The name of the presiding officer
5. A record of all reports and motions presented, including their disposition

Only the most formal minutes will show the names of persons introducing and seconding motions and the names of those voting for and against a measure. They do not have to indicate the course of the debate. Informal minutes, however—especially those prepared for circulation to those not present—usually give the sense of the discussion.

The minutes that follow may be considered moderately formal:

FINANCE CLUB OF AMERICA, INC.

Minutes of the Regular Meeting
of the Board of Governors Held May 25, 19--

The Board of Governors of the Finance Club of America, Inc. met in regular meeting in the club rooms in the Hotel Stafford, Lexington Avenue and 49th Street, New York, N.Y. at 6:30 p.m. on May 25, 19--.

The meeting was called to order and presided over by the President, Mr. Trotter.

The Secretary, Mr. Wade, recorded the proceedings of the meeting.

Present, in addition to Messrs. Trotter and Wade, were Messrs. Behan, Brown, Everett, Fellows, Frank, Horne, Kingsley, Morris, and Swenson.

Colonel Durand was unable to be present at the meeting of the Board but attended the technical meeting later in the evening.

The Secretary announced that minutes of the meeting held on April 25, 19--, had been mailed to each member of the Board. Upon motion duly made, seconded, and carried, the minutes were approved.

The Admissions Committee submitted the following names and announced that these gentlemen were eligible for membership in the Club. Upon motion duly made, seconded, and carried, they were declared duly elected members of the Club.

Singer, John; Morgan Guarantee Trust Company
    Proposed by Mr. Frank and seconded by Mr. Fellows
Travers, Murray; Commercial Credit Corporation
    Proposed by Mr. Brown and seconded by Mr. Swenson

The Secretary announced with regret the death on May 15, 19-- of Mr. William Samuel Storer, who had been a member of the Club since December 30, 19--. Upon motion duly made, seconded, and carried, the Board expressed its regret and the Secretary was instructed to write to Mr. Storer's family accordingly.

The report of the Treasurer, Mr. Morris, was read and upon motion duly made, seconded, and carried, the report was ordered received and filed.

The Treasurer stated that he had been requested by the Merchants' Hospital to subscribe, on behalf of the Club, to an advertisement in the hospital's annual Souvenir Journal. After some discussion, it was decided that such a subscription should be made in the sum of $100.

<u>Entertainment Committee</u>

The possibility of a Club golf tournament in the vicinity of New York in June was discussed. Mr. Horne, Chairman of the Entertainment Committee, stated that in his opinion it would be impossible to secure a large enough attendance, and upon his recommendation the matter was dropped until the fall.

<u>Technical Meetings Committee</u>

Mr. Kingsley introduced a resolution expressing the thanks of the Board of Governors to Mr. Behan, Chairman of the Technical Meetings Committee, and to the members of that Committee for the interesting and instructive technical meetings they had arranged during the past winter. The resolution was duly seconded and carried unanimously, and Mr. Behan expressed his appreciation on behalf of himself and the members of his committee.

The President announced that the meeting was adjourned until Thursday, June 9.

Secretary

A less formal report of a meeting is this one, which is characteristic of a great many found in ordinary business practice:

```
Meeting of the Personnel Committee

August 23, 19--

Members of the Personnel Committee met on August 23 to
discuss a change in the provisions for tuition remission
for employees.  Present were Messrs. Gray, Fellows, and
Caldwell, and Mrs. Terry.

After considerable discussion, it was decided to recom-
mend to the Executive Committee that tuition allowances
be increased from the present limit of $700 per year to
$900 per year.  It was felt that this increase was neces-
sary to keep pace with increases in tuition instituted
in nearly all colleges in the Metropolitan Area since
the $700 figure was set four years ago.  It was agreed
that all other rules relating to tuition remission be
retained.

                              ______________________________
                              Henry Caldwell, Secretary
```

RESOLUTIONS

A resolution is the formal statement of the will or opinion of some group, adopted by a vote. Through a resolution, for example, an organization may propose an idea, endorse or condemn an act or measure, or offer condolences to the survivors of a deceased member.

The resolution often follows a verbal ritual that consists of a series of paragraphs beginning with "WHEREAS" and a final paragraph beginning "THEREFORE BE IT RESOLVED, That." A modified version of this pattern is seen in the following resolution adopted by a company's board of directors:

```
The President reported that Director Salvador Ferrari had
suggested the Corporation make a deep study of research
and development as it affects corporate earnings in the
soft goods industries, referring especially to (a) new
products, (b) new processes, (c) new markets, and (d) new
personnel; whereupon, after discussion, upon motion duly
made, seconded, and unanimously carried, it was

RESOLVED, That the idea for the study of corporate re-
search in the soft goods industries be submitted to the
staff of our Economics Department for their consideration
with the understanding that it will be reported on at the
next Board of Directors' meeting.
```

AGENDA

An agenda (this Latin plural is commonly used as a singular noun) is the official list of topics to be brought up at a meeting. In the most formal circumstances, the list will follow this pattern:

1. Call to order
2. Reading of minutes of previous meeting
3. Reports of committees
   a. Standing
   b. Special
4. Unfinished business
5. New business
6. Announcements
7. Adjournment

A less formal agenda is often drawn up for submission in advance to those expected to attend the meeting. The items are listed and numbered in the order of discussion and include any details the participants may need for an understanding of the matters to be placed before them. This is an example:

FINANCE CLUB OF AMERICA, INC.

Meeting of the Board of Governors:
Tuesday, August 9, 19--

Agenda

1. Applications for membership.

2. Matter of extending invitation to nonresident membership to Army and Navy officers stationed in the New York district and assigned to financial and accounting duties.

3. Matter of renting space in the Club to manufacturers of business machines and office equipment, affording an opportunity to them to demonstrate their products with privilege of using the main dining room between 3 and 5 p.m. to conduct classes for accountants and others.

4. Report of the House Committee.

5. Report of Mr. Harry L. Morris with reference to Field Day. Mr. Morris, chairman of the Membership Committee, believes that the Field Day will be valuable in promoting the membership campaign which he has in mind. He has discussed the matter with Mr. Horne, chairman of the Entertainment Committee, and Messrs. Morris and Horne will be prepared to submit concrete suggestions.

Secretary

CITATIONS

When it is desired to honor a member or friend of the organization, he may be given a citation. This is a formal expression of the group's regard for him and often includes a recounting of his achievements. The style ranges from very dignified to good-naturedly facetious. Often the citation is printed or hand-lettered and framed. It may be accompanied by a medal, plaque, gift, or other concrete evidence of appreciation.

The citation that follows, although written some years ago, is still notable for its informative content combined with light but affectionate touches. What do you think of the appropriateness of the allusions and the choice of words?

CITATION

Accompanying the Presentation of the Madden Memorial Award to

A. MILTON RUNYON

From Plainfield, New Jersey, to Garden City, Long Island, is but a few short miles in space, but millions of light years in mass culture. A. Milton Runyon made the trip by jet propulsion in 32 years.

Born beyond the meadows in 1905, he early showed his penchant for the literary life by planting his feet firmly on the bohemian soil of Greenwich Village, where he attended New York University's School of Commerce, Accounts, and Finance. There, surrounded by memories of Edith Wharton, Henry James, and Mark Twain, he imbibed the heady liquor of Business English and Advertising Copy. Soon he was trying his wings with little essays entitled "Final Examination" and at the same time sharpening his business sense by calculations designed to show that culture might be made to produce a buck or two if only it could be sold by the pound instead of by the point.

Accordingly, in 1926, he flew the Commerce menage with his B.C.S. degree and, after brief tenure elsewhere, became advertising manager of Doubleday and Company. There, working with fellow litterateur Nelson Doubleday, he soon realized the vast potential in the annual tonnage the book clubs were even then producing. Forthwith he gave orders to add coal to the creative fires and to increase the output. With the help of such stokers as Daphne du Maurier, Thomas B. Costain, and Somerset Maugham, one word burgeoned into a thousand, one page multiplied into a library, and one book club led to another.

Today the man who doesn't belong to a book club is as hard to find as the moral in a Mickey Spillane novel. By psychic estimate, Milton Runyon's customers in Doubleday book clubs run to some 2,000,000 families. He himself is the founder of the Mystery Guild and other successful book clubs, and the president of the Literary Guild of America—this in addition to being executive vice president of the largest book company in the world.

The School of Commerce Alumni Association is pleased to write a new chapter in the biography of A. Milton Runyon by honoring him with the Madden Memorial Award.

SUMMARY

Although short reports can perform the same functions as long reports, they cannot cover as much ground. They also look different and can play a greater variety of roles. Some are printed forms with blanks to be filled in, some take the form of letters, and most others are set up as memorandums. The heading of a memorandum will include the date and the name of the receiver; it may also include the name of the sender, and the subject. The memorandum may end with a signature, but the name is not preceded by *Very truly yours* or other complimentary close.

A common type of short report is one analyzing some internal method or procedure, with recommendations for change. Inquiry reports communicate information obtained through interrogation of external sources. Other reports give information periodically, as annually, quarterly, or monthly; still others detail the progress made in particular projects, or state the findings of official inspections, or make suggestions or proposals, or conveniently abstract a larger document, or record the minutes of a meeting, or put forward the agenda for a coming meeting. Resolutions and official citations may also be considered special types of short reports.

Short reports are often quite informal in language, but they need to be clear, concise, and well organized if they are to be of the greatest help to the reader. The listing and enumeration of coordinate details and the use of subheadings are encouraged. Tables and graphs are commonly employed in much the same manner as they are in long reports; they may be positioned either with the text or following it.

PROBLEMS

1. Assume that you keep your company's records relating to the annual September visit of the Red Cross Bloodmobile, through which employees donate blood.

   Two years ago 393 employees who signed up to donate blood gave 282 pints. The Red Cross, for various reasons postposed or declined donations from 35 applicants. Eleven applicants canceled their visits, and 65 did not keep their appointments. The year before, the comparable figures were 374, 249, 51, 14, and 60. The Bloodmobile can process 125 pints (125 donations) per day. It is now August 5. For the next visit on Tuesday, September 11, and Wednesday, September 12, you expect to have at least 375 employees signed up.

   Write a memorandum to Mrs. Dorothy Carman, your immediate superior, outlining your experience, so that she may make the necessary final arrangements with the Red Cross. With a dropout rate of 33 per cent among those who signed up to donate blood, it appears that processing can be completed during the two-day visit. Include a table showing your experience for the past two years. (For help with the table, see Chapter 12, "Graphic Presentation," pages 368–372.)

2. Assume that your employer rebates tuition and fees and the cost of books for approved evening courses taken at accredited colleges. As an employee, you have just completed two such courses—Principles of Accounting I and Organization

and Management—for which tuition came to $240 per course; the university fee was $30 for the semester. In addition, you spent $26.20 on books.

It is now February 25. Write a memorandum to Mr. Jay Williams, your company's director of education and training, asking for full reimbursement. Provide an itemized list of your expenditures for books, and enclose a copy of your official college transcript. You may assume the names and prices of the books.

3. Assume that you are the son or daughter of an employee of the Allied Insurance Company, which has put into effect the scholarship plan proposed in the memorandum on pages 355–357. You have obtained one of the scholarships and have now completed your first year of college. The plan, as finally approved, requires that each recipient report to the trustees of the fund on his or her progress during the year. Write such a report in a memorandum to Ms. Nora Bayle, a vice president of the company and one of the trustees of the scholarship fund. Stick as closely to the facts as you can, inventing necessary data only if you have not yet actually completed your first year of college.

4. A week ago, the dean of students of your college addressed the Student Council, of which you are the Secretary, on the subject of the desire of the administration to be sensitive to the needs and desires of the student body. He asked that anyone with suggestions for the improvement of services to students communicate with him. At a subsequent meeting, the Student Council passed a resolution reading, "Resolved, that the college administration install beverage and snack machines in the Student Lounge."

   In a letter report addressed to the dean (provide the name and college address), apprise the dean of the action of the Student Council. Include the information that the Council is aware of the fact that food and beverage machines were installed briefly a few years ago and that they were removed because of the messy conditions they caused. The Council believes, however, that with enough receptacles for waste and proper monitoring now regularly assigned to the lounge (there was none before), a high standard of cleanliness can be maintained. Ask courteously that the Council's resolution be implemented after giving the dean appropriate reasons.

5. Assume that you are a member of the Marketing Society of your college. You are distressed by the practice of leading food processors of constantly adding more and more chemicals to prepared, packaged foods. (Just read the label on a package of dry soup mix.) Last month, under the title of "Food Additives and Health Risk," the U.S. Food and Drug Administration (FDA) issued a report in which it was pointed out that while the new foods may offer convenience, they have less nutritive value than their traditional counterparts. They also tend to aggravate allergies and present additional hazards, even including cancer, that may not become evident for years.

   Draft a resolution to be presented for a vote at the next meeting of the Marketing Society, condemning the proliferation of chemical food additives and including the provision that a copy of the resolution be sent to leading food processors as well as to the food editors of your local newspapers. Although your club may have a small voice, you feel that it is important for business to know how young people view the trend away from natural foods.

6. Assume that you are working for a medium-size company and that Sara Playton,

the director of training, knows you are taking a college course in business communication. Conscious of the need for improved quality in the letters the company sends out, Ms. Playton plans to organize an in-service training course in business correspondence. As a former high-school English teacher, she will conduct the course herself. However, she would like some ideas on the content of the course and has asked for some suggestions from you, including topics that should be emphasized. Using the experience you have gained in the business communication course you are taking, address an appropriate memorandum to Ms. Playton.

7. The Neighborhood Consumers Protective Association (NCPA), of which you are a member, is interested in obtaining a comparison of the prices and service at three local supermarkets. As head of their Comparison Shoppers Committee, you have been delegated to make the investigation. You are to include in your survey ten common, branded products usually sold in such stores (for example, Tide, Del Monte peaches, Chicken of the Sea tuna, Jell-O).

   After comparing prices for the same items in the three competitive stores you have chosen for the survey, note the service at the checkout counter and such additional amenities as check-cashing and unit pricing, as well as flow of store traffic, adequacy of the stock on shelves, lighting, and sanitary conditions. Then write a memorandum to Mrs. Mary Wellbaum, the NCPA's president, incorporating your findings.

8. From your reading in *Business Week*, *Fortune*, or the business pages of your newspaper, select some current business leader (like the head of some very large corporation), whom your college has decided to honor with its "Business Achievement Award," a medal given each year to some outstanding business executive with a good record of public service. After finding out as much as you can about this individual through *Who's Who in America*, or articles listed in the *New York Times Index* or the *Business Periodicals Index*, write a citation (about 300 words) to accompany the medal. In a parenthetical note to your instructor, name your sources of information.

9. Write an abstract of about three hundred words of the article "The Writing Behavior of Businessmen," reproduced on pages 114–120. As an alternative assignment, you may select from a recent issue of the *Harvard Business Review* an article relating to your major field of interest and write an abstract of similar length.

10. Assume that your instructor has given you the following memorandum. Write the report called for. [*Continued on next page.*]

```
Memorandum to (Your Name):

I would like your help in a little research project I am
undertaking.  Your first-hand experience as a student
could be invaluable to me.

As you must be aware, a vast new arsenal of communication
techniques and media is available to education, as well
as to business and the arts.  I would like to learn the
extent to which the new methods are finding their way
into the classroom.

On the basis of your personal experience with college
courses this semester, will you please let me have a
formally organized report on the teaching techniques used
at this College.  Subjects that I would especially like
you to investigate and report on are:

(a)  Methods of presentation, e.g., lecture, discussion,
     recitation.
(b)  Use of printed materials, e.g., textbooks, readings,
     "handouts," cases.
(c)  Use of the computer and audio-visual media, e.g.,
     overhead projector, slides, films, tapes, records.

Please include a tabular summary and analysis of the
data, as well as your conclusions.  Finally, please con-
centrate on methods and media; exclude the names of in-
structors and make no attempt to evaluate their
performance.
```

11. The Dynamic Development Corporation of Wilmington, Delaware, is one of the largest makers of electrical components for cars, airplanes, atomic plants, and guided missiles. It has plants in many large cities. Its corporate offices are in New York where, assumedly, you are engaged in personnel development for the company.

From several of your young engineers who are interested in attending, you have learned of a graduate "retreat" in the liberal arts to be held for one week (April 14–21) at Dartmouth College in Hanover, New Hampshire. This is one of an annual series. The special purpose of the seminar is to give business people with professional undergraduate degrees an opportunity for the kind of mental stimulation which their jobs do not ordinarily afford. They would listen to specialists in such fields as literature, history, government, and science, and engage in study and discussion of these subjects afterward.

After giving some thought to the subject, you have decided that it would be desirable for your company to sponsor a week's sojourn at the seminar for a half dozen members of the engineering staff, with tuition, board, and transportation to be paid for by the company. The cost in addition to salaries would be approximately $400 per person. It is your idea that other groups could be chosen to attend the seminars in succeeding years.

You will need to present your plan to the company's president, Mr. Anthony S. Gould, for approval. Before you do this, however, there are certain questions you have to be able to answer to his satisfaction. These are: "What is a fair way to select the participants?" "What will the seminar do for the people selected?" "How will the company realize a fair return on its investment?" When you have given sufficient thought to these questions and you believe you have the answers, write a memorandum to Mr. Gould stating your plan in detail.

12. The Lincoln Corporation, manufacturers of air-conditioning equipment have seven salesmen operating from the New York office and covering New Jersey, Connecticut, and New York State, including Long Island. They sell to medium-sized business and industrial firms.

For the same area, Lincoln's two major competitors have 17 and 29 salesmen respectively. These two competitors sell approximately the same type of air-conditioning product as Lincoln. Thus, from the viewpoint of number of salesmen alone, the first competitor has more than twice the opportunity to make customer contacts as Lincoln, and the second competitor has over four times as much. Obviously, if Lincoln were to compete on an equal basis with these two competitors, Lincoln salesmen would have to make customer contacts as frequently as the two competitors. In the present situation this is impossible.

A possible solution would be to hire additional salesmen. However, these salesmen are highly trained engineers and command a subtantial salary in addition to commissions. Also, because they are in demand, they are difficult to obtain. Furthermore, a salesman's success depends to a great extent on personal contacts with accounts; and this relationship may take several years to establish and to cement. While hiring additional salesmen is a long-term proposition, this solution nonetheless merits consideration.

The customers in the three states are available only between 9 a.m. and 5 p.m., Mondays through Fridays. Lincoln salesmen spend about 35 to 40 per cent of this time (or 14 to 16 hours per week) in the New York office doing detailed presale and postsale paper work. Were it not for this fact, they could devote more time to customer contacts. If part of the presale and postsale work could be taken over by office personnel, the salesmen estimate that they could cut the time spent in the New York office to 10 per cent (as opposed to 35 to 40 per cent) of their available sales time.

If their estimate is accurate, each salesman could then have 20 to 22 more hours per week for selling and his office time would be cut by 10 to 12 hours per week. On the basis of hours, estimate how many backup employees Lincoln would need in the New York office to take care of the salesmen's detail work. Under such a plan, the salesmen would not be going to New York so frequently. How would they get the information to the New York Office so that the backup personnel could do the detail work?

Write a memorandum report to Mr. Charles Wood, manager of the New York office, explaining the problem to him in your own words and making such recommendations as you think would help to bring Lincoln's sales opportunities in line with those of the two competitors.

12
Graphic Presentation

IN ANY REPORT, whether given in speech or writing, words are advantageously supplemented by tables, graphs, and other types of exhibits. By appealing to the eye, graphic aids bring an extra dimension to the presentation and add clarity, force, and interest. Quantitative data, for example, are hard to deal with in writing and speaking without causing confusion. When, however, the figures are arranged in a table or shown in a graph, the relationships become clearer because the eye and mind of the receiver are permitted to work together. Photographs, drawings, samples of materials, and the like may serve a similar purpose.

Apart from the natural advantage that graphic display would afford in any instance, the communicator must be aware that in today's visual culture, the reader and listener are apt to be less tolerant of a wall of words than they used to be. If they do not actually demand it, they are certainly more receptive to a presentation that permits them to look as well as read or listen.

TABLES

A table is a mosaic of figures that permits easy reference and comparison. It saves words and improves understanding. Sometimes in a single sweep, the reader gains insights from a table that would otherwise take many pages and give him much more strain.

Kinds of Tables

Tables are generally classified as spot tables or reference tables. The *spot tables* are an integral part of the text and are treated in the manner shown in Figure 12-1. They serve a very limited purpose. *Reference tables* are positioned independently, either near the text to which they refer or in appendixes. Each bears a title and, if there is more than one table, a number (Figure 12-2). Reference tables are sometimes further classified as special purpose or

Last February we conducted a series of mailing tests to determine the optimum warehouse location. This test consisted of mailing packages of books each day for a week from five cities which were considered possible warehouse locations. The books were mailed to the same ten customers in each instance, with mailing addresses scattered throughout the country. The results of the test were as follows:

City	Average Mail Service All Locations, Days
Chicago	3.75
St. Louis	4.25
Long Island City	4.65
Dayton	4.81
Buffalo	5.69

FIG. 12-1. *Spot table (bottom), showing relation to text.*

general purpose tables. As the names suggest, the *special purpose tables* illustrate a particular facet of the text, whereas the *general purpose tables* have value as more inclusive reference tools. Where both types of reference tables are used, the special purpose tables are usually placed in the body of the report, and the general purpose tables are placed in appendixes.

General Design

The data in a table are arranged in rows (horizontal) and columns (vertical), so that a special relationship is shown by the figure at the juncture of a row and column. These principles apply:

TABLE 4

NUMBER AND SIZE OF CHECKS RECEIVED

January, 19--

Under $1,000	1,980
$1,000 - $4,999	690
$5,000 - $9,999	273
$10,000 - $24,999	237
$25,000 and over	116
Total	3,296

FIG. 12-2. *Reference table.*

1. Data may be arranged geographically, numerically, alphabetically, chronologically, or by class, rank, or size.
2. In general, quantities should occupy the columns, while the things being studied (the "variables") are listed in the "stubs" on the left side of the table.
3. It is better that a table be read across than down, and the shape is better long than wide, though exceptions to these guidelines should be made whenever good sense dictates.
4. When figures are arranged by size, magnitudes usually diminish from left to right or from top to bottom.
5. A column containing percentages, averages, ratios, and the like should be placed to the right of a column containing the base figures.
6. Coordinate columns—that is, columns containing the same kinds of information—should be the same width.
7. Horizontal rules are usually used to separate the column heads from the body of the table, but other horizontal rules and vertical rules between columns are used only to improve display or prevent the confusion of figures. In any case, the sides are usually left open.

Parts of the Table

The parts of a reference table are shown in Figure 12-3. Below is a description of the parts, with additional commentary on tabular techniques:

Title. The title and number are centered above the table in one or several lines. Roman numerals may be used for the table number, and full capitals may be used for the title, which should be as brief and specific as possible. Unit values, if applicable, are placed in parentheses below the title.

Columns. Each column has a descriptive heading or caption centered in one or several lines to fit the width of the column. A caption may also span several columns, each with its own subcaption. Unit values applicable to any of the columns should be included tersely in parentheses, as, for example, "(000's)," where three ciphers are to be added to the figures given.

Column totals should be placed at the top or bottom to suit the convenience of the reader. Subtotals within a column should be underlined.

Column spaces should not be left blank. If there are no figures to be supplied, the fact should be indicated by a long dash (—) or by the abbreviation "n.a." (not available).

Stubs. The headings in the left-hand column are called stubs. The stub caption is the descriptive word or phrase at the top of the column. When stubs are subdivided, the main entry is the group caption; the subentries, slightly indented, are the line captions. A space is preferably left above the group caption. If a space cannot be left below the group caption, the group caption may be underlined to separate it from the line captions. In a closely packed table, a space should be left between every five rows to make reading easier. Leaders, or spaced periods, may also be used to carry the eye from the stub to the column data. The periods should be aligned vertically.

End Data. A single footnote reference in a table may be marked by an asterisk (*). If there are several footnote references, alphabetical symbols are

TABLE VIII ← Table Number

TOTAL JOBS IN METROPOLITAN REGION ← Title

1965-1985 (in thousands) ← Subtitle

Stub → ; Column Caption →

	County or City	1965	1975	1985	Change 1965-1985 ← "Spanner" Caption	
Stub Heading →					Number	Per Cent ← Column Subcaption
Totals →	TOTALS FOR REGION	7,642.2	8,610.0	9,466.3	1,824.1	23.9
Group Caption →	NEW JERSEY SECTOR	2,040.2	2,415.1	2,783.1	742.9	36.4
	Bergen	285.2	348.5	392.8	107.6	37.7
	Essex	470.2	513.5	547.0	76.8	16.3
	Hudson	277.9	293.4	305.0	27.1	9.8
Footnote Symbol →	Mercer a/	132.8	155.8	178.6	45.8	36.5
	Middlesex	187.2	245.6	317.8	130.6	69.8
	Monmouth	120.7	175.7	245.5	124.8	103.4
	Morris	87.6	117.5	153.4	65.8	75.1
	Passaic	187.8	219.5	246.3	58.5	31.2
	Somerset	52.6	69.9	92.9	40.3	76.6
	Union	282.2	275.7	303.8	65.6	27.5
	NEW YORK SECTOR	5,294.1	5,824.1	6,259.5	965.4	18.2
Line Caption →	New York City	4,076.4	4,351.2	4,521.9	445.5	10.9
	Dutchess	67.6	83.2	105.1	37.5	55.5
	Nassau	496.1	587.0	640.1	144.0	29.0
	Orange	60.2	74.6	100.3	40.1	66.6
	Putnam	7.7	11.0	16.3	8.6	111.7
	Rockland	52.7	78.0	116.2	63.5	120.5
	Suffolk	202.9	257.0	325.8	122.9	60.6
	Westchester	330.5	382.1	433.8	103.3	31.3
	CONNECTICUT SECTOR					
	Fairfield	307.9	370.8	423.7	115.8	37.6

Footnote → a/Included in Metropolitan Region for first time.

FIG. 12-3. *The parts of a table.*

generally preferred in conjunction with figures. The following styles are acceptable:

1,956[a]	a/1,956	(A) 1,956
560[b]	b/ 560	(B) 560

The symbols are repeated at the bottom of the table before the respective footnotes.

In addition to footnotes, the end of the table may also have an explanatory note and a statement of the source of the data. The sequence and style are shown in the following example:

```
    a/Approximation, due to rounding-off.

    b/Computed with switch to straight-line method.

    Note: Present discounted values are computed as of
the end of the year in which the investment was made.

    Source: Survey of Current Business, February 1978.
```

GRAPHS

Graphs and other types of charts cannot present the detailed information found in tables, even though tables may provide the source data. The graphic exhibits do have an advantage, however, in their dramatic appeal to the eye. Like simple tables, they can be prepared not only for use in a written report, but also for display or projection in a speech presentation. Some companies have specialists draw the finished charts, but the preparation of at least the drafts is the work of the writer or researcher.

Chartmaking Materials

The following materials are useful for making simple charts:

Graph paper
Ruler
Protractor
Compass
Ruling pen
Speedball pens
Black india ink
Lettering guide
Drawing board
T-square
Triangle

Printed graph paper is available in a variety of rulings, principally 5, 6, 8, 10, and 12 to the inch. The 6 ruling corresponds to the vertical spacing on the typewriter; the 10 and 12 correspond to the horizontal spaces of pica and elite type.

Other chartmaking aids include colored cellophane tapes for use in making lines and bars, acetate film for use in shading, and alphabet packs with transferable letters and symbols. Some of the trade names under which these materials are available are Chart-Pak, Prestype, Formatt, and Letraset. The best sources are art supply stores and college bookshops.

General Techniques

1. Draw the graph in pencil on graph paper; then copy the draft on plain white paper. Keep the grid lines to a minimum. Intermediate values can be shown, where necessary, by "ticks" along the horizontal or vertical axis.
2. The use of color for lines and bars helps to emphasize distinctions but is impractical if the graphs are going to be reproduced in black and white.
3. Type the title and other data on the graph or hand draw them in block letters. The number and title of a graph are usually, but not always, placed at the bottom.
4. Explain distinctions in color, shading, or line quality by a "legend" in a convenient part of the chart (Figure 12-6).
5. Generally, time is indicated by the horizontal scale of a line or column graph, and quantity by the vertical scale. Clearly mark the points on both scales and place the index or unit of measure (examples: "1960 = 100"; "Thousands of Dollars") above the vertical scale or below the horizontal scale, as the chart requires.
6. Choose the scale or range to represent conditions accurately. Figure 12-4 shows how the choice of range may accentuate a rise or drop.
7. Be consistent in your scale. Don't, for example, show five-year intervals at the beginning of the scale and one-year intervals at the end. All the measures must be uniform.
8. Don't crowd the chart. Select carefully the few details to be shown and the few relationships to be established. Cut the number of words and figures to a minimum and make sure they are clearly visible.

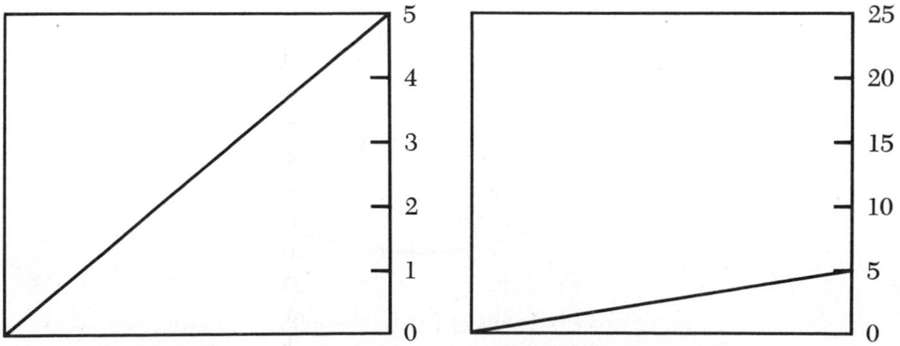

FIG. 12-4. *Visual effects of differences in scale.*

9. The most common types of charts are the pie chart, the bar chart, the column chart, and the line chart or curve. Instructions for drawing these types of charts are given below.

Pie Charts

A pie chart is a full circle that divides a whole quantity into its parts (Figure 12-5). Thus it might show the distribution of a dollar of income, the proportion of men to women in the employ of an organization, or the relative sales of a company's several product lines. To make a pie chart:

1. Convert all figures into percentages.
2. Beginning at "12 o'clock," mark off the required segments, going from the largest to the smallest, unless emphasis requires some other arrangement.
3. In allocating space, consider the circumference of the circle as 100 per cent and determine the size of each segment by using a protractor or by making a close estimate. Reasonable accuracy is possible if the circle is quartered, then each quarter halved, and each half quarter halved again. Each of the 16 segments is then equal to 6.25 per cent. If you use a pro-

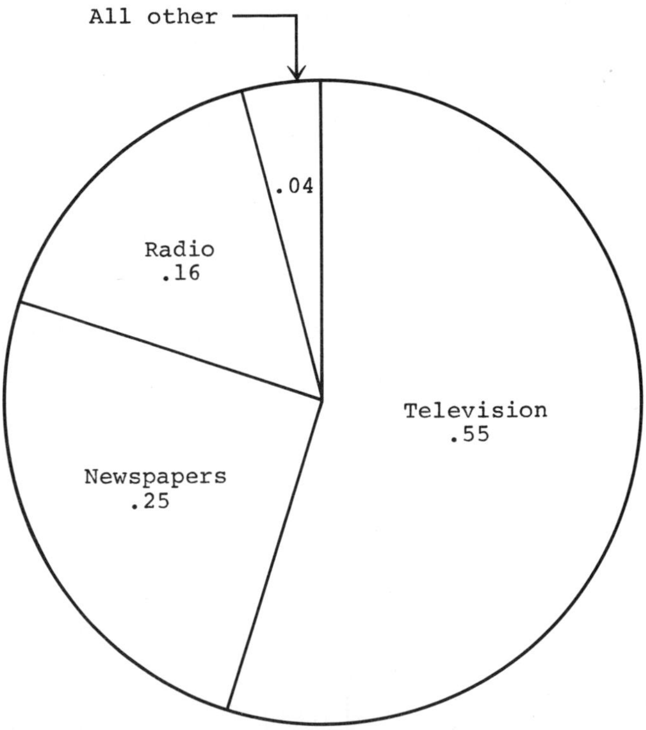

DISTRIBUTION OF ADVERTISING DOLLAR

FIG. 12-5. *Pie chart.*

tractor, keep in mind that the circumference of the circle is 360°; so 10 per cent would be 36°, 20 per cent 72°, and so on.

4. Place the segment labels and percentages inside or outside the circle, depending on the space available. Segments may be shaded for contrast.
5. Type all labels horizontally. Draw arrows, if necessary, to the segments to which they apply.

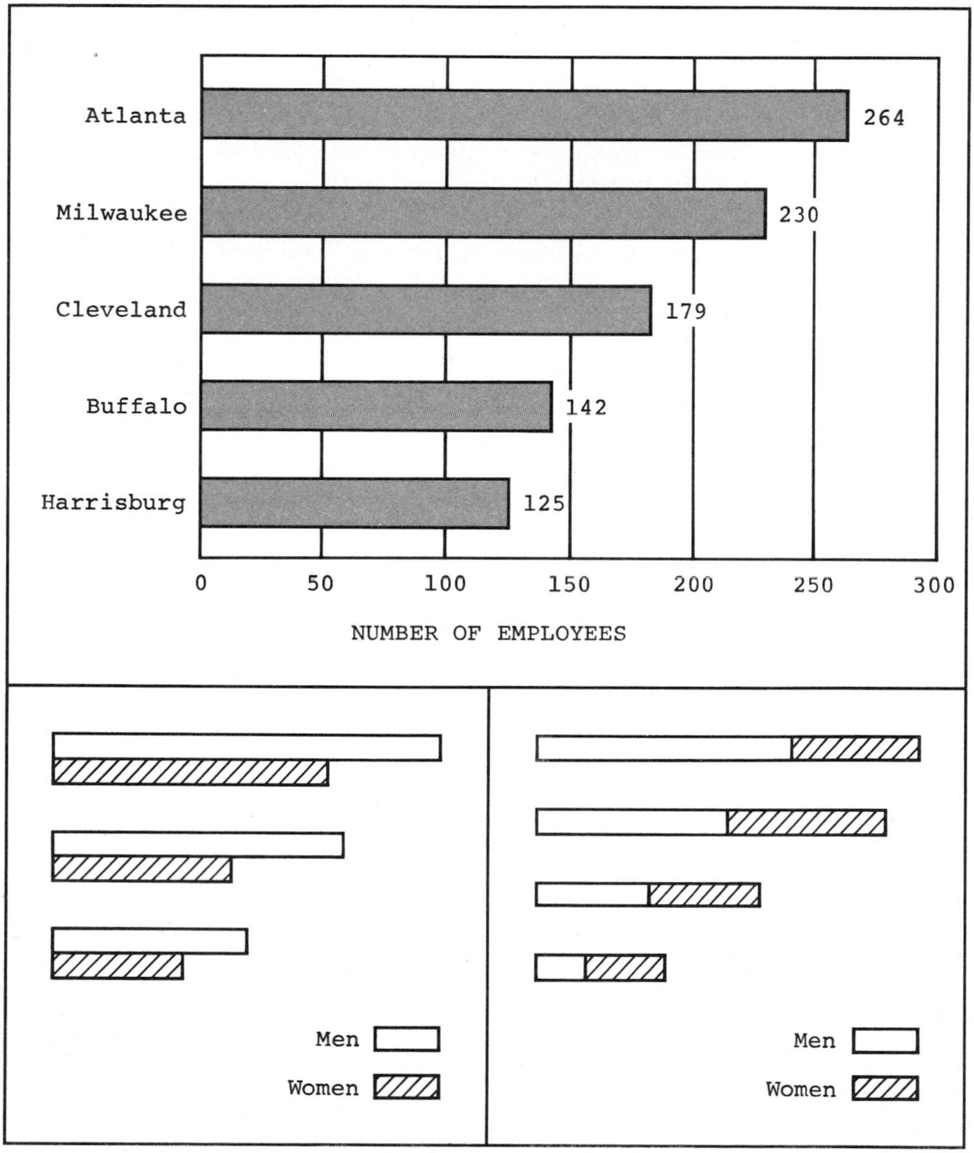

FIG. 12-6. *Bar charts.*

Bar and Column Charts

The bar chart shows the magnitude, or quantities, of different things. A sequence of dates or amounts is marked off on the horizontal axis, while the things being compared are represented by the bars extending from the vertical axis. The bars may be subdivided to show their components, or they may be clustered in groups of two or three (Figure 12-6).

Although the bar chart may be set upright to form a column chart, the column chart is technically reserved for "two-scale" representations, that is those that permit measuring both horizontally and vertically (Figure 12-7). As in bar charts, the columns may be subdivided or grouped.

The following suggestions apply to both bar and column charts:

1. Space the bars from one-half to a full bar width apart. Use narrower spaces or none at all between grouped bars.
2. Arrange the bars in ascending or descending order, or any other order consistent with the purpose of the chart or the emphasis you desire. A

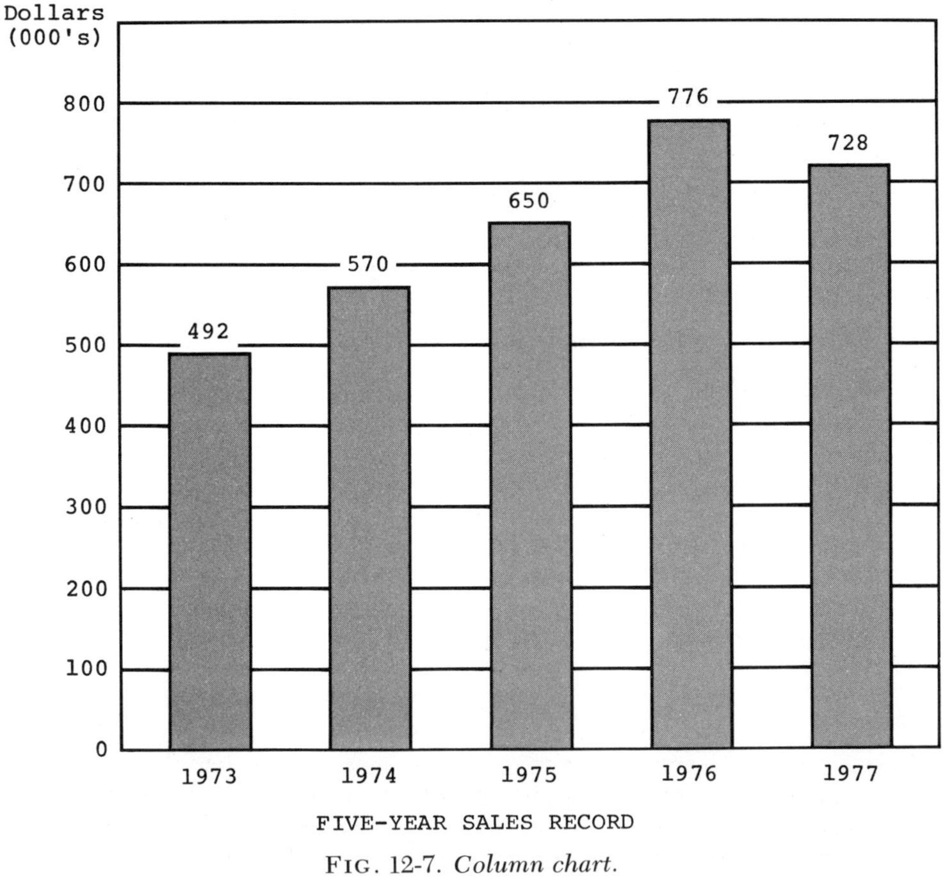

FIG. 12-7. *Column chart.*

time sequence, however, must be plotted in chronological order, beginning with the earliest period.

3. Use a consistent shading scheme for the parts of divided bars and the members of grouped bars. For simple bars and columns, draw outlines or solids.
4. A bar chart may be typewritten instead of drawn. Use conventional symbols, as shown in Figure 12-8.

```
                  EMPLOYMENT OF TEMPORARY HELP

                     October-November, 19--


      OCT.XXXX
      NOV.####                            Man-Hours

                       0    50     100     150     200     250
                       ┴─────┴──────┴───────┴───────┴───────┴

 34th Street   120     XXXXXXXXXXXXXXXXXX
    Store      179     ############################

 59th Street    96     XXXXXXXXXXXXXX
    Store      168     ##########################

 86th Street    39     XXXXXXX
    Store      109     ################
```

FIG. 12-8. *A typewritten bar chart. The upper bars are made of superimposed parentheses.*

Line Charts (Curves)

When points along a horizontal scale are too close for a column chart to be feasible, the points may be connected to form a curve (Figure 12-9). Two or three curves may also be overlaid on the same grid to show other variations in quantity over the same period. Some further suggestions:

1. If practicable, plan the chart so that it is about half again as wide as it is high; this will help prevent visual distortion.
2. Begin quantity scales at zero; otherwise a rise or fall will seem steeper than it is. If the curves begin somewhat high on the chart, the chart may be "broken" near the bottom to show the omission of part of the scale.
3. When several curves are superimposed, separate them by color or use a solid line for one and broken and dotted lines for the others.

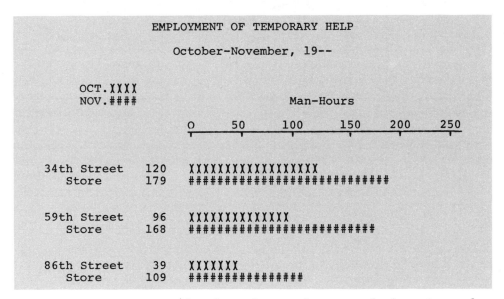

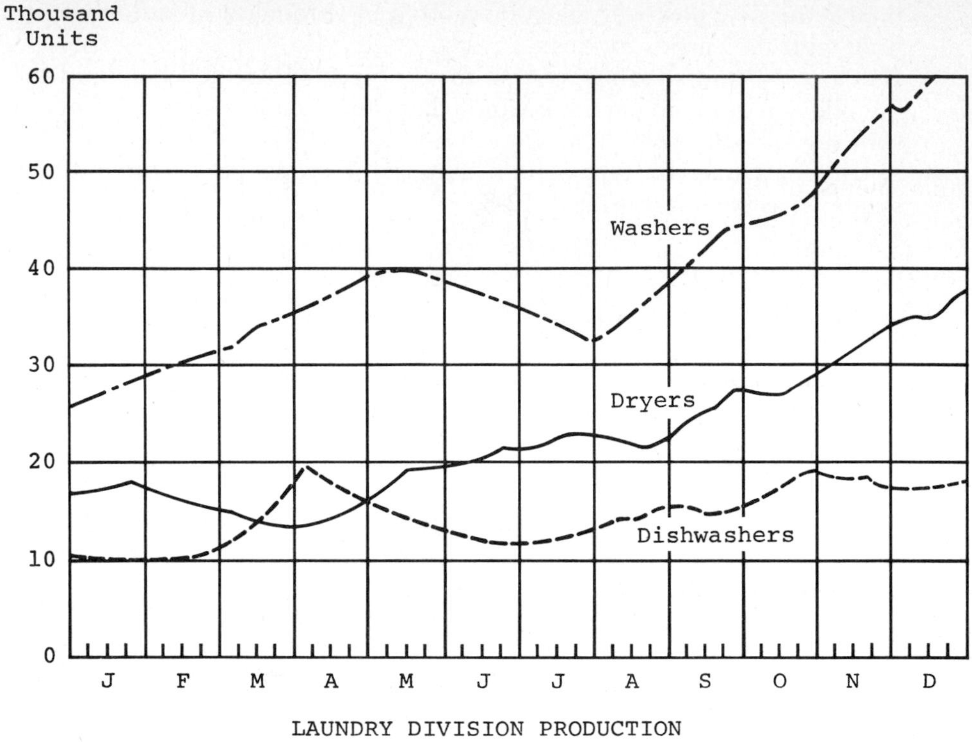

FIG. 12-9. *Line chart (curve).*

SUMMARY

Tables, graphs, and other exhibits aid clarity because they permit the eye and mind of the reader to work together.

Tables put related figures together to permit easy reference and comparison. Spot tables cover very limited ground and are an integral part of the text. Reference tables are positioned independently near the text to which they refer or at the end of the report. Reference tables are labeled at the top by number and title. Relationships in a table are pointed up at the intersections of the rows and columns. The columns contain quantities that are identified in the column heads or captions. Unit values are given tersely at the top of a column (e.g., *000's*). The things being studied (the variables) are listed in the "stubs" in the left-hand column. Captions may be divided into subcaptions and stubs may have subentries. Footnotes in a table are best shown by alphabetical symbols (*a, b, c*). Notes to the table and sources of information may also be indicated below the table.

Graphs cannot show as much data as tables, but they have greater visual appeal. The simplest kind of graph, a pie chart, divides the whole into its parts. The pie represents 100 per cent and all the figures to be represented in the pie must be converted into percentages. The pie is usually divided clockwise, beginning at the "12 o'clock" position, with the largest quantity first and the others in order of diminishing size. All parts must be properly labeled.

A bar chart shows the magnitude of different things, with the quantities indicated along the horizontal axis and the things being compared represented by bars extending from the vertical axis. Bars may be divided to show their components, or they may be clustered in groups of two or three. The column chart is similar to the bar chart except that the bars are arranged vertically for two-scale measurements. Amounts are usually listed along the vertical axis and time is indicated along the horizontal axis. The columns, like the bars, may be divided or clustered.

A line chart is used when the points along a horizontal scale are too close for a column chart to be feasible. The points are connected to form a curve. Several curves may be superimposed to show other variations during the same period.

PROBLEMS

1. In a brief report to Miss Ida Clark, director of the clerical training program, Mr. Marvin Davis, the personnel manager, assembled the following information from the July files.

   Between July 1 and July 31 he hired 247 clerical workers, mostly to staff the offices of the new building; 62 of these are men, the rest women.

   Of the new employees, 65 per cent of the women are high-school graduates, 15 per cent are graduates of 2-year business colleges, 5 per cent have college degrees, and the rest are high-school dropouts.

   Among the men he has 2 college graduates, 23 high-school graduates, 6 2-year business school graduates; the rest are high-school dropouts.

   The median age of the new women employees is 19, with a range of 17–31; the median for the men, 21, with a range of 17–26.

   From this group (men and women) he has 142 typists with 2 or more years' experience, 81 stenographers with 2 years' or more experience. The others are inexperienced or slightly inexperienced people who will have to be trained for clerical jobs. These workers have on record their employment tests in spelling, English, and mathematics, showing that they have met our minimum standards or better.

   Put as much as possible of these data into tabular and graphic form. Use as many tables and graphs as you need.

2. Figures of the U.S. Bureau of Labor Statistics show hours and earnings of workers engaged in manufacturing. The data below for the years 1960, 1965, 1967, 1968, 1969, and 1970 are averages of monthly figures and cover production workers only.

   Gross weekly earnings in 1960 were $90, while net weekly earnings of those without dependents were $73 and those with three dependents $80; the weekly hours worked were 39.7 and hourly earnings excluding overtime were $2.20. In 1965 and 1967 through 1970, the gross weekly earnings were $108, $115, $123, $130, and $134 respectively, while net weekly earnings for those with no dependents and 3 dependents respectively for the same periods were $89 and $97, $93 and $101, $98 and $107, $102 and $111, and $107 and $116. The number of weekly hours worked ranged from 41.2 in 1965 to 40.6 in 1967 to 40.7 in 1968 to 40.6 in 1969 to 39.8 in 1970. Hourly earnings for the same period were \$2.51, \$2.72, \$2.88, \$3.06, and \$3.24. Net earnings represent gross earnings less social security and income taxes.

(*a*) Put all these figures in a single table, including a title and footnotes.

(*b*) Show as much of the data as you feasibly can through the use of graphs. You may use a number of different groupings of data.

3. The United Oil Corporation has just issued the following figures covering chronologically the last six calendar years of its operations. Put each set of figures into the most suitable graphic form for use in its annual report to stockholders.

(*a*) Revenues (in thousands of dollars): \$5,078,641, \$5,517,426, \$5,886,515, \$6,473,084, \$7,092,705, \$7,572,658

(*b*) Net income per share: \$2.89, \$3.15, \$3.51, \$3.80, \$4.26, \$4.50

(*c*) Cash dividends per share: \$1.40, \$1.52½, \$1.65, \$1.85, \$2.05, \$2.25

(*d*) Distribution of revenue dollar for the last calendar year: taxes, 31¢; selling and general expenses, 11¢; costs, operating and exploration expenses, 47¢; net income 6¢; depreciation, depletion, etc., 5¢.

4. In 1950, 1960, 1965, and 1970, the number of telephones per thousand population was 281, 408, 478, and 563 respectively. The average daily telephone calls in millions for the same years were 176, 285, 367, and 462. The number of first-class and airmail pieces per capita for the same years was 168, 193, 205, and 238. Draw a separate bar graph for each set of figures. The figures on telephones come from the American Telephone & Telegraph Company. The figures on mail come from the U.S. Postal Service.

5. A survey conducted among college students by the American Association of Advertising Agencies showed that 20 per cent of those questioned thought there was too much advertising in newspapers, 56 per cent thought there was too much advertising on radio (network prime time), and 29 per cent thought there was too much advertising in magazines. Other figures were 62 per cent for billboards and 78 per cent for television (network prime time). At the same time the media department of Ketchum, McLeod & Grove, a New York advertising agency, showed that, on the average, the percentages of advertising versus the percentages of editorial or program content for the various media were 65 and 35 respectively for newspapers, 26 and 74 for radio, and 10 and 90 for television. Billboards had 100 per cent advertising content. Studies of advertising versus editorial content in a number of specific magazines showed percentages of 50–50 for *Sports Illustrated*, 51–49 for *Time*, 47–53 for *Newsweek*, and 30–70 for *Reader's Digest*.

Incorporate all of the data in a single table.

13
Elements of Persuasion

As we noted in Chapter 2, all communication is persuasive in that once the message is perceived, it brings about some change in the receiver's knowledge or attitudes. Even so, one may make a distinction between the informative elements of a message and the affective elements, between reporting and special pleading. In this chapter and the several that follow we are going to be concerned with special pleading—with those messages and those message elements by which we sell goods and services and influence in our favor the beliefs, attitudes, and habits of those with whom we communicate. Persuasion of this kind is found in sales letters, advertising, personal selling, promotion, publicity, and messages concerned with the settling of disputes. In modified form and in varying degrees it is also found in some parts of ordinary business correspondence, in business meetings, in personal conversation, and in memorandums and reports.

THE PROCESS OF PERSUASION

How do you sell an idea? What causes an individual to accept one argument and reject another? To prefer an Oldsmobile to a Chrysler? To vote for an incumbent in office and sneer at his opponent? To support one decision by an employer and sulk over another? There is no single theory of persuasion on which all authorities agree. However, we have enough knowledge of the process to see how minds can be influenced and how goods, services, and ideas can be promoted.

To begin with, persuasion is not to be regarded as simply an external force overwhelming the opposition. In most instances, the individual to be persuaded is already susceptible to the message by reason of his beliefs, his motives, his attitudes, or his experiences. It is the persuader's job to find the link between his proposition and the feelings, or "internal state," of the receiver. As an example, take the following store advertisement:

> CREATE WORKS OF PRIDE WITH NEEDLEPOINT
>
> It's easy. It's a fun way to wait out winter's end. With beautiful rewards in decorative excitement for dens, living rooms, bedrooms, family rooms. Makes a lovely hostess gift, too. All kits contain cotton canvas, yarn to complete, corduroy pillow back, piping, zipper, tapestry needle.

It is apparent that if the woman to whom the appeal is made is not already *inclined* to be creative, the advertisement would have no chance of persuading her to buy. Granted, then, that the internal state of the person to be influenced has an important bearing on the outcome, we can still identify the various functions in the persuasive process and the elements that support them. The functions that concern us are (1) attracting and holding attention, (2) providing effective motivation, (3) instilling belief, and (4) stimulating action.

ATTRACTING AND HOLDING ATTENTION

When William James stated, "What holds attention determines action," he was expressing a basic principle of persuasion. A converse principle is that the target of the message cannot be influenced by what he does not perceive.

During any given time span, we are subjected to countless stimuli that compete for attention. There are sounds, odors, tastes, sensations of feeling, visual images, and words in print. Some of these stimuli are only on the edge of our consciousness and others do not enter into the consciousness at all. Those we elect to "attend" to are usually very striking in their intensity or form, or those to which we are already disposed.

For a time Alka-Seltzer was attracting much attention with a series of amusing commercials, highly creative in their conception and production. Many viewers acknowledged that the commercials had more entertainment value than the shows they interrupted. Such pre-eminence in quality, however, is not necessary to draw the reader or listener to a commercial message.[1] The mere fact that one has insomnia, for example, will cause the listener to select a Sominex (sleeping pill) commercial for his attention, whereas others not so afflicted will use the time to pick up the crossword puzzle or go to the refrigerator.

Even when an individual is not strongly predisposed toward a message, however, repetition will eventually cause him to pay attention to it. Thus a housewife may be eminently satisfied with her present detergent and pay little or no attention to a message promoting, say, Cheer. With repetition,

[1] As a matter of fact, there is no proved relation between the creative quality of a message and its sales effectiveness. When sales fell, the Alka-Seltzer commercials reverted to the "hard sell" approach of previous, more successful sales efforts.

though, the message will register on her consciousness, and some day—should she become dissatisfied with her present detergent or fail to find it on the shelves of her supermarket—she may settle for Cheer simply because she recognizes the name. Even when repetition leads to annoyance, there is evidence to suggest that the irritation produces a high recall value and promotes sales.[2]

Nonverbal Methods

The earliest published advertisements consisted entirely of words, with little more display than one finds today in a classified announcement. Advances in printing and photography, and increased sophistication in design brought a new look to advertising, just as the typewriter brought a new look to business letters. Space—especially white space—was used more freely, and color, design, and pictures not only drew attention to the message, but helped increase its effectiveness. In broadcast advertising, these techniques have been expanded to include—variously—action, settings, voice quality, music, and sound effects. You need only turn on your radio or television set to discover how important such techniques are in attracting attention, sustaining interest, and aiding retention. It is not possible in print to convey the impact of a radio or television commercial, but one can imagine the effect of a tender, outdoor, boy-and-girl scene played against the plaintive song and off-screen announcer's voice in the following script:

CLOSE-UP TOOTHPASTE FOR THE
CLOSE-UP SMILE[3]

Singer's voice: Come a little closer baby
Smile for me, for a little while, for a little while
Look into my eyes!
Touch my hand!
I need a smile from you, I need a close-up smile.
Don't give me that faraway look
Don't tell me to phone
Don't just stand there . . . smile for me
And I won't feel alone.

Announcer: When you're close to people you need Close-Up Toothpaste. With two whiteners and a mouthwash, Close-Up gives you fresh breath. Makes your teeth their whitest white. In regular or mint flavor. Close-Up Toothpaste for the Close-Up smile.

Singer: Close-Up smile.
Close-Up smile.

[2] This is the substance of interviews by Philip H. Dougherty with a number of creators of advertising, as reported in the *New York Times*, September 29, 1971.

[3] "Close-Up" and "Close-Up Toothpaste for the Close-Up Smile" are registered trademarks of Lever Brothers Company. The song is copyrighted 1970 by Lever Brothers Company. Reprinted by permission of Lever Brothers Company.

The point that should be emphasized is that in the modern idiom of persuasion, words are still important, but the marriage of the arts to modern technology has made possible a wide range of supporting effects that no student or practitioner of persuasion can afford to ignore. It should be noted, too, that these effects may spill over from attention into every other facet of the message, from motivation to action.

Titles and Headlines

Within the text of a message, the means of attracting attention depend principally on the preoccupations, attitudes, and permanent interests of the reader whose attention you want. True, you can attract attention with some nonsense word like *Drdgsk!* which bears no relation whatever to anything the reader is thinking about; but such a device has limited application and the time during which it can hold the reader's attention must be measured in seconds.

More practical and effective is the word or thought that capitalizes on what is already in the reader's mind and may be brought to the surface. Thus the knowledge that a letter or report originated within his own company or department and that it is addressed to him gives the reader ample reason to pay attention to it. For it is through such messages that he receives information, instructions, praise, and blame; and he knows that he ignores them only on penalty of later embarrassment or personal loss. Attention to these communications is gained by fairly direct means in a title, subject line, or salutation as in these respective examples:

```
Revised Holiday and Overtime Rules

Subject: Storage of Old Correspondence

Memorandum to G. S. Smith, Plant Engineer
```

A letter going to a reader outside the immediate organization commands at least the initial attention of the *person* who receives it—good reason for addressing mail to an individual rather than an organization. In other instances, the reader's attention is controlled by a normal interest in the subject. Thus any message bearing the company's name is sure to hold some interest for a stockholder, and titles as ordinary as *Annual Report, Quarterly News for Shareholders,* and *Your Company's Products* have a ready attraction. In a similar way, such titles as *How to Carve, Notice to Theatergoers,* and *It's Your Library* may be said to select their own audiences. Other examples of selective titles and headlines are listed here:

Before You Make That Speech . . . (prospective speakers)

How Western Electric Helps to Keep Down the Cost of Telephone Service (telephone users)

Pack! Zip! Go! (travelers)

The Copymaker That Copies Everything (office managers)

Careers in the Grain Trade (agricultural-college seniors)

Thank You (new customers)

It's Easy to Be Safe With Electricity (users of electricity)

Dramatizing Attention

As the reader's interest in a subject becomes more remote, or as he develops resistance to a particular kind of message, attracting attention becomes more difficult. A reader may, for example, give his full attention to a message about a strike that prevents him from obtaining bread or transportation, but he is likely to be indifferent to similar news about a bathtub factory a thousand miles away. The same reader may attend closely to the initial announcement of a new movie, but he will pay little attention to the same announcement on its third, fourth, or tenth appearance. Under such circumstances, the writer often seeks to gain attention by dramatic methods. He may wait until he can capitalize on a timely event, or he may resort to some arresting literary treatment in the heading or opening of his message. Following are examples of varied techniques:

NEWS

Macy's warehouse sale—Friday and Saturday.

Eastern cuts the red tape on low fall fares to Florida.

Skirts may not be new—but aren't you glad they're back? (Bonwit Teller)

CURIOSITY

The ad your grandparents wouldn't let your parents read. (Metropolitan Life)

Can you find the 10 traffic hazards in this picture? (Shell Oil Company)

The odor you smell is money escaping. (Catalytic Combustion Corp.)

SHOCK

Tonight, as a public service, we're going to make you sick. (American Broadcasting Company)

If America dies, where will we bury it? (American Medical Association)

Her father gave her away when she was three years old. (Children, Incorporated)

HISTORY

Bull Run—where Stonewall Jackson earned his name. (Sinclair Oil Company)

PARADOX

We treat all our customers the same—differently. (Kidder Peabody & Co.)

PUN

Victor Hugo was writing. Renoir was painting. And Mumm was the word. (Mumm's Cordon Rouge Champagne)

Sustaining Interest

Since your objective is not only to attract attention but to hold it, the need for attention spills over from the title or headline into the body of the message. The beginning, consisting of the first paragraph or the first several paragraphs, has the principal burden of engaging the reader while the other elements of persuasion are brought into play. The immediate problem is to accomplish the often difficult transition between what attracts the reader and what is important to the purpose of the message. Here, for example, is a headline set in a field of white space:

Good night! Irene!

It attracts the reader perhaps because he recognizes that it is the title of an old song. It also attracts him because the advertisement bears the logotype of the *New York Times*. His curiosity is aroused. What is the connection? The first paragraph provides the necessary bridge:

> Now that Arlene, Beulah, Cindy, Debra, Edith, Flora, Gracie and Hannah have breezed by—keep your eye on Irene. Best way to follow her—and all the hurricanes from now to Zasu—is through the weather page of The New York Times.

The advertisement continues by describing the completeness of the weather reports to be found in the *Times*. But the opening has done its work. It has satisfied the reader's curiosity and has put his interest on a firmer footing than the headline alone could do. A similar technique is used in an advertisement for Lehigh Cement. Here, too, the reader's interest is drawn from the question raised in the headline to the answer in the opening paragraph.

> How Concrete Helps You Run Your Home
>
> Concrete dams tame rivers to provide electricity. Reservoirs made of concrete store water. Time-defying pipes of concrete deliver water to your community where it ends in your bathroom, your kitchen, your laundry.

In other instances, the early paragraphs are used, not to satisfy the reader's interest, but to heighten it. In the following example—from a sales letter for *The Time-Life Book of Family Finance*—the curiosity aroused in the first paragraph is intensified in the succeeding paragraphs, which at the same time draw the reader closer to the main point of the message.

Dear Friend:

Are there ways to save far more money than you do now? Can you increase your capital significantly by shrewd investments? What are the smart ways to buy so that you spend less and have more? How do others free dollars from taxes in ways you'd never suspect?

There are perfectly legal--and ethical--techniques for multiplying your money and its buying power. Some people know them:

> Near you, perhaps, lives a man who you suspect earns less than you. Yet he seems never to want for the good things in life. He drives an impressive car, lives in a handsome house, gives his children every advantage.

On the other hand, consider the other extreme:

> Another man may be making more than you. But you don't envy him. He's doing without some of the things you take for granted. He envies <u>you</u>. He complains that he can't get his head above water and vows that someday he's going to manage his money better.

What makes the difference between these two types?

Each manages his money differently. And the experts agree--and can prove--that the proper handling of money is the key to security. . .comfort. . . . and the rich, full life.

Do you know, for example . . .

* where you can average 9% on your investments?

* that you can save a great deal on men's clothes just by timing your purchases?

* why many car dealers would rather <u>not</u> have you pay cash for a new car?

* how to protect your retirement nest egg from inflation?

* why old-fashioned budgeting no longer makes much sense?

* how to get more insurance for less money?

If you feel that information like this would be useful, then you'll be interested in the book from which this information comes. It's a large and level-headed guide called . . .

THE TIME-LIFE BOOK OF FAMILY FINANCE

Attracting and Holding Attention

MOTIVATING THE READER

If the message has done well in engaging the reader's attention and interest, it has probably also helped the reader identify with some important problem or need. The message must now go further, however, and show how the problem can be solved or the need satisfied. The sequence is shown in the following portion of a magazine advertisement:

Attention:	Can you afford to have your son get good grades?
Need:	If your son's grades are good enough for him to get into college, will you be able to afford to send him?
Satisfaction:	Yes—if he's under the Travelers insurance umbrella. With the new Travelers Guaranteed College Fund, you can make sure there will be college money for your child whether you're around to see him graduate or not.

The satisfaction of needs is a familiar theme of modern advertising. The telephone company, for example, offers executives "a way to speed office communications." A publisher of dictionaries says that "a good vocabulary is a tremendous help toward better grades in college and success in the business world." A company selling an exercise machine states that "exercise is one of the most important factors contributing to total fitness." In the psychologist's parlance, each of these messages has an "appeal," or incentive. The appeal holds out the promise of reward. Description of the product or service shows how the promise is fulfilled. Together, the appeal and the description motivate the response.

Appeals

Appeals are found not only in advertising, but in other areas of communication as well. The teacher motivates students by appealing to their desire for good grades. The shop foreman obtains better results from workers by appealing to their pride and spirit of competition. The doctor induces patients to take a prescribed course of treatment by appealing to their desire for good health. The government official wins the cooperation of citizens by appealing to their patriotism. In every instance, one appeal can be found that, perhaps more than any other, moves the reader toward a desired goal.

Often the appeal is negative. Instead of promising a reward for following his suggestions, the writer threatens a penalty if the suggestions are not followed. Thus social ostracism is the penalty for not using a deodorant, accident and injury are the penalty for disobeying safety instructions, and loss of valuables is the penalty for not renting a safe-deposit box.

Negative appeals must be used with considerable care; otherwise the feelings they arouse may be so closely associated with the source of the message or with the general proposition that they inhibit favorable action. For many years, the makers of Lifebuoy Soap had to struggle to live down the association with B.O. (for *body odor*), a term they invented. Tire manufacturers and accident insurance companies also found that, in raising the specter of accidents, they had to suppress the more morbid details in order to avoid such revulsion that the reader would refuse even to think about tires or insurance. Research studies suggest that the reader's "defensive avoidance" of appeals to fear can be minimized by the inclusion in the message of reassuring recommendations. Such recommendations are designed to relieve the reader's emotional tension and motivate him to take constructive action.[4]

Many appeals, both positive and negative, are implied rather than stated. For example, the advertisement for a lady's suit described as "flown from Rome" leaves the reader to infer the fashion benefits. A collection notice that says merely, "Past due," appeals to the conscience of the reader and may imply penalties if payment is not made. A set of instructions tacitly promises good results if the reader follows them and the reverse if not.

The range of appeals is as broad as the spectrum of people's wants and desires. Some touch on man's elemental wish for survival. Others affect his more subtly realized feelings and emotions.

APPEALS TO BASIC NEEDS

The reader can be depended on to modify his thinking or take some action to satisfy his basic physical need for food, drink, sleep and rest, physical comfort, health, and the like. The appeal to self-preservation is evident in the road sign "Carelessness Kills." An airline employs a similar appeal when it writes to a customer who has complained about a two-hour delay in takeoff:

> Although we regret the flight was delayed, we want to assure you that it was only because we consider your safety more important than speed.

When the reader has a choice of several ways by which to satisfy a basic need, he will choose the one that most nearly conforms to his preferences. He will also on occasion modify his choices in accordance with his experience and changing tastes. The message that follows offers only one way to satisfy hunger, but it makes that way seem very appealing:

> It's Spaghetti and Beef-Stuffed Mushrooms à La Rosa. Juicy meatballs sitting pretty on Spring mushroom caps—simmered in Meat Sauce and consommé. Delicious when served with delicate strands of La Rosa thin spaghetti.

APPEALS TO EMOTIONS, FEELINGS, AND ATTITUDES

The response to a message is closely related to the kind and intensity of feeling it engenders. The reader may act through such strong emotions as fear, hate, anger, love, or despair; in response to the milder feelings of nostalgia, loneliness, affection, pride, generosity, resentment, sympathy, loyalty, and

vanity
pleasure-principle

[4] Carl I. Hovland, Irving L. Janis, and Harold H. Kelley, *Communication and Persuasion* (New Haven: Yale University Press, 1953), p. 88.

gratitude; or in accordance with his likes and dislikes, his partialities and prejudices. Thus a worker may be induced to learn a new skill under threat of losing his job; a man may buy a Lincoln for the pride of ownership it will give him; a housewife may try a special brand of soup out of gratitude for the company's television program, which she enjoys; and a citizen may vote for one candidate rather than another because of prejudice against "big business," or "starry-eyed liberals," or "reckless spenders."

The employee manual of a manufacturing company explains the rule against smoking in terms of job security:

> Smoking is strictly prohibited except in certain specified areas. Be especially careful to observe this rule because there is so much inflammable material about. A bad fire would seriously impair our work and might result in layoffs for a considerable period.

A lawyer appeals to the protective instinct of a client when he writes as follows about the desirability of a trust fund:

> A trust would also solve the problem that would arise if both you and your wife were to die while a child is a minor. If there is no trust to manage your property for a minor, the court will appoint a guardian who will be required to post bond and obtain court approval of investments and expenditures out of principal. If a trust is used, this cumbersome and expensive method is avoided because the trust can be drawn to authorize the trustee to use the principal for any purpose for which you would have used it. I am thinking particularly of the children's education, which I know is a primary concern.

The strength of the following appeal to students is apparent:

> You'll know the Galaxie's a winner the minute you see it. It's easy to type on, easy to learn on . . . helps you turn out neater homework and do it faster. You get high marks . . . and have more time for sports, clubs, all kinds of activities. And typing's plenty useful when you're through school, too.

APPEALS TO SOCIAL MOTIVES

Many of the reader's motives stem from his relation to society in general. His ambition for success, social approval, and prestige are matched by a desire to conform to approved standards of behavior, dress, and environment. In this respect, few appeals are so productive as those that cite the precedents of others. Testimonial advertising is a prominent example. Another kind of social motive is served by appeals to charity, duty, and civic pride. Fortunately for society, the citizen easily recognizes the satisfactions to be derived from his contribution to the Red Cross, his service on a Visiting Committee to his alma mater, his support of the antilitter drive, and his active participation in other good causes.

The following appeals are based on the desire for social approval:

Distinctive, classic styling identifies Weejuns as *the* important shoe on campus—just as it has been for generations.

The world over, correctly dressed men who know the quality of British woolens and the fit of London tailoring wear Daks trousers.

Pride of possession creates a bond between Rolex owners. It starts conversations and makes strangers friends. Their "badge" is their Rolex chronometer. It distinguishes each of them as a man of taste and a leader in his field.

A sublimated form of the appeal to social motives characterizes this message from the International Ladies Garment Workers Union:

BUT CAN YOU BLINDFOLD
YOUR CONSCIENCE?

Shopping for women's or children's clothing? Take a long, sharp look at style, color, fit and workmanship. But use your conscience as well as your eyes. Look also for the ILGWU label. It represents the 450,000 skilled men and women who through many years of struggle have won for themselves fair wages, the right to work in clean shops, security and a respected place in their community. They're important, too.

Procter & Gamble deal with a perennial marketing problem in this plea for fairness:

"DON'T"

embarrass your dealer. . . . Some women try to redeem coupons without buying the brands called for . . . not realizing that this is asking their dealer to violate the terms of the coupon offer. That's not playing fair. . . .

"DO"

play fair. . . . Your dealer will be happy to redeem your coupons when you buy the brands called for . . . and you will be saving money on top-quality products.

The following letter, bearing the photograph of a small child, tugged at the hearts of New Yorkers for many years.

```
May I be your guest at luncheon, Mr. Janis?

I am really not a bit fussy.  Just a warm, nourishing
lunch that will make up for some of the things Mommy
can't afford to buy now.

Your gift of $2.00 to The Children's Aid Society will
make me your guest at lunch every day for two weeks.
RSVP.

                                   Thank you!

P.S. If you can spare more, my friend could be your
guest, too.
```

Rationalization

Sometimes the reader's motives are hidden from him, and sometimes he hides them from others. An employee will refuse, for example, to take a company-given course in English on the pretext that he does not have the time; perhaps the real reason is his unwillingness to admit that he needs the course. An executive is reluctant to approve the budget for redecorating a subordinate's office. He says it is too expensive; actually, he is afraid that other employees will be jealous. In another instance, the buyer of a pretentiously expensive automobile tells his friends, "It's a good investment." In truth, he wants the world to know how successful he is. In each case, the individual is rationalizing, or substituting a merely creditable reason for the real one.

The writer can play the same game, of course. When he suspects that the reader would be offended or unmoved by a reminder of his real motives, he may offer an acceptable substitute. To overcome the employee's aversion to taking a course in English, the personnel director may call it an "Executive Skills" course, thus suggesting that it provides a path to advancement rather than a cure for English deficiency. If, even through vanity, the subordinate wants his office expensively redecorated, he will make it easier for his superior to give approval by pointing out that his office is the only part of the company many customers see and that it is therefore important to make a good impression on them. The manufacturer of the pretentiously expensive car may assist the buyer in his rationalization by stressing its durability, efficiency, and high trade-in value.

Some time ago a large bank wished to suggest to parents that for Christmas they give their children a checking account of their own, complete with 100 personally imprinted checks. It feared, however, that by seeming to encourage easy spending in already overindulged youngsters, it would arouse negative public opinion. The advertising department solved the problem by offering the plan as *a way to teach thrift.* A folder on the subject bore the title, "What a wonderful, sensible gift." This is another example of the rationalization of an emotional appeal.

Consistency of Belief

An interesting theory relating to motivation and persuasion is that advanced by a number of scholars under the general name of "consistency theory."[5] The theory proceeds on the assumption that the human organism dislikes inconsistency and that when a viewpoint is encountered in contradiction to one already held, one will try to resolve the conflict by changing his old viewpoint in favor of the new or by discrediting the new information. The more strongly the old viewpoint is held, the more difficult it is to dislodge.

This theory is utilized in a number of ways. A common practice is showing that a proposed idea is actually in harmony with the receiver's established beliefs when, in other circumstances, it might not be so considered. The promotion of checking accounts for youngsters as a way to teach thrift is an example of an attempt to reconcile an existing belief with a contrary one. In another instance, there is ample ground for belief that heavy-duty washing and drying machines use a great deal more electricity than those that take lighter loads. This fact creates a problem for the manufacturer of the heavy-duty machines during a period when the public is being urged to take measures to conserve electricity. He attempts to solve the problem, however, by arguing that his machines are "power savers" because they do in one load what another machine will take two loads to do. Thus—at least for the large family—inconsistency, or "dissonance," is avoided.

Inconsistency is invariably present when a seller promotes a product or service for which the intended customer feels no need. That is why it is good strategy to relate the product or service to some other need the prospective customer already recognizes. A man may be inclined to say, for example, "I don't need more insurance," but he does have a desire for financial security in his retirement. When the insurance salesman shows that more insurance can provide such security, the customer may resolve his inconsistency by buying more insurance. In other instances, inconsistency may be resolved by the credibility of the message source or endorser. This point will be expanded later in the chapter.

Description

The communicator, we have seen, attempts to influence the prospective customer to look favorably on the advertised product or service as a means of satisfying some need. Description plays an important part in this process, for it directs attention to the particular ways in which the product or service will fulfill the need. The two kinds of description are *physical* and *emotive.*

PHYSICAL DESCRIPTION

Physical description provides explanation and practical details regarding appearance, composition, construction, operation, procedures, stipulations,

[5] See especially Leon Festinger's *A Theory of Cognitive Dissonance* (New York: Harper & Row, 1957).

and the like—anything having to do with the intrinsic characteristics of the object or plan under discussion. Here are several examples:

> 400 pages, over 460 illustrations, with more than 125 in color.
>
> *The Pioneer Spirit* is a big book. Pictured above in actual size, it measures 8½ by 11 inches. There are eleven narrative chapters, each illustrated on almost every page with drawings, paintings, maps and photographs in color and black and white. In addition, there are four 16-page portfolios, three devoted to pictures in color and the fourth to quotations from pioneer journals and literature.
>
> The book is printed on fine coated paper by both letterpress and offset. It is strongly and attractively bound to withstand both time and frequent use. The dust jacket pictures Bierstadt's famous "Oregon Trail."

> This is one of the most powerful 3-piece systems we have ever offered. The KLH Model 51 has an all-silicon solid-state AM/FM stereo receiver with over 100 watts IHF peak power. It has a Garrard four-speed automatic turntable with a Pickering magnetic cartridge, diamond stylus, and ultra-balanced tone arm. Comes complete with two high performance KLH speaker systems and acrylic dust cover.

> Ideal for travel, sports & leisure, our exceptionally long-wearing Cavalry Twill Chino Slacks in a comfortable, no-iron blend of cotton and Dacron. Fully cut with proportioned room at seat, thigh & knee for excellent fit. Conservative legs taper slightly from knee to bottom. Ruggedly tailored with belt loops and practical watch pocket, in good-looking British tan, navy, taupe, forest green or white. Waist sizes 30 to 46, including 35.

EMOTIVE DESCRIPTION

Emotive description tells what emotional satisfactions the plan or product will provide. In a more direct way than physical description, it usually represents an extension of the primary appeal. If, for example, a message appeals to the desire for money, the physical description may explain the particular features of a course of instruction that will lead to a better-paying job; but the emotional description will tell how the extra money can be used for travel, better living, and a college education for the children. In the following examples of emotive description, you will note that interest is centered on effects rather than on any substantive information about the offering:

> If you're just looking for a job, you can probably take your pick of thousands. But if you're also looking for adventure, the field suddenly narrows. To the Navy.
>
> In the Navy, a job means more than a good paycheck. It means the opportunity to see places like Italy, Spain, Morocco, Hong Kong, the Philippines and Hawaii. It means working on some of the most advanced technical equipment devised by man. It means doing a job that really counts, with guys who count on you to do it. . . .

Navy. It's not just a job. It's an adventure.

Comfort is the hallmark of every Hilton hotel, the reason for our existence. This is what makes your hotel room a place to enjoy, and it's one of the reasons why more and more travelers make it a habit to stay Hilton.

The history of the White House—the story of those who have lived in it and changed it—is a miniature of the history of America. For this reason, as well as for its current interest, this volume will become a family treasure and an heirloom-to-be . . . a dramatic and significant record of the legacy which all Americans share.—*Doubleday & Co., Inc., promotion for "A Tour of the White House"*

COMBINED TYPES

Especially in sales writing, it is hard to find examples of either pure physical description or pure emotive description, and it is just as hard to draw a line between them. Almost invariably some amount of "hard" information is interwoven with description of the resulting satisfactions to produce the persuasive effect. Here is an example:

BEHIND ITS GOOD LOOKS
IS QUIET DEPENDABILITY

Do handsomely by your slides with this Kodak Carousel custom H slide projector.

It's good-looking so you don't have to hide it away somewhere between shows.

It's quiet so it doesn't interfere with your enjoyment. It's dependable because gravity drops each slide in place.

It's easy to use. It has push-button remote control, both forward and reverse. Autofocus, too, so you usually have to focus only the first slide.

See the custom 840H (shown) at your photo dealer's. . . .

DESCRIPTIVE STYLE

Important to good sales description is the careful selection of details and the use of colorful and lively words. The particulars should not only contribute to the reader's knowledge of the subject, but also stimulate the desire to experience the benefits offered. The language, too, should heighten interest and desire.

The following description, although not extraordinary, benefits from the use of contrast and alliteration, the choice of such words as "musclecar" and "thunderbarges," and the specific details:

It's sort of
a miniature musclecar

No, the Datsun 1200 Sport Coupe isn't one of those great, snorting thunderbarges. But it's not your run-of-the-mill economy car, either.

It's something in between. A neat little machine that handles like a sports car, goes like a bat and comes with an economy price that includes a lot of extras as standard equipment. Reclining buckets, tinted glass, whitewalls and nylon carpeting to name a few. Add to that an engine that delivers around 30 miles per gallon. It's a powerful combination at any price.

Drive a Datsun . . . then decide.

The more imaginative advertisement below derives its effect not only from its colorful words, but also from the originality of its concept and copy arrangement.

Meet
Old-fashioned
Mr. Jennings
(the ice-cream
parlor man)

Always be polite to Mr. Jennings.
He'll keep us young forever.
He doesn't care for war,
he doesn't care for jewels,
he doesn't care for architecture.
Mr. Jennings knows what counts.
Sodas.
And heavenly sweets.
Ethereal creams.
Blasphemous blendings of
delectable fruits.
(And it's a wondrous place
to spend lunchtime, dinnertime—
even suppertime.)
No matter how many years you live,
everything in Mr. Jennings' place
tastes as good as treats did
when you were a kid.
Guaranteed.

Old-fashioned
Mr. Jennings

The appeal of Australia is well documented in this picturesque description:

Australia is a continent of contrasts. It's a midnight march of Fairy Penguins on paradisal Phillip Island. A Flower Day festival in Adelaide with color, color everywhere. A leisureland of jagged mountains and orchard-dotted valleys called Tasmania. It's waltzing Matildas; towering mountain peaks; boundless plains; primeval forests; towns with tongue-twisting names like Goondiwindi, Woolloomoolo, Coonabarabran. The uncommon place—untrampled, untarnished, virtually untouched by tourists. The home of the highest-hearted people on earth.

The following description of life on board ship gains interest from the selection of details and the narrative treatment:

> . . . The first few days aboard ship, our photographer friend just wanted to relax in a deck chair and then proceed step by leisurely step through every course on our menu with a good bottle of wine within easy reach. After about 48 hours of our rest cure, the effects of sun and not-a-care-in-the-world took hold. First, he cautiously decided to take a swim in the Sundeck Pool. Then he played some shuffleboard, some deck tennis, some pingpong. At his wife's behest he went to see a brand-new movie (prerelease). At night he found the night club in the Boat 'n Bottle Bar equal to some of the better ones in the "Fifties." "Just one heck of a lot of fun," he remarked to us. His wife had only one reservation: "His dancing is terrible and I made him take lessons from the instructor on board."

INSTILLING BELIEF

So far we have been concerned largely with appeals to the reader's emotions. As any observer of advertising knows, these are often enough to produce the desired action. In many types of communications, however, appeals to the emotions are either out of place or must be supplemented by rational argument. A business report, for example, is damaged rather than helped by overt emotional appeals. An advertisement for a beauty product, on the other hand, will utilize emotional appeals even to the point of excluding the rational. In still other instances, there is a good mixture of rational and emotive argument, and also, as we shall see, what purports to be rational may really be emotive after all.

An important reason for the use of rational appeals is the need to make the message believable. No one is under the illusion that persuasion is impartial; however, a bias in favor of the message, and belief in it, can be promoted by the use of various kinds of evidence and by the psychological conditioning of the reader through other means.

Factual Evidence

The main types of evidence are facts and opinions. Factual evidence consists of personal observation and reports based on the experience of others. It includes facts and figures, test results, testimony, and specific details of construction or performance. These are examples of factual evidence:

> The American Electric Power Company used a helicopter to build 29 miles of remote power lines. In one morning, the Sikorsky helicopter carried 268,000 pounds of construction steel to distant sites.—*United Aircraft Corporation*

Three independent testing laboratories (United States Testing Laboratories, Hoboken, N.J.; City Testing and Research Laboratories, New York City; and New York Testing Laboratories, New York City) were asked to grade the Duncan Parking Meter against the meters manufactured by the three largest competitors. All meters were graded for workmanship, accuracy, security of lock, suitability for conditions of weather and environment, proof against illegal entry into the coin box and proof against jamming. Duncan scored highest in each of these three testing series, and was rated "considerably superior" to all other makes tested.—*Nautec Corporation*

Push a Cold Button and the temperature drops to—20 degrees. In just a short time you and the test car are sitting at the North Pole freezing your fenders off. This is how we test for cold weather starting. At zero degrees, we test the operation of heaters, de-foggers, defrosters, engines, and fuel systems.

Push a Hot Button . . . 240 overhead heat lamps put us right in the middle of the Sahara desert. In this 110-degree oven, we test the engine cooling system, air-conditioning, ventilation. And also, test for vapor lock.

Tests like these are tough on a car. But tough testing makes for tough cars . . . so, at Ford Motor Company, we do a lot of it.

"Long Distance helped us multiply our sales by six," says Gilbert Merrill, president, the Gilbert Merrill Steel Corp., Westbury, N.Y. "We use long distance almost exclusively to sell out-of-town customers," reports Mr. Merrill. "Our warehouse's sales have grown from $500,000 to over $3,000,000 annually. Recently, an Ohio company offered to sell us 32,000 pounds of special highgrade steel. We selected three prospects, each in a different state, and sold the steel. In one morning, those few calls brought us $12,000 in business." —*Bell Telephone System*

Facts are most convincing when they meet the following criteria:

1. *They come from reliable sources.* These sources may include the writer and his staff, government agencies, official records of professional and scientific bodies, audited or notarized statements, and such standard reference books as dictionaries, encyclopedias, and annuals.

2. *They are clearly stated.* The report that says, "4,356 contributors gave up to $10,000 each," leaves considerable doubt as to the size of individual contributions.

3. *They are verifiable.* The statement, "Mr. Jones was graduated from M.I.T. in 1968," can easily be proved or disproved, although under ordinary circumstances it is not likely that the reader would bother.

4. *They are relevant.* The fact that a millionaire bachelor built a house on certain acreage thirty years ago does little to support the argument that the same land today makes a desirable homesite for families with incomes of $20,000 a year.

Factual information is invariably a part of physical description. It qualifies as evidence when it is specific and verifiable. Thus, in addition to creating desire for the product or service, it increases credibility. This excerpt from a shoe advertisement uses specific facts to support the appeal to comfort. The persuasive effect is evident.

> You'll walk for miles—stand for hours, and be more comfortable throughout the day, less tired at the end of it, when you wear these new slip-ons. The secret is in the thoughtful way Allen Edmonds designed and constructed the sole and heel. It's made of three layers of tough, springy Micronite Crepe Rubber, a new, extremely durable rubber compound. The top layer is strong and flexible. The middle layer is a tapered wedge of spongy, resilient crepe rubber to cushion every step and virtually eliminate heel shock. The bottom layer is a durable formulation of Micronite that will wear . . . and wear . . . and wear.

Illustrations, charts, and demonstrations are always useful adjuncts to verbal claims. How a demonstration-in-print adds to the persuasiveness of an advertisement for the IBM Memory Typewriter is shown in Figure 13-1.

Opinion

An opinion is a personal belief or judgment that does not rest on positive knowledge. For example:

> The company's sales should benefit from the general economic upturn.
>
> The new laboratory building is an architectural monstrosity.

Neither of these statements can be proved. The first is a prediction that will eventually turn out to be right or wrong. The second is a judgment or personal evaluation on which there is sure to be considerably less than universal agreement. Even though these statements are not facts, however, they may yet carry some weight as evidence. The first statement, for example, will have considerable validity if it represents the opinion of the board chairman, the second if it is the expression of a respected architect.

The ideal conditions for the use of opinions as evidence may be stated as follows:

1. *The opinion comes from a person qualified as an expert.* A prediction about the state of business six months from now comes better from an economist than from the man on the street. An opinion on the best preparation for a career in law can be expected to carry more weight if offered by a judge than by a grocer.

2. *The opinion relates to the specific area in which the expert practices.* A fashion specialist is qualified to express an opinion on fashions, but his opinions on politics are no more expert than those of any other citizen.

3. *The specialist offering the opinion is unbiased.* The television performer who endorses the sponsor's lozenges can hardly be considered impartial. Neither can the manufacturer who sees national disaster in the imposition of an excise tax on the product he makes.

The opinions cited in the example below appear to meet all three tests of validity. They form part of an advertisement advocating legislation to end the expensive practice of dating containers of milk sold at retail.

. . . here is what men who are really concerned with your health and the milk you drink are saying:

Hollis S. Ingraham, M.D., First Deputy Commissioner, New York State Department of Health: "In our opinion, such a regulation is no longer necessary from the public health point of view. Dating may actually be a detriment . . ."

John D. Faulkner, Chief, Milk and Food Program, United States Public Health Service: ". . . Regulations requiring the dating of milk are more disadvantageous than advantageous in protecting the public milk supply."

A. C. Dahlberg, Professor Dairy Industry, Cornell University: ". . . There is no evidence to indicate any relationship whatever between the dating requirement and milk quality or the public health . . ."—*Metropolitan Dairy Institute*

Credibility

It is not necessary, of course, for opinions to meet all or any of the criteria listed above in order to be credible and therefore persuasive. A man planning to buy a new car may, for example, be influenced more by the experience of his next-door neighbor than by the testimony of a professional driver. At least, the neighbor is known not to have received any payment for his opinion and, in any case, his driving experience is probably closer to that of the man soliciting his advice than to the professional driver's. This also seems to be the thinking of advertisers who employ plain and often unnamed people to endorse their products; the reader or viewer finds it easy to relate to them.

In many instances a popular actor or other public figure will be chosen to give an endorsement. Though he is neither an authority nor free of bias, he may still have the confidence of the audience to whom the message is addressed. Thus an advertisement for a health insurance plan appealing especially to older citizens contained an endorsement by Art Linkletter, whom many of the citizens remembered as an ingratiating television personality. In the following statement Mr. Linkletter attempts to transfer to his insurance sponsor his own credibility among his public.[6] It should be noted that the appeal here is emotional rather than rational, although the remainder of the advertisement (not shown here) does provide the specifics the endorser omits.

> You know me. I wouldn't recommend anything I didn't honestly believe in. And I think National Home's $600-a-month plan is just about the best additional financial protection you can give your family--especially in these days of rising medical costs.
>
> That's why I'm happy to give this plan my wholehearted endorsement.
>
> I've looked over the policy very carefully. I've made a point of getting to know some of the folks at National Home. And you won't find more decent, friendly people.

[6] The *New York Times* of June 11, 1972, reported that Mr. Linkletter, elected a director of the insurance company, would earn $50,000 for five years. In later advertisements, Mr. Linkletter was identified as a member of the company's board of directors.

Because it remembers what you type and can play it back automatically, with corrections, you get letter-perfect work. Every time. Without the delay, expense, or drudgery of manual retyping and reproofing.

Typing mistakes no longer have to be messy and time-consuming. The Memory Typewriter lifts mistakes (a character, a word, or a line) right off the page with the press of a key. Which means even first drafts can be done faster, yet come out as clean and easy to read as this.

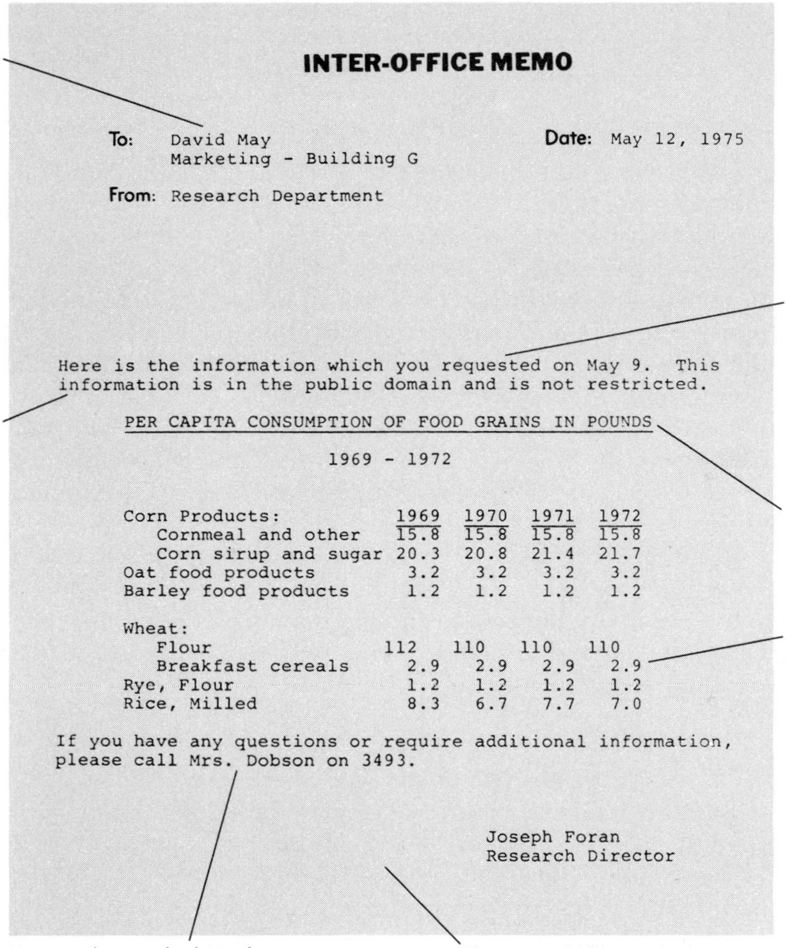

INTER-OFFICE MEMO

To: David May
Marketing - Building G

Date: May 12, 1975

From: Research Department

Here is the information which you requested on May 9. This information is in the public domain and is not restricted.

PER CAPITA CONSUMPTION OF FOOD GRAINS IN POUNDS

1969 - 1972

	1969	1970	1971	1972
Corn Products:				
Cornmeal and other	15.8	15.8	15.8	15.8
Corn sirup and sugar	20.3	20.8	21.4	21.7
Oat food products	3.2	3.2	3.2	3.2
Barley food products	1.2	1.2	1.2	1.2
Wheat:				
Flour	112	110	110	110
Breakfast cereals	2.9	2.9	2.9	2.9
Rye, Flour	1.2	1.2	1.2	1.2
Rice, Milled	8.3	6.7	7.7	7.0

If you have any questions or require additional information, please call Mrs. Dobson on 3493.

Joseph Foran
Research Director

Form material such as this can be stored in the Memory Typewriter, then played back whenever needed. When revisions are required, only the revisions have to be typed. The entire corrected page is then typed back automatically, ready for signature.

The Memory Typewriter automatically centers, aligns columns of figures, indents, even underlines. Which means complex material can be stored and played back as needed. Without errors. Without long waits. Without frayed tempers.

You get the standard 10 characters per inch unless you flip a lever. Then you get a space-saving 12 characters per inch. If the type style on this page doesn't suit you, we have over 20 others. Any one can be snapped in place in a matter of seconds.

If you would like to produce work like this, with ease like this, call the IBM Office Products Division branch near you. We'll be happy to demonstrate the Memory Typewriter for you, at your convenience.

FIG. 13-1. *Annotated chart provides a convincing demonstration of the performance of the IBM Memory Typewriter.* [Courtesy of International Business Machines Corporation.]

```
That's why I cannot imagine anybody passing up the
chance to enroll in this health plan.

We all know what a terrible thing it is to be hospital-
ized.  But what a relief it is to know there's extra
cash coming in when you need it most!  Take my advice.
Send the enrollment form below now--before you forget.

                                    Sincerely,
                                    Art Linkletter
```

Even when other measures of its value are difficult to assess, an endorsement can be useful if it helps to attract attention to the advertisement. Many products that are not easy to differentiate from competing products may obtain a distinct advantage by recruiting a well-known performer or other celebrity to speak for them, for the presence of the celebrity immediately provides an easily remembered mark of identification. That would appear to have been the motive when a glamorous actress, dressed in sequined décolleté, was presented on television as the endorser of a national auto transmission service. Certainly, there was enough interest in her voice and figure and enough incongruity in her association with auto engines to give the commercial a great deal of attention value it might not otherwise have been possible to obtain.

From the foregoing examples it may be surmised that some forms and sources of "evidence," though they have the ring of rational argument, represent essentially appeals to the senses and feelings. As such, they may still make an effective, although sometimes socially questionable, contribution to the total task of persuasion.

Reasoning

Of course, the purpose of any type of evidence is to lead the reader to a conclusion favorable to the idea or product being promoted. Sometimes this conclusion can be inferred. When, for example, a cigarette is advertised as "lowest in tar," one concludes—rightly or wrongly—that the product is less harmful to health than a cigarette with a higher tar content. In other instances, conclusions are not so easily drawn, and in any case the communicator does not wish to take the chance that the point will be missed. The tool used to bridge the gap between facts and conclusion is reasoning. In Chapter 15 we will have much to say about the formal processes of logic and reasoning, but it will be enough here to show how reasoning may be used to drive home the point of the message. For this purpose we will quote from the advertisements of two competing metals: aluminum and steel. In the first, the point to be demonstrated is the fuel-saving potential of aluminum coal cars. In the second, the reasoning is directed to showing how the magnetic attraction of steel brings about lower energy costs and cleaner cities. In neither instance would the message be as persuasive without the explanation that links causes and effects.

PROBLEM: MOVE 4 MILLION TONS OF COAL 1,700 MILES
SOLUTION: USE ALUMINUM-BODIED COAL CARS AND SAVE OVER 2,000,000 GALLONS OF DIESEL FUEL

Consider the energy-saving advantages of lightweight, long-lasting aluminum-bodied coal cars for carrying coal from mine to electric generating stations.

Aluminum-bodied coal cars offer greater payload capacity. This means fewer cars or fewer trips. Either way, there are important fuel savings. In this case, as much as over 70 million gallons during the projected 35-year life of the generating plant.

Unit trains with aluminum cars use less fuel on the empty return trip because they're lighter.

The higher initial cost for aluminum cars is quickly recovered by savings in operating and maintenance costs.

Aluminum unit train coal cars are not a new idea. There are almost 2,000 now in this service with 746 having logged more than a million miles each in 15 years of successful performance.

The significant fuel and operating savings of aluminum coal cars in unit trains can make the generation of electricity less costly for the utility. It is another reason why Alcoa says the reasons for using aluminum are found in aluminum itself.—*Alcoa*

WHAT DOES THE STEEL CAN HAVE GOING FOR IT BESIDES STRENGTH, LIGHT WEIGHT AND LOW COST?

MAGNETIC ATTRACTION

That's why steel cans, as well as other steel scrap, are so easy to reclaim and recycle.

It's all done through a new system of magnetic recovery now operating in many American communities. Here's how it works.

A giant electromagnet is brought into contact with a pile of municipal trash, and with the selectivity of a pickpocket retrieves *only* the steel.

Magnetic recovery brings big returns.

All this takes a lot less energy than making new steel from scratch. It conserves human energy, too. It means that tin cans can be thrown in with the rest of the trash instead of hauled off and sorted for recycling. Best of all, it means that communities can *make money* by selling the tin cans and other steel scrap back to the mills.

Right now magnetic separation systems are operating in a significant number of communities across the country (often as part of systems that convert refuse to energy by burning flammable trash to produce electric power). And that number grows larger each month.

The dollar return on the steel scrap reclaimed from trash gives these communities a steady and substantial source of revenue. To help reduce taxes. Or support city services. Or both.

But there's one more huge benefit of magnetic steel scrap retrieval. It encourages people to stop littering by giving them an *easy* way to put trash back to work.

Add it up: easy magnetic retrieval, energy saved, cash for trash, cleaner cities.

All thanks to steel.

It's the only packaging material that can be reclaimed magnetically.

The most ecologically logical packaging material around.—*United States Steel*

STIMULATING ACTION

No persuasion is worth the writer's trouble unless it induces the reader to form the desired attitude or take the desired action. How soon the response is required to be made, what form it will take, and how the request for a response is to be phrased vary from message to message. Some messages ask for action now; others look forward to future action at, say, election time, car replacement time, or school opening. Some ask only for sympathy or agreement; others ask for a tangible response in such form as an order, a visit, an inquiry. Some are sedate in their directives ("Exclusively at A & P Stores"); others have all the force of a bulldozer, employing direct commands ("Do it now!") and offering gifts, prizes, special price reductions, and other inducements to action.

Although a positive response is the hoped-for result of the persuasive process, response will depend largely on the specific measures taken in the message. If an advertisement for a particular shirt appeals to you because of the price, the shape, the color and design, the tailoring details, and the name of the maker; and if, further, you are in need of shirts and have waited for just such an opportunity, you are indeed ready to consummate the purchase. But obstacles may arise: If the advertisement has been placed by the manufacturer, it may not mention the stores in your community where the shirt can be bought. If it is a store advertisement, the store may be inconvenient to reach, or you may not be able to make the time to visit it. Even if you were to pass the store, you may not have sufficient cash with you or have a charge account with the store. Again, you may have decided to buy the shirts, but you put off the purchase until you had forgotten about it or lost the initial impulse. Or you may, in the meantime, see competing advertisements, which create an indecisiveness you did not experience earlier.

These are only some of the reasons why a response may fail to materialize. In such circumstances, is there anything in the power of the persuader to pin down the sale? In the instance of the manufacturer's advertisement, the names of local stores might be mentioned. If it is not possible to do so, the reader may be directed to the Yellow Pages, where the dealers' names are generally listed under the brand name of the product. A retail store might also take an advertisement adjacent to the manufacturer's to make known the availability of the advertised shirts. If the shirts are advertised by the retailer, the reader should be told at what branches, if any, the shirts are available, and in what department or on what floor. A telephone number would be helpful in obtaining phone orders, and for mail orders, a specific street address, with ZIP code, should be given. If American Express or other non-store charge cards are acceptable, the advertisement should say so. To prevent procrastination, notice should also be given if there is only a limited stock or a limited time for the offer.

It is hard to prescribe all the measures the persuader can take, but the following suggestions governing the conclusion of the message are designed to meet a variety of circumstances.

1. Arrange the message so that it reaches its climax in the stimulus to action at the end. This does not exclude the possibility of also suggesting action at the beginning or at some other point in the message.
2. If the message requires no direct action, but only the formation of an attitude, let the close express the essence of the message.

    We hope the sign of the Shell reminds you of people who never stop asking why, who never stop the quest for new ideas, new products, new and better ways to serve you.

3. If you want the reader to take some action, state clearly what it is.

    See your nearest State Mutual agent or group of representatives. Or write us here in Worcester, Mass.

    Vote as you please . . . but please VOTE election day, November 8.

    We look forward to welcoming you as a friend and customer.

4. Let the stimulus to action echo the appeal or theme of the message so that the reader will be reminded of what is at stake.

    Buckle up. Seatbelts save lives.

    Your Reynolds Aluminum Specialists can help you improve your products and reduce your costs. Call on their help today by contacting your nearest Reynolds office.

5. Make action easy. Unless it is inconsistent with the dignity or aim of the message, provide the coupon, card, order blank, envelope, etc., that will enable the reader to reply. Be sure to mention these aids in the message.

    SEND NO MONEY! Just mail the enclosed postage-paid card today. It already has your name on it.

6. See that gifts or other inducements are in harmony with the primary purpose of the message.

    Take any 3 of these books free when you join the Mid-Century Book Society.

Why not consider investing as a means to provide better for *your* future. As a starter, send the coupon below for a free copy of "Dividends Over the Years." It's a basic guide to common stock investment, and it lists over 400 companies that have paid cash dividends every year for 25 years or more.—*New York Stock Exchange*

7. If promptness is urgent, tell why.

Your immediate action will enable us to get Saturday Review's distinctive gift announcement card—specially designed and engraved by Tiffany's and signed in your name—to recipients in time for Christmas.

SUMMARY

Persuasion is closely associated with sales communications, but it is also an important part of all business messages. The functions of persuasion, which vary in their application to particular communication needs, are (1) attracting and holding attention, (2) providing motivation, (3) instilling belief, and (4) stimulating action.

Attention depends very much on the latent interests of the reader, but it is stimulated by the mechanics and content of the message, particularly the heading and initial statement.

Motivation is supplied through the use of appeals and description, which, in effect, show how the reader may satisfy some need or desire. The need the writer offers to satisfy may be as basic as the need for food and shelter; it may be related to feelings of sympathy, fear, affection, pride, and the like; or it may touch on such social motives as the desire for success, prestige, and acceptance by one's peers. Negative appeals, those that show the consequences of not taking the proposed action, may—if too strong—result in "defensive avoidance" unless they are modified. Appeals are "rationalized" when they provide a socially acceptable excuse for a purchase that may otherwise be difficult to justify. Appeals are also useful in resolving the conflict, or "inconsistency," that may arise when the communicator introduces a belief that is contrary to one the receiver already holds. Thus the appeal to the desire for career advancement may resolve the conflict of a reader who is initially reluctant to subscribe to a business magazine. Description directs a reader's wants toward a particular mode of fulfillment. It may depict an object for sale in physical terms (physical description) or it may tell how the object will give certain emotional satisfactions (emotive description).

Belief is strengthened through the offer of proof consisting of facts or opinions. Facts are verifiable reports that are most convincing when they come from reliable sources, are clearly stated, and are relevant to the issue at hand. Opinions are personal beliefs or judgments that are most effective when they come from unbiased individuals expert in those areas to which their opinions relate. Evidence that does not meet these tests may still give a message strong support, however, if it succeeds in attracting attention. If the linkage between the proof and the desired conclusion is not self-evident, logical reasoning is employed to fill the gap.

The final step in persuasion is the stimulus to action. This may be implied or expressed, weak or strong, depending on the purpose of the message. Action can be spurred by the use of premiums or other inducements, by making action easy ("send no money"; "mail the postage-free card"), and by giving specific instructions for taking action.

PROBLEMS

1. Write a headline for each of the following announcements to be printed as an advertisement in your local newspaper:
   (*a*) The opening of a nonprofit community theater
   (*b*) A preseason sale of men's overcoats
   (*c*) The winning of the 500-mile Grand Prix auto race in Cannes, France, by a Chevrolet *Corvette*
   (*d*) The Second National Bank's traditional Christmas greeting
   (*e*) The introduction of chocolate mint flavor to the Jell-O line of puddings for pies and desserts

2. Write an opening (the first paragraph or first several paragraphs) for each of the sales letters described below. You may invent any appropriate details.
   (*a*) A letter accompanying a Christmas catalog of food delicacies shipped by mail. The mailing list consists of business executives who may be expected to buy both for themselves and for gift-giving to business acquaintances.
   (*b*) A letter from your local newspaper to induce householders to order the paper for home delivery.
   (*c*) A letter from your college bookstore at term-end to influence students to sell their old textbooks. The letter will be printed as an advertisement in the college newspaper.

3. Write a short statement that will motivate the reader to take the action indicated in each of the following instances:
   (*a*) To try Stouffer's frozen macaroni and cheese
   (*b*) To buy Christmas cards in July
   (*c*) To see his dentist twice a year
   (*d*) To wear safety shoes on the job (These are shoes with concealed metal plates over the toes.)
   (*e*) To vote on election day

4. Write (1) one hundred words of predominantly physical description *and* (2) one hundred words of predominantly emotive description for *one* of the following:
   (*a*) The World Almanac and Book of Facts (latest edition)
   (*b*) A lounging chair with adjustable back and footrest
   (*c*) Your college or the company you work for

5. Write a short passage (50–100 words) of predominantly emotive description for the following:
   (*a*) Green Giant brand baby green peas
   (*b*) The Eaton line of fine social stationery
   (*c*) Miss Dior (a perfume by Christian Dior)

6. Comment on the appeal (motivation) used in each of the following advertisements. Do you consider the appeal effective? With whom?

   (*a*) The "White Dot" marks a gift of pride.
   Pride in giving, pride in receiving, pride in possessing. Never more evident than when the gift is Sheaffer. "White Dot." Crafted in the tradition of the world's finest writing instruments—the "White Dot" collection and this distinctive gold-filled presentation set. Ballpoint or pencil, $8.50. Pen, $18.00. SHEAFFER. The proud craftsmen.

   (*b*) The annual checkup. It may save your life.
   There's only one way to be sure you're in perfect health. Have an annual checkup. It gives your doctor a good chance to catch any minor ailment before it becomes a major illness. Or a fatal one.
   We want to wipe out cancer in your lifetime. Give to the American Cancer Society.

   (*c*) Looking for more than just room and bored?
   If you're tired of flashy hotels that give you four walls, a bed, and little else . . . then maybe you're ready for the Colonial Inn. We're only minutes from downtown Boston in historic Concord. Our no-nonsense menu offers tasty Yankee dishes; our Forge Lounge serves up excellent concoctions and lively company; our 60 modern rooms make you feel like you've never left home. We treat you like a guest and not just a room key. For a delightful change of pace, come see us. We promise you won't be bored.
   The Colonial Inn
   Concord, Massachusetts

   (*d*) (Classified advertisement—Vacations)
   DAVID'S FOLLY. Country living on Maine Coast. Seafood, garden vegetables, blueberry pies, coffeepot always on stove. Minerva Cutler, Brooksville, Maine.

7. Norm Thompson Outfitters, a mail-order house of Portland, Oregon, advertises the "Mule Bag," a casual, duffel-type bag that measures 24 by 18 by 12 inches, and can be folded flat for storage. Part of the description follows. Comment on the persuasive qualities of the language and the use of detail.

   The Forty-niners invented it

   Our Mule Bag has evolved from the homely but rugged bags the prospectors packed on their mules during the Gold Rush. (Hence, the name.) Those original, tough old bags had to hold everything a grubstaker needed while trudging from camp to camp. The bags took a lot of punishment and held up well, but they soaked up rainwater like a sponge.

   We've improved it

   We admit we stole the idea for our Mule Bag. But, while retaining the ruggedness of the original, we've modernized it with new materials and construction techniques. It's waterproof, for one thing, and every bit as sturdy as its predecessors. We have a friend living in the back woods up in Oregon's Cascade Mountains who ran over his Mule Bag with a D9 Cat and pretty well ruined it. But aside from mashing the Mule Bag with a tractor or poking it with the knife, it's really pretty hard to hurt it!

What it's made of

The Mule Bag is built to last. The body is 24-ounce, water-repellent cotton hose duck—same material fire hoses are made of. (If you've ever seen a fire hose at work, you know how strong the fabric must be to tolerate the tremendous water pressure, being dragged over pavement and run over—not to mention being unrolled and rolled up again and again.) Takes unusually rough handling with ease!

At the top the prospector's rope ties have been replaced with a strong heavy metal zipper—larger than those used in most luggage—which in turn is covered by a protective flap that keeps out rain, dirt and dust. The flap itself closes with heavy leather straps that buckle securely (and the straps are adjustable so you can carry a fishing rod under the flap if you like).

The strong handles are made from heavy 2-inch web, sewn all around the bag then overlapped three times and double stitched. They'll hold a heavy load safely and they're comfortable to grip. If you're packing in, leather loops sewn into the seams at either end of the top can be attached to a pack saddle or back-pack snaps.

Every inside seam is completely bound so there's not a single edge to ravel or rip. The sturdy zipper is attached with a strong double seam—won't rip out even when the Mule Bag is really stuffed. (We were testing the zipper here at the office, and stuffed the Mule Bag so full it was gapping open about five inches at the top. I got it shut, using all my strength, my right knee, and my right thumb and index finger, both of which are still numb. The strain didn't bother the zipper a bit.) All these details contribute to the Mule Bag's durability, which promises you years of service with little or no care. You'll want to air it out after it's been closed for long periods of time, and after a rainstorm or an accidental dip in the creek you'll want to let it dry out thoroughly. But that's all the "work" there is to it!—*by Parma Advertising for Norm Thompson Outfitters*

8. How convincing do you find the following advertising copy?
   (*a*) (Photograph shows two businessmen in conversation.)

"He's important to us. Let's take him to a restaurant that serves lamb."

American lamb on the menu is the mark of a fine restaurant. Hearty roast leg of lamb, elegant French lamb chops, lamb en brochette. Whether the treat's on you or on your expense account, choose a restaurant that serves lamb. It puts your guest in a receptive mood.—*American Lamb Council, Denver, Colorado*

   (*b*) Mail-order advertisement with coupon attached, including price ($28.95, including $2 postage) and money-back guarantee. Drawing shows knives on magnetized rack.

Does your lady look a little tired?

If she does, chances are that she's spending too much time in the kitchen, slowed down by inefficient tools. Now you can change all that with Tsurugi Knives. These splendid Japanese knives are forged of vanadium cutlery steel, have waterproof Permawood handles and come in their own magnetized hardwood rack. A sharpening steel to keep them honed to razor's edge is included. Strike a sharp blow for *your* woman's liberation and get her out of the kitchen fast! Give her a matchless set of Tsurugi Knives.—*Haverhill's, San Francisco, California*

9. Write three statements, each constituting a different type of evidence, designed to help sell a particular make of portable typewriter to college students throughout the country. You may invent any appropriate and reasonable details; just be sure to give enough of them to make your statements convincing.

10. Comment on the techniques used to stimulate action in each of the following closings. Try to explain why the respective techniques were chosen.

(*a*) So why not pick up a pencil and fill out our Christmas order form now? Just write in the names and addresses of all the friends you want to please . . . and tell us how you want the gift cards signed. It won't take more than a minute or two, and if you wish we will charge your order, bill you *after* Christmas. But the sooner we get your order, the better attention we can give it—and the more gifts you take care of now, the merrier you'll be feeling when the Christmas crush is on.—Sports Illustrated.

(*b*) Become a Daks [trousers] collector. At fine stores from coast to coast or write Simpson Imports, Inc., 9 East 37th Street, New York 10016, Dept. TD.

(*c*) To discharge this responsibility [the physical fitness of youth], it is essential that we guarantee youth the opportunity to develop at home and in the school. Equitable is proud of the millions of youngsters who have been given this opportunity through Living Insurance from Equitable.

(*d*) In ways like this, the Milwaukee Road constantly applies creative thinking to the safeguarding of *all* commodity shipments.

(*e*) So if your organization is sincerely interested in raising funds, act now. Simply take the reply card from the pocket below and drop it in the mail. No stamp is needed. I'll rush a full pound canister of GOLDEN BUTTER-BITS to you absolutely FREE and postpaid, together with full fund-raising facts. Then your members can sample the candy while you present our plan for their approval.

It costs you nothing to try the BUTTER-BITS plan. No experience is needed. We show you what to do and provide each member with a free book of valuable fund-raising hints that will help your group reach its goal quicker. All we ask is that your organization be sincerely interested in raising funds. You are under no obligation whatsoever. So mail the reply card NOW for full details and a pound of GOLDEN BUTTER-BITS absolutely FREE—*Master Kitchens, Inc.*

(*f*) For additional information on TWA's convenient schedules and low, low rates, just fill in the enclosed card and mail it right away . . . or make your reservations directly by simply picking up your phone and calling the number shown on the front of the card.

We are anxious to make *your* trip to the Convention swift . . . smooth . . . and enjoyable.

11. Assume that you are the sales representative at your college for *Time* magazine or some other popular periodical. Write a letter to fellow students to induce them to order through you subscriptions (or renewals of their present subscriptions). Students will be billed directly by the publisher. All you have to do is induce them to return to you an attached subscription blank that provides for a student discount of 40 per cent under the regular subscription price. Give as your address Box 311 at your college post office or student building. Small quantities of your letter, to be picked up by students, will be left at strategic points around the campus. Study carefully the magazine you are selling before you write the letter, and try to include in your letter some element of each of the four functions of persuasion mentioned in this chapter.

14
Sales and Goodwill Letters

IN THE preceding chapter we examined the functions of persuasive messages, from attracting attention, through motivating and convincing the reader, to stimulating action. We also demonstrated some of the techniques used in the performance of those functions. In this chapter we are going to see the application of those techniques to the writing of a few fairly well-defined types of sales and promotional letters. We will, in addition, turn our attention to the general category of goodwill messages, those that seek primarily to develop relationships that can serve, in various ways, the aims of the organization.

DIRECT SELLING[1]

Almost all common household products have been sold at one time or another directly by mail. With a long history of service, the mail-order catalog is still an effective merchandising medium. Letters are also used for mail-order sales of particular classes of merchandise, such as books and magazines, records and tapes, gifts, specialty foods, wearing apparel, and novelties. Among the mass media, newspapers and magazines have traditionally carried mail-order advertisements; and they have more lately been joined in force by local radio and television stations. Many of the mass-media advertisers are traditional retail outlets that seek to supplement in-person sales with telephone and mail orders.

For a number of reasons, books and magazines are ideally suited to mail-order selling. Their verbal content lends itself well to description in words;

[1] The terms *direct selling, direct-mail,* and *mail-order selling* sometimes lead to confusion. Generally, *direct selling* includes any effort to sell without salesmen; *mail-order selling* denotes the ordering and shipping of goods by mail; and *direct-mail advertising* (or simply *direct advertising*) is the use of the mails for advertising of any kind, whether mail-order or not. Direct selling and mail-order selling refer to methods of distribution, but direct-mail is an advertising medium in the same way that newspapers and magazines are.

there is often no convenient way to obtain them except through direct dealings with the publishers; and publishers are favored with lower postage rates than most other mailers. Still, publishers must usually depend on repeat sales for their mail-order profits. The reason is that advertising costs tend to be very high on initial sales, but much lower on repeat sales. Even an established magazine, for example, may get a return of not more than 2 or 3 per cent from sales letters to nonsubscribers, but the return on renewal letters may be ten to twenty times that.[2]

A factor tending to put a brake on mail-order selling is the rapidly rising postage costs. Advertisers who want to stay in business have been forced to seek more effective ways of presenting their messages, but have found it even more important to find ways of reducing the cost per mailing. The "omnibus" mailing has proved to be a popular device. Stores that send out monthly bills to charge customers have always known that the first-class postage cost is the same for a fraction of an ounce as it is for a full ounce. They have therefore followed the practice of stuffing the envelopes to bring the weight of each piece to the full ounce. The stuffers, featuring special offerings, invariably solicit mail and telephone orders, and the use of lightweight paper for both the envelope and the enclosures increases the number of advertisements that may be included. Many stores, as well as Master Charge and other credit card companies, also use the back of the return envelope for additional selling space, often with a detachable flap to be used as an order blank. These practices have also been adopted with some modification by national advertisers, who pool their cents-off and mail-order offerings and dispatch them in a single envelope to residents in selected neighborhoods and communities. The enormous saving in addressing and postage is apparent.

Two other relatively recent developments have also helped to encourage the use of direct selling. One is the computerization of mailing lists, which makes possible the selection of target markets with demographic characteristics—age, sex, income, occupation, etc.—that closely match the requirements of the seller. Such "profile matching" ensures a higher rate of efficiency and lower cost per dollar of sales than were possible by older hit-or-miss methods.

The second development is the increasing number of persons who have general purpose credit cards, for example, American Express, Master Charge, and Visa, as well as the credit cards issued by the better established oil companies. The owners of these cards make excellent mailing lists for the sale of high-priced products by mail, first because they represent stable or high-income groups and, second, because they can conveniently charge their purchases—often with installment privileges. In some instances, the credit card companies offer the use of their lists and credit machinery to responsible vendors. Products sold to credit card holders have included portable typewriters, cameras, phonographs, tape recorders, and similar items at prices ranging up to several hundred dollars.

[2] In a *New York Times* advertisement on June 14, 1972, *Reader's Digest* stated that its renewal rate is 70.4 per cent.

Mail-Order Sales Letters

Letters that sell direct by mail are a microcosm of the whole sales process. Usually the work of highly experienced writers, they are worth study because to some degree all other sales-letter types borrow their techniques from them.

The characteristics of mail-order sales letters, keyed to the functions of persuasion, may be summarized as follows:

ATTRACTING AND HOLDING ATTENTION

1. Apart from having the appearance of a letter, with a salutation and signature, a mail-order sales letter is not a personal communication and must compensate for that deficiency by its attractive display and inherent interest.
2. Selling begins on the mailing envelope which, by its size, color, use of illustration, and arresting copy invites attention to the contents.
3. In the letter itself attention is obtained through the use of similar techniques, including a headline and an attention-getting opening.

MOTIVATING THE READER

1. The sales appeal begins in the headline or letter opening and continues into the body of the letter.
2. A great deal of physical description is often required because there is no opportunity for inspection of the goods before ordering.
3. Pictures, either in the enclosures or on the letter itself, usually supplement the verbal description. The pictures show the product close up—often in various views—and in use. The satisfaction of the users is reflected in the illustrations.

INSTILLING BELIEF

1. Claims are supported by various forms of evidence, including sales figures, performance data, details of composition or construction, samples, and testimony.
2. Strong guarantees of satisfaction are used to overcome skepticism.
3. A "no-risk" offer permits examination of the goods before payment or promises money back if the customer is not satisfied.

STIMULATING ACTION

1. Specific directions for ordering must be given.
2. The "send-no-money" appeal invites quick action.
3. The offer of a desirable premium adds an incentive to ordering.
4. A return order card and postage-paid envelope make action easy.

A Specific Example

The mail-order techniques mentioned are effectively demonstrated in a letter from the Mobil Merchandise Center to sell a Royal electric portable

FIG. 14-1. A *mail-order letter.* [Reprinted by permission of the Mobil Oil Corporation.]

Mobil P. O. BOX 497
DES MOINES, IOWA 50303

...because you are a Mobil credit card customer:

You and your family may use

THE ROYAL TRAVELER FULLY ELECTRIC PORTABLE TYPEWRITER

free for 15 days

WITH ABSOLUTELY NO COST OR OBLIGATION!

Dear Mobil Credit Card Customer:

A typewriter is one of the most useful things any family can own, because every member of the family can use it.

Dad can use it to type memos, notes and reports. It's faster than writing...and unlike handwriting, typewritten work is more quickly and more easily understood.

Mom can use it to type recipes, messages, notes, letters.

The children can use it -- indeed, they should use it -- for schoolwork. Most teachers will tell you that typewritten papers are a big plus for any student.

Knowing this, we at Mobil looked for a typewriter for your family.

We didn't want to offer you just an ordinary typewriter. We wanted something special, because as a Mobil credit card customer, we think you are entitled to the best.

We found what we wanted to offer you...and we believe you'll love it.

It's a ROYAL typewriter; a name you know and trust. For over 60 years, ROYAL has been one of America's top names in fine office and portable typewriters.

It's a FULLY ELECTRIC typewriter, because electric typing is twice as fast as manual typing! Electric typing is sharper, crisper. It looks professional...no matter who does it! And it's so much easier to type when electricity does all the work!

It's a PORTABLE typewriter, so you can carry and use it in any room of your home...and take it on business trips and to club or church meetings (or let the children take it to school). Royal named it the Traveler!

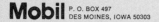

Some typewriters are partly electric...but not fully electric. FULLY ELECTRIC means that you find the same power features (yes, even an electric carriage return) that you find on office electric typewriters!

Your Royal Traveler is a FULLY ELECTRIC typewriter. Just look at the features you'll enjoy:

FULLY ELECTRIC CARRIAGE RETURN...your fingers never leave the keyboard, not even to return the carriage. Just touch a button and the carriage zips back instantly, ready for the next line.

FULLY ELECTRIC REPEAT KEYS...continuous pressure on X's, periods, dashes and underlines gives you automatic repeat action. Great for underscoring, for making forms.

FULLY ELECTRIC REPEAT SPACING...slight extra pressure on the space bar gives you automatic repeat spacing.

ELECTRIC BACKSPACE KEY...a light touch on this key moves the carriage back one full space...automatically.

FULL 88-CHARACTER KEYBOARD...even including figure "1", exclamation point, "plus" sign and "equal-sign": characters essential to students, yet rarely found anywhere except the big office typewriters!

FULL WIDTH PRE-SET TAB BAR...for indenting paragraphs, for typing in columns. Just touch the bar and the carriage moves automatically to the next pre-set tab.

RUGGED INSIDE...BEAUTIFUL OUTSIDE...has steel-framed, unitized construction for smoothness and durability--but you can't see it. What you see is the high-impact, beautifully-molded plastic case that makes your typewriter lightweight and easy to carry.

FULL 10-INCH CARRIAGE...types a No. 10 envelope and full width of standard typewriter paper.

LARGE PICA TYPE...easy to read...best for schoolwork...for business reports, for recipes and the best type for stencil cutting.

VARIABLE LINE SPACING WITH HALF-LINE SPACING...set it to type single-spaced or double-spaced lines...or 1-1/2-line spacing! Line spacing is done automatically when you press the electric carriage return button.

VARIABLE IMPRESSION CONTROL...when typing carbons, you can set the control to automatically produce heavier strokes...and better carbon copies!

TWO-COLOR RIBBON...types black or red, as you select. Can also be set to type stencils. Ribbon reverses automatically.

SPEED MARGINS, RIGHT AND LEFT...set them instantly. Bell warns when you're approaching right margin.

More? You bet there's more! Three-position paper bail with typing scale...built-in erasure table...infinite line space adjustment... margin release key...paper release...on-off switch...

Feature after feature after feature...all adding up to make this ROYAL FULLY ELECTRIC one of the finest all-purpose family typewriters we've ever seen...and so easy to use!

FIG. 14-1 (*continued*).

What's more, two important "extras" are included with your Royal fully electric portable typewriter:

A slim, handsome two-piece carrying case...custom-fitted to give your typewriter maximum protection when you store it or when you carry it. For extra security, the case has a lock and key.

A complete course on touch typing...designed by Royal to teach people who have never typed in their lives -- even children -- how to touch-type!

It takes only 20 or 30 minutes a day. The simple, clear instructions lead you along step by step. Almost before you realize it, you're typing simple words by touch...then sentences...then complete paragraphs! You've learned a skill that will be valuable to you all your life!

Your typing course even includes tips on proper typing posture...on the right form for letters...on the maintenance of your typewriter...and even a supply of typing paper and carbon paper!

AND YOU GET A BONUS GIFT TOO!

When you request your Royal fully electric portable typewriter, you will be eligible to receive, at no cost to you, a Sight 'N Sound High Intensity Lamp/Radio!

In one compact, handsome unit, your Sight 'N Sound Lamp/Radio has:

- A high-intensity desk lamp with two-level illumination and 360° swivel top to give light where you want it - and a telescoping arm as well. Use it when typing, or on your bedside table to read by.

- An all-transistor AM radio - with "instant on" high-fi sound and manual gain control...to make typing and reading even more fun.

You'll consider this most exciting gift one of your most useful items--in fact, you'll be hard-pressed to decide where to keep it: at home or at the office (unless one of your children solves the problem for you by taking it to college!) When we ship your typewriter, we'll include a Bonus Certificate for your Lamp/Radio. When you decide to keep the typewriter, simply mail the Bonus Certificate to us, and we'll ship your Sight 'N Sound Lamp/Radio at no additional charge!

We want you, and everybody in your family, to use and enjoy your ROYAL FULLY ELECTRIC PORTABLE TYPEWRITER for 15 days...WITHOUT COST AND WITHOUT OBLIGATION. Use it, and let every member of your family use it.

Then, if you don't agree that this typewriter is one of the most useful and valuable things your family could have, simply return the typewriter...and you will owe nothing.

But if you want to keep it, you can charge it to your Mobil Credit Card, just like you do your gasoline - but pay in small amounts monthly - with no interest or finance charge!

FIG. 14-1 (*continued*).

What do you think the price of this feature-filled, fully electric typewriter should be?

$159.00? - $199.00? - $179.00?

The full price--the very special Mobil price--is only $129.95...including the carrying case...including the touch-typing course...and including your gift!

If you decide to keep the typewriter, we will add just $11.54 per month to your regular Mobil account for a 12 month total of payments price (amount financed) of $138.48* which includes $8.53 for packaging and shipping.

NO MONEY DOWN, NO FINANCE CHARGE when payments are made on time**

I think you'll agree that this Mobil policy of no extra charge for extended payments is a distinctly unusual one in these days of extra high interest rates.

If you prefer a single charge, we will add the cash price of $129.95* plus the shipping and packaging charge, to your next regular Mobil account statement.

Value? Fantastic value! But you don't have to decide now whether or not you want to keep it--right now; we only want you to try it.

Simply sign and mail your Free Trial Certificate. That's all you have to do. We will send you your Royal Traveler fully electric typewriter for your family to try--with no obligation or cost--plus your Radio/Lamp Bonus Certificate!

Cordially,

H. J. Byers

H. J. Byers
Manager, Credit Card Sales
Mobil Oil Corporation

P.S.—For your prompt action, we will also include—FREE—a Webster's New World Dictionary. Yours to keep whether or not you keep the typewriter!

** STATEMENT ON FINANCE CHARGES
NO FINANCE CHARGE
when payments are made on time.

You select the terms. Pay all at once, or take 12 months to pay. You will be billed, according to your selection, on your Mobil Credit Card Account. If you select an easy monthly payment plan, there will be **NO FINANCE CHARGE** on these installments. However, a **FINANCE CHARGE** is imposed on any past due balance which is not paid within 25 days after its original billing date. The **FINANCE CHARGE** is imposed on the unpaid balance after deducting payments and credits up to the closing date of the bill.

The **FINANCE CHARGE** on such late payments is computed at a periodic (monthly) rate of 1½% on balances of $500.00 or less, and 1% per month on balances over $500.00. These are the rates for most states, and the corresponding **ANNUAL PERCENTAGE RATES** are 18% on balances of $500.00 or less, and 12% on balances over $500.00. The exceptions are as follows, with the periodic rate shown first and the annual rates shown in parentheses: Pennsylvania — 1¼% (15%) on $500.00 or less; Colorado—1¼% (15%) on $300.00 or less and 5/6% (10%) over $300.00; Indiana, Washington, New Jersey and Wisconsin — 1% (12%) on ALL balances; Ohio — 1% (12%) over $400.00; Kansas—1% (12%) over $300.00; Montana — 11/12% (11%) on $300.00 or less and 7/12% (7%) over $300.00; Missouri—¾% (9%) over $500.00; Arizona, Arkansas, Idaho—5/6% (10%) on ALL balances.

But remember—For this Special Offer you can take 12 months to pay and there is **NO FINANCE CHARGE** on any installment paid within 25 days of its original billing date. You may also pay the full amount due at any time.

*State and local taxes, if any, additional.

MOB-RL(RL)D-KM-3

FIG. 14-1 (*concluded*).

typewriter by mail to a list of Mobil credit card holders (Figure 14-1). Since the price is well over a hundred dollars, it might be expected that none but an attractive and powerful mailing could induce readers to purchase the article sight unseen. The mailing consisted of the pieces listed below. Note, however, that notwithstanding the numerous enclosures, the letter is complete in itself and describes in detail all the features of the machine as well as the exact terms of purchase.

The mailing assembly:

1. Outside window envelope, size 6¼ by 9½ inches. To the left of the window the gist of the sales message was handwritten and then repeated in typewriter type to show the difference in appearance. The copy read: "Fully electric typing is ten times faster than writing . . . twice as fast as manual typing. It's neater, cleaner, easier, too! Discover this for yourself . . . right in your own home . . . FREE!" The envelope was printed in red and blue on a white background.
2. A letter in the form of a four-page folder, size 8½ by 11 inches. The copy was printed mostly in black ink, but the main head as well as the subheads and important paragraphs were printed in red.
3. A full-color folder that opened to size 17 by 22 inches. It showed the machine in actual size, with attention drawn to the many special features. It also had a half dozen smaller color photographs of the machine in use by various members of a typical family. Insets showed the complete typing course given free, the slim carrying case, and the college dictionary the purchaser of the typewriter could keep even if he decided to return the typewriter. One panel of the folder showed the Mobil credit card; another gave specific details of the guarantees offered by both Mobil and Royal.
4. A leaflet, size 8½ by 11 inches, showing in full-color the Sight 'N Sound Lamp-Radio offered as a bonus when the purchaser decided to keep the typewriter.
5. An order card with the reader's name and address already filled in, and a place for the purchaser's signature. The name and address on the order card showed through the window of the mailing envelope and thus served as the mailing address.
6. A business-reply envelope to take care of the possibility that the reader would want to pay for the machine with his order.

Shorter Mail-Order Sales Letters

Of course, not every mail-order sales letter has to be as long as the letter just described. In some instances, the reader is already thoroughly aware of the point of the message and requires only a brief reminder. In other instances, the letter is brief while additional reliance is placed on data in the enclosures. The following letter, promoting the sale of Christmas Seals among former purchasers, was printed on one side of a single sheet. A panel to the left listed about forty well-known sponsors. On the reverse side, the reader found a fuller description of the health problem dealt with in the letter as well as instructions for making bequests and special gifts. Undoubtedly, the reader's familiarity with Christmas Seals and the predisposition to give to this cause made the sponsors feel that a short letter would do the job adequately. Another reason may have been the disparate nature of the mailing list, including people from all walks of life and all levels of reading competence.

Dear Contributor:

While you are reading this letter you will breathe in and out about 9 times . . . and never give it a thought. Do you realize how lucky you are?

Almost 1,000,000 Americans who have emphysema aren't so lucky--to them, breathing is a real effort.

Emphysema is no longer confined to the elderly--today more and more young men and women are developing it. The number of patients doubles every five years. Emphysema is the fastest growing killer disease today.

The familiar, friendly Christmas Seals enclosed are one way you help control this menace. Your Christmas Seal association fights emphysema, tuberculosis, asthma, other chronic respiratory diseases, air pollution, and smoking.

Because there's more than ever to do--won't you please try to give a little more this year?

Please return your contribution in the special envelope enclosed. You'll breathe a little easier for it--and we'll be most grateful.

Sincerely,

Christmas Seal Chairman

Magazine subscriptions are commonly sold by mail. The length of the letters varies with the amount of selling to be done—long letters for new subscriptions, shorter letters for renewals. Typical of the latter type is the following letter sent to *Atlantic* subscribers when their trial subscription expired. The letter assumes the reader's familiarity with the magazine and emphasizes the dollar savings and convenience. Also worth noting is the privileged status conferred upon the reader as an *Atlantic* "regular."

Renew now--
before your subscription expires
--and save up to $14.50

Dear Subscriber:

Your Atlantic subscription will expire shortly. As a new subscriber, you can now renew at substantial savings.

The enclosed form offers a "1st time" renewal saving of $14.50 This is only offered to new friends of The Atlantic.

The greatest savings, you'll note, are yours when you choose the three-year rate--$14.50 under the annual rate.

The savings are an incentive, of course, but most important, you are assured of receiving The Atlantic on a regular basis, without the bother of renewal notices and bills.

Remember, these rates are for "new friends" only so take advantage of them today.

A simple check mark on the enclosed card is all that is required. No need to stop and write out a check, unless you prefer. We'll bill you later. And--welcome to The Atlantic regulars.

Cordially,

Subscribers who did not reply to the original letter received a copy as a follow-up. Written in simulated handwriting across the top was the message:

> Just in case you forgot about it or misplaced your original order card, we've enclosed another. There's still time to continue your subscription without interruption and save up to $14.50 under the regular rate if you mail your card today.

SALES PROMOTION

Most sales letters are more limited in their aim than the mail-order message. Instead of trying to do the complete selling job, they are used to "promote" sales by educating the customer to the nature of the goods and services being offered and by soliciting some form of interest that can then be capitalized. The prospective customer may be asked to see the company's representative on the customer's premises, to visit the store or showroom where the goods can be seen or demonstrated, or to request additional information to help with the buying decision.

Inviting Sales Inquiries

There are many reasons for using sales letters to obtain inquiries. The advertised product or services may require more explanation than any written message can effectively convey; perhaps the nature of the product makes a demonstration mandatory; perhaps the descriptive material is too expensive to chance on an indiscriminate list of supposed prospects; and perhaps the advertiser already has an adequate sales force but needs good "leads" to keep them busy.

Since it is easier to secure inquiries than orders, the message may be relatively short and omit much of the description and evidence a mail-order appeal would require. In the following letter to book manufacturers, a power scissors is offered as an inducement "just for listening" to the company's representative. Even so, the emphasis in the letter is on the higher profits and lower costs made possible by the company's primary line of paper folders and cutters.

> Dear Sir:
>
> With profit margins decreasing and labor costs increasing at a record rate, managers throughout the graphic arts industry are looking to modern bindery equipment to help stem the tide.
>
> How about you? Even though your present folders and cutters are still operating well, are you sure they're still operating profitably? Are they capable of handling your current and future production requirements economically? If not, Bell & Howell can help bring your operation up-to-date.
>
> To help you fold and cut your way to higher profits and lower production costs, we've been conducting an intensive program to develop the right equipment for your needs. And we believe we have, with a modern new line of Baumfolders and Senator Cutters specially designed for the graphic arts industry.
>
> Your Baumfolder representative would like an opportunity to discuss this advanced equipment with you. And to make the discussion even more worthwhile, Bell & Howell will give you a cordless "Power-Cut" Power Scissors for your office...absolutely FREE...just for listening. No efficient office should be without this precision cutting tool. It cuts paper, packages, cloth, string -- even light cardboard...makes any office cutting job simpler and faster.
>
> Just mail the enclosed postage-paid reply card now. You'll receive your FREE Power Scissors from your Baumfolder representative -- just for listening to how you can fold and cut more profitably!
>
> Sincerely yours,

The letter that follows is part of a series mailed from such unlikely places as Spot, North Carolina; Wax, Kentucky; and Protection, Kansas. Through the letters, paper and paperboard manufacturers were made aware of the advantages of using 3M Company protective coatings on package materials. Readers were invited to return an enclosed card for additional details.

Spot, North Carolina

I was trailing
my wife...

through the store here in Spot the other day, when I noticed about a dozen boxes of big-name cookies on one of the shelves.

They stopped me cold.

You see, all the boxes were covered with tiny gray spots about the size of a nickel and they looked, well... dirty.

"Funny," I thought, "here a big company spends years in research to make a good product...invests millions of dollars in distribution and advertising...and when their product gets on the shelf, it's spotty and ugly!"

A little thing? I don't think so...and you probably don't either. In fact, that's why I'm writing.

If there's any question in your own mind about whether the products you package look as good on the shelf as they did in your plant, I think you'll want to consider the benefits of "Scotchban" Paper Size.

"Scotchban" Size, you see, was developed to give you permanent built-in protection against wicking by grease, oil, asphalt and wax...and has virtually no effect on your package's strength, porosity or flexibility. And naturally, "Scotchban" Size is cleared for direct food contact, even for hot-fill and storage up to 150 degrees F.

And that's only part of the story.

You can learn all the facts about "Scotchban" Paper Size and what it can do by returning the enclosed reply card. Just sign it and drop it in the mail now.

Sincerely,

Pitney Bowes, a name long associated with postage meters, used a two-letter series to announce the introduction of a copying machine to its line. The letters were personally addressed and signed, and were mounted flat in large leather-like binders. Since little information was given in the letters themselves, getting attention was a crucial function, and this was accomplished in a distinctive way. Note also the postscript to the second letter, which makes a strong competitive point.

1.

Dear Mr. Doe:

Pitney Bowes will soon introduce its exciting new plain bond copying machine.

I would like to cordially invite you to be among the first in your area to see the PBC copier at its premiere appearance.

I am particularly proud of this machine as it provides many features and excellent copy quality. I am sure you will find it will be of great interest to you.

I will advise you shortly concerning the time and place of its first showing.

Sincerely yours,

2.

Dear Mr. Doe:

Enclosed is your personal invitation to the premiere showing, in your area, of Pitney Bowes' exciting new plain bond copier, the PBC.

This special premiere is for selected friends of Pitney Bowes. As attendance will be limited, I would very much appreciate your letting me know at your earliest convenience if you or your representative will attend.

I am particularly excited about this machine, and I am sure you will find the presentation highly informative and enjoyable. We are looking forward to meeting you.

Sincerely yours,

P.S. This paper is the same fine quality, relative. inexpensive 20 lb bond that our PBC copier use.

Letters soliciting inquiries are more likely to be sent to business and industrial users than to consumers. The reason is that the products require a good deal of demonstration and missionary work. Still, letters inviting consumer inquiries are a necessary part of the selling efforts of certain types of companies. The following letter attempts to interest the homeowner in taking a second mortgage on his property. The specific figures unquestionably bring the reader visions of obtaining a large sum of cash by using the equity in his home as security. A personal quality is added to the letter by references to the reader's own street and community.

Dear Mr. Stevens:

You may not be aware that the value of your home on Yockey St. is probably much higher today than ever before.

As a matter of fact, homes all over Garden Grove are worth an average of 41% more now than they were just three years ago. This means a home that sold for about $33,000 in 1972 is now worth about $46,500.

The enclosed folder explains how an Avco Homeowner's Loan may help you turn the increased value of your home into a substantial amount of cash.

Please take a minute to read through the folder. Then, to find out exactly what an Avco Homeowner's Loan can do for you, simply give me a call at 535-2819, or drop the enclosed reply card in the mail.

I'll be looking forward to hearing from you soon.

Sincerely yours,

Some sales promotion letters "pave the way for the salesman" in the sense that they do not ask the recipients to request his call, but instead announce his coming. The letters give the advertiser the opportunity to acquaint prospects with the line and try to make the salesman welcome.

The excerpted letter that follows was one of a series of four sent to restaurant owners. Each of the four letters was accompanied by a wooden rack containing a different combination of spices packed in jars: for seafood, meat, poultry, and (with the letter quoted) salad. The advertiser, who makes internally illuminated plastic-faced outdoor signs, reported that every one of the 115 prospects reached gave the salesman the opportunity to discuss the company's "sign-identity programs."[3] You might note how closely the theme of the letters tied in with the interests of the special class of prospects solicited.

Dear Mr. Burke:

. . . .

Let us help you toss together some crisp new ideas for that most important advertising venture. Our creative group focuses on the interplay of color, shape, size and dimensional treatment. We can design from your specific instructions, or create a total concept for you.

. . . .

Wilted advertising can leave your company looking as limp as a left-over salad. Don't take a chance on less than A & E Plasti-Line/Texlite.

[3] From the records of the Direct-Mail Marketing Association.

```
If you'd care to leaf through some of our samples, a
representative will be in touch soon to show you what
we've done for well-known names across the country.  And
he can tell you even more of the unique benefits you'll
enjoy with the A & E Plasti-Line/Texlite sign program.

                              Very truly yours,
```

Answering Sales Inquiries

When prospective customers respond to sales messages or write on their own initiative, their inquiries may be answered by letter. If a booklet, sample, or other inducement has been offered, a letter will usually accompany it. Some answers are individually dictated to fit the inquiry; others are either preprinted or prepared in advance for personal typing when the inquiries are received. In the last instance, provision is sometimes made for the typing in of details relating to the specific inquiry in addition to the "canned" copy. Computerized typewriters that make possible the selection of alternative stock phrases may also be used in answering a large volume of sales inquiries.

The most important fact about a sales inquiry is that it evidences the prospective customer's interest. It is now up to the sales correspondent to turn this interest into a sale or at least to induce the prospect to take the next step, like visiting his dealer or receiving a salesman at his home or place of business. The biggest mistake the correspondent can make is to treat the inquiry in a perfunctory way and thus turn away business that his company has spent a great deal of money to attract.

A good answer will conform to these rules:

1. It should be sent promptly. Delay will only cool the inquirer's ardor and give him time to investigate a competitor's offerings.
2. The information given should fully satisfy the reader. If his questions are not answered in a form letter or the accompanying literature, a personal letter should be dictated.
3. The letter should contain any additional material necessary to convince the reader and influence his decision.
4. The letter should tell the reader how to go about obtaining further information or making a purchase. A company that sells through local distributors should provide the name of the nearest one. For example:

```
Your local Collomatic representative

 Carew-Meehan Co.
 487 Broadway
 New York, N.Y.  10013
 946-1044

is a specialist in collating problems.  A few moments
spent with him will quickly determine if there is a sound
basis for the application of a Collomatic Collator to
your work.  If so, he will be pleased to arrange an "in-
your-office" demonstration.
```

5. If the anticipated results warrant, the answer should be followed up either by a salesman's call or additional letters. In the former instance, the initial reply should give the salesman's name.

> We have asked our factory representative, Mr. Robert M. Colbert, 750 Boylston Street, Boston, Mass. 02110, to get in touch with you regarding a personal demonstration of our product.

When a company offers literature of general interest through a mass advertising medium, it will receive many requests from prospective customers as well as from readers who are not interested in the product or service itself. A brief letter or card accompanying the literature may then be used to solicit further inquiries from the prospective customers only. Here is an example from the Pitney Bowes organization mentioned earlier.

> Here's the Material You Requested
>
> And we hope you'll find some ideas in it that you can use to your profit. . . . If you would like to know how our products might be used in your business, you'll find a handy postpaid card enclosed in the booklet. Mailing it will bring a prompt response. Thank you for your interest.
>
> Sincerely yours,

A more involved follow-up system was used by United Airlines. The first letter, on page 428, is their response to an inquiry to an advertisement offering planning suggestions for a Hawaii vacation. You will note that the letter goes through all the steps of the persuasive process from attracting attention to stimulating action. A unique feature is contained in the postscript which offers a book of bonus coupons for free attractions in Hawaii. To receive it, the reader must have an enclosed certificate validated by a travel agent. In this way, the mere curiosity-seekers are separated from the genuine prospects, and the latter are put in touch directly with an agency from which United Airlines flights to Hawaii can be booked. The second letter, on page 429, is sent on receipt of the validated certificate for the coupon book.

1.

Dear Friend:

Thank you very much for requesting United's vacation planners for Hawaii.

We are delighted to enclose them along with our hope that you and your family will visit Hawaii this summer.

> If you haven't been there before, you will find the islands to be a place of breath-taking beauty and incredible diversity.
>
> If you have visited Hawaii, you know that on each island there are new charms and new delights just waiting to be discovered around each bend in the road.
>
> Our Royal Hawaiian service will pamper you with island atmosphere, giving you a touch of Hawaii even before you arrive.

And first-timer or old-timer, it is comforting to know that for all its romance and exotic flaver, Hawaii is, of course, one of the fifty states--so you can visit this "foreign" land without passports, without language problems and without the problem of wrestling with unfamiliar currencies or dollar devaluation.

The vacation planners we have enclosed will help you choose exactly the right vacation for you. As you read them, if you have any questions whatsoever, please get in touch with your travel agent. They are experts on all aspects of travel.

To make your Hawaii dream even more possible, remember that you can charge your air fare on your American Express card. And when you do, ask about the American Express extended payment plan.

We hope that United will have the pleasure and privilege of flying you to Hawaii very soon.

Sincerely,

P.S. So much of what's great about our 50th state is FREE! That's why we've put together an unusual Coupon Book that guides you to many of the famous free attractions in Hawaii you won't want to miss! We think you will find this useful when you visit the islands. We have enclosed a special flyer to tell you how you can obtain this coupon book.

2.

Dear Friend:

We're pleased to enclose your "See Hawaii Free" coupon book, with the compliments of United Airlines.

We hope we're correct in assuming that your request for this book indicates that you intend to visit the islands in the near future. And if you do, we naturally hope that United can have the pleasure and privilege of flying you there and back again.

In any case, the coupon book is yours to use however you wish. We hope it will produce some pleasant and memorable experiences for you.

Thanks again for requesting it -- and have a wonderful time!

UNITED AIRLINES

Retail Sales Letters

For large centrally located stores, the most economical advertising media are newspapers, radio, and television; for the smaller neighborhood stores, it is usually their own windows and circulars distributed from door to door. More selective advertising, however, is done through the mails. Such advertising permits a store to reach only its own customers or some specific class of customers, for example, men or women, credit customers, inactive accounts of patrons of the custom shirt department. For selective advertising of this sort, letters cannot be surpassed.

One of the common uses of retail sales letters is to announce a sale. Added interest is provided when regular customers are invited to make their selections for some days prior to public announcement. Other traditional features of the sale announcement are the following:

1. Reason for the sale: end-of-season, preseason, overstock, etc.
2. Exact dates of the sale, or at least the starting date.
3. Description or list of offerings. Is full or only partial stock available at sale prices? What is the range of sizes, colors, styles, etc.?
4. Comparative before-and-after prices, or percentages of markdown.
5. Urge to hurry for best selections.

The following letter combines all of these features into an effective sales appeal for the customers of a large clothing chain. A list of the specific merchandise offered, with a comparison of in-season and pre-season prices, was included at the point where you see the spaced periods.

Dear Customer:

Ten years ago this week our telephone never stopped ringing. One business acquaintance called up and offered to sell us a carload of snowballs. Another said he was an Eskimo and wanted to open a charge account. Several asked if we were going out of business.

The reason for all the joking was that we just sent out a letter, like this one, advertising overcoats and top-coats in August. It was an unprecedented thing to do and and a lot of people thought we were quite mad. But our reasoning--that plenty of men would buy in advance of the season if offered a sufficiently good inducement--turned out to be right. Since then, our annual Coat Event has broken its own record every year. This coming month, with better-than-ever selections and savings, we expect to reach a new high.

Beginning Saturday, August 1, we will again offer special groups of brand-new Hart Schaffner & Marx and Wallachs own overcoats and topcoats at substantial Pre-Season Savings. Pick out the coat you want now; pay for it later this Fall. This plan offers you every advantage, as you will see.
Among the <u>overcoats</u> we'll feature are:

. . . .

Along with the benefits of early selection and a special saving, you don't pay for your coat until you begin wearing it. We will make necessary alterations on the coat you select, then keep it for you in mothproof storage until the onset of cool weather.

We are advising you of this special event in advance of public announcement because, as a regular customer, we would like you to choose from the most complete selection. We think you'll agree that it does make sense to choose your coat ahead of the season, at the comfortable air-conditioned Wallachs store nearest you. Plan to be there just as soon as convenient, to select the coat you prefer at a saving you'll enjoy.

Sincerely yours,

Another common use of retail letters is to build up regular patronage by offering charge accounts. In the letter that follows, the repetition of the addressee's name in several places in the letter suggests that the letter was produced on a computer-assisted automatic typewriter. Note, too, the description of merchandise and the privileges available to the card holder. Since the store is new to the community, the paragraph before the last commendably gives assurance of its reputation. Also, the so-called "Confirmation Certificate" enclosed with the letter—really the application for credit—has an expiration date which provides a stimulus for prompt action.

I take pleasure, Mr. & Mrs. Compton

... in advising you that as of last Wednesday, a Burdine's "Charter Cardholder" charge account has been tentatively RESERVED IN YOUR NAME.

As soon as the attached Confirmation Certificate is received and approved, I'll see to it that your Burdine's Credit Card is issued promptly -- in plenty of time for you to take advantage of our Clearwater Mall GRAND OPENING SALES!

No red tape. No lengthy credit applications. Just complete the Comfirmation Certificate below, return it in the enclosed postpaid envelope (while this special opportunity is still open to you), and I'll take care of everything else.

Your Burdine's Credit Card will let the Compton family charge the latest fashions (including a wide selection of children's wear), home furnishings and housewares ... gifts, cosmetics, jewelry and much, MUCH more. Buy what you want, when you want, with never a worry about how much cash you have.

You'll also enjoy instant check-cashing privileges, free delivery, liberal returned-merchandise policy, special V.I.P. services ... plus the many other Charter Cardholder benefits described in the ENCLOSED FOLDER.

Consider, too, that for over 77 years Burdine's has served discriminating customers in Central and South Florida. And, like all Federated Department Stores -- Bloomingdale's, Foley's, Lazarus and Bullock's, to name a few -- Burdine's takes real pride in offering you unsurpassed quality and value.

Soon, I hope, it will be our privilege to add the Compton name to Burdine's roster of preferred Charter Cardholders.

Cordially,

After credit has been approved, it is customary to send a letter announcing the opening of the account. The letter on page 432, signed by the store president, is used as a follow-up to the invitational letter shown above. Though rather effusive it tries to be helpful.

Dear Mr. and Mrs. Compton:

We'd like to welcome you as a preferred customer at Burdine's. Your charge account has been opened and you'll receive your Charter Credit Card shortly before the grand opening of Burdine's beautiful, new Clearwater Mall store.

Please take a moment to read the enclosed brochure ... it will explain your CHARTER CARDHOLDER benefits, and help you to understand the important advantages you'll have as a Burdine's preferred customer.

We've been alert to the needs of the people of Central and South Florida for over 77 years...and it will be a pleasure for us to serve you and your neighbors in the W. Collingswood area as customers. We'll always try our best to assist you in every possible manner.

If ever you have any questions, suggestions, or special needs, please call us at 813/725-6117. We want to assure you of our concern for your total satisfaction and our sincere willingness to please.

Should you wish to use your Charter Card at any other Burdine's store in advance of our Clearwater opening, just drop us a line at Box 470399, Miami, Florida 33127.

Cordially,

GOODWILL MESSAGES

Unlike mail-order and sales promotion letters, goodwill letters are institutional. If they sell, they sell only indirectly. Their chief function is to cement relationships and create an atmosphere in which business can be conducted smoothly.

Goodwill letters may be used in communicating with any of the company's constituents: employees, stockholders, dealers and distributors, customers and prospective customers, and the general public, whose good opinion of the organization must always be considered a necessary asset. Here we will consider some uses of goodwill letters in customer relations.

Cultivating Good Relations

Fruitful sources of goodwill as well as business are the company's customers and prospective customers. The time and energy spent in cultivating present customers are especially rewarding. For just as it is easier to keep a running engine going than to start a cold one, so it so it takes less effort to nourish the trade one already has than to attract new trade. Yet this elementary principle is often overlooked by proprietors intent on winning over someone else's customers while at the same time they neglect their own. In recent years, consumer dissatisfactions have spread to whole industries—cars, drugs, foods and beverages, for instance—and some companies have set up emergency units—often with special addresses and toll-free telephone numbers—to receive complaints and deal with them.

One of the objectives of goodwill messages to customers is to discover and remove any causes of dissatisfaction before they become infectious; a second objective is to strengthen the relationship by demonstrations of friendship beyond those called for or expected in the normal course of business. Goodwill messages to prospective customers, also, seek business through friendly gestures rather than direct selling appeals. The idea is to bypass their natural defenses against overt salesmanship and obtain their trade by more subtle means.

A noteworthy service campaign directed to present customers was that of the Cryovac division of W. R. Grace & Co. Its aim was to help customers feel that some one individual could be counted on to handle all their orders, inquiries, and—only incidentally—complaints. First a printed flier was sent to the customers over the signature of the District Manager. At the top was a letter beginning:

> Have you got one of those little black books all men carry around? With little red stars next to the special names? You do! Great! Put a new name in it now. Marian Chambers. And call her . . . anytime. (215) 555-5555.

The bottom half featured a close-up photograph of the lady, phone in hand, with the caption in large type:

MEET MARIAN CHAMBERS
SHE'S GOT YOUR NUMBER. AND NOW YOU'VE GOT HERS.

A follow-up letter repeated the lady's first name and telephone number in a caption over her photograph. The names and photographs were changed in the mailings to match the representative to the particular group of customers she was assigned to serve. The basic letter read as follows:

> Dear Mr. Benson:
>
> I hope by this time you've put my name in your little black book...and near your telephone. I'm Marian Chambers and I'm here, eager to help you with any packaging problem from now on.
>
> I'm part of Cryovac's "ONE NUMBER-TOTAL SERVICE" program. All you have to do is dial one number...mine...and you'll get total service. Usually I'll be able to take care of the problem myself. If not, I'll know exactly who to contact to do it for you...fast.
>
> Maybe you suddenly discover you're running low on shrink film or bags and you'll need delivery fast. Just call me.
>
> Maybe you've got a shipment overdue, and you want to know where it is. Just call me.

```
Maybe you need to make some changes on your packaging
line.  Just call me.  In no time I'll make arrangements
for one of our technical specialists to pay you a visit.

So, see, now all you have to do is make one contact.  Me.
That's a promise.  Just ask for Marian, (215) 555-5555.
Anytime, and we'll get things moving.

                                 Sincerely,



P.S.  Since "ONE NUMBER-TOTAL SERVICE" is a whole new pro-
gram, I'd really like to know what you think of it.  Would
you fill out the enclosed reply card and drop it in the
mail to me?  I'll look forward to hearing from you.
```

Removing Dissatisfaction

When customers are unhappy about the treatment they receive, they are more likely to tell their friends and neighbors than to complain to the offending organization. As a result, management often does not know why sales fall off and customers fail to return. The deficiency may be remedied by systematic inquiries among present and former customers. They ask, in effect, "Have you been happy with our goods and services? Is there anything we can do to increase your satisfaction?" A television service company uses this technique in a double postcard sent immediately after repairs have been made on a customer's set. The message reads:

```
Dear RCA Victor Television Owner:

Thank you for the privilege of serving you.  We trust
that your set is once more in good working order and
operating to your satisfaction.

It is our aim to maintain the highest standards of cus-
tomer satisfaction and we ask your cooperation in help-
ing us determine whether or not we are accomplishing our
objective.  Kindly fill out the attached (postage paid)
card and drop it in the mail.  Sign your name if you like
--although it isn't necessary.

Thank you again for the opportunity of serving you, and
please call on us again when you need service.

                              Service Manager
```

A common practice is to make a list of customers who have not placed any business with the company for some time. A letter is then written to determine if the seller has been in any way at fault. Here is such a letter from the president of a retail store:

> Dear Mrs. Callan:
>
> We notice with regret that you have not used your charge account recently.
>
> We are all human, and while we strive for perfection, mistakes do occasionally occur. Won't you be equally frank with us and tell us on the reverse side of this letter if you have been displeased by any action of ours?
>
> Sincerely,

Even more important than inviting complaints is doing something about them when customers respond. After receiving two letters from her former laundry, pleading with her to tell why she discontinued her patronage, a lady answered by stating her complaint. The reply she received only worsened the already strained relations. It read:

> Dear Madam:
>
> We are in receipt of your letter telling us why you discontinued our services.
>
> As to your complaint about shirts being torn, there are no parts of the machinery or the process of washing that would cause the condition you report. If the collars had to be turned, as you claim, it was due to general wear and not to improper handling or laundering.
>
> Collars and cuffs of all shirts show signs of wear after a time. Naturally, the rest of the shirt must be weakened and would tear easily. You will find that clothes of any type after continuous usage will tear at some time.
>
> Very truly yours,

A more statesmanlike handling of the situation might have resulted in a letter like this, in addition to a generous adjustment:

> Dear Mrs. Gray:
>
> We're very glad you wrote to us about the problem you have been having with your laundered shirts.
>
> So that we may be able to correct any fault at our plant, I am asking our routeman to call on you and pick up the shirts in question. We in turn will see that you are fully compensated for the damage you report.
>
> The laundry you send to us is certainly entitled to the best of care and we want to assure you of our efforts in that direction.
>
> Sincerely,

In other situations customers respond in detail to letters inviting complaints, then do not receive an acknowledgment, let alone an adjustment. (For principles relating to the writing of adjustment letters, see Chapter 6, pages 171–180.)

Some goodwill communications are the outgrowth of the company's experience with customers' attitudes and are in fact designed to forestall complaints and criticism by acquainting customers with some basic business facts. An example is the booklet "How Your Telephone Calls Are Counted." The ostensible purpose is enlightenment of the customer, but more basically it serves to minimize complaints about overcharges by showing the extreme care that is exercised in computing bills. A hotel chain achieves a similar purpose with a pamphlet of "Tips to Travelers." By stating hotel customs with respect to reservations, credit, and checkout time, the pamphlet encourages observance and reduces misunderstandings.

Other examples of defensive as well as informative literature are the washing instructions that accompany colored sport shirts (they may fade), the package enclosure on the care of patent leather shoes (they chip, check, peel), the store sign advising on the selection of hairbrushes (they are not returnable), and the bill enclosure that defines trade terms (they are often misunderstood or ignored).

Some of the problems of big distributors are created not so much by themselves or their retail customers as they are by dealers who do not live up to the standards expected of them. The Standard Oil Company of California produced a series of mailings to dealers designed to improve their service to customers. Above the heading of the following copy was a full-color photograph of an attractively dressed woman:

> WOULD SHE USE YOUR RESTROOM?
>
> Maybe a better question is—would you want her to?
>
> Right now . . . while you're reading this . . . do you know for sure that your women's restroom would pass feminine inspection?
>
> Many women stopping at your station may or may not come back, depending on how they *feel* about the appearance of your restroom.
>
> The more women who spend dollars at your station, the more volume you'll do to bring in bigger Profit Point checks. You could really clean up!

Goodwill "Extras"

A maxim of good customer relations is never to take customers for granted. Like any other individuals they seek appreciation and attention, and they take their trade where these civilities are offered. An opportunity to pay attention to customers is afforded immediately after a first purchase. The "thank you" note or letter of welcome fills the purpose admirably. The letter that follows is sent to customers of a retail clothing store, but the same technique is used to greet new magazine subscribers, new bank depositors, and new industrial accounts.

```
Dear Mr. Sampson:

Thank you again for your recent purchase.  I hope that
your new garment is giving every bit as much pleasure
and service as you expected when you bought it from me.
If there is any detail that is not entirely satisfac-
tory, please come in and let me see what can be done to
correct it.

It was a pleasure to serve you, and I look forward to
the opportunity of doing so again.

                                  Sincerely,
```

With the customer made to feel welcome, the next step is to keep him informed. The most immediately productive means are mailed announcements of sales, special offers, new lines, and the like. Although these have a direct selling aim, they also have a great goodwill potential because they remind the customer of the seller's interest in him. As a matter of fact, once the relationship is established and confidence in the seller secured, the urgency of the sales message can often be considerably relaxed. In these instances, the emphasis is less on selling than on the desire to serve, less on direct methods of persuasion than on suggestion. Note the informality of the following letter—hardly more than a reminder—to the male customers of a large department store. The use of the legal idiom is especially appropriate in that the store is located near the city's civic center and counts many lawyers among its clientele.

```
Dear Sir:

You have heard that jury duty can be a pleasure.

Here at the Gentleman's Corner we have a very happy cal-
endar for Spring.

As befits the growing importance of this "store within
a store," we have gathered a wealth of apparel and ac-
cessories for the new season.  And we have established
a prima facie case for quality . . . with many of the
respected brands in men's wear serving as character wit-
nesses.

Court is now in session.  The attendants are eager to
be helpful.  You'll find all the evidence attractively
displayed for the "jury" of interested men who, each
day, review and approve the testimony of good taste.

Will you, too, serve on the jury?  We'll be delighted
to have your verdict.

                              Cordially,
```

Many of the goodwill messages sent to customers are "service" messages in the sense that they point up service accommodations. A retail store, for example, tells its customers about the convenience of its newly installed escalators, announces a golf demonstration in the store, invites customers to its own flower show, and offers a personal shopping service for men at Christmastime. The letter that follows extends to cash customers the privilege of opening a charge account. Note the *service* (as opposed to the *selling*) point of view.

> Dear Mrs. Blair:
>
> Wouldn't it be more convenient to shop with us if you had a charge account? In addition to the freedom of not having to carry cash with you, you will also be among the first to know about our sales and special values, many of which are advertised to charge customers only.
>
> No formalities are necessary. Just fill in and sign the acceptance card enclosed and mail it back to me personally. We look forward to the privilege of including you among our many thousands of charge customers.
>
> Sincerely,

A large metropolitan bank keeps a small staff busy on such amenities as arranging for transportation, hotel accommodations, and theater tickets for visiting customers and their families and for other bankers with whom it deals; thousands of letters a year are a necessary part of this service. The bank employs many more people to furnish its customers with credit information, advice on trusts and investments, and analyses of economic problems. Like other types of businesses, it also provides credit references for its customers and letters of introduction and recommendation. Another now-common service is banking-by-mail. The following letter is particularly effective because it shows an awareness of the customer's special situation:

> Dear Mr. Keith:
>
> Your address shows that you live at some distance from the bank.
>
> If you have not already used our Banking-by-Mail service, I should like to take this means of calling it to your attention. Your passbook is mailed back to you the same day it is received. You can make withdrawals as well as deposits. We provide the printed forms and postage both ways.
>
> One of our postage-free forms is enclosed. Why not use it the next time you find it more convenient to bank by mail?
>
> Sincerely,

Continued appreciation for a customer's business is shown not only through offers of service, but also by messages that are predominantly personal: Christmas greetings, a birthday card, a congratulatory note on the occasion of a customer's promotion or appointment to a position of honor, a letter marking an important anniversary of the beginning of business with the customer. The felicitory letters sound most sincere when they avoid effusiveness and incorporate details that apply to the reader alone. The latter ideal is especially difficult to achieve when a great many letters are to be written and the pressures of time make it imperative to copy phrases, paragraphs, and even whole letters that were used previously in similar circumstances. (See also "Official and Personal Letters" in Chapter 6, pages 180–186.) This congratulatory letter is distinctively adapted to the one person to whom it was sent:

Dear Walter:

What grand news appeared in the financial pages of the New York Times this morning--and a very good likeness, too! I am delighted to observe the fine tribute that has been paid to you in your promotion and it is with real pleasure that I applaud. I know you will shoulder your new responsibilities just as well as those you leave behind and I welcome this opportunity to extend my best wishes as you undertake them.

We miss you at Willow Lake.

Sincerely yours,

The letter that follows is individually typewritten from a standard form. A different letter is used for other anniversaries occurring at five-year intervals. All are signed by the president.

Dear Mr. Crane:

I wonder if you realize that today is the thirtieth anniversary of your company's association with us.

I do not wish to let this occasion pass without again thanking you for the business with which you have favored us and telling you how highly we value a relationship extending over so many years. I hope we may look forward to its continuance for many years to come, and that you will not hesitate to call on us whenever you feel we can be of service.

Kindest regards to you and your staff.

Sincerely,

SUMMARY

Persuasion has its most obvious application in the sale of goods and services. Sales letters, as distinguished from other message forms, either sell direct by mail or promote sales by eliciting expressions of interest that can be followed up, or by inducing customers to come to the retail store or the showroom. Mail-order sales letters go through the complete sales process of attracting attention, providing motivation, instilling belief, and inducing action. They are usually quite long and may include a number of supportive printed enclosures.

Sales letters of the promotional type are usually shorter because they are more limited in their aim. Among them are letters that invite or answer sales inquiries. When a sales inquiry is solicited, a return card is a practical necessity, and some gift or other inducement may be offered. The answer to a sales inquiry should be prompt, respond fully to the reader's questions, and give specific instructions on how to order or obtain more information. If the expense is warranted, the letter should be followed up by additional letters or a salesman's call. Sales letters in retail trade are used largely for advertising sales and special promotions, and for offering credit privileges.

Less direct forms of persuasion are found in a class of messages called goodwill letters. Like other institutional messages, they are used in promoting good relations with many different audiences, including employees, stockholders, and the general public. Sent to customers, they help to anticipate their service needs, to seek out and remove the causes of possible dissatisfactions, and to cement the business relationship—as by a seasonal greeting, an invitation to some special event, or a timely congratulatory note.

PROBLEMS

1. Write a letter to sell *Reader's Digest* by mail at the special price of ten monthly issues for $3.99 (the newsstand price would be $7.50). Attract attention and stimulate interest by reference to articles that have appeared in recent issues. You may, in addition, *invent* any reasonable evidence. Assume that a return order card and postage-paid envelope will be enclosed. Subscribers will be billed after receiving the first issue, but anyone sending cash or check with the order will have an extra issue added to the subscription.

2. Write a letter to sell this book by mail to a list of business executives. Offer as a premium for prompt action a booklet, "100 Model Letters," containing examples of letters of congratulation, recommendation, invitation, condolence, and others that fall into the category of personal letters in business. Offer the book for ten days' free trial, after which the reader will either send his check for the purchase price or return the book. He may keep the premium in any case. Assume that a postage-paid order card is enclosed. In presenting evidence, you may make any reasonable assumptions.

3. Assume that you are in the promotion department of the Pioneer Camera Company. You are at present conducting a campaign among sales executives of large companies suggesting that they offer the Pioneer Jet camera as a premium to retail customers through coupons given by dealers with regular purchases. The retail value of the camera is $10.50, but the consumer can have it for only $4.50 with the coupon.

The offer mentioned is only one in the 24-page Pioneer Premium Catalog showing dozens of self-liquidating gifts. "Self-liquidating" means that the price the purchaser pays covers the cost of the goods to the sponsoring company. The premiums can also be used for business gifts, dealer and salesman incentives, and employee-recognition awards.

Write a series of two letters designed to obtain requests for the catalog. A postage-paid reply card is to be enclosed. You may assume any reasonable details.

4. Write a third letter to those sales executives who have not responded to the first two letters mentioned in Problem 3 above. Offer the $10.50 Pioneer Jet Camera free as an inducement for sending for the premium catalog.

5. Write a letter to accompany the Pioneer Premium Catalog mentioned in Problem 3.

6. Assume that the Lions Club of Cypress Hills, a group of civic-minded businessmen, are sponsors of the Cypress Hills Volunteer Ambulance Corps. They own and operate an ambulance for emergency calls from any resident of the community. The ambulance is on call 24 hours a day. There is no charge. Each year, however, the Lions Club conducts a campaign to raise funds. Write a letter to be mailed to a selected list of businessmen and residents. Ask that checks be made out to the Lions Club of Cypress Hills and that they be mailed to William Gross, treasurer, 750 Main Street, Cypress Hills, Massachusetts 02159.

7. The Braymar Electric Company is a large corporation with administrative offices in your city. For the signature of the president, Mr. Harmon Pell, write a letter to all employees in your local offices, asking that they contribute to the Community Drive. This is the only charity appeal the company officially participates in. Employees may have contributions deducted from their salary checks. All contributions are tax deductible. The Community Drive is the main support of 74 different hospitals, clinics, homes for the aged, and other welfare services in your city. Make any other reasonable assumptions. A pamphlet describing the work of the Community Drive will be enclosed with the letter, which will be mailed to the employees' homes. Also enclosed will be a subscription card addressed to the president. Although you want employees to contribute, you do not want them to feel intimidated.

8. Assume that you are the advertising manager for Winston Club men's shirts. The shirts are part of a moderately priced line appealing to younger men and those who would like to consider themselves young. The advertisements reflect this image in their choice of photographic backgrounds, human models, and typographic treatment. Write a letter to your dealers telling them that full-page advertisements for Winston Club shirts will appear in the fall (or spring) issues of *Esquire*, *Playboy*, the *New York Times Sunday Magazine*, and *Gentlemen's Quarterly*. Impress on them the need to display the shirts in order to capitalize on the advertising. Copies of the advertisements with the advertising schedules are to be enclosed.

9. Write the copy for the face of a leaflet to be enclosed with the monthly bills being sent to charge customers of the Crane Department Store of Seattle, Washington. The copy is to feature boxed double-initial stationery at $6.95 for 50 sheets of Eaton's fine white kid finish note paper (folded size, 7¼ × 5⅛) and 50 envelopes to match. The double-initial monograms, in engraver's script, are printed at the top

of the note sheets. Four hundred twenty double-initial monograms are kept in stock, so there is no waiting for printing. All initials are available except Q, U, X, Y, and Z. Ask customers to come in, phone, or fill in and mail the coupon on the back of the leaflet. The stationery department is on the first floor. Suggest stationery for gifts as well as personal use.

10. Clark-Hudson, a local women's clothing store, is featuring a post-Christmas sale at savings of 20 per cent to 50 per cent. Some typical values:

    Fur trimmed coats—were $285, now $175
    Tweed coats—were $129, now $69
    Cashmere sweaters—were $65, now $40
    Imported English leather handbags—were $76, now $49
    Nylon hosiery—were $2.50, now $1.25
    Shoes—were $55, now $27.50

    Write a letter to all customers on your mailing list, giving them the opportunity to shop on December 26, 27, and 28, before announcement of the sale is made to the public. Charge customers will not be billed until February 1.

11. For Bentley's, a men's shop in your city, write a letter to all customers shown by your records to have bought hosiery from you. Invite then to drop in to buy long ("executive length") hose in a blend of 40 per cent wool and 60 per cent stretch nylon in a fine rib. They give mild support, resist shrinkage, and keep their shape through machine washings. Black, charcoal, navy, brown, and olive. One size (10 to 13) fits everyone. Imported from England. Usually $3.75 a pair; now featured at $2.25 each or four for $8.50. Also in anklet length at the same price. Ask the reader to look for some surprise unadvertised specials in furnishings and apparel when he drops in.

12. The Weldon Electrical Manufacturing Company is now featuring in its *Time* magazine advertisements an electronic air cleaner which fits into the air ductwork of any forced-air-heating or air-conditioning system. The device cleans the air that passes through the system from every room in the house, removing 95 per cent of airborne particles, including the tiny bits of grime ordinary filters miss. It traps dust, ash, grease, smoke, and pollen, yet the system uses no more current than a 40 watt bulb. Your advertisements offer a "detailed brochure of the Weldon Electronic Air Cleaner."
    (*a*) Write a form letter to accompany the brochure. Leave space for the name of the nearest distributor.
    (*b*) You receive a coupon from Mr. James T. Fell of 568 Doberman Street, Springfield, Illinois 62704. In an accompanying letter, Mr. Fell wants to know if the cleaner will really remove pollen; he suffers from hay fever. Write a personal letter to go with the booklet. Tell Mr. Fell that air passing through the system is freed of 99 per cent of the pollen, as measured by test methods approved by the United States Bureau of Standards. Invite Mr. Fell to discuss the installation with his local distributor, the Springfield Hardware Company, 60 Washington Avenue.
    (*c*) You receive a letter from Mr. Peter Campbell of 1965 Pleasant Street, Rochester, New York 14614. Mr. Campbell says he runs a plumbing business and would consider handling the Weldon Electronic Air Cleaner if the terms are attractive. Acknowledge his letter, send him your catalog, and tell him that you

have asked Mr. Henry Fargo of your Syracuse office to get in touch with him. You can tell Mr. Campbell that you already have 300 dealers handling the cleaner, but none in Rochester. There is a chance to make a good profit.

13. The following letter is the first of a series by the Sunkist Growers to induce food packers to try flavoring their mayonnaise and salad dressings with lemon juice. Write two more letters for the same series. Assume that a reply card is to be enclosed and that the letters are to be mailed two weeks apart.

> Dear Sir:
>
> The cherimoya is a rich tropical fruit and in season is found in some American markets. Its appearance, a cross between a pear and an artichoke, is fairly easy to describe. But not the taste. That's something you have to test for yourself. Bite into a cherimoya sometime--you're in for a pleasant surprise.
>
> And if you test lemon juice in your mayonnaise or salad dressing you'll find, we believe, another pleasant surprise.
>
> Our research information and the assistance of one of our technical men are available without obligation.
>
> Very truly yours,

14. The Liberty Hotel in your city has compiled a list of businessmen whose last stay at the hotel was more than a year ago. On behalf of the management, write a letter to these former patrons for the combined purpose of getting them to come back and learning from them if their long absence is due to any dissatisfaction with your service. Assume that a card and postage-paid envelope are enclosed for the reply.

15. For the Liberty Hotel in your city, write a letter to be sent to guests after their initial stay. Thank them for their patronage and ask if everything was satisfactory. Assume that a card and postage-paid envelope are enclosed for the reply.

16. As credit manager of Magnus & Company, San Francisco, California, an exclusive specialty shop for men and women, write a letter to a select list of local residents inviting them to open a charge account at Magnus. You may assume any reasonable details about the store.

17. As credit manager of the same store mentioned in Problem 16 above, you have received from the National Express Company a list of their credit card holders in your area. Write a letter to those card holders telling then that they may now use their National Express Cards to charge purchases in the store.

18. Assume that you are the proprietor of your local Buick agency. You keep a record of every car brought in for service and regularly put aside the names and addresses of owners of cars that are more than two years old. Write a letter to be sent to the latter customers a week following the completion of the work. Ask if the work has been done satisfactorily. Use the same letter to stress the quality of your service

and tactfully make a bid for the owner's business when he is in the market for a new car.

19. The Croesus Bank and Trust Company has 53 branches in your city. On behalf of the management, write a letter to all customers with regular checking accounts, inviting them to apply for a "Courtesy Card" that will enable them to cash checks at any of your branches. Application must be made in person to any officer at the branch at which the account is held.

20. The Neely-Tiff Company, an exclusive and highly reputed jewelry and gift shop in your city, publishes an expensive 64-page Christmas catalog. Write a covering letter to go with the catalog to all regular customers. An order blank and envelope are bound into the catalog for mail orders. Use the letter to stimulate Christmas business. You may make any reasonable assumptions about the contents of the catalog.

21. For the president of a company listed on the New York Stock Exchange, write any of the following letters assigned by your instructor:
    (*a*) To stockholders who have just received a copy of the company's annual report, a letter asking them to suggest the names of friends who might be interested in receiving a copy. Assume that a postage-paid reply card is enclosed.
    (*b*) To college professors of economics and related subjects, a letter accompanying a copy of the annual report, with the suggestion that they may want additional copies to distribute to their classes for group study. Assume that a postage-paid reply card is enclosed.
    (*c*) A letter of welcome to new stockholders.

22. The Comprehensive Auto Insurance Company, located in your city, has prepared a pamphlet called "Defensive Driving," designed to promote road safety, especially among young drivers. As part of its public relations program, the company would like to distribute the pamphlet to teen-agers. Write a letter to high-school teachers to obtain orders for the pamphlet. Assume that a copy of the pamphlet and a postage-paid return card are enclosed. There is no charge for the pamphlets.

23. The president of the Wachover Bank in your city has just learned from an item in the *New York Times* that Nathaniel Dover has been promoted from senior vice president to president and chief executive officer of the Carlton Knitting Mills, one of the bank's most important customers. Mr. Dover started with his company as an accountant twenty years ago. The bank president, who has known him in a business capacity for the last five or six years, has asked you to write a congratulatory letter to Mr. Dover for his signature.

24. Assume that you are the head of your company's Accounting Department. You have just read in your local newspaper that Mr. James Ambrose, an accountant employed in the department, has been elected president of the Parents Association of the County High School. Write a congratulatory letter to Mr. Ambrose at his home, 42 Leewood Drive, your town. Let him know that the whole department and the company are honored by his election.

25. Employees of The Fair, a department store in your city, have for many years been able to obtain a 3 per cent discount on anything they bought in the store simply by

showing their employee identification card. It is now September 15. Over the signature of the president, Mr. Roderick Stiles, write a letter for publication in the company's employee house organ announcing that from October 1 to December 31 of this year, the discount will be increased to 5 per cent. This extra benefit is in recognition of the demands put on employees during the Christmas shopping season. Take the occasion to remind employees, in a gracious way, of the special need in this season for good attendance, courtesy, cheerfulness, and helpfulness to customers and to each other.

15
Handling Controversial Issues

WHEN YOUR persuasive efforts are stalled by disagreements, you may enter the controversy with the idea of resolving the differences.

Some controversies represent fairly routine business situations: a dealer, for instance, wants a bigger discount than the supplier is willing to give him; two executives have conflicting ideas about the value of a proposed policy; a union disputes a company's plea of financial stringency as a reason for denying a wage increase; a purchasing agent threatens to boycott a supplier who is lax in meeting delivery dates.

Other controversies raise specific questions regarding the public interest. Does smoking cause cancer? Will a wage increase for steelworkers be inflationary? Does government stockpiling of grain have a deleterious effect on farm prices? Are government restraints on the oil industry increasing our dependency on foreign oil? Such questions are difficult to resolve and are sometimes argued for years. Even when there is no decisive conclusion to an argument, however, persuasion may help to win many converts and produce at least a temporary settlement. It may be years, for example, before any but a statistical link is found between smoking and cancer; still the Cancer Committee has been able to dissuade a great many persons from smoking and, by opposing efforts, the tobacco industry has undoubtedly been able to mitigate the effects of the antismoking argument. So, too, it may never be conclusively proved whether or not a specific increase in steel wages is inflationary, but the arguments on both sides help clarify the issues and bring public opinion to bear on the settlement of a strike.

ARGUMENT AND PERSUASION

The means of settling controversies, like those used in persuasion generally, are both rational and emotional. The rational means are often called *argument.* This term is not to be associated with quarreling. Argument, rather, calls for the use of logic and reasoning to reach valid conclusions, the assumption being that reasonable people seek reasonable solutions to their differences. The emotional means entail principally the arousal of feeling through psychological appeals and emotive language.

When argument is used effectively, it is convincing; it instills belief. Since the purpose of persuasion, however, is not just to instill belief, but to bring about the desired action, rational argument often needs the help of emotional techniques to turn conviction into positive response. What kinds of emotional techniques are used, and to what degree, will depend on the purpose to be served. When, for example, an issue relating to management policy is to be settled within an organization, the future of the organization would seem to dictate a wholly rational solution to the problem. When, however, the same management enters into a dispute with a supplier or a customer, it would unquestionably use emotional as well as rational means to ensure favorable action.

ANALYZING THE CONTROVERSY

Controversy often engenders so much heat that the best approach to a solution consists of analyzing the situation as rationally as possible. Although, as you will see, we will not altogether give up appeals to the emotions, we will concentrate on cases that can be resolved mostly by reason and goodwill. Certainly, that would seem to be the best approach when a controversy has already engendered some feeling and when both parties are open-minded enough to want a rational and fair solution. An orderly course is to define the problem or proposition you are arguing, study the audience, and formulate the issues. All this work is preparatory to actual writing, but it cannot be slighted without hurting the persuasiveness of the message.

The Problem

What, precisely, are you arguing for? In order to avoid going off on a tangent, you should start by identifying the main problem. In a debate this problem is called the "proposition" and is usually stated as a resolution or question. For example:

> *Resolved,* That college tuition should be deductible for Federal income tax purposes.
>
> Should college tuition be deductible for Federal income tax purposes (yes or no)?

Handling Controversial Issues

As a writer, you seldom find your topic in such a neat package. More often, you have to draw it out of a developing situation or out of a report, letter, news story, or other source. Here, for example, is a letter that raises a controversial point. It is written by the beneficiary of a trust fund to a bank, which is the trustee.

```
Dear Mr. Andrews:

I received the Christmas card signed by you in which the
Directors and Officers of the Trust Company wished me a
Merry Christmas and a Happy New Year.  Thank you very
much but I find it hard when the income from my trust
fund is only half what it used to be and my living ex-
penses have about doubled.

I do not understand why you have put such poor invest-
ments in my fund.  I have talked with one of my friends
whose husband left a trust fund for her about the same
size as mine, in another bank, and she gets a much higher
income from her trust than I get from mine.

I wish you would buy some securities that will give me
more money to pay my living expenses.

                                 Yours truly,

                                 Anna Jackson
```

Although several subordinate issues are raised in the letter, the main problem pertains to the amount of income yielded by the fund. This may be expressed as follows:

> Is the trust fund yielding the maximum income?

We shall return to Miss Jackson's letter a little farther on.

The Reader

The way in which a controversy is handled will be determined in large part by the reader or group of readers to whom the message is addressed. Public speakers often classify audiences as receptive, neutral, or antagonistic. Such a classification can also help the writer.

The *receptive reader* is already well disposed toward the writer and his point of view. Any controversy must therefore involve some third party—perhaps the government, a business rival, or some pressure group. When repeal of the 10 per cent Federal excise tax on telephone service was imminent, for example, New York State proposed to pick up the same tax and make it available to local communities. The New York Telephone Company thereupon called on its subscribers—those who would have to pay the tax—to help defeat the measure. Another time, a large discount department store asked consumers to resist the passage of a "price fixing" bill favored by some manufacturers. Usually the chief problem in writing to the receptive reader is to overcome his apathy. Appeals addressed to him may therefore use strong terms to arouse him to the threat that faces him and to encourage him to take some concrete action.

The *neutral reader* is one who has not yet taken sides in a controversy. He may be an executive called on to arbitrate a dispute, a schoolboy trying to decide whether smoking is worth the risk to his health, or a citizen still making up his mind whether a bill to provide medical aid for the aged deserves his support. The writer may help such a reader by providing him with sufficient information to enable him to arrive at a decision. If the opposition is pronounced and the stakes are high, the writer may also adopt a strongly combative attitude against the foe, with generous use of emotive language. Some of the sharpest verbal battles occur when powerful unions and large companies carry their disputes to the public.

The *antagonistic reader* is the hardest to manage. He himself may have started the controversy by objecting to policy, methods, prices, and the like, or by taking some objectionable action. Miss Jackson, quoted a few paragraphs above, is antagonistic in that she expresses dissatisfaction with the manner in which the bank is managing her trust fund. A dealer is antagonistic when he refuses to stock a product on the grounds that the discount offered him is not high enough. A policyholder who expresses a desire to cancel his life insurance may become antagonistic when the insurance company tries to dissuade him. It should be evident that the approaches suggested for writing to receptive and neutral readers will not do in these instances. Instead, the writer must seek to minimize differences and look for avenues of agreement and, if need be, compromise.

Study of the reader should reveal not only his attitude toward the controversy, but also his basic interests, for the reader can be persuaded to respond favorably only if he believes he is acting in accordance with his own beliefs and desires. You may well expect family men, for example, to favor Federal assistance in paying medical bills, yet an inherently conservative individual may be persuaded to the contrary on the grounds that the program is compulsory or socialistic or will lead to invasions of privacy. It follows that the more you know about the reader and his motives, the better you can adapt to him. Important considerations, in addition to his age and political philosophy, may include his economic position, education, family status, group affiliations, and past performance.

The Issues

Most controversies encompass several related points or issues on which the outcome of the argument depends. These points must be analyzed, sorted, accepted or rejected, and resolved. Coming back to Miss Jackson, we may summarize her case as follows:[1]

[1] In this case the reader is asked to assume a market condition in which yields from common stocks are high and those from bonds are relatively low. Changing markets would, of course, alter the specifics of the case, but the basic principles leading to the solution would be unaffected.

1. The income from her trust fund is less than what it used to be.
2. Living expenses have about doubled.
3. The trust fund suffers from "poor" investments.
4. A friend obtains a higher income from a fund of about the same size.

As we address ourselves to these issues on behalf of the trust company, we must go through a process of logical inquiry applicable to all argumentative situations:

Are the points relevant?
Are the statements true? If not, what is the truth?
Are the expressed opinions and judgments valid? If not, can we offer logical support for the opposing views?
Are any additional facts needed to put the problem in true perspective?

With these questions in mind, we can make the following observations about the points raised in Miss Jackson's letter:

Point 1 is substantially true, as the bank's records confirm; so no issue is involved. However, Miss Jackson apparently does not know that the reasons why the income is lower than it used to be have nothing to do with the competence of the administrators of the trust fund.

Point 2 is also irrelevant in that the income from the trust fund bears no relation to the cost of living and cannot be adjusted to it.

Point 3 involves an opinion with which we cannot agree. The kinds of investments the bank can make are clearly and strictly defined by the trust instrument or contract. If the yield is lower than it used to be, the reason is that the "safe" investments prescribed by the trust agreement and consisting of corporate and government bonds, pay less today than they did when the trust was effected. The important fact is that after twenty-five years the principal sum in the trust is still intact, in accordance with the wishes of Miss Jackson's father, who left the trust, and it is still yielding income.

With regard to Point 4, we would have to know more about the provisions of the friend's trust fund before we could accept the analogy as having any relevance to Miss Jackson's situation. It may be that the trust instrument permits a more liberal investment policy or that it sanctions withdrawals from the principal sum in order to provide living expenses for the beneficiary.

FORMING THE MESSAGE

Analysis of the controversial problem must inevitably be followed by the actual construction of the message. The arguments must be developed and arranged in effective order, and an opening and close must be found that will aid in securing the desired response. Below is the letter sent to Miss Jackson. After you have read it, we shall have a few observations to make about its composition.

Dear Miss Jackson:

We're glad you wrote us about the income from your trust fund because we feel both a personal and a legal obligation to see that you enjoy every benefit to which it entitles you.

Your friend is very fortunate to enjoy the high income from her trust, but her situation is not necessarily analogous to yours. As you know, the nature of the investments in any trust is severely circumscribed by the provisions of the trust instrument and State law. In your case, it was your father's wish that the principal remain intact during your lifetime. As a result, we have had to invest in so-called "legal" securities, bond issues on which interest is fixed and does not vary with the cost of living.

The fact that the income from the trust fund is now slightly less than it was some three years ago is due to the circumstance that when the various bonds matured, we had to reinvest the proceeds in other "legal" securities on which the interest was lower. We had no choice here because the bond market as a whole had advanced.

If we had been free to invest in common stocks, we might of course have been able to increase materially the principal in your trust fund and the amount available to you. Against the inherent risks in such a procedure, we have been able to preserve the principal in your fund while you have been receiving the income for some twenty-five years. Regardless of how the stock market acts, you can look forward to receiving this income for the remainder of your life.

As the condition of the bond market permits, we will reinvest the principal of the trust in securities that pay higher interest rates. That may be some time off, but in the meantime you can be confident that your regular monthly checks will continue to come in.

We hope you'll drop in some day so that we may discuss this matter in more detail.

Sincerely,

This letter has an affirmative beginning and continues by treating the issues without in any way contradicting the reader. Rather, Miss Jackson is shown that the bank carried out its obligations honorably and with due concern for her welfare. The issue regarding the friend's trust is taken up early in the letter because it leads naturally to a discussion of the terms of the Jackson trust agreement. This explanation, in turn, opens the way to discussion of the two remaining issues, of which the one relating to "poor investments" is crucial to the whole controversy. The letter ends by holding out some hope of improving the situation and, instead of shutting off debate, invites further discussion.

The general principles that guide the construction of such a message and lead to agreement are discussed below.

The Beginning

At the start, the message acquaints the reader with the problem and your attitude toward it. The amount of background information will depend on what the reader knows about the subject. If you are answering a letter, the subject will already be familiar to him and will require only brief identification. If, however, you are initiating the problem, you will have to state the proposition fully, at the same time giving the reason for bringing up the subject.

You cannot in any case escape the necessity of attracting the reader's attention. Fortunately, almost any controversial message, addressed to the right audience at the right time, has some interest that can be readily projected in the beginning. Perhaps the most important stipulation in this respect is that the opening cultivate harmonious relations with the reader. Anyone can arouse interest—as well as bad feeling—by taking an opposing view, but it takes great skill under the same circumstances to make a conciliatory approach without compromising one's own position. We shall elaborate on "the technique of agreement" a few pages farther on.

In the openings that follow, the reader's familiarity with the subject is assumed and the issue is drawn quickly, but in a friendly spirit:

> Memorandum to Mr. George C. Phillips:
>
> The proposal to centralize the advertising activities of the company has come as a surprise, especially in view of the outstanding sales performance of the past year. Since the consolidation of departments is still in the talking stage, I thought you would not mind if I put forward some ideas that may not as yet have been fully considered.

> Dear Mr. Donlon:
>
> We appreciate your frankness in giving us your reasons for canceling your order of March 8. We know how you feel when you see other dealers cutting prices on our brands, but we are not sure that you are going to make more money without our product than with it.

In a folder accompanying the monthly bill, the telephone company protested the proposed imposition by New York State of a tax the Federal government was going to drop. The part that follows is only the beginning, but it is unusually detailed because of the necessity to acquaint the reader with the subject.

TAKE ANOTHER LOOK AT THE "U.S. TAX" ON YOUR TELEPHONE BILL

It is an unfair tax—and you pay it! N.Y. State should not adopt it if the Federal government drops it.

On your monthly telephone bill you'll notice an item: "U.S. Tax." This refers to a Federal excise tax of 10%. It is a luxury sales tax on an essential service—the same sort of tax that applies on jewelry and furs.

Congress voted last year to drop the excise tax on local telephone service this coming June. It decided that the tax—the only such tax on a household utility—was unfair and discriminatory.

This would mean a 10% cut in the local telephone bills of all customers in the State.

But New York State now proposes to pick up the same tax and make it available to local communities!

A tax unfair for citizens of the country as a whole is equally unfair in New York!

Logical Supports

The principal substance of the controversial message consists of the facts, opinions, and reasoning which support the argument. These elements of persuasion, discussed in Chapter 13, apply here with special force because success in controversy depends so much on rational appeals. Later in this chapter we will have occasion to look more closely at particular methods of reasoning, but we can in the meantime demonstrate how evidence and reasoning are used in meeting controversial issues.

The issue: How extensive is false advertising on television?
Method of handling: Evidence (facts and figures)

The Federal Trade Commission last November announced an intensified campaign against false or misleading advertising on television. Since then it has issued eight complaints, all charging violations of existing law.

Two important features of the FTC's campaign against television advertising have been underplayed or ignored in most accounts published in newspapers and magazines and indeed in the FTC's own announcements: 1. Of the eight complaints, only three were directed exclusively to the television advertising of the defendants; the other five also involved advertising in newspapers or magazines or both. 2. In rigorous monitoring of television commercials, the FTC has so far found only eight cases to prosecute. Competent authorities estimate that during a year at least 7,000 different products and services are advertised nationally on television.—Broadcasting Magazine

The issue: Am I qualified for the State Assembly?
Method of handling: Evidence (expert opinion)

> The Citizens Union, a nonpartisan civic organization, in supporting me every time I was a candidate, has said: ". . . a very able alert legislator . . . liberal . . . one of the Assembly's most effective speakers . . . party spokesman on important issues . . . his votes showed unusual discrimination in the public interest."

The issue: Are limits on steel company profits in the national interest?
Method of handling: Reasoning

> Whatever figures your advisers may elect to use, however, the simple fact is that the profit left in any company, after it pays all costs, is all there is out of which to make up for the serious inadequacy in depreciation, to repay borrowings, to pay dividends and to provide added equipment. If the profit is not good enough to do these things, they cannot and will not be done; and that would not be in the national interest.—*United States Steel Corporation*

Adapting to the Reader's Point of View

An inherent weakness of even the most rational argument is that it casts the writer in the role of special pleader. He supports a point of view usually because it is in his interests to do so. When, for example, a big advertiser cancels his contract with a national magazine, he has good reasons—his sales are falling, he will save money, he will get more effective coverage elsewhere. The magazine, on the other hand, has its own reasons for wanting the contract to remain in force—it needs the revenue, it is apprehensive about the effect on other advertisers, it does not want to see the business go to its competitors. Obviously, the magazine cannot make a very good case on the basis of these arguments. Rather, it must find ways of convincing the advertiser that it is in *his* interests to continue his advertising with the magazine.

Almost everyone who engages in controversy finds a similar need to search out and present the meaning of the issues from the reader's point of view. If the reader is not personally involved, the argument must be won on behalf of fair play, the public interest, or other goals the reader can support. In the following paragraphs, for example, a public utility tries to make a rate increase palatable to the small user of electricity by explaining that the big user would be hit hardest.

> Rates are set with the aim of playing fair with everybody. Electricity, like most everything else, is sold at a quantity discount. The more you use, the less you pay per kilowatt-hour. This is a sound principle.
>
> However, the quantity discount rates for the largest users were too low in relation to the cost of supplying electricity today and the big fellows simply weren't paying their way. At the same time, as their demand for electricity increased, they were taking more and more at the lowest rates. Last year some of them were paying less than 1.5 cents per kilowatt-hour and this was below the cost of service.
>
> If you sell too cheap, the more you sell, the more you lose. The new rates

tend to correct this. Naturally, the large users are not particularly happy about the prospect of paying more. Nor do we like to charge more—but each group should pay its own fair share.
At the same time, we can well understand people asking, "Why should anyone pay higher rates?" We think a few facts will give the answer. . . .
—*Consolidated Edison Company of New York, Inc.*

When the International Business Machines Corporation proposed to build a plant in Harrison, New York, a prominent resident objected to the "intrusion" and accused the company of "an effort to break down our zoning laws." In replying, the chairman of the board showed considerable feeling for the wishes of the town residents. This is part of his letter:

I.B.M. has purchased a number of plots, varying from the old Guggenheim estate in Sands Point, which we now use for an employee country club and executive school, to some property in Yorktown Heights, where we have recently opened a corporate research center.

In each case the local community analyzes the desirability of an I.B.M. facility in the community against the obvious disadvantage of having any business activity located in a residential area. Hearings are held, at which point it becomes apparent whether or not there is substantial feeling in the community against our proposal, and we have never intruded on a community where strong feeling against us existed.

As a matter of business procedure we normally try to get some indication of the extent of such feeling prior to the purchase of property. In the case of the Harrison site, we did not obtain any feeling which would indicate that we should not purchase the property and apply for the necessary rezoning.

It would seem that the people most concerned would be those who have homes adjacent to the property concerned. We would want to be very sensitive to the wishes of the entire community.

Concluding the Argument

The end of the argumentative message makes the final bid for support. This may be a statement of the strongest argument or a bid for direct action. Other treatments include a brief summary of your position, a plea for understanding, and, if no immediate agreement is foreseen, a pledge to continue seeking a solution.

This close invites a show of interest:

If you would like more information on how the public postal service benefits both private citizens and commerce, please write to the address below.—*The Business Mail Foundation*

These closes offer reassurance:

Containing hospital costs while protecting the quality of care is one of the most complex problems facing our society. We will continue to work on this problem, as we have in the past. Meanwhile, we hope you realize that Blue Cross continues to provide better care for more people at lower cost than any agency, public or private.

We hope you'll keep these facts in mind when you read or hear about electric rates. Con Edison's aim is to provide you with all the electricity you need—now and in the years to come—at the lowest *practical* rates.

This close indicates reluctant submission:

We cannot urge you too strongly to review this matter carefully. If, after you have done so, you still wish to surrender the policy, please complete the enclosed application for surrender and return it to this office together with your policy. We hope, however, that you'll see the dollars and cents value of keeping the policy in force.

This close specifies the means of settlement:

On the table right now are two honorable and peaceful ways to end the strike. These are:

1. The way 343 other unions have already taken—accept the three-year agreement which General Electric offers.

2. Accept the Company's standing offer—until a new agreement is negotiated, re-establish the specific rates of pay and other terms and conditions of employment (except future cost-of-living escalation) including special prerogatives for the union and for union officials that were previously in effect under the union-terminated contract.

Either of these arrangements can bring this needless strike to a peaceful and immediate conclusion.—*General Electric Company*

This close promises further effort to reach an agreement:

Despite the fact that a strike has now been forced upon the union, the officers of the IUE will continue to explore every possible means of achieving a speedy, honorable settlement of this strike and the signing of a new contract that will benefit the workers, the company and the communities in which IUE members work and live.—*International Union of Electrical, Radio and Machine Workers, AFL-CIO*

LOGICAL REASONING

Reasoning plays such an important role in argument that it is time we examined the methods of reasoning and learned to judge their validity. In Chapter 13, "The Elements of Persuasion," we discussed the two main types of evidence—facts and opinions. Apart from any intrinsic value they may have, facts and opinions are important in that they permit inferences to be drawn from them. If we know that a still-growing company has paid dividends consecutively for 56 years, we can hopefully infer that dividends will continue to be paid out in the foreseeable future; if we know that the sale of soft drinks and food by vending machines is increasing, we can anticipate a corresponding increase in the sale of paper containers; if we know that a play has been endorsed by the major critics, we can look forward with reasonable confidence to enjoying it ourselves. The process by which we reach our conclusions is reasoning. The principal methods of reasoning are *induction* and *deduction.* Less disciplined, but widely employed, are *reasoning by analogy* and *causal reasoning.*

Inductive Reasoning

Through inductive reasoning, the writer reaches general conclusions from an examination of particular facts and instances. Sometimes called "the scientific method," inductive reasoning is the mainstay of the scientist, scholar, and business researcher. By way of example, let us say that you want to test the relative pulling power of two competing newspapers that you are considering as regular advertising media for your company. Your advertising objective is to obtain "leads" for your sales force. To start, you take a single advertisement bearing a coupon for replies and place it in both newspapers on the same day and in identical positions. When the returned coupons are tallied and the number is divided into the cost of the space, you find that the coupon inquiries from newspaper A cost you $2 each while those from newspaper B cost $3 each. Now you repeat the experiment with another advertisement on another day, and later you try a third and fourth advertisement. If newspaper A consistently brings inquiries at lower cost than newspaper B, it seems fair to conclude that, for your purpose at least, newspaper A will continue to be the less expensive advertising medium.

Conclusions reached inductively are not necessarily correct, but certain precautions can be taken to ensure that they are reasonably so:

1. The evidence should be sufficient to minimize the chance of a wrong conclusion. One difficulty in this respect arises from the use of a sample to arrive at a conclusion about the whole class of which it is a part. If the sample is too small, the conclusion is likely to be invalid. Thus a mail-order house that tests a letter on 100 prospective customers will find it risky to use the results in predicting the performance of the same letter mailed to a half million prospective customers. Sometimes evidence must be gathered from more than one source before a sound conclusion can be reached. One might, for instance, install new lighting in an office and, relying exclusively on the internal evidence, conclude that the installation has reduced turnover of personnel. It is possible, however, that the reduction in turnover was the result of other conditions as, for example, a scarcity of jobs or the inauguration by the company of an employee profit-sharing program. The evidence would be stronger if a control group had been established in another office where the old lighting was still being used.[2]

[2] For a classic example of this type of business investigation, see the description of the "Hawthorne Experiment" in Elton Mayo's *The Human Problems of an Industrial Civilization* (New York: Macmillan, 1933), chs. III-V.

2. *The evidence should be representative.* When a conclusion is drawn from a sample—even a large sample—the conclusion will be inaccurate if the sample is not typical. The mail-order company that selects its test mailing list from a single state, for example, when the whole list is distributed nationally, is not likely to arrive at any valuable conclusion from the test. So, too, a college alumni association falls into error (and misleads its alumni) when it reports without qualification that "72 per cent of the Class of 1967 earn over $25,000 a year." Actually, only 72 *per cent of those reporting* earn that much. The sample is unrepresentative because those who do not answer are likely to be the least successful.

3. *Negative instances should be taken into account.* Some years ago, a cigarette manufacturer had a research firm conduct tests in colleges throughout the country to determine the smoking preferences of students. Advertisements later proclaimed the preference for the manufacturer's product in college after college. One wondered how the results could be so one sided until he realized that the advertiser was reporting only the "successful" tests.

4. *The conclusion should not embrace more than the evidence warrants.* Much of the disbelief in inductive reasoning is not any distrust of the evidence, but a failure to accept the inferences. "This proves that Computer A is better than Computer B" may cause the reader to wonder whether the issue is so clear. A more acceptable conclusion might read, "The facts point to the probability that Computer A will serve us for at least the next five years, with a considerable saving over Computer B in installation and operating costs." Qualifying terms like *may, should,* and *probably* play an important part in making inductive reasoning convincing.

Deductive Reasoning

Most of our reasoning, in business and elsewhere, is deductive. Unlike inductive reasoning, which arrives at general conclusions from an examination of specific evidence, deductive reasoning takes the generalizations and uses them as a means of finding new knowledge. Thus specific research and experience leads inductively to the conclusion that "machines save labor." Deductive reasoning, however, will start with that conclusion and build upon it to reach a new conclusion applicable to a specific instance—for example, "The Magnus Electric Saw saves labor." If no evidence is given to support the initial assumption, the reason is that the evidence was found long ago and is now taken for granted.

THE SYLLOGISM

Deduced conclusions are drawn from a form of argument called a *syllogism.* In formal logic, the syllogism consists of a major premise, a minor premise, and a conclusion. The major premise is the initial broad assertion, the minor premise names a specific application, and the conclusion is the inference drawn from the two premises. A particular example would go like this:

Major premise:	All our employees are covered by group insurance.
Minor premise:	Joe Ford is an employee.
Conclusion:	Joe Ford is covered by group insurance.

In practice, the syllogism is almost invariably abbreviated, so that it takes a form such as "Joe Ford must be covered by group insurance because he's an employee" (major premise omitted); or "Joe Ford is covered by group insurance" (major premise and minor premise omitted). Even though it is not formally expressed, the syllogism is a useful means of testing the validity of a deductive argument. Basically, the validity lies in the truth of the premises and the correctness of the structure of the syllogism. Without becoming unnecessarily technical, we may list the rules of validity as follows:

1. *The premises must be true.* Reasoning may be expressed in entirely logical terms and yet be invalid because it does not conform to reality. An advocate of private power companies writes, "TVA is inconsistent with democracy." If this conclusion were to be related to the whole syllogism, the syllogism would read as follows:

Major premise:	Government ownership is inconsistent with democracy.
Minor premise:	TVA is government-owned.
Conclusion:	TVA is inconsistent with democracy.

The major premise is not true and therefore the conclusion is not true. We have many examples to prove that government ownership is practiced in democratic forms of government. A more valid premise would be that "Government ownership is competitive with free enterprise." The logical conclusion of the syllogism would then be, "TVA is competitive with free enterprise."

2. *The major premise must include all cases.* "We have to raise our prices because our labor costs have gone up" assumes the major premise, "Higher wages make higher prices necessary." But this is only sometimes true. It is possible that efficiency can be improved or that economies can be effected to make higher prices unnecessary.

3. *The premises must be so related that they lead inevitably to the conclusion.* This syllogism is badly constructed:

FAULTY

Major premise:	All businessmen pay taxes.
Minor premise:	Mr. Tobin pays taxes.
Conclusion:	Mr. Tobin is a businessman.

The fact that Mr. Tobin pays taxes does not make him a businessman. The faulty conclusion derives from a basic fault in the structure of the syllogism. If the parts are to be correctly linked, they should follow the pattern in the syllogism below:

CORRECT

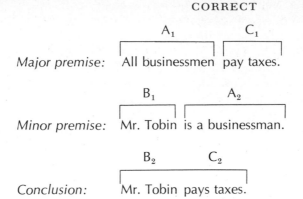

	A_1	C_1
Major premise:	All businessmen	pay taxes.
	B_1	A_2
Minor premise:	Mr. Tobin	is a businessman.
	B_2	C_2
Conclusion:	Mr. Tobin	pays taxes.

Here the subject of the major premise (A_1) is correctly echoed in the predicate of the minor premise (A_2), the subject of the minor premise (B_1) is also the subject of the conclusion (B_2), and the predicate of the major premise (C_1) agrees with the predicate of the conclusion (C_2). The common element in both premises (businessmen, businessman) is called the *middle term.* When, as in the faulty syllogism cited above, the position of the middle term (pay(s) taxes) is unchanged in both premises, there occurs the *fallacy of the undistributed middle.*

VARIATIONS OF THE BASIC SYLLOGISM

The syllogism demonstrated—called the *categorical syllogism* because the major premise makes an unqualified assertion about all members of a class—is only one of three kinds. The others are the *disjunctive syllogism* and the *hypothetical syllogism.*

The *disjunctive syllogism,* which begins with a statement of alternative possibilities, follows this pattern:

Major premises:	All customers are classified as "cash" or "credit."
Minor premise:	Mrs. Smith, a customer, does not buy on credit.
Conclusion:	Mrs. Smith is a cash customer.

An advertisement for a dictating machine reads:

> Why waste precious time? Get a Dictomat.

The implied premise is "Either you own a Dictomat or you are wasting precious time." This reasoning is invalid if—as is probable—other dictating machines will save as much time as the Dictomat.

The *hypothetical syllogism* is characterized by a major premise beginning with *if* or *when.*

Major premise: If the loans are refused, the company will have to go out of business.

Minor premise: The loans have been refused.
Conclusion: The company will have to go out of business.

Such reasoning is employed in this remark of a job interviewer:

> When a man asks a question, he proves he is alert. Simms is one smart fellow!

Here the implied minor premise is, "Simms asks questions." The syllogism is valid, although you may question the truth of the major premise.

Suppose, however, the job interviewer should say:

> When a man asks questions, he proves he is alert. Simms is a complete dullard.

The implied premise is now, "Simms does *not* ask questions." But this contradicts the conditional statement in the major premise, and the reasoning is therefore invalid.

Reasoning from Analogy

We have already described analogy as a method of literary composition (Chapter 8, pages 235–236). It is also used as a method of logical reasoning. In reasoning from analogy, the writer arrives at a conclusion about one instance on the basis of its similarities to another. He may thus reason that if his company found satisfaction in a 1975 Chevrolet truck, it would find equal satisfaction in a 1979 Chevrolet truck of similar specifications. The two trucks are not, of course, the same, but analogy permits the confidence in one to be transferred to the other. It should be apparent that the validity of such reasoning is not by any means comparable to that of other methods. If it is not always reliable, however, it is convenient and often persuasive.

An important stricture regarding analogy is that there be sufficient similarities to permit reasonable inferences. In arguing against raising postal rates to make the Post Office self-supporting, one may, for example, cite the fact that other major departments of the Federal government are traditionally run at a deficit. A question remains, however, as to whether the services performed by the Post Office are comparable to those performed by the Department of Agriculture, the Department of Labor, or the Department of State. In another instance, one may try to convince a widow, by reference to past performance, that a particular mutual fund will give her a greater return on her money than United States Savings Bonds. The argument collapses, however, in the face of the fact that mutual funds offer no guarantee of either safety of principal or certainty of dividends, whereas United States Savings Bonds guarantee both.

You can decide for yourself the validity and effectiveness of these examples of reasoning by analogy:

In 1917, Russia took all status away from its officers. It ruined the army. No titles, salutes, or privileges. Troops only followed the orders they liked. Of course, when the Russians saw the mess this made of the Army, they restored their officers' first class status completely. Orderlies, epaulettes and all. This interests us because status is also the reason many firms ask their men to fly first class. Not only so the man on the mission will have a place to work. But also as an investment in his frame of mind. A good mind is a fragile thing. A man simply cannot think "poor" on his way to a client and then think like a vice president when he gets there. Men do not turn on and off like this. We might add that first class is not even expensive any more. . . .—*From an advertisement of American Airlines*

Federation of Women Shareholders in American Business, Inc. . . . have submitted the following proposal which they state they intend to present for action at the meeting:

"Resolved: American Telephone and Telegraph stockholders, assembled in person and by proxy in annual meeting, request our Board of Directors to take such steps as may be necessary to amend the certificate of incorporation or the by-laws, or otherwise to provide for a secret ballot or method of secret voting by stockholders for the election of directors and upon resolutions appearing in our proxy statement except in those specific instances, if any, where it would be contrary to the law of the State of New York to do so."

These stockholders give the following reasons in support of the proposal: "Reasons: Shareowners are corporate citizens and should have protection against pressure, substantial or supposed, real or feared, and the same privacy accorded political citizens. Labor has a secret ballot provided by Congress in union elections, denied stockholders in corporation elections. AT&T has 250,000 employee-shareowners who must vote openly unless a stock is in street name [remaining in broker's hands]. . . ."—*Notice of Annual Meeting of Stockholders, American Telephone and Telegraph Company*

Causal Reasoning

Medical evidence shows that a large proportion of those who die of lung cancer are heavy smokers of cigarettes. Does that mean that cigarette smoking causes cancer? Medical authorities say it does. The tobacco industry, however, insists that there is no positive proof. Causal reasoning—reasoning from cause to effect, effect to effect, or effect to cause—is never conclusive, but it can be convincing. An investigator making a survey of practices in a freight yard reports:

> Orders for car moves now originate with more than one individual in the freight office. All of these persons make direct contact with the yard office. This practice has resulted in extra yard-crew moves through the issuance of conflicting orders.

The writer could document his conclusion by citing actual instances, but even if he does not, he has made an effective point. He has begun with a fact and gone on to attribute certain consequences to it. This is *reasoning from cause to effect.* A diagrammatic rendering of his argument would look like this:

Cause ⟶	*Effect* ⟶	*Effect*
Orders originate with more than one person	Conflicting orders	Unnecessary moving of yard crews

You will note that the second effect is the result of the first. This type of causal reasoning is *reasoning from effect to effect.*

In *reasoning from effect to cause,* the writer begins with an observable result and makes conjectures as to the reasons for it. The cigarette controversy, mentioned above, centers around this kind of reasoning. Another example is contained in this paragraph from a business report:

> The efficiency of the present tabulating operation at Oklahoma City is excellent. Considering the complexity of the accounting operation, the control of costs and the accuracy are among the best seen in our experience. It is our impression that the high quality of administration in this installation is due primarily to the unusual efficiency of the present tabulating supervisor.

A common fallacy in causal reasoning is attributing an effect to one cause when the cause may very well be something else. "There's a big difference in Vineland Tomato Juice," runs a radio commercial, "that makes it Chicago's best seller." In spite of the implications of better quality as the cause of the sales primacy, the fact is that it is lower priced than other major brands and may enjoy a sales edge for that reason. Much worse is this statement by a student of economics:

> Retail sales were down 5 per cent last week in comparison with the same period a year ago. This proves that people are hoarding their money.

What the student failed to consider were the heavy rains during the week as well as the Department of Labor statistics showing more unemployment and smaller paychecks than a year ago.

Another fallacy is concluding that something is necessarily a cause when it merely *precedes.* A new driver is involved in an automobile accident. His employer concludes that his inexperience was the cause when it was only a prior condition. The real cause, it turns out, was a malfunctioning brake. In another situation, the hiring of a new sales manager is immediately followed by a rising sales curve. Is the new executive responsible for the rise? He would certainly like everyone to think so, but the insiders know that the real reason for the improved showing was the introduction of a popular new line.

LANGUAGE AND TONE

However much we may want reason to prevail in the settlement of disputes, the emotions intrude. We cannot always, for instance, give sound reasons for the position we take, but we know the way we feel. When disputes occur, expressions like these are common emotional indicators:

"They had it coming to them."
"What they're getting away with is absolutely criminal."
"If he says so, it's all right with me; I trust him."
"How greedy can you get?"

In dealing with such feelings in the reader, you must examine your own attitudes carefully and just as carefully choose the words with which you express them. Otherwise, you increase the risk of alienating the neutral or sympathetic reader and hardening the position of the antagonistic reader.

The Technique of Agreement

When business engages in controversy with customers, employees, suppliers, and the public, it usually has a genuine desire to settle the dispute in such a way that a friendly continuance of the relationship is possible. This solution calls for a good measure of courtesy, tact, and sympathy, even when the company feels strongly about the justice of its own position.

A positive way to achieve these qualities is afforded by the technique of agreement. This, you will recognize, is an extension of the principle of consistency, discussed in Chapter 13, which holds that acceptance is increased when a communicator declares his views are in harmony with those of the receiver. Writer and reader are seldom at odds about every issue in a controversy. At the least, they can agree on broad aims or the desire for a fair and speedy settlement. Especially when it comes at the beginning of the message, agreement helps to loosen tension and open the reader's mind.

To a dealer who protested that the price he had to pay for a supplier's product did not give him a sufficient margin of profit, the supplier replied:

> In answering your letter of May 6, let us say at the start that we believe you are entitled to earn a good profit on our shoes. We wouldn't want you to handle them under any other conditions.

A similar approach is used in a letter to its customers from the Consolidated Edison Company of New York after a series of disastrous power failures:

> You have a right to good electric service. That's what you're paying for, and that's what we are determined to supply you.
>
> The fact that about 95 out of 100 customers had no electrical trouble this past summer is not good enough. We want to do better and, with your help, we think we can.

In some instances, agreement takes the form of an expressed willingness to do what the reader wants. Thus reassured, the reader is likely to be more receptive to an explanation of another point of view. When, for example, a lady was offended by an article in a national magazine and asked that her subscription be canceled, the publisher began his reply as follows:

> Of course, we'll cancel your subscription as you asked and give you a full refund on the remaining issues. But first, perhaps, you'll give us the opportunity to say something about the article in question.

A notable feature of the last example is the transitional second sentence, designed to lead the reader from the point of agreement to the statement of the writer's case. The transition takes longer in the following excerpt from a letter from Blue Cross announcing a substantial increase in its rates. Note the effort to alleviate in advance the impact of the bad news by describing the efforts to reduce costs and improve service.

> We have written to you before to share our concern about the spiraling cost of hospital care and to discuss its causes. At the same time, we have been busy in our constant efforts to hold down the cost of care while continuing to encourage high quality.
>
> Last year we introduced a new method for paying hospitals for the service they render to Blue Cross subscribers. This method sets payment rates in advance and builds in a clear incentive for operating efficiency. Some favorable effect is already evident. The rate of increase in hospital costs in the New York area is now considerably below the national average.
>
> On May 1 we are adding new and improved Outpatient Benefits to reduce the length and number of costly inhospital stays. Many of the services which previously were available in full only to bed patients will now be available on an ambulatory basis. This new venture should not only develop a more efficient use of hospital service but also provide a convenience for subscribers who can use them.
>
> Despite our efforts, the increase in the cost of hospital service has now exceeded our income. Currently, Blue Cross is paying out about $2½ million more each month than it receives in subscription income. To continue to serve each subscriber as he needs service and to launch the new benefit provisions, an adjustment in rates is necessary.

Even when the writer is in other respects combative, he may find it advantageous to concede something to his opponent. To give in on a minor or obvious point, to take part of the loaf instead of the whole one, helps to show a reasonable attitude and thus eases the path to agreement. Although expressing strong disapproval of credit buying, the Bowery Savings Bank was still able to make this concession:

> Now we don't mean to imply that borrowing money is necessarily a mistake anywhere, any time.
>
> Federal, state and local governments are sometimes forced to borrow—to finance defense, or to build a new schoolhouse, for example. Sound businesses often borrow. And few families could pay for houses of their own without mortgage money.
>
> However, the finance charge paid by such borrowers normally is true annual interest at the going rate, even if monthly payments are involved.
>
> We *do* want to give you an idea of what it costs to buy now—and pay later out of income you haven't yet received.

When, finally, there is no point on which agreement exists, the communicator may be able to show the receiver that the action proposed or taken is relatively superficial and poses no threat to him. Thus a company that initiates new work rules may forestall criticism by noting that the new rules affect only a small number of employees, or that the rules are fully consistent with previously announced policies, or that they will in fact tend to distribute the work load more equitably. In the Vietnamese War, a succession of American presidents claimed with every change in our military posture that no new policy was involved. One reason was to keep Congress off their back, but another was to reassure a public prone to protest.

Argumentative Connotations

We have already noted (Chapter 3) how words may be selected to connote favor or disfavor. The possibilities of using words to win or prejudice the reader in a controversy are especially tempting. Apart from the obvious ethical consideration, however, the writer must also contend with the danger of arousing resentment or disbelief. In the circumstances, the writer's responsibility, at the least, is to see that affective words support facts and logic, but do not take their place.

Some years ago General Electric succeeded in combating a strike by one of its unions. A principal factor in its success was a publicity campaign designed to discredit the union's president. In the following excerpt from one of its newspaper advertisements, note especially the connotation of the words *"gimmick," counterfeit, lawbreaking, red herring, bribe,* and *deals.* Some observers seriously questioned the use of the *ad hominem* argument, that is, an argument directed against a person rather than the issues.

> Mr. Carey's latest "gimmick" was a counterfeit truce proposal. In effect, he would call off his law-breaking tactics at defense and essential plants in return for the Company's giving in to some extra demands.
>
> The truce offer was another red herring. It is an attempt to get General Electric, in effect, to pay a bribe so that Mr. Carey will stop interfering with the livelihood of thousands of employees who want to work. Mr. Carey should not be so bribed by anyone in return for simply obeying the law. Nor should IUE agents be bribed by special truce deals to get them to stop violence on the picket lines.

In another vein, the Business Mail Foundation opened an appeal for the principle of postal subsidies by trading on the universally favorable opinion surrounding the name of Benjamin Franklin.

> Since Benjamin Franklin's tenure as Postmaster in Colonial Philadelphia, the Post Office has been the arm of Government serving the most people at the least cost. No American home, no matter how remote is without mail service.
>
> Eighty-six Congresses, from the first one to the one now serving, have endorsed the Franklin concept of service to all at low cost. In recent years, however, the true worth and purpose of this Nation's magnificent postal system have been obscured by persistent efforts to transform this public service into a business by consistently raising its rates and fees.
>
> It would be nice if it did not cost anything to run the postal service. It would be even nicer if the Post Office earned a profit sufficient to permit a general tax cut. But a break-even or profit-making Post Office must remain an impractical dream UNLESS Franklin's blueprint is to be scrapped and history reversed.

The American Medical Association was long opposed to the use of the Social Security system to finance medical care for the aged. In the following excerpted statement, note the connotation of the words the Association used to describe "what we favor" as opposed to the connotation of the words describing "what we reject." Now, in retrospect, you may decide for yourself whether the prejudicial language used in describing the "rejected" program, known today as Medicare, was warranted.

> MEDICAL AID FOR THE AGED
>
> *Here's what we favor:*
>
> As Americans, we believe that our aged citizens who need medical care should get it, whether or not they can afford to pay for it.
>
> The medical profession favors a program of medical aid for the aged sensibly designed to *help those who need* help.
>
> Such a program was enacted by Congress last year. It's the Kerr-Mills law which has the enthusiastic support of America's doctors. Specifically, the law provides for Federal grants-in-aid to the individual states, enabling them to provide health care for those among the elderly who need help. The benefits of this locally administered program also include the 2½ million Americans eligible for Old Age Assistance . . . and protect all other senior citizens who cannot meet the costs of a serious or long-lasting illness.
>
> The Kerr-Mills law represents a common-sense approach to solving a problem that concerns us all. Doctors support it; their first consideration is the health and life of their patients. As Americans, we endorse it because helping those who need help is the obligation of all decent people. . . .
>
> *Here's what we reject:*
>
> As Americans, we are deeply concerned about the dangers of Socialized Medicine. And we are not crying "wolf" when we apply that term to the cur-

rently proposed legislation which would establish a COMPULSORY health-care program for everyone covered by Social Security (regardless of need). The Socialist Party itself calls this Socialized Medicine. And we believe them more expert on socialist definitions than those who describe the Social Security approach as "just a method of financing aid for the aged."

This COMPULSORY health-care program adds up to nothing more than Socialized Medicine—controlled by a bureau of the Federal government . . . paid for by increased Social Security taxes, burdening both present and future generations. Confined at first to the aged, it would inevitably be expanded to cover all Americans.

Moreover, when the Federal government enters the privacy of the examination room—controlling both standards of practice and choice of practitioner—the cost includes loss of freedom. Your doctor's freedom to treat you in an individual way. Your freedom to choose your own doctor. We must all recognize that when the physician is socialized, his patient is socialized as well. . . .

The American Medical Association's consistent opposition to what others considered enlightened social policies gained for it much ill will, even among many of its own members. In consequence it dropped its older, negative public relations techniques and embarked on a more positive campaign to acquaint the public with the asset it has in the American Medical Association. One advertisement in the new campaign is quoted below. Note the specific use of facts to bring about public understanding as well as to win the goodwill of doctors themselves.

ANATOMY OF A DOCTOR

What makes a doctor tick?

Basically, knowing what's good for you. And behind that knowing lies a lot of work.

Even before he hangs out his shingle, he will have gone through about 12 years of medical education and training.

But research is forever uncovering new things that are good for you. Which is why your doctor can never really stop going to school.

We, the American Medical Association, help him in his education from the day he walks into medical school till the day he retires.

We help set and supervise the standards of education in America's medical schools.

We're working to streamline schooling so it will take less time for a doctor to enter practice.

We're helping more people to become doctors. Through our Education and Research Foundation, we guarantee loans to students, interns and residents (over $50 million worth so far).

Every year we sponsor more than 1,000 conferences and study sessions where doctors can exchange ideas.

AMA Councils on everything from drug abuse to nutrition get the latest scientific information into doctors' hands. And so do the many medical journals we publish.

Altogether, the AMA spent $20 million on scientific and health education. For doctors. And for their patients.

Knowing what's good for you.

It's what being a good doctor is all about.

SUMMARY

Opinion change is a function of persuasion that seeks to settle disagreements by converting an individual or group from a belief already held to one that the communicator offers as a substitute. When rational methods are used, the process is often referred to as argument.

The writer of an argumentative message starts by analyzing the problem, the reader, and the issues, and then composing a message that is well supported by the evidence and expressed in a way that is most likely to bring an affirmative response. The problem, or "proposition," is best put in words as a guide to the writer, for example, "An investment tax credit is essential to promote capital spending." Classification of the reader as receptive, neutral, or antagonistic helps in the selection of content and language as well as in the arrangement of the message parts. The issues are the particular points around which the controversy revolves. These must be examined for their relevance and validity and, if necessary, new facts should be introduced to put the problem in perspective.

In constructing the message, the writer should begin with points of agreement, if possible, or some affirmation of the reader's rights or his entitlement to an equitable settlement of the issues. The body of the message should consist of facts, opinions, and reasoning—all designed to show not only the merits of the writer's point of view, but also his concern for the interests of the reader. The close may ask for direct action or, if the reader is not considered ready for such action, the close may take a conciliatory stance, offer more information, or otherwise give the reader some time to think over his decision.

The use of logical reasoning in argument is inevitable. Logical reasoning is either inductive or deductive. Inductive reasoning, or "the scientific method," proceeds from an examination of specific data to conclusions drawn from those data. Deductive reasoning draws a conclusion from a broad assertion known to be true (the major premise) and a specific fact (minor premise) through a form of argument called a syllogism. (Example: All men are mortal; Smith is a man; Smith is mortal.) Less valid, but not necessarily less persuasive forms of reasoning are reasoning from analogy and reasoning from cause to effect.

All controversy involves the emotions, and it is therefore difficult (and often undesirable) to keep emotion out of the argumentative presentation. Although prejudicial terms may be used to win support from a sympathetic audience, however, they will not win points with the opposition and they may even be turned against the user.

PROBLEMS

1. Make a list of what you consider to be changing trends in public opinion with respect to dress, life-styles, race relations, preservation of the environment, urban living, and/or any other aspects of our social, spiritual, or political climate. Then, for each trend that you note, comment on the ways in which the mass communication media contribute to public opinion. Give specific evidence wherever possible.

2. To what extent, if any, do you think the advertising for five of the following products has contributed to changes in our way of living? Where you consider advertising responsible for such changes, explain what persuasive tools were used to bring them about. Cite particular advertisements or advertising campaigns in your answer.
   (*a*) Soaps and cleansers
   (*b*) Cars
   (*c*) Tobacco
   (*d*) Drugs and cosmetics
   (*e*) Toys
   (*f*) Candy, cake and cake mixes, and ice cream
   (*g*) Air travel
   (*h*) Beer and liquor
   (*i*) Gas and oil
   (*j*) Household appliances
   (*k*) Soft drinks

3. Take some pressing local or national problem that does not lend itself to a popular solution, and suggest some specific and socially acceptable techniques by which public opinion might be strengthened in one direction or another.

4. Find support, both emotional and rational, for or against one of the following propositions, or some other one suggested by your instructor:
   (*a*) The highest income groups should be asked to bear a larger share of the tax burden than they now do.
   (*b*) The government should share the cost of controlling pollution caused by industry.
   (*c*) Crime will be reduced when the penal system is reformed.
   (*d*) Conflicts of interest among legislators are a national disgrace.
   (*e*) Regulation of the (oil, lumber, drug, or other) industry is endangering the public interest.

5. Mr. Julian Cranmoor is the personnel director of the Metropolitan Bank and Trust Company. His difficulties with both present and prospective employees are aggravated by the false notion that banks pay notoriously low salaries in nonexecutive jobs. He has asked you to investigate this subject and draft for his signature a memorandum which he can send to other bank officers so that they will be prepared to speak up whenever the question of salaries is raised. On the basis of talks with others in the bank, you have made these notes:
   (*a*) Harry Delos, the bank's salary administrator, compared salaries for all clerical jobs at Metropolitan with figures reported by 400 businessmen to the City Chamber of Commerce. On two-thirds of the jobs, Metropolitan salaries were

equal to or better than the prevailing wages of comparable jobs. On some jobs, however, especially those requiring a low level of skill (e.g., clerks and pages) Metropolitan paid lower than prevailing wages.

(*b*) Newspaper stories about salaries earned by truck drivers and workers in some manual trades make bank salaries look low in comparison. But it is difficult to compare work done by truck drivers and factory hands with that done in banks. Bank people probably would not like to be truck drivers at any salary. Besides, salaries that make the news headlines are not typical of those earned by even blue-collar workers.

(*c*) The expansion of the American economy experienced since 1939 has worked to the disadvantage of clerical workers, and especially those older workers who have reached their maximum salary ranges for their kind of work. This fact explains why disillusionment with bank salaries is particularly strong among senior employees. High-school students queried by the bank's recruiters also believed bank salaries were low.

(*d*) Stenographic and clerical salaries in a large bank are sometimes compared with those in small companies hiring only one or two such employees at salary scales that are out of line. But employees in small companies have less security and fewer benefits than a large bank can offer.

In preparing your memorandum, use these and any other relevant and reasonable arguments, which you may assume.

6. Assume that you are the manager of the Universal Broadcasting Company. You have a contract with the Wilson Manufacturing Company, (executive offices in Tulsa, Oklahoma 74103) for the sponsorship of 32 half-hour programs of news commentary by Barry Brown. The contract calls for payment of $1,250,000. On the April 6 program Mr. Brown featured a story involving the indictment of one of the officers of the Wilson Manufacturing Company for mail fraud. Today (April 9) you received the following letter from Mr. Carroll Wilson, the president:

April 7, 19--

Gentlemen:

I do not think that any rule of broadcasting forced you to use our program time for the story of Stephen Q. Lawrence's indictment. Both you and Mr. Brown must have realized that the story could only injure a valued sponsor in the public mind and subject him to the ridicule of our competitors. There were certainly plenty of other stories that could have commanded your attention.

Before you raise any cry about freedom of speech, you might consider also the good old American adage that no one is guilty until proved so. By trying Mr. Lawrence on national television, you have certainly prejudiced the case against him.

I cannot conceive that my stockholders will stand for the continued expenditure of company money for such harmful publicity. As of today, you will please cancel the remaining 28 programs in the Wilson series.

Very truly yours,

Write the reply to Mr. Wilson. You will not cancel the contract, which gives you full freedom to decide what will be discussed in the program. You personally approved the story in consultation with Mr. Brown. The story was of such great public interest that it could not be ignored in any review of the week's news. Most newspapers in the country had already featured the story on their front pages, and the two minutes it took to tell on the air gave it far less emphasis than it deserved. Besides, the telling was entirely objective, with no attempt to influence public opinion one way or the other. A sponsor may have much to say about other types of programs, but news programs must remain inviolate, and all contracts with sponsors of news programs give the station full control over them. You doubt that, on reflection, Mr. Wilson would want it any other way. Far from subjecting the company to ridicule, the program strengthened respect for it among listeners. Among dozens of letters so far received, all had praise for both the network and the sponsor. Use these and any other relevant arguments to alter Mr. Wilson's attitude.

7. Assume that you are the Sales Manager of the Syracuse office of the Weldon Electrical Manufacturing Company mentioned in Problem 12(c), Chapter 14. Mr. Fargo, your representative, has called on Peter Campbell, who is in the plumbing business in Rochester, New York, and has taken an order for four units at $650 each, less the regular 40 per cent discount and a 3 per cent discount for cash. Today, a week later, you receive the following letter from Mr. Campbell.:

September 14, 19--

Gentlemen:

I've been thinking over the order I gave your Mr. Fargo, and I feel maybe I acted a little hastily.

These electronic air cleaners of yours are certainly outstanding, but nobody around here knows about them, and I'm going to have to put a lot of effort into selling them. It seems to me that this effort is going to be worth more than a 40 per cent discount.

If you're willing to raise the discount to 50 per cent, I'll let the order stand. Otherwise, please cancel it until I can see where the business is going to come from.

Very truly yours,

Peter Campbell

Try to convince Mr. Campbell that he ought to take the air cleaners on your terms. The price is already set low to attract new business, and you cannot grant any further concessions. Mr. Campbell must have had a pretty good idea where the business would come from when he ordered the units; why should the situation be different now? Since the electronic air cleaner is a new product, every house-owning customer is a prospective purchaser. Furthermore, air cleaner business should lead to other plumbing contracts. The advertising campaign in *Time* has already produced hundreds of inquiries, all of which have been forwarded to local dealers for follow-up. Your advertising campaign will be stepped up next month, with full pages in *Reader's Digest* and *Better Homes and Gardens.* Since you offer exclusive distribution to only one dealer in a community, you will have to consider another distributor in Rochester if Mr. Campbell insists on canceling his order. Now answer Mr. Campbell's letter.

8. Assume that you are the Commissioner of the Purchasing Department of a large city. On September 28 you opened the sealed bids for lumber to be supplied to the city. The contract award normally goes to the lowest bidder. If, in your opinion, not enough companies enter bids or if the bids are not low enough, you may set them aside and announce another bid opening through advertisements in the *City Record.* Today you receive the following letter dated October 20:

> Dear Sir:
>
> In response to an invitation to bid, we submitted our prices for lumber on the bidding date of September 28.
>
> Reports indicated that we were the low bidder, but on inquiry we learned that no award was made because there were not enough bidders and that another bidding date was to be scheduled.
>
> It has now come to our attention that new bids were advertised for and were opened on October 19. Since we were the low bidder on the previous quotation and expressed our willingness then to quote prices on your lumber requirements, we are surprised that no new invitation to bid was sent us.
>
> We feel that we should have been asked and that the City should have the benefit of our consistently low prices.
>
> May we ask that no awards be made on this particular bid and that we be asked to quote when the bidding date is rescheduled.
>
> Your consideration will be greatly appreciated.
>
> Very truly yours,
>
> Maple Lumber Company

These are the facts: The Maple Lumber Company was one of two bidders on the September 28 opening, and it was the absence of sufficient competition that made necessary a second advertisement for bids. The new opening, which was to take place on October 19, was advertised in the *City Record* on each of the five days preceding. You are not obliged to invite individual suppliers to bid, although you sometimes do so when the circumstances permit. It is the responsibility of prospective bidders to follow the bid advertisements.

Write a letter to the Maple Lumber Company refusing to readvertise for bids.

9. As a member of the legislature in the State of Pacifica, you were instrumental in having a contract for $356,000 awarded to a company in your political district for carpets in the State Capitol and legislative office buildings. For a week now, newspaper stories have been saying that the carpets will be made by nonunion workers in an out-of-state factory and that some are to be imported from Hong Kong. This

charge, if true, is especially harmful politically because one of the country's leading carpet mills, a union shop, is located in Bristol, right in your own state.

The facts are these: The Bronston Rug Company of Carville was the low bidder. Since they are not manufacturers, they tried to obtain the carpeting from the Bristol Mills. They were refused the carpets, however, on the ground that Bristol dealt only through exclusive agencies in various parts of the country and that since Bronston was not such an agency, the carpeting could not be distributed through them. In the circumstances, Bronston placed the order with the Belfast Carpet Company, a maker of excellent repute, with plants in other states. All the plants have contracts with the local unions of the Carpet Workers of America. With respect to the charge that some of the carpeting is being made in Hong Kong, the fact is that only 400 square yards of a total of 15,000 square yards is involved. The smaller yardage represents a centerpiece bearing the State seal. This is to be entirely handwoven. The cost of such weaving in this country would be prohibitive.

Write a letter to be sent to the editors of all newspapers in your state, setting forth the facts.

10. As personnel director of the Famous Insurance Company, you are concerned about talk among some junior executives that higher officers of the company, who are in a position to hire and promote on their own authority, have been making private investigations of the wives and home life of the men under consideration. One high executive has publicly expressed the view that a wife should be good looking and charming, but also ambitious for her husband's success and willing to make personal sacrifices to help him achieve it. One of the sacrifices cited was having him away from home a good deal.

It is your feeling that the stories about "personnel tests" for wives are injurious to morale within the company and to the "image" the company wishes to project in public. The whole idea is distasteful to you personally, who have always believed that a man should be judged on his own merits.

Write a memoradum explaining your views to the president of the company, Mr. Merrill T. Snyder. Try to find support for your views in current writing on the subject.

11. You are in the public relations department of the Metropolitan Light and Power Company, a public utility serving Metropolitan City. In last Tuesday's *Metropolitan Press,* there appeared an editorial castigating your company for the clouds of dense smoke pouring from the chimneys of your Riverside Power Plant. The editorial said that the people would not tolerate this nuisance much longer and that if it persisted, it was up to the State Public Service Commission to take legal action.

Here are the facts: Your company bought the Riverside Power Plant from the city two years ago, after the city turned over to Metropolitan the task of providing power for the city-operated transit system. In the twenty-two years the city operated the plant, it never did anything to correct the smoke nuisance. Your company, on the other hand, has spent ten million dollars in the last five years to correct smoke conditions at its four power plants. The other three plants are now fully converted to new equipment, which produces power without noxious smoke. Equipment for the Riverside plant has been on order since the company took over the facility, but it takes time to design and manufacture such equipment. Delivery is expected in about six months. The cost of converting this plant alone will come to three million dollars. Your company does not object to the cost, but it would like to get some credit for the constructive things it is doing for the people of Metropolitan City.

Write a letter to the editor of the *Metropolitan Press* explaining your company's position.

12. You are assistant to Mr. Grant T. Fellows, sales manager of a large office supply and stationery company. A fellow worker has suggested to Mr. Fellows that the company give Christmas gifts to its customers and those employees of customers whose goodwill the stationery company depends on for continued sales. The gifts would be rather expensive, ranging from leather billfolds and cigarette lighters to liquor and baskets of gourmet foods. Although in the past the company has sent Christmas cards, it has never made it a policy to give presents as a consideration for continued patronage. Before making a decision, Mr. Fellows wants you to present counter arguments. He is worried not only about the expense—several thousand dollars—but also about the ethics involved. Address a memorandum on the subject to him. See if you can find support for your point of view in published statements on the subject.

13. Some time ago, your company established a rule forbidding employees to accept gifts or gratuities of any kind from your suppliers, which number several hundred. Your purchasing agents and other employees are familiar with the rule and, as far as you know, observe it. On the other hand, they are often embarrassed by offers of gifts and the necessity of refusing them. To help them and to aid enforcement of your rule, you propose to write a letter to all suppliers asking them to refrain from offering gifts. Make it clear that relations with your company depend on meeting your needs for quality, service, and price, rather than on gratuities. You may, if you see fit, also point out that committees of company officers, who cannot be influenced by gifts, regularly review all relations with suppliers.

14. The president of a large corporation, Synfoil, Inc., has asked you to prepare for his signature a letter to all stockholders asking them to write to their Congressional representatives to protest against a measure for the withholding of taxes on corporate dividends at the source. The practice would cost the company many thousands of dollars for administration and record keeping, and is also inimical to the interests of stockholders who depend on dividends to meet their living costs. Assume that a list of all Congressmen identified by state and Congressional district is to be enclosed with the letter.

15. The Clothing Council, a trade organization to which your company belongs, is disturbed by what it considers to be the "sloppy" dress of college students. The suggestion has been made that an educational campaign be undertaken to correct the situation. Draft an "open letter" to be sponsored by the Council and published as an advertisement in college newspapers throughout the country. You are, naturally, expected to consider the college student's psychology in developing your appeal.

16. Assume that you are an assistant treasurer of the Claremont National Bank of your city. Today you received a telephone call from Mr. Herbert S. Grotman regarding a bill for $60 for the preparation of his income tax returns for last year. Your bank manages some property for Mr. Grotman, his only source of income. You prepare his income tax returns merely as a convenience to him.

Mr. Grotman says he thinks the charge is exorbitant and will not pay it. Since you do not have the facts at hand, you tell Mr. Grotman that you will look into the matter and get in touch with him promptly.

You have now consulted your bank's accounting department and learn that the sum charged Mr. Grotman covers the analysis of his account, the preparation of all income tax forms, and the payment of taxes as they fall due. You make no profit from this service and consider the bill reasonable.

You could if necessary charge the $60 against Mr. Grotman's account, but that would antagonize the customer. Write a letter to induce Mr. Grotman to accept the charge willingly. He lives at 40 Jefferson Street South.

17. Comment on the validity of the reasoning in each of the following passages:

(*a*) We asked 100 company officers, "How many magazines, books, and newspapers have you read in the past week?" The total of their answers: magazines, 338; books, 53; newspapers, 1,490.

Then we asked 100 men in the same age group whose salaries had never quite reached $7,500 a year. 229 magazines for them—and only 28 books. That's about a fourth of a book apiece. The conclusion is as clear as print. *Men who read more achieve more.—International Paper Company*

(*b*) Have you fully realized how big an advertising job direct mail could do for you? You *would* if you were our client American Airlines. When American introduced its new Jet Flagships an announcement mailing was sent to 700,000 businessmen. Over 140,000 responded. On top of this, a readership study showed that over 66% of those addressed—more than 450,000—read the mailing. In anyone's book that's proof-positive of direct-mail's effectiveness.—*Dickie-Raymond*

(*c*) Cities Service gasolines actually protect as they power your car . . . work *with* your car to give you trouble-free driving and long mileage. No matter what the going distance, your engine gives maximum efficiency . . . you'll get all the mileage you're entitled to from every gallon.

Why handicap your car with ordinary brands when these superior Cities Service gasolines cost no more!

(*d*) Manifestly telephone progress depends on an economic climate that will stimulate savings and investment, and on the willingness of regulatory commissions to encourage earnings that maintain and augment the financial strength of business.—*Bell Telephone System*

(*e*) Blue Cross and Blue Shield provide more benefits and services because they are nonprofit and sponsored by hospitals and physicians. Blue Cross and Blue Shield have low administrative costs; pay no commissions; have no brokers or agents; and are governed by nonsalaried Boards of Directors.

(*f*) Our tables won't start making money for you until you start selling them.

That's why we urge you to unpack them immediately upon arrival and put them on display.

(*g*) When "public power" wins—you lose! Every time the lobby for Federal "public power" pushes another government electricity project through, *you* are taxed to pay the bill.—*America's Independent Light and Power Companies*

(*h*) The sad case of the happy investor.

For a time he was happy, for he had bought some stocks on a tip that they would go up. And they did—for a short while. But then the rumor that caused the rise proved unfounded—and his stocks declined with a sickening speed.

To avoid such losses, get your information from a RELIABLE SOURCE.

Here at Darby and Yates, we are constantly gathering and evaluating information on companies and industries. You can invest with the confidence that comes from *knowing* rather than *hoping*.

18. During recent Congressional hearings, the relationship between large companies and their retail agencies was explored, with considerable criticism directed at oil companies for "dictatorial" practices.

As one of the companies subject to criticism, the Majestic Oil Company undertook a review of its dealer policies. Of its 25,000 dealer outlets (service stations) from Maine to Louisiana, about 10 per cent are owned by Majestic Oil Company and leased to dealers, another 20 per cent are owned by private interests, leased by the Majestic Oil Company and, in turn, subleased to dealers. Seventy per cent are either owned by the dealer himself or leased by him from others. Majestic enters into arrangements with all dealers to provide them with gasoline, oil, tires, batteries, and accessories, all marketed under the Majestic label. There is nothing in the franchise agreement to prevent dealers from selling other brands if they desire. Figures show that 933 dealers have been selling Majestic products for 30 years or more; 3,021 for 20 years or more; and 4,385 for 10 years or more.

In the light of the Congressional testimony and mounting criticism from its dealers, the Majestic Oil Company has decided to issue a statement of policy to all its dealers. As the person in the organization who will have to write this document, you recently had a talk with the company's vice president for marketing. A tape recording of his remarks runs as follows:

You can always depend on dealers to complain about something. For example, we put some company-operated stations on the Turnpikes, and they say we're taking away business that ought to be theirs. Outside of these Turnpike stations, we operate only 43 of our own stations, and this is done just to train personnel and give us some direct contact with the gas-buying public.

Dealers who lease from us often forget that we're in business to make money, just as they are; and if a station isn't selling as much of our stuff as we think they ought to, we have a perfectly legitimate right not to renew. The fact is that in many cases we lease on a commission basis until the operators are able to take over on their own. In other cases we make concessions on rent until a dealer gets on his feet. On the other hand, when these dealers become able to pay what the property is worth, we think we ought to be able to raise the rent without getting howls to the effect that we're taking advantage of the situation.

Sure we've disenfranchised dealers, but we've got a reputation to maintain, too. What are we supposed to do when a dealer has filthy rest rooms and gives inefficient and discourteous service? Don't forget, too, that the dealer's signs and pumps and a lot of other equipment are our property—we just lend them to our dealers—and we think they ought to be properly cared for. In spite of the pressures on us, we're going to keep selling to the dealers who prove they can sell our products to our credit and theirs, and we'll get rid of those dealers who are slipshod in their management and discredit the Majestic name.

We're not really fighting our dealers. We consult with groups of them about our products and the problems involved in selling them profitably. As far as the rents being out of line is concerned, we have all property analyzed by experts before we put any rental value on it. The point is we like to be fair and cooperative, but we expect a little fairness and cooperation in return. Furthermore, when a dealer has a complaint, he'd do a whole lot better by coming to us instead of to a Congressional committee.

From what you have learned draft a statement of policy to be included in a small booklet to be distributed to all service-station dealers. Naturally, you want it to promote good company-dealer relations.

16
Speech Communication

SO FAR we have dealt with communication particularly as it is practiced in writing. Although most of what we have had to say is also applicable to speech, there remain certain differences between writing and speaking. Study of these differences can help improve the performance of writers as well as speakers. But there is yet another reason why this chapter is included. Recent changes both in media technology and management thinking have given speech communication a new importance that no writer can afford to ignore.

Despite the many advantages of writing, management today recognizes the necessity of face-to-face meetings and encourages the use of conference and discussion as tools in accomplishing the communication objectives of the organization. At the same time, the ready availability of the overhead projector, the videotape recorder, and other sophisticated visual and auditory aids makes possible more interesting and successful meetings than ever before. What remains is the need for communicators who can recognize the opportunities in speech communication and have the resources and training to take advantage of them.

SPEECH SETTINGS IN ORGANIZATIONS

Apart from the ordinary face-to-face speaking that occurs between individuals all the time, organizations also offer other, more formal opportunities for speech communication.

Interviews

An interview may be said to take place when one person seeks out another for the purpose of getting information or solving a problem. Thus a reporter on the staff of a company's house magazine may conduct an interview with a staff worker in order to obtain information for an article. Another familiar type of informational interview is the job-application interview, in which the applicant is called on to answer questions about himself and his job aims. Interviews that attempt to solve problems include the interview given a worker who has a grievance and the job-evaluation interview in which a supervisor and worker discuss the latter's performance on the job. Problem solving is also the aim of the interviews with workers conducted by the methods and systems analyst intent on finding more efficient work procedures.

Small-Group Conferences

Every organization has a number of activity and decision-making centers held together by communication links. Within each center and between centers, communication is often carried on through meetings of various sorts. Small groups may come together to obtain information, pool ideas, solve common problems, or make recommendations to management. In some instances, the groups are formed into committees. A *standing committee* is one that meets on a regular basis. An *ad hoc committee* is one appointed on an interim basis to deal with a specific problem. The head of a committee is usually known as the chairman or chairperson; the committee may also have other officers, such as vice chairman, secretary, and treasurer; and subcommittees may be appointed to deal with specific tasks or problems and to bring their recommendations to the full committee. Most of the speaking in small-group meetings is done informally across the table; however, specific occasions may call for a standing presentation with a full panoply of visual aids.

Large Meetings

Conferences on a large scale may consist of assemblies of employees, executives, stockholders, dealers, and distributors, and civic and consumer groups. Such meetings may be held at the request of management or of the representatives of those who constitute the audience. In the former case, the presumption is that management has something important to communicate to the audience and that the best way is to call them together and address them in person. Questions and opinions may be invited from the audience, but the aim is usually not so much a search for solutions as it is a clarification of actions, decisions, or policies already formulated. When the meeting is called at the request of representatives of the audience, the purpose may be a quest for information or the alleviation of grievances. Large-scale meetings often use a panel of speakers to treat different parts of the subject and to answer questions in their respective areas of competence. Effectiveness is increased by the use of professionally prepared visual aids and handouts of printed material for reference after the meeting.

PUBLIC SPEECH SETTINGS

The businessman's opportunities for speaking are by no means confined to his own organization. Ordinarily, the business person will belong to a number of trade or professional organizations which hold meetings and conventions. If he is active, he will attend the meetings, participate in the discussions, and on occasion be called on to address a meeting on a subject on which he is expert by reason of his research or firsthand experience. It is not unlikely that such an individual will also belong to local civic clubs and other groups devoted to social causes and community betterment. But whether or not he is a member of any of these groups, he may speak to them as a representative of his company. For there is always a need for able speakers to fulfill the requests of local organizations for help in presenting interesting and informative programs. Similar opportunities exist on programs broadcast by radio or television. The participating businessman helps his community and his employer at the same time. If the public relations department does not itself arrange the speech engagements, it likes to be informed about them, and often it will publicize the events in the company's publications and in the trade and community press.

Public meetings take a number of forms. Zelko lists the following:[1]

Group Discussion. Here there is a free exchange among all members of the group, who are usually seated around a table or in some other informal setting.

Forum. The program is turned over to the audience for questions and comments after the conclusion of the formal program.

Panel-Forum. Several participants, constituting the "panel," hold an informal but organized discussion in the presence of a larger audience. After the conclusion of the panel discussion, the audience may be invited to engage the panel with comments and questions.

Symposium-Forum. This is similar to the Panel-Forum except that the panel give prepared talks on different phases of the same subject and each member usually speaks in a standing position from the center of the platform.

Debate. Two teams, usually consisting of two persons each, take opposing views on a controversial subject in the presence of an audience. Debate is not true discussion because both sides have set views to be defended with no thought that either side will change its mind.

Lecture. A single speaker presents a subject on which he is expert. Ideally, the talk should be followed by questions from the audience.

Radio and Television. The broadcast media may provide an outlet for any of the methods of public presentation already described, although the panel is probably the most spontaneous and therefore the most interesting. Radio and television are also ideal media for interviews, especially on news and public events programs.

[1] Harold P. Zelko, *The Business Conference: Leadership and Participation* (New York: McGraw-Hill, 1969), pp. 231–236.

PREPARING TO SPEAK

In any setting, effective speech requires some degree of preparation. A few basic suggestions follow:

1. Confidence in yourself can be your most important asset. Such confidence must come from a sure knowledge of your subject, a sympathetic understanding of the needs of the audience, and a sincere desire to share your ideas and feelings with them.
2. Even if you have a natural talent for speaking (as who has not?), solid preparation will pay generous dividends. Research your topic and your audience thoroughly, plan your talk step by step in advance, and pay special attention to the need for visual aids and to their preparation.
3. If you can, carefully check in advance the physical setting in which you will speak. Comfortable seating and good ventilation are conducive to a receptive attitude on the part of the audience. If your presentation needs special equipment like a blackboard or screen or table, be sure it is available. And if you are going to use a movie or slide projector, be sure an electrical outlet is handy and that the room can be conveniently darkened.

DELIVERY TECHNIQUES

Once you are in the presence of your audience, you need to ensure that they receive your message with interest and respond favorably. Here you will have to rely on a variety of delivery techniques, of which some may come to you instinctively and others may have to be learned and applied consciously. Certainly, the more coordinated you are, the better your reception will be.

Volume

Your first objective is to be heard distinctly by every person in your audience. So whether you speak from your seat or from the platform, you should speak as loud as conditions dictate. A large room naturally requires more volume than a small one, although noise interference and the acoustics of the chamber need to be considered also. If a moving truck outside can be heard through the open windows, raise your voice until the vehicle has passed; similarly you should speak louder if there is noise coming from the back of the meeting room or from outside the door.

Even when you speak loud enough, however, you may still not be heard because you do not have the attention of the audience. It is well, therefore, not to plunge into your speech until you have attention. On the platform, it is usually enough to look directly at the audience and wait a moment before speaking. If you are engaged in a group discussion, you may get attention by raising your hand and being recognized by the chairman; or you may preface your remarks with a statement like, "I see another side to the question," and then pause briefly before continuing.

Articulation

If you are going to be heard and understood, you must not only speak loud enough to an attentive audience; you must also articulate clearly. What is sought here is not a false refinement of speech, but an ordinary regard for the sound of the language. When *reliability* sounds like *liability, being* like *bing, acetic* like *acidic,* and *death* like *debt,* there is real danger that you will be misunderstood. But articulation has a social dimension, too. If a speaker says *dis* and *dat* for *this* and *that, pitcher* for *picture,* and *f'rinstance* for *for instance,* he creates in his audience an attitude similar to that which a misspelled word would cause in written communication. The result is a loss of acceptance that can seriously reduce the speaker's ability to hold and influence his audience.

Variety

A good speaker avoids a monotone. By variations in rate, pitch, and force, he enlivens his delivery and brings out subtleties of meaning. The speaker may also vary the tone of his voice so that the mood it conveys—amusement, sadness, reflection, enthusiasm, and so on—is consistent with the nature of the message.

Eye Contact

The most direct link between the speaker and the audience is through the eyes. If you care about your audience, you will look right at them, directing your eyes momentarily to one person then another. You will not look over their heads or out the window or down at the floor.

Eye contact is important in getting your message across to the audience, but it is also a way of receiving feedback. By noting the response of the audience—whether it be interest, boredom, or confusion—you are in a position to determine whether to continue in the same vein or to make adjustments in the content and delivery of your speech. One difficulty in maintaining eye contact arises when you are using notes or visual aids. Notes should be as brief as possible and once you glance at them, you should return your attention to your audience. If you point to a chart, fix your eyes on the chart as you ask the audience to do the same, but then remove the chart as soon as you are through with it.

Posture and Movement

There are no fixed rules on how to stand or sit when you talk, but it is expected that a speaker will look alert and interested in what he is saying. That means that the speaker will not slouch over a table on his elbows or keep both hands in his back pockets while his stomach protrudes over the platform. Sitting or standing, his best position is erect but not stiff. A stand-up speaker will look most comfortable with both feet solidly on the floor and a trifle apart, and his hands at his sides. Unnecessary movement, like fidgeting with the hands or shifting the weight from one foot to another, is distracting and should be avoided. Meaningful movement, on the other hand, will add interest to the presentation. Thus, to emphasize a point, the speaker may gesture with one or both hands or move closer to the audience. As he progresses from one point to another, he may also move a few steps to the right or left of the platform, as if to call attention to the change in ideas. The movement, incidentally, helps the speaker relieve some of his tension, but in a constructive way.

VISUAL AND AUDIO AIDS

The fact that we are living in an age of mechanical sound and images makes it all the more important that the speaker consider using such adjuncts if he wishes his speech to be effective. The audience, in any case, has only a limited capacity for reception through the ear, but reception can be infinitely enhanced by multi-media techniques. Most of us are already aware of many of the presentation methods available. These methods not only help to give a speech clarity and interest, but also result in better retention by the listener. Some kinds of data, like statistics and technical description, cannot adequately be presented without graphics.

Types Available

Visual and audio aids are now available to meet almost any need. The choice must depend on the point to be demonstrated, the availability of the materials or equipment, and the ability of the speaker to handle the aids smoothly while he talks. Some of the aids now commonly used may be listed as follows:

Direct Visual Aids

Three-dimensional objects: products, models, mock-ups
Pictures: photographs and drawings
Chalkboard, including the familiar blackboard
Magnetic board. Allows progressive buildup of points.
Charts: graphs and diagrams, simple tables
Handouts: samples, printed materials, programs

Projected Visual Aids

Overhead projector. Requires transparencies. Speaker can face audience and add or remove details at will.

Opaque projector. Projects directly from pictures and other graphics. Machine is cumbersome and blower used to dispel heat is noisy.

Slide projector. A day or two are needed for processing slides, but results are sharp and realistic.

Motion picture projector. Requires operator; has limited usefulness in speech presentations, though a film may become the basis for discussion afterward.

Videotape playback. Provides instantaneous replays of videotape recordings. Possibilities for instructional use not yet completely realized, but the opportunities seem infinite.

Audio Aids

Amplifying system
Tape player
Phonograph

The direct visual aids have an advantage in that they require no special processing and can be shown in full light. However, they may be too small to be seen by any but a small audience. The projected visual aids, except for the overhead projector and videotape player, require a darkened room, which inhibits the taking of notes. They also tend to subordinate the speaker to the visuals, though there is no doubt that they can be effective in their own right. The audio aids, which of course include the sound portions of motion pictures and videotapes, have obviously limited applications in "live" presentations.

Effective Use

Unless they are properly used, visual and audio aids can hinder the presentation rather than help it. The following guidelines should be helpful:

1. Use a visual aid only when it is closely related to the purpose of the speech and its presentation is coordinated with your remarks.
2. Charts and pictures should be large and bold enough to be seen by everyone in the audience. If good visibility cannot be obtained otherwise, the use of slides or transparencies should be considered.
3. Avoid using any visual material that cannot be handled conveniently. A hand-held picture that flops over is distracting to both the speaker and the audience. It would be better to mount it and set it on an easel. For another example, if you are going to have to turn your back to the audience for a long time while you put notes or a diagram on a chalkboard, perhaps it would be better instead to prepare the material in advance on display cards or a flip-chart.
4. A speaker is usually limited to the equipment available on the premises or to that which he can conveniently obtain and transport himself. In any case, there may still be some question about the availability of an electrical outlet or the ability to darken a room. Because of such obstacles as these, a speaker may choose simple charts or pictures instead of more sophisticated types of visual aids.
5. If the presentation requires such equipment as a slide projector or tape player, be sure the equipment is set up in advance and that you are practiced in using it efficiently. You don't want to be fumbling with a recalcitrant machine when you should be making an important point about your subject.
6. Be sure to erase the chalkboard or put away the visuals after you are through referring to them, so that they will not divert the listener as you continue to talk.
7. Unless handouts are required for reference during the speech, they should not be given out until after the speech. Otherwise they may occupy your audience while you are talking about other matters.

LANGUAGE REQUIREMENTS OF SPEECH

In earlier chapters we have given considerable space to matters of language and the organization of information. Our chief concern in those chapters was meeting the needs of written communication. As we turn now to the language of speech communication, we find that the general standards of language are similar, but that particular differences in expression do exist. The differences are occasioned by the speech setting and the fact that the appeal is primarily to the ear.

A speech is designed to be delivered orally to a specific audience, usually face-to-face, and within a limited time. Generally, it favors (1) informality, (2) a limitation on technical detail, (3) an abundance of illustration and narrative, (4) a simple pattern of organization, and (5) special attention to the beginning and the end. Here we will discuss these qualifications in order.

Informality

Although state occasions demand ceremonial speech, most speech gains effectiveness when it sounds like plain talk. The language should be direct, simple, natural, and personal. Contractions like *don't, aren't,* and *can't* are encouraged. An occasional colloquialism or slang expression gives color to the presentation even when the expression is somewhat less than original. Thus a speaker might use words like *woozy, blooper,* and *emcee* and express himself in such terms as "Then what happened? The market sat on its hands for a spell." The informality also extends to the use of direct address and personal reference to oneself and others.

Technical Detail

A written statement can be read at one's own pace, pondered over, and reread; and words that are not immediately understood can be looked up in the dictionary. The spoken message does not offer the listener these luxuries. He must understand the message while it is being uttered, at the pace decreed by the speaker, or the meaning will be lost. In the circumstances, the speaker must be highly selective, omitting those details that will clutter the presentation or obscure the meaning. The allowable degree of difficulty must of course be determined by the kind of audience, but there are limits to the comprehension of even knowledgeable listeners. When technical terms cannot easily be avoided in a speech to laymen, care must be taken to define the terms and to illustrate them by analogy or otherwise. In sum, the spoken word must be somewhat lighter in content than an equivalent presentation in writing.

Illustration and Narrative

The loss of technical detail is compensated in speech by generous fleshing out with human interest material. This includes especially anecdote, narrative, and concrete illustration. Such material is suitable for the beginning and the end, and as an accompaniment to each major point in the speech. This technique permits the listener time to savor and absorb each idea in its turn.

The more pertinent and interesting the material, the more effective it is. Narrative is especially recommended for its ability to hold the audience. When the narrative is personal or humorous, the interest is even keener.

Organizational Pattern

Because of the difficulties of listening, the organization of a speech must necessarily be simple. The listener must know almost from the start the purpose of the speech and the direction in which the speaker intends to take him. He must then be aware of each step in the presentation and its relation to the others as he is carried forward to the conclusion. The pattern should be easy to follow as, for example, the problem—the solution; causes—effects; advantages—disadvantages; and plenty of time should be taken to introduce each part and show its relation to the others. In this task topic and transitional statements, enumeration, and summaries can be extremely useful.

Beginning and Ending

Time is needed to get the attention of the audience and gain their interest. An anecdote or analogy is useful for this purpose. The speaker must also use the opening to clarify his purpose, show the importance of his subject to his listeners, and perhaps give some history or background and establish his authority to deal with the subject. Sometimes the use of a large card or projection bearing the title of his talk is helpful. This may be followed by another visual listing the points the speaker intends to cover. In this way the pattern of the talk can be established firmly in the listeners' minds and their comprehension improved. The closing is best given to a summary, or a list of recommendations and an urge to action. A simple "thank you" may be added or, if a question period is to follow, the speaker may say, "Now I'll be glad to answer your questions."

CONFERENCE PARTICIPATION

The conference is gaining widespread popularity as a basic tool for accomplishing the communication objectives of an organization.[2] It serves not only the needs of the organization, but those of the participants as well, for it provides abundant opportunities for individual development, personal recognition, human interaction, and the acquisition of information. In addition, each group usually has a self-perpetuating function which may involve (1) electing officers, (2) adopting rules for its own conduct, (3) maintaining records, and (4) giving recognition to those who serve it well, as through a gift, a citation, a vote of thanks, a testimonial dinner.

The ability to express yourself on the platform is a desirable goal and should be developed. On the other hand, for every opportunity to give a stand-up speech, you will have perhaps fifty to engage in group discussion. Such discussion can seem deceptively easy because of the informal environment, but

[2] Zelko, p. 33.

actually it demands much of both the leader and the participants if the desired outcome is to be achieved.

Conference Objectives and Patterns

The outcome of a meeting will depend on its objective and the steps taken to achieve that objective. In general terms, a meeting may be called for the purpose of instruction, problem solving, or persuasion.

Instruction. Attendees come to learn about new administrative procedures, changes in organizational personnel, and new developments in their professional or technical specialty. All briefing and training sessions are included in this category. The customary sequence follows these lines:

1. The subject is announced
   - Value explained
   - Interest aroused
2. Information is developed
   - Presentation by leader
   - Contributions from group
   - Use of visual aids, cases, role playing, etc.
3. Acceptance is sought
   - Questions raised and answered
   - Understanding promoted
4. Applications are discussed
   - Uses of information explained
   - Follow-up procedures announced
   - Summary and conclusion

Problem solving. An administrator may seek the advice of his peers or subordinates before making a decision. A committee or other group may meet to make decisions for which the whole group is responsible. Two sides with opposing views—labor and management, for example—may get together to reach a settlement. In such instances a deliberative pattern is followed.

1. The problem or difficulty is exposed
   - Its origin
   - Its timeliness
   - Its importance
2. The problem is analyzed
   - The issues separated and defined
   - Attitudes considered
   - Questions raised
3. Possible solutions are proposed
   - Brainstorming (uninhibited suggestions) encouraged
   - Criteria for solutions established
   - Most likely alternatives weighed
4. Best solutions are arrived at and tested
   - Critical examination encouraged
   - Operation and application determined
5. A decision is made

Persuasion. When persuasion is the objective, the meeting becomes a marketplace for ideas, services, or products. Here advocates plead their cause in one-sided presentations. Sales representatives and advertising agencies hold persuasive meetings with clients and prospective clients. Diplomats, politicians, attorneys, executives, creative people, and other advocates use similar techniques to "sell" their ideas. Their meetings follow a pattern similar to that used in sales writing.

1. Attention and interest are aroused
2. The need is shown
   - Appeals to reason
   - Appeals to the emotions
3. The idea, product, or service is presented as a way of meeting the need
   - Description
   - Models and other visual aids
   - Practical applications
4. Belief is instilled
   - Logical reasoning
   - Testimony
   - Demonstration
5. Questions and objections are resolved
6. Action is urged

Duties of Leaders and Conferees

Any conference will be a better conference if the leader and other participants know their roles and exercise them competently.

The leader performs these duties:

1. He makes advance arrangements. These include setting the goals of the meeting, preparing the program, attending to the physical arrangements, and sending out announcements of the meeting. Whether or not the leader has any control over the selection of the participants, he will study the roster carefully and, if he considers it necessary, ask particular individuals to be prepared with certain types of data.

2. He starts the conference and keeps it moving toward its objectives. Thus he introduces the subject of the meeting, establishes the procedure with the consent of the group, and directs the discussion. Occasionally, he may ask a question; at other times he will attempt to find relationships in seemingly disparate ideas. He will also make frequent summaries as he helps the group reach valid conclusions within the alloted time.

3. He maintains a firm but friendly rein on the proceedings. The leader should always be in control of the situation, curbing conflicts and rivalries among the participants and preventing any single member of the group from talking too long. Throughout, however, he should be friendly and informal, and avoid giving the impression of coercion. Because of his position of leadership, his suggestions or opinions may carry considerable weight; for that reason he should avoid expressing his personal views in the hope that they will come from someone else in the group. If they do not, he may offer an idea in the form of a question, for example, "Should we be concerned with the effects on our suppliers?" Or he may attribute an idea to someone else, as in "One of our executives has suggested. . . ." Thus he can promote a view without seeming to exert undue pressure.

4. He follows through. It is the leader's responsibility to see that the decisions and recommendations of the group are carried out or communicated to the concerned individuals. This may entail merely distributing the minutes or other report of the meeting, or delegating responsibility for follow-up action, or making arrangements for conferences with those whose further help is required. He will then report back to the original group on the progress that has been made. In this way, the results of the meeting will not be dissipated, as so often happens, with resulting cynicism about the usefulness of all meetings. The importance of follow-up suggests that the possible implementation of the group's decisions be carefully considered before a meeting is called.

The responsibilities by the leader are complemented by those of the conferees. James N. Holm offers these suggestions for productive participation:[3]

1. Be prompt and regular in attendance.
2. Realize that the conference belongs to you, and its success depends in part on you.
3. Enter enthusiastically into the conference, giving freely of your experience.
4. Stick to the point and problem.
5. Say what you think, but don't make speeches.
6. Keep your remarks impersonal and free from prejudice.
7. Listen attentively to understand others.
8. Keep an inquiring mind; appreciate the views of others.
9. Avoid monopolizing the discussion.
10. Assist in reaching conclusions.
11. Ask questions freely.
12. Be a good sport when the discussion goes against you.

SPEAKING FROM MANUSCRIPT

Speeches on formal occasions are often read from manuscript. The written speech permits the communication of complex ideas and technical material with great precision and with the most effective organization and choice of words. Slides and other visual aids can also be woven into the speech more smoothly than when delivery is extemporaneous. When exact timing is important and when there is danger of misunderstanding or misquotation, the manuscript speech is especially desirable.

Since there is bound to be a loss of spontaneity in the delivery from manuscript, the speaker must seek to minimize the loss. Nothing is so dull as words spoken weakly, monotonously, and too rapidly, and with the speaker's face buried in the script before him. The suggestions that follow are intended to give the speech maximum effect:

[3] *Productive Speaking for Business and the Professions* (Boston: Allyn & Bacon, 1967), pp. 278–283.

1. Have the speech typed, double-spaced, on one side of 5½ by 8½ file cards held horizontally. Number the cards prominently in the upper right. The shallow depth of the cards will help you keep your head up and maintain eye contact with your audience.
2. Rehearse the speech thoroughly before you get on the platform. Determine where the stresses and pauses should be placed and which phrases may be read fairly rapidly and which others should be read more slowly for emphasis. To indicate stresses and pauses, mark the manuscript as shown in Figure 16-1. With the help of the marked manuscript, you should be able to control your delivery so that you never run out of breath.
3. When you get on the platform, face your audience. Begin when you have their attention. It is always good to have some informal remarks so that you can start without reference to your manuscript. An alternative is to memorize the first paragraph or so, so that you may have the advantage of eye contact with your audience at this important juncture. As you continue, you will find that the better you know your manuscript, the more often you will be able to glance away from it and look directly at your audience. You may also find it possible to depart from the manuscript occasionally in order to introduce, informally, some narrative or brief elaboration of a point in the script.
4. A lectern, or high stand, for your manuscript is probably best because it permits the least bending over. Even though it prevents movement on

> Like óther áreas,|the Wést enjóys todáy|the económic bénefits|from thóse résources|it has devéloped--|and has encóuntered álso|the environméntal|and sócial problems| assóciated with rápid grówth. | In fúture years,| Wéstern státes|and the nátion|can derive even gréater benefits| from devélopment of the Wést's|substántial cóal,|uránium,| and shále óil reserves. | But along with thís,| there is néed|for thóughtful|and thórough plánning|to assure ór-derly grówth.|
>
> To the lasting crédit|of the Wéstern státes,|the basic appróaches|for déaling with grówth|are being crè-ated|and útilized. . . .

FIG. 16-1. *Portion of a speech manuscript marked for stresses and pauses. (From "Developing Western Energy Resources," by Randall Meyer, President, Exxon Company, U.S.A.)*

the platform, it is better than fumbling with sheets or cards held in one's hands.

5. Following your marked manuscript, consciously pace your delivery so that you speak distinctly and with enough force and variety in speed and pitch to bring out most effectively the meaning you want to impart.

LISTENING

Speaking presumes the presence of a listener. But the listener might as well be a wall if he does not attend to what is being said. Such a condition poses a problem for the speaker, of course, but it also poses a problem for the listener. In recent years considerable attention has been given to the relation of listening to communication effectiveness and to techniques for improving one's listening capability.

When a person does not listen, he shuts himself off from incoming ideas, including feedback from his own utterances, and thus reduces his ability to make sound judgments. Moreover, his lack of receptivity is communicated to the speaker, with a resulting impairment of the latter's performance and the creation of an atmosphere inimical to good relations. Listening, however, is not merely hearing; it is a state of receptivity that permits understanding of what is heard and grants the listener full partnership in the communication process.

Good listening thus begins with an open mind. It requires also a willingness to give up temporarily the role of sender and assume that of receiver. This may be an especially difficult assignment for those in positions of authority, but it is also difficult for everyone else. Most people speak at the rate of about 125 words per minute, yet it is believed that the brain can process information at about 500 words per minute.[4] Listening can thus be a tedious chore, with plenty of time for the mind to wander. The poorer the speaker, and the less organized his remarks, the greater the tendency of the listener to withhold attention. Nevertheless, listening skill can be developed. These specific suggestions are offered:

1. Concentrate on what the speaker is saying. Look directly at him and attend to his speech as well as his movement and gestures. Regardless of any hindrance he may put in your way through bad expression or poor organization of ideas, try to understand the speaker's objectives and relate his statements to that objective. Don't make the mistake of turning over in your mind your own remarks or rebuttal while the speaker is talking. Obviously, you can't concentrate on your thoughts and the speaker's at the same time. Another suggestion: If you must take notes, make them brief or you will find yourself missing the speaker's second and third points while you are still writing up his first.

2. Learn from the speaker. An important part of your job as listener is to evaluate what you hear and judge its usefulness to you. What is the speaker trying to tell you? If you have trouble in understanding him, is it because he is

[4] Ralph G. Nichols, "Listening Is a 10-Part Skill," *Nation's Business*, July 1957.

unclear or because you are not paying close attention? If the exposition is tough or dry, don't be put off; it may have considerable value to you. On the other hand, be alert for flaws in fact or reasoning. Also examine the speech for clues to the speaker's motives, character, and background. They may help to explain what the words themselves do not. Finally, look to the speaker for feedback from your own utterances so that you will learn to what extent you have succeeded in getting *your* points across.

3. *Listen without bias.* There is a tendency to "turn off" or even show hostility toward a speaker who says things with which we do not agree or which threaten our complacency or security. As a good listener, you should control your feelings at least until you have heard the speaker out. You may find that your views or policies have been wrong and that, benefiting from the speaker's remarks, you can take some action to improve your position. Even if the speaker does not eventually change your mind, you will by your patience and courtesy avoid antagonizing him.

4. *Act on what you hear.* Just as you want feedback from your remarks, so the speaker wants feedback from his. You can provide the feedback by your attentiveness, of course, but also by a nod, smile, laugh, frown, or other appropriate gesture or sound. There may also be an opportunity to ask a question or pay a compliment. From another point of view, you can also take action on your own behalf. If you have listened at all, it should have been for the purpose of benefiting from the speaker's remarks. What has he said that is of value? What can you do to capitalize on your newly acquired knowledge? You may make a decision to invest in some stock, engage in further study, write to a friend, make a suggestion to management, or issue an order to the workers under your direction. Whatever you do, your role as listener will have had a useful and perhaps personally rewarding result.

SUMMARY

Speech is such an important part of business communication that even a writer should be aware of its possibilities. The structured speech settings in organizations include interviews, small-group conferences, and large meetings. The interviews seek and provide information, or help to settle a grievance or solve a problem. Small-group meetings are mainly informal gatherings designed to pool ideas, solve problems, or make recommendations to management. A basic form of the small group is the committee, with a chairman as head. Subcommittees may be designated to perform specific tasks. Large meetings are assemblies of employees or other groups usually called together by management. Feedback here is minimal, though questions from the audience may be invited. Panels of speakers may be used to present different aspects of a problem.

Public settings—those outside the organization—include trade and professional meetings and provide the businessman with opportunities to give his ideas a wider hearing than they could otherwise obtain. Group discussion, panel, lecture, and radio and television broadcasts are only some of the forums available to public speakers.

A speaker in any setting should be well prepared in his subject and be mindful of the audience he is addressing. In delivering his talk, he should speak loud enough to be heard, articulate clearly, avoid a monotone, maintain eye contact with his audience, stand straight, and use gesture and body movement only to add emphasis or meaning. Visual and audio aids give additional dimensions to the speaker's presentation, and he should select and use them with care. They should have a direct and specific relation to the purpose of the speech, should be clearly visible or audible, and should be easy to use without fumbling. The equipment should be checked in advance, as should the location of electric outlets and the facilities for darkening the room if necessary.

The language of speech is usually less formal than that of writing. It is plain, and favors contractions, colloquialisms, and occasional slang. Personal references to oneself and others may provide additional interest. Because of the fleeting nature of the spoken word, technical details must be limited and the content of the speech must be somewhat lighter than an equivalent presentation in writing. The loss should be made up by a generous use of anecdote, narrative, and concrete illustration. To help the listener, the speaker should also use a simple pattern of organization and make sure that the audience knows at every step what he is up to. A good beginning is especially helpful in showing the listener the path on which he is to be taken. The close should summarize the main points and, if appropriate, recommend some form of action.

As opposed to the platform speech, conference participation involves the speaker in a far greater degree of interaction with the audience. Conferences may be called for instructional purposes, problem solving, or persuasion. A conference leader makes advance arrangements for the meeting, keeps the meeting moving toward its objectives, and follows through after the meeting to make sure its recommendations are carried out. A good participant arrives promptly, engages actively in the discussion, but also listens to others, asks questions, and assists in reaching final conclusions.

Occasionally, circumstances will dictate that a speech be read from manuscript. Despite the need to read, the speaker should make every effort to maintain eye contact with his audience. Marking the manuscript for stresses and pauses will aid in the delivery.

Listening is the counterpart of speaking. Cultivating good listening habits adds to one's knowledge and helps in the formation of sound judgments. A good listener concentrates closely on what the speaker is saying, examines the speech for the information and clues it contains, keeps an open mind, and responds in ways that provide feedback to the speaker and, possibly, profit to himself.

PROBLEMS

1. Engage in one of the following role-playing situations with other members of your class whom we shall call B and C.
   (*a*) B is a prospective employer. He has already received from you your resume and

job application (Chapter 7) and has called you in for an interview. Submit to the interview.

(*b*) You and B are at the opposite ends of a telephone line. You would like to enlist the aid of B, a fellow student, in soliciting funds from recent alumni for your college alumni fund. All contributed small sums last year. You offer to supply B with a list of ten names to follow up by telephone. The alumni in question have already received several mail solicitations but have not yet responded.

(*c*) Now assume the role of B as described in Problem 1(*b*) above, and make one of the telephone calls to C, an alumnus on your list. C tells you that he is disgusted with the admissions policies of the college. He had recommended a friend's brother for admission, but the application was denied. The boy's scholastic average may have been a little low, C tells you, but he had qualities of character and determination that would unquestionably have made him a desirable student.

2. From the list of "Selected Books for Reference" following this chapter (or from some other source recommended by your instructor), choose some technical point of severely limited scope and, in a three-minute talk from notes only, explain it to your classmates. Use the blackboard, charts, or other means of communicating visually.

3. Sit with a panel of several classmates—one of them acting as chairman—and present to the class a symposium on some current topic of general interest. The subject should be divided so that each member of the panel covers one particular segment. At the end of the formal presentations, which should take about five minutes for each speaker, members of the panel should submit to questions from the class.

4. Choose an idea that is likely to be unpopular with your classmates, and in a five-minute presentation, try to win some degree of acceptance.

5. Write a 90-second editorial (about 250 words) on some subject in the news and read it assumedly for transmission on a local radio or television outlet after the evening news broadcast. Follow a persuasive pattern, progressing from attention and motivation to conviction and an urge to action.

6. Select a passage of about 300 words from a current speech, book, or article and after marking it for delivery as shown in Figure 16-1, read the passage to the class.

7. After submitting the topic to your instructor for his approval, develop an informative or persuasive speech on a subject on which you have special knowledge. Count on taking ten minutes for the presentation unless your instructor indicates otherwise. Write an outline for the speech and type it in duplicate. Give one copy to the instructor when you get up to speak and keep the other for reference as you speak. No other notes are to be used. You will, of course, be expected to employ any audio or visual aids that will help make your speech effective.

8. Your instructor will announce a subject and appoint a student to chair a class discussion. After a proper orientation, the chairman will divide the class into buzz groups. Each buzz group will select its own leader. At the conclusion of a discussion period of fifteen minutes, the leaders of the buzz groups will report the consensus of their groups. The chairman will end the meeting with a summation.

Selected Books for Reference

BUSINESS COMMUNICATION: SCOPE AND CONCEPT (CHAPTERS 1 AND 2)

BERELSON, BERNARD, and STEINER, GARY A. *Human Behavior* (Shorter Edition). New York: Harcourt Brace Jovanovich, 1967.

BERLO, DAVID K. *The Process of Communication.* New York: Holt, Rinehart and Winston, 1960.

BORMANN, ERNEST G., and others. *Interpersonal Communication in the Modern Organization.* Englewood Cliffs, N.J.: Prentice-Hall, 1969.

BRENNAN, LAWRENCE D. *Modern Communication Effectiveness.* Englewood Cliffs, N.J.: Prentice-Hall, 1962.

CAMPBELL, JAMES H., and HEPLER, HAL W. (eds.) *Dimensions in Communication: Readings.* 2d ed. Belmont, Calif.: Wadsworth, 1970.

CHERRY, COLIN. *On Human Communication.* 2d ed. Cambridge: Massachusetts Institute of Technology Press, 1966.

COFFEE, ROBERT E.; ATHOS, ANTHONY G.; and RAYNOLDS, PETER A. *Behavior in Organizations: A Multidimensional Approach.* 2d ed. Englewood Cliffs, N.J.: Prentice-Hall, 1975.

HALL, EDWARD T. *The Silent Language.* Garden City, N.Y.: Doubleday, 1959.

HANEY, WILLIAM V. *Communication and Organizational Behavior.* 3d ed. Homewood, Ill.: Richard D. Irwin, 1973.

HUSEMAN, RICHARD C.; LOGUE, CARL M.; and FRESHLEY, DWIGHT L. (eds.) *Readings in Interpersonal and Organizational Communication.* 2d ed. Boston: Holbrook Press, 1976.

LEAVITT, HAROLD J. *Managerial Psychology.* 3d ed. Chicago: University of Chicago Press, 1972.

MCLUHAN, MARSHALL. *Understanding Media: The Extensions of Man.* New York: McGraw-Hill, 1964.

MERRIHUE, WILLARD V. *Managing by Communication.* New York: McGraw-Hill, 1960.

ROGERS, EVERETT M., and AGARWALA-ROGERS, REKHA. *Communication in Organizations.* New York: The Free Press, 1976.

RUESCH, JURGEN, and BATESON, GREGORY. *Communication: The Social Matrix of Psychiatry.* New York: W. W. Norton, 1951.

SCHNEIDER, ARNOLD E.; DONAGHY, WILLIAM C.; and NEWMAN, PAMELA JANE. *Organization Communication.* New York: McGraw-Hill, 1975.

THAYER, LEE. *Communication and Communication Systems in Organization, Management, and Interpersonal Relations.* Homewood, Ill.: Richard D. Irwin, 1968.

THE LANGUAGE OF BUSINESS (CHAPTER 3)

BROWN, ROGER W. *Words and Things.* New York: The Free Press, 1958.
CHASE, STUART. *The Power of Words.* New York: Harcourt Brace Jovanovich, 1953.
FLESCH, RUDOLF. *The ABC of Style: A Guide to Plain English.* New York: Harper & Row, 1965.
GOWERS, SIR ERNEST. *Plain Words: Their ABC.* New York: Knopf, 1954.
HAYAKAWA, S. I. *Language in Thought and Action.* 3d ed. Harcourt Brace Jovanovich, 1972.
JOHNSON, WENDELL. *People in Quandaries.* New York: Harper & Row, 1946.
KEITHLEY, ERWIN M., and THOMPSON, MARGARET H. *English for Modern Business.* 3d ed. Homewood, Ill.: Richard D. Irwin, 1976.
LEE, IRVING J. *Language Habits in Human Affairs.* New York: Harper & Row, 1941.
MILLER, GEORGE A. *Language and Communication.* New York: McGraw-Hill, 1951.
PERRIN, PORTER G., and EBBITT, WILMA R. *Writer's Guide and Index to English.* 5th ed. Glenview, Ill.: Scott, Foresman, 1972.
STRUNK, WILLIAM J., and WHITE, E. B. *The Elements of Style.* 2d ed. New York: Macmillan, 1971.
U.S. General Accounting Office. *The Language of Audit Reports.* Washington, D.C.: U.S. Government Printing Office, 1957.

BUSINESS LETTERS AND REPORTS (CHAPTERS 4–12)

BECKMAN, THEODORE N., and FOSTER, RONALD S. *Credits and Collections.* 8th ed. New York: McGraw-Hill, 1969.
BROWN, LELAND. *Communicating Facts and Ideas in Business.* 2d ed. Englewood Cliffs, N.J.: Prentice-Hall, 1970.
———. *Effective Business Report Writing.* 3d ed. Englewood Cliffs, N.J.: Prentice-Hall, 1973.
EWING, DAVID. *Writing for Results in Business, Government, and the Professions.* New York: John Wiley, 1974.
GALLAGHER, WILLIAM J. *Report Writing for Management.* Reading, Mass.: Addison-Wesley, 1969.
JANIS, J. HAROLD. *The Business Research Paper: A Manual of Style.* New York: Hobbs, Dorman, 1967.
LESIKAR, RAYMOND V. *Business Communication: Theory and Application.* 3d. ed. Homewood, Ill.: Richard D. Irwin, 1976.
———. *Report Writing for Business.* 4th ed. Homewood, Ill.: Richard D. Irwin, 1973.
MEASURES, HOWARD. *Styles of Address.* 2d ed. New York: Thomas Y. Crowell, 1969.
MENNING, JACK H.; WILKINSON, CLYDE W.; and CLARKE, PETER B. *Communicating Through Letters and Reports.* 6th ed. Homewood, Ill.: Richard D. Irwin, 1976.
MEYERS, CECIL H. *Handbook of Basic Graphs: A Modern Approach.* Belmont, Calif.: Dickenson Publishing Co., 1970.
MILLER, DONALD E., and RELKIN, DONALD B. *Effective Credit and Collection Practices.* New York: Macmillan, 1970.

ROBINSON, DAVID M. *Writing Reports for Management Decisions.* Columbus, O.: Charles E. Merrill, 1969.

ROGERS, ANNA C. *Graphic Charts Handbook.* Washington, D.C.: Public Affairs Press, 1961.

SCHMID, CALVIN F. *Handbook of Graphic Presentation.* New York: Ronald Press, 1954.

SIGBAND, NORMAN B. *Communication for Management.* 2d ed. Glenview, Ill.: Scott, Foresman, 1976.

SPEAR, MARY ELEANOR. *Practical Charting Techniques.* New York: McGraw-Hill, 1969.

U.S. General Services Administration, National Archives and Records Service. *Managing Correspondence: Form and Guide Letters.* Washington, D.C.: U.S. Government Printing Office, 1974.

WOLFE, MORRIS P., and AURNER, ROBERT R. *Effective Communication in Business.* 6th ed. Cincinnati: South-Western, 1974.

PERSUASION: INFLUENCING SALES AND ATTITUDES (CHAPTERS 13–15)

BAKER, RICHARD M., and PHIFER, GREGG. *Salesmanship: Communication, Persuasion, Perception.* Boston: Allyn & Bacon, 1966.

BEARDSLEY, MONROE C. *Thinking Straight: Principles of Reasoning for Readers and Writers.* 4th ed. Englewood Cliffs, N.J.: Prentice-Hall, 1975.

BETTINGHAUS, E. O. *Persuasive Communication.* New York: Holt, Rinehart and Winston, 1968.

BROADBENT, DONALD E. *Perception and Communication.* New York: Pergamon Press, 1958.

BROWN, J. A. C. *Techniques in Persuasion.* Baltimore: Penguin Books, 1963.

CANFIELD, BERTRAND R., and MOORE, H. FRAZIER. *Public Relations: Principles, Cases, and Problems.* Homewood, Ill.: Richard D. Irwin, 1973.

EISENSON, JON; AUER, J. JEFFREY; and IRWIN, JOHN V. *The Psychology of Communication.* New York: Appleton-Century-Crofts, 1963.

FESTINGER, LEON. *A Theory of Cognitive Dissonance.* New York: Harper & Row, 1957.

HOVLAND, CARL L. (ed.) *Order of Presentation in Persuasion.* New Haven, Conn.: Yale University Press, 1958.

———; JANIS, IRVING L.; and KELLEY, HAROLD H. *Communication and Persuasion.* New Haven, Conn.: Yale University Press, 1953.

HUFF, DARRELL. *How to Lie with Statistics.* New York: W. W. Norton, 1954.

MASLOW, ABRAHAM (ed.). *Motivation and Personality.* 2d ed. New York: Harper & Row, 1970.

MINNICK, WAYNE C. *The Art of Persuasion.* 2d ed. Boston: Houghton Mifflin, 1968.

ROBERTSON, THOMAS S. *Consumer Behavior.* Glenview, Ill.: Scott, Foresman, 1970.

SCHRAMM, WILBUR (ed.). *The Process and Effects of Mass Communication.* Urbana, Ill.: University of Illinois Press, 1954.

SIMONS, HERBERT W. *Persuasion: Understanding, Practice, and Analysis.* Reading, Mass.: Addison-Wesley, 1976.

STEINBERG, CHARLES S. *The Creation of Consent: Public Relations in Practice.* New York: Hastings House, 1975.

SPEECH COMMUNICATION (CHAPTER 16)

AUGER, B. Y. *How to Run Better Business Meetings.* New York: American Management Association, 1973.

DUKER, SAM (ed.). *Listening: Readings.* New York: Scarecrow Press, 1966.

FLUHARTY, GEORGE W., and ROSS, HAROLD R. *Public Speaking.* New York: Harper & Row, 1966.

HOWELL, WILLIAM S. and BORMANN, ERNEST G. *Presentational Speaking for Business and the Professions.* New York: Harper & Row, 1971.

MILLER, GERALD R. *An Introduction to Speech Communication.* Indianapolis: Bobbs-Merrill, 1972.

MORRISEY, GEORGE L. *Effective Business and Technical Presentations.* Reading, Mass.: Addison-Wesley, 1975.

NICHOLS, G., and STEVENS, LEONARD A. *Are You Listening?* New York: McGraw-Hill, 1957.

OLBRICHT, THOMAS H. *Informative Speaking.* Glenview, Ill.: Scott, Foresman, 1968.

TACEY, WILLIAM S. *Business and Professional Speaking.* 2d ed. Dubuque: William C. Brown, 1975.

ZELKO, HAROLD P. *The Business Conference: Participation and Leadership.* New York: McGraw-Hill, 1969.

Style Manual

This manual is a concise statement, with examples, of the rules of business composition. It may be used for self-study and review as well as for revising papers. A complete key to the rules will be found inside the back cover. There you will also find a list of correction symbols, which the instructor may use either in place of or in conjunction with the rule numbers.

When you find a rule number or correction symbol on your paper, your instructor is signifying need for improvement. Look up the rule in each case, and—where indicated—read the related pages in the body of the text. In this way you will discover how to make the necessary changes. Then revise or rewrite the paper as your instructor directs.

No person in business achieves success as a writer without a great deal of practice. Whether in writing or rewriting, your own efforts will be more rewarding if you let this manual help you.

MESSAGE EFFECTIVENESS

Attitude

1. Consider the impression on the reader.

1a. Obtain the reader's point of view (pp. 88–89).

NOT: We need your new address for our records.
BUT: Will you please let us have your new address so that we will know where to send your dividend checks.

1b. Where appropriate, use a direct, personal approach (pp. 72–74, 89–90).

NOT: Next week our customers will receive . . .
BUT: Next week you will receive . . .

NOT: It has been learned that . . .
BUT: We have learned that . . .

1c. Express yourself naturally. Avoid clichés (pp. 62–63, 91–93).

NOT: Receipt is hereby acknowledged of yours of recent date.
BUT: We have received your recent letter.

NOT: We will leave no stone unturned to find a solution for this problem.
BUT: We will do all we can to find a solution to this problem.

1d. Favor affirmative ideas (pp. 61–62, 96–97).

NOT: We trust there will be no recurrence of this unfortunate incident.
BUT: We assure you that we will try to handle future transactions more efficiently.

1e. Show courtesy (p. 93).

NOT: We have your check.
BUT: Thank you for your check.

NOT: Surely you must have known that the price has since been increased.
BUT: As you know, our prices have since been increased.

1f. Phrase "touchy" ideas tactfully (pp. 93, 95–96).

NOT: You obviously ignored our instructions to return the goods by air freight.
BUT: Our instructions were to return the goods by air freight.

1g. Be sincere. Do not bluff or exaggerate (p. 96).

NOT: You couldn't do better at ten times the price.
BUT: Comparison will show that our power lathe outmatches the performance of any other in its price range.

Clearness

2. Write so that the reader understands you.

2a. Be sure that you know your subject well enough to explain it to the reader. Research the subject thoroughly and familiarize yourself with its terminology. It is usually a good idea to have more information than you can use.

2b. Keep sentences reasonably short and simple (pp. 67–68).

FAULTY: The first requirement of good internal control is incorporated in the present procedure in that each office maintains a list of institutions to be examined and it is the responsibility of the Assistant Chief Examiner in each office to see that the examinations are conducted except in those instances where responsibility has been delegated to a subordinate who is responsible for assigning examiners, as in the case of currency exchanges and credit unions. (One sentence of 73 words.)

IMPROVED: The first requirement of good internal control is incorporated in the present procedure. Each office maintains a list of institutions to be examined, and it is the responsibility of the Assistant Chief Examiner to see that the examinations are conducted. In some instances, however—notably those involving currency exchanges and credit unions—the responsibility for assigning examiners has been delegated to a subordinate. (Three sentences averaging 21 words each.)

2c. Use specific words (pp. 51–53).

NOT: Delivery will be delayed for a time because of operational difficulties.
BUT: Delivery will be delayed until April 24 because of a shortage of valves needed for the assembly.

2d. Use exact words (pp. 49–51).

NOT: Thank you for your prompt remittance of the information we asked for.
BUT: Thank you for sending us so promptly the information we asked for.

2e. Avoid ambiguity (p. 51).

NOT: This chair will eliminate tired employees.
BUT: This chair will reduce fatigue.

2f. Adapt to the vocabulary of the reader (pp. 53–57).

Simple but exact words are usually best. When, however, you are writing to persons on a technical subject in their own area of interest, you may find it desirable to employ the specialized vocabulary they use themselves.

Conciseness

3. Practice economy in phrasing.

3a. Leave out unnecessary details (pp. 65–67, 99–101).

NOT: If you hadn't reported the loss so promptly, we would be unable to do anything for you. However, in your case, we are glad to tell you . . .
BUT: Because you were so prompt in reporting the loss, we are glad to tell you . . .

3b. Don't repeat (p. 65).

NOT: We have your letter of May 10 asking how to transfer ownership of your certificates. In order to effect the transfer, it will be necessary for you to . . .
BUT: In order to transfer ownership of the certificates mentioned in your letter of May 10, it will be necessary for you to . . .

3c. Shorten wordy phrases, and eliminate unnecessary ones (pp. 100–101.)

NOT: Your check in the amount of $26 payable to the order of James Smith . . .
BUT: Your check for $26 payable to James Smith . . .

NOT: I wish to take this opportunity to thank you for . . .
BUT: Thank you for . . .

NOT: We regret the inconvenience caused you in this matter.
BUT: We regret the inconvenience caused you.

Coherence

4. Organize ideas for easy comprehension.

4a. Put ideas in logical and effective order. (See "Order" in Index.)

Have a plan before you write, and follow it through. For long compositions, make a formal outline. In every case, use the order that will most effectively help the message accomplish its purpose.

4b. Show the relationship between ideas (pp. 237–242).

As the composition permits, use an introductory statement, informative headings and subheadings, topic sentences, transitional words and phrases, and parallel structure.

Development

5. Cover the important points thoroughly enough to accomplish the purpose of the message.

5a. Divide the subject systematically into its classes or parts, and develop each in turn (pp. 214–222).

> Traditionally, the markets for steel have fostered fundamentally two types of companies: those which produce in sufficient volume to meet the incredible demands of certain broad segments of the economy and those which produce smaller volumes of specialty steels required in both large and small industries throughout the economy. The first . . . The second . . . —Steelways

5b. Expand and clarify ideas by the use of definition, details, examples, and comparison and contrast (pp. 231–237).

5c. Give little or no space to the less important ideas. Avoid negative ideas and any others that defeat the purpose of the message.

Force

6. Let the important ideas stand out.

6a. Stick to a single main idea (pp. 97–98, 257–258).

Competing ideas dissipate the reader's attention and weaken response. Make sure that all the details of the message contribute to your one big purpose. Suppress any unrelated ideas.

6b. Attract attention from the beginning. (See "Beginning" in Index.)

Find a point of contact with the reader's interests and hold his attention firmly as you proceed to the core of the message.

6c. End your message decisively. (See "Ending" in Index.)

If there is something you want the reader to do, tell him specifically what it is. If no action is necessary, you may end by echoing the theme of the message or by adding a summary sentence or paragraph. Short, informative messages often require no formal close at all.

6d. Use fresh, vivid language (pp. 62–65, 72–75).

You may achieve force by the use of concrete nouns and verbs, figures of speech, and direct, uncomplicated sentences. Avoid weak phrasing especially in the beginning and end.

SENTENCE EFFECTIVENESS

Simplicity

7. Strive for simplicity and smoothness in sentence structure.

7a. Regulate sentence length (pp. 67–68).

Use short sentences for attention and action; longer sentences for conciliation, persuasion, or exposition. Variety in length adds interest, but try to keep average length to 18–22 words and avoid single sentences of 40 words or more, especially when the structure is complex.

7b. Maintain sentence unity (pp. 69–70).

Separate unrelated ideas or establish relationship by subordinating one idea to another.

NOT: We are glad to have you as a customer, and please call on us whenever we can be of help.
BUT: We are glad to have you as a customer. Please call on us whenever we can be of help.

NOT: The company does an import and export business and was organized in 1970 under the laws of New York.
BUT: The company, which does an import and export business, was organized in 1970 under the laws of New York.

7c. Avoid unnecessary shifts in grammatical subject or structure.

NOT: Any information you *can give* [active] us *will be appreciated* [passive] and we *assure* [active] you that discretion *will be exercised* [passive] in its use. [Note differences in the underlined subjects and the indiscriminate use of passive- and active-voice verbs.]
BUT: We *will appreciate* any information you *can give* us and [we] *assure* you that we *will use* it with discretion. [Use of the active voice throughout permits retention of the subject *we* in the dominant clauses.]

7d. Put coordinate ideas in parallel structure (pp. 71–72, 240–242).

NOT: Check each account and making sure it is a good risk.
BUT: Check each account and make sure it is a good risk.
OR: Check each account, making sure it is a good risk.

7e. Favor the active voice (p. 69).

NOT: The canceled check was returned by us to you by air mail.
BUT: We returned the canceled check to you by air mail.

Order and Connection

8. Put words in clear relationship to each other.

8a. Keep related parts together (pp. 69–71).

NOT: We would appreciate your sending us permission to pay this bill by mail or cable. [Meaning not intended.]
BUT: We would appreciate your sending us permission by mail or cable to pay this bill. [Meaning intended.]

8b. Avoid "dangling" sentence elements.

A "dangler" is a modifying phrase or clause that does not seem to relate to the word it should or—in some instances—to any other word in the sentence. Especially when you begin a sentence with a phrase containing a verb form ending in *-ing,* be sure that the phrase logically modifies the following subject.

NOT: Knowing your interest in the test results, you will shortly receive the complete report from us. [Misrelated.]
BUT: Knowing your interest in the test results, we will shortly send you the complete report.

NOT: While visiting your Akron plant, a number of instances of pilfering were reported to us. [Misrelated.]
BUT: While visiting your Akron plant, we were told of a number of instances of pilfering.
OR: While we were visiting your Akron plant, a number of instances of pilfering were reported to us.

NOT: As agents for the Atlantic Steamship Line, full refunds are granted on reservations canceled two weeks before the sailing date. [Related to a word not expressed in the sentence.]
BUT: As agents for the Atlantic Steamship Line, we are authorized to grant full refunds on reservations canceled two weeks before the sailing date.

NOT: The need for good English doesn't end after being hired. [Related to a word not expressed in the sentence.]
BUT: The need for good English doesn't end after you are hired.

8c. Use exact connectives to show the relationship between ideas (pp. 69–70, 239).

NOT: The weather was bad and we lost a lot of business.
BUT: We lost a lot of business because the weather was bad.
OR: The bad weather cost us a lot of business.

Emphasis

9. Begin and end sentences with important words. See especially that there is no letdown in the close.

NOT: There are three courses open to us.
BUT: Three courses are open to us.

NOT: The figures were unfortunately transposed, as you can see.
BUT: As you can see, the figures were unfortunately transposed.

Grammatical Completeness

10. See that every sentence is a complete and independent grammatical unit.

10a. Do not use a fragment (a dependent sentence element) as a sentence. Rephrase the fragment to make it a grammatically complete sentence, or join the fragment to another sentence.

NOT: During the last five years, sales of white shirts have declined by 20 per cent. While sales of colored shirts have increased by 34 per cent. [The underscored words form a subordinate clause, not a grammatically complete sentence.]
BUT: During the past five years, sales of white shirts have declined by 20 per cent. At the same time, sales of colored shirts have increased by 34 per cent. [The substitution of a prepositional phrase for the subordinate conjunction *while* now makes the underscored word group above a complete sentence.]
OR: During the past five years, sales of white shirts have declined by 20 per cent, while sales of colored shirts have increased by 34 per cent. [The subordinate clause is joined to the preceding main clause, to which it is related.]

Note: Fragmentary sentences are sometimes used for stylistic effect, especially in advertising copy.

> In this gray flannel world, you're glad you're born female. And you dress in Diane's sleek, frankly feminine clothing, so they'll never forget the woman underneath. The fit, the perfection. Because Diane's dresses are designed to slim and skim the body. The fabric, an Italian acrylic that feels like a silky second skin. The print, a brilliant starburst on the reversible wrap, in black or bright blue and white. . . .—*Bonwit Teller*

10b. Use a period or semicolon, not a comma, between independent clauses *not* joined by a coordinate conjunction (*and, but, for, or, nor*).

NOT: The colored seal on genuine notes has sharp sawtooth points around the rim, on bogus money the points are usually broken off.
BUT: The colored seal on genuine notes has sharp sawtooth points. On bogus money the points are usually broken off.
OR: The colored seal on genuine notes has sharp sawtooth points; on bogus money the points are usually broken off.

10c. Do not omit words necessary for grammatical completeness.

NOT: The goods were ordered on May 9 and confirmation [*were?*] received on May 13.
BUT: The goods were ordered on May 9 and confirmation was received on May 13.
OR: The order was sent on May 9 and confirmation received on May 13. [*Was* is understood.]
OR: We sent the order on May 9 and received confirmation on May 13.

NOT: You cannot compare conditions in 1950 with today.
BUT: You cannot compare conditions in 1950 with those of today.

GRAMMATICAL AGREEMENT

Subject and Verb

11. Make the verb agree with its subject.

11a. See that the verb agrees with its subject in person.

NOT: I, like everyone else, is expected to participate.
BUT: I, like everyone else, am expected to participate.

NOT: It is I who is going.
BUT: It is I who am going. [*Who,* like its antecedent *I*, is in the first person. See Rule 12.]

11b. See that the verb agrees with its subject in number.

(1) Do not be influenced by words that come between the subject and the verb.

NOT: The retention of a major portion of net earnings have helped build up working capital.
BUT: The retention of a major portion of net earnings has helped build up working capital.

(2) Singular subjects joined by *and* generally take plural verbs. An exception is made when the subjects stand for the same thing.

RIGHT: Our review of the situation and our recommendation for dealing with it were forwarded to management.
RIGHT: A skilled technician and administrator is needed in this position.

(3) When subjects are joined by *or* or *nor,* the verb agrees with the nearer one. If awkwardness results, recast the sentence.

NOT: Neither the fans nor the air conditioner were working.
BUT: Neither the fans nor the air conditioner was working.
OR: Neither the air conditioner nor the fans were working.

(4) A modifying phrase beginning with words like *including, together with, as well as* and *in addition to* does not influence the number of the subject.

NOT: The engineer as well as the plant manager were consulted.
BUT: The engineer as well as the plant manager was consulted.

(5) Pronouns in the class of *either, neither, each, everyone, anyone, anything,* and *someone* regularly take singular verbs.

RIGHT: Neither of them is ready to show his hand.
Everybody was agreeable to the change in plan.
Anyone is eligible to join.

(6) The pronoun *none* takes either a singular or plural verb depending on the sense.

RIGHT: When an exception to the rules was sought, none was found.
None of the files are now available to us.

(7) A subject modified by the words *each* or *every* is singular.

RIGHT: Each one of you has his responsibilities.
Every discharged worker was given a terminal interview.

(8) A verb following a relative pronoun agrees in number with the antecedent of the pronoun. (The antecedent is usually the immediately preceding noun.)

RIGHT: He is one of the six employees *who* have been with us for more than forty years.
RIGHT: His is one of the few engineering firms *that* have been approved by the U.S. Government.

(9) Singular collective nouns (the names of groups of things) and nouns denoting fixed quantities usually take singular verbs. An exception is made in the instance of a collective noun representing the members of the group as individual participants.

RIGHT: The committee has issued its report.
Ten dollars is not much to pay for a good stapling machine.
BUT (ALSO RIGHT): The committee are divided on the solution to the problem.
The full dozen were intact.

Note: The number generally takes a singular verb; *a number,* a plural verb.

RIGHT: The number of overdue accounts is small.
A number of problems are still unsolved.

(10) In some constructions, the subject follows the verb.

NOT: There is six boxes missing from the shipment.
BUT: There are six boxes missing from the shipment.
OR (BETTER): Six boxes are missing from the shipment.

(11) A predictate noun (a noun following the verb *to be* and representing the same thing as the subject) does not affect the agreement of the subject and verb.

NOT: The cause of the accident were three loose bolts.
BUT: The cause of the accident was three loose bolts.

(12) You may have some difficulty in determining whether some words are singular or plural. Whenever in doubt, consult your dictionary.

RIGHT: The news is good.
The acoustics are bad.
Statistics is a branch of mathematics.
The statistics are incontrovertible.

Pronoun and Antecedent

12. Make the pronoun agree with its antecedent in person, number, and gender.

12a. When the sentence contains several nouns, be sure the pronoun agrees with its real antedecent.

NOT: If you want the gist of the complaints, I will give them to you.

BUT: If you want the gist of the complaints, I will give it to you.

12b. A pronoun relating to a singular noun or pronoun should also be singular. [See Rules 11b(5)–11b(9).]

NOT: Everyone is reporting to their own supervisor.
BUT: Everyone is reporting to his own supervisor.

NOT: The task force is almost ready to make their report.
BUT: The task force is almost ready to make its report.

Note: Although it is inconsistent to refer to a collective noun as singular and plural in the same context, the practice is common in business in order to avoid awkwardness or the necessity of making corrections in copy already dictated.

AWKWARD: The B. C. Gray Company has inquired [singular] about the new line. We wrote *it* [singular] that it would not be ready until September 22.
ACCEPTABLE: The B. C. Gray Company has inquired [singular] about the new line. We wrote *them* [plural] that it would not be ready until September 22.
CORRECT: The B. C. Gray Company have inquired [plural] about the new line. We wrote *them* [plural] that it would not be ready until September 22.

12c. When both a singular and plural antecedent are joined by *or* or *nor*, the pronoun preferably agrees with the nearer one.

QUESTIONABLE: I suggest you ask either the auditors or Mr. Thomas for their advice.

AWKWARD: I suggest you ask either the auditors or Mr. Thomas for his advice.

BETTER: I suggest you ask either Mr. Thomas or the auditors for their advice.

OR: I suggest you ask either the auditors or Mr. Thomas for advice.

Reference of Pronouns

13. See that every pronoun has a clear and definite antecedent.

13a. The reference of the pronoun should be unambiguous.

AMBIGUOUS: Mr. Wells said that while Mr. Farmer was agreeable, he remained unconvinced of his sincerity. [*Who* remained unconvinced of *whose* sincerity?]

BETTER: Mr. Wells said that Mr. Farmer was agreeable but not convincing in his sincerity.

13b. Avoid using a pronoun that refers not to a noun antecedent but to a whole clause or sentence. Either give the pronoun a noun antecedent or recast the sentence.

VAGUE: Tooling costs for a new model are extraordinarily high, which is necessary to ensure maximum efficiency in production.

ALSO VAGUE: Tooling costs for a new model are extraordinarily high. This is necessary to ensure maximum efficiency in production.

BETTER: (1) Tooling costs for a new model are extraordinarily high—an expense [which is] necessary to ensure maximum efficiency in production.
(2) Tooling costs for a new model are extraordinarily high. This expense is necessary to ensure maximum efficiency in production.
(3) A new model requires extraordinarily high tooling costs to ensure maximum efficiency in production.

13c. Avoid using a pronoun that has no antecedent.

NOT: In Dallas, they keep a complete stock of the bearings.
BUT: Our Dallas warehouse keeps a complete stock of the bearings.

13d. Avoid using a pronoun to refer to a word in subordinate syntax, that is, one that has a grammatically minor role and therefore does not stand out as an antecedent.

NOT: He had no experience with machine dictation, but he bought one anyway. [*Machine* is only a qualifying word and is therefore not immediately recognized as an antecedent.]
BUT: He had no experience with a dictating machine, but he bought one anyway.

14. See that the case of every noun and pronoun correctly expresses the grammatical relationship of the word to the rest of the sentence.

The three cases are the *nominative, possessive,* and *objective.* Nouns and many pronouns have the same form for the nominative and objective cases. In the instance of all the personal pronouns (except *you* and *it*) and the pronoun *who,* the nominative and objective forms are different. The following table shows the case forms of these pronouns:

NOM.: *I, you, he, she, it, we, they, who*
POSS.: *my, mine; your, yours; his; her, hers; its; our, ours; their, theirs; whose*
OBJ.: *me, you, him, her, it, us, them, whom*

With the exceptions noted in the table above, the possessive case of nouns and pronouns is regularly formed by the addition of *'s* in both the singular and plural. When, however, the plural noun already ends in *s,* only the apostrophe is added.

SING.:	*company's*	*child's*	*someone's*
PLURAL:	*companies'*	*children's*	[no plural]

14a. Use the nominative case for the subject of a verb and the complement following the verb *to be* (predicate noun or pronoun).

CORRECT: Mr. Graves and I will represent the company. [Subject of verb.]
CORRECT: The two representatives will be Mr. Graves and I. [Predicate noun and predicate pronoun following verb *will be.*]
CORRECT: I do not know who will sign the voucher. [Subject of *will sign.*]
CORRECT: Give the key to whoever will occupy the office. [Subject of *will occupy.*]

Note: "It's me," although a departure from the rule, is well established in informal usage.

14b. Be sure to use the apostrophe where it is required to show the possessive case and to leave it out where it is not required.

NOT: We placed the mens hats back in the box.
BUT: We placed the men's hats back in the box.

NOT: I believe the payment is your's.
BUT: I believe the payment is yours.

Caution: Do not confuse *its* (possessive) with *it's* (contraction of *it* and *is*), or *your* (possessive) with *you're* (contraction of *you* and *are*), or *whose* (possessive) with *who's* (contraction of *who* and *is*).

14c. There are logical grounds for not attributing possession to inanimate objects. Note, however, that the apostrophe and *s* are used in certain idiomatic constructions where possession is not involved.

DOUBTFUL: the machine's parts
BETTER: the parts of the machine
CORRECT: a day's pay, a month's work, a dollar's worth

14d. A noun or pronoun preceding a gerund (an *ing* form of the verb used as a noun) is usually possessive. Exceptions are made, however, to prevent awkwardness.

CORRECT: We objected to his going.
CORRECT: Mr. Cortland approved of Mr. Grant's postponing the trip.
CORRECT: I shudder whenever I think of a fire destroying our records. [It would be awkward to say "a fire's destroying our records."]
CORRECT: I observed him carrying a briefcase. [Here *him* is the object of the verb *observed*, and *carrying* is a participle (verbal adjective) modifying *him*.]

14e. Use the objective case for a direct object, indirect object, and object of a preposition.

CORRECT: He selected Tom Ehrlich and me for the job. [Direct object.]
CORRECT: Please give them and us the benefit of your advice. [Indirect object.]
CORRECT: The choice was between me and him. [Object of preposition.]
CORRECT: To whom shall we deliver the bonds? [Object of preposition.]

14f. Use the objective case for the subject and complement of an infinitive.

CORRECT: I asked him to come with me.
It turned out to be her.

14g. A pronoun in apposition with a noun or other pronoun takes the same case as the word with which it is in apposition.

CORRECT: We two—Mr. Sully and I—will make the arrangements.
CORRECT: They were talking about the account executive—me, that is.

14h. In determining the case of a pronoun in an incomplete comparative clause beginning with *than* or *as*, consider the function of the pronoun in relation to the whole cause.

CORRECT: He is as enthusiastic as I. [*I* is the subject of *am* understood.]
CORRECT: I would rather he had praised Miss Teller than me. [*Me* is the object of *had praised* understood.]

Verbs

15. Use the correct form of the verb.

15a. Use the correct tense form.

Regular verbs follow the pattern of I *walk*, I *walked*, I *have walked*. Irregular verbs vary—for example, I *run*, I *ran*, I *have run;* I *know*, I *knew*, I *have known*. In case of doubt, consult your dictionary.

ILLITERATE: He begun work on March 24.
I have drawed the check to your order.
Production was delayed when the steam pipe bust.
CORRECT: He began work on March 24.
I have drawn the check to your order.
Production was delayed when the steam pipe burst.

15b. Learn to use *shall* and *will*, and *should* and *would* correctly.

According to the formal rules, *shall* is used in ordinary discourse in the first person singular and plural (I shall go, we shall go), and *will* is used in the second and third persons (you will go, he will go, they will go). *Should* and *would* follow the same pattern (I should be glad, you would be glad, etc.). To express, determination, the positions of *shall* and *will* are reversed (I will go, you shall go, etc.). In questions, *shall* or *will* is used, depending on the form expected in the answer (Shall you be going? Will I be expected to attend?) Although these distinctions are still observed by many discerning writers, the following observations probably reflect current business usage more accurately:

(1) The writer or speaker who uses *will* and *would* in all persons is following general practice and is rarely subject to censure.

ACCEPTABLE: I will appreciate your comments.
We will be glad to make the adjustment.
They will mail the contract tomorrow.
I would be delighted to have you call on us.

(2) In questions, *shall* is generally used in the first person and *will* in the second and third.

ACCEPTABLE: Shall I wrap this package for you?
Will you please sign the card?
Will he be able to attend?

(3) *Should* is correctly used in all persons to suggest obligation (I should attend the meeting). Hence many writers object to its use in ordinary discourse. To them, "I should be glad to hear from you" suggests, "I ought to be glad to hear from you [but I'm not]." They therefore prefer, "I would be glad to hear from you."

(4) No dispute surrounds the use of *would* in all persons to indicate habitual action.

CORRECT: When I was a salesman, I would call on them regularly.
They would make the same error time after time.

15c. Let the tenses of the verbs show the proper relationships in time.

NOT: I have seen him at five o'clock yesterday.
BUT: I saw him at five o'clock yesterday.

NOT: He claimed they placed the order on April 10.
BUT: He claimed they had placed the order on April 10.

NOT: By next May, he will be serving us for 25 years.
BUT: By next May, he will have served us for 25 years.

Note: Use the present infinitive to denote action occurring at the same time as the verb.

NOT: I wanted to have gone with him.
BUT: I wanted to go with him.

15d. Do not shift unthinkingly from one tense to another.

NOT: We ordered the display on September 17 and were promised delivery on November 15 last. Then on November 1, the manufacturers write to tell us . . .
BUT: . . . Then on November 1, the manufacturers wrote to tell us . . .

15e. Use the subjunctive mood when the sense requires.

The subjunctive form of the verb *to be* is *be* in all forms of the present tense and *were* in all forms of the past tense (He asked that I be removed from the committee; I wish he were a member). The principal characteristic of the subjunctive mood forms of other verbs occurs in the third person singular of the present tense, which drops the *-s* ending (NOT "I asked that he writes," BUT "I asked that he write").

The uses of the subjunctive mood are confined mainly to (1) a conditional statement (one beginning with *if*) that is untrue or unlikely of accomplishment, (2) a wish or prayer, and (3) a "that" clause expressing a request, command, or resolution.

CORRECT: If he were opposed to the plan, he would have said so.
CORRECT: If he was opposed to the plan, I didn't know it. [Indicative mood because the opposition expressed by the verb is not necessarily untrue.]
CORRECT: I wish Mr. Cannon were here.
CORRECT: We requested that he appear in person.
CORRECT: RESOLVED, That an invitation be extended to all members.

Adjectives and Adverbs

16. Distinguish carefully between adjectives and adverbs, and use the proper form. If in doubt about the correct form, consult the dictionary.

16a. Use the correct part of speech. Adjectives regularly modify nouns and pronouns. Adverbs modify adjectives, verbs, and other adverbs.

NOT: This offer is real attractive. [Adjective]
BUT: This offer is really attractive. [Adverb]

NOT: Mr. Hahn works very diligent. [Adjective]
BUT: Mr. Hahn works very diligently. [Adverb]

16b. Use the comparative degree in comparing only two persons or things. Use the superlative in comparing three or more units.

The *comparative degree* is regularly formed by the addition of the suffix *-er* (warm, warmer) or by the use of the words *more* or *less* (more sure, less sure); the *superlative* is regularly formed by the addition of the suffix *-est* (warmest) or by the use of the words *most* or *least* (most sure, least sure). Words irregularly compared include *good* (better, best), *bad* (worse, worst), and *well* (better, best).

NOT: Jim Taylor is the best candidate [of two].
BUT: Jim Taylor is the better candidate.

NOT: With a choice of rail, road, and water transportation, shipping by water is by far the less expensive method.
BUT: . . . shipping by water is by far the least expensive method.

16c. After certain verbs—among them, *look, feel, prove, remain, see, smell, taste, sound*—use an adjective, not an adverb, to describe the subject.

CORRECT: The offer looks good to us.
CORRECT: The grapes in this shipment taste sweeter than usual.
CORRECT: If the arrangement proves profitable, we will renew the contract.
CORRECT: I hope you are feeling well. [*Well* is an adjective in this context. See your dictionary.]

16d. The use of the comparative and superlative degrees of certain adjectives that are already absolute in meaning is not approved in formal writing.

NOT: This is the most unique product of its kind.
BUT: This product is unique.

NOT: If we could buy a more perfect machine, we would.
BUT: If we could buy a better machine, we would.

WORD USE

Good Usage

17. Use words correctly.

Have a good college dictionary and use it often. Among those that can be recommended are the *American Heritage Dictionary of the English Language, Random House College Dictionary, Webster's New Collegiate Dictionary,* and *Webster's New World Dictionary.* If you question a point of usage in one dictionary, see what other dictionaries say about the same point. Helpful auxiliary tools include *Roget's Thesaurus,* the *Webster-Merriam Dictionary of Synonyms,* and Wilson Follett's *Modern American Usage.*

17a. Let appropriateness be your guide to correctness.

There is no single standard of good usage in business—no more than there is in journalism or in the home or classroom. The best personal equipment you can have in this respect is a thorough knowledge of words (including a knowledge of all shades of opinion regarding disputed usages) and sound judgment in choosing words for your own purposes. Such judgment entails consideration of the character of the source and the reader, the purpose of the message, the communication medium, and your own tastes and inclinations.

Some usages are so barbarous that no moderately literate businessman will support them. For example:

We can't hardly agree with you.
You could of seen that the contract was carried out.
Everything considered, he done pretty well for himself.
Mr. Jarvis got an invite to the meeting.
We'll do it irregardless of the competition.

Other usages are at worst questionable. For example, all of the underscored expressions in the following sentences have some "taint," which a knowledgeable writer will be familiar with, even if he decides for good reasons to use the expressions anyway. The objection to each expression—an objection not uniformly supported by arbiters of good usage—is noted in the brackets.

Due to the circumstances, they were forced to cancel the performance. [*Due to* should not be used as a preposition. Use *because of*.]

Please contact us at the first opportunity. [*Contact* is, in general usage, a noun, not a verb.]

Our salesmen will travel even further next year. [*Farther*, not *further*, should be used to express geographic distance.]

There are less pages in these books than there used to be. [*Fewer*, not *less*, should be used to denote number.]

Other questionable expressions including the following:

amount (for *number*)
and etc. (for *etc.*)
as per (for *in accordance with*)
balance (for *remainder*)
being that (for *because*)
but what (for *but that*)
can (for *may*)
enthuse (for *to become enthusiastic*)
expect (for *suppose*)
gotten (for *got*)
former (for *first*, when three or more are named)
infer (for *imply*)
in regards to (for *in regard to*)
kind of a (for *kind of*)
leave (for *let*)
lay (for *lie*)
prefer rather than (for *prefer to*)
reason is because (for *reason is that*)
seldom ever (for *seldom if ever*)

17b. Maintain a consistent level of diction.

Although slang and colloquial words are appropriate for some purposes, be careful not to let the intrusion of such words destroy the mood of your message. If you are not sure of the usage level of the word, look the word up in the dictionary to see if there is a qualifying label.

INCONSISTENT: We strongly believe that the company is in a sound financial position and will soon be going places saleswise.

IMPROVED: . . . and will soon be showing a good improvement in sales.

INCONSISTENT: There's a lively 101-horsepower engine up front that's mighty nice to have, too. Most other compacts simply don't offer this much oomph except at additional expenditure.

IMPROVED: . . . except at additional cost.

17c. Consult the dictionary for the correct spelling of a word. If alternate spellings are given, the spelling listed first is preferred.

The following words are among those commonly misspelled in business:

accidentally	customer	length	quiet
accommodate	definitely	maintenance	receive
advertisement	disastrous	manufacturer	schedule
all right (two words)	eighth	occurred	separate
among	embarrass	organization	similar
argument	equipment	personnel	surprise
believe	financier	persuade	tremendous
business	height	practice	truly
calendar	incidentally	privilege	undoubtedly
committee	independent	probably	writing
convenience	indispensable	procedure	written
	irrelevant	pursue	

17d. Do not confuse words that look or sound alike, but are different in meaning. Some examples:

accept, except	later, latter
affect, effect	lead, led
all ready, already	loose, lose
all together, altogether	moral, morale
appraise, apprise	passed, past
biannual, biennial	personal, personnel
calender, calendar	practical, practicable
capital, Capitol	practice, practise
complement, compliment	precedence, precedents
continually, continuously	principal, principle
correspondence, correspondents	receipt, recipe
credible, creditable	respectfully, respectively
flaunt, flout	stationary, stationery
formally, formerly	than, then
forth, fourth	therefor, therefore

17e. Distinguish carefully between the singular and plural of certain foreign words.

SING.	PLURAL	SING.	PLURAL
agendum	agenda*	analysis	analyses
alumna	alumnae	basis	bases
alumnus	alumni	criterion	criteria

datum	data*	phenomenon	phenomena
diagnosis	diagnoses	stratum	strata
medium	media (sometimes *mediums*)	synopsis	synopses
parenthesis	parentheses	thesis	theses

* Common practice condones the use of these plurals as singular nouns also.

Effective Usage

18. Use words that most effectively convey your meaning.

Good usage is but one of the two major criteria of word selection. The other is effectiveness—a quality embracing precision, suggestion, and force. (See also Rules 1c and 2c–2f.)

18a. Short, simple specific words are usually best (pp. 49–57).

NOT: The agency attributed its operational deficiencies to a lack of personnel resulting from budget limitations.
BUT: The agency said it could not do a good job because it did not have enough money to hire enough people.—*The Language of Audit Reports* (U.S. General Accounting Office)

18b. Use words that have the connotation you desire (pp. 59–62).

NOT: We ask you to try this piece of Eraso-Bond Paper.
BUT: We ask you to try this sheet of Eraso-Bond Paper.

NOT: In this position I was an underling to Mr. Porter.
BUT: In this position I was an assistant to Mr. Porter.

18c. Use concrete (not flat or dull) language. Favor colorful nouns and strong verbs (pp. 62–65, 72).

GOOD: When the "draw works" [machinery that powers a drilling rig] is loaded onto a truck, 50 tons crush down on the rear tires. This squeeze forces the cab as much as 6 feet into the air. As the load is drawn forward, the driver rides his truck back to earth, then starts his tortuous trip across roads made of oak boards nailed together with 60-penny spikes.—*B. F. Goodrich Company*

18d. Do not "mix" figures of speech (pp. 64–65).

INCONSISTENT: Be an early bird. If you miss the boat, you'll have to pay through the nose to get your hands on some of these bargains.
CONSISTENT: Like most successful Wall Streeters, he relies mainly on blue chips. Hence a periodic visit to Barney's when he's in the market for clothing. Barney's specializes in the blue chips of America's clothing industry . . . forty distinguished brands in all. With over twenty times as many individual items as the New York Stock Exchange lists, business on the block-long floor at Barney's is rather brisk. Newcomers sometimes approach us a little bearishly. They fear a degree of speculation in such vital

matters as, for example, fit. But by the time our master tailors—we have 76 of them—complete the final custom touches, the skeptics, invariably become our most bullish enthusiasts. We'll repress the obvious remarks about dividends. But shopping at Barney's IS a little like clipping coupons.

PUNCTUATION

End Punctuation (Period, Question Mark, Exclamation Point)

19. Use the appropriate punctuation at the end of a sentence or abbreviation.

19a. Use a period after a declarative or imperative sentence, or one containing an indirect question.

The truss wall-frame will be welded rather than bolted.
Safety glasses must be used on the job.
Please wait for an answer.
Mr. Ruden asked if we would be able to meet him at the airport.

19b. Use a period for abbreviations.

Mr.	Capt.	St.	a.m.	qt.	lb.
Mrs.	Dr.	Ave.	p.m.	pt.	oz.

Note: The period is not uniformly used in the punctuation of letters standing for the names of government agencies and private organizations, and in other abbreviations consisting of the first letters of words.

GM, G.M.; TVA, T.V.A.; NAM, N.A.M.
FTC, UN, ASCAP, IBM, AFL-CIO, NATO

19c. Use three spaced periods (an ellipsis) to show the omission of words from a quoted passage. If the omission comes at the end of a sentence, use the three periods plus any other required punctuation marks.

Even if the worker joins the union in fear . . . he is doing something not only emotional, but also rational. He wants to live with the people in his department in peace. . . .—T. V. Purcell in *Industrial Man* (W. Lloyd Warner and Norman H. Martin, eds.)

19d. Use a question mark at the end of a direct question.

What price would you offer for the lot?
Shall we send the contract directly to you?
Have you received the catalog we recently sent you? May we help you?

Note 1: A period is commonly used after a question of courtesy.

Will you please sign the card and return it to me.
May we ask you to keep the matter confidential for a while.

Note 2: Occasionally the question mark is used before the sentence is completed.

What does he want? is a question that only he can answer.

19e. A question mark in parentheses is used to indicate doubt regarding a preceding figure or statement.

The strength of the steel was given as 50,000 psi (?).

19f. Use an exclamation point at the end of a statement expressing strong feeling.

Free! Full-Color Brochure.
Don't wait. Mail the order card now!
He has already interviewed twelve candidates for the job—what fortitude!

The Comma

20. Use commas to separate or enclose words, phrases, and clauses.

20a. Use a comma to separate coordinate clauses joined by *and, but, for, or, nor,* or *yet.*

Methods are now available to measure indirect labor costs, and management is finding that simple and direct control is best.

Management applies pressure to improve overall performance, but workers apply pressure to get more pay.

Note: An exception to this rule is sometimes made when the coordinate clauses are short and closely related in thought.

We tried out the card process and we are now ready to accept it in our company-wide operations. [No comma]

20b. Use commas to separate sentence elements in a series. When the last two elements of a series of three or more are joined by *and* or *or,* use of the comma before the conjunction is generally recommended, although it is conventionally omitted in journalistic writing.

Available in small, medium, large, and extra large.

By next year we will need three additional clerks, a cashier, and a wrapper.

With conventional equipment, different machines are needed to read and process employee payroll data, write a payroll register, punch new-employee earning cards, and accumulate totals.

Note: Two or more adjectives in a series are not punctuated when each is thought of as modifying the whole phrase that follows.

They have just occupied a new 25-story stone-and-steel building.

As a result we purchased a Bolnes two-cylinder cross-head Type L diesel.

20c. Use a comma after an introductory sentence element that (1) contains a verb or part of a verb, or (2) runs noticeably long, or (3) functions as a connective.

If you want us to make the purchase for you, please let us know. [Introductory adverbial clause]

Noticeably distressed, he asked if we would reconsider our decision. [Introductory participial phrase]

In the space of little more than three years, they became one of the major producers. [Long introductory prepositional phrase]

In the interim, we will look around for another man. [Introductory connecting phrase]

Note 1: A short prepositional phrase at the beginning of a sentence is not ordinarily punctuated.

CORRECT: In a few days you will receive the remainder of the order.

Note 2: An adverbial clause following a main clause is not ordinarily set off by a comma.

CORRECT: Mr. Hanes flew down to the plant because he wanted to see for himself how the repairs were going.

20d. *Yes, no, oh, certainly,* and other mild interjections are set off by commas when they begin a sentence.

Yes, we knew about the arrangement all the time.
Certainly, you are aware of the legal implications.

20e. Use a comma in order to prevent misreading.

NOT: Ever since the relations between us have been most cordial.
BUT: Ever since, the relations between us have been most cordial.

20f. Use commas to set off direct quotations, parenthetic or interrupting words and phrases, and nonrestrictive clauses. A nonrestrictive clause is one that is not necessary to the sense of the sentence.

The report concluded, "In our opinion, the expense of microfilming the records is entirely justified." [Quotation]

Thomas Reed, the noted lawyer, was also a member of the committee. [Appositive phrase]

Here, for example, is the experience of Fawcett & Co. [Connecting phrase]

We cannot be responsible, however, for merchandise not claimed within thirty days. [Conjunctive adverb]

Mr. Parker, we are sure you have been with us long enough to know the high regard we have for you. [Noun in direct address]

We asked for Model T95, not S40. [Contrasting element]

The customer, who had already had a bad experience with us, vowed that he would take his business elsewhere. [Nonrestrictive clause]

Note: A restrictive clause—one that helps in identifying the word it modifies and is essential to the sense of the sentence—is *not* set off by commas.

CORRECT: A customer who has had one bad experience is apt to be especially cautious in his future dealings. [If the underscored clause were left out, the sentence remaining would not retain the intended sense.]

20g. Use commas to set off titles and the parts of dates and addresses.

Memorandum to Mr. Arthur Fellows, Vice President.

We refer to your letter of December 27, 19—, with which you enclosed your application for an account with us.

Please send the order to Mrs. Eleanor Travis, care of Goldring, 247 West 16th Street, Cleveland, Ohio 44114.

The Semicolon

21. Use the semicolon for longer stops than those provided by the comma.

21a. Use the semicolon to separate main clauses not joined by a conjunction.

The agent works on a contingent basis; he collects a fee only if the client is pleased.

Note: In the same construction, you may use a period, but not a comma.

RIGHT: The agent works on a contingent basis. He collects a fee only if the client is pleased.

WRONG: The agent works on a contingent basis, he collects a fee only if the client is pleased.

21b. Use a semicolon (not a comma) to separate main clauses joined by *however, therefore, accordingly, furthermore, moreover, thus, hence,* and other conjunctive adverbs.

Our survey confirms the need for rented computer services; however, we disagree that banks lack the flexibility to provide such services.

Note: You may use a period in the same construction. Either way, it is usually desirable to give less emphasis to the connective by moving it away from its position at the beginning of the clause.

CORRECT: Our survey confirms the need for rented computer services. We disagree, however, that banks lack the flexibility to provide such services.

21c. Use semicolons instead of commas to separate sentence elements already internally punctuated by commas.

The company has factories in Springfield, Illinois, and Kansas City, Missouri; a warehouse in Portland, Oregon; and sales offices in twelve cities in this country, three in South America, and five in Europe.

Featured on the menu are quiche Lorraine, a savory of ham, cream, and cheese; saucisson en croute, a delicious sausage in puff paste, hot from the oven; quenelles de brochet, pike dumplings with aurora sauce; and duckling a l'orange or Montmorency.

Quotation Marks

22. Use double quotation marks (" ") to enclose a direct quotation, single quotation marks (' ') to enclose a quotation within a quotation.

22a. Use quotation marks to enclose any words taken without change from another source.

The notice on the invoice states, "All transactions are FOB factory."

We have received the following telegram from our Cincinnati office: "EXPECT TO SHIP ELLIOT ORDER ON THURSDAY MAY 14."

Their message said, "Please interpret the notation, 'No imports,' on your Order No. 4365."

Note: Do not use quotation marks to enclose an indirect quotation.

CORRECT: Our Cincinnati office telegraphed that you can expect shipment on Thursday, May 14.

However, quotation marks may be used to enclose one or more of the words to show that they are given exactly as in the source.

CORRECT: The contract explicitly forbids the marketing of a "competitive" product.

22b. Use quotation marks to enclose words used facetiously or in a special sense.

We have just heard from our "friendly" competitors.

The insurer reserves the right to cancel on written notice coverage on any accounts specifically named in "extraordinary coverage" and "increased coverage" endorsements.

22c. Use quotation marks to enclose the quoted titles of articles, the names of chapters or sections of books, and the names of other short literary works. (See Rule 31a.)

Have you seen the article, "Behind the Publishing Scene," in the January 19 issue of the *Saturday Review*?

Chapter 3, "Employee Benefits in Non-Profit Organizations," is not yet completed.

22d. When a direct quotation consists of more than one paragraph, put a quotation mark at the beginning of each paragraph, but at the end of only the last paragraph.

On April 22 we sent you the following letter:

"Please refer to File No. 4325 relating to the estate of William Squire.

"We need to know immediately what Federal income taxes were paid on this estate in 19—. May we have your reply on the copy of this letter which we are enclosing.

"Thank you for your trouble."

22e. At the end of a quotation, put a comma or period inside the quotation mark, a semicolon or colon outside the quotation mark, and an exclamation point or question mark either inside or outside the quotation mark, depending on the sense.

"I will meet you at your office," he wrote.

The rubber-stamp notice read, "Past due. Please remit."

The door of the office is marked "Private"; that's a word we respect around here.

Here are your "orders": Take the next week off, go to some balmy resort, and play golf until you can't stand the sight of a fairway.

He has a habit of yelling "Ouch!" before he's hurt.

You must not toss around packages marked "Fragile"!

We ask, "When did you receive this notification?"

Shall we write "we suggest" or "we request"?

22f. When *he said* or a similar element breaks into a quotation, put a comma before the interruption and a comma, semicolon, or period after it, depending on the structure of the quotation.

"I will pay you," he wrote, "as soon as I have the money." [A comma follows the interrupting phrase when the quotation calls for a comma or no punctuation at all at the break.]

"Our order books are already closed," they said; "however, we will accommodate you if we receive a cancellation." [A semicolon follows the interrupter when the quotation calls for a semicolon at the break.]

"Consumer spending on durables was up 1 per cent," the report said. "Net exports declined." [A period follows the interrupter when the break in the quotation marks the division between two sentences.]

The Colon

23. Use the colon to direct attention to a following statement.

23a. Use a colon after a formal introduction to a list, an example or explanation, or a quotation. After the colon, use a capital letter except for a phrase that may be considered part of the whole statement.

Please send us the following: [List follows.]

This is how the plan works: You order as many . . .

I quote from the report: "The basic factors shaping the profit trend remain virtually unchanged from the last quarter."

We carry all sizes: small, medium, large, and extra large.

Note: Do not use a colon when the words that follow are not formally introduced and are an integral part of the sentence.

NOT: The colors available are: rose, green, and canary.
BUT: The colors available are rose, green, and canary.

23b. Use a colon between two independent clauses when the second clause amplifies or explains the first. In this usage, the word following the colon may begin with a small letter.

We need to take to heart the lesson out of last month's development in Canada: excesses in government spending and cheap money are more likely to lead to crises of confidence than to full employment.—*Citibank, New York*

23c. Use a colon after the salutation of a business letter and in expressions of time.

Dear Mr. MacGregor:
the 5:30 express; 10:15 a.m.; 11:00 p.m.

The Apostrophe

24. Use the apostrophe to show possession, to denote the omission of letters in a contraction, and to form certain plurals.

24a. Use the apostrophe to show possession or some other relationship that can be expressed by an "of" phrase. (See Rule 14.)

an employee's records — the company's problems — Mr. Jones's order
our employees' pensions — the season's greetings [greetings of the season]

24b. Use the apostrophe in a contraction to stand for the omitted letters. Contractions should not be used where formality is desired.

isn't (is not) — they've (they have)
can't (can not) — haven't (have not)
it's (it is, it has) — won't (will not)

24c. Use the apostrophe and *s* to form the plural of numerals, letters, symbols, and words referred to as words. The expression, but not the *'s*, is usually underlined or set in italics.

Your sentences have too many *and*'s
His *3*'s look like *8*'s
Type a series of *X*'s at the end of the story.

Note: In financial writing, the apostrophe and underlining are often omitted in such an expression as "the Treasury 4s" (4 per cent Treasury bonds).

The Hyphen

25. Use hyphens to join words or parts of words that belong to the same expression.

25a. Hyphenate words that form a single name.

secretary-treasurer — son-in-law
director-producer — sergeant-at-arms

25b. Hyphenate compound numbers from twenty-one to ninety-nine and all but simple fractions. Do not use more than one hyphen in a fraction.

thirty-two members — six twenty-fifths
one hundred and forty-five dollars — sixty-five hundredths

25c. Hyphenate words forming a compound adjective followed by a noun.

an ill-conceived project
a well-informed employee
a satin-smooth foundation

a high-and-mighty attitude
a peaches-and-cream complexion
a two-months' delay
a third-rate mechanic

BUT (CORRECT):

The project was ill conceived. [No noun following.]
It is good to see an employee well informed.
The foundation was satin smooth.

Note 1: Do not hyphenate compounds consisting of two proper nouns or those containing an adverb ending in *-ly*.

a New York statute
a fully packed container

Note 2: Use the "suspension hyphen" as in this example:

They deal in first-, second-, and third-line tires.

25d. Use the hyphen between the parts of a word to prevent confusion or awkwardness.

NOT: belllike, recover (cover again)
BUT: bell-like, re-cover
CORRECT: recover (regain), preeminent, reentry

The Dash

26. Use the dash to indicate an abrupt change in thought. (On the typewriter, a dash is formed by two hyphens; leave no space before or after.)

26a. Use the dash or dashes to mark a break or an interruption in the thought of a sentence.

What we meant was—but why rake over old coals?

A few years ago—I think it was before the merger—we did a great deal of business with the Donalds.

26b. For emphasis or clarity, use dashes instead of commas to set off an explanatory or appositive phrase or a summary statement.

He predicted that the unemployment rate then prevailing—"around 6.5 to 7 per cent"—might turn out to be the lowest it would ever get.

The control device "reads" its instructions—just as a teletype machine "reads" the news, or a player piano "reads" the music on a roll—and, in effect, produces a finished part direct from the original blueprint.

Improved technology in production means a higher standard of living as well as more leisure—shortened working hours, longer vacations, and earlier retirements.

New products, new markets, new jobs—these are the promises of the scientific revolution.

26c. Use the dash before a word or phrase to which you want to give special emphasis.

Mail the order card—now!

A tax cut would provide new thrust to the economy by stimulating expansion, modernization, and the undertaking of new business ventures—not just next year, but for years to come.

Parentheses

27. Use parentheses around incidental signs, words, and phrases where commas and dashes are either not suitable or not desired. Punctuation marks follow the parentheses when the same punctuation would otherwise be required where the parenthetic remark begins. Note the use of punctuation and capitalization with the parentheses in the following examples:

The maximum tax rates on additional income (i.e., "marginal rates") provide an index to the extent to which various nations go on discouraging people from earning additional taxable income. [No punctuation follows the parentheses because the sentence requires no punctuation at the point where it is interrupted by the parenthetic element.]

Thus the added value of the incentive is $190,000 (that is, $1,390,000 minus $1,200,000), not $1,300,000 (that is $2,500,000 minus $1,200,000). [A comma and period follow the respective parentheses because these marks would otherwise be placed at the points where the parenthetic remarks begin.]

They can improve the quality of our existing services (this statement is especially true for smaller banks). [No capital is seen at the beginning of the parenthetic remark because the parentheses are inside the sentence.]

They can improve the quality of our existing services. (This statement is especially true for smaller banks.) [Capital and period are inside the parentheses because the parenthetic remark is separated from the preceding statement by a period.]

Brackets

28. Brackets are used by an editor to enclose his own corrections or explanatory remarks in a quoted passage.

Said Mr. Griswold, "They [the banks] just don't have enough work to keep their machines busy 24 hours a day."

MECHANICS

Manuscript Form

29. Submit papers in correct form. Be guided by the requirements of the problem, the wishes of your instructor or employer, and the impression you want to make on the ultimate reader.

29a. Use 8½ × 11 in. white paper of substantial weight (not tissue). Leave adequate margins. Write or type legibly and neatly on one side only. Clearly identify your work. Number pages and fasten them securely together.

29b. Submit letters in correct mechanical form. Pay attention to margins and the conventions of the date, inside address, salutation, complimentary close, signature, and other parts (pp. 81–87).

Capitals

30. Capitalize proper nouns and the first word of every sentence.

30a. Use a capital letter at the beginning of every sentence, including quoted sentences and questions.

> An income tax installment is due on January 15.
> The advertisement said, "All quoted prices are effective at once."
> Would they carry out their threat? Of course.

30b. Capitalize proper nouns, and adjectives derived from proper nouns. (A proper noun is the name of a particular person, place, or thing.)

PERSONS: George, Mary Sackett, Kaufman, Henry Marsden
ORGANIZATIONS: Burroughs Corporation, American Red Cross, Federal Reserve Board, Harvard University, the Advertising Council, Department of Commerce.
PLACES: New York, Sante Fe, Lake Erie, South America, the Catskills
DERIVATIVES OF PROPER NAMES: American, Cuban, African, European
RACES AND RELIGIONS: Negro, Caucasian, Protestant, Moslem
MONTHS, DAYS, PERIODS: Sunday, Monday, January, October, the Mauve Decade, the Great Depression, World War II

Note 1: Words like *company, department,* and *university* are not capitalized when they are used in a generic sense. Compare:

> We received a reply from one company yesterday.
> We received a reply from the A. S. Brown Company yesterday.

Note 2: Words like *company, department,* and *sales department* are generally capitalized when they refer to the writer's own organization, but they are not capitalized when they designate some other company or a department in another company.

> I will write to the company for more information.
> Last year the Company [the writer's] expanded its foreign operations.
> We will soon look into the operations of the Sales Department. [The writer is referring to his own company.]
> Their sales department has lately taken on more help.

Note 3: In addressing a letter, omit the article *the* before a proper name, unless the article is an integral part of the name. Do not capitalize the article *the* before a proper name in the text unless the article begins a sentence or forms an integral part of the name.

Radio Corporation of America	The Custom Shop
30 Rockefeller Plaza	716 Fifth Avenue
New York, N.Y. 10022	New York, N.Y. 10022

> We have written to the Radio Corporation of America.
> We have written to The Custom Shop.

30c. Capitalize a title of respect when it precedes a name; also capitalize a title when it follows a name in the envelope address, inside address, or signature of a letter.

Mr. George Thomas
Captain Erwin Tanner
Chairman Jones

Very truly yours,
Roy S. Cramer
Chairman of the Board

Mr. Samuel E. Elofson, Director
Metal Research Institute
895 Park Avenue
New York, N.Y. 10026

Note 1: When a title follows a name in the text or when the title is used alone, it is capitalized only to show great respect.

Walter C. Evans, Secretary of Commerce; Roy S. Cramer, chairman of the board; the Secretary of Commerce; the chairman of the board.

Note 2: Writers often capitalize the titles of officers of their own company, but not of others.

I spoke to the Controller [of our company] yesterday.
I spoke to the controller [of another company] yesterday.

30d. Capitalize *North, East, Southeast,* etc., when they refer to geographical divisions, but not when they refer to direction.

CORRECT: He arrived here from the West.
You must travel east to hit the big population centers.

30e. Capitalize a name that describes a following numeral.

Economics 31
Room 1405

Order No. 5074B
File 95

Note: The word *page* is not so capitalized.

CORRECT: You will find the reference on page 374.

30f. Capitalize the first and last word in a title or heading, and all other words except articles and prepositions and conjunctions with fewer than four or five letters.

A Study of the Efficiency of the Transcription Department
Conclusions and Recommendations
The Case Against the Proposed Tariff
A Box to Put Things In

Underlining

31. Underline words in manuscript (or typescript) that the printer would normally set in italics.

31a. Underline for italics the names of books, plays, magazines, newspapers, musical compositions, works of art, ships, trains, and planes.

Peter Drucker's The Age of Discontinuity

the musical play, Fiddler on the Roof

the Saturday Review

the New York Times or the New York Times

Verdi's Aida

Rodin's The Thinker

the next sailing of the Queen Elizabeth 2

United's Golden Hawk to Los Angeles

Note 1: This rule is not uniformly applied in practice. In informal writing, especially, quotation marks are often substituted for underlining (or italics) and sometimes neither quotation marks nor underlining (or italics) is used.

The ad originally appeared in the Rochester "Times."

To reach these families, more advertisers are putting more money in Redbook.

Note 2: In accordance with Rule 22c, the titles of chapters in a book or articles in a magazine are put in quotation marks.

Have you seen the article, "Crisis in the Airlines," in this week's Advertising Age?

31b. Underline foreign words and phrases not completely absorbed into English (see your dictionary for help), and words, letters, and figures referred to as such.

Only at the annual dinner is the tuxedo de rigueur.*

He will be paid on a per diem† basis.

The word writing was misspelled.

His 7 looked like a t.

* A French phrase not considered part of the English language.
† A Latin phrase adopted into English.

Note: In informal writing quotation marks are often used for words and symbols used as such, and foreign terms are treated without underlining or quotation marks.

```
The word "writing" was misspelled.

The tuxedo is de rigueur.
```

31c. Underline words which require special emphasis. Except in the more strident advertisements, underlining for emphasis should be used sparingly.

```
    The report makes the point that businessmen prefer
their cars to air travel for distances up to 500 miles,
but it doesn't explain why.
    Clorox bleach gives suds the added cleaning power they
need to give you the cleanest possible wash.
```

Numbers

32. Observe the rules of correctness and consistency in writing numbers and amounts.

32a. In general, use figures to express exact numbers and amounts, except at the beginning of a sentence. Numbers that can be expressed in one or two words are often written out.

> We have your order of October 20 for 36 dozen of our Softex nylon ribbed hosiery at $5.50 per dozen.
>
> Ten thousand dollars was the price asked.
>
> They will need three extra clerks for Christmas.

32b. Recast a sentence, if necessary, to avoid beginning it with a figure.

NOT: $431.75 is the full amount past due.
BUT: The full amount past due is $431.75.

32c. Spell out numbered street names up to and including ten; use figures for house numbers, dates, catalog numbers, page numbers, room numbers, sizes, measures, mixed amounts, decimals and percentages, and fractions that are appended to whole numbers or cannot be written in one or two words.

> 575 Eighth Avenue; 29 West 12th Street; August 6; Cat. No. 47568; page 95, Room 1806; Size 16; 36 degrees; 9 by 12 feet; $15\frac{1}{2}$; $86.50; 79,863 shares; 2 per cent; $15\frac{1}{2}$; one-half; $^{5}/_{32}$.

Note: The names of numbered streets are usually followed by the endings *-st, -nd, -rd,* and *-th;* the days of the month are not followed by these endings except in such expressions as the *3rd of October* and *your letter of the 24th.*

RIGHT: 265 West 24th Street
Your letter of September 3 [not *3rd*]
April 22, 19—[not *22nd*]

32d. Except in a series, do not place two sets of figures in succession. Either write out one of them, or change the sentence order.

NOT: When you reach 65, $15,000 will be placed in your account by the trustees.
BUT: When you reach 65, the trustees will place $15,000 in your account.

NOT: 100 15-cent stamps
BUT: 100 fifteen-cent stamps
OR: one hundred 15-cent stamps

32e. Round numbers are often spelled out or, in the instance of numbers exceeding a million, expressed in words and figures.

a population of ten million; fifty years; a thousand dollars; assets of $1.2 million; 59 million dial telephones

32f. In writing a series of figures containing both mixed amounts and even-dollar amounts, add the decimal point and two ciphers to the even-dollar amounts.

The price rose from $18.60 in 19—, to $18.85 in 19—, to $21.00 in 19—. [Not $21]

32g. In writing amounts of less than a dollar, use figures and the word *cents* or the cents sign (¢), not the dollar sign and decimal point.

NOT: The account is short $.89.
BUT: The account is short 89 cents.

NOT: Please deposit $.05.
BUT: Please deposit 5¢.

Note: This rule does not hold in a column containing mixed amounts.

CORRECT:

CORRECT:	$29.75
	3.50
	.45
	$33.70

32h. Place a comma after each three digits counting from the right, except in dates, serial numbers, catalog numbers, etc.

a population of 180,463
a deficit of $2,462,195
May 15, 1975
No. 463592
Room 4086

Abbreviations

33. Use abbreviations sparingly but correctly.

Abbreviations are more frequently used in catalogs, business forms, and technical writing than in ordinary business correspondence and reports. For the correct form of an abbreviation, consult your dictionary.

33a. It is correct to use abbreviations in the following instances:

Before proper names: Mr., Ms., Mrs., Dr., Messrs.*
After proper names: Jr., Sr., M.D., Esq.*
With hours, dates, or numerals: A.M. (or a.m.). P.M. (or p.m.) B.C., A.D., No.

* *Messrs.* is occasionally used with the name of a professional partnership, as in law or accounting. *Esq.* is correct in addressing an attorney. Note that the title *Mr.* is omitted when *Esq.* follows the name.

NOT: Messrs. International Business Machines Corporation
BUT: Messrs. Field and Williams

NOT: Mr. George B. Stone, Esq.
BUT: George B. Stone, Esq.

NOT: I will see you tomorrow a.m. about a No. of problems.
BUT: I will see you tomorrow at 9 a.m. about a number of problems. [The abbreviations must be used with specific figures.]

33b. Other, less common abbreviations may be used provided they are known to the reader or are initially defined for him.

Technical terms: LIFO* (last in, first out); GNP (gross national product)
Organizational names: BBD&O (Batten, Barton, Durstine and Osborne); IBM (International Business Machines Corporation); BLS (Bureau of Labor Statistics)

* For the use of the period with abbreviations, see Rule 19b.

33c. Some words, which may be abbreviated in addresses, tables, footnotes, and on printed forms and elsewhere to conserve space, are generally written out in formal composition.

Milwaukee, Wisconsin [not *Wis.*]
2756 Forest Avenue [not *Ave.*]
September 30, 19— [not *Sept.*]
Tuesday, May 3 [not *Tues.*]
page 275 [not *p.*]

33d. The words *Honorable, Reverend, Professor, Captain,* and similar titles may be abbreviated only when they precede a person's full name, not the last name alone.

NOT: Hon. Compton, Rev. Palmer, Prof. Smith, Capt. Long
BUT: Hon. Arthur B. Compton, Rev. Allen Palmer, Prof. Helen V. Smith, Capt. Elmer S. Long

ALSO CORRECT: Honorable Arthur B. Compton (but NOT Honorable Compton), Reverend Allen Palmer or, if the title applies, Reverend Dr. Palmer (but preferably NOT Reverend Palmer), Professor Helen V. Smith or Professor Smith, Captain Elmer S. Long or Captain Long

33e. In addressing a person or organization, adopt the style used in the addressee's own signature or letterhead.

NOT: Prof. Jack H. Janis
BUT: Professor J. Harold Janis

NOT: Peat, Marwick, Mitchell and Company
BUT: Peat, Marwick, Mitchell & Co.

33f. On envelope addresses, the U.S. Postal Service recommends the following two-letter state abbreviations to facilitate the electronic processing of mail.

Alabama	AL	Kentucky	KY	Ohio	OH
Alaska	AK	Louisiana	LA	Oklahoma	OK
Arizona	AZ	Maine	ME	Oregon	OR
Arkansas	AR	Maryland	MD	Pennsylvania	PA
California	CA	Massachusetts	MA	Puerto Rico	PR
Colorado	CO	Michigan	MI	Rhode Island	RI
Connecticut	CT	Minnesota	MN	South Carolina	SC
Delaware	DE	Mississippi	MS	South Dakota	SD
District of Columbia	DC	Missouri	MO	Tennessee	TN
Florida	FL	Montana	MT	Texas	TX
Georgia	GA	Nebraska	NE	Utah	UT
Guam	GU	Nevada	NV	Vermont	VT
Hawaii	HI	New Hampshire	NH	Virginia	VA
Idaho	ID	New Jersey	NJ	Virgin Islands	VI
Illinois	IL	New Mexico	NM	Washington	WA
Indiana	IN	New York	NY	West Virginia	WV
Iowa	IA	North Carolina	NC	Wisconsin	WI
Kansas	KS	North Dakota	ND	Wyoming	WY

Word Division

34. At the ends of lines, divide words only when necessary to preserve an even margin. Always divide words according to dictionary practice.

34a. Divide a word only between the main parts or syllables. It is usually correct to divide a word after the prefix, before the suffix, or between a double consonant; or at any point where the word regularly requires a hyphen. If you do not know where the division should take place, look up the word in your dictionary.

CORRECT: sub/stantial, acknowledg/ment, col/lection

34b. Try not to divide a proper name.

BAD: William/son, Por/ter, Pough/keepsie

34c. Do not divide a word after a single letter or before only one or two letters; also avoid any division that may result in a misreading of the word.

BAD: a/mong, e/lusive, tack/y, improper/ly
ope/rate, read/just, dynamo/meter

34d. Do not divide a word that is already hyphenated.

BAD: self-ser/vice, mid-Cen/tury, re-de/signed

Documentation

35. In formal writing, identify direct quotations and other source material by means of footnotes and a bibliography.

In informal writing, references to source material may be integrated with the text. The purpose of documentation is (1) to give due credit for material you have borrowed and (2) to provide support for your statements. Failure to identify your sources could lead to charges of plagiarism.

35a. A bibliography of works used in research should be appended to the research paper. Entries should be clear, concise, and consistent in form (see the model bibliography on page 536).

(1) List works alphabetically according to the author's last name, where given; otherwise, according to title.
(2) Give the place of publication, the name of the publisher, and the date of publication (last copyright date).
(3) If the entry takes more than a line, indent succeeding lines. Use double spacing between entries.
(4) In a long bibliography, list books, periodicals, and "miscellaneous" sources separately in that order.
(5) The use of underlining for the names of books and periodicals and quotation marks for the names of articles, chapters, etc., accords with the rules in this Style Manual (Rules 22c and 31a).

35b. Footnotes are used to identify the source of particular quotations and statements in the text. The form is only slightly different from that used in the bibliography.

BIBLIOGRAPHICAL ENTRY
Longman, Kenneth A. *Advertising.* New York: Harcourt Brace Jovanovich, 1971.

FOOTNOTE
[1] Kenneth A. Longman, *Advertising* (New York: Harcourt Brace Jovanovich, 1971), p. 119.

35c. For initial footnote references, follow these rules:

(1) List footnotes consecutively on page-bottoms to agree with references in the text.*
(2) Identify authors with given names first.
(3) Put facts of publication (place, publisher, and date) in parentheses.
(4) Give exact page references.

* The practice is growing of putting all footnotes at the end of a paper in a manner similar to that shown on page 120. The footnotes, arranged alphabetically, also serve as the bibliography.

BIBLIOGRAPHY

American Management Association. Financing East-West Business Transactions. AMA Bulletin, No. 119, 1968.

Bradt, William R. Organizing for Effective Public Affairs: How Companies Structure Their Corporate Unit. NICB Studies in Public Affairs, No. 5. New York: National Industrial Conference Board, 1969.

"A Cold War for Press Freedom." Time, Dec. 20, 1976.

Haney, William V. Communication and Organizational Behavior. Rev. ed. Homewood, Ill.: Richard D. Irwin, 1967.

Janis, J. Harold. "A Rationale for the Use of Common Business-Letter Expressions." Journal of Business Communication, 4 (October 1966), 3-11.

______. Writing and Communicating in Business. 3d ed. New York: Macmillan, 1978.

Kay Herbert. "Do We Really Know the Effects of Using Fear Appeals?" Journal of Marketing, 36 (April 1972), 55-57.

Patton, Arch. "Why Incentive Plans Fail." Harvard Business Review, May-June 1972, pp. 58-65.

Pigors, Paul, and Meyers, Charles A. Personnel Administration: A Point of View and Method. New York: McGraw-Hill, 1956.

Rogers, Everett M., and Agarwala-Rogers, Rekha. Communication in Organizations. New York: The Free Press, 1976.

U.S. House of Representatives, Committee on Ways and Means. Hearings on the Investment Tax Credit. 87th Cong., 2d Sess. (1962).

Whyte, W. F. Human Relations in the Restaurant Industry. New York: McGraw-Hill, 1968.

Correct Form of a Bibliography

Note the style of the following footnotes:

BOOK (ONE AUTHOR)

[2] Marshall McLuhan, *The Mechanical Bride: Folklore of Industrial Man* (New York: Vanguard, 1951), p. 46.

BOOK (TWO AUTHORS)

[3] Wassily Leontief and Herbert Stein, *The Economic System in an Age of Discontinuity* (New York: New York University Press, 1976), pp. 64–65.

EDITED WORK

[4] Wilbur Schramm (ed.), *The Science of Human Communication* (New York: Basic Books, 1963), p. 117.

BOOK (SECOND OR LATER EDITION)

[5] S. I. Hayakawa, *Language in Thought and Action,* 3d ed. (New York: Harcourt Brace Jovanovich, 1972), pp. 21–25.

CHAPTER OR ARTICLE IN A COLLECTIVE WORK

[6] Lee Thayer, "Communication and Organizational Theory," in *Human Communication Theory,* Frank E. X. Dance, ed. (New York: Holt, Rinehart and Winston, 1967), pp. 70–115.

ARTICLE IN A LEARNED JOURNAL

[7] Charles Winick, "The Social Contexts of Humor," *Journal of Communication,* 26 (Summer 1976), 113. [The first number following the name of the periodical is the volume number; the last is the page number.]

SIGNED MAGAZINE ARTICLE

[8] Peter Gillman, "Supersonic Bust." *Atlantic,* January 1977, pp. 75–76.

UNSIGNED NEWSPAPER ARTICLE

[9] *New York Times,* Aug. 11, 1977.

ARTICLE IN ENCYCLOPEDIA

[10] "Scientific Management," *Encyclopaedia Britannica,* vol. 20, 14th ed.

VOLUME IN A SERIES

[11]. Norman E. Pflomm, *Managing Company Cash* (New York: National Industrial Conference Board, 1961), Studies in Business Policy No. 99, p. 83.

PAMPHLET

[12] *Manual of Style* (Garden City, N.Y.: Doubleday, n.d.), p. 12. A booklet published for the guidance of the Doubleday organization.

SPEECH, LECTURE, ETC.

[13] Speech by John J. Jones, president, A.B.C. Company, at the Sales Executives Club, New York, Aug. 7, 1978, as reported in the *New York Times,* Aug. 8, 1978.

[14] Statement by John J. Jones, president, A.B.C. Company, personal interview, Aug. 7, 1978.

[15] From lecture notes taken in class of Dr. Lawrence D. Brennan, Graduate School of Business Administration, New York University, October 13, 1977.

[16] Letter from John J. Jones, president, A.B.C. Company, April 23, 1978.

35d. Subsequent footnote references should be brief, but clear. Latin terms should be used sparingly, if at all. Note these examples:

FIRST REFERENCES

[17] L. Roy Blumenthal, *The Practice of Public Relations* (New York: Macmillan, 1972), p. 75.

[18] Julian L. Simon, *The Management of Advertising* (Englewood Cliffs, N.J.: Prentice-Hall, 1971), pp. 18–19.

SUBSEQUENT REFERENCES

[19] Simon, loc. cit. [Same passage as cited above.]

[20] Ibid., p. 65. [Same work, but another page.] or (preferred)

[21] Simon, p. 65.

[22] Blumenthal, *Public Relations*, p. 172. [This form, with shortened title is useful when footnotes cite more than one work for an author.]

[23] Simon, op. cit., p. 145. [This is a variant of footnote 21; the Latin abbreviation is usually considered unnecessary.]

35e. Below are some common abbreviations used in the documentation of sources. It is no longer the practice to underline (for italics) abbreviations of Latin terms.

anon.	anonymous.
ca. (*circa*)	about. Used where the exact date is unknown (as in "ca. 1930").
ch., chs.	chapter, chapters.
ed.	edition, editor, edited by.
et al. (*et alii*)	and others, as in "Carl I. Hovland et al."
f., ff.	and the following page, pages, as in "pp. 17ff."
ibid. (*ibidem*)	in the same (immediately preceding) footnoted work.
infra	below.
loc. cit. (*loco citato*)	in the place cited. Used with the author's name to refer to the same passage cited in an earlier footnote.
n.d.	no date of publication given.
op. cit. (*opere citato*)	in the work cited. Usually superfluous.
p., pp.	page, pages.
passim	here and there. Denotes scattered references, as in pp. 132–155 passim."
rev.	revised by, revised.
supra	above.
vol., vols.	volume, volumes.

Index

Numbers in **boldface** refer to rules in the Style Manual, pp. 500–538. A key to the Manual and a list of correction symbols will be found inside the back cover.

A

Index

D

H

I

J

L

P

Q

R

S

XYZ

KEY TO THE STYLE MANUAL

(A Concise Reference to the Style Manual on Pages 500–538)